BGP Design and Implementation

Randy Zhang, CCIE No. 5659
Micah Bartell, CCIE No. 5069

Cisco Press

Cisco Press
800 East 96th Street, 3rd Floor
Indianapolis, IN 46240 USA

BGP Design and Implementation

Randy Zhang, CCIE #5659

Micah Bartell, CCIE #5069

Copyright © 2004 Cisco Systems, Inc.

Cisco Press logo is a trademark of Cisco Systems, Inc.

Published by:
Cisco Press
800 E. 96th St., 3rd Floor
Indianapolis, IN 46240

Printed in the United States of America 1 2 3 4 5 6 7 8 9 0

First Printing December 2003

Library of Congress Cataloging-in-Publication Number: 202105327

ISBN: 1-58705-109-5

Trademark Acknowledgments

All terms mentioned in this book that are known to be trademarks or service marks have been appropriately capitalized. Cisco Press or Cisco Systems, Inc. cannot attest to the accuracy of this information. Use of a term in this book should not be regarded as affecting the validity of any trademark or service mark.

Warning and Disclaimer

This book is designed to provide information about Border Gateway Protocol (BGP). Every effort has been made to make this book as complete and accurate as possible, but no warranty or fitness is implied.

The information is provided on an "as is" basis. The authors, Cisco Press, and Cisco Systems, Inc. shall have neither liability nor responsibility to any person or entity with respect to any loss or damages arising from the information contained in this book or from the use of the discs or programs that may accompany it.

The opinions expressed in this book belong to the authors and are not necessarily those of Cisco Systems, Inc.

Feedback Information

At Cisco Press, our goal is to create in-depth technical books of the highest quality and value. Each book is crafted with care and precision, undergoing rigorous development that involves the unique expertise of members of the professional technical community.

Reader feedback is a natural continuation of this process. If you have any comments regarding how we could improve the quality of this book, or otherwise alter it to better suit your needs, you can contact us through e-mail at feedback@ciscopress.com. Please be sure to include the book title and ISBN in your message.

We greatly appreciate your assistance.

Corporate and Government Sales

Cisco Press offers excellent discounts on this book when ordered in quantity for bulk purchases or special sales. For more information, please contact:

U.S. Corporate and Government Sales   1-800-382-3419   corpsales@pearsontechgroup.com

For sales outside of the U.S. please contact: **International Sales**   1-317-581-3793   international@pearsontechgroup.com

Publisher	John Wait
Editor-In-Chief	John Kane
Cisco Representative	Anthony Wolfenden
Cisco Press Program Manager	Sonia Torres Chavez
Cisco Marketing Communications Manager	Tom Geitner
Cisco Marketing Program Manager	Edie Quiroz
Acquisitions Editor	Amy Moss
Managing Editor	Patrick Kanouse
Development Editor	Dayna Isley
Project Editor	Marc Fowler
Copy Editor	Gayle Johnson
Technical Editors	Juan Alcaide
	Jonathan Looney
	Vaughn Suazo
Team Coordinator	Tammi Barnett
Book Designer	Gina Rexrode
Cover Designer	Louisa Adair
Production Team	Octal Publishing, Inc.
Indexer	Tim Wright

CISCO SYSTEMS

Corporate Headquarters
Cisco Systems, Inc.
170 West Tasman Drive
San Jose, CA 95134-1706
USA
www.cisco.com
Tel: 408 526-4000
    800 553-NETS (6387)
Fax: 408 526-4100

European Headquarters
Cisco Systems International BV
Haarlerbergpark
Haarlerbergweg 13-19
1101 CH Amsterdam
The Netherlands
www-europe.cisco.com
Tel: 31 0 20 357 1000
Fax: 31 0 20 357 1100

Americas Headquarters
Cisco Systems, Inc.
170 West Tasman Drive
San Jose, CA 95134-1706
USA
www.cisco.com
Tel: 408 526-7660
Fax: 408 527-0883

Asia Pacific Headquarters
Cisco Systems, Inc.
Capital Tower
168 Robinson Road
#22-01 to #29-01
Singapore 068912
www.cisco.com
Tel: +65 6317 7777
Fax: +65 6317 7799

Cisco Systems has more than 200 offices in the following countries and regions. Addresses, phone numbers, and fax numbers are listed on the
Cisco.com Web site at www.cisco.com/go/offices.

Argentina • Australia • Austria • Belgium • Brazil • Bulgaria • Canada • Chile • China PRC • Colombia • Costa Rica • Croatia • Czech Republic
Denmark • Dubai, UAE • Finland • France • Germany • Greece • Hong Kong SAR • Hungary • India • Indonesia • Ireland • Israel • Italy
Japan • Korea • Luxembourg • Malaysia • Mexico • The Netherlands • New Zealand • Norway • Peru • Philippines • Poland • Portugal
Puerto Rico • Romania • Russia • Saudi Arabia • Scotland • Singapore • Slovakia • Slovenia • South Africa • Spain • Sweden
Switzerland • Taiwan • Thailand • Turkey • Ukraine • United Kingdom • United States • Venezuela • Vietnam • Zimbabwe

About the Authors

Randy Zhang, Ph.D., CCIE No. 5659, is a network consulting engineer at Cisco Systems Advanced Services (AS), supporting Cisco strategic service provider and enterprise customers. He has helped many of these customers in large-scale BGP and MPLS designs, migrations, and implementations. Before joining the AS group, he was a senior software QA engineer for IP routing and MPLS for Cisco 6x00 series IP DSL switches, among many other projects. He has written more than 30 publications on a variety of subjects.

Micah Bartell, CCIE No. 5069, is a network consulting engineer at Cisco Systems. He is a member of the ISP Experts team in Advanced Services, providing support to Cisco strategic service provider and enterprise customers. He is a recognized expert in the area of large-scale IP network design, with a strong focus on BGP, IS-IS, and IP multicast. He is involved in standards work through the International Standards Organization (ISO) and the Internet Engineering Task Force (IETF). He most recently served as editor for ISO/IEC IS 10589.

About the Technical Reviewers

Juan Alcaide joined Cisco in 1999 in a joint effort with Duke University to study BGP scalability. Since then, he has been working in the routing protocol team at the Cisco Technical Assistance Center. Currently, he works as a consultant, offering support to large ISPs.

Jonathan Looney, CCIE No. 7797, is a senior network engineer for Navisite, Inc., where he designs and implements custom network solutions for customers as well as the 15 data centers the company owns. He has more than five years of experience implementing and maintaining BGP in both enterprise and service provider environments. Before working for Navisite, he worked for both an ISP and a large university, where he designed and maintained the company's networks.

Vaughn Suazo, CCIE No. 5109, is 12-year veteran in the technology field with experience in server technologies, LAN/WAN networking, and network security. He has achieved certifications as a dual CCIE for Routing and Switching and Security. His career at Cisco began in 1999, where he worked directly with network service provider customers and provided engineering support. Before working at Cisco, he worked with technology companies, providing customers with network design consulting, pre- and post-deployment support, and network audits for many enterprise and commercial companies in the Tulsa and Oklahoma City areas.

Dedications

Randy Zhang:

To Susan, Amy, and Ally, for their enduring love, support, and patience.

Micah Bartell:

To my parents, Merlin and Marlene, for all their support over the years.

Acknowledgments

This book has been the result of the efforts of many for whom we are ever so grateful. We would like to express our deep gratitude to many colleagues who provided detailed technical reviews within tight schedules—specifically, Rudy Davis, Tony Phelps, Soumitra Mukherji, Eric Louzau, and Chuck Curtiss. We also want to thank Mike Sneed and Dave Browning for their encouragement and support.

We are very thankful to the kind folks at Cisco Press who made this book a reality. John Kane has patiently guided us throughout the project at every stage. John's encouragement and guidance have made the project a bit less challenging. Dayna Isley and Amy Moss, two talented editors, helped put various editing and reviews in the proper process and provided us with detailed comments and suggestions in revising the manuscript. We also want to thank Brett Bartow, Chris Cleveland, and Tammi Ross for their support and coordination in the initial part of the project.

Our thanks also go to the three technical reviewers—Juan Alcaide, Jonathan Looney, and Vaughn Suazo. Their helpful comments and suggestions resulted in much improvement.

Randy Zhang: My special thanks go to my family, friends, colleagues, and many others for their help and encouragement over the years.

Micah Bartell: I would like to thank my family and friends—specifically, Adam Sellhorn and Jeff McCombs—for their support during this project. I would also like to thank Tom Campbell and the rest of the guys from the Global Internet NOC for making networking so much fun right from the start. Finally, and most importantly, I would like to thank God for giving me the talent and opportunity to write this book.

Contents at a Glance

Table of Contents

Chapter 6   Internet Connectivity for Enterprise Networks   221

Introduction

Border Gateway Protocol (BGP) is one of the most widely deployed protocols in networks today and is the de facto routing protocol in the Internet. BGP is a flexible protocol, in that a variety of options are available to network designers and engineers. Furthermore, extensions and implementation enhancements make BGP a powerful and complex tool.

The purpose of this book is to go beyond the basic protocol concepts and configurations and to focus on providing practical design and implementation solutions. BGP is treated as a useful tool in designing and implementing complex networks. Using a hands-on approach, details on Cisco IOS implementation are provided, with extensive examples and case studies throughout the book.

Who Should Read This Book?

This book is intended to cover advanced BGP topics in designing and implementing networks. Although basic concepts are reviewed, this book's emphasis is not on BGP or basic BGP configurations. Practical design and implementation guidelines are provided to help network engineers, administrators, and designers build a scalable BGP routing architecture. This book can also be used by anyone who wants to understand advanced BGP features that are available in Cisco IOS and to prepare for Cisco certification exams.

How This Book Is Organized

The chapters in this book can be roughly grouped into four parts.

Part I, "Understanding Advanced BGP," discusses and reviews some of the fundamental components and tools in BGP:

- Chapter 1, "Advanced BGP Introduction," discusses the characteristics of BGP and compares BGP to IGP.

- Chapter 2, "Understanding BGP Building Blocks," lays a foundation for the book by reviewing various components that are relevant to BGP.

- Chapter 3, "Tuning BGP Performance," presents a detailed discussion of how to tune BGP performance, with emphasis on recent developments in IOS.

- Chapter 4, "Effective BGP Policy Control," presents common policy control techniques that have made BGP so flexible.

Part II, "Designing BGP Enterprise Networks," focuses on how to leverage BGP characteristics when designing an enterprise network:

- Chapter 5, "Enterprise BGP Core Network Design," discusses various options in designing an enterprise core network using BGP.

- Chapter 6, "Internet Connectivity for Enterprise Networks," presents design options for an enterprise network to connect to Internet Service Providers (ISPs) for Internet connectivity.

Part III, "Designing BGP Service Provider Networks," focuses on BGP network designs for service providers:

- Chapter 7, "Scalable iBGP Design and Implementation Guidelines," details the two options that are available to increase iBGP scalability: route reflection and confederation.

- Chapter 8, "Route Reflection and Confederation Migration Strategies," presents several step-by-step procedures on network migrations between a fully meshed BGP network and networks that are based on route reflection and confederation.

- Chapter 9, "Service Provider Architecture," discusses various BGP design options available for a service provider.

Part IV, "Implementing BGP Multiprotocol Extensions," focuses on the multiprotocol extensions to BGP:

- Chapter 10, "Multiprotocol BGP and MPLS VPN," discusses the BGP multiprotocol extension for MPLS VPNs and various design and implementation options to build complex VPN solutions.

- Chapter 11, "Multiprotocol BGP and Interdomain Multicast," provides design options for how BGP is used for interdomain multicast.

- Chapter 12, "Multiprotocol BGP Support for IPv6," presents the BGP extension for IP version 6.

Part V, "Appendixes," provides the following information:

- Appendix A, Multiprotocol BGP Extensions for CLNS Support

- Appendix B, Matrix of BGP Features and Cisco IOS Software Releases

- Appendix C, Additional Sources of Information

- Appendix D, Acronym Glossary

Icons Used in This Book

Cisco uses the following standard icons to represent different networking devices.
You will encounter several of these icons within this book.

Router

Multilayer Switch

Switch

Firewalls

ATM Switch

Content Switch

Route/Switch
Processor

Cisco 7500
Series Router

ISDN/Frame
Relay switch

Hub

Bridge

Intrusion Detection
System

Load Balancer

Access
Server

CiscoSecure
Scanner

IP/TV
Broadcast
Server

Cisco
CallManager

Cisco
Directory Server

PC

Laptop

Cisco Works
Workstation

Web
Browser

Web
Server

Network Cloud

Concentrator

Gateway

Fax

File Server

Printer

VPN Concentrator

Phone

Cache or
Content Engine

Multilayer Switch
with Load Balancer

SSL Offloader

Tape Subsystem

Fibre Channel
Switch

DWDM-CWDM

Storage Subsystem

Command Syntax Conventions

The conventions used to present command syntax in this book are the same conventions used in the IOS Command Reference. The Command Reference describes these conventions as follows:

- Vertical bars (|) separate alternative, mutually exclusive elements.

- Square brackets ([ ]) indicate optional elements.

- Braces ({ }) indicate a required choice.

- Braces within brackets ([{ }]) indicate a required choice within an optional element.

- **Bold** indicates commands and keywords that are entered literally as shown. In actual configuration examples and output (not general command syntax), bold indicates commands that are manually input by the user (such as a show command).

- *Italic* indicates arguments for which you supply actual values.

Addressing Conventions

To simplify the discussion, private IP addressing (RFC 1918) is commonly used in this book. Where relevant, simple subnetting is used. Any such addressing and subnetting schemes are used for demonstration only and should not be construed as recommendations.

The AS numbering schemes used typically are in the hundreds, such as 100, 200, 300, and so on. When appropriate, private autonomous systems are used as well. Unless specifically indicated, these AS numbers are used for demonstration only and should not be construed as recommendations.

Cisco bugs are often used as a tool to document new IOS features. Where appropriate and relevant, Cisco bug IDs are provided. To access these bugs, you need registered access to the Cisco Systems website (www.cisco.com).

Understanding Advanced BGP

This chapter covers the following topics:

- Understanding BGP characteristics
- Comparing BGP and IGP

CHAPTER 1

Advanced BGP Introduction

Border Gateway Protocol (BGP) is a routing protocol that is used to exchange network layer reachability information (NLRI) between routing domains. A routing domain is often called an *autonomous system (AS)* because different administrative authorities control their respective domains. The current Internet is a network of interconnected autonomous systems, where BGP version 4 (BGP4) is the de facto routing protocol.

Understanding BGP Characteristics

The Internet has grown significantly over the past several decades. The current BGP table in the Internet has more than 100,000 routes. Many enterprises have also deployed BGP to interconnect their networks. These widespread deployments have proven BGP's capability to support large and complex networks.

The reason BGP has achieved its status in the Internet today is because it has the following characteristics:

- Reliability
- Stability
- Scalability
- Flexibility

The following sections describe each of these characteristics in more detail.

Reliability

You can examine BGP's reliability from several perspectives:

- Connection establishment
- Connection maintenance
- Routing information accuracy

BGP takes advantage of the reliable transport service provided by Transmission Control Protocol (TCP). This eliminates the need in BGP to implement update fragmentation, retransmission, acknowledgment, and sequencing, because TCP takes care of these functions. Additionally, any authentication scheme used by TCP may be used for BGP.

After the session is established, BGP uses regular keepalives to maintain session integrity. Update messages also reset the hold timer, which is typically three times the keepalive timer. A BGP session is closed if three consecutive keepalives are missed and no Update messages are received.

Accurate routing information is important for reliable forwarding. BGP uses several measures to increase accuracy. When updates are received, *AS_PATH* (a BGP attribute that lists the autonomous systems the route has traversed) is checked to detect loops. Updates sourced from the current AS or that have passed through the AS are denied. Inbound filters can be applied to all updates that ensure conformance to local policies. Reachability of the next hop is regularly verified before a BGP route is considered valid.

To maintain the accuracy of the routing information, it is also important to remove unreachable routes in a timely manner. BGP withdraws them promptly from the peers as the routes become unreachable.

Stability

A routing protocol's stability is critical for large networks. Given the size of the current Internet, flapping of large numbers of routes can be catastrophic.

By implementing various timers, BGP suppresses the impact of interface or route up/down events on the network. For example, a BGP speaker can generate updates up to only the Minimal Advertisement Interval. In Cisco IOS software, the interval is 30 seconds for external BGP (eBGP) sessions and 5 seconds for internal BGP (iBGP) sessions, plus some jitters to avoid synchronization of updates. The subject of eBGP versus iBGP is discussed in Chapter 2, "Understanding BGP Building Blocks."

Route dampening is another BGP feature that suppresses instability. The router tracks a route's flapping history. Unstable routes are penalized and are subject to suppression. Route dampening is discussed in several chapters of this book.

Stability can be increased if sessions do not have to be reset when a policy changes. Features such as soft reconfiguration and route refresh, both of which are covered in Chapter 3, "Tuning BGP Performance," are useful for changing BGP policy without resetting the BGP session. Both of these features allow new updates to be requested or sent dynamically.

If a session must be reset, all BGP routing and forwarding information for that session is cleared. This might lead to packet loss until a new forwarding database is built. Nonstop Forwarding (NSF) or Graceful Restart allows a router to continue forwarding with the existing information (retained from the previous session) while the session is being reset. NSF is discussed in detail in Chapter 3.

Convergence is the process in which a network synchronizes to the same routing information after a change in the network. A network that is not converged can lead to packet loss or forwarding loops. However, stability can be reduced if a network is in a constant state of convergence. A proper balance of stability and convergence can be dependent on the services a network provides. For example, when BGP is used to provide virtual private network (VPN) services over a shared Multiprotocol Label Switching (MPLS) network, there might be more emphasis on convergence. Chapter 10, "Multiprotocol BGP and MPLS VPN," provides detailed discussions of this subject. The discussion of BGP convergence tuning is presented in detail in Chapter 3.

Scalability

You can evaluate BGP's scalability in two areas: the number of peer sessions and the number of routes. Depending on the configuration, hardware platform (CPU and memory), and Cisco IOS release, BGP has been proven to support hundreds of peer sessions and to maintain well over 100,000 routes.

Several measures are available to increase BGP scalability. These measures reduce either the number of routes/paths to be maintained or the number of updates to be generated.

As a form of distance vector protocol, BGP updates its peers only with the paths it uses. In other words, only the best paths are advertised to its peers. When the best path changes, the new path is advertised, which lets peers know to replace the previous best path with the new best path. This action is an implicit withdrawal of the previous best path.

When BGP is used to exchange reachability information within the same AS, all BGP speakers are required to be fully meshed. Because fully meshed networks tend to limit scalability because of the number of sessions that must be maintained on each router and the number of updates that must be generated, route reflection and confederation are two methods that increase the scalability of BGP networks. Detailed discussions of these methods are included in Chapter 7, "Scalable iBGP Design and Implementation Guidelines," Chapter 8, "Route Reflection and Confederation Migration Strategies," and Chapter 10.

Aggregation of routes is another tool that BGP uses to reduce the number of prefixes to be advertised and increase stability. Proper aggregation is, in fact, a requirement in the Internet, as discussed in Chapter 6, "Internet Connectivity for Enterprise Networks."

Lowering the number of updates to be generated reduces CPU utilization and enables faster convergence. In IOS, peers that have the same outbound policy can be grouped in a peer group or update group. One update is generated and then replicated for the entire group. The subject of performance improvement using update grouping is discussed in detail in Chapter 3.

Flexibility

BGP is a path vector protocol, a form of distance vector protocol that constructs an abstract graph of autonomous systems for each destination. BGP's flexibility is demonstrated in the number of path attributes that can be used to define policies. BGP path attributes are parameters that describe characteristics of a BGP prefix. Because the attributes are what make BGP unique, they are discussed throughout this book.

You can define two types of policies for BGP: routing and administrative. These policies often overlap in their functionality.

You can define a BGP routing policy for either the inbound or outbound direction to affect route or path selection. For example, an inbound filtering policy can be defined to accept routes that originate only from the immediate upstream provider and customers of that provider. With proper setting of some attributes, one path can be made to be preferred over others. Detailed examples of setting routing policies are provided in the rest of this book.

A BGP administrative policy defines administrative controls for routes coming into the AS or leaving the AS. For example, an AS might intend to protect its border routers by limiting the maximum number of prefixes it allows itself to receive. On the outbound side, as another example, a border router of a multihomed AS might choose to set its attribute in such a way that only locally originated routes are advertised.

To enforce policies, BGP uses a three-step process:

1 Input policy engine

2 Path selection

3 Output policy engine

Figure 1-1 illustrates this process.

Figure 1-1   *BGP Policy Engines and Path Selection: A Conceptual Model*

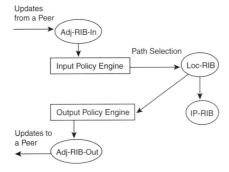

As updates are received from a peer, they are stored in a Routing Information Base (RIB) for that peer (Adj-RIB-In). The updates are filtered by the Input Policy Engine. A path selection algorithm is then performed to determine the best path for each prefix, as discussed in detail in Chapter 2.

The resulting best paths are stored in the local BGP RIB (Loc-RIB) and then are submitted to the local IP routing table (IP-RIB) for installation consideration. Chapter 2 discusses the IP-RIB installation process.

When multipath is enabled, the best path plus all equal-cost paths are submitted for IP-RIB consideration.

In addition to the best paths received from peers, the Loc-RIB also contains BGP prefixes injected by the current router (called *locally sourced*) that are selected as the best paths. The content of the Loc-RIB must pass through the Output Policy Engine before being advertised to other peers. The routes that successfully pass through the Output Policy Engine are installed in the output RIB (Adj-RIB-Out).

This discussion of RIBs is a conceptual overview. Actual update processing can vary depending on the BGP implementation and configuration. In Cisco IOS, the BGP table or the BGP RIB (the output of **show ip bgp**) contains all the routes that are permitted by the Input Policy Engine, including routes that are not selected as the best paths. When the Inbound Soft Reset IOS feature (soft reconfiguration) is enabled, routes that are denied by the Input Policy Engine are also retained (marked as *Receive only*) but are not considered in the path-selection process. The use of soft reconfiguration is discussed in Chapter 3.

Comparing BGP and IGP

When discussing BGP, it is important to understand the difference between an Interior Gateway Protocol (IGP) and BGP (an example of an Exterior Gateway Protocol). An IGP is designed to provide reachability information within a single routing domain.

Three types of IGPs are commonly used in networks today:

- Distance vector protocols such as Routing Information Protocol (RIP) and Interior Gateway Routing Protocol (IGRP)

- Link-state protocols such as Open Shortest Path First (OSPF) and Intermediate System-to-Intermediate System (IS-IS)

- Hybrid protocols such as Enhanced IGRP (EIGRP)

Although these protocols are designed with different goals and behave differently, the common goal is path optimization within a routing domain—that is, finding an optimal path to a given destination.

An IGP has some or all of the following characteristics:

- It performs topology discovery
- It strives to achieve fast convergence
- It requires periodic updates to ensure routing information accuracy
- It is under the same administrative control
- It assumes a common routing policy
- It provides limited policy control capability

Because of these characteristics, an IGP is not suitable to provide interdomain routing. For example, an interdomain routing protocol should be able to provide extensive policy control, because different domains often require different routing and administrative policies. As another example, periodic refresh of IGP routes is not scalable when the number of prefixes is at the Internet level.

From the start, BGP was designed to be an interdomain protocol. Two of the most important design goals were policy control capability and scalability. However, BGP typically is not suitable to replace an IGP because of its slower response to topology changes. When BGP is used to provide intradomain reachability, such as in an MPLS VPN, BGP tunings are often needed to reduce the convergence time.

Both IGP and BGP have their place. When designing networks, it is important to use both types of protocols appropriately. A more detailed comparison of BGP and IGP is provided in Chapter 2.

This chapter covers the following topics:

- Comparing the control plane and forwarding plane
- BGP processes and memory use
- BGP path attributes
- Understanding internal BGP
- Path decision process
- BGP capabilities
- BGP-IGP routing exchange
- Routing information base
- Switching paths

CHAPTER 2

Understanding BGP Building Blocks

The purpose of this chapter is to lay the groundwork for the rest of this book. No attempt is made to cover all the basics of BGP, but some of the fundamental BGP components and concepts are highlighted in this chapter to give you the proper perspective. Wherever appropriate, updated information is provided. Specifically, this chapter tries to achieve the following objectives:

- Provide an overview of Cisco's implementation of BGP, such as BGP processes in IOS. A case study on how to estimate BGP memory use in Cisco routers is presented near the end of this chapter.

- Review fundamental BGP components, such as BGP attributes, the BGP decision process, BGP capabilities exchange, the Routing Information Base (RIB), and so on.

- Discuss some of the basic BGP concepts, such as iBGP and BGP and IGP routing exchange.

- Provide an overview of the major switching paths available in Cisco IOS software and how they relate to the performance of BGP and routers because of resource contention.

Comparing the Control Plane and Forwarding Plane

A router consists of two logical components: the control plane and the forwarding plane. The *control plane* is responsible for building a RIB, which the *forwarding plane* can use to classify and forward packets.

A router's performance is closely tied to the performance of both of these planes and how effectively they coordinate. In a routing architecture design, it is important to understand the interactions of both planes in regards to packet forwarding and resource contention.

The interaction of the control plane and the forwarding plane and the resulting effect on BGP performance can be shown in the following example. Processing of BGP protocol packets involves a lot of computation and data manipulation, especially during convergence. Thus, BGP competes for CPU time with other processes running on the router. Reducing the number of transit packets (those not directed to the router) being process-switched (a CPU-intensive operation) by the router can improve BGP performance, especially during initial convergence. This is because more CPU cycles are available for BGP.

A router can use many sources of information to build its RIB. In an internetworked environment such as the Internet, routing information is exchanged via a variety of dynamic routing protocols, which can be Interior Gateway Protocols (IGPs) or Exterior Gateway Protocols (EGPs). Timely distribution of correct routing information throughout the network is a major component in building a reliable network. Later chapters examine various techniques to optimize BGP routing architectures for convergence, policy control, and scalability.

Within the forwarding plane are two major functions: packet classification and packet forwarding. *Packet classification* is the process of condensing the RIB into a forwarding information base (FIB). A typical FIB is organized around destination prefixes, with each prefix associated with a next-hop address, outgoing interface, and so on. Actual *packet forwarding* is performed by the switching component of the forwarding plane. Specifically, the router uses the prefix as the key to perform a lookup operation to produce the next-hop address, outgoing interface, and Layer 2 header, which depends on the type of outgoing interface.

BGP Processes and Memory Use

Cisco IOS software has three main BGP processes:

- I/O
- Router
- Scanner

Figure 2-1 shows the three BGP processes and the interactions among all the major BGP components in IOS.

Figure 2-1 *BGP Processes in IOS*

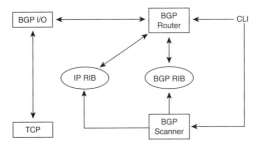

The BGP I/O process handles reading, writing, and executing BGP messages. It provides the interface between TCP and BGP. On one hand, it reads messages from the TCP socket and puts them into the BGP input queue (InQ) to be processed by the BGP Router process.

On the other hand, messages accumulated in the output queue (OutQ) are moved by the BGP I/O to the TCP socket.

The BGP Router process is a main BGP process that is responsible for initiating other BGP processes, maintaining BGP sessions with neighbors, processing incoming updates from peers and locally sourced networks, updating the IP RIB with BGP entries, and sending updates to peers. Specifically, the BGP Router process receives commands entered from Common Line Interface (CLI) via the parser. It interacts with the BGP I/O process for update processing (sending and receiving) using per-neighbor queues, as shown in Example 2-1. After all valid paths are installed into the BGP RIB, the BGP Router runs the path selection and installs the best paths into the IP RIB. Events happening in the IP RIB and the BGP RIB can also trigger appropriate actions in the BGP Router process. For example, when a route needs to be redistributed from another protocol to BGP, IP RIB notifies the BGP Router to update the BGP RIB.

Example 2-1 *BGP Queues*

```
router#show ip bgp summary
BGP router identifier 192.168.100.6, local AS number 100
BGP table version is 8, main routing table version 8
4 network entries and 7 paths using 668 bytes of memory
3 BGP path attribute entries using 180 bytes of memory
6 BGP rrinfo entries using 144 bytes of memory
1 BGP AS-PATH entries using 24 bytes of memory
0 BGP route-map cache entries using 0 bytes of memory
0 BGP filter-list cache entries using 0 bytes of memory
BGP activity 4/74 prefixes, 11/4 paths, scan interval 60 secs

Neighbor        V    AS MsgRcvd MsgSent   TblVer  InQ OutQ Up/Down  State/PfxRcd
192.168.100.4   4   100    1120    1119        8    0    0 17:12:34            3
192.168.100.5   4   100    1114    1111        8    0    0 00:07:35            3
```

The primary function of the BGP Scanner process is BGP housekeeping. Specifically, the BGP Scanner performs periodic scans of the BGP RIB to determine if prefixes and attributes should be deleted and if route map or filter caches should be flushed. This process also scans the IP RIB to ensure that all the BGP next hops are still valid. If the next hop is unreachable, all BGP entries using that next hop are removed from the BGP RIB. BGP dampening information is also updated in each cycle. General scanning is performed every 60 seconds. BGP Scanner also accepts commands from CLI via the parser to change its scan time.

Example 2-2 is a snapshot of the BGP processes and memory use in a Cisco 12000 router. The Allocated column shows the total number of bytes allocated since the creation of the process. The Freed column provides the number of bytes the process has freed since its creation. The Holding column shows the actual memory that is being consumed by the process at the moment. In this example, the BGP router process holds more than 34 MB of memory, whereas BGP I/O and BGP Scanner hold 6 KB each.

Example 2-2 *BGP Processes and Memory Use*

```
router#show process memory | include BGP

PID TTY  Allocated     Freed    Holding   Getbufs   Retbufs Process
  99   0  171331064  28799944   34023220         0         0 BGP Router
 100   0     131064  22748136       6796         0         0 BGP I/O
 101   0          0   6814116       6796         0         0 BGP Scanner
```

As indicated in the example, the BGP Router process accounts for the majority of BGP's memory use (the Holding column). The memory use for both the BGP I/O and BGP Scanner processes are insignificant. Three major components in the BGP Router process account for the bulk of its memory use:

- BGP RIB
- IP RIB for BGP learned prefixes
- IP switching component for BGP learned prefixes

The information held in the BGP RIB includes network entries, path entries, path attributes, and route map and filter list caches. The memory used to store this information can be found in the **show ip bgp summary** output.

BGP learned prefixes in the IP RIB are stored in two types of structures:

- Network Descriptor Blocks (NDBs)
- Routing Descriptor Blocks (RDBs)

Each route in the IP RIB requires one NDB and one RDB per path. If the route is subnetted, additional memory is required to maintain the NDB. The direct memory use for IP RIB can be shown using the **show ip route summary** command.

The third major element of the BGP Router process with significant memory demand is the IP switching component, such as FIB structures. Switching paths are discussed later in this chapter.

The BGP Router process also requires a small amount of memory for its own operation in addition to what is required to store the routing information; however, the amount of memory for the process alone is approximately 40 KB and therefore is insignificant compared to the overall memory consumed by the BGP router process. The case study near the end of this chapter provides a detailed examination of these components' memory use.

BGP Path Attributes

BGP path attributes are a set of parameters describing the characteristics of a BGP prefix. Because BGP is foremost a routing policy tool, BGP makes extensive use of these attributes in influencing the path selection. Effective use of these attributes is critical in designing an effective BGP routing architecture. This section highlights some of the common BGP attributes, with more-detailed discussion in later chapters.

The following attributes currently are supported in Cisco IOS software:

- ORIGIN
- AS_PATH
- NEXT_HOP
- MULTI_EXIT_DISC
- LOCAL_PREF
- ATOMIC_AGGREGATE
- AGGREGATOR
- COMMUNITY
- ORIGINATOR_ID
- CLUSTER_LIST
- Multiprotocol Reachable NLRI (MP_REACH_NLRI)
- Multiprotocol Unreachable NLRI (MP_UNREACH_NLRI)

The following is a brief overview of some of the more common BGP attributes. Additional attributes are discussed in later chapters.

ORIGIN

This attribute indicates a prefix's source. There are three possible origins:

- **IGP**—ORIGIN of 0
- **EGP**—ORIGIN of 1
- **INCOMPLETE**—ORIGIN of 3

A prefix with a lower ORIGIN value is preferred during a path selection. A prefix's ORIGIN attribute is automatically defined when a prefix is injected into BGP but can be modified through the use of a route map. For example, if a prefix is redistributed into BGP using the **redistribute** command, its ORIGIN is set to 3; if a prefix is injected into BGP via the **network** command, its origin is set to 0. In effect, routes originated by the **network** command are preferred over those that are redistributed.

AS_PATH

AS_PATH lists in reverse order the autonomous systems traversed by a prefix, with the last AS placed at the beginning of the list. The primary purpose of the AS_PATH is to provide loop prevention for inter-AS routing. The accepted number of autonomous systems in the list is between 1 and 255. Prepending the same AS number to the list is a common method of influencing inbound path selection, because the path with the shortest list is preferred. Four types of AS segments within the AS_PATH are supported in Cisco IOS software:

- AS_SET
- AS_SEQUENCE
- AS_CONFED_SET
- AS_CONFED_SEQUENCE

The difference between SET and SEQUENCE is that the list of autonomous systems is unordered (with regard to the autonomous systems traversed in the path) in a SET and is ordered in a SEQUENCE. The latter two apply only to paths originated within the local confederation. Additionally, they are counted differently in path selection, as discussed in the section "Path Decision Process."

NEXT_HOP

This attribute defines the next-hop IP address to reach a prefix from the BGP point of view. This does not necessarily mean that the next hop is directly connected. If the BGP next hop is not the immediate next hop, a recursive route lookup in the IP RIB is needed. A prefix must have a reachable next hop before BGP considers it in the best path selection. In other words, the next hop must be under a prefix in the routing table, including the 0.0.0.0/0. There are three points at which the next-hop attribute for a BGP path is commonly set:

- When the prefix is first injected into BGP, the next hop is set by the BGP speaker that injects the prefix. The next hop's value depends on how the prefix is injected. If the prefix is injected by the **aggregate-address** command, the prefix's BGP next hop is the BGP speaker doing the aggregation. If the prefix is injected by the **network** command or redistribution, the IGP next hop before the injection becomes the BGP next hop. For example, if an OSPF prefix is redistributed into BGP, the BGP next hop is not necessarily the BGP speaker doing the redistribution, but rather is the original next hop of the OSPF prefix. Thus, in this case, it is advisable to reset the next hop at the redistribution point to the BGP speaker itself. If the IGP next hop does not exist (such as in the case of a route pointing to the Null0 interface), the next hop is the BGP speaker itself. If the local BGP speaker becomes the next hop, the next-hop field in the BGP RIB is 0.0.0.0. The next hop in the outgoing updates is set to the local BGP peering address.

- When the prefix is advertised via eBGP, the next hop is automatically set to the IP address of the eBGP peer that is sending the prefix. If three or more peers are sharing the same multiaccess network, however, the advertising speaker sets the original speaker on the same segment as the next hop, rather than itself. This is called *third-party next hop*.

- The next hop is manually changed through the use of a route map or **next-hop-self** command. Note that the next hop is not changed by default for a BGP session within the same AS.

MULTI_EXIT_DISC

The MULTI_EXIT_DISC (MED) attribute is typically used on inter-AS links to discriminate among multiple exit/entry points to the same neighboring AS. Cisco IOS software also allows you to compare MEDs among different autonomous systems using the **bgp always-compare-med** command. MED values are expressed as metric values. In a manner consistent with metrics, the path with a lower MED is preferred.

In Cisco IOS software, the following are some of the rules on MED setting and advertisement:

- If a route is learned from an iBGP peer, the border router removes the MED before advertising the route to an eBGP peer. To force the border router to advertise the MED in such a case, the route-map **set metric-type internal** command can be configured for that eBGP peer.

- Routes injected into BGP locally on a border router are advertised to an eBGP peer with MED. The metric values are determined as follows:
  - If the injected BGP route, using the **network** or **redistribute** command, is from an IGP, the BGP MED is derived from the IGP metric.
  - If the injected BGP route (using the **network** or **redistribute** command) is from a connected route, the BGP MED is set to 0.
  - If the route is injected by the **aggregate-address** command, MED is not set.

LOCAL_PREF

LOCAL_PREF is an attribute used by an iBGP speaker to calculate a degree of preference for each external route. It is exchanged between iBGP peers to set a preferred exit point out of an AS. The path with a higher LOCAL_PREF is preferred. This attribute is not included in eBGP prefix advertisements (typically set administratively in incoming eBGP updates) and is used only inside an AS for path selection manipulation. In comparison, MED is sent from one AS to another neighboring AS on an eBGP link to affect the outbound policy of the receiving AS.

NOTE   In Cisco IOS software, another parameter, WEIGHT, can also influence path selection. This parameter is Cisco-proprietary and is local to the router on which it is configured. That is, the WEIGHT setting is not exchanged between routers.

COMMUNITY

A *community* is defined as a group of prefixes that share a common property. Multiple communities can be applied to a prefix, each community being 4 bytes. Two types of communities exist:

- **Well-known communities**—When receiving prefixes with these communities, peers take actions automatically based on the predefined meanings of the communities. No additional configurations are needed. In RFC 1997, the well-known communities fall in the range of reserved values, which are from 0xFFFF0000 through 0xFFFFFFFF.

- **Private communities**—Communities can be defined by the administrators and must be coordinated between peers of the different autonomous systems. Actions must be specifically configured. Private communities have values outside the reserved range.

Currently, four well-known communities are supported in Cisco IOS software:

- **NO_EXPORT**—Prefixes with this community should not be advertised to eBGP peers but can be sent to subautonomous systems within the same confederation. The value of this community is 0xFFFFFF01.

- **LOCAL_AS**—Do not advertise these prefixes outside the local AS. With confederation, only peers within the same sub-AS are allowed to receive these prefixes. Without confederation, LOCAL_AS is treated the same as NO_EXPORT. In RFC 1997, NO_EXPORT_SUBCONFED (0xFFFFFF03) is defined for this purpose.

- **NO_ADVERTISE**—Do not advertise prefixes with this community to any peer, internal or external. The value of this community is 0xFFFFFF02.

- **INTERNET**—Advertise the prefixes to the Internet community. In other words, there are no restrictions. This well-known community is not specifically defined in RFC 1997. In Cisco IOS software, the INTERNET community (with a value of 0) is one that every prefix is part of.

More commonly used communities are private communities. The main objective of using them is to attach administrative tags to prefixes so that proper policies can be created. The private community uses the format of *AS:number*, where *AS* is the local AS number or a peer AS and *number* is an arbitrary number administered locally or with peers to represent a community grouping to which a policy may be applied. This user-friendly format is enabled by **ip bgp-community new-format** in global configuration mode.

ORIGINATOR_ID

ORIGINATOR_ID is used as a loop-prevention mechanism inside an AS when route reflectors (RRs) are deployed. It is created by the first RR and is not modified by subsequent RRs. ORIGINATOR_ID is the router ID of either of the following:

- The BGP speaker that originates the route in the local AS, such as routes injected using the **network** command.
- The BGP border router of the same AS if the route is learned via eBGP.

The ORIGINATOR_ID is 32 bits long and should be received only from iBGP peers. On an RR, the ORIGINATOR_ID is used in place of the router ID in the path selection. When an iBGP speaker receives updates containing its own ORIGINATOR_ID, it discards the routes, breaking the routing information loop. A BGP speaker should not create an ORIGINATOR_ID attribute if one already exists.

CLUSTER_LIST

CLUSTER_LIST is another loop-prevention mechanism inside an AS when RRs are deployed. This attribute records the list of CLUSTER_IDs that a prefix has traversed in an RR environment. When an RR reflects a route from its clients to nonclients outside the cluster, from nonclients to clients, or from one client to another client, it prepends the local CLUSTER_ID to the CLUSTER_LIST. If the update has an empty CLUSTER_LIST, the RR creates one. Using this attribute, an RR can identify if the routing information is looped back to the same cluster. If the local CLUSTER_ID is found in the CLUSTER_LIST, the update is discarded, breaking the routing information loop. A detailed discussion of the configuration and design of CLUSTER_LIST and CLUSTER_ID is presented in Chapter 7, "Scalable iBGP Design and Implementation Guidelines."

Understanding Internal BGP

BGP was designed to provide a loop-free path among a series of autonomous systems on the Internet. The mechanism to ensure a loop-free topology is the AS_PATH attribute. Consider Figure 2-2, in which three autonomous systems are interconnected. If router R1 in AS 65000 advertises a prefix to R3 in AS 65001, R1 prepends 65000 to the AS_PATH list for the prefix when it sends the prefix to R3. If that same prefix is received by AS 65000 again, a border BGP speaker rejects the prefix, because it detects a loop in the AS_PATH attribute.

Figure 2-2 *Prefix Propagation in a Multi-AS Topology*

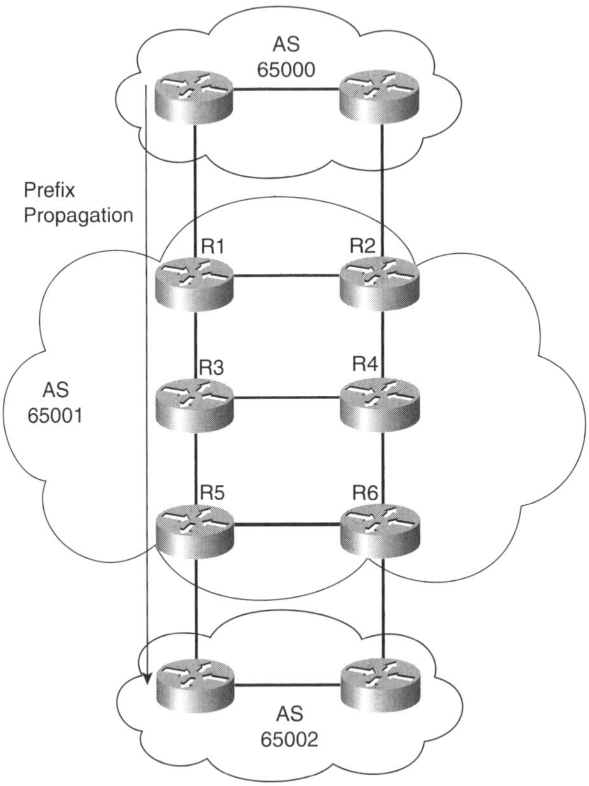

Continuing with Figure 2-2, assume that R3 needs to propagate the prefix to R7 in AS 65002. There are a couple of options to achieve that.

One option is to have R3 redistribute all the BGP prefixes into the IGP, which advertises them to R4, R5, and R6. Next, have R5 and R6 redistribute these prefixes back into BGP, and advertise them to their respective eBGP neighbors, R7 and R8. There are a few issues with this strategy.

IGPs were not designed to handle the number of routes that would be involved. The full Internet table has more than 100,000 prefixes. The periodic refresh of prefix information that many IGPs require could further result in network instability, additional system resource consumption, and significant bandwidth requirements on a regular basis for routing updates. The increased number of prefixes results in a greater probability of route flapping, which can lead to significant stability and convergence issues.

BGP information that is redistributed into the IGP results in a loss of all BGP attributes, including the AS_PATH. The loss of the AS_PATH attribute defeats the BGP loop-prevention mechanism. For example, when the prefix is redistributed back into BGP in R4, the same prefix is sent back to R2, because the AS_PATH contains only 65001. Redistribution also results in the loss of any policy attributes that have been set for the BGP learned prefixes.

The preferred option is to use internal BGP (iBGP). When R3 advertises the prefixes to R5 via iBGP, R3 does not add its own AS number in the AS_PATH. In fact, Cisco IOS software does not even check for AS_PATH loops if updates come from an iBGP peer. Without the additional AS_PATH information, a routing information loop can form within the iBGP domain.

The loop is avoided if R3 is allowed to advertise the prefix to R5 but R5 is not allowed to advertise a prefix learned via iBGP to another iBGP peer, such as R4 and R6. However, this solution requires that all iBGP speakers be fully meshed. For example, R3 is required to have iBGP sessions with R4, R5, and R6. In an AS that has a large number of iBGP speakers, a full mesh can present a scalability issue. Solutions to this issue involving route reflection and confederation are covered in detail in Chapter 7.

The use of iBGP to transport prefix information brings to light another issue. Is an IGP even needed if BGP can transport all the prefixes?

An IGP is definitely required. In Figure 2-2, R3 is not directly connected to R6. How will R3 form an iBGP session without some form of routing information to reach R6? The answer is to have an IGP provide infrastructure reachability inside the autonomous system. Internal BGP was never designed to exist without an IGP, but in conjunction with an IGP. An iBGP route is often recursively resolved using an IGP. Table 2-1 shows a few ways in which iBGP differs from an IGP.

Table 2-1   *Comparison of iBGP and IGP*

IGP	iBGP
Changes a prefix's next hop at each router to point to a directly connected address.	Does not change a prefix's next-hop attribute.
Automatically discovers and forms neighbor relationships.	Requires manual configuration.
Provides information about how to traverse a given AS or reach a given location.	Provides information about what is available at a location, without indicating how to reach it.

After you examine the differences between iBGP and IGPs, it is also important to understand the fundamental differences between iBGP and eBGP (see Table 2-2).

Table 2-2 *Comparison of iBGP and eBGP*

iBGP	eBGP
Peering inside an AS must consist of a full mesh, because an iBGP speaker is not allowed to pass on prefixes learned from one iBGP peer to another iBGP peer.	Has no full-mesh requirement.
Advertises the LOCAL_PREF attribute, which eBGP does not. Does not modify the next hop and AS_PATH (exceptions are discussed in Chapter 7). Next-hop reachability within the AS is provided by an IGP.	Modifies next-hop and AS_PATH attributes.
Does not require direct connectivity, because iBGP uses an IGP to allow reachability to a remote next hop.	Requires direct connectivity by default. In almost all cases, a common IGP is not shared between eBGP peers. Cisco IOS software provides a workaround to this requirement with the use of eBGP multihop.
Requires prefix synchronization between iBGP and IGP to prevent routing loops and black-holing of traffic. *Prefix synchronization* means that a prefix learned via iBGP is not included in the best-path selection unless that same prefix exists in the IGP. If the IGP is OSPF, the router ID for the prefix in the IGP must also match the router ID of the BGP peer advertising the prefix. Synchronization may be disabled if this AS does not provide transit for another AS or if all routers in the transit path are running BGP. It is generally a good practice to disable prefix synchronization.	Has no synchronization requirement.
Routes from iBGP are not redistributed into an IGP by default, even if the redistribution from BGP into the IGP is configured, because this could result in routing loops. If it is mandatory that iBGP prefixes be redistributed into an IGP, IOS provides the **bgp redistribute-internal** command.	Has no such restriction.

Path Decision Process

BGP steps through a complex algorithm to determine the best path and updates the BGP RIB and IP RIB. As mentioned earlier, BGP is a policy tool. The significance of this is best shown by how BGP uses attributes and other parameters to select the best path.

When multiple valid BGP paths to a particular destination exist, IOS lists them in the reverse order in which they were received. That is, the newest path is listed at the beginning, and the oldest path is listed at the end. In the output of **show ip bgp**, the newest path is listed at the top, and the oldest path is listed at the bottom. To select the best path for a given destination, BGP generally uses a sequential comparison method. It assigns the first path (the newest path) as the current best path. It then compares the current best path to the next path in the list until it reaches the end of the list of valid paths. For example, for three paths received sequentially—1, 2, and 3—BGP first compares paths 3 (received last) and 2. The resulting best path is then compared to path 1 (received first). The best path of the second comparison becomes the final best path for the destination.

A path is not a valid candidate in the best-path selection process if it meets any of the following conditions:

- The path's next hop is unreachable
- The path is not synchronized, and synchronization is enabled
- The path is denied by inbound BGP policies, and inbound soft reset is configured
- The route is dampened

Path selection in Cisco IOS software currently has 13 steps (www.cisco.com/warp/customer/459/25.shtml). Each step is evaluated sequentially until a preference is found:

1 WEIGHT is the first parameter considered. The path with the highest WEIGHT is preferred. WEIGHT is a Cisco-proprietary parameter and is local to the router on which it is configured. By default, paths originated locally have an equal WEIGHT of 32768, and all other paths have a WEIGHT of 0.

2 The path with the highest LOCAL_PREF is preferred. The default LOCAL_PREF is 100 in Cisco IOS software.

3 The routes are evaluated based on the origination, with preference to the path that was sourced locally on the router. Here is the complete order with decreasing preference: **default-originate** (configured per neighbor), **default-information originate** (configured per address family), **network**, **redistribute**, **aggregate-address**.

4 The length of AS_PATH is evaluated, with preference to the path with the shortest AS_PATH list. However, the configuration of **bgp bestpath as-path ignore** (a hidden command) bypasses this step.

Keep the following in mind when evaluating the path length:

- An AS_SET is counted as 1, no matter how many autonomous systems are in the set.
- The AS_CONFED_SEQUENCE is not included in the AS_PATH length.

5 The route's ORIGIN is evaluated here, with preference to the path with the lowest ORIGIN type. IGP is lower than EGP, and EGP is lower than INCOMPLETE.

6 MED is evaluated. The path with the lowest MED wins. By default, this comparison is done only if the first (neighboring) AS is the same in the two paths; any confederation subautonomous systems are ignored. In other words, MEDs are compared only if the first AS in the AS_SEQUENCE is the same for multiple paths. Any preceding AS_CONFED_SEQUENCE is ignored. If **bgp always-compare-med** is enabled, MEDs are compared for all paths, regardless of whether they come from the same AS. If you enable this option, you should do so over the entire AS to avoid routing loops. Note the following MED modification options:

- With **bgp deterministic-med**, the result of a MED comparison is consistent regardless of the order in which prefixes are being received. With this configuration, all paths are grouped based on AS_PATH. Within each group of the AS_PATH, paths are sorted by MED. A path with the lowest MED is selected for each group. The final best path is the path with the lowest MED among all the selected paths. This is the recommended configuration if MED is present.

- If **bgp bestpath med-confed** is enabled, MEDs are compared for all paths that consist only of AS_CONFED_SEQUENCE—that is, paths originated within the local confederation. Note that if a path consists of any external autonomous systems, this path is not considered in the comparison, and its MED is passed unchanged inside the confederation.

- Paths received with no MED are assigned a metric of 0, unless **bgp bestpath missing-as-worst** is enabled, in which case they are assigned a value of 4,294,967,294 (the maximum). This is for compatibility with the old standard.

7 External (eBGP) paths are preferred over internal (iBGP) paths. Paths containing AS_CONFED_SEQUENCE are local to the confederation and therefore are treated as internal paths. There is no distinction between Confederation External and Confederation Internal in path selection.

8 BGP prefers the path with the lowest IGP metric to the BGP next hop. This step allows the local topology to be taken into consideration.

9 If **maximum-paths** [**ibgp**] *n* is enabled, where *n* is between 2 and 6, and multiple equal-cost paths exist (the results from Steps 1 through 6 are the same among the paths, and AS_PATH is identical), BGP inserts up to *n* received paths in the IP routing table. This allows BGP multipath load sharing. Without the optional keyword **ibgp**, multipath applies only to eBGP or confederation external paths from the same neighboring AS or sub-AS. The default value of *n*, when this option is not enabled, is 1.

10 When both paths are external, BGP prefers the path that was received first (the oldest one). This step minimizes route flap, because a newer path does not replace an older one, even if it is the preferred route based on additional decision criteria, as described in steps 11, 12, and 13.

This step is skipped if any of the following are true:

- The **bgp bestpath compare-routerid** command is enabled.

- The router ID is the same for multiple paths, because the routes were received from the same router.

- There is no current best path. An example of losing the current best path occurs when the neighbor advertising the path goes down.

11 BGP prefers the route coming from the BGP router with the lowest router ID. The router ID is the highest IP address on the router, with preference given to loopback addresses. It can also be set statically using the **bgp router-id** command. If a path contains RR attributes, the ORIGINATOR_ID is substituted for the router ID in the path selection process.

12 If the originator or router ID is the same for multiple paths, BGP prefers the path with the minimum CLUSTER_LIST length. This is present only in BGP RR environments. When peered with RRs or clients in other clusters, a client can use the CLUSTER_LIST length to select the best path. To take advantage of this step, the client must be aware of the RR-specific BGP attributes.

13 BGP prefers the path coming from the lowest neighbor address. This is the IP address used in the BGP **neighbor** configuration, and it corresponds to the remote peer used in the TCP connection with the local router.

BGP Capabilities

BGP, as defined in RFC 1771, can carry only IPv4 reachability information between peers. To exchange network prefix information other than IPv4, BGP must be extended. This is accomplished by the capabilities exchange and attribute extension. This section covers only the capabilities exchange. Various attribute extensions are covered starting in Chapter 10.

As defined in RFC 1771, BGP supports the following four types of messages:

- **Open**—This type of message is used to set up the initial BGP connections.

- **Update**—These messages are used between peers to exchange network layer reachability information.

- **Notification**—These messages are used to communicate error conditions.

- **Keepalive**—These messages are exchanged periodically between a pair of peers to keep the session up.

Within the Open message is a field for Optional Parameters where additional optional information can be negotiated during session setup. The addition of the Capabilities Optional Parameter (Parameter Type 2) in RFC 3392 allows a pair of BGP speakers to negotiate a common set of capabilities.

Here are some of the capabilities that are supported in Cisco IOS software:

- Capability code 1, Multiprotocol extension
- Capability code 2, Route refresh
- Capability code 64, Graceful restart
- Capability code 128, Old form of route refresh
- Capability code 130, Outbound Route Filter (ORF)

The subject of multiprotocol BGP is covered in Chapter 10 through Appendix A. Route refresh, graceful restart, and ORF are covered in Chapter 3, "Tuning BGP Performance."

To support addresses other than IPv4, various address families (AFs) are defined (RFC 1700). Examples of supported address families are IPv4 and IPv6. Within each address family, subsequent address family identifiers (SAFIs) are further defined. Within the IPv4 address family, for example, the following SAFIs are defined:

- Unicast, SAFI code 1
- Multicast, SAFI code 2
- IPv4 Label, SAFI code 4
- Labeled VPNv4 Unicast, SAFI code 128

Within each supported capability, a peer may advertise the AFs and SAFIs that are supported. Only the common capabilities are used during session setup.

Example 2-3 shows an example of BGP capabilities as part of the **show ip bgp neighbor** output. Four capabilities are exchanged (advertised and received): route refresh (both old and new forms), IPv4 Unicast, IPv4 Label, and IPv4 ORF (shown under IPv4 address family).

Example 2-3 *Example of BGP Capabilities*

```
router#show ip bgp neighbor | begin cap
  Neighbor capabilities:
    Route refresh: advertised and received(old & new)
    Address family IPv4 Unicast: advertised and received
    IPv4 MPLS Label capability: advertised and received
  Received 1355 messages, 0 notifications, 0 in queue
  Sent 1354 messages, 0 notifications, 0 in queue
  Default minimum time between advertisement runs is 30 seconds

 For address family: IPv4 Unicast
  BGP table version 5, neighbor version 5
  Index 1, Offset 0, Mask 0x2
  AF-dependant capabilities:
    Outbound Route Filter (ORF) type (128) Prefix-list:
      Send-mode: advertised, received
      Receive-mode: advertised, received
```

Example 2-3   *Example of BGP Capabilities (Continued)*

```
     Route refresh request: received 1, sent 1
     Sending Prefix & Label
     1 accepted prefixes consume 48 bytes
     Prefix advertised 6, suppressed 0, withdrawn 0
 ...
```

NOTE   Because capabilities currently are negotiated only during session setup, capabilities
configured after the session are unavailable until the next session reset.

Example 2-4 shows another example of BGP capabilities exchanged between a pair of
routers. Four capabilities are exchanged (advertised and received): route refresh (both old
and new forms), IPv4 Unicast, VPNv4 Unicast, and IPv4 Multicast. For each of the three
address families, more information is provided in its respective section.

Example 2-4   *Another Example of BGP Capabilities*

```
router#show ip bgp neighbor 192.168.100.2 | begin cap
  Neighbor capabilities:
    Route refresh: advertised and received(old & new)
    Address family IPv4 Unicast: advertised and received
    Address family VPNv4 Unicast: advertised and received
    Address family IPv4 Multicast: advertised and received
  Received 1356 messages, 0 notifications, 0 in queue
  Sent 1370 messages, 0 notifications, 0 in queue
  Default minimum time between advertisement runs is 5 seconds

 For address family: IPv4 Unicast
  BGP table version 11, neighbor version 11
  Index 1, Offset 0, Mask 0x2
  Route refresh request: received 0, sent 0
  Sending Prefix & Label
  0 accepted prefixes consume 0 bytes
  Prefix advertised 10, suppressed 0, withdrawn 4

 For address family: VPNv4 Unicast
  BGP table version 1, neighbor version 1
  Index 1, Offset 0, Mask 0x2
  Community attribute sent to this neighbor
  Route refresh request: received 0, sent 0
  0 accepted prefixes consume 0 bytes
  Prefix advertised 0, suppressed 0, withdrawn 0

 For address family: IPv4 Multicast
  BGP table version 1, neighbor version 1
```

continues

Example 2-4 *Another Example of BGP Capabilities (Continued)*

```
   Index 1, Offset 0, Mask 0x2
     Uses NEXT_HOP attribute for MBGP NLRIs
   Route refresh request: received 0, sent 0
   0 accepted prefixes consume 0 bytes
   Prefix advertised 0, suppressed 0, withdrawn 0
...
```

Example 2-5 shows the output of **debug ip bgp** during session establishment. Within the Open message, a Capabilities field is included in the Option parameter. Within the field, all supported capabilities are exchanged. The following capabilities are exchanged:

- Multiprotocol extension, code 1: IPv4 Unicast (AF/SAFI codes 1/1), VPN IPv4 (1/128), IPv4 Multicast (1/2)
- Old form route refresh, code 128
- New form route refresh, code 2

Example 2-5 *Output of* **debug ip bgp** *for Session Establishment*

```
*Oct 16 16:00:06.682: BGP: 192.168.100.2 went from Idle to Active
*Oct 16 16:00:06.694: BGP: 192.168.100.2 open active, delay 7887ms
*Oct 16 16:00:14.602: BGP: 192.168.100.2 open active, local address 192.168.100.1
*Oct 16 16:00:14.654: BGP: 192.168.100.2 went from Active to OpenSent
*Oct 16 16:00:14.654: BGP: 192.168.100.2 sending OPEN, version 4, my as: 100
*Oct 16 16:00:14.674: BGP: 192.168.100.2 send message type 1, length
  (incl. header) 69
*Oct 16 16:00:14.802: BGP: 192.168.100.2 rcv OPEN, version 4
*Oct 16 16:00:14.802: BGP: 192.168.100.2 rcv OPEN w/ OPTION parameter len: 32
*Oct 16 16:00:14.802: BGP: 192.168.100.2 rcvd OPEN w/ optional parameter type 2
  (Capability) len 6
*Oct 16 16:00:14.802: BGP: 192.168.100.2 OPEN has CAPABILITY code: 1, length 4
*Oct 16 16:00:14.802: BGP: 192.168.100.2 OPEN has MP_EXT CAP for afi/safi: 1/1
*Oct 16 16:00:14.802: BGP: 192.168.100.2 rcvd OPEN w/ optional parameter type 2
  (Capability) len 6
*Oct 16 16:00:14.802: BGP: 192.168.100.2 OPEN has CAPABILITY code: 1, length 4
*Oct 16 16:00:14.802: BGP: 192.168.100.2 OPEN has MP_EXT CAP for afi/safi: 1/128
*Oct 16 16:00:14.802: BGP: 192.168.100.2 rcvd OPEN w/ optional parameter type 2
  (Capability) len 6
*Oct 16 16:00:14.802: BGP: 192.168.100.2 OPEN has CAPABILITY code: 1, length 4
*Oct 16 16:00:14.802: BGP: 192.168.100.2 OPEN has MP_EXT CAP for afi/safi: 1/2
*Oct 16 16:00:14.802: BGP: 192.168.100.2 rcvd OPEN w/ optional parameter type 2
  (Capability) len 2
*Oct 16 16:00:14.802: BGP: 192.168.100.2 OPEN has CAPABILITY code: 128, length 0
*Oct 16 16:00:14.802: BGP: 192.168.100.2 OPEN has ROUTE-REFRESH capability(old)
  for all address-families
*Oct 16 16:00:14.802: BGP: 192.168.100.2 rcvd OPEN w/ optional parameter type 2
  (Capability) len 2
*Oct 16 16:00:14.802: BGP: 192.168.100.2 OPEN has CAPABILITY code: 2, length 0
```

Example 2-5 *Output of* **debug ip bgp** *for Session Establishment (Continued)*

```
*Oct 16 16:00:14.802: BGP: 192.168.100.2 OPEN has ROUTE-REFRESH capability(new)
  for all address-families
*Oct 16 16:00:14.802: BGP: 192.168.100.2 went from OpenSent to OpenConfirm
*Oct 16 16:00:14.882: BGP: 192.168.100.2 went from OpenConfirm to Established
*Oct 16 16:00:14.882: %BGP-5-ADJCHANGE: neighbor 192.168.100.2 Up
```

BGP-IGP Routing Exchange

Routing exchange between BGP and an IGP can occur in two directions: from the IGP to BGP, and from BGP into the IGP. There are two common ways to inject routes from an IGP into BGP:

- Using the **redistribute** command
- Using the **network** command

IGP routes can be dynamically injected into BGP using the **redistribute** command. You should use proper filtering and summarization whenever you do this to reduce the impact of IGP instability on BGP. Even with these measures, dynamic redistribution of IGP routes into BGP is not encouraged because of its dynamic nature and thus its lack of administrative control.

NOTE   When you redistribute routes into BGP using the **redistribute** command, only the classful networks are redistributed by default. To have all routes redistributed individually, you must disable BGP **auto-summary** (otherwise, an automatic classful summary is created). A new default behavior was introduced in recent Cisco IOS software releases in which **no auto-summary** is automatically enabled.

The BGP **network** command operates differently from an IGP **network** command in Cisco IOS software. In most IGP configurations, the **network** command binds a local interface to a routing protocol and injects the interface address into the IGP. With BGP, the **network** command creates the route in the BGP table only if the route is already present in the IP routing table. This allows IGP routes to be injected into BGP semistatically. It is semistatic because the route is injected into BGP only when it already exists in the IP routing table.

Redistribution of BGP routes into an IGP should be used with only a small subset of the BGP Internet routes or when the number of BGP routes is small. Proper filtering should be deployed during redistribution to minimize the prefix count in the IGP. Various filtering techniques are discussed in Chapter 4, "Effective BGP Policy Control."

Routing Information Base

The IP RIB, or IP routing table, is a critical database that provides a vital link between the control plane and the forwarding plane, as mentioned earlier in the section "Comparing the Control Plane and Forwarding Plane." On one hand, various routing sources/protocols such as BGP and IS-IS populate the RIB with their paths. On the other hand, RIB provides information to build the forwarding database (some switching methods use the RIB directly for forwarding).

As each routing protocol receives updates and other information, it chooses the best path to any given destination and attempts to install this path into the routing table. When multiple paths for the same prefix/length exist, the router decides whether to install the routes based on the administrative distances of the protocols involved. IOS has predefined but configurable administrative distances for various routing protocols/sources. The prefixes from a routing source that has a lower administrative distance are preferred. Backup routes are still maintained by the protocol, if supported, and are used as the best routes when existing best routes fail.

NOTE   When BGP fails to install a route into the IP RIB, a RIB failure is reported in the route's BGP RIB. The failure code indicates the reason. Check out Appendix B, "Matrix of BGP Features and Cisco IOS Software Releases," for additional information.

The IP RIB is organized as a collection of Network Descriptor Blocks (NDBs). Each NDB is a single entry in the routing table and represents a network prefix obtained via one of three sources:

- An address/mask pair configured on a local interface on the router. This becomes a connected route, which has the highest preference, or an administrative distance of 0.

- A static route configured on the router. A static route has a default administrative distance of 1.

- A dynamic routing protocol such as BGP.

NDBs contain information about the network address, mask, and administrative distance, as well as information needed for the operation of dynamic routing protocols, such as route redistribution. Because each prefix in an NDB can be potentially reached through multiple paths, Routing Descriptor Blocks (RDBs) are also used. One or more RDBs can be linked to each NDB to store the actual next-hop information. An NDB currently may have up to eight RDBs, which sets the upper limit to the number of load-shared links per destination (that is, eight). Note that because NDBs are controlled by individual routing protocols, the routing protocols determine how many RDBs to associate with an NDB.

The packet-forwarding database is built based on the information contained in the IP RIB and IP Address Resolution Protocol (ARP) table. A prefix lookup in the RIB is performed to determine the next-hop address and the outgoing interface. The actual Layer 2 header is built based on the information from the IP ARP table. Frame Relay and ATM maps are other examples used to map Layer 3 addresses to Layer 2 addresses. Two general types of RIB lookup operations are supported in Cisco IOS software:

- **Classless**—The longest matching prefix is looked up. If no matching prefixes are found, the default route, if present, is used. IP classless lookup has been the default (although it is still shown in the running configuration) since Cisco IOS software Release 11.3.

- **Classful**—Longest-match lookup. Supernets and the default route are not considered if the routing table contains a subnet of the destination major network (the classful network of the address being resolved).

Switching Paths

Within Cisco IOS software, three general switching paths are supported, dependent on the hardware platforms and configurations:

- Process switching
- Cache-based switching
- Cisco Express Forwarding (CEF)

The next sections discuss each switching path in greater detail.

Process Switching

Process switching is the most basic form of switching and is universally available on all Cisco routers. *Process switching* refers to the fact that the CPU is directly involved in the process required to forward the packet. The packet is switched at the process level within IOS. In other words, the forwarding decision is made by a process scheduled by the IOS scheduler and running as a peer to other processes on the router, such as routing protocols. Processes that normally run on the router are not interrupted to process-switch a packet. For IP packets, the forwarding process is IP Input.

Figure 2-3 shows the main components of typical IP process switching. The following list outlines the process:

1   An IP packet received from the inbound interface is queued in the Synchronous Dynamic RAM (SDRAM) packet memory.

2   The processor copies the packet to the system buffer area in Dynamic RAM (DRAM), where the IP Input process begins its Layer 3 and Layer 2 processing of the packet.

3 Using the destination IP address in the packet header, the process first checks the RIB to determine the outbound interface. It then consults the ARP cache to build the Layer 2 header.

4 At this point, the packet is rewritten with the new Layer 2 header and is copied back into the packet memory or system memory for forwarding to the outbound interface.

Figure 2-3 *IP Process Switching*

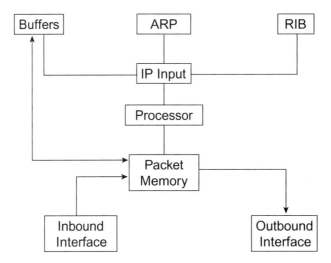

Process switching is CPU-intensive and might result in low system performance if a large number of packets need to be examined at the process level. The following CPU-intensive tasks are involved in process-switching an IP packet:

- Memory copy of the packet from the receive buffer to a shared memory system buffer.

- Routing table lookup. This task has generally become less of a problem over the years because of more-efficient algorithms used to store information.

- Memory copy of the packet from the shared memory system buffer to the transmit buffer.

The limitation of process switching is exacerbated if the router needs to handle large numbers of packets in an unstable network, such as the environment on the Internet. Process switching is also not an efficient switching mechanism, because packet information is never reused. Process switching involves performing prefix lookups directly into the RIB, which is not optimized for route table lookups.

It is important to note that packets directed to the router, such as BGP packets, are process-switched. When a packet is destined for the router, the IP Input process queues the packet for the next-higher layer for processing; in the case of BGP, that layer is TCP. The efficiency of this process can directly affect the BGP performance. During convergence, for example, TCP might receive a large number of ACK packets. If these packets are not delivered to TCP in time, sessions might not be established. Chapter 3 goes into detail on how to tune various parameters to avoid this type of situation.

Cache-Based Switching

Cache-based switching is a more efficient switching mechanism that takes advantage of the information gained from the first packet switched by a scheduled process. In this type of switching, the IOS process currently running on the processor is interrupted to switch the packet. Packets are switched on demand, rather than being switched only when the IP Input process can be scheduled, as in the case of process switching.

The processor switches the first packet at the process level and creates an entry in the route cache so that subsequent packets with the same destination address are switched based on the cache entry. Switching packets based on the route cache requires less processing, which allows the packet to be switched at the interrupt level. This is why cache-based switching is also called *interrupt context switching*.

Compared to process switching, cache-based switching has the following advantages:

- It switches packets as they arrive without the need to wait for the forwarding process to be scheduled, which reduces delay.

- Only the first packet to a destination needs to be process-switched to populate the route cache, minimizing the amount of time spent performing CPU-intensive tasks.

- Subsequent packets are switched based on the information in the route cache.

Several forms of cache-based switching are currently available in Cisco routers:

- Fast switching

- Optimum switching

- Distributed optimum switching

- NetFlow switching

The cache-based switching paths differ in how the information is stored in the cache. The following sections briefly review these switching paths and their shortcomings.

Fast Switching

Fast switching stores the forwarding information and MAC header rewrite string (the new MAC header) using a binary tree for quick lookup and reference. You can display the content of the fast cache using **show ip cache verbose**.

Figure 2-4 shows the components of fast switching. The following list outlines the process:

1 As a packet arrives from an inbound interface, a lookup is performed to determine if a cached entry exists for the packet.

2 If none exists, the packet is process-switched.

3 Information gained from switching the first packet creates an entry in the fast cache.

4 If an entry already exists when the packet arrives, the packet is rewritten with the new Layer 2 information for the outbound interface and is forwarded to that interface. The packet is not copied to the system buffer, as in process switching.

Figure 2-4 *IP Fast Switching*

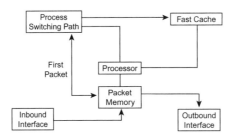

Optimum Switching

Optimum switching stores the forwarding information and the MAC header rewrite information in a 256-way radix tree. Using a 256-way tree reduces the number of steps that must be taken when looking up a prefix, although more memory is needed. Optimum switching is supported only on platforms based on the Route Switch Processor (RSP).

Distributed Optimum Switching

Distributed optimum switching seeks to offload the packet-switching function from the main CPU by moving the routing decision to the interface processors. This is possible only on routing platforms that have dedicated CPUs per interface, such as Versatile Interface Processors (VIPs). In the case of VIP, for example, the optimum cache is populated by the RSP. When a packet is received, the VIP attempts to make the routing decision based on that table. If the VIP can locate an entry on its local route cache, it switches the packet without interrupting the RSP. If it fails, it enqueues the packet for the next configured switching path (optimum switching, and then fast switching, and then process switching). With distributed switching, access lists are copied to the VIPs, which allows the VIP to check the packet against the access list without RSP intervention.

NOTE   Both optimum switching and distributed optimum switching are no longer supported beginning with Cisco IOS software Release 12.0.

NetFlow Switching

NetFlow switching is another form of cache-based switching. The NetFlow cache is built by processing the first packet of a flow through the standard switching mechanism. As a result, each flow is associated with an incoming and outgoing interface and with a specific security access permission and encryption policy. The cache also includes entries for traffic statistics that are updated with the switching of subsequent packets.

A *flow* is defined as a specific conversation between two hosts. Source and destination addresses, ports, and the IP packet type define a flow. For TCP communication, a conversation starts and stops with various TCP control messages. For UDP, a conversation is considered to have ceased after a timer has expired. Subsequent packets that match the flow tag are considered to be members of the same flow and are simply switched through the outbound interface, bypassing further checking against access lists, queuing, and so on.

NetFlow switching is designed to provide a highly efficient mechanism with which to process extended or complex access lists without paying as much of a performance penalty as with other switching methods. With NetFlow switching, detailed accounting information is collected for each flow. In fact, information collection has become so important that in newer IOS releases, NetFlow switching is being used exclusively for that purpose and is no longer used to switch packets.

NOTE   With both CEF and NetFlow switching enabled, CEF provides the switching path for IP packets and populates the flow cache. NetFlow is used to export the statistics to a flow collector. The flow information includes per-user, per-protocol, per-port, and per-type of service statistics, which can be used for a wide variety of purposes, such as network analysis and planning, accounting, and billing.

Shortcomings of Cached-Based Switching Methods

The following are some of the shortcomings of the cache-based switching methods:

- They are all traffic-driven, in that they are dependent on receipt of the first packet to populate the cache. This packet is switched in the slow path, leading to low performance and high CPU usage. In a network with large and constantly changing traffic patterns, such as the Internet, the processing of the first packet can cause significant system degradation. Thus, cache-based switching has scalability problems for Internet core routers. As another example, the efficiency of NetFlow switching depends on the flow's length. If there are large numbers of short flows, new entries are created constantly, resulting in lower efficiency and performance.

- It is possible for caches to grow larger than routing tables, such as when multiple equal-cost paths exist. As a result, fast cache can consume significant amounts of memory.

- Periodic aging of the cache entries can consume large amounts of CPU time if the cache is large.

- Cache invalidation because of a route flap relies on process switching to repopulate the cache with valid entries. When the route table changes, the affected old entries must be invalidated, and traffic previously using the cache entries is process-switched as the cache is rebuilt. If there are a large number of flaps, which occur frequently on the Internet, significant cache invalidation is seen, reducing the effectiveness of the cache-based switching mechanism. This can also result in contention for system buffers and loss of control traffic, contributing to network instability.

- Cache-based switching is unable to do per-packet load sharing at an interrupt level. Because cache-based switching is entirely destination-based, load sharing occurs only on a per-destination basis.

Cisco Express Forwarding

As discussed in the preceding section, although cache-based switching mechanisms improve forwarding performance over process switching, their performance is nondeterministic. Both process switching and cache-based switching are data-driven or demand-driven. In other words, the switching components are in place only after the packets enter the router, and they are removed when such packets are not being forwarded by the router. If there are large numbers of packets with unpredictable patterns, switching performance is degraded significantly. Obviously these switching paths are not scalable at the Internet level.

CEF was created to avoid the problems inherent in cache-based switching mechanisms. It is designed to best accommodate the changing network dynamics and traffic characteristics resulting from increasing numbers of short duration flows typically associated with web-based applications and interactive TCP sessions.

CEF offers the following benefits:

- **Scalability**—CEF is topology-driven and relates closely to the routing table. CEF also offers full switching capacity at each line card when Distributed CEF mode is active. CEF supports hardware-assisted forwarding, necessary to offer line rate switching on high-capacity line cards.

- **Improved performance**—CEF is less CPU-intensive than route caching. More CPU processing power can then be dedicated to Layer 3 services, such as processing BGP updates.

- **Resilience**—CEF offers better switching consistency and stability in large dynamic networks. In such networks, fast switching cache entries are frequently invalidated because of routing changes. These changes can cause traffic to be process-switched using the routing table rather than fast-switched using the route cache. Because the CEF lookup table contains all known routes that exist in the routing table, it eliminates route cache maintenance and the fast switch/process switch forwarding scenario. CEF can switch traffic more efficiently than typical demand caching schemes.

NOTE   Because entries are maintained for all the routes in the IP RIB whether they are used or not, more memory might be required by CEF than for other switching methods.

CEF is a topology-driven switching mechanism whose forwarding table is tied to the routing table. Whenever there are routing table changes, the CEF forwarding table is updated. While entries are created, packets are switched in a slower switching path. CEF splits the function of the route cache into two main components:

- Forwarding information base (FIB)
- Adjacency table

FIB

The *FIB* contains all IP prefixes from the routing table. If different routing tables are maintained, such as in an MPLS VPN environment, each VPN has its own FIB. The FIB is not data-driven. Rather, it is created and updated by the routing table. The FIB subsystem is responsible for ensuring that all recursive routes (routes are not associated with immediate next hops) are resolved.

To increase consistency and decrease lookup time, FIB is organized in a multiway data structure called mtrie. In an *mtrie data structure*, the tree structure is used to locate the desired data, but the data itself is stored elsewhere. In contrast, an *mtree data structure* stores the actual data within the tree structure itself. For example, in the optimum switching mtree cache, the MAC header data used to forward packets is actually stored inside the mtree.

Two types of mtrie structures are commonly used in Cisco routers:

- **8-8-8-8**—This form is also called *256-way mtrie*, because the four-octet IPv4 address is mapped to four 8-bit structures. Thus, the maximum number of lookups for a prefix is four. This form is used on most Cisco routers.

- **16-8-8**—This is a three-level mtrie, where the root level has 65,536 entries. Thus, the maximum number of lookups is three. In other words, the first lookup resolves the first two octets, and at most two more lookups are needed to resolve the last two octets. This form is used only on Cisco 12000 series routers.

Each level of the mtrie is called a node. The final node is called a *leaf*. The leaf points to the *adjacency table* or to another load-sharing structure when multiple paths to the same destination exist. The content of the IP FIB can be displayed with the **show ip cef** command.

Some of the FIB entries are as follows:

- **Attached**—The prefix is configured to be directly reachable via the interface. No IP next hop is needed to create the adjacency. This is the network that local interfaces belong to.

- **Connected**—The interface is configured using the **ip address** *address mask* configuration command. All connected FIB entries are attached, but not all attached entries are connected.

- **Receive**—The prefix is a host address (/32) corresponding to one of the addresses that the router always receives (as a host). There are generally three of these per interface: the actual interface address plus the all-0 subnet and the all-1 broadcast addresses.

- **Recursive**—A prefix is flagged as recursive when the output interface is not specified by the routing protocol or static configuration. A recursive FIB entry may be unresolved when no FIB entry is found for the next-hop IP address. So, the flag actually is associated with a next hop rather than a FIB entry.

Adjacency Table

An *adjacency table* is created to contain all connected next hops. An *adjacent node* is a node that can be reached in one link layer hop. As soon as a neighbor becomes adjacent, a link layer header, called a MAC string or MAC rewrite, used to reach that neighbor is created and stored in the table. On an Ethernet segment, for example, the header information is destination MAC address, source MAC address, and EtherType, in that order.

Example 2-6 shows a MAC header for Ethernet. In this example, 00044EB31838 is the MAC destination address, 0003E4BB2000 is the source MAC address, and 0800 is the EtherType for IP.

Example 2-6 *Adjacency Information*

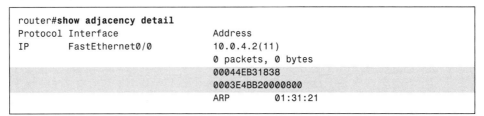

```
router#show adjacency detail
Protocol Interface              Address
IP        FastEthernet0/0        10.0.4.2(11)
                                 0 packets, 0 bytes
                                 00044EB31838
                                 0003E4BB20000800
                                 ARP        01:31:21
```

As soon as a route is resolved, it points to an adjacent next hop. If an adjacency is found in the adjacency table, a pointer to the appropriate adjacency is cached in the FIB element. If multiple paths (that is, multiple next hops or adjacencies) exist for the same destination, a pointer to each adjacency is added to the load-sharing structure. With CEF, load sharing per packet is available at the interrupt level.

Several types of exception adjacencies exist. When prefixes are added to the FIB, prefixes that require exception handling are cached with special adjacencies. The following are some special adjacencies:

- **Null**—For packets destined for Null 0 interfaces that are to be dropped.

- **Glean**—For destinations that are attached via a broadcast network but for which MAC rewrite strings are unavailable. Consider the router directly connected to a subnet with several hosts. The FIB table on the router maintains a prefix for the subnet instead of individual host prefixes. This subnet prefix points to a glean adjacency. When packets need to be forwarded to a specific host, the adjacency database is gleaned for the specific prefix. This incurs the cost of an additional lookup.

- **Punt**—Packets are forwarded for handling by the next-slower switching path if CEF is not supported for these packets.

- **Drop**—Drops the packets because they cannot be CEF-switched or cannot be punted to other paths.

- **Discard**—Similar to drop adjacency but applies only to Cisco 12000 routers.

Figure 2-5 ties all the CEF components together.

Figure 2-5 *CEF Components*

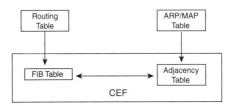

Distributed CEF

To increase scalability, FIB can also be distributed to line cards for Cisco 7500 and 12000 routers. In fact, Distributed CEF (dCEF) is the only switching mechanism supported in the 12000 series routers (Gigabit Switch Routers [GSRs]). The route processor (RP), RSP in 7500 or Gigabit RP (GRP) in 12000, uses the information from the IP routing table to build the master FIB table, which is used to fully repopulate the line cards that are booted, inserted, or cleared. When a line card is synchronized with the RP, the RP sends only incremental updates to the individual line cards. Updates are sent only when changes in the routing topology occur.

When dCEF is enabled, line cards maintain an identical copy of the FIB and adjacency table. The line cards perform the express forwarding between port adapters, relieving the RP of involvement in the switching operation. dCEF uses Inter-Process Communication (IPC) to ensure synchronization of FIBs and adjacency tables between the route processor and line cards. The IPC mechanism provides a reliable and orderly delivery of messages. The delivery mechanism is a simple sliding-window protocol, with a window size of 1.

Figure 2-6 shows the components of dCEF.

NOTE   dCEF is enabled by default on the Cisco 12000 routers and should not be disabled; otherwise, packets will be dropped. The CLI keyword **distributed** is not supported on GSR line cards, because it is the default. Depending on the implementation, forwarding in a line card can be done by software or hardware.

Even though IPC is a reliable communication mechanism for CEF, databases can get out of sync between the RP and line cards during large updates. Inconsistency in CEF can cause forwarding problems. Since Cisco IOS software Releases 12.0(15)S, 12.0(14)ST1, and 12.1(7), a CEF inconsistency checker has been implemented. This feature is on by default but can be disabled with **no ip cef table consistency-check**. Various parameters of the checker can be modified with **ip cef table consistency-check type** *type* [**period** *seconds*] [**count** *count*], where *type* is the type of consistency checker to be modified, *seconds* is how often the FIB table is scanned, and *count* is the number of prefixes to be sent to the RP.

Figure 2-6   *dCEF Components*

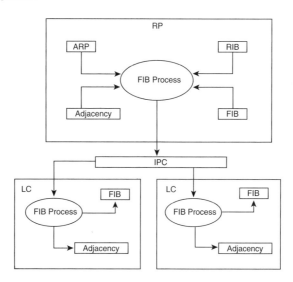

There are four types of consistency checkers:

- **lc-detect**—The line card sends any addresses of packets to the RP for which it could not forward packets. If the RP detects that it has the relevant entries, an inconsistency has been detected, and an error message is printed. The RP sends a signal back to the line card confirming the inconsistent prefixes.

- **scan-lc**—Line cards scan their FIB tables on a periodic basis (60 seconds by default, but this can be configured) and send the next *n* prefixes to the RP. *n* currently is 100 but can be configured. The RP does an exact lookup. If it finds any prefixes missing, it reports an inconsistency. Signaling to the line card happens as just described.

- **scan-rp**—This is the opposite of scan-lc, with the RP doing the scanning. This time the line card signals any verified inconsistencies to the RP.

- **scan-rib**—RP scans the IP RIB periodically to ensure that entries are also present in the RP FIB table. This checker also works in nondistributed CEF.

In all cases, the error messages are reported on the RP only. The consistency-check infrastructure always keeps statistics on the detection mechanisms, as well as recording detailed information for a number of confirmed inconsistencies (currently four). The result of the inconsistency check can be displayed with **show ip cef inconsistency**. You can use the following methods to clear the inconsistency:

- If a prefix is missing from a line card, use **clear cef linecard** *slot*.

- If a prefix is missing from the RP, use **clear ip route ***.

- To reset the consistency checkers, use **clear ip cef inconsistency**.

NOTE   Resetting the routing table and CEF tables might cause brief packet drops.

Load Sharing

CEF has two forms of load sharing:

- **Per-session load sharing**—This is commonly, although incorrectly, called per-destination load sharing. This form of load sharing is the default behavior and does not require special configuration. A session is a traffic flow that has the same source and destination IP addresses.

- **Per-packet load sharing**—Load is shared on a per-packet basis. To enable it, enter **ip cef load-sharing per-packet** in interface configuration mode. For per-packet load sharing to work properly, all outgoing interfaces must have the command configured.

Per-Session Load Sharing

Per-session load sharing allows the router to use multiple paths to distribute the traffic. Packets for a given source-destination host pair are guaranteed to take the same path, even if multiple paths are available. Traffic destined for different pairs tends to take different paths. Per-session load sharing is enabled by default when you enable CEF; it's the method of choice in most situations. Because per-session load sharing depends on the statistical distribution of traffic, load sharing becomes more effective as the number of source-destination pairs increases. Per-session load balancing can be used to ensure that packets for a given host pair arrive in order, because all packets for the same host pair are routed over the same link (or links).

For each session of the source and destination addresses, an active path is assigned. Each path carries an equally loaded number of sessions. A hash function using the source and destination addresses, number of active paths, and router ID is run to assign sessions to paths. Sixteen hash buckets are numbered 0 through 15. Evenly filled buckets are assigned to paths depending on the number of paths and each path's weight.

In Example 2-7, 16 buckets from 0 through 15 are evenly filled with three equal paths (0 through 2). (Bucket 15 is not used in this example.)

Example 2-7   *Load Sharing for Three Paths*

```
Bucket number  0    1    2    3    4    5    6    7    8    9    10   11   12
        13     14   15
Path number    0    1    2    0    1    2    0    1    2    0    1    2    0
         1      2
```

Unequal weight load sharing is also possible. The weight is assigned by the routing protocols with different traffic share counts. IOS currently supports a maximum of eight paths per prefix.

Per-session load sharing has the potential problem of traffic polarization. In other words, traffic would always use the same link if the same hash function is used on all the routers. A new algorithm is integrated into Cisco IOS software Releases 12.0(11)S2 and later to allow a unique ID for each router. The ID is automatically generated or can be fixed with the optional keyword id. The ultimate goal is that the hash functions in each router are completely different and independent.

```
ip cef load-sharing algorithm universal [id]
```

To see the ID, use **show ip cef detail**. Example 2-8 shows a snapshot of the output.

Example 2-8 *CEF Detail*

```
router#show ip cef detail
IP CEF with switching (Table Version 5), flags=0x0
  5 routes, 0 reresolve, 0 unresolved (0 old, 0 new), peak 0
  8 leaves, 11 nodes, 12400 bytes, 8 inserts, 0 invalidations
  0 load sharing elements, 0 bytes, 0 references
  universal per-destination load sharing algorithm, id 24D5ED01
  2(0) CEF resets, 0 revisions of existing leaves
  Resolution Timer: Exponential (currently 1s, peak 1s)
  0 in-place/0 aborted modifications
  refcounts:  796 leaf, 795 node
```

Per-Packet Load Sharing

Per-packet load sharing allows the router to send successive data packets over paths without regard to individual hosts or user sessions. It uses the round-robin method to determine which path each packet takes to the destination. Per-packet load sharing ensures more even balancing over multiple links.

Per-packet load sharing is most effective when the bulk of the data passing through parallel links is for a single session. Per-session load sharing in this case overloads a single link while other links have very little traffic. Enabling per-packet load sharing allows you to use alternative paths for the same busy session.

Although path utilization with per-packet load sharing is better, packets for a given source-destination host pair may take different paths. This can introduce reordering of packets, which might be inappropriate for certain types of data traffic that depend on packets arriving at the destination in sequence, such as voice over IP traffic.

Comparison of Switching Mechanisms

Table 2-3 compares the different switching methods available in Cisco routers.

Table 2-3 *Comparison of Switching Path Support in Cisco Routers for Transit Packets*

Switching Path	Configurations to Enable the Switching Path	Low to Medium Range*	Cisco 7200/ 7100 series	Cisco 7500 series	Cisco 12000 series
Process switching	**no ip route-cache** under an interface	Yes	Yes	Yes	No
Fast switching	**ip route-cache** under an interface	Yes (the default)**	Yes (the default)	Yes	No
Optimum switching***	**ip route-cache optimum** under an interface	No	Yes	Yes	No
Distributed optimum switching	**ip route-cache distributed** under a VIP interface	No	No	Yes, with VIPs	No
NetFlow switching	**ip route-cache flow** under an interface	Yes	Yes	Yes	Yes****
CEF	**ip route-cache cef** under an interface **ip cef** in global configuration	Yes	Yes	Yes (the default for IP)	No
dCEF	**ip cef distributed** in global configuration	No	No	Yes, with VIPs	Yes (the default); cannot be disabled globally

*   Includes all other router platforms not specifically listed here.

**   The default switching path for a platform may vary between different IOS releases and is dependent on the hardware support and the type of protocol to be switched.

***   Optimum switching and distributed optimum switching are no longer supported for IOS releases beginning with Release 12.0.

****   For collecting traffic statistics only; not for packet switching.

Several commands display which path the interface uses and how the traffic is being switched:

- **show ip interface**
- **show interface statistics**
- **show cef interface**
- **show interface switching**

The portion of CPU cycles used to switch the packets at the interrupt level is shown in **show process cpu**. Some sample command outputs are provided in the following examples.

Example 2-9 shows what switching paths are enabled at an interface level. In this example, both Fast Switching and CEF are enabled.

Example 2-9   *Example of* **show ip interface**

```
router#show ip interface FastEthernet 0/0
...
  IP fast switching is enabled
  IP fast switching on the same interface is disabled
  IP Flow switching is disabled
  IP CEF switching is enabled
  IP Fast switching turbo vector
  IP CEF switching with tag imposition turbo vector
  IP multicast fast switching is enabled
  IP multicast distributed fast switching is disabled
  IP route-cache flags are Fast, CEF
...
```

Example 2-10 shows per-interface CEF status. In this example, CEF is enabled, and per-packet load sharing is not enabled.

Example 2-10 *Example of* **show cef interface**

```
router#show cef interface FastEthernet 0/0
FastEthernet0/0 is up (if_number 2)
  Internet address is 10.0.4.1/24
  ICMP redirects are always sent
  Per packet load-sharing is disabled
  IP unicast RPF check is disabled
  Inbound access list is not set
  Outbound access list is not set
  IP policy routing is disabled
  Hardware idb is FastEthernet0/0
  Fast switching type 1, interface type 18
  IP CEF switching enabled
  IP Fast switching turbo vector
  IP CEF switching with tag imposition turbo vector
  Input fast flags 0x0, Output fast flags 0x0
  ifindex 1(1)
  Slot 0 Slot unit 0 VC -1
  Transmit limit accumulator 0x0 (0x0)
  IP MTU 1500
```

Example 2-11 shows the interface switching statistics. In this example, all the packets are process-switched.

Example 2-11 *Example of* **show interface statistics**

```
router#show interface statistics

Serial5/0
          Switching path    Pkts In   Chars In   Pkts Out   Chars Out
               Processor    1512063   80735470    1512064    80865400
             Route cache          0          0          0           0
                   Total    1512063   80735470    1512064    80865400
```

The command shown in Example 2-12 gives more detail and lists information for each protocol. Three types of protocols are listed: IP, CDP, and others. All packets are process-switched in this example.

Example 2-12 *Example of* **show interface switching**

```
router#show interface switching

Serial5/0
...
      Protocol      Path    Pkts In   Chars In   Pkts Out   Chars Out
         Other   Process          0          0     951854    15229544
           Cache misses          0
                    Fast          0          0          0           0
              Auton/SSE          0          0          0           0
            IP   Process     480877   35602293     480869    35727362
           Cache misses        100
                    Fast          0          0          0           0
              Auton/SSE          0          0          0           0
           CDP   Process      79323   29903377      79331    29907805
           Cache misses          0
                    Fast          0          0          0           0
              Auton/SSE          0          0          0           0
```

Case Study: BGP Memory Use Estimation

The purpose of this case study is to demonstrate the interdependency of various components that contribute to BGP memory use, specifically with regard to the BGP Router process. The case study also establishes a simple method to estimate the BGP memory requirements based on a defined number of prefixes and paths. An experimental approach is used to determine the various relationships between BGP components and their memory use. The total memory consumed by BGP is the sum of memory use for BGP networks (prefixes), BGP paths, BGP path attributes, IP NDB, IP RDB, and IP CEF. The results should provide a reasonable estimate of BGP memory use in Cisco Internet routers.

Methods

To simulate BGP memory use, a Cisco 12012 and four network simulation tools are used. The GSR is the device under test. It is running Cisco IOS software Release 12.0(15)S1. The network simulation tool can simulate BGP and OSPF sessions. The test topology is shown in Figure 2-7.

Figure 2-7   *Test Network Topology*

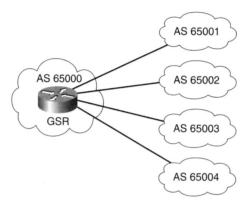

The GSR is running OSPF and BGP. The GRP has 128 MB of DRAM. Its version and relevant configuration are shown in Examples 2-13 and 2-14.

Example 2-13   *Output of* **show version**

```
GSR#show version
Cisco Internetwork Operating System Software
IOS (tm) GS Software (GSR-P-M), Version 12.0(15)S1, EARLY DEPLOYMENT RELEASE
  SOFTWARE (fc1)
...GSR uptime is 1 hour, 8 minutes
...
cisco 12012/GRP (R5000) processor (revision 0x05) with 131072K bytes of memory.
...
1 eight-port FastEthernet/IEEE 802.3u controller (8 FastEthernet).
9 Ethernet/IEEE 802.3 interface(s)
507K bytes of non-volatile configuration memory.

20480K bytes of Flash PCMCIA card at slot 0 (Sector size 128K).
8192K bytes of Flash internal SIMM (Sector size 256K).
Configuration register is 0x2102
```

Example 2-14 *GSR's Running Configuration*

```
GSR#show running-config

...
hostname GSR
!
ip subnet-zero
!
interface FastEthernet10/0
 ip address 172.16.1.1 255.255.255.0
 no ip directed-broadcast
!
interface FastEthernet10/1
 ip address 172.16.2.1 255.255.255.0
 no ip directed-broadcast
!
interface FastEthernet10/2
 ip address 172.16.3.1 255.255.255.0
 no ip directed-broadcast
!
interface FastEthernet10/3
 ip address 172.16.4.1 255.255.255.0
 no ip directed-broadcast
!
router bgp 65000
 neighbor 172.16.1.2 remote-as 65001
 neighbor 172.16.2.2 remote-as 65002
 neighbor 172.16.3.2 remote-as 65003
 neighbor 172.16.4.2 remote-as 65004
!
...
```

Each test tool is assigned a different AS, from 65001 through 65004. All prefixes advertised are in /24, from two to six Class C networks. All other BGP configurations are the default settings.

NOTE   The route map, filter list, community, and route reflection parameters are not considered in this test. For example, more memory can be used if inbound soft reconfiguration is used.

To provide a reasonable distribution of memory use and number of prefixes in the test results, the 11 pairs of BGP networks and paths shown in Table 2-4 were simulated.

Table 2-4   *Test Network and Path Combinations*

Networks (in thousands)	7	20	40	60	80	100	100	100	100	120	130
Paths (in thousands)	14	30	70	67	160	100	200	310	400	170	180

For each network/path pair, memory allocation for the BGP RIB, IP RIB, and IP CEF is collected, together with memory use reported for the BGP router, IP CEF table, and BGP and IP tables. For the BGP RIB, memory use is reported for BGP networks, BGP paths, and path attributes. For IP RIB, data is reported for the NDB and RDB. IP CEF memory data includes both FIB structures and the mtrie used to store BGP networks.

For each component, the memory is plotted against BGP networks or paths, depending on the correlation. A linear regression is conducted to obtain an estimation model for that component. The linear model is expressed in the format of

$$y = b + a\,x$$

where y is a type of component memory to be estimated, x is either the number of network entries or path entries, b is the line's intercept (the value of y when x is 0), or an estimation deviation in this case, and a is the line's slope, indicating how sensitive the memory is to the changes of prefixes and paths. The result of the regression is the values of a and b for each linear model.

The precision of each regression to the actual data is expressed by R^2, the *coefficient of determination*. Mathematically, R^2 is the ratio of the sum of squares because of regression over the total sum of squares. It is also called the square of the *correlation coefficient*. The value of R^2 is between 0 and 1, with 0 being the worst or no correlation and 1 being the best correlation or a perfect fit.

Estimation Formulas

Using the method described in the preceding section, various estimation formulas are produced. The following section begins with the memory use before BGP is enabled.

Free Memory Before BGP Is Enabled

After booting up but before any routing protocols are configured, the free memory is 99.8 MB out of the 128 MB DRAM on the GRP, as shown in Example 2-15. The memory is primarily consumed by expanding the IOS image into DRAM. The processes use another 12.3 MB, leaving 87.5 MB free at this point.

Example 2-15 *Memory Use Summary*

```
GSR#show memory summary
              Head    Total(b)    Used(b)    Free(b)  Lowest(b) Largest(b)
Processor  620D3CE0   99795744   12295416  87500328   87426704   87500136
     Fast  620B3CE0     131092     128488      2604       2604       2396
```

With OSPF enabled and 442 OSPF routes, the free memory is down to 86.4 MB, as shown in Examples 2-16 and 2-17.

Example 2-16 *Memory Use Summary for IP RIB*

```
GSR#show ip route summary
Route Source    Networks    Subnets    Overhead    Memory (bytes)
connected       0           9          504         1368
static          1           0          56          152
ospf 1          0           442        24752       67184
   Intra-area: 442 Inter-area: 0 External-1: 0 External-2: 0
   NSSA External-1: 0 NSSA External-2: 0
internal        3                                  3516
Total           4           451        25312       72220
```

Example 2-17 *Memory Use for Processes*

```
GSR#show process memory | include Total
Total: 99795744, Used: 13410184, Free: 86385560
```

Within the 1.1 MB used (13.4 minus 12.3), OSPF contributes directly to about 390 KB, as shown in Example 2-18. The rest is consumed by existing processes.

Example 2-18 *Memory Use for OSPF Processes*

```
GSR#show process memory | include OSPF
PID TTY  Allocated    Freed    Holding    Getbufs    Retbufs Process
  2   0        476        0       7272          0          0 OSPF Hello
 98   0     452420    11024     379468          0          0 OSPF Router
```

Memory Use for BGP Networks

Figure 2-8 shows the memory used to store all BGP network entries in the BGP RIB. Memory use is plotted against the number of network entries (shown as Actual); these are actual measurements. The Regression line is then overlaid on to the graph to create a visual comparison between the actual and the modeled memory usage. The Regression line is

memory (in bytes) = 214196.9 + 114.9 network entries

with an R^2 of 0.996. The correlation between memory use for networks and path entries is insignificant in this case. (The data isn't shown; from now on, only significant regressions are mentioned.)

Figure 2-8   *Memory Use for BGP Networks*

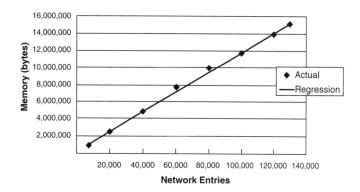

Memory Use for BGP Paths

Figure 2-9 shows the memory used to store all the BGP path entries in the BGP RIB. The Regression line is

memory (in bytes) = –20726.5 + 44.0 path entries

with an R^2 of 1.000.

Figure 2-9   *Memory Use for BGP Paths*

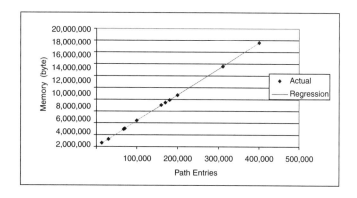

Memory Use for BGP Path Attributes

Figure 2-10 shows the memory used to store all the BGP attributes in the BGP RIB. The Regression line is

memory (in bytes) = $-146792.2 + 6.1$ path entries

with an R^2 of 0.908.

Figure 2-10 *Memory Use for BGP Path Attributes*

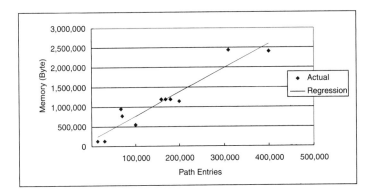

Memory Use for IP NDB

Figure 2-11 shows the memory used for NDB. The Regression line is

memory (in bytes) = $-47765.9 + 172.5$ network entries

with an R^2 of 1.000.

Figure 2-11 *Memory Use for IP NDBs*

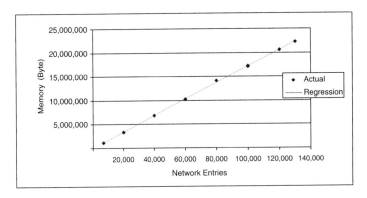

Memory Use for IP RDB

Figure 2-12 shows the memory used for RDB. The Regression line is

memory (in bytes) = 21148.5 + 76.1 network entries

with an R^2 of 0.996.

Figure 2-12 *Memory Use for IP RDBs*

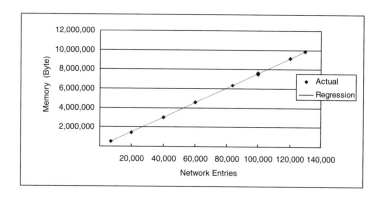

Memory Use for IP CEF

Figure 2-13 shows the memory used for IP CEF. The Regression line is

memory (in bytes) = 32469.1 + 151.9 network entries

with an R^2 of 0.999.

Figure 2-13 *Memory Use for IP CEF*

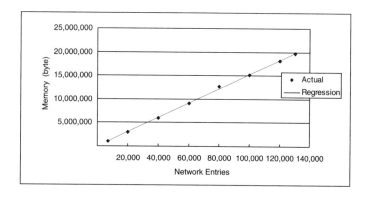

Total BGP Memory Use

The total memory use for the BGP Router process is the sum of memory used for all the components. Using the equations just described, you can estimate the memory use for each component. By adding the memory use for all six components, you can obtain the total memory use estimate.

For example, assume that the BGP RIB has 103,213 network entries and 561,072 path entries. Table 2-5 shows the estimated memory use for each component. The total memory use for the BGP router is the sum of all the memory use estimates—81.5 MB.

Table 2-5 *Memory Use Estimate Example*

	Networks	Paths	Path Attributes	IP NDB	IP RDB	IP CEF	Total
Memory Use (MB)	12.1	24.5	3.6	17.8	7.8	15.7	81.5

Table 2-6 summarizes all the slopes.

Table 2-6 *Slopes for the Regression Lines*

Memory Models	Slope
Networks	114.9
Paths	44.0
Path attributes	6.1
IP NDB	172.5
IP RDB	76.1
IP CEF	151.9

Analysis

Cisco IOS software keeps track of three structures related to BGP: the BGP RIB, the IP RIB, and the IP CEF. The BGP RIB is used to store prefixes received via BGP in addition to their associated attributes, which include communities, AS_PATH, and so on. A BGP speaker may have multiple BGP sessions with an assortment of iBGP and eBGP peers, resulting in the potential for multiple paths per prefix. Each unique prefix is stored in the BGP network table, and all the paths for the same prefix are stored as BGP path entries. The amount of memory that each prefix (or network) and path entry consumes may vary from release to release.

The **show ip bgp summary** output provides memory use for certain BGP components. With Cisco IOS software Release 12.0(15)S1, each unique prefix uses 129 bytes, and each additional path consumes another 36 bytes. For example, if the BGP RIB has 100 prefixes and 200 paths, the total memory for these entries is (100 * 129) + (100 * 36) = 16,500 bytes.

The output also contains the memory use for path attributes, community, caches, and so on, depending on the BGP configuration and prefixes received from peers. Note that these numbers are smaller than what are estimated (as shown in Table 2-6). This is because the memory numbers in the **show ip bgp summary** output does not include the memory overhead. The results in this case study were obtained directly from the output of **show memory**, which includes all memory usage.

If BGP inbound soft reconfiguration is enabled locally, all denied routes are still retained as receive-only routes, leading to higher memory use for the BGP RIB. Because the receive-only routes are excluded from the best-path selection, they do not affect the memory use for IP RIB and IP CEF. With the route refresh feature available since the 12.0 release, inbound policy changes are updated dynamically to peers, so inbound soft reconfiguration is no longer required. The route refresh feature is on automatically for supported releases. To verify whether it is supported, execute the **show ip bgp neighbor** command.

Memory use for caching route maps and filter lists is not considered in this test. For a typical Internet router with 100,000 routes and six different BGP paths, this portion of memory use could be in the vicinity of 2 MB, and the total BGP memory use is about 80 MB. Combined memory use for BGP Scanner, BGP I/O, and BGP Router process maintenance is generally well under 50 KB.

In this case study, only static memory use is estimated for BGP. Static memory here refers to the memory use when BGP is in a steady state—that is, when prefixes are converged. However, BGP might use additional memory during convergence. This type of memory is called *transient memory use*. The size of transient memory is difficult to track and can vary according to factors such as how updates are sent and received, the state the BGP Router process is in, and the IOS releases. For example, peer groups allow updates to be replicated from a peer group leader to other members of the group, so less memory is needed to hold the messages. Update packing is another method to reduce the number of update packets sent to peers. These and other performance tuning techniques are discussed in detail in Chapter 3.

The BGP Router process can be in one of three states, depending on the IOS releases, BGP, and router states, with increasing functionality and memory use:

- **Read-only**—BGP accepts updates only from peers. It does not calculate the best path, nor does it install routes into the routing table. This reduces transient memory use. During initial router bootup, BGP is typically in this mode.

- **Calculating the best path**—BGP accepts updates and runs through the path-selection process, which generally is associated with the caching of some structures and thus increased transient memory use. This typically is the transition mode.

- **Read and write**—BGP accepts updates, calculates the best path, installs the routes into the IP routing table, and generates updates to be sent to peers. More transient memory is needed. This is the normal BGP mode.

A best-practice guideline during capacity planning is to increase another 20% of the static memory use to account for the transient memory and any other variables. Another number to watch out for is the minimum largest block of DRAM available in the system. If that number is 20 MB or less, more resources are needed.

All best network/path entries in the BGP RIB are installed into IP RIB, resulting in memory use for NDB and RDB structures. If a major network is subnetted, in fixed or variable length, an additional entry is created in IP RIB for the major network. Each entry uses 1172 bytes of memory, depending on the IOS release. The memory use for subnetted entries is shown as internal in **show ip route summary**. This value is the total number of entries in **show ip route**, with *prefix* subnetted or variably subnetted. Because only two to six major networks were used in this test, the memory use for subnetted entries in IP RIB is less than 7 KB.

Another important contributor to BGP memory use in IP RIB and IP CEF that is not considered in this test is BGP load sharing. By default, BGP installs one best path into the IP RIB. With BGP multipath, multiple entries per BGP prefix may be installed into the IP routing table, resulting in increased memory use by IP RIB and IP CEF.

BGP prefixes installed in the IP RIB are populated in the FIB table. Memory allocation for IP CEF is generally in line with what is reported by **show ip cef summary**. For line cards running dCEF, this is the only memory use for BGP, because line cards do not maintain the BGP RIB or the IP RIB. Besides the number of prefixes, memory use by CEF is also related to prefix length. For example, if the prefix is /16, the memory use for this prefix is 1 KB on top of the 1 KB used by the root of mtrie. If the prefix is /24, another 1 KB is used. If the prefix is longer than /24, another 1 KB is used. Internet prefix distribution generally shows 9% for prefixes /16 and shorter, 83% for prefixes between /17 and /24, and 8% for prefixes longer than /24. With the goal of establishing a simple method without losing accuracy, the prefixes used in this test were all /24.

Summary

This chapter started by examining the relations between the control plane and the forwarding plane; both are fundamental functions of a router. As a routing protocol, BGP is a part of the control plane. However, BGP's performance can be affected by the forwarding plane's performance, because both planes might compete for the same resources, such as CPU and memory. BGP processes in Cisco IOS software were discussed, with emphasis on memory use and the interactions among the processes. The case study provided a simple method to estimate BGP memory use in Cisco Internet routers. To build a solid foundation for the rest of the book, this chapter reviewed some of BGP's essential components. These include BGP attributes, path selection, capabilities exchange, iBGP, BGP-IGP routing exchange, and RIB.

On the forwarding plane, all common switching paths in IOS were discussed, with an emphasis on CEF. Process switching and cache-based switching were reviewed as well. As the high-performance switching mechanism in IOS, CEF was presented in detail, with its components, structure, load sharing, and distributed form.

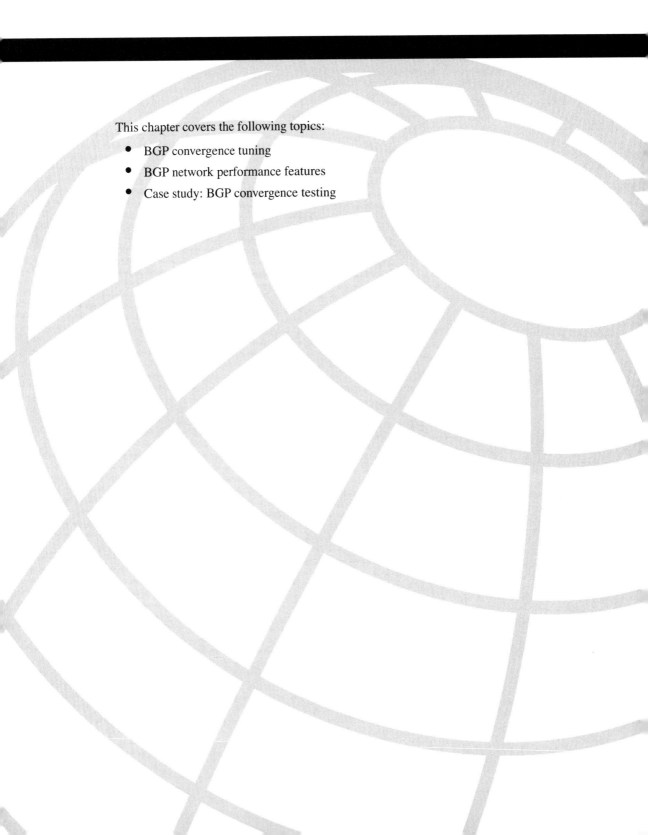

This chapter covers the following topics:

- BGP convergence tuning
- BGP network performance features
- Case study: BGP convergence testing

CHAPTER 3

Tuning BGP Performance

The focus of this chapter is tuning BGP performance. There is some ambiguity as to what exactly is meant by BGP performance, because BGP performance has several aspects. This chapter divides BGP performance tuning into two major categories:

- BGP convergence from an uninitialized state
- BGP network performance

BGP convergence from an uninitialized state is an aspect of BGP performance concerned with how quickly BGP can converge from an empty Routing Information Base (RIB). Performance tuning is focused on optimizing the transport mechanisms and updating generation facilities.

BGP network performance focuses on reduction of routing information through intelligent filter handling, managing network and routing instability, and convergence timing issues between the IGP and BGP. The BGP network performance topics covered in this chapter are

- BGP fast external fallover
- IGP/BGP convergence time deltas
- BGP Non-Stop Forwarding
- BGP route flap dampening
- Soft reconfiguration and route refresh
- Transmit side loop detection
- Outbound route filtering

This chapter concludes with a case study on BGP convergence optimization. Through the use of lab testing, this case study examines in depth the impact of peer groups, queue optimization, TCP tuning, and efficient BGP update packing.

BGP Convergence Tuning

This section examines performance aspects of BGP convergence from an uninitialized state. This state is typical for a router that has just been reloaded or is newly deployed. BGP convergence from an uninitialized state is of special interest because of the significant impact on the network.

NOTE	The term *BGP convergence* requires clarification to ensure that a common definition is being used. A BGP router is said to have converged when the following criteria have been met: • All routes are accepted. • All routes are installed in the routing table. • The table version counter for all peers must equal the table version of the BGP table. • The BGP InQ and OutQ for all peers must be 0. This chapter defines convergence as the amount of time it takes from the establishment of the first peer until the router has a fully populated RIB and has updated all its BGP peers.

The placement of the initializing router in the network is significant in determining the scope of impact on convergence. The focus is on convergence internal to the network. The following examples describe three different BGP convergence scenarios:

- **Scenario 1: The edge router initializes**— An edge router is an ISP router that is used for customer aggregation. A more-detailed explanation of the BGP topology for an edge router is provided in Chapter 9, "Service Provider Architecture." An edge router initializes its BGP sessions with the customers and with its two upstream route reflectors. The route reflectors send down the full internal table of 125,000 prefixes. The edge router sends upstream 500 prefixes, received from the customers, to the route reflectors. The edge router receives approximately 250,000 paths and advertises 500 prefixes to both the route reflectors.

- **Scenario 2: The peering router initializes**— A peering router is an ISP router that is used for connecting to another ISP, a special case of the edge router. A more-detailed explanation of peering is provided in Chapter 9. A peering router initializes its BGP sessions with the external peers and its two upstream route reflectors. If the peering router receives 80,000 unique prefixes from its various peers, they are sent upstream to the route reflectors. The route reflectors advertise the internal table, which consists of 125,000 prefixes, to the peering router.

The decision process on the router reflectors could result in prefixes being withdrawn and updated across the entire network for a subset of those 80,000 prefixes received from the peering router. The peering router also runs the decision process and might withdraw prefixes from the route reflectors based on the decision process outcome.

This BGP scenario results in the peering router's receiving 80,000 paths from the peers and 250,000 paths from the upstream route reflectors (125,000 from each). The route reflectors each receive 80,000 prefixes. If 25 percent of these are installed in the routing table on the route reflectors, this results in 20,000 update messages being sent to all iBGP peers and route reflector clients on those route reflectors. A total of 50 peering sessions on the route reflectors would result in 1 million advertised paths per route reflector.

- **Scenario 3: The route reflector initializes**—A route reflector initializes its BGP sessions with its regular iBGP peers and route reflector clients. The route reflector might receive 400,000 paths, which results in 125,000 prefixes installed in the routing table from its nonclient iBGP peers. The 125,000 prefixes are advertised to all its client sessions. If the route reflector has 50 clients, 7.5 million prefixes are advertised. If the route reflector has 100 clients, there are 15 million prefix advertisements. This provides a best-case number. If the sessions come up staggered over a period of time, the best path could change several times, resulting in a significant increase in advertisements.

Each of these scenarios results in different behavior on the network. The concentration of update generation varies based on the source of prefix information for that BGP speaker. The edge router scenario injects very small amounts of new prefix information into the network, resulting in a much smaller scope of impact. The peering router injects significantly more new prefix information, which greatly increases the scope of impact on the network. The route reflectors, however, are the real workhorses for distributing BGP prefix information. The route reflectors send the most significant number of prefix updates, regardless of where the route initialization takes place.

The commonality in the initialization scenarios is that BGP works with large amounts of prefix information. Changes in that information can result in very large amounts of data generation and advertisement. This section focuses on tuning BGP to deliver large amounts of information as efficiently as possible. The areas in which tuning is performed are as follows:

- **TCP operation**—The underlying transport for BGP is TCP. The operation of TCP provides opportunities for improving BGP convergence.

- **Router queues**—The route reflectors generate a moderate amount of data per peer, but aggregate for all the peers results in a significant amount of data generation. The operation of TCP requires that the peers respond to the route reflectors to acknowledge receipt of the TCP packets. This many-to-one data flow can overload the route reflector with more information than it can process immediately.

- **Data packaging**—BGP information can be packaged for transmission in multiple ways. Optimizations are available when commonalities in data or remote peer attributes are leveraged. These commonalities take advantage of the BGP update packaging mechanism to drastically reduce the number of packets required.

The following sections examine each of these aspects of the BGP update process, identify bottlenecks, and recommend features that can improve performance. These aspects are interdependent. This section concludes with a discussion of the interdependencies.

TCP Protocol Considerations

The two main parameters that affect TCP's performance are the maximum segment size (MSS) and the TCP window size. The TCP MSS controls the size of the TCP segment, or packet, and the TCP window size controls the rate at which packets can be sent.

TCP MSS

The TCP MSS for a session is determined at session initiation. This value is advertised using a TCP option, as described in RFC 793. The TCP MSS option is carried only in the SYN packet and the corresponding SYN/ACK. The TCP MSS that is used for the TCP session is the smallest of the advertised TCP MSS options in the SYN packets, as shown in Figure 3-1.

Figure 3-1 *TCP Session Establishment and MSS Determination*

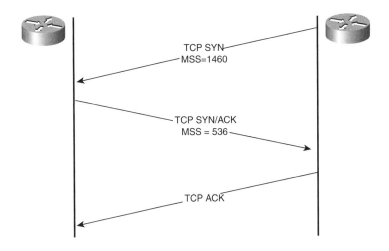

A Cisco router uses a default MSS of 536. This is based on the requirement in RFC 791 that a host not send a packet larger than 576 bytes unless it is certain that the destination can accept packets larger than 576 bytes. The MSS value of 536 results from the 576-byte requirement minus 20 bytes for the IP header and 20 bytes for the TCP header.

The assurance that the destination can accept packets that are larger than 576 also implies that the packets can reach the destination without being fragmented. Any performance gains achieved by a larger MSS would be drastically reduced, if not completely negated, by excessive fragmentation in the delivery path.

The main issue with the TCP MSS value defaulting to 536 is the number of packets that are required to send large amounts of BGP prefix information. Typically, a TCP ACK is sent for every other packet. This is a two-to-one ratio of BGP update packets to TCP ACKs.

Increasing the TCP MSS from 536 bytes to 1460 bytes, which is based on a maximum transmission unit (MTU) of 1500 minus 40 bytes of IP and TCP headers, provides a reduction in update packets of 272%! This update packet reduction in turn reduces the number of acknowledgments by two-thirds.

TCP Window Size

The *TCP window size* is the mechanism that TCP uses to control the rate at which it sends packets. The TCP window default value in Cisco is 16 KB. There is a command-line interface (CLI) command to configure the TCP window value. However, this value is not applied to the BGP sessions, which continue to use the 16 KB default. The role of TCP window size is examined in more detail in the section "Queue Optimization."

Path MTU Discovery

The Path MTU Discovery (PMTUD) feature is defined in RFC 1191. This feature determines what the MTU is over the path between two nodes. This allows the TCP session to set the maximum possible MSS to improve TCP performance for large data transfers without causing IP fragmentation.

PMTUD is based on trial and error. The first packet is built to the size of the MTU of the next-hop interface to the destination. The Don't Fragment (DF) bit is set, and the IP packet is sent. If the packet reaches the destination, the session forms.

However, if the packet does not reach the destination, the intermediary hop that discards the packet because of an MTU conflict responds with an ICMP Packet Too Big message, which contains the MTU of the link that could not accommodate the packet. The sending host then issues another packet that is sized to the MTU in the ICMP message. This process repeats until the packet reaches the destination.

The MSS value is set to the MTU minus the 40 bytes of IP and TCP overhead. The 40-byte values assumes that additional TCP options are not being used, which is the default behavior. This provides the 1460-byte MTU. It is possible to have even larger MTU sizes, especially internal to the network. The Packet over SONET (POS) link has an MTU of 4470. If two BGP peers use PMTUD and are connected only by POS or ATM links with MTUs of 4470, the MSS could be as large as 4430, which provides an even greater reduction in update packets and TCP ACK messages.

There is a major caveat to be aware of when the MSS derived from PMTUD is greater than 1460. Figure 3-2 shows the initial network topology, with the path of the BGP TCP session.

Figure 3-2   *Path MTU Discovery Path Change Scenario*

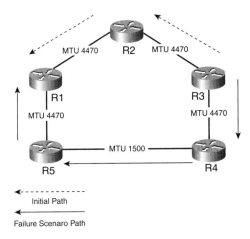

If the link between R2 and R3 fails, the TCP session is rerouted and sent over the link between R3 and R5. This path has a Fast Ethernet segment, which reduces the path MTU to 1500. The result is that large BGP updates are fragmented on R5, which reduces performance and increases convergence time.

However, the impact that BGP update fragmentation has depends heavily on network events. If no major routing changes happen, there is minimal to no impact. If major routing churn occurs, this can significantly impair convergence, especially if the link failure results in a large number of BGP sessions experiencing this impact.

This issue is resolved by using Gigabit Ethernet and jumbo frames. It is also becoming much less common to see Fast Ethernet as part of the core infrastructure in large BGP environments. A typical large-scale BGP network is composed of POS and Gigabit Ethernet.

Queue Optimization

The purpose of queue optimization is to minimize packet loss. This most often occurs on a router with a large fan-out of BGP sessions. The root cause is the stream of acknowledgments that are received from a large number of peers simultaneously. The router is unable to process all the TCP ACKs, causing the input queues to overflow, resulting in packet loss. This packet loss causes TCP retransmissions and loss of peer group synchronization. Peer group synchronization is discussed in the section "Peer Groups." A better understanding of queue optimization first requires an understanding of what queues are involved in the packet reception process.

Packet Reception Process

The packet reception process for BGP packets has three major components:

- **Input hold queue**—This is not an actual queue, but a counter that is assigned to an interface. When a packet bound for the processor is received on an interface, the input hold queue is incremented by 1. After that packet has been processed, the input hold queue is decremented to reflect that the packet is no longer in the queue. Each input queue has a maximum queue depth.

- **Selective Packet Discard (SPD) Headroom**—SPD Headroom is a counter that allows the input hold queues to exceed their configured maximum size. The total value of the SPD Headroom is shared by all the interfaces. This headroom is used to store high-priority packets, such as routing control traffic, above and beyond the input hold queue. The SPD feature is discussed in detail in the section "Selective Packet Discard."

- **System buffers**—The system buffers store the incoming packets being sent to the process level. A packet destined for the processor is removed from the interface buffer and is put in the system buffer. These buffers can be seen with the **show buffers** command.

The packet reception process is as follows:

1 A BGP packet is received on an interface.

2 The switching process requests a system buffer.

   a. If no system buffer is available, the packet is discarded, and the input drop counter is incremented.

   b. If a system buffer is available, the input hold queue is checked. If the queue is full, the packet's priority is checked.

   c. If the packet has IP Precedence 6 or is an L2 Keepalive, the SPD Headroom is checked. If there is room, the packet is kept, and the input hold queue is incremented. If the SPD Headroom is full, the packet is dropped, and the input drop counter is incremented.

  d. If the packet is normal priority, the packet is dropped, and the input drop counter is incremented.

  e. If the input hold queue is not full, the packet is kept, and the input hold queue counter is incremented.

3 The packet is processed.

4 The input hold queue is decremented.

The three major components of the packet-reception process are each a possible discard location. The queue optimization involves tuning each of these components to minimize dropping legitimate packets.

Hold Queue Optimization

The input hold queue has a default value of 75. In an environment with a larger number of BGP sessions, this is insufficient to hold a rush of incoming TCP ACKs. The following interface configuration command is used to change the size of the input hold queue:

hold-queue *value* **in**

The size change is *nonimpacting*, meaning that it can be configured without causing negative impact on a running router. The size of the input hold queue is shown in the output of the **show interfaces** command.

In determining the value to use when configuring the input hold queue, use the worst-case scenario to ensure that the hold queue size is sufficient. You can determine the maximum possible number of TCP ACKs that will be waiting to be processed by checking the following TCP parameters for the BGP sessions:

- **TCP window size and TCP MSS**—TCP window size is a static 16 KB. The TCP window is the amount of information a TCP session can transmit before it must receive an ACK. TCP MSS indicates how much data is sent in each packet.

  The TCP MSS and the TCP window size together determine the maximum number of outstanding TCP packets requiring acknowledgment.

  The TCP window size of 16,000 and a default TCP MSS of 536 indicate that 29 packets can be sent before an acknowledgment is required. A TCP MSS of 1460 allows 10 unacknowledged packets, and a TCP MSS of 4430 allows three packets.

  To optimize TCP ACK generation, only every other TCP packet generates a TCP ACK. The TCP ACK acknowledges all the TCP packets received up to the sequence number in the TCP ACK. This reduces the TCP ACK count to 50% of the TCP data packet count.

- **Number of BGP sessions terminated on the router**—There is a single TCP session for each BGP peering session.

The following hold queue sizing formula helps you determine the worst-case scenario:

$$\begin{matrix} \text{Hold} \\ \text{Queue} \\ \text{Size} \end{matrix} = \frac{\text{Window Size}}{2 * \text{MSS}} * \text{Peer Count}$$

This is a worst-case formula for the number of acknowledgments that can be sent to a single BGP router at one time. The window size divided by the MSS times 2 provides the maximum number of TCP segments that can be unacknowledged at any point. Cisco IOS software sends one TCP ACK per two TCP segments, so the maximum number of acknowledgments is one-half the maximum number of segments that can be outstanding. The maximum number of outstanding acknowledgments per peer can be multiplied by the route's peer count to obtain the maximum number of outstanding TCP ACK messages for a particular BGP router.

Table 3-1 shows results for various TCP MSS values.

Table 3-1   *Worst-Case Input Queue Values for BGP Traffic*

TCP MSS (in Bytes)	Window Size (in Bytes)	Session Count	Hold Queue Size
536	16000	50	700
1460	16000	50	200
4430	16000	50	50
536	16000	100	1400
1460	16000	100	400
4430	16000	100	100

The values in Table 3-1 are the worst-case values for the BGP packets. This does not include any other traffic destined for the route processor that also needs a place in the hold queue. The common recommendation is to set the input hold queue to a value of 1000 in heavy BGP environments. This accounts for additional traffic, such as management traffic and other control plane traffic.

SPD

The SPD feature is a queue-management mechanism that operates on the input hold queues for traffic destined for the route processor. The SPD process can distinguish between high- and normal-priority traffic, allowing it to better manage system resources in the input queue. The SPD function is specifically for managing input queue congestion.

The SPD process divides the queue to the route processor into a general packet queue (GPQ) and a priority queue. The packets in the GPQ are subject to the preemptive discard mechanism in SPD. The GPQ is for IP packets only, and it is a global queue, not a per-interface queue. The packets in the priority queue are not subject to this discard process.

The SPD random discard process is done through the SPD state check on the GPQ. Two thresholds determine the GPQ's SPD state: the minimum threshold and the maximum threshold. There are three SPD queue states:

- Normal state:

  GPQ depth <= minimum threshold

- Random Drop state:

  minimum threshold < GPQ depth <= maximum threshold

- Full Drop state:

  maximum threshold < GPQ depth

The SPD state check uses the queue's state to determine the action to take on the packet. When the queue is in a Normal state, packets are not discarded. If the queue depth crosses the minimum threshold, the SPD process is in Random Drop state. At this point, SPD begins discarding normal-priority packets randomly. If the queue depth crosses the maximum threshold, the SPD process is in Full Drop state. All normal-priority packets are discarded until the queue depth drops below the maximum threshold.

In Random Drop state, SPD can operate in two modes: normal and aggressive. When operating in aggressive mode, SPD drops malformed IP packets. In normal mode, SPD does not pay attention to whether packets are malformed.

The minimum and maximum thresholds are determined by the smallest hold queue on the router. The minimum threshold is 2 less than the size of the queue. The maximum threshold is 1 less than the size of the queue. This is to ensure that no interface will be throttled, which is what occurs when the input queue is completely full.

In addition to providing queue management, the SPD process is also used to protect high-priority traffic. Although Random Drop state and Full Drop state drop only normal-priority traffic, two additional extensions to the input queue are available to high-priority traffic: SPD Headroom and SPD Extended Headroom.

SPD Headroom allows the input queue to exceed the configured input hold queue. If the input hold queue is 75 and the SPD Headroom is 100, which are the default values, the input hold queue can hold 175 packets. As soon as the input hold queue reaches its maximum depth of 75, only high-priority packets are accepted, until the input queue reaches an overloaded depth of 175. Packets considered high-priority are IP Precedence 6 traffic (BGP), IGP packets, and L2 keepalives.

The second extension is the SPD Extended Headroom, which allows further extension to the input queue beyond the combined value of the input hold queue and the SPD Headroom. The default value for the SPD Extended Headroom is 10, which results in the input queue's having a maximum depth of 185. The SPD Extended Headroom is only for IGP packets and L2 keepalives. These packets are crucial to maintaining a stable network.

The complete picture of the input queue is shown in Figure 3-3.

Figure 3-3 *Input Hold Queue Layout*

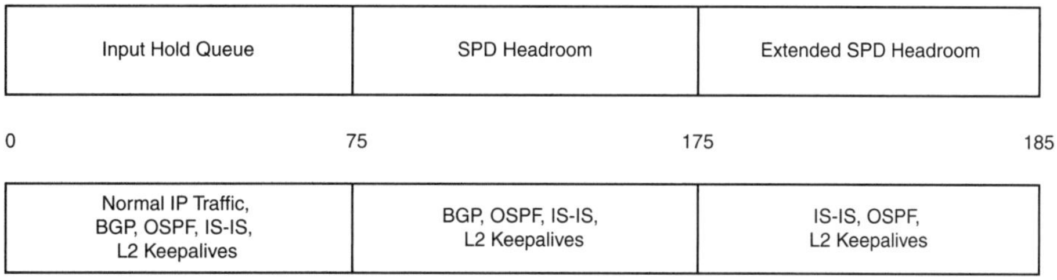

Input Hold Queue	SPD Headroom	Extended SPD Headroom

| 0 | 75 | 175 | 185 |

Normal IP Traffic, BGP, OSPF, IS-IS, L2 Keepalives	BGP, OSPF, IS-IS, L2 Keepalives	IS-IS, OSPF, L2 Keepalives

The maximum input queue actually consists of three values: the input hold queue, the SPD Headroom, and the SPD Extended Headroom. Each is more specific and is tailored toward preserving higher-priority traffic from being crowded out.

The default size of the SPD Headroom has been increased in Cisco IOS Release 12.0(19)S to accommodate the needs of large-scale BGP networks. The new default, 1000, is specific to 12.0S and is the same as the standard suggested size for the input hold queue. This is because in the worst-case scenario of tuning the input hold queue, it was determined that 1000 TCP ACKs was a reasonable expectation. If the input hold queue is full of regular IP traffic for some reason, the SPD Headroom of 1000 is sufficient to hold the influx of TCP ACK messages.

The sizing of the SPD Headroom is to prevent packet loss for high-priority traffic. Aggressive sizing of the SPD Headroom is not a problem, because only high-priority traffic is allowed to use the SPD Headroom to increase the input queue depth beyond the configured input hold queue.

It is also common practice to enable SPD aggressive mode. If the input queue has become congested, maintaining malformed IP packets is a poor use of system resources. The standard recommended SPD configuration is as follows:

- **ip spd mode aggressive**
- **ip spd headroom 1000**
- **ip spd queue min-threshold 998**
- **ip spd queue max-threshold 999**

You can verify the SPD parameters with the command **show ip spd**, as shown in Example 3-1.

Example 3-1   *Command Output for* **show ip spd**

```
Router#show ip spd
Current mode: normal.
Queue min/max thresholds: 73/74, Headroom: 100, Extended Headroom: 10
IP normal queue: 0, priority queue: 0.
SPD special drop mode: none
```

The SPD Headroom is not a queue of its own, just like the input hold queue is not an actual queue, but a counter. The SPD Headroom and SPD Extended Headroom are extensions to the input hold queue counter.

System Buffers

The last component of the data path to the process level is the system buffers. These buffers are where the actual data is stored for the processor. System buffers are created and destroyed as needed. The memory used to allocate system buffers is the main processor memory. The system buffer information on the router is shown with the **show buffers** command in Exec mode. A sample portion is provided in Example 3-2 for only the small buffers. The small buffers are the system buffers that are used for packets less than 104 bytes.

Example 3-2   *System Buffer Information for Small Buffers*

```
Small buffers, 104 bytes (total 150, permanent 150):
    140 in free list (30 min, 250 max allowed)
    564556247 hits, 148477066 misses, 16239797 trims, 16239797 created
    29356200 failures (0 no memory)
```

The small buffers are of most interest from a BGP tuning perspective. The handling of a large influx of TCP ACK messages is the main thrust of queue optimization. A TCP ACK is 64 bytes, so it is stored in the small buffers. Table 3-2 explains each field shown in Example 3-2.

Table 3-2   *Explanation of the Fields in Example 3-2*

Field	Description
total	The total number of buffers currently in the pool, both used and unused.
permanent	The minimum number of buffers that will always be present in the pool. Buffers will not be trimmed below this number.
free list	The number of buffers that are currently available in the pool and are unused.
min	The number of buffers the router should try to keep in the free list. If the free list drops under this number, more buffers should be created.
max allowed	The maximum number of buffers the router is allowed to keep in the free list. If the free list increases beyond this number, the router should trim buffers.
hits	The number of buffers successfully allocated from the free list.
misses	The number of times a buffer was requested but none were available in the free list.
trims	The number of buffers trimmed from the free list because max allowed was exceeded.
created	The number of buffers created because the free list dropped below min.
failures	The number of failures to grant a buffer under interrupt processing. The number of failures represents the number of packets dropped because of buffer shortage.
no memory	The number of times the router tried to create a new buffer, but there was not enough free memory.

The default values for system buffers are for an average environment. They are not optimal for a large BGP deployment. The main area of concern is the low number of small buffers. A value of 150 for the Permanent value results in severe packet loss with a huge influx of TCP ACK messages on a route reflector with 50 to 100 peers. The number of small buffers eventually will be created, but only after a significant number of TCP ACKs have been lost.

You must check the amount of free memory before changing buffer settings to ensure that there is adequate free memory for the new buffers. This is done with the **show memory summary** command.

You need to tune three parameters when modifying the small buffers to handle the TCP ACKs:

- **Permanent buffers**—The number of permanent buffers should be sufficient to handle the worst-case scenario number of TCP ACK messages. This ensures that the router has the available buffers to handle a sudden influx of packets.

- **Min-free setting**—Increase the Min-free setting to prompt the router to create more buffers before the free list reaches a critical level. This number should be approximately 25% of the permanent buffers.

- **Max-free setting**—The Max-free setting should be more than the permanent buffers plus the Min-free value. This helps prevent buffers from being trimmed prematurely.

The configuration commands for small-buffer tuning are shown in Example 3-3.

Example 3-3 *Buffer Tuning Configuration*

```
buffer small permanent 1000
buffer small min-free 250
buffer small max-free 1375
```

Buffer tuning should be done with care. The buffer tuning performed here is specific to route reflectors that are subject to massive influxes of TCP ACKs. If a large number of TCP retransmissions are seen on the BGP sessions with significant buffer failures, buffer tuning is a possible option. When performing buffer tuning, it is best to involve the Cisco Technical Assistance Center (TAC).

BGP Update Generation

The focus of this chapter so far has been on reducing the bottlenecks in the transport of BGP updates. The first section focused on optimizing the TCP aspects of the transport, and the second section focused on ensuring that the router can handle the amount of traffic delivered. The most significant performance gains in achieving fast BGP convergence are found in the manner in which updates are generated.

The bottlenecks in the default TCP and queue configurations are not a significant factor if the router is unable to generate BGP update messages efficiently. This section focuses on the following methods of improving update generation, which are the basis for any BGP convergence tuning:

- Peer groups
- BGP dynamic update peer groups
- Update packing enhancement
- BGP read-only mode

Peer Groups

Peer groups provide the foundation for optimizing BGP convergence. Peer groups provide a mechanism for BGP peers that have the same outbound policy to be associated with each other. This feature has two major benefits: configuration reduction and the ability to replicate updates between peers.

The most common reason for deploying peer groups is configuration reduction. The peer group is formed, and the common outbound policy is applied to the peer group. Each peer that has the same outbound policy is assigned to the peer group, which can greatly reduce redundant configuration on routers that have a large number of BGP peers. Example 3-4 shows a sample BGP configuration without peer groups.

Example 3-4 *BGP Neighbor Configuration*

```
router bgp 100
 ...
 neighbor 10.1.1.1 version 4
 neighbor 10.1.1.1 remote-as 100
 neighbor 10.1.1.1 password cisco
 neighbor 10.1.1.1 route-reflector-client
 neighbor 10.1.1.1 update-source loopback0
 ...
```

Five lines of configuration are needed for every route reflector client in Example 3-4. In Example 3-5, this configuration is done using peer groups.

Example 3-5 *BGP Neighbor Configuration with Peer Groups*

```
router bgp 100
 ...
 neighbor RR_CLIENTS peer-group
 neighbor RR_CLIENTS version 4
 neighbor RR_CLIENTS password cisco
 neighbor RR_CLIENTS route-reflector-client
 neighbor RR_CLIENTS update-source loopback0
 neighbor RR_CLIENTS remote-as 100
 neighbor 10.1.1.1 peer-group RR_CLIENTS
 ...
```

In Example 3-5, the initial peer group configuration takes six lines. The addition of a new route reflector client takes only a single line of configuration. This reduces the configuration's size, increases configuration readability, and reduces the probability of configuration errors. Inbound configuration can be applied to the peer group and to the individual neighbors. The inbound policy for members of a peer group does not need to be consistent.

If peer groups were purely a configuration enhancement feature, the restriction of all peers sharing the same outbound policy would not make sense. However, the main benefit of peer groups—the ability to replicate updates across peers—is derived from this requirement.

Because all the peers have the same outbound policy, the update messages they send are the same. This means that the BGP update message is generated once for each peer group and then is reused for all the neighbors.

In a nonpeer group environment, the BGP process must walk the entire BGP table for every peer, creating updates for each peer independently. If there are 100,000 prefixes and 100 iBGP peers, the router walks through 10,000,000 prefixes.

In a peer group environment, the BGP process walks the entire BGP table only once for each peer group. A peer group leader is elected for each peer group based on the lowest IP address. The BGP process walks the table for the peer group leader, creating the BGP update messages. These update messages are replicated for all other members in the peer group. If the 100 iBGP peers are all in the same peer group, the router walks 100,000 prefixes instead of 10,000,000. This optimization reduces both the processor and memory requirements.

A peer group member must be in sync with the peer group leader for replication to take place. A peer group member is synchronized with the leader if the set of BGP paths advertised to the leader has also been advertised to the peer group member. A peer group member that is initialized after the peer group has begun to converge will not be in sync with the peer group. This requires the router to format update messages for the nonsynchronized peer just like a nonpeer group member until that peer becomes synchronized with the peer group leader.

The command to examine the replication statistics is **show ip bgp peer-group**, as shown in Example 3-6.

Example 3-6   *Command Output for* **show ip bgp peer-group**

```
Router#show ip bgp peer-group
BGP peer-group is regular_group, peer-group leader 10.1.1.2, external
 Index 1, Offset 0, Mask 0x2
  BGP version 4
  Neighbor NLRI negotiation:
    Configured for unicast routes only
  Minimum time between advertisement runs is 30 seconds
  Update messages formatted 2714375, replicated 4174650

BGP peer-group is filter_group, peer-group leader 10.1.1.17, external
 Index 2, Offset 0, Mask 0x4
  BGP version 4
  Neighbor NLRI negotiation:
    Configured for unicast routes only
  Minimum time between advertisement runs is 30 seconds
  Update messages formatted 1904858, replicated 3145550
```

In the example, for peer group regular_group, the number of update messages that are formatted is 2714375, and the number replicated is 4174650. The number of peers is not shown; however, there are 55 peers in regular_group. If the number of replicated messages is divided by the number of formatted messages, the result is the replication rate—in this case, 1.54. In an optimal situation, the replication rate is 1 less than the total number of peers. The number of updates per peer is 125,255. If the replication had been perfect, 125,255 updates would have been formatted for the peer group leader, and 6,763,770 updates would have been replicated for the other 54 peer group members.

BGP Dynamic Update Peer Groups

The BGP dynamic peer group feature, first introduced in Cisco IOS Release 12.0(24)S, identifies peers that have the same outbound policy and optimizes update generation and replication across those peers. Before this feature, these peers had to be manually grouped with traditional peer groups. The use of traditional peer groups limited the available outbound policy that could be defined and the ability to have session-specific configuration. Dynamic peer groups separate the peer group configuration from update replication through two new features:

- Peer templates
- Update groups

The next sections discuss both dynamic peer group features in more detail.

Peer Templates

The traditional peer group model was focused on update replication. This constrained the ability to configure outbound policy for the peer group to those features that would allow update replication. Traditional peer groups from a configuration perspective had two major disadvantages:

- All neighbors in a peer group must have the exact same outbound routing policy.
- All neighbors in a peer group must be in the same address family.

Fulfilling these requirements allowed update replication to be performed across a peer group.

The configuration feature of peer templates allows a set of configuration options to be applied to a set of neighbors. Peer templates are reusable and support inheritance, giving you much more power and flexibility in generating concise BGP configurations.

The peer template model allows you to develop the needed policies without the restrictions imposed by the update replication requirements. Update groups, which handle the update replication, are covered in the next section.

There are two types of peer templates:

- Peer session templates
- Peer policy templates

Peer session templates are used to build a template of general session configuration. This does not include any policy type attributes, but is focused on session attributes. Peer session templates support the following commands:

- **description**
- **disable-connected-check**

- **ebgp-multihop**
- **local-as**
- **password**
- **remote-as**
- **shutdown**
- **timers**
- **translate-update**
- **update-source**
- **version**

The commands supported are all general session commands. These commands apply across all address families.

Peer policy templates are used to build a template of policy information. This includes aspects of the BGP session related to manipulating actual BGP prefix information, such as filtering, capabilities, and route reflection. Peer policy templates support the following commands:

- **advertisement-interval**
- **allowas-in**
- **as-override**
- **capability**
- **default-originate**
- **distribute-list**
- **dmzlink-bw**
- **filter-list**
- **maximum-prefix**
- **next-hop-self**
- **next-hop-unchanged**
- **prefix-list**
- **remove-private-as**
- **route-map**
- **route-reflector-client**
- **send-community**
- **send-label**
- **soft-reconfiguration**

- **unsuppress-map**
- **weight**

Many of the commands are not applicable across address families. For example, a prefix list assigned to IPv4 sessions does not apply to an IPv6 session.

Peer templates provide inheritance capabilities to maximize template reusability. You can build a general template containing the basic attributes, and then you can build more-specific templates containing only additional information. Example 3-7 defines a general session template. The attributes configured are true for all peers, both internal and external. The internal-session template and external-session template are built using the base-session template as a foundation.

Example 3-7 *Session Inheritance Configuration*

```
router bgp 100
...
neighbor 10.1.1.1 inherit peer-session internal-session
...
template peer-session base-session
 password cisco
 version 4
 exit-peer-session
!
template peer-session internal-session
 inherit base-session
 update-source loopback0
 remote-as 100
 exit-peer-session
!
template peer-session external-session
 inherit base-session
 password customer
 remote-as 65001
 exit-peer-session
!
```

In the base-session template, the password is defined as cisco, but in the external-session it is changed to customer. When processing a template, any inherited templates are processed first, and then the configuration specific to that template occurs. In this case, the password setting of cisco is overwritten for the external-session with the password customer.

Templates are applied to BGP peering sessions using the inheritance concept. A neighbor has its default settings as its "base" configuration. The neighbor is configured to inherit a peer template, which modifies those settings. In the example, the BGP session 10.1.1.1 inherits the internal session template. Any configuration settings at the neighbor level take precedence over peer template settings.

A BGP session cannot be associated with both a peer group and peer templates. The peer templates feature is expected to ultimately replace the peer group feature. However, they will continue to coexist for quite some time.

Update Groups

The update replication aspect of traditional peer groups is where the dynamic aspect of dynamic peer groups comes into play. Peer templates provide a highly flexible replacement for peer group configuration. However, this is based on relaxing the requirements that make update replication across a peer group possible.

The router builds update groups dynamically based on examining the outbound policy of the configured BGP sessions. The router dynamically assigns BGP peers to update groups that have the same outbound policy configuration. No configuration is required for this feature.

When changes are made to the outbound policy of BGP peers, the router automatically recalculates the update groups. If any changes are required, the router automatically triggers a soft clear outbound for all affected BGP peers.

You can obtain information about BGP update groups with the **show ip bgp update-group** command, as shown in Example 3-8.

Example 3-8 *Command Output for* **show ip bgp update-group**

```
Router#show ip bgp update-group
...
BGP version 4 update-group 4, external, Address Family: IPv4 Unicast
  BGP Update version : 0, messages 9482/0
  Update messages formatted 11134, replicated 1002060
  Number of NLRIs in the update sent: max 0, min 0
  Minimum time between advertisement runs is 30 seconds
  Has 91 members (* indicates the members currently being sent updates):
   10.0.101.1      *10.0.101.100   *10.0.101.11    *10.0.101.12
  *10.0.101.13     *10.0.101.14    *10.0.101.15    *10.0.101.16
  *10.0.101.17     *10.0.101.18    *10.0.101.19    *10.0.101.20
... <TRUNCATED>
```

The output from Example 3-8 shows the essential information about the update group. The truncated information consists of the rest of the IP addresses for update group members. In this example, the update group 4 consists of IPv4 unicast eBGP peers. The replication statistics provided include the number of BGP Update messages formatted and replicated. The number of peers in the update group is given, along with a listing of those peers. An asterisk next to a peer's IP address indicates that updates are still being sent to that peer.

You can get a summary view of replication statistics for all update groups using the **show ip bgp replication** command, as shown in Example 3-9.

Example 3-9 *Command Output for* **show ip bgp replication**

```
Router#show ip bgp replication
BGP Total Messages Formatted/Enqueued : 9490/0

    Index    Type  Members      Leader   MsgFmt  MsgRepl  Csize  Qsize
        1 external     100  10.0.101.201        0        0      0      0
        2 external     100  10.0.101.101      289    28611      4      0
        3 external       9  10.0.101.10     20646   165168      0      0
        4 external      91   10.0.101.1     11134  1002060   9482      0
        5 internal       2  10.0.102.51      302      302      4      0
```

The general BGP replication statistics for the entire BGP router are provided, followed by the statistics for each update group. The update group index and update group leader are listed to identify the group, followed by the number of messages formatted and the number of messages replicated. Csize and Qsize indicate how many messages are in the Update Cache and the Update Write Queue, respectively. Nonzero values indicate that the update group is still converging.

In contrast to the previous section about peer groups, where the replication rate was 1.54, update group 3 in Example 3-9 has nine peers. The replication rate is 8. This shows optimal replication. Updates were formatted for the update group leader and were replicated for all eight of the other peers.

Update Packing Enhancement

A BGP update message consists of a BGP attribute combination followed by all the network layer reachability information (NLRI) that matches that attribute combination. The router walks through the BGP table for a certain period of time, building updates. The router transmits all the updates that have been created. This does not allow BGP to walk the entire table each time it sends updates, because the BGP table can be huge. The NLRI found for a particular attribute combination is not necessarily all the NLRI for that attribute combination. Multiple updates need to be sent for each attribute combination. This is not the most efficient method of handling update generation.

Cisco IOS Release 12.0(19)S brought about a significant enhancement to how Cisco IOS handles packing NLRI into BGP update messages. The solution is to build an update cache for each peer or update group. The NLRI for each attribute combination can then be packed in to create a single update for each attribute combination. This provides 100% efficiency for the update packing process and greatly reduces the number of BGP Update messages that must be formatted and replicated.

BGP Read-Only Mode

Originally, when BGP peers came online and accepted prefixes, the path-selection process would begin running before all the path information had been received from a peer. The BGP process would begin advertising prefix information to peers based on the outcome of the decision process. As more path information was received, the outcome from the decision process for a particular prefix resulted in best-path changes. This in turn resulted in multiple updates for the same prefix as the best path changed, which was inefficient.

Another similar issue is that the BGP process can begin advertising NLRI with a specific attribute set, but not all NLRI has been received for that attribute combination. This reduces the efficiency of the update packing.

This inefficiency can be removed by having a BGP peer remain in read-only mode until it stops receiving updates. As soon as the full path information has been received from a remote peer, the decision process can choose the best path for a prefix before sending any BGP Updates. A BGP peer in read-only mode only receives updates; it doesn't advertise any prefixes. An upper bound of 2 minutes is placed on a BGP peer remaining in read-only mode, based on the session initiation.

The addition of read-only mode also allows for optimal update packing. If the BGP router is sending updates before receiving full path information from all peers, all the NLRI for a particular attribute combination might not have been received before the BGP router begins sending updates. After the BGP peer finishes receiving the initial routing information from a peer, the BGP session changes to read-write mode. This allows the BGP router to run the decision process and send updates. You can configure the maximum amount of time that BGP stays in read-only mode using the command **bgp update-delay** *RO_Limit*.

RO_Limit is a limit on how long a BGP peer can remain in read-only mode. The BGP process automatically leaves read-only mode when it receives a BGP keepalive, which indicates that the initial routing update has completed. The end of the initial routing update can be detected because the Cisco BGP implementation sends the entire routing update before sending a BGP keepalive. The arrival of the first BGP keepalive signals the end of the initial routing update. As soon as the BGP decision process has completed, the IP routing table and CEF table are appropriately updated.

Performance Optimization Interdependencies

The convergence tuning described in this section should not be deployed in a piecemeal fashion. Each aspect is an optimization that builds on other aspects, with many interdependencies:

- The foundation for convergence tuning is the peer group feature or, in later versions, update groups. The update replication behavior greatly increases the amount of BGP update information a router can generate.

- The optimization of the queuing system on the router is performed to handle the additional load generated by the update replication.

- The TCP MSS manipulation with Path MTU Discovery is done to maximize the size of the BGP updates, reducing the number of BGP update messages and corresponding TCP ACKs.

- The read-only mode and update packing efficiencies maximize the effectiveness of each BGP update.

These features all enhance BGP's behavior independently; however, maximum impact is gained through the interdependency of the enhancements themselves.

BGP Network Performance Features

The topic of BGP performance is not solely about optimizing the BGP update process. Converging BGP on the network from a cold start is a very important aspect; however, the handling of network-affecting events is also an important topic. This section focuses on mitigating the impact of network failures and prefix update optimizations.

Network Failure Impact Mitigation

The failure of a node or link in the network is inevitable. Detecting the failure quickly and minimizing its impact is important for maintaining high network availability. In addition to handling failures quickly, the interaction between IGP and BGP can result in problematic recovery scenarios. This section covers the following features of failure mitigation:

- **BGP fast external fallover**—The BGP fast external fallover feature provides a mechanism for BGP to quickly tear down an eBGP session without waiting for the hold timer to expire.

- **IGP/BGP convergence time deltas**—The rate at which the IGP and BGP converges can create situations in which traffic loss is incurred. Mechanisms available in both IS-IS and OSPF help mitigate this issue.

- **BGP Non-Stop Forwarding (NSF)**—This feature is also called *graceful restart*. It is designed to make the restart of the BGP process invisible to the rest of the network.

BGP Fast External Fallover

The default behavior for tearing down a BGP session is to require the hold timer to expire, which by default is 180 seconds. The BGP fast external fallover function triggers the teardown of an eBGP session immediately when the link to that eBGP peer fails.

This quick fallover improves the speed at which the Adj-RIB-In for that peer is removed. This feature is only for external peers. If the link to an internal peer fails, it is usually possible to route around the failed link.

Tearing down iBGP peerings because the next-hop link failed can introduce significant network instability. A network failure that severs connectivity to the iBGP peers typically also results in loss of reachability to the next-hop addresses for prefixes learned from those peers. The BGP Scanner process removes those prefixes from the BGP decision process. Refer to Chapter 2, "Understanding BGP Building Blocks," for an explanation of the Scanner process.

The BGP fast external fallover feature is enabled globally, not on a per-peer basis. This feature is enabled by default. To disable this feature, under the BGP router process, configure the command **no bgp fast-external-fallover**.

The ability to apply greater granularity to this command is provided in Cisco IOS Releases 12.0ST and 12.1. The following interface configuration command was added. The default setting is to comply with the global setting:

```
ip bgp fast-external-fallover [permit | deny]
```

When using BGP fast external fallover, a link that is flapping repeatedly can result in BGP prefix dampening. The link stays down a couple of seconds and then comes back up. If BGP fast external fallover is used, the BGP session is torn down every couple of minutes, only to be restarted a couple of seconds later. It is even possible that the BGP session will have difficulty fully reconverging before it is torn down again.

However, BGP fast external fallover is useful for a customer edge router with multiple eBGP sessions to upstream providers. If the links are stable and the customer requires very fast fallover, this feature triggers BGP to act at the moment of link failure. This feature does not work with eBGP multihop, and the peering address must be the same as the physical interface address.

IGP/BGP Convergence Time Deltas

In general, the return of a router to service is not considered a potential cause of traffic loss. The common focus is on detecting the failure of a router and converging around the failed router. However, in a BGP network, a newly recovered router can result in traffic loss for a period equal to the BGP reconvergence time. Figure 3-4 shows the flow of traffic through the BGP network from the customer in AS 65000 to a destination in AS 200.

Figure 3-4 *IGP/BGP Convergence Scenario*

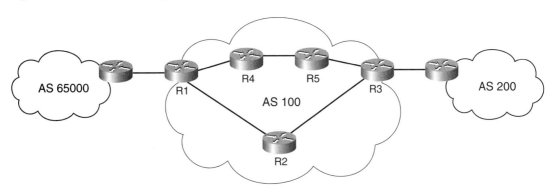

If R2 fails, the traffic reroutes, taking the longer path through R4, R5, and R3. The issue arises when R2 returns to service. The IGP reconverges, and the next hop on R1 for prefixes in AS 200 is R2. However, BGP has not reconverged on R2, which means that R2 does not know how to reach any destinations in AS 200. Traffic destined for AS 200 from AS 65000 is sent to R2. However, without the necessary routing information, the traffic is discarded until R2 learns the prefix information for AS 200.

The solution is to have a method for a router that has just rebooted to advertise in the IGP that it should not be used as a transit router. This means that the newly rebooted router must be a leaf on the Shortest Path Tree. The only traffic that should be sent to this router is traffic destined for a directly connected prefix. The prefixes on the router itself must be reachable, or the BGP sessions can't form.

The IS-IS and OSPF routing protocols both provide a transient black hole avoidance mechanism.

IS-IS Overload Bit

The IS-IS protocol provides a feature called the *Overload bit (OL-bit)*. The OL-bit is a value in the Link State PDU (LSP) that was originally intended to signal that the router was having a problem, such as resource starvation, and to specify that the router should not be included in the topology as a transit-capable router. However, the directly connected prefix information still can be reached through a router with the OL-bit set, much like a router acting as a multihomed host. This allows for remote router management.

The issue of IGP convergence black-holing traffic presents another use of the OL-bit. The OL-bit can be set for the newly rebooted router, which allows the BGP sessions to form and BGP to reconverge. The router, however, is not be used for transit. After the BGP sessions converge, the router issues a new copy of its LSP with the OL-bit removed. The fully converged router then becomes part of the transit topology.

There are two options. The first is to configure the router to set the OL-bit on startup for a predefined amount of time. This feature is configured as follows:

```
router isis
    set-overload-bit on-startup timeout
```

The only problem is that BGP might converge much faster than the configured time. The second option is to use the following configuration:

```
router isis
    set-overload-bit on-startup wait-for-bgp
```

This option allows BGP to signal to IS-IS that it is converged and to remove the OL-bit. If BGP does not signal IS-IS in 10 minutes, the OL-bit is removed. This prevents IS-IS from becoming stuck in an overloaded state. This feature was added to Cisco IOS Release 12.0(7)S. For information on integration into other Cisco IOS trains, reference Cisco DDTs CSCdp01872. It is recommended that you use the **wait-for-bgp** option.

OSPF Maximum Metric on Startup

The OSPF protocol does not have an OL-bit. In OSPF, the OL-bit functionality provided by IS-IS needs to be simulated through the manipulation of metrics. An OSPF router can set all metrics in its router link-state advertisement (LSA) and can network LSA to the maximum metric. This ensures that the router will not be used as a transit path but will still be reachable for BGP session formation. The configuration options are as follows:

```
router ospf 100
    max-metric router-lsa on-startup timeout
```

The OSPF max-metric feature can operate in cooperation with BGP using the following command:

```
router ospf 100
    max-metric router-lsa on-startup wait-for-bgp
```

The OSPF router reissues its router LSA and any network LSAs after notification from BGP that BGP is converged. If BGP does not notify OSPF in 10 minutes, the router LSA and network LSAs are regenerated with the proper metrics to prevent the router from becoming stuck in a nontransit state. You can verify the OSPF maximum metric on-startup feature with the **show ip ospf protocol** command, as shown in Example 3-10.

Example 3-10 *Verifying the OSPF Maximum Metric on Startup*

```
Routing Process "ospf 100" with ID 10.1.1.1
    Supports only single TOS(TOS0) routes
    Supports opaque LSA
    It is an area border and autonomous system boundary router
    Redistributing External Routes from,
        static, includes subnets in redistribution
    Originating router-LSAs with maximum metric, Time remaining: 00:01:18
        Condition: on startup while BGP is converging, State: active
    SPF schedule delay 5 secs, Hold time between two SPFs 10 secs
```

Example 3-10 *Verifying the OSPF Maximum Metric on Startup (Continued)*

```
        Minimum LSA interval 5 secs. Minimum LSA arrival 1 secs
        Number of external LSA 7. Checksum Sum 0x47261
        Number of opaque AS LSA 0. Checksum Sum 0x0
        Number of DCbitless external and opaque AS LSA 0
        Number of DoNotAge external and opaque AS LSA 0
        Number of areas in this router is 2. 1 normal 0 stub 1 nssa
        External flood list length 0
          Area BACKBONE(0)
             Number of interfaces in this area is 1
             Area has no authentication
             SPF algorithm executed 3 times
             Area ranges are
             Number of LSA 8. Checksum Sum 0x474AE
             Number of opaque link LSA 0. Checksum Sum 0x0
```

The OSPF max-metric feature was integrated into Cisco IOS Release 12.0(15)S. The IS-IS OL-Bit setting and OSPF max-metric setting provide identical functionality. They both allow the router to be reachable but removed from the transit path.

BGP Non-Stop Forwarding

When a BGP router restarts, the BGP peering session goes down. After the restart, the session reforms. This transition results in prefixes being withdrawn and then readvertised, which is called *route flapping*. Route flapping causes additional BGP route computation, update message generation, and forwarding table churn.

The current generation of middle to high-end routers has separated control plane processing from data plane processing. The route processor generates the forwarding table and programs it into the forwarding engines on the line cards. The route processor is not a required part of the forwarding path.

The BGP Non-Stop Forwarding (NSF) or graceful restart (BGP-GR) feature takes advantage of the independence of the data plane and control plane processing. The concept of BGP NSF is that the data plane can continue forwarding for a period of time while BGP restarts. This BGP restart could be in the form of a route processor reload, route processor switchover, or, in the future, a restart of the BGP process. When a BGP router goes down, it does not notify its peers that it is restarting. Following the restart, the BGP process forms new TCP sessions, resynchronizes its RIB, and performs any updates needed to the FIB. This entire process is visible only to the BGP peers of the restarting BGP router. Two additions to BGP provide this functionality:

- End-of-RIB marker
- Graceful restart capability

These new mechanisms are discussed in the next two sections.

End-of-RIB Marker

The end-of-RIB marker indicates to a BGP peer that the initial routing update has completed after session initiation. This feature is valuable for BGP convergence independently of BGP-GR. For general convergence, the end-of-RIB marker can serve as a trigger for BGP to run the best-path algorithm. This allows BGP to remain in read-only mode until the end-of-RIB marker is received for all peers. The best-path algorithm creates the local RIB. The BGP updates are built, efficiently packed, and sent to the remote peers.

For IPv4, the end-of-RIB marker is a BGP Update message with no reachable NLRI and empty withdrawn NLRI. Additional address families indicate the end-of-RIB with a BGP Update containing only the MP_UNREACH_NLRI attribute with no withdrawn routes for that AFI/SAFI. Although Cisco IOS does not send a keepalive until after the initial routing update, not all vendors conform to this behavior. The end-of-RIB provides an interoperable method of indicating the end of the initial routing update. This functionality is independent of BGP-GR can be used even when BGP-GR is not being used.

Graceful Restart Capability

The graceful restart capability, shown in Figure 3-5, is sent one time, as part of the capabilities negotiation process discussed in Chapter 2, in the section "BGP Capabilities." The graceful restart capability carries several important pieces of information. The existence of this capability indicates that the peer intends to use the end-of-RIB marker. This capability also contains the Restart State, Restart Time in the Restart Flags, and Forwarding State for each AFI/SAFI, as part of the Address Family flags.

Figure 3-5 *BGP Graceful Restart Capability*

Restart Flags (4 Bits)
Restart Time in Seconds (12 Bits)
Address Family Identifier (16 Bits)
Subsequent Address Family Identifier (8 Bits)
Flags for Address Family (8 Bits)
...
Address Famlly Identifier (16 Bits)
Subsequent Address Family Identifier (8 Bits)
Flags for Address Family (8 Bits)

The Restart State indicates that the router restarted. This prevents two adjacent restarting routers from deadlocking while waiting for an end-of-RIB marker. After a router restarts and reforms its BGP sessions, it waits until it has received the initial routing update from each of its peers before running the best-path algorithm and sending its own updates. If the Restart State is set to 1, they don't wait for that peer to send the initial routing update.

The Restart Time indicates how long a peer of the restarting router should maintain prefix information received from the restarting router. For example, suppose Router A indicates a Restart Time of 180 seconds to Router B. If Router A restarts but does not reform the session to Router B within 180 seconds, Router B assumes that there was a problem with Router A's restarting. Router B then removes all the stale prefix information in its RIB from Router A, removing Router A from the forwarding path.

The Forwarding State indicates if a router successfully maintained forwarding state over the restart. Not all platforms can maintain state information over a route processor restart. This must be indicated in the graceful restart capability after a router restarts. If a BGP router is capable of BGP-GR, but it cannot maintain forwarding state over a restart, it cannot restart gracefully itself. It only participates in a supporting role. This means that if the router that is incapable of maintaining forwarding state fails, it does not gracefully restart. However, if one of its peers that is capable of maintaining forwarding state restarts, it participates in updating the restarting router's BGP RIB.

A BGP router advertises the BGP-GR capability using BGP's dynamic capability negotiation feature at session initiation. The reception of a BGP-GR capability with no AFI/SAFI information indicates that the sending peer supports the end-of-RIB marker and can support peers that can maintain forwarding state and that want to utilize BGP-GR. The reception of a BGP-GR capability with AFI/SAFI information indicates that the sending peer wants to perform BGP-GR for the included AFI/SAFIs.

The restart time should be less than the holdtime for the BGP peer. In the following sections, the "restarting BGP router" is the router on which BGP has been restarted, and the "receiving BGP router" is the BGP router that is peered with the restarting BGP router.

When the BGP router restarts, the forwarding information base (FIB) should be marked as stale. The stale forwarding information is used to forward packets. The "stale" designation allows the router to update the forwarding information after restart.

After the BGP router restarts, the Restart State must be set to 1 to reestablish the peering session with the receiving BGP router. After the BGP session has reformed, the restarting BGP router waits until it has received the full initial routing update, as denoted by the end-of-RIB marker from the receiving BGP router. The restarting BGP router then runs the BGP decision process, refreshes the forwarding table, and updates the receiving BGP router with the Adj-RIB-Out terminated by the end-of-RIB marker.

When the BGP router restarts, the receiving BGP router might or might not detect the session failure. The receiving BGP router still might have the BGP session in an Established state when the restarting BGP router attempts to initiate a new BGP session with the receiving BGP router. The receiving BGP router accepts the new session and closes the old TCP connection. The receiving router does not send a BGP NOTIFICATION, as per the normal behavior.

The receiving BGP router sends the BGP-GR capability to the restarting BGP router, with the Restart State set to 0, unless the receiving BGP router also is reset. The receiving BGP router receives a BGP-GR capability from the restarting BGP router with a Restart State of 1. This triggers the receiving BGP router to send the initial routing update, followed by the end-of-RIB marker.

The receiving router maintains the "stale" routing information until one of three events occurs:

- The receiving router detects that forwarding state is not kept on the restarting router via the Forwarding State bit received in the BGP-GR capability.

- The receiving router receives the end-of-RIB marker from the restarting router.

- The receiving router has a failsafe timer expire that ensures that the "stale" information does not remain in use.

An important distinction to make is between the first BGP peering session, where the BGP-GR capability is established, and the first restarting session. The first session initiated with the BGP-GR capability tells the peers that they should maintain its prefixes if it goes down. The capability is received for the second time after the restart. This reestablishes that the peers should maintain the BGP prefix information for future restarts. It also indicates that the forwarding state was maintained over the restart, preventing an impact on data traffic.

The BGP NSF feature is enabled globally and not on a peer-by-peer basis. It is enabled with the following configuration:

```
router bgp ASN
  bgp graceful-restart
```

The BGP restart time is configured with the command **bgp graceful-restart restart-time** *value* with a granularity of seconds.

You can also configure the stale path timer with a granularity in seconds for BGP NSF. The stale path timer determines how long a router holds onto the paths received from a gracefully restarted peer. You configure this timer with the command **bgp graceful-restart stale-path-time** *value*.

The BGP NSF feature can be verified using the output from **show ip bgp neighbors**. You also can verify that the graceful restart capability has been advertised and received. The BGP NSF feature was integrated into Releases 12.0(22)S and 12.2.15T.

Prefix Update Optimization

Prefix update optimization is focused on preventing instabilities in prefix advertisement and minimizing the impact of new policy application. This involves detecting instabilities external to the network and filtering the instabilities to the internal network. Another aspect is minimizing the impact of making policy changes and reducing the amount of prefix information advertised. The following features cover the available prefix-handling optimizations:

- **Route flap dampening**—This feature monitors routing information for signs of instability. Prefixes that demonstrate instability are dampened until they stabilize.

- **Soft reconfiguration and route refresh**—The soft reconfiguration and route refresh features are designed to minimize the impact of applying new policy through reducing the impact on unaffected prefixes.

- **Transmit (TX) side loop detection**—Transmit side loop detection is focused on reducing prefix information sent to an external peer. If the prefix information will be rejected by the remote peer because of the AS_PATH loop-detection mechanism, the update process can be optimized by suppressing the advertisement of those prefixes.

- **Outbound Route Filtering (ORF)**—The ORF capability is similar in concept to the TX side loop detection in that it focuses on reducing the prefix information advertised by a peer based on inbound policy configuration on the remote peer. The ORF feature specifically focuses on offloading the inbound prefix filtering on the transmitting peer.

Route Flap Dampening

The route flap dampening feature is described in RFC 2439. It has three major goals:

- Provide a mechanism to reduce router processing load caused by unstable routes.

- Prevent sustained route oscillations.

- Provide increased route stability without sacrificing route convergence time for generally well-behaved routes.

Route dampening maintains a route flap history for each prefix. The dampening algorithm has several parameters:

- **History state**—After a single route flap, the route is assigned a penalty, and the dampening state for the route is set to History.

- **Penalty**—Each time the route flaps, the penalty increases. The default penalty increase for a route flap is 1000. If the route attributes are the only change, the penalty increase is 500. This value is hard-coded.

- **Suppress limit**—If the penalty exceeds the suppress limit, the route is dampened. The route state is changed from History to Damp. The default suppress limit is 2000. The suppress limit can be configured.

- **Damp state**—When a route is in the Damp state, the router does not consider this path for best-path selection and therefore does not advertise this prefix to its peers.

- **Half life**—The penalty for a route is decreased based on the half-life period, which by default is 15 minutes. The penalty on the route is reduced every 5 seconds. The half life can be configured.

- **Reuse limit**—The penalty on a route decreases over time. When the penalty falls below the reuse limit, the route is unsuppressed. The default reuse limit is 750. The router checks for prefixes to unsuppress every 10 seconds. The reuse limit can be configured. When the penalty reaches one-half of the reuse limit, the history is cleared for that prefix to make more efficient use of memory.

- **Maximum suppress limit**—This is an upper bound for prefix suppression. If a route exhibits extreme instability for a short period of time and then stabilizes, the penalty accrued might result in the route's being dampened for an excessive period of time. This is essentially an upper bound on the penalty. If the route exhibits continuous instability, the penalty remains at its upper bound, which keeps the route dampened. The default maximum suppress limit is 60 minutes. The maximum suppress limit can be configured.

When a route flaps, a penalty is assigned to the route, and the route is marked as having a history of instability. Successive route flaps increase the penalty. When the penalty increases above the suppress limit, the route is suppressed, or dampened.

Figure 3-6 shows route dampening for a prefix.

Figure 3-6   *BGP Route Dampening*

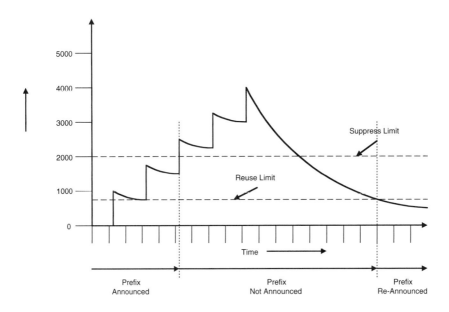

The default suppress limit is 2000; however, it takes three route flaps to trigger suppression. The penalty assigned for each flap is 1000; however, the penalty begins to decay immediately. The decay between the first and second flaps keeps the penalty below the suppress limit of 2000 until the third flap.

The penalty assigned to a route decays over time. When the penalty for the route drops below the reuse limit, it is again advertised to peers. This mechanism allows well-behaved routes to converge quickly; however, routes that exhibit instability are dampened until the instability subsides.

Example 3-11 shows the route-dampening feature configuration.

Example 3-11 *Route Dampening Configuration*

```
router bgp 100
  bgp dampening half-life reuse-limit suppress-limit maximum-suppress-time
```

The configuration of BGP dampening parameters can result in unexpected behavior if care is not taken when determining the values. The maximum penalty that can be assigned to a prefix is determined through a formula. If the maximum penalty is not larger than the suppress limit, prefixes will never achieve a high-enough penalty to be suppressed, effectively rendering BGP dampening useless. The formula is as follows:

$$\text{max-penalty} = \text{reuse-limit} * 2\left(\frac{\text{max-suppress-time}}{\text{half-life}}\right)$$

The following is an example of BGP dampening parameters that will prove ineffective:

bgp dampening 30 750 3000 60

The suppress limit is 3000, and the maximum penalty assigned to a route is 3000. The penalty for a route must exceed the suppress limit. In this case, the penalty is equal to the suppress limit.

The following is an example of the default values for BGP dampening that are effective:

bgp dampening 15 750 2000 60

This results in a suppress limit of 2000 and a maximum penalty of 6000. Always check parameters to ensure that they will actually engage the BGP dampening feature for flapping routes.

The BGP dampening feature affects only external BGP routes. If BGP dampening were applicable to internal prefixes, disparate dampening parameters could provide inconsistent forwarding tables throughout the network. Dampening the prefixes at the edge removes them from the internal network, effectively providing internal dampening. The BGP dampening feature operates on routes on a per-path basis. If a prefix has two paths, and one is dampened, the other prefix is still available and is advertised to BGP peers.

The BGP dampening feature allows a route map to be applied to the dampening process. This provides graded dampening, in which different dampening parameters can be applied to different types of prefixes based on assorted matching criteria. This concept is covered in Chapter 9.

BGP Soft Reconfiguration

When BGP policy is changed, the BGP session needs to be reset for the new policy to take effect. The resetting of a BGP session results in route churn and route flapping. Excessive resetting of BGP peers can even trigger route flap dampening.

The BGP soft reconfiguration and route refresh features are both methods to clear a BGP session in an unintrusive manner, providing a "soft" clear as opposed to the normal "hard" clear. A soft clear does not actually reset the BGP session. It triggers reprocessing of prefix information through the appropriate inbound or outbound policy configuration when soft reconfiguration is enabled.

Soft reconfiguration outbound does not require any additional resource. The BGP router can process the Adj-RIB-Loc through the outbound policy for the particular peer, creating a new Adj-RIB-Out. The remote peer can be updated by any changes with BGP Update messages.

The soft reset of an inbound connection presents more of a difficulty. When prefix information for a remote peer is rejected because of inbound policy, that prefix information is not maintained in the BGP table. This is intended to optimize resource utilization on a BGP router that has a large number of prefixes.

The BGP soft reconfiguration feature lets a BGP peer maintain all prefix information learned from the remote peer, even if it is rejected because of inbound policy filtering. This feature increases the memory resource requirements; however, the router can reprocess all inbound prefixes through an updated inbound configuration.

The BGP soft reconfiguration feature is enabled on a per peer basis. The configuration for enabling soft reconfiguration is

```
router bgp xxxxx
    neighbor address or peer group soft-reconfiguration-inbound
```

Prefix information that is denied by inbound policy configuration but is stored in the BGP table because the soft reconfiguration feature is marked as received-only. These prefixes are not allowed in the BGP decision process.

Route Refresh Feature

The route refresh feature is a replacement for the soft reconfiguration feature. Route refresh is a capability that is negotiated at session initiation. The route refresh feature allows a BGP router to request that a remote peer resend its BGP Adj-RIB-Out. This allows the BGP router to reapply the inbound policy.

Example 3-12 shows the verification of route refresh support for a particular BGP session.

Example 3-12 **show** *Command Output for Route Refresh Capability Verification*

```
Router#show ip bgp neighbor peer address | include [Rr]oute [Rr]efresh
....
  Neighbor capabilities:
    Route refresh: advertised and received(old & new)
....
```

If BGP soft reconfiguration is enabled for a particular neighbor, route refresh is operational for that neighbor. These features are mutually exclusive. Route refresh is handled on a per-address family basis.

Transmit Side Loop Detection

Transmit (TX) loop detection must be implemented manually. A BGP router advertises prefixes to a peer with that peer's autonomous system number (ASN) in the AS_PATH, relying on the peer to perform loop detection by checking for its own ASN in the AS_PATH. The idea is that preventing the prefixes from being advertised in the first place reduces the size of the BGP update, providing an optimized set of prefixes for the receiving peer to process.

The TX loop-detection configuration is applicable only to external peers. The configuration is minimal and can be applied using a route map or a filter list. A configuration example is provided in Example 3-13.

Example 3-13 *TX Side Loop-Detection Configuration*

```
router bgp 100
  ...
  neighbor 10.1.1.1 remote-as 1
  neighbor 10.1.1.1 filter-list 1 out
  ...
!
ip as-path 1 deny _1_
ip as-path 1 permit any
!
```

The as-path list matches on the existence of the remote ASN in the AS_PATHs of the advertised prefixes and denies them. All other prefixes are explicitly permitted.

NOTE	In some scenarios, TX-side loop detection is undesirable—specifically, in MPLS-VPN environments. This used to be the default behavior when peer groups were not used; however, it was removed for MPLS-VPN support.

Outbound Route Filtering

The BGP ORF feature uses BGP ORF send and receive capabilities to minimize the number of BGP updates sent between peer routers. Configuring this feature can help reduce the number of resources required for generating and processing routing updates by filtering unwanted routing updates on the transmit side.

The BGP ORF feature is enabled through the advertisement of ORF capability to BGP peer routers. This capability indicates that a BGP-speaking router accepts a prefix list from a neighbor and applies the prefix list outbound to that peer. The BGP ORF feature can be configured with send, receive, or send and receive ORF capabilities. The BGP router continues to apply the inbound prefix list to received updates after the BGP router has pushed the inbound prefix list to the remote peer.

A sample configuration is provided in Example 3-14.

Example 3-14 *BGP ORF Capability Configuration*

```
router bgp 100
  ...
  neighbor 10.1.1.1 remote-as 10
  neighbor 10.1.1.1 capability prefixlist-orf both
  ...
!
```

In Example 3-14, the BGP ORF advertises the capability with both the send and receive options. Instead of the **both** keyword, either **send** or **receive** can be used to allow one-way ORF. The **send** and **receive** keywords indicate the ability to send or receive the prefix list. They do not refer to the advertisement of routes.

The BGP ORF feature cannot be used with BGP peer groups when a peer group member is receiving a prefix list. The dynamic nature of the outbound policy prevents update replication. Peer group members can send policies. The BGP ORF capability was introduced in Releases 12.0(6)S and 12.0(7)T.

Case Study: BGP Convergence Testing

The topic of BGP convergence tuning was covered earlier in this chapter. The discussion examined the bottlenecks in the BGP update process and presented configuration options to remove them. This case study focuses on providing empirical data to support the convergence-tuning recommendations provided earlier in this chapter.

Test Scenario

The equipment used in performing the convergence testing is

- Cisco 7206VXR

- NPE 300 network processor

- 256 MB DRAM

Two versions of Cisco IOS are used in the testing. All the tests except the update enhancement test are performed using Release 12.0(15)S1. The update enhancement test is performed using Release 12.0(23)S. This change in code is required for update packing and BGP read-only mode.

The Unit Under Test (UUT) is configured with a single eBGP peering session to supply the prefix information. This information is then sent to 50 iBGP peers. The prefix count ranges from 70,000 to 140,000 in 10,000-prefix increments.

The BGP tables used are specially built to represent the standard Internet routing tables in prefix length distribution and attribute combination distribution. The same BGP table is used for each test for a specific prefix count.

The BGP process on the UUT is said to have converged when the BGP table version for all peers is equal to the BGP table version for the router and the BGP InQ and OutQ for every peer is 0. The output from **show ip bgp summary** is used to determine when a converged state has been reached. The convergence time for the UUT is the amount of time from the first BGP peering session's initiating until the BGP router reaches a converged state.

Baseline Convergence

The baseline convergence is performed using a default configuration. The BGP feature status is as follows:

- Peer groups are not enabled.

- Path MTU Discovery is disabled (TCP MSS 536).

- The input hold queue is 75.

- Update packing is not supported.

Figure 3-7 shows the results of the testing.

Figure 3-7   *Baseline BGP Convergence Statistics*

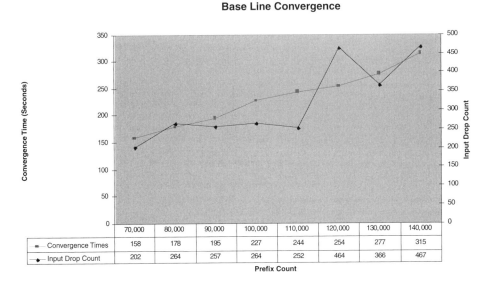

Base Line Convergence

	70,000	80,000	90,000	100,000	110,000	120,000	130,000	140,000
Convergence Times	158	178	195	227	244	254	277	315
Input Drop Count	202	264	257	264	252	464	366	467

Prefix Count

Convergence Times
Input Drop Count

The BGP convergence time is reasonably linear. The network takes 158 seconds to converge
with 70,000 prefixes and 315 seconds with 140,000 prefixes. The input drop count is reasonably low; however, note that it remains low until the 120,000 prefix mark, at which point
it increases dramatically. This can be accounted for by TCP's engaging its congestion-
management mechanisms. The initial packet loss causes TCP to back off. The reduction in
packet loss causes TCP to increase its rate again, causing further loss.

Peer Group Benefits

The peer group feature is the first deployed. As stated in the section "Peer Groups," this
feature is the foundation for all performance tuning. The rest of the testing performed
includes BGP peer groups.

The BGP feature status is as follows:

- Peer groups are enabled.
- Path MTU Discovery is disabled (TCP MSS 536).
- The input hold queue is 75.
- Update packing is not supported.

Figure 3-8 shows the results of the testing.

Figure 3-8   *Peer Group Convergence Statistics*

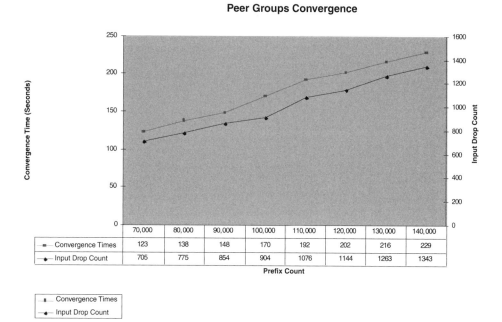

Peer Groups Convergence

Prefix Count	70,000	80,000	90,000	100,000	110,000	120,000	130,000	140,000
Convergence Times	123	138	148	170	192	202	216	229
Input Drop Count	705	775	854	904	1076	1144	1263	1343

The convergence time for the BGP peers continues to be linear. The convergence time has decreased with the deployment of peer groups by an average of 22%. The input drop rate, however, has increased dramatically. This increase in the input drop rate is a result of the update replication improving to the router's update generation efficiency.

Peer Groups and Path MTU Discovery

The Path MTU Discovery (PMTUD) feature is enabled in addition to peer groups. This should reduce the number of BGP update packets required and also the number of input drops.

The BGP feature status is as follows:

- Peer groups are enabled.
- Path MTU Discovery is enabled (TCP MSS 1460).
- The input hold queue is 75.
- Update packing is not supported.

Figure 3-9 shows the results of the testing.

Figure 3-9 *Peer Group and Path MTU Convergence Statistics*

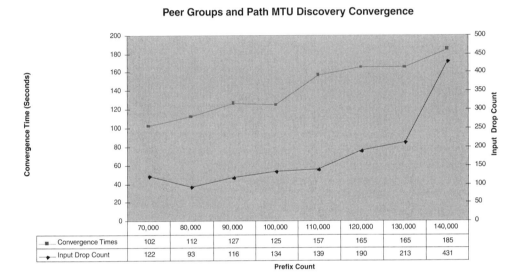

The deployment of PMTUD should reduce the number of BGP updates by approximately 63%, which significantly reduces the number of input queue drops. The reduction in input queue drops improves the TCP throughput on the BGP sessions. The increase in packet size provides on average a 20% decrease in convergence time over peer groups.

Peer Groups and Queue Optimization

The input hold queues have been optimized to prevent input drops in addition to peer groups. This optimization allows the TCP transport for the BGP peering sessions to operate without retransmissions.

The BGP feature status is as follows:

- Peer groups are enabled.
- Path MTU Discovery is disabled (TCP MSS 536).
- The input hold queue is 1000.
- Update packing is not supported.

Figure 3-10 shows the results of the testing.

Figure 3-10 *Peer Group and Queue Optimization Statistics*

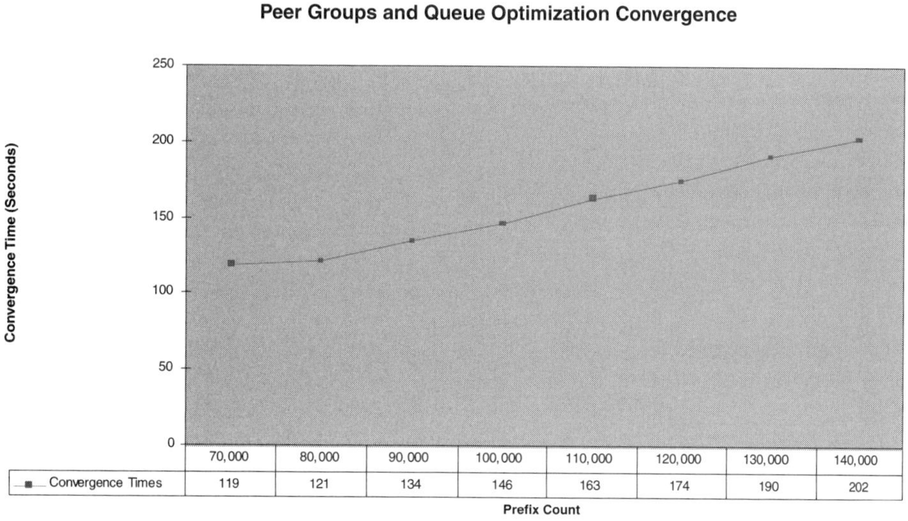
Peer Groups and Queue Optimization Convergence
Convergence Time (Seconds)
250
200
150
100
50
0
70,000
80,000
90,000
100,000
110,000
120,000
130,000
140,000
Convergence Times
119
121
134
146
163
174
190
202
Prefix Count

The input packet drops fell to 0, so they were removed from the graph. The convergence time with optimized queues decreases by 12% when compared to just peer groups.

Pre-Release 12.0(19)S Feature Comparison

Figure 3-11 compares decreases in convergence time for the various feature combinations.

This graph shows the impact of stacking the BGP convergence features. The improvement over peer groups for deploying both PMTUD and queue optimization is a 29% decrease in convergence time on average.

Figure 3-12 compares a fully optimized pre-Release 12.0(19)S router and the baseline convergence.

The available features before Release 12.0(19)S provide a decrease in BGP convergence time of 45% over the default configuration. This increase in BGP performance is available as early as 12.0(13)S.

Figure 3-11 *Peer Group, PMTUD, and Queue Optimization Statistics*

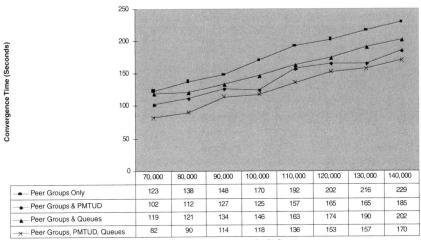

Peer Groups/PMTUD/Queues Comparison

	70,000	80,000	90,000	100,000	110,000	120,000	130,000	140,000
──■── Peer Groups Only	123	138	148	170	192	202	216	229
──◆── Peer Groups & PMTUD	102	112	127	125	157	165	165	185
──▲── Peer Groups & Queues	119	121	134	146	163	174	190	202
──✕── Peer Groups, PMTUD, Queues	82	90	114	118	136	153	157	170

Prefix Count

Figure 3-12 *Baseline and Optimal Pre-Release 12.0(19)S Comparison*

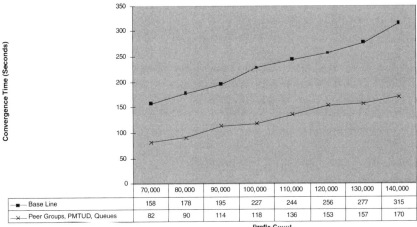

Base Line and Optimal Pre-12.0(19)S Configuration Comparison

	70,000	80,000	90,000	100,000	110,000	120,000	130,000	140,000
──■── Base Line	158	178	195	227	244	256	277	315
──✕── Peer Groups, PMTUD, Queues	82	90	114	118	136	153	157	170

Prefix Count

Post-Release 12.0(19)S BGP Enhancements

The final test scenario involves upgrading the UUT to Cisco IOS Release 12.0(23). This enables the use of BGP Update Packing and BGP read-only mode. These enhancements are coupled with all the previously discussed features in this case study for determining the optimal BGP convergence times.

The BGP feature status is as follows:

- Peer groups are enabled.
- Path MTU Discovery is enabled (TCP MSS 1460).
- The input hold queue is 1000.
- Update packing is enabled.

Figure 3-13 provides three important convergence scenarios: Baseline, Optimal Pre-12.0(19)S, and Optimal Post-12.0(19)S.

Figure 3-13 *Baseline, Pre-12.0(19)S, and 12.0(23)S Comparison*

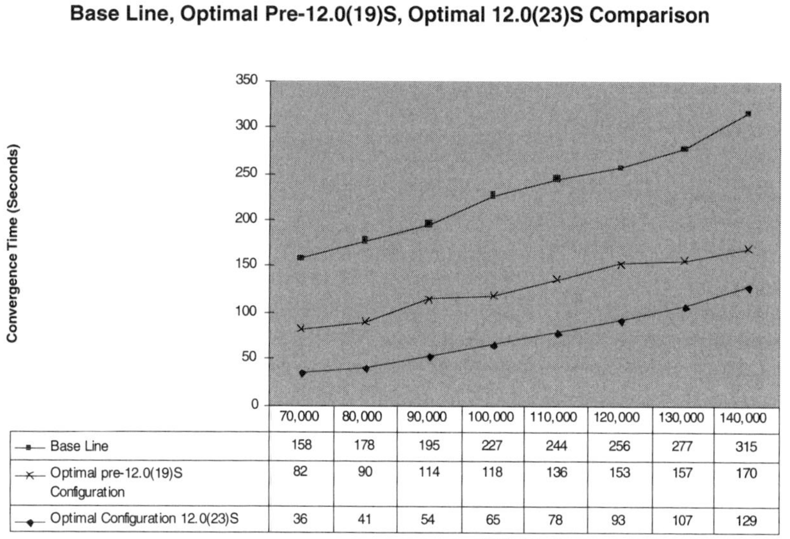

Base Line, Optimal Pre-12.0(19)S, Optimal 12.0(23)S Comparison

	70,000	80,000	90,000	100,000	110,000	120,000	130,000	140,000
Base Line	158	178	195	227	244	256	277	315
Optimal pre-12.0(19)S Configuration	82	90	114	118	136	153	157	170
Optimal Configuration 12.0(23)S	36	41	54	65	78	93	107	129

Prefix Count

As previously stated, the improvement for optimal pre-Release 12.0(19)S over the baseline is 45% on average. The improvement for optimal post-Release 12.0(19)S over optimal pre-Release 12.0(19)S is an additional 43% on average.

The decrease in convergence time for an optimal configuration post-Release 12.0(19)S over the baseline is 69% on average.

Case Study Summary

This case study examined the input drops in the particular test scenarios where input drops occurred. The number of input drops provided insight into the number of BGP packets being generated. The larger the number of BGP updates, the more incoming TCP ACKs there are. Figure 3-14 shows the input hold queue drops.

Figure 3-14 *Final Summary Input Drop Counts*

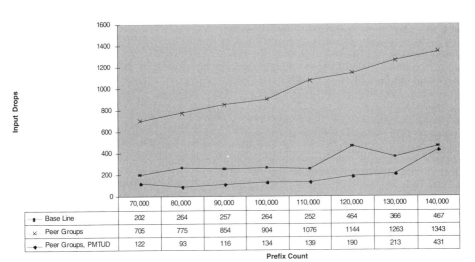

The major point from the input drop counts is the massive increase when peer groups are enabled. This increase indicates the impact that peer groups have on increasing update generation through replication.

Figure 3-15 shows the convergence times for all six test scenarios to summarize the impact of BGP convergence tuning and the interdependencies between the various aspects of convergence tuning.

Throughout this case study, the improvements in convergence time have been discussed as percentages. Table 3-3 compares all the prefix counts and the relevant scenarios.

Figure 3-15 *Final Summary Convergence Times*

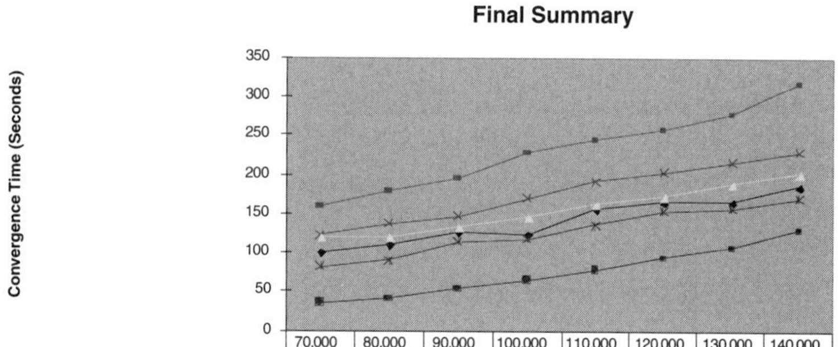

Final Summary

	70,000	80,000	90,000	100,000	110,000	120,000	130,000	140,000
Base Line	158	178	195	227	244	256	277	315
Peer Groups	123	138	148	170	192	202	216	229
Peer Groups, PMTUD	102	112	127	125	157	165	165	185
Peer Groups, Queues	119	121	134	146	163	174	190	202
Peer Groups, PMTUD, Queues	82	90	114	118	136	153	157	170
Peer Groups, PMTUD, Queues, 12.0(23)S	36	41	54	65	78	93	107	129

Prefix Count

Table 3-3 *Convergence Improvements Over Various Scenarios*

Control	Improvement	70,000	80,000	90,000	100,000	110,000	120,000	130,000	140,000	Avg.
Baseline	Peer group	22.15%	22.47%	24.10%	25.11%	21.31%	21.09%	22.02%	27.30%	22.15%
Peer group	PG and PMTUD	17.07%	18.84%	14.19%	26.47%	18.23%	18.32%	23.61%	19.21%	19.49%
Peer group	PG and queues	3.25%	12.32%	9.46%	14.12%	15.10%	13.86%	12.04%	11.79%	11.49%
Peer group	PG, PMTUD, queues	33.33%	34.78%	22.97%	30.59%	29.17%	24.26%	27.31%	25.76%	28.52%
Baseline	PG, PMTUD, queues	48.10%	49.44%	41.54%	48.02%	44.26%	40.23%	43.32%	46.03%	45.12%
PG, PMTUD, queues	Optimal	56.10%	54.44%	52.63%	44.92%	42.65%	39.22%	31.85%	24.12%	43.24%
Baseline	Optimal	77.22%	76.97%	72.31%	71.37%	68.03%	63.67%	61.37%	59.05%	68.75%

This table shows what the control scenario was and the improvement that was made. The percentage increase in performance is shown for each prefix count tested. A number of combinations were performed to show the relationship between the various optimizations. The control time is the amount of time the test took to run with the optimization set defined in the Control column. The improvement time is the amount of time the test took to run with the optimization set defined in the Improvement column. The improvement percentages were derived by dividing the delta between the control time and improvement time by the control time. This reflects the improvement based on the control time.

Summary

This chapter covered two major aspects of BGP performance tuning: BGP convergence tuning and BGP network performance turning. The first section covered the major features that dramatically improve BGP convergence. The case study provided empirical evidence to complement the conceptual explanation.

The section on BGP network tuning focused on reducing the scope of network-affecting events and reducing the amount of BGP information advertised.

The challenge of BGP performance tuning is ongoing as networks increase in both node count and prefix count. The sheer amount of information involved in large BGP networks provides many areas for optimization that, if not capitalized on, can result in network-wide meltdowns. Deploying BGP convergence optimizations should be considered a common best practice for all BGP networks.

This chapter explores the various aspects of BGP policy control:

- Policy control techniques
- Conditional advertisement
- Aggregation and deaggregation
- Local AS
- QoS policy propagation
- BGP policy accounting
- Case study: AS integration via the Local AS

CHAPTER 4

Effective BGP Policy Control

Throughout this book, you have learned that BGP is first and foremost a policy tool. This results in BGP's being used to build very complex policy-based architectures. The protocol itself provides a list of attributes through which you can set policies. Additionally, Cisco IOS software further expands and enhances what is available with additional tools and knobs. This chapter examines these tools and how you can use them to build complex and effective BGP policies.

Policy Control Techniques

BGP employs many common policy control techniques. This section starts with regular expressions and then describes various forms of filter lists, route maps, and policy lists.

Regular Expression

A *regular expression* is a formula for matching strings that follow a certain pattern. It evaluates text data and returns an answer of true or false. In other words, either the expression correctly describes the data, or it does not.

A regular expression is foremost a tool. For example, a regular expression can help extract the needed information from a large IOS output quickly, as shown in Example 4-1.

Example 4-1 *Regular Expression to Extract All Neighbors' Maximum Data Segment Sizes*

```
R2#show ip bgp neighbors | include max data segment
Datagrams (max data segment is 1460 bytes):
Datagrams (max data segment is 1460 bytes):
Datagrams (max data segment is 1460 bytes):
```

As a formula, a regular expression allows pattern matching in BGP AS_PATH and community policy settings. Example 4-2 shows the use of a regular expression to describe an AS_PATH pattern that matches all AS_PATHs that are originated from the neighboring AS 100.

Example 4-2 *Regular Expression Matches AS_PATH Patterns*

```
ip as-path access-list permit ^(100_)+$
```

Components of a Regular Expression

A regular expression consists of two types of characters:

- Characters to be matched, or regular characters
- Control characters or metacharacters that have special meanings

To really make good use of regular expressions, it is critical to understand the control characters and how they are used. Control characters can be grouped into three types:

- **Atom characters, or atoms**—An atom is an independent control character or placeholder character that defines or expands the regular characters that are before or after it. Some atoms can be standalone, without regular characters.

- **Multiplier characters, or multipliers**—A multiplier follows an atom or a regular character and is used to describe repetitions of the character immediately before it. Except for the dot (.) character, all other atom characters must be grouped with regular characters before a multiplier is appended.

- **Range characters**—Range characters (brackets) specify a complete range.

Table 4-1 lists the common atom characters.

Table 4-1 *Common Atom Characters and Their Usage*

Atom Character	Usage
.	Matches any single character, including white space.
^	Matches the beginning character of a string.
$	Matches the ending character of a string.
_	Underscore. Matches a comma (,), left brace ({), right brace (}), the beginning of an input string, the end of an input string, or a space.
|	Pipe. It is an OR, meaning that it matches either of two strings.
\	An escape character to turn a control character that immediately follows into a regular character.

Some simple examples are listed in Table 4-2.

Table 4-2   *Examples of Atoms*

Regular Expression	Usage
^a.$	Matches a string that begins with character a and ends with any single character, such as ab, ax, a., a!, a0, and so on.
^100_	Matches 100, 100 200, 100 300 400, and so on.
^100$	Matches 100 only.
^100_500_	Matches 100 500, 100 500 500, and so on.
100$|400$	Matches 100, 2100, 100 400, 400, 100 100, 1039 2400, 600 400, and so on.
^\(65000\)$	Matches (65000) only.

Table 4-3 shows the common multiplier characters.

Table 4-3   *Multipliers and Their Usage*

Multiplier	Usage
*	Any sequence of the preceding character (zero or more occurrences).
+	One or more sequences of the preceding character (one or more occurrences).
?	Matches a preceding character with zero or one occurrences.

A multiplier can be applied to a single-character pattern or a multicharacter pattern. To apply a multiplier to a multicharacter pattern, enclose the pattern in parentheses. Some simple examples are shown in Table 4-4.

Table 4-4   *Examples of Multipliers*

Regular Expression	Usage
abc*d	Matches abd, abcd, abccd, abcccd, and so on.
abc+d	Matches abcd, abccd, abcccd, and so on.
abc?d	Matches abd, abcd, abcdf, and so on.
a(bc)?d	Matches ad, abcd, cabcd, and so on.
a(b.)*d	Matches ad, ab0d, ab0b0d, abxd, abxbxd, and so on.

The characters [ ] describe a range. Only one of the characters within the range is matched. You can make the matching exclusive by using the caret (^) character at the start of the range to exclude all the characters within the range. You can also specify a range by providing only the beginning and the ending characters separated by a dash (-). Some simple examples are shown in Table 4-5.

Table 4-5 *Examples of Ranges*

Regular Expression	Usage
[aeiouAEIOU]	Matches a, aa, Aa, eA, x2u, and so on.
[a-c1-2]$	Matches a, a1, 62, 1b, xv2, and so on.
[^act]$	Matches d, efg*, low2, actor, path, and so on, but not pact.

How to Use Regular Expressions in Cisco IOS Software

Regular expressions in IOS are only a subset of what is available from other operating systems. The use of regular expressions within IOS can be generally described in two categories:

- Filtering the command output
- Pattern matching to define policies

Regular expressions can be used in filtering outputs of **show** and **more** commands. The entire line is treated as one string. Table 4-6 shows the three types of filtering that can be done on an output.

Table 4-6 *Regular Expressions Used to Perform Three Types of Output Filtering*

Keyword	Usage
begin	Begins output lines with the first line that contains the regular expression.
include	Displays output lines that contain the regular expression.
exclude	Displays output lines that do not contain the regular expression.

To filter the output, send the output with a pipe character (|) followed by the keyword and a regular expression. For example, **show run | begin router bgp** shows the part of the running configuration that begins with **router bgp**. To interrupt the filtered output, press **Ctrl-^** (press Ctrl, Shift, and 6 at the same time). Example 4-3 shows an example of filtering **show ip cef** output to show all the prefixes associated with the interface Ethernet0/0.

Example 4-3   *Filtering* **show ip cef** *Output with a Regular Expression*

```
R1#show ip cef | include Ethernet0/0
172.16.0.0/16       192.168.12.2       Ethernet0/0
192.168.12.0/24     attached           Ethernet0/0
192.168.12.2/32     192.168.12.2       Ethernet0/0
192.168.23.0/24     192.168.12.2       Ethernet0/0
192.168.25.0/24     192.168.12.2       Ethernet0/0
192.168.36.0/24     192.168.12.2       Ethernet0/0
```

NOTE   To type a question mark in a regular expression on the router, first press **Ctrl-V** (Escape for CLI), and then you can enter **?**.

Regular expressions are used extensively in pattern matching to define BGP policies, such as AS_PATH filtering. The AS_PATH attribute lists, in reverse order, the AS numbers, separated by blank spaces, that the prefix has traversed. You can use the command **show ip bgp regexp** to verify the result of the configured regular expressions.

Table 4-7 shows some examples of common AS_PATH pattern matching using regular expressions.

Table 4-7   *Examples of AS_PATH Pattern Matching Using Regular Expressions*

AS_PATH Pattern	Usage
.*	Matches all path information—for example, no filtering.
^$	Matches updates originated from the local AS.
^200$	Matches all paths that start and end with AS 200—that is, only updates originated and sent from AS 200 (no AS prepending and no intermediary). For example, this does not match 200 200.
_200$	Matches all routes originated from AS 200, including those prepended with 200.
^200	Matches any updates received from the neighboring AS 200, such as 200, 200 100, 200 300 100, 2001, and so on.
_200_	AS_PATH contains AS 200 (the prefix passed through AS 200 but not necessarily originated by or received directly from AS 200), such as 200, 200 100, 300 200 100, and so on.
^100(_100)*(_400)*$	Matches paths from AS 100 and its immediate neighbor AS 400, such as 100, 100 100, 100 400, 100 400 400, 100 100 100 400 400, and so on.

Filter Lists for Enforcing BGP Policies

Filter lists are used extensively in BGP to define policies. This section covers prefix lists, AS path lists, and community lists.

Prefix Lists

Prefix lists are used to filter IP prefixes and can match both the prefix number and the prefix length. Compared to regular access lists, use of prefix lists provides higher performance (fewer CPU cycles).

NOTE   Prefix lists cannot be used as packet filters.

A prefix list entry follows the same general format as an IP access control list (ACL). An IP prefix list consists of a name for the list, an action for the list (permit/deny), the prefix number, and the prefix length. Here is the basic format of an IP prefix list:

```
ip prefix-list name [seq seq] {deny | permit} prefix/length
```

NOTE   A distribute list is another way to filter BGP routing updates. It uses access lists to define the rules and is mutually exclusive with the prefix list.

Any prefixes entered are automatically converted to match the length value entered. For example, entering 10.1.2.0/8 results in 10.0.0.0/8. Example 4-4 shows a simple example of matching 172.16.1.0/24. As with an access list, a deny-all entry is implied at the end of the list.

Example 4-4   *Matching 172.16.1.0/24*

```
ip prefix-list out-1 permit 172.16.1.0/24
```

Optionally, a sequence number can be supplied for each entry. By default, the sequence numbers are automatically generated in increments of 5. They can be suppressed with the command **no ip prefix-list seq**. Entries are processed sequentially based on the sequence number. The use of sequence numbers offers flexibility when modifying a portion of a prefix list.

With the basic form of the prefix list, an exact match of both prefix number and prefix length is assumed. In Example 4-4, the prefix list matches only the prefix 172.16.1.0/24. The prefixes 172.16.1.128/25 and 172.16.1.0/25, for example, are not matched.

To match a range of prefixes and lengths, additional optional keywords are needed. When a range ends at /32, the greater-than-or-equal-to (**ge**) can be specified. The value of **ge** must be greater than the length value specified by prefix/length and not greater than 32. The range is assumed to be from the **ge** value to 32 if only the **ge** attribute is specified. If the range does not end at 32, another keyword, **le**, must be specified. The use of **le** is discussed later in this section.

NOTE   A prefix consists of a prefix number and a prefix length. When a range is specified for a prefix list, the prefixes are matched for a range of prefix numbers and prefix lengths. For example, if a prefix list is **172.16.1.0/24 ge 25**, the matched range of the prefix numbers is 172.16.1.0 255.255.255.0 (representing a network mask in this case). The range of the matched prefix lengths falls between 25 and 32, inclusive. Thus, prefixes such as 172.16.1.128/25 and 172.16.1.0/30 are included. As another example, if the prefix list is **172.16.1.0/24 ge 27**, the matched range of the prefix numbers is still the same—that is, 172.16.1.0 255.255.255.0. The difference between the two is the range of the matched prefix lengths is smaller in the second example.

Example 4-5 shows an example of matching a portion of 172.16.0.0/16. Notice that the range is between /17 and /32, inclusive. Thus, the network 172.16.0.0/16 is excluded from the match. The legacy extended ACL version is also included for comparison.

Example 4-5   *Matching a Portion of 172.16.0.0 255.255.0.0*

```
ip prefix-list range-1 permit 172.16.0.0/16 ge 17
!
access-list 100 permit ip 172.16.0.0 0.0.255.255 255.255.128.0 0.0.127.255
```

NOTE   Standard ACLs do not consider prefix lengths. To filter classless routing updates, you can use extended ACLs. The source address, together with wildcard bits, specifies the prefix number. The field of destination address in an extended ACL is used to represent the actual netmask, and the field of destination wildcard bits is used to denote how the netmask should be interpreted. In other words, the fields of destination address and wildcard masks indicate the range's prefix lengths. The following are some examples.

This denies the prefix 172.16.0.0/24 only (not a range):

```
access-list 100 deny ip host 172.16.0.0 host 255.255.0.0
```

This permits 172.16.0.0 255.255.0.0 (the entire class B range):

```
access-list 100 permit ip 172.16.0.0 0.0.255.255 255.255.0.0 0.0.255.255
```

This denies any updates with lengths of 25 bits or longer:

```
access-list 100 deny ip any 255.255.255.128 0.0.0.127
```

Besides numbered ACLs, named extended IP ACLs can also be used for this purpose.

The range can also be specified by the less-than-or-equal-to (**le**) attribute, which goes from the length value specified by prefix/length to the **le** value, inclusive. Example 4-6 shows an example of matching the entire range of 172.16.0.0/16—that is, 172.16.0.0 255.255.0.0 using the regular mask or 172.16.0.0 0.0.255.255 using the inverted mask. If you want to specify a range that does not start from the length, you must specify another keyword, **ge**, as discussed next.

Example 4-6   *Matching the Entire Class B Range of 172.16.0.0/16*

```
ip prefix-list range-2 permit 172.16.0.0/16 le 32
```

Example 4-7 shows another example. Both the prefix list and the ACL versions are shown.

Example 4-7   *Matching 172.16.0.0 255.255.224.0*

```
ip prefix-list range-3 permit 172.16.0.0/19 le 32
!
access-list 100 permit ip 172.16.0.0 0.0.31.255 255.255.224.0 0.0.31.255
```

When both **ge** and **le** attributes are specified, the range goes from the **ge** value to the **le** value. A specified **ge** value and/or **le** value must satisfy the following condition:

length < ge value <= le value <= 32

The expanded prefix list format follows. Note that the **ge** attribute must be specified before the **le** value:

```
ip prefix-list name [seq #] deny | permit prefix/length [ge value] [le value]
```

Example 4-8 shows an example of using both **ge** and **le** attributes to match a portion of 172.16.1.0/24. The ACL version is also included.

Example 4-8 *Matching a Portion of 172.16.1.0 255.255.255.0*

```
ip prefix-list range-3 permit 172.16.1.0/24 ge 25 le 31
!
access-list 100 permit ip 172.16.1.0 0.0.0.255 255.255.255.128 0.0.0.126
```

Note that 172.16.1.0/24 is not in the range, nor are all the /32s. The matched ranges include all the following prefixes:

- **Two /25s**—172.16.1.0/25, 172.16.1.128/25
- **Four /26s**—172.16.1.0/26, 172.16.1.64/26, ..., 172.16.1.192/26
- **Eight /27s**—172.16.1.0/27, 172.16.1.32/27, ..., 172.16.1.224/27
- **16 /28s**—172.16.1.0/28, 172.16.1.16/28, ..., 172.16.1.240/28
- **32 /29s**—172.16.1.0/29, 172.16.1.8/29, ..., 172.16.1.248/29
- **64 /30s**—172.16.1.0/30, 172.16.1.4/30, ..., 172.16.1.252/30
- **128 /31s**—172.16.1.0/31, 172.16.1.2/31, ..., 172.16.1.254/31

Table 4-8 shows more examples of prefix lists.

Table 4-8 *Additional Examples of Prefix Lists*

Prefix List	What It Matches
0.0.0.0/0	Default network
0.0.0.0/0 le 32	Any address that has a length between 0 and 32 bits, inclusive

AS Path Lists

AS path filters are used to filter the BGP AS_PATH attribute. The attribute pattern is defined by a regular expression string, either permitted or denied per the list's action. With regular expressions and AS path filters, you can build complex BGP policies.

The AS path list is defined by the **ip as-path access-list** command. The **access-list-number** is an integer from 1 to 500 that represents the list in the global configuration:

```
ip as-path access-list access-list-number {permit | deny} as-regular-expression
```

The filter can be applied in a BGP **neighbor** command using a filter list or in a route map (discussed in the later section "Route Maps"). Example 4-9 shows the use of an AS path filter to allow incoming routes from peer 192.168.1.1 that are only originated in AS 100.

Example 4-9 *Path Filter to Permit Only Routes Originated from AS 100*

```
neighbor 192.168.1.1 filter-list 1 in
!
ip as-path access-list 1 permit _100$
```

Community Lists

Community lists are used to identify and filter routes by their common community attributes. There are two forms of community lists: numbered and named. Within each category, there are also standard and expanded formats. A standard format allows actual community values or well-known constants, and an expanded format allows communities to be entered as a regular expression string. There is a limit of 100 for either format of the numbered lists (1 to 99 for the standard format and 100 to 199 for the expanded format), but named lists have no limit. The general formats are as follows:

- Standard numbered list:

    ```
    ip community-list list-number {permit I deny} community-number
    ```

- Expanded numbered list:

    ```
    ip community-list list-number {permit I deny} regular-expression
    ```

- Standard named list:

    ```
    ip community-list standard list-name {permit I deny} community-number
    ```

- Expanded named list:

    ```
    ip community-list expanded list-name {permit I deny} regular-expression
    ```

By default, the *community-number* value is a 32-bit number between 1 and 4294967295. If you enter it in the *aa:nn* format (the new format), the resulting format is converted to a 32-bit number. If you enable the new format globally using **ip bgp-community new-format**, the new format is displayed. This change is immediate. Note that the format you choose is important, because the filtering using a regular expression in an expanded list can have different results for different formats.

NOTE   The new community format splits the 32-bit number into two 16-bit numbers, *aa:nn*. Each number is expressed in decimal format. Typically, aa is used to represent an AS number, and *nn* is an arbitrary 16-bit number to denote a routing or administrative policy. Methods to design a coherent community-based policy are discussed in more detail in Chapter 9, "Service Provider Architecture."

One or more community numbers (separated by a space) can be entered per entry, or multiple entries can be entered per list number or name. When multiple communities are entered into the same entry, a match is found only when all communities match the condition—that is, an AND comparison. When multiple entries are entered for the same list number or name, a match is found when any entry matches—that is, an OR comparison. Example 4-10 shows two forms of community lists.

Example 4-10 *Two Ways of Entering Community Lists*

```
ip community-list 1 permit 100:1 100:2
ip community-list 2 permit 100:1
ip community-list 2 permit 100:2
```

With **list 1**, a match is found only when both community values of 100:1 and 100:2 are attached to a prefix. For **list 2**, a match is found if a prefix has a community with either 100:1 or 100:2 or both. Note that the rules stated here apply only to matching community values. They do not indicate whether a community is permitted or denied. For example, if the community list 2 in Example 4-10 is changed to deny 100:1 and 100:2 and to permit all other community values, a prefix with a community of 100:1 and 100:2 results in a match, and the prefix is denied.

NOTE   To announce community settings to a peer, you must configure the command **neighbor send-community** for that peer. The result of this command is to send the peer with the communities permitted by the local outbound policies of the best paths.

Besides private communities, there are four well-known communities, as discussed in Chapter 2, "Understanding BGP Building Blocks"—**internet**, **no-export**, **local-as**, and **no-advertise**.

Community values for a prefix can be set or reset in two ways:

- Use a **set** clause within a route map to set a community value, to add a community value (**additive**), or to remove all community values:

    set community {*community-value* [**additive**]} | **none**

- Use a **set** clause within a route map to selectively remove some community values:

    set comm-list *community-list-number* **delete**

    This route map **set** command removes communities from the community attribute of an inbound or outbound update. Each community that matches the given community list is removed from the community attribute. When used with this command, each entry of a standard community list should list only one community.

NOTE   When both the **set community** and **set comm-list delete** commands are configured in the same instance of a route map, the delete operation is performed before the set operation.

Route Maps

A route map is a flexible and powerful way to set BGP policies. It can set and reset both prefixes and BGP attributes based on predefined conditions. A route map is often used to define policies toward a BGP peer or during route generation. A route map can filter updates based on prefix, AS_PATH, communities, metrics, next hop, ORIGIN, LOCAL_PREF, WEIGHT, and so on. A route map often uses policy control lists to define BGP policies.

A route map is a named group of filters consisting of one or more instances. Each instance is identified by a unique sequence number that determines the order of processing. Instances are applied sequentially. If a match is found, the rest of the route map is skipped. If the route map is finished without a match, a deny action is performed. When used in the **neighbor** command, only one route map per type per direction is allowed for each neighbor.

Within each instance, you can set conditions using the **match** clause and set actions using the **set** clause. Example 4-11 shows a simple route map named Set-comm, which resets communities to 200:100 when updates are originated from AS 100.

Example 4-11 *Simple Route Map Example*

```
ip as-path access-list 1 permit _100$
!
route-map Set-comm permit 10
 match as-path 1
 set community 200:100
route-map Set-comm permit 20
```

The second instance (with sequence number 20) is important, because without it, all other updates that don't match the first instance are not accepted. When no match clause is specified under an instance, the result is to permit any. This instance basically means that no action should be taken for prefixes that do not match the conditions in the first instance.

NOTE   The **deny** keyword in a route map is equivalent to a **no** keyword for other commands, but it does not necessarily indicate to deny something. The exact meaning depends on the route map's purpose. For example, if a route map is to suppress a route, **deny** is used to unsuppress that route. The same concept also applies to other forms of filtering of BGP prefixes and attributes.

There are two ways to match more than one condition. You can enter multiple conditions in the same **match** command or in different **match** commands. The processing rules are as follows:

- An OR function is performed between multiple **match** parameters defined in the same **match** command, regardless of the type of **match** commands.

- An OR function is performed when there are multiple **match** commands of the same type. Actually, IOS converts this form into the form discussed in the preceding bullet.

- An AND function is performed if there are multiple **match** commands of different types in the same route map instance.

Example 4-12 shows how the preceding rules work. The route map foo matches either community 100:1 or 100:2. With the route map foo2, a match is found only when the prefix and both communities are matched.

Example 4-12 *Processing Example When Multiple Conditions Are Set with* **match** *Commands*

```
ip community-list 1 permit 100:1
ip community-list 2 permit 100:2
ip community-list 3 permit 100:1 100:2
!
ip prefix-list 1 seq 5 permit 13.0.0.0/8
!
route-map foo permit 10
 match community 1 2
!
route-map foo2 permit 10
 match ip address prefix-list 1
 match community 3
```

You can use a route map in the following BGP commands:

- **neighbor**
- **bgp dampening**
- **network**
- **redistribute**

Additionally, you can use route maps in various commands for specific purposes:

- **suppress-map**
- **unsuppress-map**
- **advertise-map**
- **inject-map**
- **exist-map**
- **non-exist-map**
- **table-map**

Policy Lists

Complex route maps often have more than one match clause of different types. In a medium to large network, many of the same match clauses are reused repeatedly by different route maps. If the same sets of match clauses can be extracted from a route map, they can be reused by more than one route map or in different instances of the same route map. These independent match clauses are called *policy lists*.

A policy list is a subset of route maps that contains only match clauses. When a policy list is referenced in another route map, all the match clauses are evaluated and processed as if they were configured directly in the route map. Match clauses are configured in policy lists with permit or deny statements. The route map evaluates and processes each match clause and permits or denies routes based on the configuration in the referenced policy list.

A policy list is configured with the **ip policy-list** command and is referenced within another route map using the **match policy-list** command. Two or more policy lists can be referenced within a route map, and each entry can contain one or more policy lists. When multiple policy lists are configured in the same **match policy-list** command, it is an OR operation; when multiple **match policy-list** statements are configured, it is an AND operation. The policy lists and all other match and set options within a route map instance can coexist.

Example 4-13 shows a route map configuration using policy lists. Two policy lists are configured: as100 and as200. In as100, a match is found when both the AS path starts with AS 100 and the community is 300:105. In as200, a match is found when the AS path starts with AS 200 and the community is 300:105. With the route map foo, first a match is made to select the prefix to be 10.0.0.0/8, and then an OR operation is made for the two policy lists. The final action is to change the local preference to 105 for the updates that match.

Example 4-13 *Example of Policy List Configuration*

```
ip prefix-list 1 permit 10.0.0.0/8
ip as-path access-list 1 permit ^100_
ip as-path access-list 2 permit ^200_
ip community-list 1 permit 300:105
!
ip policy-list as100 permit
 match as-path 1
 match community 1
!
ip policy-list as200 permit
 match as-path 2
 match community 1
!
route-map foo permit 10
 match ip address prefix-list 1
 match policy-list as100 as200
 set local-preference 105
route-map foo permit 20
```

Filter Processing Order

When multiple filters are configured per neighbor, each filter is processed in a specific order, as shown in Figure 4-1. For inbound updates, the filter list is processed first, followed by the route map. The distribute list or prefix list is processed last. On the outbound side, the distribute list or prefix list is processed first, and then the prefix list received via Outbound Route Filtering (ORF), and then the filter list. The route map is processed last.

Figure 4-1   *Filter Processing Order*

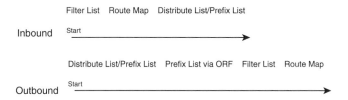

An update has to pass through all the filters. One filter does not take precedence over another. If any filter does not match, the update is not permitted. For example, if an inbound update is permitted by the filter list and the route map but is denied by the prefix list, the update is denied. The same rule applies on the outbound side.

When a policy for a neighbor is configured in the **neighbor** command but the policy is not defined, the following are the default behaviors:

- For distribute lists and prefix lists, permit any.
- For filter lists and route maps, deny any.

Conditional Advertisement

BGP by default advertises the permitted best paths in its BGP routing information base (RIB) to external peers. In certain cases, this might be undesirable. Advertisement of some routes might depend on the existence and nonexistence of some other routes. In other words, the advertisement is conditional.

In a multihomed network, some prefixes are to be advertised to one of the providers only if information from the other provider is missing, such as a failure in the peering session or partial reachability. The conditional BGP announcements are in addition to the normal announcements that a BGP router sends to its peers.

NOTE   A conditional advertisement does not create routes; it only withholds them until the condition is met. These routes must already be present in the BGP RIB.

Configurations

Conditional advertisement has two forms: advertisement of some prefixes when some other prefixes do not exist and advertisement of some prefixes when they do exist. The prefixes to be advertised are defined by a special route map called **advertise-map**. The condition is defined by a route map called **non-exist-map** for conditions that do not exist or by a route map called **exist-map** for conditions that do exist.

The first form of conditional advertisement is configured as follows:

```
neighbor advertise-map map1 non-exist-map map2
```

The route map associated with the non-exist-map specifies the prefix (or prefixes) that the BGP speaker tracks. Only permit is accepted; any deny is ignored. When a match is made, the status of the advertise-map is Withdraw; when no match is made, the status becomes Advertise.

Within the non-exist-map, a match statement for the prefix is required. You can configure it with a prefix list or a standard access list. Only an exact match is supported. Additionally, AS_PATH and community can be matched.

The route map associated with the advertise-map defines the prefix (or prefixes) that are advertised to the specific neighbor when the prefixes in the non-exist-map no longer exist— that is, when the status is Advertise. When the status is Withdraw, the prefix or prefixes defined in the advertise-map are not advertised or withdrawn. Note that the advertise-map applies only on the outbound direction, which is in addition to the other outbound filters.

The second form of conditional advertisement is configured as follows:

```
neighbor advertise-map map1 exist-map map2
```

In this case, the route map associated with the exist-map specifies the prefix (or prefixes) that the BGP speaker tracks. The status is Advertise when the match is positive—that is, when the tracked prefix exists. The status is Withdraw if the tracked prefix does not exist. The route map associated with the advertise-map defines the prefix (or prefixes) that are advertised to the specific neighbor when the prefix in the exist-map exists. Prefixes in both route maps must exist in the local BGP RIB.

Examples

Figure 4-2 shows a topology of a conditional advertisement that tracks the nonexistence of a prefix. AS 100 is multihomed to AS 200 and AS 300, with the link to AS 300 as the primary connection. The address block of AS 100 is assigned from AS 300, within the range of 172.16.0.0/16. The address block 172.16.1.0/24 is not to be advertised to AS 200 unless the link to AS 300 fails. AS 300 sends 172.16.2.0/24 to AS 100, and it is tracked by the non-exist-map on R1. Example 4-14 shows R1's BGP configuration. Note that the community 100:300 is set and matched for the prefix to be tracked to ensure that the prefix is indeed from AS 300.

Figure 4-2   *Conditional Advertisement in a Primary-Backup Scenario*

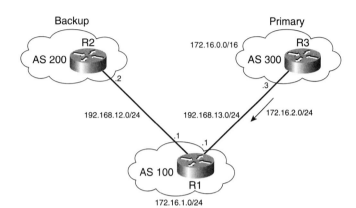

Example 4-14 *Sample BGP Configuration for Conditional Advertisement on R1*

```
router bgp 100
 network 172.16.1.0 mask 255.255.255.0
 neighbor 192.168.12.2 remote-as 200
 neighbor 192.168.12.2 advertise-map AS200-out non-exist-map AS300-in
 neighbor 192.168.13.3 remote-as 300
 neighbor 192.168.13.3 route-map Set-comm in
!
ip community-list 1 permit 100:300
ip prefix-list AS300-track seq 5 permit 172.16.2.0/24
ip prefix-list Local-prefix seq 5 permit 172.16.1.0/24
!
route-map AS300-in permit 10
 match ip address prefix-list AS300-track
 match community 1
!
route-map Set-comm permit 10
 set community 100:300
!
route-map AS200-out permit 10
 match ip address prefix-list Local-prefix
```

When prefix 172.16.2.0/24 is present in R1's BGP RIB, 172.16.1.0/24 is not advertised to R2, as shown in Examples 4-15 and 4-16.

Example 4-15 *Advertisement Status in R1 Under Normal Conditions*

```
R1#show ip bgp 172.16.2.0
BGP routing table entry for 172.16.2.0/24, version 3
Paths: (1 available, best #1, table Default-IP-Routing-Table)
  Advertised to non peer-group peers:
  192.168.12.2
  300
    192.168.13.3 from 192.168.13.3 (192.168.13.3)
      Origin IGP, metric 0, localpref 100, valid, external, best
      Community: 100:300

R1#show ip bgp neighbor 192.168.12.2 | include Condition-map
  Condition-map AS300-in, Advertise-map AS200-out, status: Withdraw
```

Example 4-16 *R2 Does Not Have 172.16.1.0 Under Normal Conditions*

```
R2#show ip bgp 172.16.1.0
% Network not in table
```

When the session between R1 and R3 is down, 172.16.2.0/24 is removed from R1's BGP RIB. R2's advertisement status is now Advertise, as shown in Example 4-17. The prefix 172.16.1.0/24 is now available in R2, as shown in Example 4-18. For this design to work, it is important to ensure that the right prefix from the provider is being tracked.

Example 4-17 *Advertisement Status During Primary Link Failure*

```
R1#show ip bgp neighbor 192.168.12.2 | include Condition-map
  Condition-map AS300-in, Advertise-map AS200-out, status: Advertise
```

Example 4-18 *Prefix 172.16.1.0 Is Present on R2 During a Primary Link Failure*

```
R2#show ip bgp 172.16.1.0
BGP routing table entry for 172.16.1.0/24, version 14
Paths: (1 available, best #1, table Default-IP-Routing-Table)
  Not advertised to any peer
  100
    192.168.12.1 from 192.168.12.1 (192.168.13.1)
      Origin IGP, metric 0, localpref 100, valid, external, best
```

Figure 4-3 shows a topology of conditional advertisement to track the existence of a prefix. Within AS 100, R1 is the only BGP speaker, and it has an eBGP session with R3 in AS 300. All routers within AS 100 communicate using OSPF. The internal address block 10.0.0.0/16 is translated into a public block 172.16.0.0/16 on R2. The policy is that R1 should not advertise 172.16.0.0/16 to R3 unless 10.0.0.0/16 is available.

Figure 4-3   *Conditional Advertisement to Track the Existence of a Prefix*

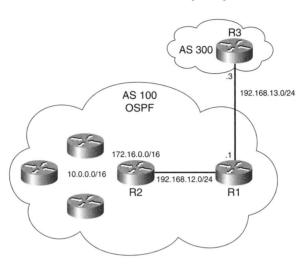

Example 4-19 shows a sample BGP configuration on R1. Both the prefix to be advertised (172.16.0.0) and the prefix tracked (10.0.0.0) are injected into the BGP RIB. The private prefix is then blocked from being advertised to R3 with the prefix list Block10. The exist map Prefix10 tracks the existence of 10.0.0.0/16, which is learned from OSPF. When the match returns true (status: Advertise), AS300-out is executed. When 10.0.0.0/16 is gone from OSPF (status: Withdraw), 172.16.0.0/16 is not advertised or withdrawn.

Example 4-19 *Sample BGP Configuration on R1*

```
router bgp 100
 network 10.0.0.0 mask 255.255.0.0
 network 172.16.0.0
 neighbor 192.168.13.3 remote-as 300
 neighbor 192.168.13.3 prefix-list Block10 out
 neighbor 192.168.13.3 advertise-map AS300-out exist-map Prefix10
 no auto-summary
!
ip prefix-list Block10 seq 5 deny 10.0.0.0/16
ip prefix-list Block10 seq 10 permit 0.0.0.0/0 le 32
ip prefix-list adv-out seq 5 permit 172.16.0.0/16
ip prefix-list Private10 seq 5 permit 10.0.0.0/16
!
route-map Prefix10 permit 10
 match ip address prefix-list Private10
!
route-map AS300-out permit 10
 match ip address prefix-list adv-out
```

Example 4-20 shows what happens when 10.0.0.0/16 is available on R1's BGP RIB. The prefix 172.16.0.0/16 is advertised to R3.

Example 4-20 *Advertisement of 172.16.0.0/16*

```
R1#show ip bgp 10.0.0.0
BGP routing table entry for 10.0.0.0/16, version 2
Paths: (1 available, best #1, table Default-IP-Routing-Table)
  Not advertised to any peer
  Local
    192.168.12.2 from 0.0.0.0 (192.168.13.1)
      Origin IGP, metric 20, localpref 100, weight 32768, valid, sourced, local,
  best

R1#show ip bgp 172.16.0.0
BGP routing table entry for 172.16.0.0/16, version 4
Paths: (1 available, best #1, table Default-IP-Routing-Table)
  Advertised to non peer-group peers:
  192.168.13.3
  Local
    192.168.12.2 from 0.0.0.0 (192.168.13.1)
      Origin IGP, metric 20, localpref 100, weight 32768, valid, sourced, local,
  best

R1#show ip route 10.0.0.0
Routing entry for 10.0.0.0/8, 1 known subnet
O E2    10.0.0.0/16 [110/20] via 192.168.12.2, 00:36:47, Ethernet0/0

R1#show ip bgp neighbor 192.168.13.3 | include Condition-map
  Condition-map Prefix10, Advertise-map AS300-out, status: Advertise

R3#show ip bgp 172.16.0.0
BGP routing table entry for 172.16.0.0/16, version 12
Paths: (1 available, best #1, table Default-IP-Routing-Table)
  Not advertised to any peer
  100
    192.168.13.1 from 192.168.13.1 (192.168.13.1)
      Origin IGP, metric 20, localpref 100, valid, external, best
```

Example 4-21 shows what happens when 10.0.0.0 is not available on R1.

Example 4-21 *No Advertisement When 10.0.0.0 Is Down*

```
R1#show ip bgp neighbor 192.168.13.3 | include Condition-map
  Condition-map Prefix10, Advertise-map AS300-out, status: Withdraw

R3#show ip bgp 172.16.0.0
% Network not in table
```

Example 4-22 shows the output of **debug ip bgp update** on R1 when 10.0.0.0/16 is down. Example 4-23 shows a similar output when 10.0.0.0/16 is up again.

Example 4-22 *Output of* **debug ip bgp update** *on R1 When 10.0.0.0 Is Down*

```
*Jul 29 21:37:39.411: BGP(0): route 10.0.0.0/16 down
*Jul 29 21:37:39.411: BGP(0): no valid path for 10.0.0.0/16
*Jul 29 21:37:39.411: BGP(0): nettable_walker 10.0.0.0/16 no best path
*Jul 29 21:37:39.411: BGP(0): 192.168.13.3 computing updates, afi 0, neighbor
  version 4, table version 5, starting at 0.0.0.0
*Jul 29 21:37:39.411: BGP(0): 192.168.13.3 update run completed, afi 0, ran for
  0ms, neighbor version 4, start version 5, throttled to 5
*Jul 29 21:38:20.331: BPG(0): Condition Prefix10 changes to Withdraw
*Jul 29 21:38:20.331: BGP(0): net 172.16.0.0/16 matches ADV MAP AS300-out: bump
  version to 6
*Jul 29 21:38:20.379: BGP(0): nettable_walker 172.16.0.0/16 route sourced locally
*Jul 29 21:38:20.379: BGP(0): 192.168.13.3 computing updates, afi 0, neighbor
  version 5, table version 6, starting at 0.0.0.0
*Jul 29 21:38:20.379: BGP(0): 192.168.13.3 172.16.0.0/16 matches advertise map
  AS300-out, state: Withdraw
*Jul 29 21:38:20.379: BGP(0): 192.168.13.3 send unreachable 172.16.0.0/16
*Jul 29 21:38:20.379: BGP(0): 192.168.13.3 send UPDATE 172.16.0.0/16 --
  unreachable
*Jul 29 21:38:20.379: BGP(0): 192.168.13.3 1 updates enqueued (average=26,
  maximum=26)
*Jul 29 21:38:20.379: BGP(0): 192.168.13.3 update run completed, afi 0, ran for
  0ms, neighbor version 5, start version 6, throttled to 6
```

Example 4-23 *Output of* **debug ip bgp update** *on R1 When 10.0.0.0 Is Up*

```
*Jul 29 21:40:10.679: BGP(0): route 10.0.0.0/16 up
*Jul 29 21:40:10.679: BGP(0): nettable_walker 10.0.0.0/16 route sourced locally
*Jul 29 21:40:10.679: BGP(0): 192.168.13.3 computing updates, afi 0, neighbor
  version 6, table version 7, starting at 0.0.0.0
*Jul 29 21:40:10.679: BGP(0): 192.168.13.3 update run completed, afi 0, ran for
  0ms, neighbor version 6, start version 7, throttled to 7
*Jul 29 21:40:20.539: BPG(0): Condition Prefix10 changes to Advertise
*Jul 29 21:40:20.539: BGP(0): net 172.16.0.0/16 matches ADV MAP AS300-out: bump
  version to 8
*Jul 29 21:40:21.119: BGP(0): nettable_walker 172.16.0.0/16 route sourced locally
*Jul 29 21:40:37.639: BGP(0): 192.168.13.3 computing updates, afi 0, neighbor
  version 7, table version 8, starting at 0.0.0.0
*Jul 29 21:40:37.639: BGP(0): 192.168.13.3 172.16.0.0/16 matches advertise map
  AS300-out, state: Advertise
*Jul 29 21:40:37.639: BGP(0): 192.168.13.3 send UPDATE (format) 172.16.0.0/16,
  next 192.168.13.1, metric 20, path
*Jul 29 21:40:37.639: BGP(0): 192.168.13.3 1 updates enqueued (average=51,
  maximum=51)
*Jul 29 21:40:37.639: BGP(0): 192.168.13.3 update run completed, afi 0, ran for
  0ms, neighbor version 7, start version 8, throttled to 8
```

Aggregation and Deaggregation

Aggregation of prefix information reduces the number of entries BGP has to carry and store. There are two common ways prefixes can be aggregated in BGP:

- Using the **network** command to enter an aggregate address and a static route to Null0
- Using the **aggregate-address** command to create an aggregate

Because the first method is straightforward, this section focuses on the second method—using the **aggregate-address** command. Here is the full command with its various options:

```
aggregate-address address mask [as-set] [summary-only] [suppress-map map1]
   [advertise-map map2] [attribute-map map3]
```

The creation of an aggregate in the BGP RIB is dependent on the existence of at least one component route in the local BGP RIB. Without any options specified, BGP attributes of the individual components are not included in the aggregate. The aggregate prefix has the following default attributes:

- **NEXT_HOP**—0.0.0.0 (local)
- **AS_PATH**—i (blank AS_PATH; origin code IGP)
- **MED**—Not set
- **LOCAL_PREF**—100
- **WEIGHT**—32768
- **AGGREGATOR**—Local
- **ATOMIC_AGGREGATE**—Tagged to the aggregate

By default, both the aggregate and its components are advertised. When **summary-only** is enabled for the aggregate, only the aggregate is advertised, and all the specific component routes are suppressed. The aggregate still maintains the default attributes just listed. If only a subset of the components are to be suppressed, you can define the subset with **suppress-map**. If a subset of suppressed routes needs to be made available, you can unsuppress those routes on a per-neighbor basis using the **neighbor unsuppress-map** command.

The option **as-set** allows AS path loop detection for the aggregate. Additionally, some of the attributes of components are included additively with the aggregate, even if they conflict. For example, if one component prefix has community set to 100:200 and another has it set to **no-export**, the community of the aggregate is 100:200 and **no-export**. The aggregate is not advertised to an eBGP peer.

The option **attribute-map** (a form of route map for setting BGP attributes) is used to clean up the aggregate's attributes. Using the previous community example, if an attribute map resets the community to 100:300, the previous two community values are replaced with 100:300, and the aggregate is advertised to an eBGP peer with 100:300. If only a subset of components are to be used to form the aggregate's attributes, these components can also be defined by an **advertise-map**. Note that the aggregate's AS_SET is inherited only from the components that are defined in the map.

A common route aggregation practice is to group as large an address space as possible into as few prefix entries as possible. This is desirable in reducing the number of prefixes carried by the Internet, but it's detrimental to adjacent networks that have multiple connections to the aggregating network. One result of aggregation is that routing accuracy of neighbors is lost. In this situation, more-specific routes can be generated to better identify a prefix's address subsets across multiple connections. Deaggregation is a BGP feature that reconstructs components from a received aggregate prefix.

Deaggregation is accomplished by using the conditional injection feature. *Conditional injection* is the creation of more-specific components when an aggregate exists. These components are injected into the local BGP RIB to provide more-specific routing information in the local AS than the aggregate. These components can be installed in the IP RIB and advertised to other BGP peers within the AS.

Conditional route injection is configured as follows:

```
bgp inject-map map1 exist-map map2 [copy-attributes]
```

BGP tracks the prefix (the aggregate) in the exist-map to determine whether to install a prefix or prefixes as specified in the inject-map. The exist-map must have at least two match clauses:

- **match ip address prefix-list** specifies the aggregate based on which to inject more specifics. Only one exact match is allowed.

- **match ip route-source** specifies the neighbor that sent the aggregate. The component inherits the attributes from the aggregate if the option **copy-attributes** is specified; otherwise, they are treated as locally generated routes for some of the attributes. The NEXT_HOP is always the eBGP peer that originated the aggregate. Additional matches can be made for AS_PATH and community.

Within the inject map, use **set ip address prefix-list** to define the prefixes to be injected into the local BGP RIB. The injected prefixes can be displayed with the **show ip bgp injected-path** command.

Figure 4-4 shows a sample topology that takes advantage of conditional injection to achieve deaggregation. Both AS 300 and AS 400 are customers of AS 200 and receive address blocks assigned by AS 200. The prefix block is 172.16.1.0/24 for AS 300 and 172.16.2.0/24 for AS 400. When announcing to AS 100, border routers of AS 200 summarize their address space to a single aggregate, 172.16.0.0/16.

Because AS 100 follows a best-exit policy (sometimes called *cold-potato routing*), it attempts to optimize its exit points. With a single aggregate, however, traffic destined for AS 300 might be exiting the AS via R3. If more-specific prefixes are available, you can control the traffic flows with better granularity.

Figure 4-4 *Example of Conditional Injection*

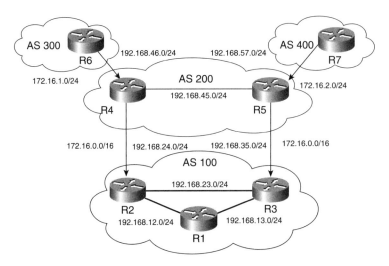

With traffic statistics analysis, AS 100 determines that the best exit for 172.16.1.0/24 is via R2. It is also found that the best exit to 172.16.2.0/24 is via R3. In an effort to optimize the exit points, conditional injection is deployed on R2 and R3. The network address for each link is specified in Figure 4-4, with each router's number as the host address.

Example 4-24 shows a sample BGP configuration on R2. The route map **AS200-aggregate** matches the incoming aggregate from R4. If the match is positive, create 172.16.1.0/24 in the local BGP RIB. To prevent the injected routes from leaking back out, a community of **no-export** is set for the injected route. Also, a community of 100:200 is tagged for the route to indicate that it is a locally injected specific from AS 200.

Example 4-24 *Sample BGP Configuration on R2*

```
router bgp 100
 bgp inject-map AS200-specific exist-map AS200-aggregate
 neighbor 192.168.12.1 remote-as 100
 neighbor 192.168.12.1 send-community
 neighbor 192.168.23.3 remote-as 100
 neighbor 192.168.23.3 send-community
 neighbor 192.168.24.4 remote-as 200
!
ip bgp-community new-format
ip prefix-list AS200-R4 seq 5 permit 192.168.24.4/32
ip prefix-list Aggregate seq 5 permit 172.16.0.0/16
ip prefix-list Specific seq 5 permit 172.16.1.0/24
!
route-map AS200-specific permit 10
```

Example 4-24 *Sample BGP Configuration on R2 (Continued)*

```
 set ip address prefix-list Specific
 set community 100:200 no-export
 !
route-map AS200-aggregate permit 10
 match ip address prefix-list Aggregate
 match ip route-source AS200-R4
```

Example 4-25 shows a similar configuration on R3. Another way to inject the specific components is to inject both specifics into routers R2 and R3 simultaneously. A preference can be set for one of the two.

Example 4-25 *Sample BGP Configuration on R3*

```
router bgp 100
 bgp inject-map AS200-specific exist-map AS200-aggregate
 neighbor 192.168.13.1 remote-as 100
 neighbor 192.168.13.1 send-community
 neighbor 192.168.23.2 remote-as 100
 neighbor 192.168.23.2 send-community
 neighbor 192.168.35.5 remote-as 200
 !
ip bgp-community new-format
ip prefix-list AS200-R5 seq 5 permit 192.168.35.5/32
ip prefix-list Aggregate seq 5 permit 172.16.0.0/16
ip prefix-list Specific seq 5 permit 172.16.2.0/24
 !
route-map AS200-specific permit 10
 set ip address prefix-list Specific
 set community 100:200 no-export
 !
route-map AS200-aggregate permit 10
 match ip address prefix-list Aggregate
 match ip route-source AS200-R5
```

Example 4-26 shows the BGP RIB on R1. Note that the BGP next hops are border routers that announce the aggregate and not the routers that inject the specifics. With the more-specific information, R1 directs traffic to R4 for 172.16.1.0 and to R5 for 172.16.2.0. The aggregate is used for all other traffic to 172.16.0.0.

Example 4-26 *BGP RIB on R1*

```
R1#show ip bgp
BGP table version is 38, local router ID is 192.168.14.1
Status codes: s suppressed, d damped, h history, * valid, > best, i - internal,
              r RIB-failure
Origin codes: i - IGP, e - EGP, ? - incomplete
```

continues

Example 4-26 *BGP RIB on R1 (Continued)*

```
     Network          Next Hop         Metric LocPrf Weight Path
   * i172.16.0.0      192.168.35.5            100      0 200 400 i
   *>i                192.168.24.4            100      0 200 300 i
   *>i172.16.1.0/24   192.168.24.4            100      0 ?
   *>i172.16.2.0/24   192.168.35.5            100      0 ?
```

Example 4-27 shows the BGP RIB on R2. Note that communities of 100:200 and **no-export** are attached to the injected prefixes.

Example 4-27 *BGP RIB on R2*

```
R2#show ip bgp
BGP table version is 34, local router ID is 192.168.24.2
Status codes: s suppressed, d damped, h history, * valid, > best, i - internal,
              r RIB-failure
Origin codes: i - IGP, e - EGP, ? - incomplete

     Network          Next Hop         Metric LocPrf Weight Path
   * i172.16.0.0      192.168.35.5            100      0 200 400 i
   *>                 192.168.24.4                     0 200 300 i
   *> 172.16.1.0/24   192.168.24.4                     0 ?
   * i                192.168.35.5                     0 ?
   *>i172.16.2.0/24   192.168.35.5            100      0 ?

R2#show ip bgp 172.16.1.0
BGP routing table entry for 172.16.1.0/24, version 34
Paths: (2 available, best #1, table Default-IP-Routing-Table, not advertised to
  EBGP peer)
  Advertised to non peer-group peers:
  192.168.12.1 192.168.23.3
  Local, (aggregated by 200 192.168.46.4), (injected path from 172.16.0.0/16)
    192.168.24.4 from 192.168.24.4 (192.168.46.4)
      Origin incomplete, localpref 100, valid, external, best
      Community: 100:200 no-export
  Local, (aggregated by 200 192.168.57.5), (injected path from 172.16.0.0/16)
    192.168.35.5 (metric 20) from 192.168.23.3 (192.168.35.3)
      Origin incomplete, localpref 100, valid, internal
      Community: 100:200 no-export

R2#show ip bgp 172.16.2.0
BGP routing table entry for 172.16.2.0/24, version 32
Paths: (1 available, best #1, table Default-IP-Routing-Table, not advertised to
  EBGP peer)
  Not advertised to any peer
  Local, (aggregated by 200 192.168.57.5)
    192.168.35.5 (metric 20) from 192.168.23.3 (192.168.35.3)
      Origin incomplete, localpref 100, valid, internal, best
      Community: 100:200 no-export
```

When the link between R2 and R4 is down, the aggregate from R4 is removed. Under this condition, R2 stops the injection of the prefix 172.16.1.0/24. This is shown in the BGP RIB on R1 in Example 4-28. When the link between R3 and R5 is down as well, both 172.16.0.0 and 172.16.2.0 are also removed from AS 100 (not shown).

Example 4-28 *BGP RIB on R1 When the Link Between R2 and R4 Is Down*

```
R1#show ip bgp
BGP table version is 56, local router ID is 192.168.14.1
Status codes: s suppressed, d damped, h history, * valid, > best, i - internal,
              r RIB-failure
Origin codes: i - IGP, e - EGP, ? - incomplete

   Network          Next Hop            Metric LocPrf Weight Path
*>i172.16.0.0       192.168.35.5                 100      0 200 400 i
*>i172.16.2.0/24    192.168.35.5                 100      0 200 400 i
```

Local AS

When two ISPs merge their networks, many challenges related to BGP design arise. When one AS is being replaced by another AS, its former peering autonomous systems might not honor the new AS and might continue to insist on the previous peering agreements. For example, if ISP A has a private peering agreement with ISP B, and if ISP A is acquired by ISP C, ISP B might not want to peer with ISP C but might honor the previous peering agreement with ISP A.

An ISP generally has various peering agreements with other ISPs. Changing the AS number on a large scale might be too disruptive to its peering sessions with other ISPs. Also, changing the AS number on all the routers in one large AS during one maintenance window might not be feasible or recommended. During the migration, both autonomous systems must coexist and continue to communicate. The BGP Local AS feature helps reduce these challenges.

With the Local AS feature, a BGP speaker can be physically in one AS and acts as such to some neighbors while it appears to be another AS to other neighbors. When sending and receiving AS_PATH to and from neighbors with Local AS configured, BGP prepends the Local AS to the real AS. For these neighbors, BGP uses the Local AS as the remote AS in the configuration. Thus, the Local AS number appears as if it were another AS inserted between the two real autonomous systems.

Figure 4-5 shows an example. When AS 2 is configured on AS 200 as a Local AS, the AS_PATH is prepended with AS 2 for updates from AS 100. When AS 100 receives updates from AS 200, the AS_PATH is prepended with AS 2.

Figure 4-5 *AS_PATH Updates with Local AS*

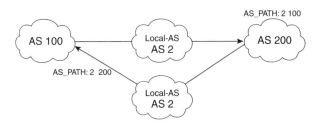

NOTE   Local AS can be used together with peer groups, but it cannot be customized for individual peers in a peer group. Local AS cannot have the local BGP AS number or the remote peer's AS number. The **local-as** command is valid only if the peer is a true eBGP peer. It does not work for two peers in different member autonomous systems in a confederation.

Example 4-29 shows a sample BGP configuration in AS 200 border routers for Figure 4-5. 192.168.1.1 is the IP address of a BGP speaker in AS 100. On 192.168.1.1, 2 instead of 200 is configured as the remote AS (not shown).

Example 4-29 *Sample Local AS Configuration in AS 200*

```
router bgp 200
 neighbor 192.168.1.1 remote-as 100
 neighbor 192.168.1.1 local-as 2
```

Figure 4-6 shows another example of Local AS. In this case, AS 200 is configured with Local AS with two remote autonomous systems, AS 100 and AS 300. When AS 200 border routers advertise prefix 172.16.0.0/16 to AS 300, the AS_PATH is 2 200 2 100. Because loop detection is done only for incoming updates from an eBGP peer, this AS_PATH is not considered a condition of a loop. AS 300 accepts the prefix because it does not detect any loop of AS 300. Similarly, AS 100 accepts prefix 10.0.0.0/8. Multiple occurrences of the Local AS number in the eBGP updates indicate more than one point of Local AS sessions.

Figure 4-6 *Local AS in Two Connections*

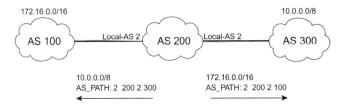

NOTE   When Local AS is used, the AS_PATH length becomes longer. If AS_PATH length is used as a deciding factor in selecting preference, AS_PATH prepending might be needed on other paths so that path selection is not affected.

During AS migration, it is possible that some routers are in the original AS and others are in the new AS. When a border router is migrated to the new AS and is configured with Local AS to remote peers, the updates from this border router to other routers that are still in the old AS are denied, because the other routers detect an AS_PATH loop.

Figure 4-7 shows what happens. Before the migration, both R1 and R3 are in AS 2. When R1 is migrated to AS 200 (the new AS), the Local AS is configured with R2 in AS 100. When R3 receives the prefix 172.16.0.0/16, it detects its own AS in the AS_PATH, and the update is denied. Example 4-30 shows the output of **debug ip bgp update** in on R3.

Figure 4-7   *Updates Denied on R3 with Local AS on R1*

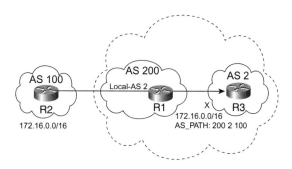

Example 4-30 *Loop Detection on R3 as Captured by* **debug ip bgp update in**

```
*Apr 22 04:59:32.563 UTC: BGP(0): 192.168.13.1 rcv UPDATE w/ attr: nexthop
  192.168.13.1, origin i, originator 0.0.0.0, path 200 2 100, community , extended
  community
*Apr 22 04:59:32.563 UTC: BGP(0): 192.168.13.1 rcv UPDATE about 172.16.0.0/16 --
  DENIED due to: AS-PATH contains our own AS;
```

As mentioned previously, loop detection is performed on the inbound of an eBGP session. Because the session between R1 and R3 is now eBGP, this detection is enforced.

The solution to the problem is to add the **no-prepend** option to the **local-as** command. With this option, R1 does not prepend its Local AS number to the update received from R2. For this example, the AS_PATH to R3 is then 200 100. The update is acceptable to R3. The case study near the end of this chapter provides a more-detailed discussion of how to migrate an AS using the Local AS feature.

QoS Policy Propagation

Cisco Express Forwarding (CEF) and the forwarding information base (FIB) were discussed in Chapter 2. A FIB leaf has three policy parameters:

- Precedence
- QoS-group ID
- Traffic index

All three parameters can be used to provide differential treatment to an IP packet in forwarding or accounting. The precedence is as defined in the IPv4 header. After it is reset in IP packets, it can influence QoS treatment in other routers. The other two parameters are used by the local router only to differentiate traffic.

BGP can set these parameters when certain BGP prefixes and attributes are matched. With this information in CEF, policies can be created and accounted. Policy accounting using BGP is discussed in the section "BGP Policy Accounting."

QoS Policy Propagation via BGP (QPPB) lets you map BGP prefixes and attributes to CEF parameters that can be used to enforce traffic policing. Compared to other QoS methods, QPPB allows BGP policy set in one location of the network to be propagated via BGP to other parts of the network, where appropriate QoS policies can be created.

Configuring QPPB generally involves the following steps:

Step 1   Identify BGP prefixes that require preferential treatment, and tag them with appropriate BGP attributes.

Step 2   Set appropriate FIB policy parameters for each type of traffic.

Step 3   Configure FIB address lookups for the tagged prefixes as packets are received on an interface, and set appropriate QoS policies.

Step 4   Enforce policing based on the lookups and settings done in Step 3 for packets received or transmitted.

The following sections describe each step in greater detail. Configuration examples appear later.

Identifying and Tagging BGP Prefixes That Require Preferential Treatment

Figure 4-8 shows how this process works. Assume that AS 100 wants to create a special forwarding policy for traffic between AS 200 and AS 300 for prefix 172.16.0.0/16. When the prefix is first received from R1 via BGP, R2 tags the prefix with special BGP attributes, such as a specific community value.

Figure 4-8 *How QoS Policy Propagation via BGP Works*

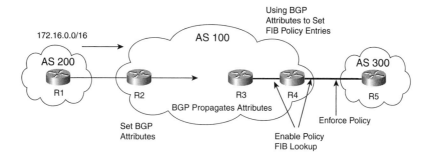

Setting FIB Policy Entries Based on BGP Tagging

As the prefix is propagated via BGP inside AS 100 to R4, the attributes are propagated as well. When R4 receives the prefix with the matching attributes, it can set various FIB policy entries using the **table-map** command in BGP. For QPPB, either or both Precedence and QoS-group ID (a parameter internal to the router) can be set. The Precedence can have eight values, 0 to 7, and the QoS-group ID can have 99 values, 1 to 99. Each value or a combination of both values can represent one class of traffic. Note that these settings have no impact on traffic forwarding until they are used to classify and police the traffic (as discussed next).

NOTE   Changes to the FIB/RIB tables are made when the IP RIB is cleared using **clear ip route ***, the BGP session is reset, or a router is reloaded. All of these actions can be disruptive to the traffic.

Within the FIB entry for the prefix 172.16.0.0/16, the following mappings are possible, depending on the table map configuration:

*   172.16.0.0 Precedence
*   172.16.0.0 QoS-group ID
*   172.16.0.0 Precedence and QoS-group ID

Configuring Traffic Lookup on an Interface and Setting QoS Policies

The next step is to classify the incoming traffic from an interface based on the FIB policy entries. The definition of the incoming interface depends on the traffic's direction. If traffic is destined for 172.16.0.0/16 from AS 300, the incoming interface is the link between R4 and R5; if the traffic is destined for AS 300 from 172.16.0.0/16 (the return traffic), the incoming interface is the link between R3 and R4. On the incoming interfaces on R4, enable FIB policy lookup using the following command:

```
bgp-policy {source | destination} {ip-prec-map | ip-qos-map}
```

The keywords **source** and **destination** indicate whether to use the source or the destination IP address of an incoming packet to look up the FIB entries. On the link between R4 and R5, the incoming traffic is destined for 172.16.0.0/16, so you should use **destination**. On the link between R3 and R4, the incoming traffic is sourced from 172.16.0.0/16, so you should use **source**.

With this configuration command, appropriate QoS policies are also set if there is a match for both the address and QoS parameters. The interface map keyword specifies which of the two policy FIB entries to set for the packet. If **ip-prec-map** is specified, the IP precedence bits are set for the matching packets; if **ip-qos-map** is specified, the QoS-group ID is set. Note that setting IP precedence bits here might affect the QoS treatment of these packets on other routers.

Enforcing Policing on an Interface as Traffic Is Received and Transmitted

The last step of QPPB configuration is to create traffic policing on the interface to AS 300. This can be accomplished by using Committed Access Rate (CAR) and Weighted Random Early Detection (WRED). The policing can be done on the input to the router for traffic destined for 172.16.0.0 or on the output from the router for the return traffic sourced from 172.16.0.0. The policing is created based on the result of the policy lookup and settings done previously.

An Example of QPPB

Figure 4-9 shows a simple topology that demonstrates how to configure QPPB. Within AS 100, special treatment is needed for traffic between AS 200 and AS 300 to and from the prefix 172.16.0.0/16. On R2, prefix 172.16.0.0/16 from R1 is tagged with a community of 100:200, and the prefix is propagated to R3 via iBGP. The FastEthernet 10/0 interface on R3 is used to demonstrate how QoS policing can be set for traffic destined for 172.16.0.0/16.

Figure 4-9   *Example of QoS Policy Propagation*

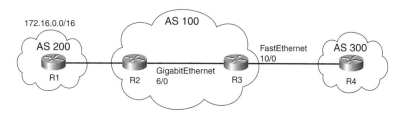

Example 4-31 shows a sample BGP configuration on R3. The router number is used as the host address. The route map Set-policy sets the FIB QoS-group ID to 2 for prefixes matching the community 100:200, which is tagged for 172.16.0.0/16 by R2.

Example 4-31 *Sample BGP Configuration on R3*

```
router bgp 100
 table-map Set-policy
 neighbor 192.168.23.2 remote-as 100
 neighbor 192.168.34.4 remote-as 300
!
ip community-list 1 permit 100:200
!
route-map Set-policy permit 10
 match community 1
 set ip qos-group 2
```

Examples 4-32 and 4-33 show the IP RIB and FIB entries, respectively. Note that prefix 172.16.0.0/16 is now set with qos-group 2.

Example 4-32 *IP RIB Entry for 172.16.0.0*

```
R3#show ip route 172.16.0.0
Routing entry for 172.16.0.0/16
  Known via "bgp 200", distance 200, metric 0, qos-group 2, type internal
  Last update from 192.168.23.2 00:32:34 ago
  Routing Descriptor Blocks:
  * 192.168.23.2, from 192.168.23.2, 00:32:34 ago
      Route metric is 0, traffic share count is 1
      AS Hops 1, BGP network version 0
```

Example 4-33 *FIB Entry for 172.16.0.0*

```
R3#show ip cef 172.16.0.0
172.16.0.0/16, version 23, cached adjacency 192.168.12.2
0 packets, 0 bytes, qos-group 2
  via 192.168.23.2, 0 dependencies, recursive
    next hop 192.168.23.2, GigabitEthernet6/0 via 192.168.23.2/32
    valid cached adjacency
```

To enable FIB lookup for the traffic destined for 172.16.0.0/16, policy lookup is enabled on the interface of FastEthernet 10/0. The keyword **destination** is used in the command. If there is a match for the destination address, a check is made into the FIB to determine if there are any matching QoS entries. In this example, ip-qos-map is configured for the interface, and QoS-group ID is set to 2 in FIB, which means that the QoS-group ID can be used to set QoS policies. An input CAR is configured for traffic matching a QoS-group ID of 2. A sample configuration is shown in Example 4-34.

Example 4-34 *Sample Interface Configuration for QPPB*

```
interface FastEthernet10/0
 ip address 192.168.34.3 255.255.255.0
 no ip directed-broadcast
 bgp-policy destination ip-qos-map
 rate-limit input qos-group 2 5000000 4000 8000 conform-action transmit
  exceed-action drop
```

Example 4-35 shows the IP interface status. Example 4-36 shows traffic policing using CAR. A similar configuration can be made for the traffic sourced from 172.16.0.0 to AS 300 (not shown). The incoming interface then is GigabitEthernet 6/0. An outbound CAR should be configured on the interface of FastEthernet 10/0 to enforce the QoS policy.

Example 4-35 *IP Interface Status of FastEthernet 10/0*

```
R3#show ip interface FastEthernet 10/0 | include BGP
  BGP Policy Mapping is enabled (output ip-qos-map)
```

Example 4-36 *Interface CAR Status*

```
R3#show interface FastEthernet 10/0 rate-limit
FastEthernet10/0
  Input
    matches: qos-group 2
      params:  5000000 bps, 4000 limit, 8000 extended limit
      conformed 112 packets, 168448 bytes; action: transmit
```

Example 4-36 *Interface CAR Status (Continued)*

```
            exceeded 0 packets, 0 bytes; action: drop
            last packet: 1300ms ago, current burst: 0 bytes
            last cleared 00:13:15 ago, conformed 1694 bps, exceeded 0 bps
```

BGP Policy Accounting

BGP policy accounting (BPA) is another BGP feature that takes advantage of the FIB policy parameters. In this case, the parameter is traffic index. Traffic index is a router internal counter within a FIB leaf with values between 1 and 8. Think of the traffic index as a table of eight independent buckets. Each can account for one type of traffic matching certain criteria. The number of packets and bytes in each bucket of an interface is recorded.

You can use this feature to account for IP traffic differentially on an edge router by assigning counters based on BGP prefixes and attributes on a per-input interface basis.

Configuration of BPA generally involves the following steps:

Step 1   Identify BGP prefixes that require preferential treatment and tag them with appropriate BGP attributes.

Step 2   Set a FIB traffic index for each type of traffic.

Step 3   Enable BPA on an incoming interface.

Figure 4-10 shows how BGP policy accounting works. As prefix 172.16.0.0/16 is propagated from AS 200 to AS 300, certain BGP attributes are modified. On R4, a traffic index number can be set when a match is made for the attributes using the **table-map** command. A total of eight traffic classes can be accounted.

Figure 4-10 *How BGP Policy Accounting Works*

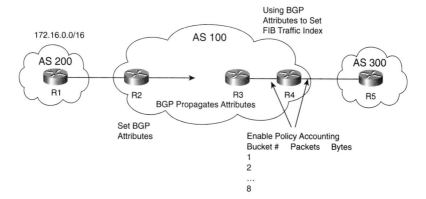

NOTE   Remember that changes to the FIB/RIB tables are updated when the IP RIB is cleared using **clear ip route ***, the BGP session is reset, or a router is reloaded. All these actions can be disruptive to the traffic.

On each incoming interface, you can enable policy accounting by using the command **bgp-policy accounting**. With this command, using destination IP addresses, traffic matching the criteria is accounted for in its respective bucket. The **show cef interface policy-statistics** command displays the per-interface table of traffic counters. The counters can be cleared using the **clear cef interface policy-statistics** command.

Using the topology shown in Figure 4-9, an example of BGP policy accounting is demonstrated here. For the prefix 172.16.0.0/16, the BGP community is set as before. On R3, a route map is created to update the FIB traffic-index, as shown in Example 4-37.

Example 4-37 *Sample BGP Configuration on R3*

```
router bgp 100
 table-map Set-policy
 neighbor 192.168.23.2 remote-as 100
 neighbor 192.168.34.4 remote-as 300
!
ip community-list 1 permit 100:200
!
route-map Set-policy permit 10
 match community 1
 set traffic-index 1
```

The updated FIB for the prefix is shown in Example 4-38. To account for the prefix, policy accounting is enabled on FastEthernet 10/0. This is the incoming interface for traffic destined for 172.16.0.0. Note that this interface doesn't account for the return traffic, because the matching is done on the destination address. To account for the return traffic, policy accounting must be enabled on GigabitEthernet 6/0, and appropriate criteria must be set using the addresses of AS 300. Example 4-39 shows the accounting statistics on FastEthernet 10/0.

Example 4-38 *FIB Traffic Index for 172.16.0.0*

```
R3#show ip cef 172.16.0.0
172.16.0.0/16, version 23, cached adjacency 192.168.23.2
0 packets, 0 bytes, traffic_index 1
  via 192.168.23.2, 0 dependencies, recursive
    next hop 192.168.23.2, GigabitEthernet6/0 via 192.168.23.2/32
    valid cached adjacency
```

Example 4-39 *Policy Accounting Statistics on FastEthernet10/0*

```
R3#show cef interface policy-statistics | begin FastEthernet10/0
FastEthernet10/0 is up (if_number 19)
  Corresponding hwidb fast_if_number 19
  Corresponding hwidb firstsw->if_number 19
BGP based Policy accounting is enabled
   Index          Packets           Bytes
      1           867256          86725600
      2                0                 0
      3                0                 0
      4                0                 0
      5                0                 0
      6                0                 0
      7                0                 0
      8                0                 0
```

Case Study: AS Integration via the Local AS

This case study shows you how to integrate two existing autonomous systems (AS 100 and AS 2) into one AS (AS 2) using the Local AS feature. A simple topology is shown in Figure 4-11. AS 100 is multihomed to three different autonomous systems: 200, 300, and 2. The prefix 172.15.0.0/16 is generated and advertised to neighboring autonomous systems. AS 100 also receives the prefix 172.16.0.0/16 generated by AS 400.

Figure 4-11 *Network Topology for the Case Study*

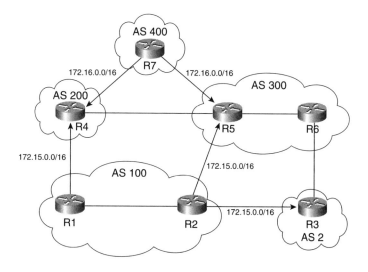

For the purposes of this case study, the last octet of an IP address indicates the router number. Basic BGP configurations for R1 and R2 are shown in Examples 4-40 and 4-41, respectively.

Example 4-40 *BGP Configuration on R1*

```
router bgp 100
 no synchronization
 bgp log-neighbor-changes
 network 172.15.0.0
 neighbor 192.168.12.2 remote-as 100
 neighbor 192.168.14.4 remote-as 200
 no auto-summary
```

Example 4-41 *BGP Configuration on R2*

```
router bgp 100
 no synchronization
 bgp log-neighbor-changes
 network 172.15.0.0
 neighbor 192.168.12.1 remote-as 100
 neighbor 192.168.23.3 remote-as 2
 neighbor 192.168.25.5 remote-as 300
 no auto-summary
```

Examples 4-42 and 4-43 show the BGP RIB.

Example 4-42 *BGP RIB on R1*

```
R1#show ip bgp
BGP table version is 3, local router ID is 192.168.14.1
Status codes: s suppressed, d damped, h history, * valid, > best, i - internal,
              r RIB-failure
Origin codes: i - IGP, e - EGP, ? - incomplete

   Network          Next Hop            Metric LocPrf Weight Path
* i172.15.0.0       192.168.12.2             0    100      0 i
*>                  0.0.0.0                  0          32768 i
* i172.16.0.0       192.168.25.5                 100      0 300 400 i
*>                  192.168.14.4                          0 200 400 i
```

Example 4-43 *BGP RIB on R2*

```
R2#show ip bgp
BGP table version is 3, local router ID is 192.168.25.2
Status codes: s suppressed, d damped, h history, * valid, > best, i - internal,
              r RIB-failure
```

Example 4-43 *BGP RIB on R2 (Continued)*

```
Origin codes: i - IGP, e - EGP, ? - incomplete

   Network          Next Hop        Metric LocPrf Weight Path
 * i172.15.0.0      192.168.12.1        0    100     0 i
 *>                 0.0.0.0             0          32768 i
 *   172.16.0.0     192.168.23.3                      0 2 300 400 i
 * i                192.168.14.4            100       0 200 400 i
 *>                 192.168.25.5                      0 300 400 i
```

Now AS 100 and AS 2 decide to merge into a single AS 2. All BGP speakers in AS 100 are to be migrated to AS 2. Because a common IGP must be used in the same AS, IGP must be migrated first (migrating the IGP is outside the scope of this book and thus isn't covered here). To reduce migration risk and the impact on the peers, migration is to take a gradual approach, with R2 being migrated first.

Local AS is configured on R2 on the session with R5. To maintain the current forwarding architecture, a higher WEIGHT is set on R2 to prefer the path from R5. The outbound AS_PATH is prepended twice on R3 toward R6 and once on R1 toward R4. The **no-prepend** option on R2 is needed so that R1 accepts the path via R5, because now there is an eBGP session between R1 and R2.

Examples 4-44, 4-45, and 4-46 show the configurations on R1, R2, and R3, respectively.

Example 4-44 *BGP Configuration on R1*

```
router bgp 100
 network 172.15.0.0
 neighbor 192.168.12.2 remote-as 2
 neighbor 192.168.14.4 remote-as 200
 neighbor 192.168.14.4 route-map Path-200 out
!
route-map Path-200 permit 10
 set as-path prepend 100
```

Example 4-45 *BGP Configuration on R2*

```
router bgp 2
 network 172.15.0.0
 neighbor 192.168.12.1 remote-as 100
 neighbor 192.168.23.3 remote-as 2
 neighbor 192.168.25.5 remote-as 300
 neighbor 192.168.25.5 local-as 100 no-prepend
 neighbor 192.168.25.5 weight 100
```

Example 4-46 *BGP Configuration on R3*

```
router bgp 2
 neighbor 192.168.23.2 remote-as 2
 neighbor 192.168.36.6 remote-as 300
 neighbor 192.168.36.6 route-map Path-300 out
!
route-map Path-300 permit 10
 set as-path prepend 2 2
```

The new BGP RIB on R1, R2, and R7 is shown in Examples 4-47, 4-48, and 4-49, respectively.

Example 4-47 *BGP RIB on R1*

```
R1#show ip bgp
BGP table version is 3, local router ID is 192.168.14.1
Status codes: s suppressed, d damped, h history, * valid, > best, i - internal,
              r RIB-failure
Origin codes: i - IGP, e - EGP, ? - incomplete

   Network          Next Hop          Metric LocPrf Weight Path
*  172.15.0.0       192.168.12.2           0             0 2 i
*>                  0.0.0.0                0         32768 i
*  172.16.0.0       192.168.12.2                         0 2 300 400 i
*>                  192.168.14.4                          0 200 400 i
```

Example 4-48 *BGP RIB on R2*

```
R2#show ip bgp
BGP table version is 5, local router ID is 192.168.25.2
Status codes: s suppressed, d damped, h history, * valid, > best, i - internal,
              r RIB-failure
Origin codes: i - IGP, e - EGP, ? - incomplete

   Network          Next Hop          Metric LocPrf Weight Path
*  172.15.0.0       192.168.12.1           0             0 100 i
*>                  0.0.0.0                0         32768 i
*> 172.16.0.0       192.168.25.5                   100 300 400 i
*                   192.168.12.1                         0 100 200 400 i
* i                 192.168.36.6               100         0 300 400 i
```

Example 4-49 *BGP RIB on R7*

```
R7#show ip bgp
BGP table version is 4, local router ID is 192.168.57.7
Status codes: s suppressed, d damped, h history, * valid, > best, i - internal,
              r RIB-failure
```

Example 4-49 *BGP RIB on R7 (Continued)*

```
Origin codes: i - IGP, e - EGP, ? - incomplete

   Network          Next Hop          Metric LocPrf Weight Path
*  172.15.0.0       192.168.57.5                       0 300 100 2 i
*>                  192.168.47.4                       0 200 100 100 i
*> 172.16.0.0       0.0.0.0              0         32768 i
```

The resulting topology is shown in Figure 4-12.

Figure 4-12 *Topology After R2 Is Migrated to AS 2*

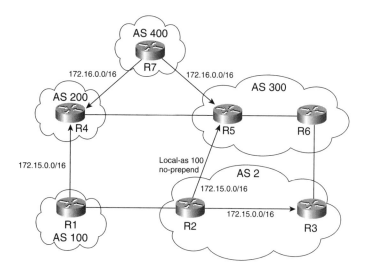

The next step is to migrate R1 to the new AS. Local AS is configured on R1 on the session with R4. AS_PATH prepending is now removed on R1. The LOCAL_PREF is modified to prefer the path via R4. The reason that LOCAL_PREF is used instead of WEIGHT is that R2 would also prefer the path via R1 for 172.16.0.0/16 if the link between R2 and R5 failed. The new BGP configurations on R1 and R2 are shown in Examples 4-50 and 4-51, respectively.

Example 4-50 *BGP Configuration on R1*

```
router bgp 2
 network 172.15.0.0
 neighbor 192.168.12.2 remote-as 2
 neighbor 192.168.14.4 remote-as 200
 neighbor 192.168.14.4 local-as 100
```

continues

Example 4-50 *BGP Configuration on R1*

```
 neighbor 192.168.14.4 route-map Set-lpref in
!
route-map Set-lpref permit 10
 set local-preference 120
```

Example 4-51 *BGP Configuration on R2*

```
router bgp 2
 network 172.15.0.0
 neighbor 192.168.12.1 remote-as 2
 neighbor 192.168.23.3 remote-as 2
 neighbor 192.168.25.5 remote-as 300
 neighbor 192.168.25.5 local-as 100 no-prepend
 neighbor 192.168.25.5 weight 100
```

The BGP RIB is shown in Examples 4-52, 4-53, and 4-54 for R1, R2, and R7, respectively.

Example 4-52 *BGP RIB on R1*

```
R1#show ip bgp
BGP table version is 3, local router ID is 192.168.14.1
Status codes: s suppressed, d damped, h history, * valid, > best, i - internal,
              r RIB-failure
Origin codes: i - IGP, e - EGP, ? - incomplete

   Network          Next Hop          Metric LocPrf Weight Path
* i172.15.0.0       192.168.12.2           0    100      0 i
*>                  0.0.0.0                0          32768 i
*> 172.16.0.0       192.168.14.4              120      0 100 200 400 i
* i                 192.168.25.5              100      0 300 400 i
```

Example 4-53 *BGP RIB on R2*

```
R2#show ip bgp
BGP table version is 5, local router ID is 192.168.25.2
Status codes: s suppressed, d damped, h history, * valid, > best, i - internal,
              r RIB-failure
Origin codes: i - IGP, e - EGP, ? - incomplete

   Network          Next Hop          Metric LocPrf Weight Path
* i172.15.0.0       192.168.12.1           0    100      0 i
*>                  0.0.0.0                0          32768 i
* i172.16.0.0       192.168.14.4              120      0 100 200 400 i
*>                  192.168.25.5                  100 300 400 i
* i                 192.168.36.6              100      0 300 400 i
```

Example 4-54 *BGP RIB on R7*

```
R7#show ip bgp
BGP table version is 5, local router ID is 192.168.57.7
Status codes: s suppressed, d damped, h history, * valid, > best, i - internal,
              r RIB-failure
Origin codes: i - IGP, e - EGP, ? - incomplete

   Network          Next Hop          Metric LocPrf Weight Path
*> 172.15.0.0       192.168.57.5                       0 300 100 2 i
*                   192.168.47.4                       0 200 100 2 i
*> 172.16.0.0       0.0.0.0                0         32768 i
```

Now AS 2 can convince AS 300 to change its peering and, thus, R5's configuration. Local
AS is not needed on R2. However, AS 200 will only honor its previous peering agreement
with AS 100. Local AS is still needed between R1 and R4. To maintain the same forwarding
policy, R2 now needs to prepend its AS_PATH outbound to R5. The final configuration of
R2 is shown in Example 4-55. The BGP RIB on R7 is shown in Example 4-56.

Example 4-55 *BGP Configuration on R2*

```
router bgp 2
 network 172.15.0.0
 neighbor 192.168.12.1 remote-as 2
 neighbor 192.168.23.3 remote-as 2
 neighbor 192.168.25.5 remote-as 300
 neighbor 192.168.25.5 weight 100
 neighbor 192.168.25.5 route-map Path-300 out
!
route-map Path-300 permit 10
 set as-path prepend 2
```

Example 4-56 *BGP RIB on R7*

```
R7#show ip bgp
BGP table version is 10, local router ID is 192.168.57.7
Status codes: s suppressed, d damped, h history, * valid, > best, i - internal,
              r RIB-failure
Origin codes: i - IGP, e - EGP, ? - incomplete

   Network          Next Hop          Metric LocPrf Weight Path
*  172.15.0.0       192.168.47.4                       0 200 100 2 i
*>                  192.168.57.5                       0 300 2 2 i
*> 172.16.0.0       0.0.0.0                0         32768 i
```

Figure 4-13 shows the final topology.

Figure 4-13 *Final Topology*

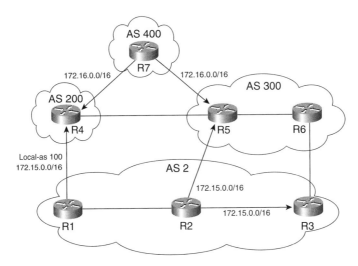

Summary

This chapter presented various techniques you can use to create complex and effective BGP policies. The chapter started with one of the fundamental techniques, regular expressions. Regular expressions are used extensively in IOS for pattern matching in parsing command outputs and in defining AS_PATH and community patterns.

A variety of filtering tools also were discussed. They include prefix lists, community lists, AS_PATH lists, route maps, and policy lists, all of which are used extensively in creating BGP policies. Additionally, more-complex policy tools were presented, including conditional advertisement, aggregation, deaggregation, Local AS, QoS policy propagation, and policy accounting. The chapter ended with a case study on AS merging using the Local AS feature.

PART II

Designing BGP Enterprise Networks

This chapter explores the various aspects of designing an enterprise BGP core network:

- Using BGP in the enterprise core
- BGP network core design solutions
- Remote site aggregation
- Case study: BGP core deployment

CHAPTER 5

Enterprise BGP Core Network Design

Enterprises have typically favored the use of IGPs to provide company-wide IP connectivity. The case for BGP is often made when an enterprise has reached scalability limitations within its IGP. BGP provides enhanced scalability when there are high prefix counts and improves the enterprise's ability to divide administrative control.

Network scalability is improved through increasing network hierarchy and better prefix summarization. Summarization in many networks can be very challenging because of past address assignments that do not provide adequate summarization boundaries. However, BGP can increase scalability by adding hierarchy in the network core.

Enterprises also face the challenge of diversified administrative control. An enterprise might have separate engineering and operations centers in different geographic regions, each with administrative control over a portion of the network. An enterprise network also can consist of a central core network with any number of individual networks, each under the control of different administrative groups. When control is distributed in this fashion, having a common IGP process can present significant operational issues. As mentioned in earlier chapters, BGP was designed with the goal of diverse administrative control.

This chapter examines when you should consider BGP as a solution and how to implement such a solution in an enterprise core network. You'll see extensive examples that demonstrate how you should use BGP to develop stable and scalable core network architectures.

Using BGP in the Enterprise Core

Enterprise engineers and architects often ask, "When should I use BGP in the enterprise core?" Although this is a very common question, the answer is not an easy one. Many factors go into determining the correct routing architecture for an enterprise network, as discussed in the next sections.

Defining the Problem

The design process begins with accurately defining the problem. The following questions help you lay the groundwork:

- What specific problem am I trying to solve?
- What is the root cause of the problem?
- How will BGP resolve this problem?
- Does BGP resolve the root cause or just resolve symptoms?

If BGP resolves only the symptoms, focus on addressing the actual root cause. Using BGP to treat symptoms can allow the underlying problem to continue to grow. A common example is the number of prefixes carried in the IGP.

If prefixes are assigned in an ad hoc manner that does not allow summarization, BGP can provide a temporary patch, but the root of the problem needs to be addressed as well. A proper numbering scheme that allows for efficient summarization should be developed and deployed, even though renumbering a network is time-consuming and often difficult.

If the root cause is not treated, it might become a chronic problem, and it won't become any easier to resolve as the network grows. A network should never be allowed to evolve in an uncontrolled manner. Network expansion should be controlled growth that is consistent with the well-defined and documented network architecture. If the network outgrows a particular architecture, a new architecture should be developed, and continued expansion should be based on this new architecture.

Determining the Solution

In determining if BGP is the appropriate solution, you must examine its strengths and weaknesses. BGP is just one more tool that is at the disposal of network engineers and architects. Deploying BGP is not a panacea, but it can help engineers resolve difficult policy and scaling issues if used correctly. However, there are trade-offs.

BGP Strengths

The following BGP strengths are important in designing an enterprise network:

- **Routing policy control**—BGP is not so much a routing protocol as a policy definition tool. The BGP protocol does carry NLRI, which allows for routing functionality; however, the main intent is to give the network administrator flexibility in defining routing policy. This is in contrast to IGPs, where the main intent is to provide reachability and fast reconvergence.

- **Diverse administrative control**—BGP was designed to provide interconnection of many diverse networks, all under different administrative control. An autonomous system in BGP is an independently controlled unit. BGP's ability to define the scope of administrative boundaries is actually an extension of policy control. BGP autonomous systems can be used to divide administrative control of a network.

- **Handling large prefix counts**—BGP was designed to scale with the growth of the global Internet routing table. Initially, this meant carrying only 10,000 prefixes. However, the mechanisms on which BGP is built have allowed it to scale to carry more than 200,000 prefixes in production networks and more than 500,000 in laboratory tests. The number of prefixes that can be maintained is primarily limited by memory.

BGP Weaknesses

Although BGP does have several benefits, you must also remember its weaknesses:

- **Increased convergence time**—BGP does not react quickly to network changes and is not optimized for fast convergence. Although the convergence time can be tuned, BGP is slower than an IGP.

- **Increased complexity**—BGP is not intended for use in lieu of an IGP. Rather, it is to act in a complementary fashion with an IGP. With BGP acting in tandem with the IGP, there are additional dependencies, which increase the network's complexity.

NOTE Protocol design, much like network design, is a series of trade-offs. When BGP was designed, sacrifices had to be made to achieve the primary design goals. The sacrifices made when BGP was designed are the very features that are taken for granted in IGPs.

Keep in mind that adding BGP to the network is likely to increase the operational complexity. This translates into additional knowledge requirements for the support staff and adds complexity to the troubleshooting process.

Assuming that BGP is the appropriate solution, the rest of this chapter shows you how to effectively design and implement a BGP routing architecture for enterprise networks. Specifically, various architectures are explored for designing a BGP-based enterprise network core.

BGP Network Core Design Solutions

Three primary options are available for a BGP network core design, all of which provide the ability to significantly reduce prefix count in the IGP processes with varying degrees of routing and administrative control:

- **Internal BGP (iBGP) architecture**—This architecture uses a single BGP AS in the network core. The primary benefit gained by deploying this architecture is the reduction of routing information in the IGP. The defining characteristic of this architecture is the complete lack of external BGP sessions, with BGP being used almost exclusively for prefix transport as opposed to routing policy. This design option provides the least administrative control for defining routing policy through the core.

- **External BGP (eBGP) architecture**—Each distinct portion of the network has its own AS. An AS peers only with those autonomous systems to which it is directly connected. In some cases, there also might be some iBGP sessions in regions with multiple core routers. The defining characteristic of this architecture is the extensive eBGP peering that ties together all the regions. This design option provides a more distinct delineation of administrative control between the regional autonomous systems.

- **Internal/external BGP architecture**—The network core is its own AS and runs iBGP on all core routers. The rest of the network is broken into separate autonomous systems that each attach to the network core to receive transit to other diverse network resources. The defining characteristic of this architecture is the use of iBGP to build the core, with eBGP providing connectivity to the core AS via eBGP. This design provides the cleanest delineation of administrative control between the regional networks.

For each of the three BGP architectures presented, the following criteria are applied to evaluate the strengths and weaknesses of each:

- **Path selection**—What key BGP attributes will be used to determine path selection? How can the BGP decision process be manipulated to provide the desired routing policy?

- **Failure and recovery scenarios**—How will the network react to a link or router failure? What is involved in network reconvergence?

- **Administrative control**—How can BGP be used to define the scope of administrative control? How does this affect troubleshooting and network expansion?

- **Routing policy**—How can routing policy be defined in this architecture? How flexible is this architecture?

Throughout the discussion of BGP core architectures, the path-selection process is discussed in great detail. Instead of reiterating the router ID assignments, they are provided in Table 5-1. A standard addressing scheme is used to set the router ID for all devices in the sample discussion network topologies. The router ID for each device is 172.16.X.1, where X is the router number. The 172.16.13.0/24 prefix is subnetted to provide addressing for all network core links.

Table 5-1   *Router ID Assignment Conventions*

Router Name	Router ID	Router Name	Router ID
R1	172.16.1.1	R7	172.16.7.1
R2	172.16.2.1	R8	172.16.8.1
R3	172.16.3.1	R9	172.16.9.1
R4	172.16.4.1	R10	172.16.10.1
R5	172.16.5.1	R11	172.16.11.1
R6	172.16.6.1	R12	172.16.12.1

Internal BGP Core Architecture

The internal BGP core architecture, shown in Figure 5-1, makes use entirely of iBGP sessions, with no eBGP. The primary benefit of this design is to limit the number of prefixes carried in the regional IGP domains. However, this design scenario does not provide a clear delineation between the core resources and the regional resources.

Figure 5-1   *Core Architecture Using iBGP*

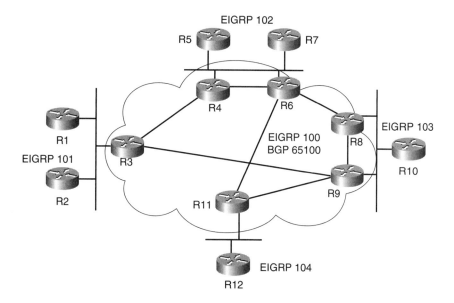

The edge of the regional networks and the core network share the same routers. This results in the core routers running all three routing processes in each region: the regional IGP process, the core IGP process, and the core BGP process. The region number corresponds with the regional IGP's EIGRP process number. One point to keep in mind is that, with all three processes sharing the same resources, instability in one routing process might affect other routing processes if there is a resource shortage.

The regional IGP process provides reachability throughout the entire regional network. This process carries full routing and topological information for the region. The regional IGP process terminates on the core routers in this architecture. A default route should be injected into the regional IGP process on the core routers to provide reachability to the core and other regions.

The core IGP process is responsible for maintaining connectivity among the core routers. This IGP process should only carry prefixes and topology information for the core routers, core links, and loopback interfaces on the core routers. There should be no redistribution between the core IGP process and any other routing process. The core IGP process provides reachability between the loopback interfaces to allow the iBGP sessions to form and provides next-hop reachability for the BGP learned prefixes. The peering for all iBGP sessions is with the loopback interfaces, and the **next-hop-self** command is used.

The BGP process running on each core router should peer via iBGP with every other core router, creating a full mesh of iBGP sessions. The BGP process is responsible for propagating prefix information between the core routers at each region. The iBGP sessions should be sourced from the loopback interfaces on the core routers to ensure that BGP sessions remain active even if a link fails, unless the core router becomes isolated.

The preferred method of injecting regional prefix information into the BGP process is through the use of **network** statements. However, redistribution may be done from the regional IGP in a controlled fashion (that is, with proper filtering). The prefixes from BGP should not be redistributed into the regional IGP, because this would drastically reduce any scalability improvements obtained by deploying BGP in the first place.

Path Selection

BGP path selection typically is resolved by comparing the IGP metrics to the routers from which it received the prefix. The assumption is made that no extra policy is applied except when explicitly mentioned or shown in configuration examples. It should be assumed that **bgp bestpath compare-routerid** is configured on all routers to ensure deterministic path selection.

If each region has only a single core router, only a single path exists, and it is installed in the routing table. If redundant routers are deployed for each region, one copy of each prefix from each core router exists in the originating region.

Consider Figure 5-2. Region 102 has two core routers, and both inject 10.2.0.0/16 into the iBGP core. All the core routers in the other regions see two paths for 10.2.0.0/16—one from each core router in region 102, as shown in Example 5-1. BGP by default selects one best path to install in the routing table.

Figure 5-2   *Path Advertisement into the Network Core for 10.2.0.0/16*

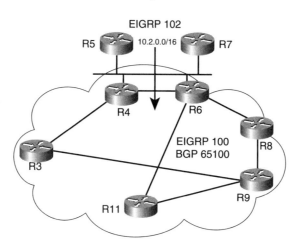

The path chosen by R11 in Example 5-1, based on the BGP attributes, indicates that the path received from R6 is the best path, because this path has a lower IGP metric.

Example 5-1   *BGP Path Information for 10.2.0.0/16 on R11*

```
R11#show ip bgp 10.2.0.0
BGP routing table entry for 10.2.0.0/16, version 3
Paths: (2 available, best #2, table Default-IP-Routing-Table)
  Not advertised to any peer
  Local
    172.16.4.1 (metric 2323456) from 172.16.4.1 (172.16.4.1)
      Origin IGP, metric 307200, localpref 100, valid, internal
  Local
    172.16.6.1 (metric 2297856) from 172.16.6.1 (172.16.6.1)
      Origin IGP, metric 307200, localpref 100, valid, internal, best
```

From the BGP table on R3 in Example 5-2, the path chosen originates from R4. Again, the decision is made based on the IGP metric to the next hop.

Example 5-2   *BGP Path Information for 10.2.0.0/16 on R3*

```
R3#show ip bgp 10.2.0.0
BGP routing table entry for 10.2.0.0/16, version 4
Paths: (2 available, best #1, table Default-IP-Routing-Table)
  Not advertised to any peer
  Local
    172.16.4.1 (metric 2297856) from 172.16.4.1 (172.16.4.1)
      Origin IGP, metric 307200, localpref 100, valid, internal, best
```

continues

Example 5-2 *BGP Path Information for 10.2.0.0/16 on R3 (Continued)*

```
Local
   172.16.6.1 (metric 2323456) from 172.16.6.1 (172.16.6.1)
     Origin IGP, metric 307200, localpref 100, valid, internal
```

Assuming that the default values of parameters such as Weight, LOCAL_PREF, and MED are not changed, the first point at which there is a difference in the paths is the IGP metric to reach the prefix's next hop. This is a definite advantage of using iBGP for the network core. Choosing the best path based on the IGP metric results in the decision's being non-arbitrary. The path installed causes the traffic to take the shortest path through the network automatically.

The core routers each choose the path with the lowest IGP metric in a consistent manner. This does not mean that they all choose the same path. Instead, it means that each router sends the packet to another router that has chosen the same path, which means that the destination remains consistent as the packet traverses the network. This behavior results in deterministic traffic patterns and prevents routing loops from occurring.

If the IGP metrics are the same, the next most common path-selection point is the router ID of the originating router. In this scenario, no additional information exists about which path is actually better. It can be argued that choosing the best path based on router ID is arbitrary because the router ID has no bearing on the path's quality.

NOTE   The decision is *deterministic*, meaning that the same router is always chosen. However, the actual path chosen is based on the luck of the draw with respect to router ID, unless the effect on BGP path selection is taken into account during the address assignment.

Other attributes can be used, but care must be taken to ensure that all routers receive identical information, or there can be potential routing loops. To prevent potential routing loops, a general rule is to modify attributes only when you originate a route, not between iBGP peerings.

As soon as the BGP router has selected a path to install into the IP routing table, the router does a recursive route lookup to determine the IGP next hop. This recursive lookup is done using the core IGP routing process, because that is the routing process that should contain the prefix for the iBGP peer where this prefix was originated.

If there are multiple equal-cost paths in the IGP to the BGP next hop, multiple entries are inserted into the routing table, and traffic is load-shared. Some IGPs, such as EIGRP, support load sharing over paths with unequal costs. The use of IGP metric for path selection allows tuning of the IGP link costs to route traffic optimally.

Failure and Recovery Scenarios

There are two types of failure: link failure and device failure. There are also two locations for a failure to occur: the regional network and the core network. Both of these locations are discussed in the next sections.

Regional Network Failure

The speed of network reconvergence around a link or device failure in the regional network is directly related to how quickly the regional IGP can reconverge. The failure should be seen in the core only if a portion of the network becomes disconnected and summarization is not employed. If the network failure is large enough, it might be seen in the core if the prefixes for an entire summary are disconnected.

When recovering from a failure, the reconvergence time should again be directly related to the IGP reconvergence time. If the prefix must be readvertised in BGP, an additional delay occurs as the regional core routers advertise the prefix to all the other core routers.

Core Network Failure

A link or device failure in the core should provide reconvergence at the speed at which the core IGP reconverges. If the link between R11 and R6 fails, as shown in Figure 5-3, R11 can no longer use this link to send traffic to 10.2.0.0/16.

Figure 5-3   *Physical Core Topology and Link Failure*

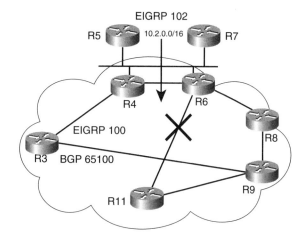

Example 5-3 shows the BGP and routing table for 10.2.0.0/16 before the link failure.

Example 5-3   *Network State Before the Failure*

```
R11#show ip bgp 10.2.0.0
BGP routing table entry for 10.2.0.0/16, version 3
Paths: (2 available, best #2, table Default-IP-Routing-Table)
  Not advertised to any peer
  Local
    172.16.4.1 (metric 2323456) from 172.16.4.1 (172.16.4.1)
      Origin IGP, metric 307200, localpref 100, valid, internal
  Local
    172.16.6.1 (metric 2297856) from 172.16.6.1 (172.16.6.1)
      Origin IGP, metric 307200, localpref 100, valid, internal, best
```

After the failure, the IGP metric in the BGP table has increased as a result of the IGP next-hop change, as shown in Example 5-4.

Example 5-4   *Network State After the Failure*

```
R11#show ip bgp 10.2.0.0
BGP routing table entry for 10.2.0.0/16, version 3
Paths: (2 available, best #2, table Default-IP-Routing-Table)
  Not advertised to any peer
  Local
    172.16.4.1 (metric 2861056) from 172.16.4.1 (172.16.4.1)
      Origin IGP, metric 307200, localpref 100, valid, internal
  Local
    172.16.6.1 (metric 2835456) from 172.16.6.1 (172.16.6.1)
      Origin IGP, metric 307200, localpref 100, valid, internal, best
```

Because the iBGP peer still can be reached, the iBGP session is still intact. Also, the best path is still from R6, because the new metric to R6 is still less than that to R4, as shown in Example 5-4. However, if the link between R6 and R8 also fails (two simultaneous failures), the BGP best path is affected, because now R11 needs to reach R6 via R4, making R4 the preferred BGP next hop for 10.2.0.0/16. This is shown in Example 5-5.

Example 5-5   *BGP Path Information with Multiple Failures*

```
R11#show ip bgp 10.2.0.0
BGP routing table entry for 10.2.0.0/16, version 7
Paths: (2 available, best #2, table Default-IP-Routing-Table)
Flag: 0x240
  Not advertised to any peer
  Local
    172.16.6.1 (metric 3347456) from 172.16.6.1 (172.16.6.1)
      Origin IGP, metric 307200, localpref 100, valid, internal
  Local
    172.16.4.1 (metric 3321856) from 172.16.4.1 (172.16.4.1)
      Origin IGP, metric 307200, localpref 100, valid, internal, best
```

After the IGP has reconverged, the BGP path-selection process replaces the path from R6, with the path from R4 as the new best path, based on the lowest IGP metric.

NOTE   The iBGP session between R11 and R6 is still intact. Until the BGP Scanner detects the metric change and, thus, a new path is selected, R6 is still the best path. When traffic reaches R4 en route to R6, it follows the EIGRP route into the regional network rather than continuing to R6. This is because R4 has the EIGRP route to 10.2.0.0/16.

If the link failure causes a core router to be disconnected from the core, the prefixes advertised by that core router have an unreachable next hop. The BGP Scanner removes these prefixes from the BGP path-selection process. This is equivalent to a device failure in the core. The reconvergence time does not depend on BGP withdrawal or update messages during a failure.

During link or device recovery, reconvergence to the optimal path is delayed by the time it takes for the iBGP sessions to reform and advertise their prefixes. This cannot occur until the IGP has reconverged, so the total reconvergence time is additive. Traffic loss might occur during recovery because of the delta between the IGP and BGP reconverging. This issue is discussed in Chapter 3, "Tuning BGP Performance."

Administrative Control

Administrative control is not well-divided in this scenario, because no clear boundaries are created. The core routers all run the core IGP process in addition to running the regional IGP process. The use of shared resources requires all administrative groups to have access to those resources.

If the core IGP and BGP processes are administered by a group other than the one that administers regional IGP processes, both groups require access to the regional core routers. IGPs are not designed with the expectation of administrators having access to only a subset of the routers. BGP also was not designed with the expectation of having disparate groups administering the same AS.

Routing Policy

It is sometimes desirable to prevent two regions from communicating with each other. In this design, however, every core router must have full routing information, because it might be acting as a transit router between two other regions. This disallows the use of route filtering to block connectivity between two regions. The best method of limiting connectivity is inbound packet filtering on the core router interfaces connecting with the regional network.

External BGP Core Architecture

The external BGP design primarily uses eBGP sessions between regions. A limited use of iBGP may be employed if there are redundant core routers in each region. The primary benefit of this architecture is the reduction of prefixes in the regional IGP processes and delineation of administrative control. An example is shown in Figure 5-4.

Figure 5-4 *Network Topology for External BGP Architecture*

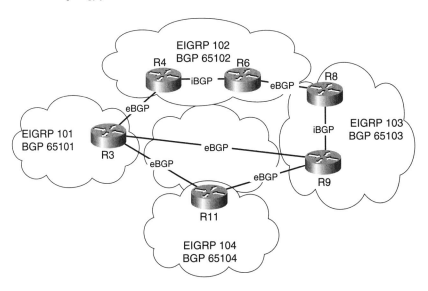

Each region has two routing processes on the core routers: the regional IGP processes and the core BGP processes. There is no core IGP process.

The regional IGP process provides reachability throughout the entire regional network. This process carries full routing and topological information for the region. The regional IGP process terminates on the core routers in this architecture. A default route should be injected into the regional IGP process on the core routers.

This BGP architecture, although it has fewer sessions, is more complex than the previous one. Each region is its own BGP AS. If a region has multiple core routers, they should be connected via iBGP, using the regional IGP to provide next-hop resolution for iBGP learned prefixes. It is essential that all routers providing transit between multiple core routers in a region also run iBGP to prevent routing loops.

If iBGP sessions are used between core routers in a region, they should be sourced from a loopback interface, with the loopback interfaces included in the regional IGP. To resolve possible next-hop resolution issues, the iBGP sessions should be configured with **next-hop-self**.

There is no core IGP routing process, because eBGP sessions between autonomous systems are tied directly to connected interfaces. Each core router has an eBGP peering session only with each directly connected AS.

Path Selection

In this design, BGP path selection is primarily influenced by two parameters: the AS_PATH length and the neighbor router ID. Without modifications, the path chosen by the best path-selection algorithm might not be the optimal path. All BGP routers are configured with the **bgp bestpath compare-routerid** command to ensure deterministic path selection based on lowest router ID.

The prefix advertisement in this design is best illustrated with an example. In Figure 5-5, the prefix 10.2.0.0/16 is first injected into BGP in AS 65102 on R4 and R6. Both routers advertise the prefix to each other via iBGP and to the eBGP peers in AS 65101 and AS 65103, respectively.

Figure 5-5   *Initial Prefix Advertisements for 10.2.0.0/16*

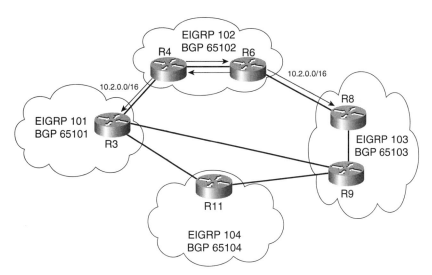

R3 receives the prefix in AS 65101 via the eBGP session with R4 in AS 65102. R3 installs the prefix in the routing table because at this point it is the only path for prefix 10.2.0.0/16. Then R3 advertises the prefix via eBGP to R9 in AS 65103 and R11 in AS 65104. This process is shown in Figure 5-6.

Figure 5-6 *Second Set of Prefix Advertisements for 10.2.0.0/16*

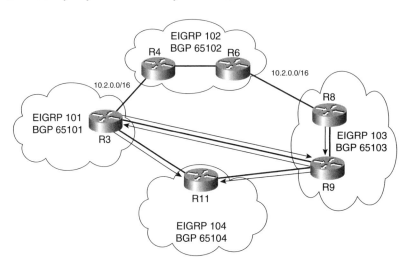

Separately, R8 receives the prefix in AS 65103 via the eBGP session with R6 in AS 65102. The prefix is installed in R8's routing table and then is advertised via iBGP to R9. The path received by R9 from R8 is installed in its routing table and is advertised to R11 in AS 65104 and to R3 in AS 65101. This is also shown in Figure 5-6.

R11 receives the prefix in AS 65104 from both R3 in AS 65101 and R9 in AS 65103. The path received from R3 is installed in the routing table on R11 because of lowest router ID. R11 advertises the prefix in AS 65104 to R9 in AS 65103 via eBGP. Figure 5-7 shows the complete flow of advertisement for prefix 10.2.0.0/16.

Figure 5-7 *Complete Prefix Advertisement Scenario for 10.2.0.0/16*

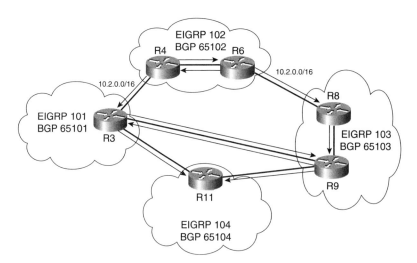

Table 5-2 summarizes the path-selection process for each router.

Table 5-2   *Path-Selection Summarization*

ASN	Router	Path Information and Selection Criteria

65101	R3	**(R9) 65103 65102**
		    172.16.13.2 from 172.16.13.2 (172.16.9.1)
		      Origin IGP, localpref 100, valid, external
		(R4) 65102
		    172.16.13.6 from 172.16.13.6 (172.16.4.1)
		      Origin IGP, metric 307200, localpref 100, valid, external, best
		
		The path from R4 has the shortest AS_PATH.

65102	R4	**(R6)** Local
		    172.16.6.1 (metric 409600) from 172.16.6.1 (172.16.6.1)
		      Origin IGP, metric 307200, localpref 100, valid, internal
		(R4) Local
		    172.17.2.1 from 0.0.0.0 (172.16.4.1)
		      Origin IGP, metric 307200, localpref 100, **weight 32768**, valid,
		      sourced, local, best
		
		The path is locally sourced, and WEIGHT is set to 32768.

65102	R6	**(R4)** Local
		    172.16.4.1 (metric 409600) from 172.16.4.1 (172.16.4.1)
		      Origin IGP, metric 307200, localpref 100, valid, internal
		(R6) Local
		    172.17.2.1 from 0.0.0.0 (172.16.6.1)
		      Origin IGP, metric 307200, localpref 100, **weight 32768**, valid,
		      sourced, local, best
		
		The path is locally sourced, and WEIGHT is set to 32768.

65103	R8	**(R6)** 65102
		    172.16.13.13 from 172.16.13.13 (172.16.6.1)
		      Origin IGP, metric 307200, localpref 100, valid, external, best
		
		Only one path is received—the de facto winner.

65103	R9	**(R11) 65104 65101 65102**
		    172.16.13.18 from 172.16.13.18 (172.16.11.1)
		      Origin IGP, localpref 100, valid, external
		(R8) 65102
		    172.16.8.1 (metric 409600) from 172.16.8.1 (172.16.8.1)
		      Origin IGP, metric 307200, localpref 100, valid, internal, best
		(R3) 65101 65102
		    172.16.13.1 from 172.16.13.1 (172.16.3.1)
		      Origin IGP, localpref 100, valid, external
		
		The path from R8 has the shortest AS_PATH.

65104	R11	**(R9)** 65103 65102
		    172.16.13.17 from 172.16.13.17 (**172.16.9.1**)
		      Origin IGP, localpref 100, valid, external
		(R3) 65101 65102
		    172.16.13.9 from 172.16.13.9 (**172.16.3.1**)
		      Origin IGP, localpref 100, valid, external, best
		
		The path from R3 has the lowest ROUTER_ID.

At the beginning of this section, it was mentioned that suboptimal routing is quite possible with this architecture. This is because the path selection outlined in Table 5-2 is the same regardless of link speeds. If all links in the core are the same bandwidth, a satisfactory path selection is achieved. However, if the links between R11 and R4 via R3 are all DS3s, and the links between R11 and R6 via R8 and R9 are OC-12s, for example, there is the potential for poor use of available bandwidth.

Assume that the path from R11 to R9 is preferable to the path from R11 to R3 for traffic destined for 10.2.0.0/16. This can be accomplished by manually applying an inbound route map on R11 to the eBGP session with R9 that changes the local preference attribute to prefer prefixes received via AS 65103. The configuration is shown in Example 5-6, and the result is shown in Example 5-7.

Example 5-6 *BGP Configuration Preferring Prefixes via AS 65103*

```
router bgp 65104
 no synchronization
 bgp log-neighbor-changes
 network 10.4.0.0 mask 255.255.0.0
 neighbor 172.16.13.9 remote-as 65101
 neighbor 172.16.13.17 remote-as 65103
 neighbor 172.16.13.17 route-map LPREF in
 no auto-summary
!
route-map LPREF permit 10
 set local-preference 120
!
```

NOTE   The same result can be achieved in this scenario by applying a higher WEIGHT to prefixes received from R9, because AS 65104 has only one BGP speaking router.

Example 5-7 *Prefix 10.2.0.0/16 with Modified LOCAL_PREF*

```
R11#show ip bgp 10.2.0.0
BGP routing table entry for 10.2.0.0/16, version 20
Paths: (2 available, best #1, table Default-IP-Routing-Table)
Flag: 0x208
  Advertised to non peer-group peers:
  172.16.13.17
  65103 65102
    172.16.13.17 from 172.16.13.17 (172.16.9.1)
      Origin IGP, localpref 120, valid, external, best
  65101 65102
    172.16.13.9 from 172.16.13.9 (172.16.3.1)
      Origin IGP, localpref 100, valid, external
```

When modifying the default BGP behavior, you must understand the full implications to avoid undesired side effects. As shown in Example 5-8, the prefix 10.1.0.0/16 originates in AS 65101. R11 receives two paths via BGP, from R3 and R9. Modifying LOCAL_PREF to incoming paths from R9 causes the traffic destined for AS 65101 to be sent via AS 65103. Assuming that AS 65104 wants to use the direct connection to AS 65101 via the link between R3 and R11, this new behavior is undesirable.

Example 5-8 *Prefix 10.1.0.0/16, Originated in AS 65101*

```
R11#show ip bgp 10.1.0.0
BGP routing table entry for 10.1.0.0/16, version 22
Paths: (2 available, best #1, table Default-IP-Routing-Table)
Flag: 0x208
  Advertised to non peer-group peers:
  172.16.13.9
  65103 65101
    172.16.13.17 from 172.16.13.17 (172.16.9.1)
      Origin IGP, localpref 120, valid, external, best
  65101
    172.16.13.9 from 172.16.13.9 (172.16.3.1)
      Origin IGP, metric 307200, localpref 100, valid, external
```

This problem can be solved by applying an as-path list to the route map to match only prefixes originated by AS 65102 to modify the local preference. The new route map configuration is shown in Example 5-9.

Example 5-9 *BGP and Route Map Configuration on R11*

```
!
ip as-path access-list 1 permit _65102$
!
route-map LPREF permit 10
 match as-path 1
 set local-preference 120
!
route-map LPREF permit 20
!
```

The final result is shown in Example 5-10 for prefix 10.1.0.0/16 and in Example 5-11 for prefix 10.2.0.0/16.

Example 5-10 *Path Information for 10.1.0.0/16*

```
R11#show ip bgp 10.1.0.0
BGP routing table entry for 10.1.0.0/16, version 45
Paths: (2 available, best #2, table Default-IP-Routing-Table)
  Advertised to non peer-group peers:
  172.16.13.17
  65103 65101
```

Example 5-10 *Path Information for 10.1.0.0/16 (Continued)*

```
        172.16.13.17 from 172.16.13.17 (172.16.9.1)
          Origin IGP, localpref 100, valid, external
    65101
        172.16.13.9 from 172.16.13.9 (172.16.3.1)
          Origin IGP, metric 307200, localpref 100, valid, external, best
```

Example 5-11 *Path Information for 10.2.0.0/16*

```
R11#show ip bgp 10.2.0.0
BGP routing table entry for 10.2.0.0/16, version 57
Paths: (2 available, best #1, table Default-IP-Routing-Table)
  Advertised to non peer-group peers:
  172.16.13.9
  65103 65102
    172.16.13.17 from 172.16.13.17 (172.16.9.1)
      Origin IGP, localpref 120, valid, external, best
  65101 65102
    172.16.13.9 from 172.16.13.9 (172.16.3.1)
      Origin IGP, localpref 100, valid, external
```

To summarize these path-selection exercises, it is obvious that the external BGP core architecture does not include the IGP metric in the path-selection process. This is because no
common IGP runs throughout the network core. The result is that the BGP path-selection
process is performed without visibility into the physical topology and link bandwidth. This
can be overcome through manually modifying BGP attributes. Care must be taken to ensure
that modifications are done precisely to avoid creating additional instances of suboptimal
routing.

Failure and Recovery Scenarios

A couple of failure scenarios are of interest in this architecture. Device failure in the regional
autonomous systems is handled by the regional IGP, making this failure uninteresting from
a BGP standpoint.

The failure of a core link causes the BGP session traversing it to be torn down. How long
this takes depends on the link failure detection and BGP hold timer. If the router detects the
link failure, the session that is sourced off that interface is torn down immediately provided
that **bgp fast-external failover** is enabled, which is the default.

If the peers are connected via a multiaccess broadcast medium, such as Fast Ethernet, the
failure of one link might not mean the failure of the other link. This results in the peer that
has the link failure tearing down the session, whereas the other peer remains in the Established state. The peer that does not detect the link failure does not tear down the session
until the holdtime expires.

When a BGP session is torn down, the BGP paths received from that peer are removed from the Adj-RIB-In, and the path-selection process is run. When the selection process is complete, the BGP speaker updates its peers with the new BGP reachability information in the form of withdrawals and advertisements. This process continues hop by hop until all BGP speakers have been updated in all BGP autonomous systems that are affected by the failure.

Consider Figure 5-8, in which 10.2.0.0/16 is advertised from AS 65102 to AS 65103 and AS 65101. When the link between R6 and R8 fails, the eBGP session between AS 65102 and AS 65103 is torn down, and 10.2.0.0/16 is removed from the BGP RIB on R8.

Figure 5-8 *Path Updates on Link Failure Between R8 and R6*

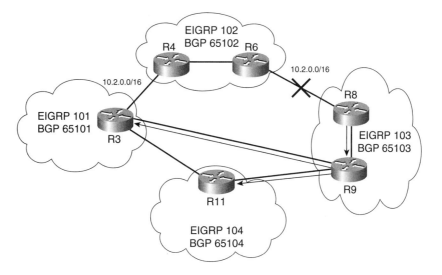

A withdrawal message is sent to R9, which in turn sends a withdrawal for 10.2.0.0/16 to R3 in AS 65101 and R11 in AS 65104. The best path for 10.2.0.0/16 on R9 is now from R3, because its AS_PATH is shorter than the path from R11. The new path is advertised to R8 via iBGP and to R11 via eBGP.

The section, "External BGP Core Architecture," examined the potential for suboptimal routing through the use of a route map setting local preference. If this same route map were in place, to reach 10.2.0.0/16, the traffic would traverse R9 to reach R3 and then R4, which in the failure scenario might not be optimal. It is important to keep in mind what additional effects might be seen in failure scenarios.

The as-path list used in Example 5-12 matches all prefixes that are originated by AS 65102. If connectivity between AS 65102 and AS 65103 becomes severed, AS 65104 still prefers AS 65103 for reachability to AS 65102, as shown in Example 5-13. This undesirable traffic pattern can be resolved by making the as-path list more specific, in that it modifies only the local preference for prefixes that are originated in AS 65102 and advertised directly to AS 65103 by requiring the AS_PATH to contain the sequence 65103 65102. The new configuration is shown in Example 5-14, and the resulting path information is shown in Example 5-15.

Example 5-12 *R11 Route Map Configuration*

```
ip as-path access-list 1 permit _65102$
!
route-map LPREF permit 10
 match as-path 1
 set local-preference 120
!
route-map LPREF permit 20
 !
```

Example 5-13 *R11 Path Information for 10.2.0.0/16*

```
R11#show ip bgp 10.2.0.0
BGP routing table entry for 10.2.0.0/16, version 59
Paths: (2 available, best #1, table Default-IP-Routing-Table)
Flag: 0x208
  Advertised to non peer-group peers:
  172.16.13.9
  65103 65101 65102
    172.16.13.17 from 172.16.13.17 (172.16.9.1)
      Origin IGP, localpref 120, valid, external, best
  65101 65102
    172.16.13.9 from 172.16.13.9 (172.16.3.1)
      Origin IGP, localpref 100, valid, external
```

Example 5-14 *Corrected Route Map on R11*

```
ip as-path access-list 1 permit _65103_65102$
!
route-map LPREF permit 10
 match as-path 1
 set local-preference 120
!
route-map LPREF permit 20
 !
```

Example 5-15 *R11 Path Information for 10.2.0.0/16*

```
R11#show ip bgp 10.2.0.0
BGP routing table entry for 10.2.0.0/16, version 63
Paths: (2 available, best #2, table Default-IP-Routing-Table)
Flag: 0x208
```

Example 5-15 *R11 Path Information for 10.2.0.0/16 (Continued)*

```
Advertised to non peer-group peers:
172.16.13.17
65103 65101 65102
  172.16.13.17 from 172.16.13.17 (172.16.9.1)
    Origin IGP, localpref 100, valid, external
65101 65102
  172.16.13.9 from 172.16.13.9 (172.16.3.1)
    Origin IGP, localpref 100, valid, external, best
```

The failure of a core router has an effect similar to a core link failure, only amplified. When the core router fails, every BGP session to that router fails. In Figure 5-9, R9 fails. The similarity of a router failure to a link failure becomes more obvious when viewed from the perspective of the other routers. R3 sees a link failure to R9, R11 sees a link failure to R9, and R8 sees a link failure to R9.

Figure 5-9   *Network Topology Core Router Failure*

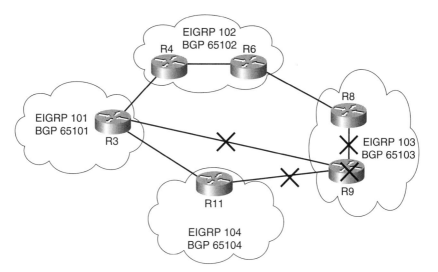

For example, consider 10.2.0.0/16, which originates in AS 65102. Only R11 is actively using the path received from R9. When R11 detects the failure, the path received from R9 is removed from the BGP RIB, and the path from R3 is used.

A more interesting scenario is the reroute of prefix 10.3.0.0/16, which is originated by AS 65103. When R3 detects the failure of the BGP session to R9, it removes the prefix from its BGP RIB. Then R3 installs the path received from R4 and advertises this path to R11, which causes R11 to replace the previous path.

An important point to note from this section is that not taking advantage of an IGP for its ability to react to network changes quickly has a slight effect on the speed at which the network can reconverge. The amount of time required to reconverge can also be additive. This additive effect is a result of each BGP speaker upon receiving the new path information having to run the path-selection process and then withdraw and advertise based on the outcome.

Administrative Control

This architecture provides clear points at which administrative authority can be divided. The easiest way to divide administrative control from a routing perspective is to introduce eBGP sessions. When eBGP is used, the next hop on advertised prefixes is changed to the address of the advertising router. Only a single BGP session is required at each interconnection point. Not all the autonomous systems need an eBGP session directly between them — only those with a direct physical connection.

Routing Policy

It is sometimes desirable to prevent two regions from communicating with each other. In this design, however, every core router must have full routing information, because it might be acting as a transit router between two other regions. This disallows the use of route filtering to block connectivity between two regions. The best method of limiting connectivity is inbound packet filtering on the core router interfaces connecting with the regional network.

Internal/External BGP Core Architecture

The internal/external BGP core architecture employs an iBGP core, with external BGP as the mechanism by which regions attach to the core. Figure 5-10 shows an example. This architecture provides prefix reduction in regional IGP processes, clear delineation of administrative boundaries, and flexible policy control. It also bounds the scope of regional IGP instabilities.

The internal/external BGP scenario at first appears to be the most complex scenario because of the number of components. However, the end result is a BGP architecture that is easier to work with when defining policy, troubleshooting, or expanding the network.

The regional IGP process provides reachability throughout the entire regional network. This process carries full routing and topological information for the region. The regional IGP process also provides next-hop resolution for the iBGP-learned prefixes between the regional border routers in addition to reachability for the iBGP peers, as required in redundant regional environments. A default route is injected into the regional IGP process on each of the regional border routers.

Figure 5-10 *Internal/External BGP Architecture*

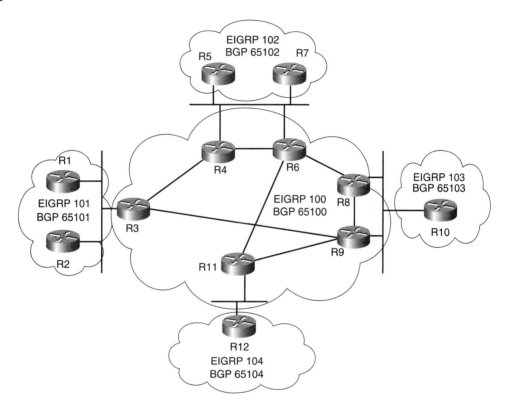

The regional border router is a new concept introduced in this architecture. The DMZ between the core and a region is the connection between the regional border router and the core router. The regional border router exists entirely in the region and connects to the network core via eBGP. This separates regional routing from core routing. In the previous architectures, the regional border router functionality was shared with the core router functions on the same device.

The core IGP is used to provide next-hop resolution and reachability for the iBGP peering sessions between core routers. The core IGP contains only the core routers, core links, and loopback interfaces on the core routers. The core IGP process does not participate in any redistribution between protocols.

There are multiple aspects to the BGP portion of this architecture. There is a full iBGP mesh between the core routers. These iBGP sessions are sourced from the loopback interfaces on the core routers and are configured with **next-hop-self**. The use of **next-hop-self** removes the need to inject the subnets on the links connecting to the regional border routers for next-hop resolution. Sourcing the iBGP sessions from the loopback interfaces allows the sessions to remain active in the case of a core link failure that can be routed around.

Each region has its own BGP AS, and the core has its own AS. Network prefixes for each region are injected into the regional BGP process using **network** statements on the regional border routers. The use of **network** statements allows for controlled injection of prefixes that can be reached in the IGP. It is possible to directly redistribute from the IGP into BGP on the regional border routers. Although this practice is discouraged, if the number of prefixes involved makes using **network** statements administratively unfeasible, redistribution becomes an option. It cannot be stressed enough that prefix filtering should be applied any time redistribution is performed between protocols. Another option is to aggregate the prefixes with a static route to Null0 and use the **network** command to inject the aggregate.

The regional BGP autonomous systems connect to the BGP core AS through the use of eBGP. Each regional border router peers via eBGP with all the core routers it is directly connected to when redundant routers are in place.

Path Selection

The path selection in the core routers is very similar to that in the iBGP-only architecture scenario. The BGP decision process typically uses the IGP metric to the next hop as the decision point.

The prefix 10.2.0.0/16 is injected by both R5 and R7 into BGP 65102. The prefix is then advertised by R5 to both R4 and R6 via eBGP. The prefix is also advertised by R7 to R4 and R6 via eBGP. The routers R4 and R6 both have to make a path selection, which results in a decision based on router ID, unless the path-selection process is manipulated through modification of one of the BGP attributes, or the BGP multipath feature is enabled. The prefix advertisements are shown in Figure 5-11. Examples 5-16 and 5-17 show the path selection. Both R4 and R6 select the path from R5.

Figure 5-11 *Prefix Advertisements*

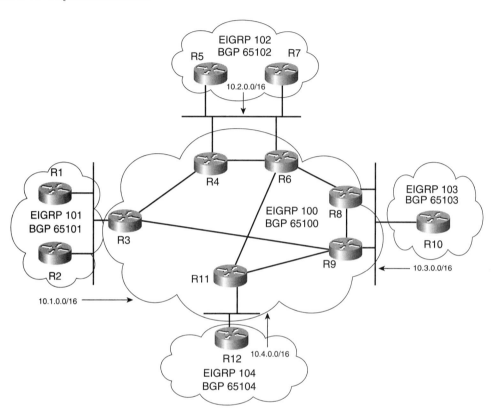

Example 5-16 *R4 Selecting the Path from R5*

```
R4#show ip bgp 10.2.0.0
BGP routing table entry for 10.2.0.0/16, version 6
Paths: (3 available, best #3, table Default-IP-Routing-Table)
Flag: 0x200
  Advertised to peer-groups:
    internal
  Advertised to non peer-group peers:
  172.17.2.2
```

continues

Example 5-16 *R4 Selecting the Path from R5 (Continued)*

```
65102
  172.16.6.1 (metric 409600) from 172.16.6.1 (172.16.6.1)
    Origin IGP, metric 0, localpref 100, valid, internal
65102
  172.17.2.2 from 172.17.2.2 (172.16.7.1)
    Origin IGP, metric 0, localpref 100, valid, external
65102
  172.17.2.1 from 172.17.2.1 (172.16.5.1)
    Origin IGP, metric 0, localpref 100, valid, external, best
```

Example 5-17 *R6 Selecting the Path from R5*

```
R6#show ip bgp 10.2.0.0
BGP routing table entry for 10.2.0.0/16, version 8
Paths: (3 available, best #3, table Default-IP-Routing-Table)
Flag: 0x210
  Advertised to peer-groups:
    internal
  Advertised to non peer-group peers:
  172.17.2.2
  65102
    172.17.2.2 from 172.17.2.2 (172.16.7.1)
      Origin IGP, metric 0, localpref 100, valid, external
  65102
    172.16.4.1 (metric 409600) from 172.16.4.1 (172.16.4.1)
      Origin IGP, metric 0, localpref 100, valid, internal
  65102
    172.17.2.1 from 172.17.2.1 (172.16.5.1)
      Origin IGP, metric 0, localpref 100, valid, external, best
```

Enabling eBGP multipath on both R4 and R6 allows traffic to be load-shared between R5 and R7 instead of only one of them being chosen to receive all traffic inbound to AS 65102. Examples 5-18 and 5-19 show the changes.

Example 5-18 *R4 Load-Balancing Between R5 and R7*

```
R4#show ip bgp 10.2.0.0
BGP routing table entry for 10.2.0.0/16, version 10
Paths: (3 available, best #2, table Default-IP-Routing-Table)
  Advertised to peer-groups:
    internal
  Advertised to non peer-group peers:
  172.17.2.1
  65102
    172.16.6.1 (metric 409600) from 172.16.6.1 (172.16.6.1)
      Origin IGP, metric 0, localpref 100, valid, internal
```

Example 5-18 *R4 Load-Balancing Between R5 and R7 (Continued)*

```
65102
   172.17.2.2 from 172.17.2.2 (172.16.7.1)
      Origin IGP, metric 0, localpref 100, valid, external, multipath, best
65102
   172.17.2.1 from 172.17.2.1 (172.16.5.1)
      Origin IGP, metric 0, localpref 100, valid, external, multipath
```

Example 5-19 *R6 Load-Balancing Between R5 and R7*

```
R6#show ip bgp 10.2.0.0
BGP routing table entry for 10.2.0.0/16, version 11
Paths: (3 available, best #1, table Default-IP-Routing-Table)
  Advertised to peer-groups:
     internal
  Advertised to non peer-group peers:
  172.17.2.1
  65102
     172.17.2.2 from 172.17.2.2 (172.16.7.1)
        Origin IGP, metric 0, localpref 100, valid, external, multipath, best
  65102
     172.16.4.1 (metric 409600) from 172.16.4.1 (172.16.4.1)
        Origin IGP, metric 0, localpref 100, valid, internal
  65102
     172.17.2.1 from 172.17.2.1 (172.16.5.1)
        Origin IGP, metric 0, localpref 100, valid, external, multipath
```

The routers R4 and R6 advertise the prefix 10.2.0.0/16 via iBGP to the routers R3, R8, R9, and R11. The path selection on these routers is based on the IGP metric to the next-hop addresses, which are the loopback interfaces on R4 and R6. When the IGP metric is equal, the path selection is based on the lowest router ID.

The path-selection process in the regional border routers varies depending on the redundancy in that region, as shown in Figure 5-12.

In AS 65104, R12 receives only a single path for 10.2.0.0/16. Figure 5-13 shows the topology for the DMZ between AS 65104 and AS 65100. The result is that R12 installs the path received from R11 for 10.2.0.0/16.

Figure 5-12 *Prefix Advertisement for 10.2.0.0/16 to Regions*

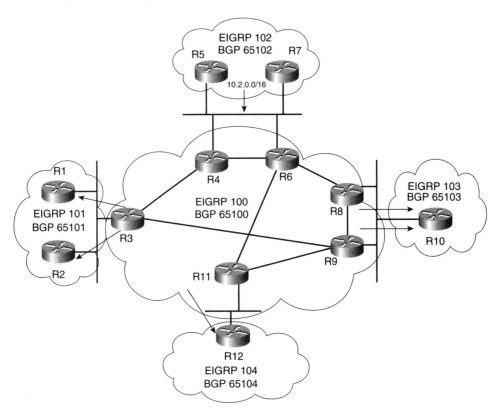

Figure 5-13 *Detailed DMZ Between AS 65100 and AS 65104*

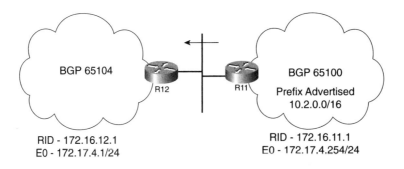

In AS 65101, both R1 and R2 receive a path for the prefix 10.2.0.0/16 from R3. Figure 5-14 shows the topology for the DMZ between AS 65101 and AS 65100. R1 and R2 each install the path they learned via eBGP from R3 and advertise that path via iBGP to each other. The path-selection process should result in the final path selection on R1 and R2 being the externally learned path. This path is chosen based on the internal versus external step in the decision algorithm, with the assumption that no eBGP policies are applied.

Figure 5-14 *Detailed DMZ Between AS 65100 and AS 65101*

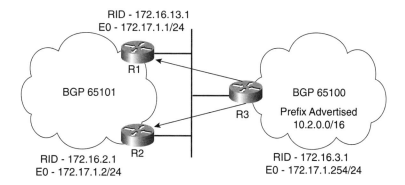

AS 65103 has a slightly different scenario. Figure 5-15 shows the topology for the DMZ between AS 65103 and AS 65100. R10 receives two paths, which appear to be identical from R8 and R9. The only difference is the router ID. This results in R10 basing its path selection on the lowest router ID and selecting either R8 or R9.

Figure 5-15 *Detailed DMZ Between AS 65100 and AS 65103*

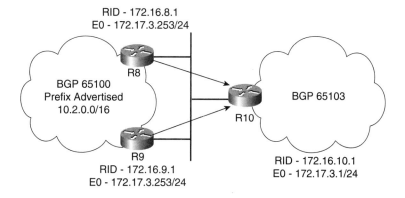

This can have an interesting effect on traffic patterns in the network. An example is sending traffic for prefix 10.4.0.0/16, which is originated by AS 65104 via R8 instead of R9. This means that the traffic pattern is R10→R8→R9→R11 instead of R10→R9→R11. This is only slightly suboptimal in this case; however, it is the concept that is of interest, as shown in Example 5-20.

Example 5-20 *Suboptimal Path Selection Favoring R8*

```
R10#show ip bgp
BGP table version is 10, local router ID is 172.16.10.1
Status codes: s suppressed, d damped, h history, * valid, > best, i - internal
Origin codes: i - IGP, e - EGP, ? - incomplete

   Network          Next Hop          Metric LocPrf Weight Path
*  10.1.0.0/16      172.17.3.254                        0 65100 65101 i
*>                  172.17.3.253                        0 65100 65101 i
*  10.2.0.0/16      172.17.3.254                        0 65100 65102 i
*>                  172.17.3.253                        0 65100 65102 i
*> 10.3.0.0/16      0.0.0.0                0        32768 i
*  10.4.0.0/16      172.17.3.254                        0 65100 65104 i
*>                  172.17.3.253                        0 65100 65104 i
```

Two issues are involved. The first issue is that all traffic is destined for a single core router, R8. The second issue is that traffic might be suboptimal. The first issue can be resolved by using eBGP multipath on R10. This solution does not address the concern of suboptimal routing, however. The other solution is to provide R10 with the topological information associated with each prefix. Setting an outbound route map on R8 and R9 to set the MED to the IGP metric provides the topological information that R10 needs to make the optimal decision. Example 5-21 shows the outbound MED configuration on R8 and R9. Example 5-22 shows the new BGP path information with MED.

Example 5-21 *Outbound MED Configuration on R8 and R9*

```
router bgp 65100
 neighbor 172.17.3.1 route-map SET_MED out
!
route-map SET_MED permit 10
 set metric-type internal
!
```

Example 5-22 *New BGP Path Information with MED*

```
R10#show ip bgp
BGP table version is 11, local router ID is 172.16.10.1
Status codes: s suppressed, d damped, h history, * valid, > best, i - internal
Origin codes: i - IGP, e - EGP, ? - incomplete
```

Example 5-22 *New BGP Path Information with MED (Continued)*

```
      Network         Next Hop         Metric LocPrf Weight Path
  *> 10.1.0.0/16    172.17.3.254      2297856           0 65100 65101 i
  *                 172.17.3.253      2323456           0 65100 65101 i
  *  10.2.0.0/16    172.17.3.254      2323456           0 65100 65102 i
  *>                172.17.3.253      2297856           0 65100 65102 i
  *> 10.3.0.0/16    0.0.0.0                 0       32768 i
  *> 10.4.0.0/16    172.17.3.254      2297856           0 65100 65104 i
  *                 172.17.3.253      2323456           0 65100 65104 i
```

This allows router R10 to intelligently choose what traffic to send to each core router. Traffic is sent to the correct core router to provide optimal routing, and traffic is distributed across the core routers.

A similar scenario is seen in AS 65102, which has two core routers, each with differing costs to reach remote locations. This is another example in which advertising IGP metrics via BGP MEDs can optimize traffic flow. In general, because AS 65100 is under the same administrative control, the MED settings can be trusted. Setting the MED values to the IGP metric for all advertisements to the regional BGP speakers helps ensure optimal routing, as a general design guideline.

Failure and Recovery Scenarios

A couple of interesting failure scenarios should be examined with this architecture. Of primary interest is the failure of the regional border routers, core routers, and core links. The regional IGP process handles failures that occur within the region.

There are multiple aspects to network reconvergence following the failure of a regional border router. The first aspect is the default route that is originated. The regional IGP process handles the removal of the now-defunct default route. Figure 5-16 shows a failure in AS 65102 of the regional border router R7.

The other aspect is tearing down the eBGP session between the core router and the failed regional border router and withdrawing the prefixes from the core. This affects the inbound traffic flow. Until these prefixes are removed from the BGP RIB on the core router and are withdrawn from the rest of the core, traffic is black-holed on the core router that is peering with the regional border router. If the interface on the core router transitions down, the BGP process tears down the BGP session with R7 and removes the path information for that peer.

Figure 5-16 *Regional Border Router Failure Scenario*

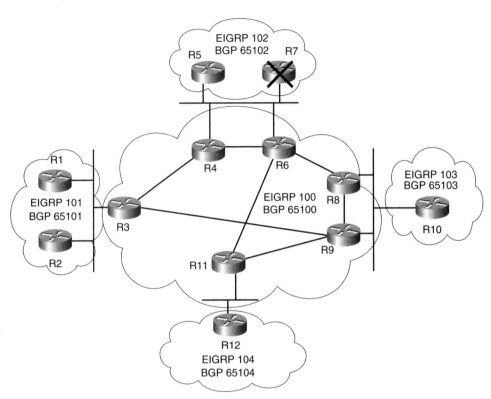

However, it is unlikely that the interface on the core router will transition down. In this example, the connection between the regional border routers and the core routers is a multiaccess broadcast medium. The failure of router R7 leaves three devices still active on this multiaccess medium. The result is that the BGP session must time out through the BGP holdtime mechanism. This greatly increases the amount of time to reconverge the network following a device failure. After the BGP session expires, the paths received from that BGP peer are invalidated, and the path-selection process installs a new path, if possible, for any affected prefixes.

The iBGP sessions in the core are all tied down to loopback interfaces. The failure of a core link causes the IGP to reroute traffic to other available links. This also results in an update to the IGP metric value for the paths in the BGP RIB. When the BGP Scanner process runs, the BGP table is updated if needed based on the new set of IGP metrics for each prefix.

Network reconvergence after the failure of a core router is very similar to the failure of a regional border router. The core IGP redirects the traffic flow from the failed router, and the

BGP process removes the prefixes from the routing table because of next-hop resolution failure. The delay for BGP to remove the prefixes because of next-hop resolution depends on when BGP Scanner runs. This could result in a maximum delay of 60 seconds. The regional border router will continue to advertise the default route into the region. Traffic destined to the unavailable prefixes will follow the default route to the regional border router, at which point that traffic will be discarded due to the next-hop information continuing to point toward the failed upstream core router.

Administrative Control

The internal/external BGP architecture provides a very clean way to divide administrative control. The eBGP sessions provide very clear delineation between the regions and the core. Each region can easily administer its own portion of the network, with the core being handled by a separate group of administrators. The core network is essentially a service provider entity for the regional networks.

The boundaries for the BGP autonomous systems are concurrent with the boundaries for the IGP processes. The regional IGP processes do not extend to the core routers; neither does the core IGP process extend to the regional border routers. The lack of shared resources between the regions and the core allows for a clean separation of administrative control. The connections between the regional border routers and the core routers form a clear DMZ.

Routing Policy

This architecture is significantly different from the previous two architectures in that the core network and the regional network are distinct entities. In the previous architectures, the core network and regional networks were blended on the core routers.

The creation of this boundary allows for routing policy to be applied at the border of each network. The core network has its set of prefixes, and the regional network has its own. In the previous architectures, the core routers did not have this separation from their geographic region because of the termination of the regional IGP on the core routers for route injection into the BGP core.

In Figure 5-17, suppose the desired policy is to block AS 65103 from sending traffic to 10.2.0.0/16 and to block AS 65102 from sending traffic to 10.3.0.0/16. The core routers would be configured to block the advertisement of 10.2.0.0/16 from being sent via eBGP by R8 and R9 to R10. The core routers R4 and R6 also need to be blocked from sending 10.3.0.0/16 to R5 and R7. This prevents traffic flow in both directions. It is assumed that the core routers do not advertise a default to the regional routers.

Figure 5-17 *Prefix Advertisement and Filtering*

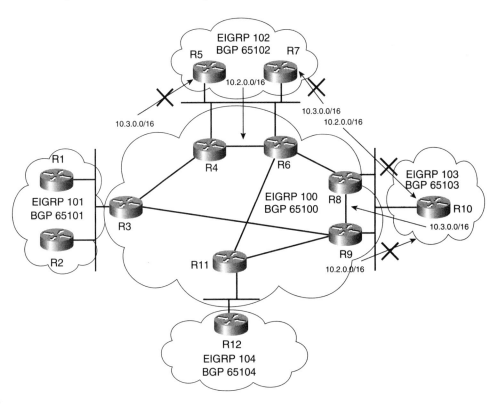

Figure 5-18 shows that AS 65104 requires transit through R8 and R9 to reach AS 65102. The separation of the regional prefix information from the core prefix information allows R8 and R9 to still contain reachability information for 10.2.0.0/16 and to provide transit services, even though the directly connected region is blocked from communicating with AS 65102.

The core can block prefix information from being sent to a particular regional network without affecting the ability of the core routers in that region to be transit routers for other regions sending traffic to that prefix.

Figure 5-18 *Network Topology for Remote Site Aggregation*

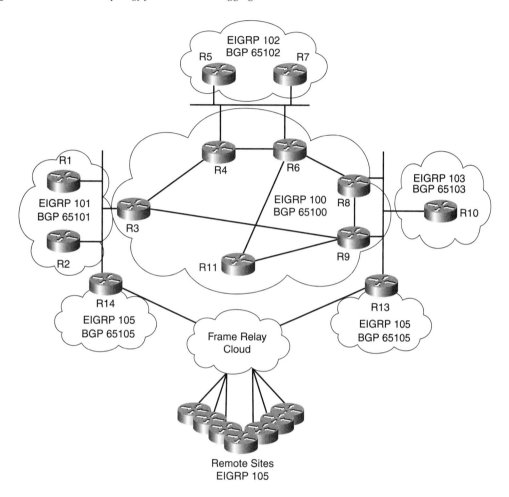

In the examples so far, for the sake of clarity, each region has been summarized into a single prefix. However, there is no requirement that the prefixes in a region must be summarized before being injected into BGP. In the previous example, with a single prefix, it is very easy to perform the prefix filtering using a prefix list. If there were a large number of prefixes, it is possible that using a filter list to block prefix advertisements based on AS would be more appropriate. Previous architectures required packet filtering, which is more resource-intensive and tends to have higher administrative complexity because of the access control list semantics.

Remote Site Aggregation

In the enterprise, it is very common to have a significant number of hub-and-spoke connections, often used to connect retail locations, manufacturing locations, and remote offices. When a BGP core is not employed, there is typically a single IGP for the entire network, which makes handling remote site aggregation with geographically diverse backup connectivity relatively simple. The addition of the BGP core results in breaking the network into multiple regional IGP processes. If the remote site's primary connectivity and backup connectivity terminate in different regions, the situation becomes more complicated.

It is common for remote site routers to be resource-constrained. This is because they are responsible for handling low traffic rates. It does not make sense to run multiple routing processes on the remote site routers.

The easiest and cleanest solution is to make the remote sites a separate region. It can operate in its own IGP, which is responsible only for maintaining the hub-and-spoke topology. The hub routers connect directly to the core routers and run eBGP with them. This separation of the remote sites into their own IGP helps isolate the impact of link failure to remote sites.

The core routers should originate the default route via BGP to the hub routers, which in this case are R13 and R14. The hub routers should redistribute this default into the IGP. This redistribution point should be filtered to allow only the default route to be injected into the IGP.

The method used to inject routes into BGP on the hub routers is a bit different than that used for the standard regions. The standard regions often can summarize their prefixes and then inject the summary into BGP using a network statement. The hub routers have a large number of prefixes, possibly numbering in the thousands, depending on the number of remote sites. The hub routers should redistribute the IGP into BGP, making use of route filters to prevent any unwanted routes from entering BGP, such as the default route, which was injected into the IGP from BGP.

The hub routers should issue a default route to the remote site routers via the IGP instead of allowing full routing information to propagate. This results in a significant increase in scalability in the remote site's region by reducing the route propagation load in the hub routers. It also prevents remote site router resources from bounding the size of the remote site's region. If only the resources available at the hub sites bound the size of the remote site's region, upgrading only the hub routers can increase the region's size.

Another benefit of allowing only the default route to the remote sites is that remote sites do not act as transit for each other in a failure situation. The amount of bandwidth to a remote site is often tailored to that site's needs by sizing the PVC. If that remote site acts as a transit device to reach another remote site, this could overload the PVC and degrade performance for the transiting remote site.

The remote site prefixes should not be summarized in BGP. The summarization of these prefixes can create an issue where traffic would be black-holed unless all the hub routers are physically connected. Figure 5-19 shows a scenario in which R1 and R2 are the hub routers, and R3 and R4 are the remote site routers. The remote sites are each dual-homed to R1 and R2 via Frame Relay PVCs.

Figure 5-19 *Remote Site Connectivity Black Hole Example*

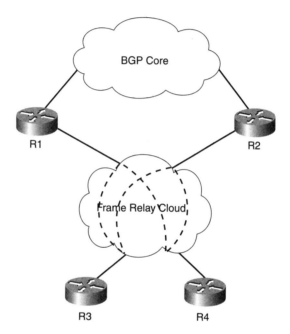

Routing information to the remote sites is filtered to allow only the default route to be sent from the hub router to the remote site. The remote site advertises only its local prefixes to the hub router. Assume that both remote sites have primary connectivity through router R1 and that R1 advertises a summary prefix that aggregates the prefixes for both R3 and R4 into the BGP core network, setting the MED such that the prefix originated by R1 is the preferred path. If the PVC between R3 and R1 fails, traffic still is directed at R1 because of the summary for R3 and R4. The link to R3 is down, which results in the traffic's being routed Null0, following the nailed up static used to create the summary.

If the hub routers are physically connected, an iBGP session can be created between them, which allows R1 to send the traffic destined for R3 via R2 and down the backup PVC to R3. However, if the hub routers are not physically connected, an iBGP session should not be created between the two, based on the IGP design used in this example. To build the iBGP session, the loopback addresses would have to be advertised between the hub routers, via the remote sites to provide reachability for the iBGP session to form. This would result in the remote sites being used as transit for reachability between the hub routers. As previously discussed, this is undesirable because of PVC sizing and isolating impact during failure scenarios. This could also result in routing loops.

The solution is to not summarize prefixes and redistribute them directly into BGP. The MED is set to the IGP metric, providing the core with topological information about which hub router to send the traffic to for each prefix. This allows R3 to use R1 as primary and R4 to use R2 as primary. The hub routers do not need to be directly connected, nor do they need iBGP between them.

As a general rule, it is desirable to summarize as much as possible whenever possible, but in some scenarios summarization can create a great deal more complexity with little realized benefit. If there are 5000 prefixes, summarizing these into a single prefix in BGP results in a savings of less than 5 MB of RAM. It is much more important to reduce prefix count in the IGP than in BGP.

Case Study: BGP Core Deployment

This case study examines a typical enterprise network and seeks to address the challenges that network engineers face as they work to scale their network. The design requirements are detailed, and a BGP architecture is selected based on the requirements identified. After the appropriate architecture is determined, the different components of the network are examined individually to determine how best to integrate them. A migration strategy is then developed and executed. The case study finishes with a look at the final configurations.

This case study was created with complex requirements and a large number of routers. The intent is to bring together the concepts discussed in this chapter in a realistic scenario.

BGP Core Design Scenario

The current network consists of a single EIGRP AS, AS100. It is very common to see Stuck In Active (SIA) messages and very high CPU loads for the EIGRP process. There are approximately 7000 EIGRP prefixes in the routing table and 900 Layer 3 devices in the network. The entire network is currently numbered using the RFC 1918 address space of 10.0.0.0/8. Prefix assignment was not performed in a consistent manner, allowing for hierarchy and summarization. Figure 5-20 shows the initial topology for the network.

Design Requirements

The current instability has reached the point at which it is no longer acceptable, because it is visibly affecting productivity. The CIO has sponsored an initiative to increase reliability; however, the project is being done on a shoestring budget, which does not permit a whole-sale upgrade. Service-Level Agreements (SLAs) have been created between IT and the operating divisions in the company. These agreements will be active in 30 days.

Figure 5-20 *Initial Network Topology*

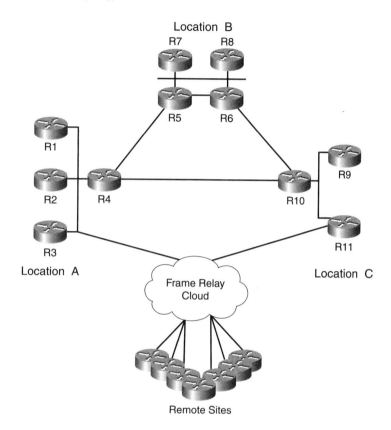

The company is planning an aggressive acquisition strategy. It is expected that each acquisition will continue to manage its own IT infrastructure, but full connectivity must be established internally. Each major center and data center will manage its own local infrastructure, with a team of individuals from various locations being responsible for the interconnectivity between the locations.

To reduce expenses, the Internet connectivity in each location is being consolidated. Internet connectivity will be consolidated to the two data centers. The current design involves the use of proxy servers. The company has sponsored an initiative to migrate to a NAT-based design to decommission the proxy servers. This means the transition from specific IP addresses for the proxy servers to a default route for Internet connectivity.

Here's a summary of the requirements:

- Low budget, no wholesale upgrades
- Increasing stability is the top priority

- Project completion in 30 days
- Diverse administration
- Accommodate an aggressive acquisition strategy
- Accommodate a new Internet connectivity design

Potential Solutions

The key issue is the network's instability. This instability is actually a result of uncontrolled growth of the network without a clear architectural goal. The number of prefixes in the network and lack of summarization are a recipe for disaster. The real fix for this network is to clean up the addressing and EIGRP design.

Stability is not the only issue. The time frame does not permit enough time to clean up the EIGRP and addressing. A single EIGRP process across the network does not allow the administrative separation that is needed to accommodate the aggressive acquisition strategy.

Requirements Analysis

The requirements need to be compared against the available BGP architectures. The first three requirements would be satisfied equally well by any of the three architectures. The last three are the determining factors in choosing a design.

The internal BGP core architecture does not allow for a clean delineation of administrative control. The aggressive acquisition strategy can also result in rapid iBGP mesh expansion.

The internal/external BGP core architecture provides the best solution to the design requirements. The external BGP core architecture requires the team of individuals managing the intersite connectivity to have control over the core routers in each region. The IT staff at each regional site must also have control over these same routers to manage regional routing, which does not provide good administrative control.

In this scenario, the internal/external BGP core architecture is chosen because of better reconvergence characteristics and the use of an IGP in the core to provide optimized routing based on link speed. There is also less administrative overhead when troubleshooting connectivity between two locations that are not directly connected. This architecture also provides the greatest amount of flexibility for future policy requirements.

Solution Description

The new architecture with the BGP core in place is shown in Figure 5-21. This new topology involves the creation of six BGP autonomous systems (65100 through 65105). The network core is one AS, each major center is its own AS, the remote site aggregation is another AS, and the Internet connectivity is the final AS.

Figure 5-21 *Network Topology with the BGP Core*

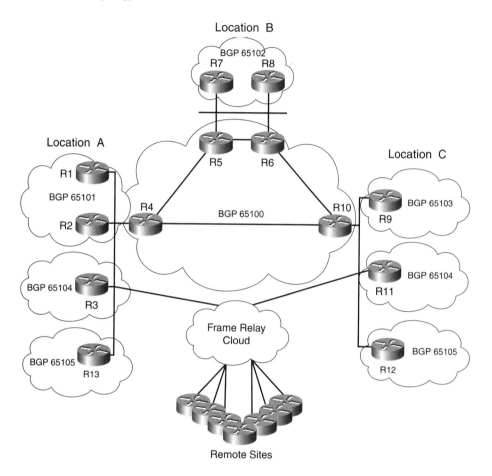

Core Design

The new network core in this topology consists of four routers—R4, R5, R6, and R10. The core itself is built using iBGP, with a full mesh between these routers. The peering sessions are sourced from the loopback interfaces. A core EIGRP AS is configured only on these four routers to provide reachability between the loopback interfaces. Each iBGP session is configured with **next-hop-self** to remove the need to carry the prefixes for the DMZ Ethernet segments. The BGP AS for the network core is 65100. The core issues a default route to major centers and the remote site aggregation routers.

Major Center Attachment

This network has three major centers, each in its own BGP AS. The BGP autonomous systems for the major centers are AS65101, AS65102, and AS65103. The major centers connect to the BGP core through eBGP sessions. Each major center runs its own EIGRP process, with connectivity external to the center provided by the network core. The border routers for AS65101 are R1 and R2. The border routers for AS65102 are R7 and R8. The border router for AS65103 is R9. The BGP peering sessions between the major center border routers and the core are sourced from the physical link addresses of the Ethernet DMZ. When there are multiple border routers in a major center, they are connected with iBGP sourced from the loopback interfaces with **next-hop-self** configured for the iBGP sessions.

Remote Site Aggregation

This network has approximately 400 remote site routers. The remote sites are dual-homed via Frame Relay PVCs to hub routers in different major centers for redundancy. The hub routers are not part of the major center BGP or EIGRP routing processes. The BGP and IGP design for the remote site aggregation is based on the earlier discussion of remote site connectivity.

The hub routers, which are physically located in Location A and Location C, connect via eBGP to the physically colocated core routers. This means that R3 is eBGP peered with router R4 and R11 is eBGP peered with R10. The hub routers are not iBGP peered because there is no direct connectivity between them except through the remote sites. To scale the remote site EIGRP process, only the default route is advertised via EIGRP to the remote site router. The only prefixes advertised by a remote site router are the prefixes at that remote site.

The bandwidth from each remote site to the hub routers might vary, which is common when the dual PVCs are designed to act as a primary PVC and secondary PVC. The hub routers will redistribute routes directly from EIGRP into BGP and will set the MED outbound for the prefixes to the IGP metric for that prefix. This provides the core with information about which PVC is preferred as the primary path and allows remote sites to have primary connectivity to either R3 or R11.

The default route will be injected into EIGRP from BGP. The redistribution into EIGRP will be filtered to allow only the default route. The redistribution from EIGRP into BGP will be filtered to block the default route.

Internet Connectivity

The actual Internet connections to the provider's network are terminated on routers that are not shown. The internal network design is separate from the Internet connectivity. However, the Internet resource must be announced to the internal network to provide routing information for reaching Internet destinations. Internet connectivity is provided in Location A and Location C. The public Internet DMZ is located outside firewalls.

In Location A, R13 connects to the firewall, which leads to the external DMZ. In Location C, R14 connects to a firewall, which leads to the other external DMZ. The network core will announce full internal routing information via eBGP to routers R13 and R12. Routers R13 and R12 originate the default route into the network core, which is disseminated to the major centers and remote site aggregation autonomous systems. The routers R13 and R12 have default routes pointing toward the firewalls to provide full reachability.

The same AS is used for both Internet connectivity sites even though there is no iBGP session between R12 and R13. Usually, it is unacceptable to have multiple BGP routers in the same AS that are not connected via iBGP. However, in this scenario, they act as a stub AS. They do not require connectivity to each other. There is no reason for R12 to ever send traffic to R13, and vice versa.

Migration Plan

The migration plan is designed to first provide the supporting infrastructure that will be needed for the BGP sessions. The BGP portion will then be overlaid on the network, allowing verification of proper prefix propagation. The EIGRP adjacencies between the border routers and the core routers will then be broken, allowing the BGP-learned prefixes to take effect. The EIGRP core process should then be renumbered to prevent misconfiguration, leading to accidental reformation of EIGRP adjacencies between the border routers and the core routers. The migration plan is designed to allow for deployment of a BGP core with minimal impact on the network's normal operation.

Supporting Infrastructure

The supporting infrastructure involves creating the loopback interfaces. The loopback address on each router will also serve as the router ID. The loopback interfaces are first configured according to a predefined scheme and are then included in the EIGRP routing process. The 172.16.0.0/16 address space will be used for the loopback addressing to provide easy identification of loopback addresses when examining the routing table. The loopback addressing scheme is 172.16.X.1/24, where X is the router number. Table 5-3 shows the addressing that will be used.

Table 5-3 *Loopback Address Assignments*

Router Name	Loopback Address	Router Name	Loopback Address
R1	172.16.1.1/24	R8	172.16.8.1/24
R2	172.16.2.1/24	R9	172.16.9.1/24
R3	172.16.3.1/24	R10	172.16.10.1/24
R4	172.16.4.1/24	R11	172.16.11.1/24
R5	172.16.5.1/24	R12	172.16.12.1/24
R6	172.16.6.1/24	R13	172.16.13.1/24
R7	172.16.7.1/24	—	—

NOTE It is not necessary to use a /24 for each loopback. In fact, it is considered a good practice to use a /32. However, it is common for /24s to be used for loopback interfaces in the enterprise environment. /24s are used in this example for clarity.

Example 5-23 shows the configuration template that should be used on each router.

Example 5-23 *Configuration Template for the Supporting Infrastructure*

```
!
interface Loopback0
  ip address 172.16.X.0 255.255.255.0
!
router eigrp 100
  no auto-summary
  network 10.0.0.0
  network 172.16.0.0
!
```

The new Internet routers should also be installed during this stage to provide origination of the default route when BGP is configured. The Internet routers do not need to join the EIGRP AS. They only need to be connected to what will be the DMZ Ethernet segment in each location with Internet connectivity. At this point, the proxy-based Internet connectivity is still being used.

Overlay BGP and Inject Prefixes

The next part of the migration involves deploying the BGP configuration and injecting the prefixes from EIGRP into BGP. The administrative distance for BGP is configured to be higher than EIGRP's administrative distance to ensure that EIGRP learned prefixes continue to be used until the BGP learned prefix information is validated. The administrative distance for BGP will be set to 200 for eBGP prefixes and to 220 for iBGP learned prefixes. The BGP configurations for all the routers are provided in Examples 5-24 through 5-36.

Example 5-24 *BGP Configuration for R1*

```
router bgp 65101
 no auto-summary
 no synchronization
 redistribute eigrp 100 route-map DENY_DEFAULT
 neighbor 172.16.2.1 remote-as 65101
 neighbor 172.16.2.1 update-source loopback0
 neighbor 10.1.1.4 remote-as 65100
 neighbor 10.1.1.4 route-map SET_MED out
 distance bgp 200 220 220
 bgp bestpath compare-routerid
!
ip prefix-list NO_DEFAULT seq 5 deny 0.0.0.0/0
ip prefix-list NO_DEFAULT seq 10 permit 0.0.0.0/0 le 32
!
route-map DENY_DEFAULT permit 10
 match ip address prefix-list NO_DEFAULT
!
route-map SET_MED permit 10
 set metric-type internal
!
```

Example 5-25 *BGP Configuration for R2*

```
router bgp 65101
 no auto-summary
 no synchronization
 redistribute eigrp 100 route-map DENY_DEFAULT
 neighbor 172.16.1.1 remote-as 65101
 neighbor 172.16.1.1 update-source loopback0
 neighbor 10.1.1.4 remote-as 65100
 neighbor 10.1.1.4 route-map SET_MED out
 distance bgp 200 220 220
 bgp bestpath compare-routerid
!
ip prefix-list NO_DEFAULT seq 5 deny 0.0.0.0/0
ip prefix-list NO_DEFAULT seq 10 permit 0.0.0.0/0 le 32
!
route-map DENY_DEFAULT permit 10
 match ip address prefix-list NO_DEFAULT
!
route-map SET_MED permit 10
 set metric-type internal
!
```

Example 5-26 *BGP Configuration for R3*

```
router bgp 65104
 no auto-summary
 no synchronization
 redistribute eigrp 100 route-map DENY_DEFAULT
 neighbor 10.1.1.4 remote-as 65100
 neighbor 10.1.1.4 route-map SET_MED out
 distance bgp 200 220 220
 bgp bestpath compare-routerid
!
ip prefix-list NO_DEFAULT seq 5 deny 0.0.0.0/0
ip prefix-list NO_DEFAULT seq 10 permit 0.0.0.0/0 le 32
!
route-map DENY_DEFAULT permit 10
 match ip address prefix-list NO_DEFAULT
!
route-map SET_MED permit 10
 set metric-type internal
!
```

Example 5-27 *BGP Configuration for R4*

```
router bgp 65100
 no auto-summary
 no synchronization
 neighbor internal peer-group
 neighbor internal update-source loopback0
 neighbor internal remote-as 65100
 neighbor 172.16.5.1 peer-group internal
 neighbor 172.16.6.1 peer-group internal
 neighbor 172.16.10.1 peer-group internal
 neighbor 10.1.1.1 remote-as 65101
 neighbor 10.1.1.2 remote-as 65101
 neighbor 10.1.1.3 remote-as 65104
 neighbor 10.1.1.13 remote-as 65105
 distance bgp 200 220 220
 bgp bestpath compare-routerid
!
```

Example 5-28 *BGP Configuration for R5*

```
router bgp 65100
 no auto-summary
 no synchronization
 neighbor internal peer-group
 neighbor internal update-source loopback0
 neighbor internal remote-as 65100
 neighbor 172.16.4.1 peer-group internal
 neighbor 172.16.6.1 peer-group internal
```

Example 5-28 *BGP Configuration for R5 (Continued)*

```
 neighbor 172.16.10.1 peer-group internal
 neighbor 10.1.2.7 remote-as 65102
 neighbor 10.1.2.7 route-map SET_MED out
 neighbor 10.1.2.8 remote-as 65102
 neighbor 10.1.2.8 route-map SET_MED out
 distance bgp 200 220 220
 bgp bestpath compare-routerid
 !
route-map SET_MED permit 10
 set metric-type internal
 !
```

Example 5-29 *BGP Configuration for R6*

```
router bgp 65100
 no auto-summary
 no synchronization
 neighbor internal peer-group
 neighbor internal update-source loopback0
 neighbor internal remote-as 65100
 neighbor 172.16.4.1 peer-group internal
 neighbor 172.16.5.1 peer-group internal
 neighbor 172.16.10.1 peer-group internal
 neighbor 10.1.2.7 remote-as 65102
 neighbor 10.1.2.7 route-map SET_MED out
 neighbor 10.1.2.8 remote-as 65102
 neighbor 10.1.2.8 route-map SET_MED out
 distance bgp 200 220 220
 bgp bestpath compare-routerid
 !
route-map SET_MED permit 10
 set metric-type internal
 !
```

Example 5-30 *BGP Configuration for R7*

```
router bgp 65102
 no auto-summary
 no synchronization
 redistribute eigrp 100 route-map DENY_DEFAULT
 neighbor 172.16.8.1 remote-as 65102
 neighbor 172.16.8.1 update-source loopback0
 neighbor 10.1.2.5 remote-as 65100
 neighbor 10.1.2.5 route-map SET_MED out
 neighbor 10.1.2.6 remote-as 65100
 neighbor 10.1.2.6 route-map SET_MED out
 distance bgp 200 220 220
```

continues

Example 5-30 *BGP Configuration for R7 (Continued)*

```
 bgp bestpath compare-routerid
 !
ip prefix-list NO_DEFAULT seq 5 deny 0.0.0.0/0
ip prefix-list NO_DEFAULT seq 10 permit 0.0.0.0/0 le 32
 !
route-map DENY_DEFAULT permit 10
 match ip address prefix-list NO_DEFAULT
 !
route-map SET_MED permit 10
 set metric-type internal
 !
```

Example 5-31 *BGP Configuration for R8*

```
router bgp 65102
 no auto-summary
 no synchronization
 redistribute eigrp 100 route-map DENY_DEFAULT
 neighbor 172.16.7.1 remote-as 65102
 neighbor 172.16.7.1 update-source loopback0
 neighbor 10.1.2.5 remote-as 65100
 neighbor 10.1.2.5 route-map SET_MED out
 neighbor 10.1.2.6 remote-as 65100
 neighbor 10.1.2.6 route-map SET_MED out
 distance bgp 200 220 220
 bgp bestpath compare-routerid
 !
ip prefix-list NO_DEFAULT seq 5 deny 0.0.0.0/0
ip prefix-list NO_DEFAULT seq 10 permit 0.0.0.0/0 le 32
 !
route-map DENY_DEFAULT permit 10
 match ip address prefix-list NO_DEFAULT
 !
route-map SET_MED permit 10
 set metric-type internal
 !
```

Example 5-32 *BGP Configuration for R9*

```
router bgp 65103
 no auto-summary
 no synchronization
 redistribute eigrp 100 route-map DENY_DEFAULT
 neighbor 10.1.3.10 remote-as 65100
 neighbor 10.1.3.10 route-map SET_MED out
 distance bgp 200 220 220
 bgp bestpath compare-routerid
```

Example 5-32 *BGP Configuration for R9 (Continued)*

```
!
ip prefix-list NO_DEFAULT seq 5 deny 0.0.0.0/0
ip prefix-list NO_DEFAULT seq 10 permit 0.0.0.0/0 le 32
!
route-map DENY_DEFAULT permit 10
 match ip address prefix-list NO_DEFAULT
!
route-map SET_MED permit 10
 set metric-type internal
!
```

Example 5-33 *BGP Configuration for R10*

```
router bgp 65100
 no auto-summary
 no synchronization
 neighbor internal peer-group
 neighbor internal update-source loopback0
 neighbor internal remote-as 65100
 neighbor 172.16.4.1 peer-group internal
 neighbor 172.16.5.1 peer-group internal
 neighbor 172.16.6.1 peer-group internal
 neighbor 10.1.3.9 remote-as 65103
 neighbor 10.1.3.11 remote-as 65104
 neighbor 10.1.3.12 remote-as 65105
 distance bgp 200 220 220
 bgp bestpath compare-routerid
!
```

Example 5-34 *BGP Configuration for R11*

```
router bgp 65104
 no auto-summary
 no synchronization
 redistribute eigrp 100 route-map DENY_DEFAULT
 neighbor 10.1.3.10 remote-as 65100
 neighbor 10.1.3.10 route-map SET_MED out
 distance bgp 200 220 220
 bgp bestpath compare-routerid
!
ip prefix-list NO_DEFAULT seq 5 deny 0.0.0.0/0
ip prefix-list NO_DEFAULT seq 10 permit 0.0.0.0/0 le 32
!
route-map DENY_DEFAULT permit 10
 match ip address prefix-list NO_DEFAULT
!
route-map SET_MED permit 10
 set metric-type internal
!
```

Example 5-35 *BGP Configuration for R12*

```
router bgp 65105
 no auto-summary
 no synchronization
 neighbor 10.1.3.10 remote-as 65100
 neighbor 10.1.3.10 default-originate
 distance bgp 200 220 220
 bgp bestpath compare-routerid
 !
```

Example 5-36 *BGP Configuration for R13*

```
router bgp 65105
 no auto-summary
 no synchronization
 neighbor 10.1.1.4 remote-as 65100
 neighbor 10.1.1.4 default-originate
 distance bgp 200 220 220
 bgp bestpath compare-routerid
 !
```

After the BGP configurations are in place, the BGP infrastructure must be validated to ensure that routing information will be available to provide full reachability when the EIGRP adjacencies over the Ethernet DMZ in each location are torn down. This stage creates additional memory requirements on the BGP speaking routers, because they will carry multiple copies of each prefix. The prefixes will exist in BGP and in EIGRP on these routers. Also, the prefixes will be injected into BGP in multiple places. If the BGP learned prefixes were being injected into the routing table, this could cause severe routing problems, but the higher administrative distance for BGP will prevent this.

In the sample configurations, the MED is set to Internal for all prefix advertisements via eBGP from the border routers to the core routers. This results in the core routers selecting the optimal path for each prefix in the BGP decision process, as follows:

Step 1 Validate that all BGP sessions reach the Established state using the **show ip bgp summary** command.

Step 2 Verify that prefix advertisement is consistent. Choose prefixes from each location, and verify in the core routers that the prefix is in the BGP table and is correctly chosen by the BGP decision process. This is done with the **show ip bgp** command. Confirm that the correct next hop is set for these prefixes in the BGP table.

The next hop for every iBGP learned prefix in the four core routers should be a loopback address in the 172.16.0.0/16 network. The next hop for every eBGP learned prefix in the core routers should be the IP address of one of the directly connected border routers. The border routers in each major location and remote connectivity hub routers should have the default route in the BGP table with an AS_PATH of 65100 65105.

Step 3   Verify that the number of prefixes in BGP is approximately the same as in EIGRP. Also, save the output from **show ip route summary** on each of the core routers and border routers. This will be used for further validation after the cutover to the BGP core has been made.

BGP Core Activation

This step activates the BGP core from a packet-switching perspective. The intent is to segment the network into separate EIGRP domains by breaking the EIGRP adjacency formation over the Ethernet DMZ in each location. To accomplish this, on all the routers, R1 through R13, configure passive interface under the EIGRP router process for the interface connecting to the Ethernet DMZ in that location. It is important to verify full connectivity after EIGRP and BGP have reconverged.

Collect the output from **show ip route summary** on each of the core routers and border routers. Compare the number of routes in the combined EIGRP and BGP processes with those collected before breaking the EIGRP adjacencies. The total number of routes in the tables on these routers should be the same. This validates that full routing information is received.

The distribution of routes between EIGRP and BGP will vary from location to location. The core routers will be almost entirely BGP routes. The border routers will be a combination, depending on how many routes are originated in that location being in EIGRP and the prefixes originated elsewhere being in BGP.

Final Cleanup

The final step in the migration is to clean up artifacts from the migration. After full connectivity has been verified, the administrative distance for BGP should be returned to the default values by removing the **distance** command from the BGP router process configuration. The **clear ip route** command must be issued for the new administrative distance to take effect.

The last step is to renumber the core EIGRP process. This can be accomplished by configuring an identical EIGRP process with a different ASN on each core router. The old EIGRP process can then be removed. The old EIGRP process should not be removed until the new EIGRP process has been configured on every core router and proper adjacency establishment has been confirmed using the **show ip eigrp neighbor** command.

Final Scenario

The final configurations for all the routers involved in the BGP core are shown in Examples 5-37 through 5-49.

Example 5-37 *Final Configuration for R1*

```
hostname R1
!
interface Loopback0
 ip address 172.16.1.1 255.255.255.0
!
interface Ethernet0/0
 ip address 10.1.1.1 255.255.255.0
!
interface Ethernet1/0
 ip address 10.1.101.1 255.255.255.0
!
!
router eigrp 100
 redistribute bgp 65101 route-map DEFAULT_ROUTE
 network 10.0.0.0
 network 172.16.0.0
 default-metric 10000 100 255 1 1500
 no auto-summary
 no eigrp log-neighbor-changes
!
router bgp 65101
 no synchronization
 bgp log-neighbor-changes
 redistribute eigrp 100 route-map DENY_DEFAULT
 neighbor 10.1.1.4 remote-as 65100
 neighbor 10.1.1.4 route-map SET_MED out
 neighbor 172.16.2.1 remote-as 65101
 neighbor 172.16.2.1 update-source Loopback0
 no auto-summary
 bgp bestpath compare-routerid
!
ip prefix-list DEFAULT seq 5 permit 0.0.0.0/0
ip prefix-list DEFAULT seq 10 deny 0.0.0.0/0 le 32
ip prefix-list NO_DEFAULT seq 5 deny 0.0.0.0/0
ip prefix-list NO_DEFAULT seq 10 permit 0.0.0.0/0 le 32
!
route-map DENY_DEFAULT permit 10
 match ip address prefix-list NO_DEFAULT
!
route-map DEFAULT_ROUTE permit 10
 match ip address prefix-list DEFAULT
!
route-map SET_MED permit 10
 set metric-type internal
!
```

Example 5-38 *Final Configuration for R2*

```
hostname R2
!
interface Loopback0
 ip address 172.16.2.1 255.255.255.0
!
interface Ethernet0/0
 ip address 10.1.1.2 255.255.255.0
!
interface Ethernet1/0
 ip address 10.1.101.2 255.255.255.0
!
router eigrp 100
 redistribute bgp 65101 route-map DEFAULT_ROUTE
 passive-interface Ethernet0/0
 network 10.0.0.0
 network 172.16.0.0
 default-metric 10000 100 255 1 1500
 no auto-summary
 no eigrp log-neighbor-changes
!
router bgp 65101
 no synchronization
 bgp log-neighbor-changes
 redistribute eigrp 100 route-map DENY_DEFAULT
 neighbor 10.1.1.4 remote-as 65100
 neighbor 10.1.1.4 route-map SET_MED out
 neighbor 172.16.1.1 remote-as 65101
 neighbor 172.16.1.1 update-source Loopback0
 no auto-summary
 bgp bestpath compare-routerid
!
ip prefix-list DEFAULT seq 5 permit 0.0.0.0/0
ip prefix-list DEFAULT seq 10 deny 0.0.0.0/0 le 32
ip prefix-list NO_DEFAULT seq 5 deny 0.0.0.0/0
ip prefix-list NO_DEFAULT seq 10 permit 0.0.0.0/0 le 32
!
route-map DENY_DEFAULT permit 10
 match ip address prefix-list NO_DEFAULT
!
route-map DEFAULT_ROUTE permit 10
 match ip address prefix-list DEFAULT
!
route-map SET_MED permit 10
 set metric-type internal
!
```

Example 5-39 *Final Configuration for R3*

```
hostname R3
!
interface Loopback0
 ip address 172.16.3.1 255.255.255.0
!
interface Ethernet0/0
 ip address 10.1.1.3 255.255.255.0
!
interface Serial2/0
 ip address 10.1.104.5 255.255.255.252
!
router eigrp 100
 redistribute bgp 65104 route-map DEFAULT_ROUTE
 passive-interface Ethernet0/0
 network 10.0.0.0
 network 172.16.0.0
 default-metric 10000 100 255 1 1500
 no auto-summary
 no eigrp log-neighbor-changes
!
router bgp 65104
 no synchronization
 bgp log-neighbor-changes
 redistribute eigrp 100 route-map DENY_DEFAULT
 neighbor 10.1.1.4 remote-as 65100
 neighbor 10.1.1.4 route-map SET_MED out
 no auto-summary
 bgp bestpath compare-routerid
!
ip prefix-list DEFAULT seq 5 permit 0.0.0.0/0
ip prefix-list DEFAULT seq 10 deny 0.0.0.0/0 le 32
ip prefix-list NO_DEFAULT seq 5 deny 0.0.0.0/0
ip prefix-list NO_DEFAULT seq 10 permit 0.0.0.0/0 le 32
!
route-map DENY_DEFAULT permit 10
 match ip address prefix-list NO_DEFAULT
!
route-map DEFAULT_ROUTE permit 10
 match ip address prefix-list DEFAULT
!
route-map SET_MED permit 10
 set metric-type internal
!
```

Example 5-40 *Final Configuration for R4*

```
hostname R4
!
interface Loopback0
```

Example 5-40 *Final Configuration for R4 (Continued)*

```
 ip address 172.16.4.1 255.255.255.0
 !
interface Ethernet0/0
 ip address 10.1.1.4 255.255.255.0
 !
interface Serial2/0
 ip address 10.1.100.5 255.255.255.252
 !
interface Serial3/0
 ip address 10.1.100.1 255.255.255.252
 !
router eigrp 101
 passive-interface Ethernet0/0
 network 10.0.0.0
 network 172.16.0.0
 no auto-summary
 no eigrp log-neighbor-changes
 !
router bgp 65100
 no synchronization
 bgp log-neighbor-changes
 neighbor internal peer-group
 neighbor internal remote-as 65100
 neighbor internal update-source Loopback0
 neighbor internal next-hop-self
 neighbor 10.1.1.1 remote-as 65101
 neighbor 10.1.1.2 remote-as 65101
 neighbor 10.1.1.3 remote-as 65104
 neighbor 10.1.1.13 remote-as 65105
 neighbor 172.16.5.1 peer-group internal
 neighbor 172.16.6.1 peer-group internal
 neighbor 172.16.10.1 peer-group internal
 no auto-summary
 bgp bestpath compare-routerid
 !
```

Example 5-41 *Final Configuration for R5*

```
hostname R5
 !
interface Loopback0
 ip address 172.16.5.1 255.255.255.0
 !
interface Ethernet0/0
 ip address 10.1.2.5 255.255.255.0
 !
interface Ethernet1/0
 ip address 10.1.100.9 255.255.255.252
```

continues

Example 5-41 *Final Configuration for R5 (Continued)*

```
!
interface Serial2/0
 ip address 10.1.100.6 255.255.255.252
!
router eigrp 101
 passive-interface Ethernet0/0
 network 10.0.0.0
 network 172.16.0.0
 no auto-summary
 no eigrp log-neighbor-changes
!
router bgp 65100
 no synchronization
 bgp log-neighbor-changes
 neighbor internal peer-group
 neighbor internal remote-as 65100
 neighbor internal update-source Loopback0
 neighbor internal next-hop-self
 neighbor 10.1.2.7 remote-as 65102
 neighbor 10.1.2.7 route-map SET_MED out
 neighbor 10.1.2.8 remote-as 65102
 neighbor 10.1.2.8 route-map SET_MED out
 neighbor 172.16.4.1 peer-group internal
 neighbor 172.16.6.1 peer-group internal
 neighbor 172.16.10.1 peer-group internal
 no auto-summary
 bgp bestpath compare-routerid
!
route-map SET_MED permit 10
 set metric-type internal
!
```

Example 5-42 *Final Configuration for R6*

```
hostname R6
!
interface Loopback0
 ip address 172.16.6.1 255.255.255.0
!
interface Ethernet0/0
 ip address 10.1.2.6 255.255.255.0
!
interface Ethernet1/0
 ip address 10.1.100.10 255.255.255.252
!
interface Serial2/0
 ip address 10.1.100.13 255.255.255.252
!
router eigrp 101
 passive-interface Ethernet0/0
```

Example 5-42 *Final Configuration for R6 (Continued)*

```
   network 10.0.0.0
   network 172.16.0.0
   no auto-summary
   no eigrp log-neighbor-changes
   !
 router bgp 65100
  no synchronization
  bgp log-neighbor-changes
  neighbor internal peer-group
  neighbor internal remote-as 65100
  neighbor internal update-source Loopback0
  neighbor internal next-hop-self
  neighbor 10.1.2.7 remote-as 65102
  neighbor 10.1.2.7 route-map SET_MED out
  neighbor 10.1.2.8 remote-as 65102
  neighbor 10.1.2.8 route-map SET_MED out
  neighbor 172.16.4.1 peer-group internal
  neighbor 172.16.5.1 peer-group internal
  neighbor 172.16.10.1 peer-group internal
  no auto-summary
  bgp bestpath compare-routerid
  !
 route-map SET_MED permit 10
  set metric-type internal
  !
```

Example 5-43 *Final Configuration for R7*

```
hostname R7
!
interface Loopback0
 ip address 172.16.7.1 255.255.255.0
!
interface Ethernet0/0
 ip address 10.1.2.7 255.255.255.0
!
interface Ethernet1/0
 ip address 10.1.102.7 255.255.255.0
!
router eigrp 100
 redistribute bgp 65102 route-map DEFAULT_ROUTE
 network 10.0.0.0
 network 172.16.0.0
 default-metric 10000 100 255 1 1500
 no auto-summary
 no eigrp log-neighbor-changes
!
router bgp 65102
 no synchronization
```

continues

Example 5-43 *Final Configuration for R7 (Continued)*

```
 bgp log-neighbor-changes
 redistribute eigrp 100 route-map DENY_DEFAULT
 neighbor 10.1.2.5 remote-as 65100
 neighbor 10.1.2.5 route-map SET_MED out
 neighbor 10.1.2.6 remote-as 65100
 neighbor 10.1.2.6 route-map SET_MED out
 neighbor 172.16.8.1 remote-as 65102
 neighbor 172.16.8.1 update-source Loopback0
 no auto-summary
 bgp bestpath compare-routerid
 !
ip prefix-list DEFAULT seq 5 permit 0.0.0.0/0
ip prefix-list DEFAULT seq 10 deny 0.0.0.0/0 le 32
ip prefix-list NO_DEFAULT seq 5 deny 0.0.0.0/0
ip prefix-list NO_DEFAULT seq 10 permit 0.0.0.0/0 le 32
 !
route-map DENY_DEFAULT permit 10
 match ip address prefix-list NO_DEFAULT
 !
route-map DEFAULT_ROUTE permit 10
 match ip address prefix-list DEFAULT
 !
route-map SET_MED permit 10
 set metric-type internal
 !
```

Example 5-44 *Final Configuration for R8*

```
hostname R8
!
interface Loopback0
 ip address 172.16.8.1 255.255.255.0
 !
interface Ethernet0/0
 ip address 10.1.2.8 255.255.255.0
 !
interface Ethernet1/0
 ip address 10.1.102.8 255.255.255.0
 !
router eigrp 100
 redistribute bgp 65102 route-map DEFAULT_ROUTE
 network 10.0.0.0
 network 172.16.0.0
 default-metric 10000 100 255 1 1500
 no auto-summary
 no eigrp log-neighbor-changes
 !
router bgp 65102
 no synchronization
 bgp log-neighbor-changes
```

Example 5-44 *Final Configuration for R8 (Continued)*

```
 redistribute eigrp 100 route-map DENY_DEFAULT
 neighbor 10.1.2.5 remote-as 65100
 neighbor 10.1.2.5 route-map SET_MED out
 neighbor 10.1.2.6 remote-as 65100
 neighbor 10.1.2.6 route-map SET_MED out
 neighbor 172.16.7.1 remote-as 65102
 neighbor 172.16.7.1 update-source Loopback0
 no auto-summary
 bgp bestpath compare-routerid
!
ip prefix-list DEFAULT seq 5 permit 0.0.0.0/0
ip prefix-list DEFAULT seq 10 deny 0.0.0.0/0 le 32
ip prefix-list NO_DEFAULT seq 5 deny 0.0.0.0/0
ip prefix-list NO_DEFAULT seq 10 permit 0.0.0.0/0 le 32
!
route-map DENY_DEFAULT permit 10
 match ip address prefix-list NO_DEFAULT
!
route-map DEFAULT_ROUTE permit 10
 match ip address prefix-list DEFAULT
!
route-map SET_MED permit 10
 set metric-type internal
!
```

Example 5-45 *Final Configuration for R9*

```
hostname R9
!
interface Loopback0
 ip address 172.16.9.1 255.255.255.0
!
interface Ethernet0/0
 ip address 10.1.3.9 255.255.255.0
!
interface Ethernet1/0
 ip address 10.1.103.9 255.255.255.0
!
router eigrp 100
 redistribute bgp 65103 route-map DEFAULT_ROUTE
 passive-interface Ethernet0/0
 network 10.0.0.0
 network 172.16.0.0
 default-metric 10000 100 255 1 1500
 no auto-summary
 no eigrp log-neighbor-changes
```

continues

Example 5-45 *Final Configuration for R9 (Continued)*

```
!
router bgp 65103
 no synchronization
 bgp log-neighbor-changes
 redistribute eigrp 100 route-map DENY_DEFAULT
 neighbor 10.1.3.10 remote-as 65100
 neighbor 10.1.3.10 route-map SET_MED out
 no auto-summary
 bgp bestpath compare-routerid
!
ip prefix-list DEFAULT seq 5 permit 0.0.0.0/0
ip prefix-list DEFAULT seq 10 deny 0.0.0.0/0 le 32
ip prefix-list NO_DEFAULT seq 5 deny 0.0.0.0/0
ip prefix-list NO_DEFAULT seq 10 permit 0.0.0.0/0 le 32
!
route-map DENY_DEFAULT permit 10
 match ip address prefix-list NO_DEFAULT
!
route-map DEFAULT_ROUTE permit 10
 match ip address prefix-list DEFAULT
!
route-map SET_MED permit 10
 set metric-type internal
!
```

Example 5-46 *Final Configuration for R10*

```
hostname R10
!
interface Loopback0
 ip address 172.16.10.1 255.255.255.0
!
interface Ethernet0/0
 ip address 10.1.3.10 255.255.255.0
!
interface Serial2/0
 ip address 10.1.100.14 255.255.255.252
!
interface Serial3/0
 ip address 10.1.100.2 255.255.255.252
!
router eigrp 101
 passive-interface Ethernet0/0
 network 10.0.0.0
 network 172.16.0.0
 no auto-summary
 no eigrp log-neighbor-changes
!
router bgp 65100
 no synchronization
```

Example 5-46 *Final Configuration for R10 (Continued)*

```
bgp log-neighbor-changes
neighbor internal peer-group
neighbor internal remote-as 65100
neighbor internal update-source Loopback0
neighbor internal next-hop-self
neighbor 10.1.3.9 remote-as 65103
neighbor 10.1.3.11 remote-as 65104
neighbor 10.1.3.12 remote-as 65105
neighbor 172.16.4.1 peer-group internal
neighbor 172.16.5.1 peer-group internal
neighbor 172.16.6.1 peer-group internal
no auto-summary
bgp bestpath compare-routerid
!
```

Example 5-47 *Final Configuration for R11*

```
hostname R11
!
interface Loopback0
 ip address 172.16.11.1 255.255.255.0
!
interface Ethernet0/0
 ip address 10.1.3.1 255.255.255.0
!
interface Serial3/0
 ip address 10.1.104.9 255.255.255.252
!
router eigrp 100
 redistribute bgp 65104 route-map DEFAULT_ROUTE
 passive-interface Ethernet0/0
 network 10.0.0.0
 network 172.16.0.0
 default-metric 10000 100 255 1 1500
 no auto-summary
 no eigrp log-neighbor-changes
!
router bgp 65104
 no synchronization
 bgp log-neighbor-changes
 redistribute eigrp 100 route-map DENY_DEFAULT
 neighbor 10.1.3.10 remote-as 65100
 neighbor 10.1.3.10 route-map SET_MED out
 no auto-summary
 bgp bestpath compare-routerid
!
ip prefix-list DEFAULT seq 5 permit 0.0.0.0/0
ip prefix-list DEFAULT seq 10 deny 0.0.0.0/0 le 32
```

continues

Example 5-47 *Final Configuration for R11 (Continued)*

```
ip prefix-list NO_DEFAULT seq 5 deny 0.0.0.0/0
ip prefix-list NO_DEFAULT seq 10 permit 0.0.0.0/0 le 32
!
route-map DENY_DEFAULT permit 10
 match ip address prefix-list NO_DEFAULT
!
route-map DEFAULT_ROUTE permit 10
 match ip address prefix-list DEFAULT
!
route-map SET_MED permit 10
 set metric-type internal
!
```

Example 5-48 *Final Configuration for R12*

```
hostname R12
!
interface Loopback0
 ip address 172.16.12.1 255.255.255.0
!
interface Ethernet0/0
 ip address 10.1.3.12 255.255.255.0
!
interface Serial2/0
 no ip address
 shutdown
 no fair-queue
!
router bgp 65105
 no synchronization
 bgp log-neighbor-changes
 neighbor 10.1.3.10 remote-as 65100
 neighbor 10.1.3.10 default-originate
 no auto-summary
 bgp bestpath compare-routerid
!
```

Example 5-49 *Final Configuration for R13*

```
hostname R13
!
interface Loopback0
 ip address 172.16.13.1 255.255.255.0
!
interface Ethernet0/0
 ip address 10.1.1.13 255.255.255.0
!
router bgp 65105
```

Example 5-49 *Final Configuration for R13 (Continued)*

```
 no synchronization
 bgp log-neighbor-changes
 neighbor 10.1.1.4 remote-as 65100
 neighbor 10.1.1.4 default-originate
 no auto-summary
 bgp bestpath compare-routerid
!
```

As discussed in the section "Defining the Problem," the root cause of the problem should be addressed. After the network has been migrated to a BGP core, the underlying issue of address assignment and prefix summarization should be resolved.

The number of prefixes involved in this case study made the use of **network** statements unfeasible, requiring direct redistribution. After the addressing and prefix summarization issue has been resolved, the BGP configurations on the border routers should be changed to inject prefixes using **network** statements, and the redistribution should be removed. This does not include the remote site aggregation, because of the issue of black-holing traffic, unless a physical circuit directly connects the hub routers and iBGP connectivity is established between the hub routers.

Summary

This chapter provided an overview of when to use BGP in an enterprise core network. It was stressed that BGP should not be used as a patch to solve a problem without also addressing the problem's root cause. This is most often seen in networks where BGP is used to resolve address assignment issues that prevent summarization. The deployment of BGP achieves better scalability at the price of increased convergence times.

Three common BGP core architectures were presented, and each was examined in depth. The internal-only BGP core architecture and the external-only BGP core architecture are most commonly seen in small- to medium-sized networks. They become increasingly difficult to manage as the network grows. The internal/external BGP core architecture is the most common architecture and is very well-suited to scale as the network expands.

Finally, a case study was provided to examine how to migrate from an IGP-only network to a BGP network core. The network requirements were complex and realistic, providing a real-world scenario. The steps in the migration were detailed, and extensive configuration information was provided.

This chapter discusses various aspects of connecting to the Internet:

- Determining what information to accept from upstream providers
- Multihoming
- Route filtering
- Load balancing
- Additional connectivity concerns
- Case study: load balancing in a multihoming environment

CHAPTER 6

Internet Connectivity for Enterprise Networks

The integration of day-to-day business communication with the Internet has made highly redundant Internet connectivity a mission-critical service. The use of e-mail and the web have become tightly integrated into the world economy and the way business is done. It is in this capacity—connecting to the Internet—that BGP is most commonly seen in enterprise environments.

This chapter presents the design options that are available and explains the central concepts of each option. The caveats associated with each design are also presented, in addition to any requirements, such as needing a unique public autonomous system number (ASN).

Determining What Information to Accept from Upstream Providers

Questioning what information to accept from upstream providers is very common. When you make routing decisions, the availability of more-specific information provides the potential for increased optimization in determining which path to use in reaching a destination. However, this increase in information results in the trade-off of higher resource requirements, both system and administrative. Three options are explored here:

- Default route only
- Default plus partial routes
- Full Internet tables

Default Route Only

The option of default routing only can be used with or without BGP. The default route is either statically defined or received via BGP from the provider. The default route is injected into the IGP, directing traffic to the closest border router. The use of default routing requires minimal system resources but can result in suboptimal routing.

Default Plus Partial Routes

The use of partial routes is the most common. It provides a fair amount of specific information to allow routing optimization but has lower resource requirements than full tables. Partial tables can be sent by the provider or defined by the enterprise. When partial tables are defined by the enterprise, full tables are requested from the provider, and inbound filtering is applied. When partial tables are sent by the provider, it is often the provider's local routes and their customers, filtering out prefixes received from peers or upstream transit providers. When partial routes are used, the default route is used in conjunction to ensure full reachability.

Full Internet Tables

The enterprise accepts full Internet routing tables from the provider(s). This method provides the most specific information, with the trade-off of being the most resource-intensive. The availability of specific information for every reachable prefix allows for the greatest amount of routing optimization. The use of default routing is not required when full tables are used, because any destination without a specific prefix is not reachable.

Multihoming

The term *multihoming* has become quite common. So what does it mean to be multihomed with respect to Internet connectivity? A network is multihomed when it has more than one path to reach the Internet. This might be multiple paths to a single provider or multiple paths to different providers. There are two primary reasons for multihoming:

- **Reliability**—Internet connectivity has become a mission-critical service in many environments. Multihoming when done correctly provides the redundancy needed to ensure reliable service.

- **Optimal routing**—The performance of Internet connectivity can be enhanced through multihoming. This is commonly done through the use of different providers to offer a more diverse selection of paths to reach destinations.

The following sections examine methods to provide Internet connectivity for an enterprise:

- Stub network single-homed
- Stub network multihomed with single or multiple border routers
- Standard multihomed network with single or multiple border routers

Stub network design scenarios present options where there is a single upstream provider. A single-homed network is by definition a stub network. Nonstub network design scenarios present options where there are multiple upstream providers. The discussion about multiple sessions to the ISP focuses on when multiple links are used between two routers to provide additional bandwidth.

Stub Network Single-Homed

The stub network design, shown in Figure 6-1, is most commonly seen in small businesses. This design often provides very little, if any, redundancy. When Internet connectivity is not vital to business operations, this design option can provide a low-cost solution.

Figure 6-1   *Enterprise Border Stub Router Architecture*

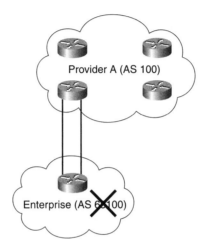

A single-homed stub network does not require the use of BGP. The provider configures a static route for the customer's prefix. The enterprise configures a static default route.

If multiple circuits are used between the provider router and customer router, multiple static routes are used. The use of multiple connections in this design assumes that they are all connected to the same routers. The level of redundancy provided is minimal and protects only against circuit failure. Router failure results in full loss of connectivity.

Stub Network Multihomed

The stub network multihomed design option is often used by small- to medium-sized businesses. The enterprise is connected to a single upstream provider, but instead of connecting to the provider at a single point, the enterprise connects to the provider in multiple places. This provides an increased level of redundancy in that failure of a provider router is protected in addition to circuit failure.

It is common to use BGP in a stub environment when multihoming is employed. In the stub environment, the enterprise typically receives a default route and, at most, partial prefixes. There is very seldom a reason to receive full routing information in a stub environment.

The design options for a multihomed stub network are using a single border router for the enterprise edge and using multiple routers. These design scenarios are described in detail in the following sections.

Single Border Router

The single border router design scenario, shown in Figure 6-2, involves the use of a single router at the enterprise border, with multiple connections to the same provider. These connections are terminated at the provider in diverse locations.

Figure 6-2 *Stub Multihomed Single Border Router Architecture*

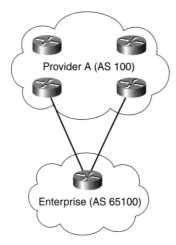

Provider A (AS 100)

Enterprise (AS 65100)

When this design is deployed, BGP should be used to provide additional control for possible load sharing. The use of a single upstream provider allows for the use of a private AS. This means that the enterprise does not need to obtain a unique and publicly visible ASN from its regional registry. The upstream provider can remove the private ASN from the updates.

The use of BGP in this design can give the enterprise a greater degree of influence over the inbound traffic patterns and better control over its outbound traffic flow. This can be especially useful if the links are unequally sized, where routing policy can be used to obtain load sharing in proportion to the links' size.

Multiple Border Routers

The use of a single enterprise border router leads to a single point of failure. The addition of one or more border routers removes the last single point of failure. This design option has multiple border routers in the enterprise network, each with one or more connections to the upstream provider. In this design, a single upstream provider is still used.

| **NOTE** | It could be argued that the single upstream provider is a single point of failure. However, that is only a matter of perspective. If the upstream provider has redundancy in its network, multiple failures are required to trigger a failure for the enterprise customer. |

This design scenario is shown in Figure 6-3.

Figure 6-3   *Stub Multihomed Multiple Border Router Architecture*

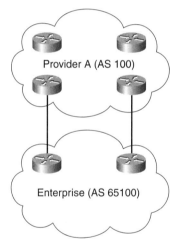

It is recommended that BGP be used with this design option. It is possible for the provider and enterprise to use static routes. However, this does not let the enterprise influence traffic patterns. This ability is especially important if the links to the upstream provider are unequally sized or terminate in globally diverse locations, such as in different continents.

The enterprise can still use a private AS in this design. The main advantage of running a private ASN is that the enterprise does not need to go through the process of acquiring one. The purpose of running BGP is to provide the enterprise with additional support for defining inbound and outbound policies. In addition to the eBGP sessions to the upstream provider, the enterprise should build a full iBGP mesh between the border routers, as well as between all Layer 3 devices that might be involved in providing transit between the border routers. This requirement ensures that traffic will not be sent to a device that does not have routing information for the destination address.

The enterprise should then originate a default route from each border router. To prevent traffic from following a default route to a border router with a failed upstream circuit, the default origination should be conditional on the circuit's being up and active. This conditional advertisement can be based on a static default pointed at the interface, or it can be received from BGP and redistributed into the IGP. In this context, conditional advertisement does not refer to the conditional advertisement feature. If additional prefix information is received from the upstream provider, do not redistribute this into any IGP process running on the border routers.

Standard Multihomed Network

The standard multihomed network design scenario described in this section is what is most commonly referred to when multihoming is discussed. This design scenario involves the enterprise connecting to multiple upstream providers.

This design scenario requires the enterprise to obtain its own ASN from its regional registry. The enterprise also needs a block of address space that is large enough to pass standard peering filters. An example of standard peering filters is discussed in detail in the later section "Peering Filters." The enterprise can usually obtain the required address space from one or more of its upstream providers.

It is also possible to obtain an address space assignment from a regional registry; however, significant justification is usually required. It is much easier to obtain an ASN than an IP address space. The regional registries assign both ASNs and IP address space. There are currently three regional registries:

- **American Registry for Internet Numbers (ARIN)**—www.arin.net
- **Asia Pacific Network Information Centre (APNIC)**—www.apnic.net
- **Réseaux IP Européens (RIPE)**—www.ripe.net

The following sections describe the single border router and multiple border router options for enterprise edge Internet connectivity.

Single Border Router

The standard multihomed network with a single border router design involves the use of multiple upstream providers, all terminated on a single enterprise border router (see Figure 6-4). This provides redundancy for protection against circuit failure and upstream provider failures. This design also provides the additional potential for optimizing outbound traffic flow.

Figure 6-4   *Multihomed Single Border Router Architecture*

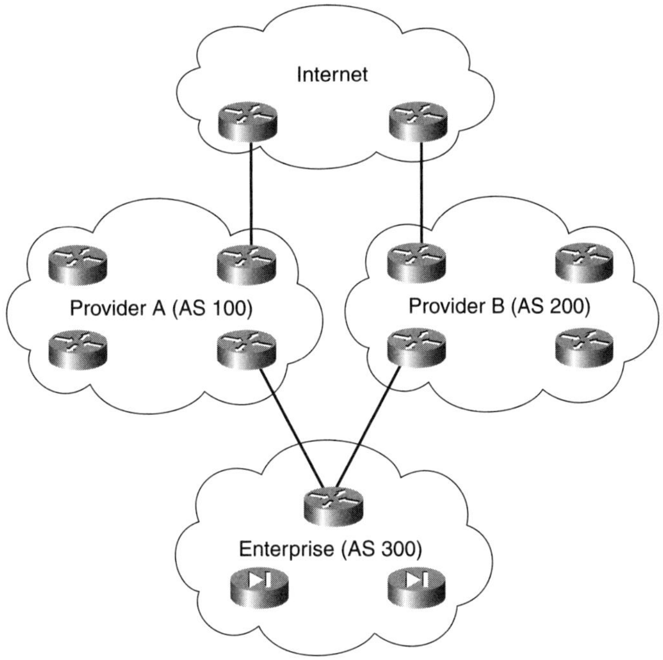

In this design, the enterprise border router is eBGP peered with both upstream providers. The information received by the enterprise border router can vary from none to full tables from both providers. The eBGP peering is required in this design scenario to allow the enterprise's IP address space to be consistently originated. If BGP were not used, both Provider A and Provider B would be seen as originating the same prefix, which does not make sense. Advertising a prefix from multiple originating autonomous systems is called inconsistent advertisement. Inconsistent prefix advertisement works just fine but is frowned upon because of the ambiguity of the origination point.

The first option for configuring routing information is for the enterprise border router to deny all prefixes and configure static default routes to the outbound interfaces. If a link goes down, the enterprise's address space is no longer advertised to that provider. The default route pointing at the failed link is removed from the routing table. This provides very even load sharing of outbound traffic, assuming equal-sized links. The problem with this scenario is that traffic destined for Provider A could be sent out the link to Provider B.

The next option is to receive partial routing information. The enterprise can request that the upstream providers send only their locally originated prefixes and those prefixes for their customers. This lets the enterprise correctly route traffic destined for either provider. A default route directed at each provider is still required to reach any destinations that are beyond the immediate upstream providers and their customers.

The enterprise can also receive full tables from both providers. This allows the enterprise border router to send traffic to the upstream provider that is logically closest to the destination. This logical distance is derived from the AS_PATH. If the AS_PATH is the same length, the traffic is sent to the upstream provider whose path has the lowest ROUTER_ID.

Multiple Border Routers

The standard multihomed network with multiple border routers design, shown in Figure 6-5, is the most common for medium and large businesses. The highest level of redundancy is provided through multiple providers, multiple circuits, and multiple enterprise border routers.

Figure 6-5 *Multihomed Multiple Border Router Architecture*

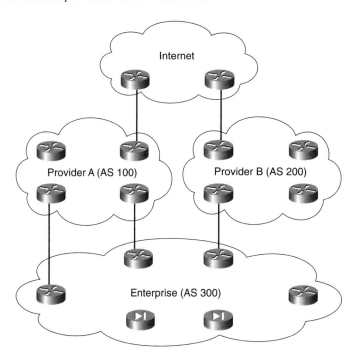

In this design, the enterprise border routers are eBGP peered with their upstream providers. There is a full iBGP mesh between all enterprise border routers and any other Layer 3 devices that might provide transit between the enterprise border routers. The amount of prefix information received can vary from default information only to full tables. The scenarios for receiving prefix information are the same as when a single enterprise border router is used.

The most common schemes involve the use of partial routing information. This can mean requesting partial routes from all upstream providers and using these in conjunction with default routes or requesting full tables and modifying the inbound filtering to achieve reasonable load sharing. Ultimately, the method used depends on the specific goals of the enterprise. The simplest method uses one link for primary connectivity and the other links for purely backup connectivity. The most difficult task is achieving fairly even load sharing over multiple links.

Route Filtering

The importance of properly filtering routing information cannot be stressed enough. This section provides a short overview of the filtering you should use between the enterprise border and the service provider.

Inbound Filtering

Two primary groups of prefixes should be filtered out of prefix information received from the upstream providers—Martian address space and your own prefix information.

Martian address space is address space that should never be globally advertised. The following is a list of Martian address spaces:

- **RFC 1918 addressing**—RFC 1918, Address Allocation for Private Internets, specifies private addressing. This addressing is intended for use in private networks. As a result, many networks might use the same netblocks. This address space, including 10.0.0.0/8, 172.16.0.0/12, and 192.168.0.0/16, should never be advertised globally.

- **System local addressing**—The 127.0.0.0/8 address space is reserved for use internal to a system. For instance, the 127.0.0.1 address is often used as an internal system address to simulate loopback functionality in hosts.

- **End node autoconfiguration block**—The 169.254.0.0/16 network block is intended for automatic address assignment when a DHCP server is unavailable.

- **0.0.0.0/8 addressing**—The 0.0.0.0 through 0.255.255.255 address space is used internally by some systems. It is not assigned and should not be used. This does not include the default route 0.0.0.0/0.

- **Test network addressing**—The 192.0.2.0/24 address space is reserved for test networks. This prefix is intended for use in documentation and sample code.

- **Class D and E address space**—Class D addresses are not actual host addresses; they represent IP multicast groups. These groups are not advertised by unicast routing protocols and should not be received via BGP. The Class D address space is 224.0.0.0/4. The Class E address space, 240.0.0.0/4, is reserved and not in use.

The other block of address space that you should never receive an advertisement for is your own address space. This includes prefix advertisements that are equal to or longer than your netblock. This does not include advertisements that are shorter than your netblock, because this could represent an aggregate of which your netblock is a component. Example 6-1 shows a sample filter. Note that the last statement permits any prefixes that have not been explicitly denied.

Example 6-1 *Inbound Martian Prefix Filtering*

```
Router#show running-config | begin prefix
ip prefix-list MARTIAN seq 5 deny 0.0.0.0/8 le 32
ip prefix-list MARTIAN seq 10 deny 10.0.0.0/8 le 32
ip prefix-list MARTIAN seq 15 deny 172.16.0.0/12 le 32
ip prefix-list MARTIAN seq 20 deny 192.168.0.0/16 le 32
ip prefix-list MARTIAN seq 25 deny 127.0.0.0/8 le 32
ip prefix-list MARTIAN seq 30 deny 169.254.0.0/16 le 32
ip prefix-list MARTIAN seq 35 deny 192.0.2.0/24 le 32
ip prefix-list MARTIAN seq 40 deny 224.0.0.0/4 le 32
ip prefix-list MARTIAN seq 50 deny 240.0.0.0/4 le 32
ip prefix-list MARTIAN seq 55 permit 0.0.0.0/0 le 32
!
```

Outbound Filtering

The prefix information that is sent to your upstream providers should also be carefully filtered to ensure that only the enterprise networks are advertised to the upstream providers. If the enterprise network is multihomed to different providers, it could provide transit for the two providers if outbound filters are not applied.

It is typically advised that you provide multiple layers of outbound filtering to protect against misconfiguration. The first layer is prefix filtering using either prefix lists or distribute lists. The second layer of filtering uses a filter list to filter on AS_PATH so that only prefixes originated by the enterprise AS are sent to the upstream provider.

Load Balancing

The biggest challenge with Internet connectivity is making optimal use of the available bandwidth. The fact that BGP always chooses a single path instead of load balancing like an IGP can result in very uneven traffic patterns. When optimizing traffic flow, inbound traffic flow is independent of outbound traffic flow. The mechanisms used to control traffic flow in each direction are independent of each other, as discussed in the next sections.

Inbound Traffic Load Balancing

There are a few tactics for controlling traffic flow inbound. The methods available depend on the form of multihoming that is being used:

- If an enterprise is multihomed to the same provider, it has the most options available for controlling traffic flow inbound.

- If there are two connections to the upstream provider, the address space is divided in half.

- If the enterprise has a /21 that is assigned by the provider, the enterprise divides it into two /22 networks. One /22 is announced on one link, and the other /22 is announced on the other link. Additionally, the /21 is announced on both links. If this does not provide the desired balance, the network can be further broken down, with different networks being advertised out each link until the desired traffic flow is achieved. It is also important to note that if the circuits being load-balanced over are unequal in size, splitting the prefix in half might not be the most optimal division.

The real difficulty in balancing traffic comes when an enterprise network is multihomed to two different providers. Announcing more-specific prefixes, as discussed in the previous example, is not always an option. Obtaining a balanced traffic flow in this environment is an iterative process.

The summary prefix is announced out both providers, and link utilization is monitored. It is important to keep in mind that perfect balancing is not a reasonable goal; the goal is fairly close load sharing. If traffic heavily favors one of the links, prepend your ASN to the path with the heaviest utilization. Continue to monitor link utilization. If traffic is still favoring the same link, you can perform additional AS_PATH prepending. Remember, increasing the AS_PATH length by even one ASN can have a drastic impact on traffic flow, so increase the AS_PATH a single ASN at a time.

As soon as traffic has been split between the two links as closely as possible with AS_PATH prepending, very few options are left to further balance traffic. The only remaining option is to make use of any communities that the upstream provider has available. The communities that are available vary from provider to provider. Chapter 9, "Service Provider Architecture," provides a detailed discussion of how service providers set up their community policies.

Outbound Traffic Load Balancing

Many more control options are available for balancing traffic outbound. This is because there is the potential to accept more than 120,000 specific pieces of routing information, or prefixes defining the remote destinations. When balancing inbound, only a few prefixes are advertised. The granularity at which traffic can be manipulated is based on the number of prefixes being used.

The simplest method of balancing traffic is to use default routes only. This provides an even traffic balance; however, it creates a very high probability of suboptimal routing. If the enterprise is multihomed to a single upstream provider, using default routes is quite likely the simplest solution.

When the enterprise is multihomed to different upstream providers, more creativity is required to obtain adequate load sharing. The simplest method is to request partial routes from both upstream providers, which can be combined with static default routes to provide full reachability. This in itself might provide acceptable load sharing, in addition to a reasonable level of routing optimization.

If using provider-advertised partial routes in conjunction with default routes does not provide adequate load sharing, the next step is to request full Internet tables from the upstream providers. The enterprise should then perform inbound filtering to create its own partial tables. The most effective form of filtering is AS_PATH filtering. Just make sure you do not block the AS directly upstream, meaning your provider's AS. Also, use a default route in conjunction with your specially created partial tables, or you might have only partial connectivity!

A slight modification to this method is to lower the local preference on the nonpreferred prefixes instead of filtering them. This shifts traffic to the higher-preference prefixes and retains the backup paths that have lower preference. This method removes the need for the presence of default routes to maintain reachability during a failure scenario.

Multiple Sessions to the Same Provider

When the enterprise connects to the upstream provider via BGP and uses multiple links for additional bandwidth between the two routers, there is the potential for only one of those links to be used. This scenario has multiple links between a single enterprise edge router and a single provider edge router.

It is considered a best practice to tie eBGP sessions directly to physical interfaces. If a single eBGP session is used, the next hop of the prefixes received is the IP address of that interface on the provider router, and only that link is used. If that link fails, the eBGP session is torn down, even though other links between the two routers might still be operational.

If multiple BGP sessions are used, for example, one for each link, the practice of using BGP to choose a single path results in only a single link's being used. If a link fails, traffic fails over to another link, but multiple links are not used.

There are two popular options for load sharing over multiple links—EBGP multihop and EBGP multipath. They are examined next.

EBGP Multihop Solution

The first solution is to use the eBGP multihop feature. This solution uses a single eBGP session between the two routers, with the eBGP session being sourced from a loopback instead of a physical interface. A static route to the remote loopback is configured for each interface. This provides the next-hop resolution and load balancing through recursive routing to the next hop. This scenario is shown in Figure 6-6. The router configuration and resulting output are shown in Examples 6-2 and 6-3.

Figure 6-6 *Multiple Connections Using EBGP Multihop*

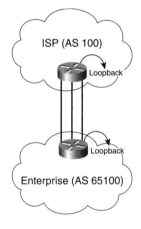

Example 6-2 *Configuration on the Enterprise and Provider Routers*

```
Enterprise#show running-config | begin bgp
router bgp 65100
 no synchronization
 bgp log-neighbor-changes
 network 172.18.0.0
 neighbor 172.16.2.1 remote-as 100
 neighbor 172.16.2.1 ebgp-multihop 2
 neighbor 172.16.2.1 update-source Loopback0
```

continues

Example 6-2 *Configuration on the Enterprise and Provider Routers (Continued)*

```
 no auto-summary
 !
 ip classless
 ip route 172.16.2.1 255.255.255.255 10.1.1.10 Serial0
 ip route 172.16.2.1 255.255.255.255 10.1.1.6 Serial1
 ip route 172.16.2.1 255.255.255.255 10.1.1.2 Serial2
 ip route 172.18.0.0 255.255.0.0 Null0

 Provider#show running-config | begin bgp
 router bgp 100
  no synchronization
  bgp log-neighbor-changes
  network 172.19.0.0
  neighbor 172.16.1.1 remote-as 65100
  neighbor 172.16.1.1 ebgp-multihop 2
  neighbor 172.16.1.1 update-source Loopback0
  no auto-summary
 !
 ip classless
 ip route 172.16.1.1 255.255.255.255 10.1.1.1 Serial0
 ip route 172.16.1.1 255.255.255.255 10.1.1.5 Serial1
 ip route 172.16.1.1 255.255.255.255 10.1.1.9 Serial2
 ip route 172.19.0.0 255.255.0.0 Null0
```

Example 6-3 *Recursive Routing Information*

```
 Enterprise#show ip route 172.19.0.0
 Routing entry for 172.19.0.0/16
   Known via "bgp 65100", distance 20, metric 0
   Tag 100, type external
   Last update from 172.16.2.1 00:05:04 ago
   Routing Descriptor Blocks:
   * 172.16.2.1, from 172.16.2.1, 00:05:04 ago
       Route metric is 0, traffic share count is 1
       AS Hops 1

 Enterprise#show ip route 172.16.2.1
 Routing entry for 172.16.2.1/32
   Known via "static", distance 1, metric 0
   Routing Descriptor Blocks:
   * 10.1.1.10
       Route metric is 0, traffic share count is 1
     10.1.1.6
       Route metric is 0, traffic share count is 1
     10.1.1.2
       Route metric is 0, traffic share count is 1
```

The **ebgp-multihop** command must be configured, or the BGP session will not form. The multihop number should be set to 2. It is a common misconfiguration to set the multihop value to 255, which can result in the session's forming through a very roundabout path in a failure scenario.

EBGP Multipath Solution

The eBGP multipath feature provides another solution to load sharing over multiple links. An eBGP session is configured between the two routers for each link. The eBGP sessions are tied directly to the interface addresses. The result is that both routers receive multiple paths, one for each link. They are identical except for the neighbor address from which the path was received. The eBGP multipath feature allows the router to install all paths up to the maximum-paths value configured. This solution is shown in Figure 6-7. The configuration and resulting output are shown in Examples 6-4 and 6-5.

Figure 6-7   *Multiple Connections Using EBGP Multipath*

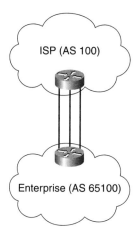

Example 6-4   *Configuration on the Enterprise and Provider Routers*

```
Enterprise#show running-config | begin bgp
router bgp 65100
 no synchronization
 bgp log-neighbor-changes
 network 172.18.0.0
 neighbor 10.1.1.2 remote-as 100
 neighbor 10.1.1.6 remote-as 100
 neighbor 10.1.1.10 remote-as 100
```

continues

Example 6-4 *Configuration on the Enterprise and Provider Routers (Continued)*

```
 maximum-paths 3
 no auto-summary
 !

 Provider#show running-config | begin bgp
 router bgp 100
  no synchronization
  bgp log-neighbor-changes
  network 172.19.0.0
  neighbor 10.1.1.1 remote-as 65100
  neighbor 10.1.1.5 remote-as 65100
  neighbor 10.1.1.9 remote-as 65100
  maximum-paths 3
  no auto-summary
 !
```

Example 6-5 *Multipath Routing Information from the Provider*

```
 Enterprise#show ip route 172.19.0.0
 Routing entry for 172.19.0.0/16
   Known via "bgp 65100", distance 20, metric 0
   Tag 100, type external
   Last update from 10.1.1.2 00:03:03 ago
   Routing Descriptor Blocks:
   * 10.1.1.10, from 10.1.1.10, 00:03:03 ago
       Route metric is 0, traffic share count is 1
       AS Hops 1
     10.1.1.6, from 10.1.1.6, 00:03:03 ago
       Route metric is 0, traffic share count is 1
       AS Hops 1
     10.1.1.2, from 10.1.1.2, 00:03:03 ago
       Route metric is 0, traffic share count is 1
       AS Hops 1
```

This solution requires the multipath feature to be configured on both the enterprise border router and the provider router. It is quite possible the provider will not want to enable BGP multipath on the router, because this feature can result in significant memory requirements, thus requiring the eBGP multihop solution to be used. The reason is that the command to enable this feature is not specific to a particular peer or group of peers, but to all BGP prefixes on the router.

Additional Connectivity Concerns

Different factors that cannot be directly controlled by the engineers operating the enterprise network can affect connectivity. This section looks at two primary issues:

- Provider-based summarization
- Prefix filtering at private peering points

Provider-Based Summarization

Provider-based summarization is when the provider assigns address space to a number of customers and then aggregates those address blocks into a single summary that it announces to its upstream transit providers and peers. In general, it is considered good practice for providers to perform this summarization, because it reduces the size of the global routing table. However, in some instances it is beneficial to advertise some of the more-specific prefixes in addition to the summary route.

In Figure 6-8, for example, the enterprise has two upstream providers. Provider A assigns 100.16.0.0/20 to the enterprise. The enterprise advertises this prefix via BGP to both Provider A and Provider B. Provider A summarizes the prefix into 100.16.0.0/16 and advertises only the summary to its peers and upstream transit. Provider B does not own the address space, so it does not perform any summarization, but it advertises the 100.16.0.0/20 directed to its peers and upstream transit providers.

The result of these advertisements is that all route lookups, except in Provider A's network, prefer the path through Provider B because of the longest match. This means that the enterprise sees the vast majority of traffic inbound on the link to Provider B. The only traffic that is inbound from Provider A is traffic from Provider A itself and its customers. In fact, it is very possible that traffic from any of Provider A's multihomed customers would use Provider B to reach the enterprise.

The solution to this problem is for Provider A to advertise the prefix 100.16.0.0/20 in addition to 100.16.0.0/16. This provides a much closer balance for the inbound traffic flow to the enterprise. It is important that you communicate with your upstream providers about your intentions to multihome. This allows them to make the necessary changes for your multihoming to be successful.

Figure 6-8 *Prefix Advertisement for a Multihomed Enterprise*

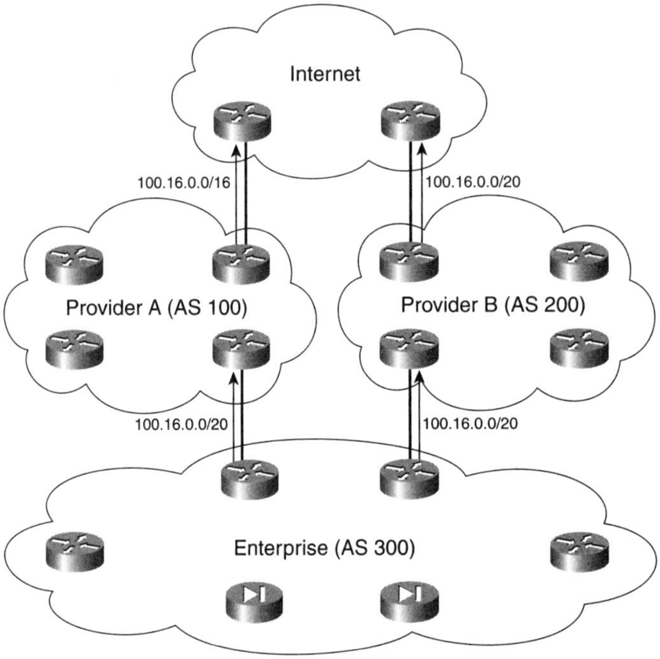

Peering Filters

To reduce their routing tables, almost all service providers perform filtering at public and private peering points. The filtering is to disallow prefixes that are too specific, because reachability can still be achieved through the use of shorter summary routes. A common peering filter might look like this:

- In the traditional Class A address space, allow prefixes that are of /21 or shorter.
- In the traditional Class B address space, allow prefixes that are of /22 or shorter.
- In the traditional Class C address space, allow prefixes that are of /24 or shorter.

It is common for peering filters to be based on the allocation sizes that the registries use. In the traditional Class A address space, the longest prefix allocations are /20 networks. In the traditional Class B address space, the longest prefix assignments are /21 networks. In the traditional Class C address space, the longest assignments are /24 networks.

Assume that the enterprise has been assigned 100.16.0.0/24 by Provider A. The enterprise is multihomed to Provider A and Provider B. The enterprise advertises its /24 network to both providers. Provider A summarizes the prefix and advertises 100.16.0.0/16. Provider B is unable to summarize and advertises the prefix 100.16.0.0/24.

The 100.16.0.0 network is in the traditional Class A address space. This means that standard peering filters permit only /21 or shorter advertisements. Provider A announces a /16, which is accepted. Provider B announces a /24, which is denied. This is shown in Figure 6-9.

NOTE   What are considered "standard" peering filters changes over time. It is becoming more common for ISPs to accept any prefix that is a /24 or shorter.

Figure 6-9   *Prefix Advertisement for a Multihomed Enterprise*

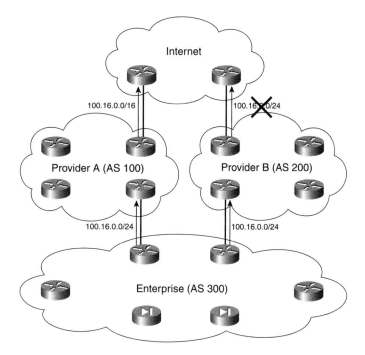

The enterprise has connectivity through Provider A. There is very little traffic through Provider B. Another problem arises if there is a link failure between Provider A and the enterprise. The advertisement from Provider B is blocked, which results in loss of connectivity because the prefix 100.16.0.0/24 is not propagated beyond the network for Provider B.

The solution to this problem is for the enterprise to obtain an address assignment from Provider A or Provider B that is large enough to fit through standard peering filters. When multihoming is desired, discussing your intentions with your upstream providers can often avoid scenarios such as this.

Case Study: Load Balancing in a Multihoming Environment

This case study examines the process of balancing traffic in a multihoming environment. A standard enterprise DMZ network is presented, with a focus on the Internet connectivity aspects and defining traffic flow policies. The security aspects of deploying Internet connectivity are outside the scope of this discussion.

Scenario Overview

The enterprise is currently single-homed, with no redundancy. The enterprise does not have its own ASN and uses a single static default route pointing toward the upstream ISP.

Internet connectivity has been identified as a mission-critical service. A new multihomed Internet connectivity design must be deployed that provides fault-tolerant service. The new connectivity design will make use of multiple border routers with diverse upstream providers. This new design is shown in Figure 6-10.

Figure 6-10 *Multihomed Enterprise Network Scenario*

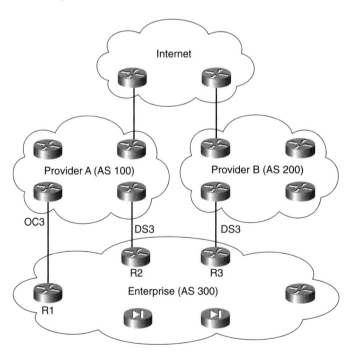

The enterprise has obtained ASN 300 and will multihome to AS 100 and AS 200. There are two connections to AS 100—an OC-3 (155 Mbps) and a DS3 (45 Mbps). The OC-3 connects to R1, and the DS3 connects to R2. There is a single DS3 to AS 200.

Traffic Flow Requirements

The primary link for most traffic should be through the OC-3 on R1 to AS 100. The DS3 on R2 should be used only if the OC-3 on R1 is down. The DS3 to AS 200 should be used for traffic local to AS 200, instead of traversing whatever peering, either direct or indirect, might exist between AS 100 and AS 200.

Failure Scenarios

If the OC-3 fails, traffic should be distributed fairly even between both DS3s. Traffic should be optimally routed to the degree that traffic destined for AS 200 is not sent to AS 100 and vice versa.

If either DS3 fails, traffic should continue to be sent to the OC-3. The DS3 to AS 100 should be used only if the OC-3 to AS 100 fails. If the DS3 to AS 200 fails, traffic should fail over to the OC-3.

Initial Configurations

Table 6-1 shows the IP addressing used. Serial addressing refers to the OC-3 and DS3 interfaces. Loopback addressing is used for iBGP sessions. The address space used by the enterprise is 172.160.0.0/16. The initial router configurations are provided in Examples 6-6, 6-7, and 6-8.

Table 6-1   *Address Assignment for Enterprise Border Routers*

Router Name	Remote Serial Address	Loopback Address
R1	100.100.100.2/30	172.160.1.1/32
R2	100.100.150.2/30	172.160.1.2/32
R3	200.200.200.2/30	172.160.1.3/32

Example 6-6   *Initial Configuration for R1*

```
R1#show running-config | begin bgp
router bgp 300
 no synchronization
 bgp log-neighbor-changes
 network 172.160.0.0
```

continues

Example 6-6 *Initial Configuration for R1 (Continued)*

```
 neighbor 172.160.1.2 remote-as 300
 neighbor 172.160.1.2 update-source loopback0
 neighbor 172.160.1.3 remote-as 300
 neighbor 172.160.1.3 update-source loopback0
 neighbor 100.100.100.1 remote-as 100
 no auto-summary
 !
```

Example 6-7 *Initial Configuration for R2*

```
R2#show running-config | begin bgp
router bgp 300
 no synchronization
 bgp log-neighbor-changes
 network 172.160.0.0
 neighbor 172.160.1.1 remote-as 300
 neighbor 172.160.1.1 update-source loopback0
 neighbor 172.160.1.3 remote-as 300
 neighbor 172.160.1.3 update-source loopback0
 neighbor 100.100.150.1 remote-as 100
 no auto-summary
 !
```

Example 6-8 *Initial Configuration for R3*

```
R3#show running-config | begin bgp
router bgp 300
 no synchronization
 bgp log-neighbor-changes
 network 172.160.0.0
 neighbor 172.160.1.1 remote-as 300
 neighbor 172.160.1.1 update-source loopback0
 neighbor 172.160.1.2 remote-as 300
 neighbor 172.160.1.2 update-source loopback0
 neighbor 200.200.200.1 remote-as 200
 no auto-summary
 !
```

Inbound Traffic Policy

The initial configuration does not provide any preference to inbound traffic flows. Traffic takes the optimal path into the network based on AS_PATH when deciding between using AS 100 and AS 200. This could result in overloading the DS3 link from AS 200. Traffic entering through AS 100 takes either the DS3 or the OC-3, depending on the IGP metric to the next-hop address, which could overload the DS3 link from AS 100.

Shifting the traffic pattern inbound to make use of the OC-3 exclusively for traffic from AS 100 can be achieved by AS_PATH prepending on the DS3 link to AS 100. R2 prepends twice. This causes AS 100 to prefer the path from R1 and to make use of the OC-3 link exclusively.

To prevent the DS3 link in AS 200 from becoming overloaded, the majority of traffic is shifted to AS 100. The AS_PATH prepending mechanism is used to prepend outbound to AS 200 twice.

After adding the AS_PATH prepends, the traffic flow is given time to settle down to the new policy. For some reason, all inbound traffic enters through the OC-3, and none enters through either of the DS3s. This is not quite the desired policy. Traffic originating in AS 200 should enter through that DS3. After checking with the upstream provider for AS 200, you discover that they have direct peering with AS 100 and are receiving the prefix 172.160.0.0/16 with an AS_PATH of 300 100, which is being preferred over the AS_PATH 300 300 300, which you are advertising to them.

After discussing your intentions for traffic flow, it is suggested that you continue sending the prefix to AS 200 over the DS3 with the two prepends. In addition, you will send them the community 200:120, which will cause them to set a higher local preference for the prefix and then prefer it over the prefix received from AS 100. Setting this community is based on a predefined policy of AS 200, which allows the following communities to be used:

    200:80 = Set LOCAL_PREF 80
    200:100 = Set LOCAL_PREF 100 (default)
    200:120 = Set LOCAL_PREF 120

After you apply the community, traffic begins to flow inbound over the DS3 link from AS 200. At this point, the inbound traffic flow is consistent with the desired policy when all circuits are active. The next step is to check the failure scenarios.

Because no traffic is flowing inbound over the DS3 from AS 100, turning down this circuit does not affect traffic flow. Turning down the DS3 to AS 200 causes the path from AS 100 to be the only remaining path, and the OC-3 will be used for all traffic. So far, everything looks good.

The last failure scenario is turning down the OC-3 link to AS 100. This makes the prepended path from R2 take precedence in AS 100. The desired behavior is for traffic to flow over both DS3 links, to AS 100 and AS 200 in a fairly even manner. Perfect load balancing is not possible. However, after turning down the OC-3 link, the DS3 to AS 200 runs at about 35 Mbps, and the DS3 to AS 100 runs at about 12 Mbps. This distribution is not in line with the desired inbound traffic policy.

The LOCAL_PREF attribute that is being set in AS 200 does not have an effect outside AS 200, so it should not affect traffic balancing. This appears to be a result of AS 200's being better connected than AS 100, which means that a majority of autonomous systems on the Internet have a shorter AS_PATH to AS 200 than AS 100. Based on this assumption, the AS_PATH prepending on R2 over the DS3 to AS 100 is reduced from 2 to 1, and the BGP session is cleared to allow the new policy to take effect. The use of a BGP soft clear is the preferred method, preventing prefix flapping.

The result is that more traffic flows over the DS3 from AS 100, with about 25 Mbps from AS 100 and 22 Mbps over the DS3 from AS 200. The OC-3 link is brought back online, and traffic flow restabilizes. The traffic flow returns to the prefailure pattern. This policy satisfies the enterprise's traffic flow policy requirements. The final configuration for the inbound policy is shown in Examples 6-9, 6-10, and 6-11.

Example 6-9 *Inbound Policy Configuration for R1*

```
R1#show running-config | begin bgp
router bgp 300
 no synchronization
 bgp log-neighbor-changes
 network 172.160.0.0
 neighbor 172.160.1.2 remote-as 300
 neighbor 172.160.1.2 update-source loopback0
 neighbor 172.160.1.3 remote-as 300
 neighbor 172.160.1.3 update-source loopback0
 neighbor 100.100.100.1 remote-as 100
 no auto-summary
 !
```

Example 6-10 *Inbound Policy Configuration for R2*

```
R2#show running-config | begin bgp
router bgp 300
 no synchronization
 bgp log-neighbor-changes
 network 172.160.0.0
 neighbor 172.160.1.1 remote-as 300
 neighbor 172.160.1.1 update-source loopback0
 neighbor 172.160.1.3 remote-as 300
 neighbor 172.160.1.3 update-source loopback0
 neighbor 100.100.150.1 remote-as 100
 neighbor 100.100.150.1 route-map AS100_OUT_POLICY out
 no auto-summary
 !
route-map AS100_OUT_POLICY permit 10
 set as-path prepend 300
 !
```

Example 6-11 *Inbound Policy Configuration for R3*

```
R3#show running-config | begin bgp
router bgp 300
 no synchronization
 bgp log-neighbor-changes
 network 172.160.0.0
 neighbor 172.160.1.1 remote-as 300
 neighbor 172.160.1.1 update-source loopback0
 neighbor 172.160.1.2 remote-as 300
 neighbor 172.160.1.2 update-source loopback0
 neighbor 200.200.200.1 remote-as 200
 neighbor 200.200.200.1 send-community
 neighbor 200.200.200.1 route-map AS200_OUT_POLICY out
 no auto-summary
 !
route-map AS200_OUT_POLICY permit 10
 set community 200:120
 set as-path prepend 300 300
 !
```

Outbound Traffic Policy

The default configuration does not apply any preference to the outbound policy. In the preceding section about inbound policy, you discovered that AS 200 was better connected. If full Internet tables were accepted, it is quite likely that the majority of traffic would be sent outbound over the DS3 link to AS 200. This is undesirable, because it would leave the OC-3 to AS 100 underutilized, and the DS3 to AS 200 would be overutilized.

The desired outbound policy is for the majority of traffic to flow over the OC-3 link. If the traffic is destined for AS 200, it should be sent directly over the DS3 on R3 to AS 200.

The first cut at applying this policy is to request partial routes plus the default over all three BGP sessions. The prefixes received on R1 and R2 from AS 100 should be pretty much the same. After requesting this from the upstream providers, the traffic balances over all three links; however, too much traffic follows the default routes over the DS3 to AS 100 and the DS3 to AS 200.

The solution to this outbound policy issue is to set LOCAL_PREF inbound on the OC-3 to 120. This ensures that the only default route used is the one from the OC-3. The more specific prefixes received from AS 200 on R3 result in traffic destined for AS 200 being sent directly there.

The primary failure scenario is that of the OC-3. The failure of the OC-3 results in two default prefixes. Traffic sent to R3 is sent to AS 200, and traffic sent to R2 is sent to AS 100. The partial routes ensure that traffic destined for AS 100 is not sent to AS 200 and vice versa.

Final Configurations

So far in this case study, you have focused on defining traffic policy. In this section, you learn the route filtering required to prevent acceptance of Martian address space and to prevent the enterprise from providing transit service. To provide a complete scenario, the route filtering will be added to the final configurations. The Martian prefix filters are shown in Example 6-12. The prefix filters for Class D and Class E have been condensed into a single rule. In an actual deployment, this route filtering would be part of the initial configuration. The final configurations are shown in Examples 6-13, 6-14, and 6-15.

Example 6-12 *Martian Prefix Filtering*

```
Router#show running-config | begin prefix
ip prefix-list MARTIAN seq 5 deny 0.0.0.0/8 le 32
ip prefix-list MARTIAN seq 10 deny 10.0.0.0/8 le 32
ip prefix-list MARTIAN seq 15 deny 172.16.0.0/12 le 32
ip prefix-list MARTIAN seq 20 deny 192.168.0.0/16 le 32
ip prefix-list MARTIAN seq 25 deny 127.0.0.0/8 le 32
ip prefix-list MARTIAN seq 30 deny 169.254.0.0/16 le 32
ip prefix-list MARTIAN seq 35 deny 192.0.2.0/24 le 32
ip prefix-list MARTIAN seq 40 deny 224.0.0.0/3 le 32
ip prefix-list MARTIAN seq 50 deny 172.160.0.0/16 le 32
ip prefix-list MARTIAN seq 55 permit 0.0.0.0/0 le 32
!
```

Example 6-13 *Final Configuration for R1*

```
R1#show running-config | begin bgp
router bgp 300
 no synchronization
 bgp log-neighbor-changes
 network 172.160.0.0
 neighbor 172.160.1.2 remote-as 300
 neighbor 172.160.1.2 update-source loopback0
 neighbor 172.160.1.3 remote-as 300
 neighbor 172.160.1.3 update-source loopback0
 neighbor 100.100.100.1 remote-as 100
 neighbor 100.100.100.1 route-map LPREF_IN in
 neighbor 100.100.100.1 prefix-list MARTIAN in
 neighbor 100.100.100.1 filter-list 10 out
 neighbor 100.100.100.1 prefix-list PFX_OUT out
 no auto-summary
!
route-map LPREF_IN permit 10
  set local-preference 120
!
ip as-path access-list 10 permit ^$
!
ip prefix-list PFX_OUT seq 5 permit 172.160.0.0/16
ip prefix-list PFX_OUT seq 10 deny any
```

Example 6-14 *Final Configuration for R2*

```
R2#show running-config | begin bgp
router bgp 300
 no synchronization
 bgp log-neighbor-changes
 network 172.160.0.0
 neighbor 172.160.1.1 remote-as 300
 neighbor 172.160.1.1 update-source loopback0
 neighbor 172.160.1.3 remote-as 300
 neighbor 172.160.1.3 update-source loopback0
 neighbor 100.100.150.1 remote-as 100
 neighbor 100.100.150.1 route-map AS100_OUT_POLICY out
 neighbor 100.100.150.1 prefix-list MARTIAN in
 neighbor 100.100.150.1 filter-list 10 out
 neighbor 100.100.150.1 prefix-list PFX_OUT out
 no auto-summary
!
route-map AS100_OUT_POLICY permit 10
 set as-path prepend 300
!
ip as-path access-list 10 permit ^$
!
ip prefix-list PFX_OUT seq 5 permit 172.160.0.0/16
ip prefix-list PFX_OUT seq 10 deny any
```

Example 6-15 *Final Configuration for R3*

```
R3#show running-config | begin bgp
router bgp 300
 no synchronization
 bgp log-neighbor-changes
 network 172.160.0.0
 neighbor 172.160.1.1 remote-as 300
 neighbor 172.160.1.1 update-source loopback0
 neighbor 172.160.1.2 remote-as 300
 neighbor 172.160.1.2 update-source loopback0
 neighbor 200.200.200.1 remote-as 200
 neighbor 200.200.200.1 send-community
 neighbor 200.200.200.1 route-map AS200_OUT_POLICY out
 neighbor 200.200.200.1 prefix-list MARTIAN in
 neighbor 200.200.200.1 filter-list 10 out
 neighbor 200.200.200.1 prefix-list PFX_OUT out
 no auto-summary
!
route-map AS200_OUT_POLICY permit 10
 set community 200:120
 set as-path prepend 300 300
```

continues

Example 6-15 *Final Configuration for R3 (Continued)*

```
!
ip as-path access-list 10 permit ^$
!
ip prefix-list PFX_OUT seq 5 permit 172.160.0.0/16
ip prefix-list PFX_OUT seq 10 deny any
```

Summary

This chapter provided a detailed discussion of the various ways for an enterprise to connect to the Internet. The requirements for each method were discussed, such as having an officially assigned ASN and registered address space, in addition to the general methodology for defining traffic policy. Additional issues that can arise when multihoming, such as provider summarization and peer filtering, were also explained.

The case study showed how to deploy a complicated Internet connectivity scenario that included multiple providers with various-sized connections to the upstream providers. A complex traffic policy was implemented with a simple configuration. Multihoming itself is not difficult when the desired traffic policy is well-defined and you understand the available tools.

PART III

Designing BGP Service Provider Networks

This chapter explores the various aspects of iBGP design and implementation:

- Issues of iBGP scalability
- Route reflection
- Confederation
- Confederation versus route reflection

CHAPTER 7

Scalable iBGP Design and Implementation Guidelines

In a typical ISP environment, an AS contains many BGP-speaking routers. Fully meshing all these iBGP speakers would result in both a high BGP session count and high resource consumption per router. This chapter focuses on two common solutions—route reflection and confederation. Using these two solutions, this chapter demonstrates practical guidelines with extensive examples of how to design a scalable iBGP routing architecture. Through four case studies in Chapter 8, "Route Reflection and Confederation Migration Strategies," which contain step-by-step migration procedures, you will further explore the subject of iBGP scalability.

Issues of iBGP Scalability

As you recall, the subject of loop prevention mechanisms in BGP was introduced in Chapter 2, "Understanding BGP Building Blocks." When BGP is used to distribute reachability information among a series of autonomous systems, as is the case with eBGP, the BGP attribute AS_PATH is used as the loop-prevention mechanism. An eBGP speaker discards any BGP updates it receives from an eBGP peer that contains its own AS number. Because the AS_PATH attribute is preserved within the same AS, a different loop-prevention mechanism must be employed for iBGP. The rule is simply that an iBGP speaker does not relay or readvertise reachability information received via iBGP from one iBGP speaker to another iBGP speaker. For example, if routers R1, R2, and R3 are all iBGP-only speakers within the same AS, and R2 receives a prefix from R1, R2 does not send that prefix via iBGP to R3.

The loop-prevention mechanism within iBGP forces all iBGP speakers to have BGP sessions with each other. In other words, they are fully meshed so that all BGP speakers can receive full routing information. In the example given in the preceding paragraph, fully meshed means that R1 needs to have BGP sessions with R2 and R3. Also, R2 and R3 must peer with each other via iBGP. The total number of iBGP sessions among n iBGP routers is $n(n-1)/2$, with each router having $(n-1)$ sessions. Figure 7-1 shows the relationship between the total number of iBGP sessions and the number of fully meshed iBGP routers, commonly called the n^2 relationship. For example, when the number of iBGP routers increases from 10 to 100, the total number of iBGP sessions increases from 45 to 4950!

Figure 7-1   *n^2 Issues for Full iBGP Mesh*

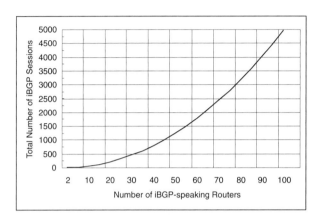

Two effective approaches to solve the iBGP scalability issue are route reflection (RFC 2796) and confederation (RFC 3065). Route reflection is based on relaxing the iBGP loop-prevention requirement for certain types of routers, whereas confederation is a method of breaking a large AS into a number of smaller member autonomous systems. Either way, the number of iBGP sessions can be reduced to a manageable level.

Route Reflection

This section discusses various aspects of route reflection:

* How route reflection works
* Rules for prefix advertisement
* Clustering
* Loop-prevention mechanisms
* Hierarchical route reflection
* Route reflection design examples

How Route Reflection Works

Route reflection involves creating a special group of routers called route reflectors (RRs). The iBGP loop-prevention rule is relaxed for these routers, in that with certain restrictions they are allowed to readvertise or reflect routes from one iBGP speaker to another iBGP speaker. Under this new structure, iBGP speakers are classified into three groups:

- Route reflectors (RRs)
- Route reflector clients (also known as clients or client peers)
- Regular iBGP speakers (also known as nonclients or nonclient peers)

NOTE The concept of clients and nonclients is always in the context of the RRs that serve or do not serve them. A client of one RR can be an RR of another client. A nonclient with respect to one RR can be an RR of another client.

Route reflectors, although acting like regular iBGP speakers with other regular iBGP speakers and with each other, can reflect routes between clients and nonclients. This includes reflecting routes from one client to another client—in other words, client-to-client reflection. With route reflection, the full iBGP mesh is required only between RRs and between RRs and nonclients.

Consider the topology shown in Figure 7-2, which shows three interconnected autonomous systems. Within AS 200, R5 is an RR, with R6 and R7 as its clients. Routers R3 and R4 are nonclients and are fully meshed with R5. Clients R6 and R7 have iBGP sessions only with R5. The total number of iBGP sessions within AS 200 is 5. Without route reflection, the total number of iBGP sessions within AS 200 would be 10.

Route reflection provides another scalability feature—an RR reflects only the best path of each prefix. When an RR receives multiple paths for the same destination, it first steps through the path-selection process to determine the best path for that destination. It then reflects the best path. Abstraction of routing information by RRs reduces the size of the BGP RIB in the domain. Note that this abstraction is different from BGP prefix summarization, although both reduce the size of the routing entries. One side effect of the RR's abstraction of routing information, however, is that inconsistent route selection between RRs and their peers might result in a loss of routing information or routing loops. This chapter details how to avoid this type of problem when implementing RR designs.

To maintain consistent BGP topology, RRs do not modify certain BGP path attributes during route reflection. These attributes include NEXT_HOP, AS_PATH, LOCAL_PREF, and MED. Two additional attributes are introduced to help prevent routing information loops in an RR environment, ORIGINATOR_ID and CLUSTER_LIST. Both are discussed later. A routing information loop, also discussed later, is a phenomenon that a router receives and accepts the routing information originated by itself.

Figure 7-2 *BGP Route Reflection Components*

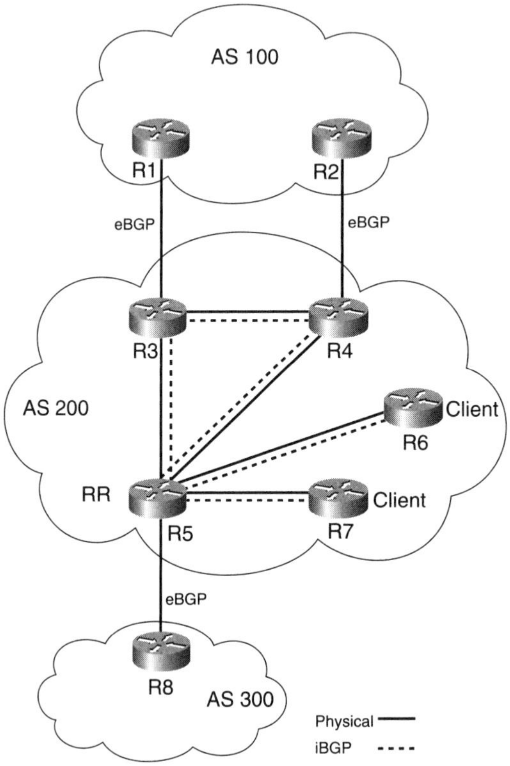

Rules for Prefix Advertisement

Before discussing the rules for prefix advertisement, a definition is in order. As a special form of prefix advertisement, reflection is the advertisement made by an RR for prefixes learned from one client to another client, from a client to a nonclient, or from a nonclient to a client. In this definition, the following advertisements are not examples of reflection: from an external peer to an RR, from an RR to an external peer, or from an RR to an internal peer (client or nonclient) for a prefix learned from an external peer. In summary, reflection is a concept that is introduced with RRs and is used as a subset of the advertisement concept.

To avoid creating routing information loops, certain rules must be followed during prefix advertisement involving RRs:

- **Rule 1**—An RR advertises or reflects only its best path.
- **Rule 2**—An RR always advertises to eBGP peers.

- **Rule 3**—An RR client follows the regular iBGP loop-prevention rule when advertising prefixes.

- **Rule 4**—Additional rules must be followed if advertising to iBGP peers, clients, or nonclients (see Rules 5, 6, and 7). When advertising to iBGP peers, the rules are dependent on where the prefix is learned.

- **Rule 5**—If an RR learns a prefix from an external peer, it advertises to all its clients and nonclients.

  Consider Figure 7-3, in which the RR (R5) receives the prefix 172.16.0.0/16 from an eBGP peer (R8). It advertises the route to both its clients, R6 and R7. R5 also advertises the route to its nonclients, R3 and R4. Both R3 and R4 are iBGP peered and are not allowed to readvertise the route to each other.

Figure 7-3 *Prefix Advertisement for External Peers*

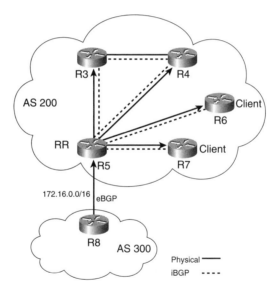

- **Rule 6**—If the prefix comes to an RR through a nonclient iBGP peer, the RR reflects the route to all its clients.

  Figure 7-4 shows the prefix advertisement. The prefix 172.16.0.0/16 is advertised to R5 via iBGP from R3. R5 reflects the prefix to its clients, R6 and R7. An RR does not reflect the route it learns from an iBGP peer to another nonclient iBGP peer, such as R4 (standard iBGP requirement). Because R3 and R4 are iBGP peered, R4 receives the prefix from R3 directly. As indicated in Rule 2, an RR always advertises to an external peer, such as R8.

Figure 7-4 *Prefix Advertisement for Internal Peers*

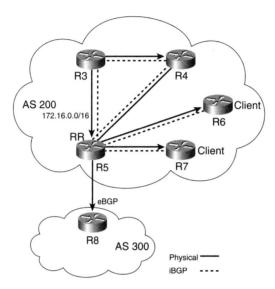

- **Rule 7**—If a prefix comes to an RR from a client, the RR reflects the route to all other clients and nonclients.

  In Figure 7-5, the prefix 172.16.0.0/16 is advertised to R5 (RR) by R7 (client), and R5 readvertises or reflects the prefix to R6 (client), R3 (nonclient), and R4 (nonclient). As always, R5 advertises the prefix to its external peer, R8 (Rule 2).

Figure 7-5 *Prefix Advertisement for RR Clients*

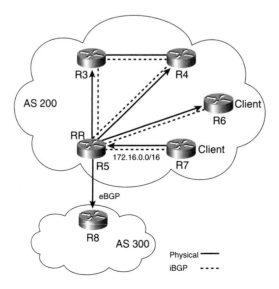

NOTE   If all clients are in the same peer group, an RR reflects the prefix received from a client to
        all clients, including the client that sources the prefix. Route reflection and peer groups are
        discussed later in this chapter.

Clustering

Clustering is introduced to provide redundancy in an RR environment. In a traditional
clustering design, multiple RRs are used to serve one or more clients. These RRs are configured with an identical CLUSTER_ID, which is a 4-byte BGP attribute that commonly
takes the form of an IP address and defaults to the BGP router ID. If two routers share the
same CLUSTER_ID, they belong to the same cluster. An advertisement that bears the same
CLUSTER_ID is ignored by the receiving RR in the same cluster. Example 7-1 shows
the output of **debug ip bgp update** as captured on an RR that has the same CLUSTER_ID
(10.0.0.100) as its peer (192.168.12.1).

Example 7-1   *Updates from an RR That Has the Same CLUSTER_ID Are Denied*

```
*Jul  3 22:48:51.899: BGP: 192.168.12.1 RR in same cluster. Reflected update
  dropped
*Jul  3 22:48:51.899: BGP(0): 192.168.12.1 rcv UPDATE w/ attr: nexthop
  192.168.14.4, origin i, localpref 100, metric 0, originator 192.168.24.4,
  clusterlist 10.0.0.100, path , community , extended community
*Jul  3 22:48:51.899: BGP(0): 192.168.12.1 rcv UPDATE about 11.0.0.0/8 -- DENIED
due to: reflected from the same cluster;
```

Over the years, the concept of RR clustering has been expanded to improve redundancy and
design flexibility. Now an RR cluster can include one or more RRs, each with one or more
clients. Figure 7-6 shows two forms of RR clustering. Routers R1, R2, R3, and R4 form one
cluster, as identified by the CLUSTER_ID of 192.168.1.3. Clients R1 and R2 can use either
R3 or R4 to reach other clusters. Note that because R3 and R4 discard the advertisements
sent to each other, R1 and R2 must form iBGP sessions with both R3 and R4.

Figure 7-6 also shows the other form of RR clustering. Both R5 and R6 have R7 as the
client, but R5 and R6 belong to different clusters. Routers R5 and R7 are in the cluster of
192.168.1.1, whereas routers R6 and R7 are in the cluster of 192.168.1.2. It is acceptable
for a client to be in multiple clusters simultaneously. Router R7 can use either R5 or R6 to
reach the other cluster. Prefixes advertised bctween R5 and R6 are accepted by the receiving
RR because they are not in the same cluster. In this form of clustering, clients must understand RR attributes to prevent potential routing information loops. This can be accomplished by having a certain level of IOS release, such as 12.0 or later. Clustering design
is presented later as an example.

Figure 7-6 *RR Clustering*

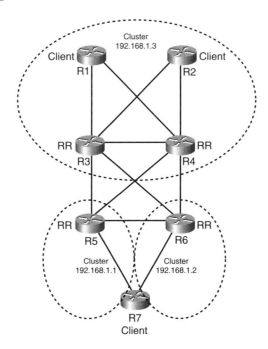

Loop-Prevention Mechanisms

It is important here to differentiate between two types of loops: routing information and routing. With a routing information loop, the reachability information is received and accepted by a router that has advertised the information. This type of loop is relevant to a routing protocol, such as BGP. A routing information loop can cause suboptimal routing and routing loops and can waste system resources. The routing information loop is the primary concern here.

Routing loops, on the other hand, can directly affect the forwarding plane. A routing loop occurs when a device receives the same packets that were originally transmitted from that same device. Routing loops cause IP packets to be sent back and forth among two or more devices, never reaching their final destination. These packets eventually are discarded when TTL reaches 0.

With the easing of the iBGP loop-prevention requirement in the RR environment, there is the potential to develop a routing information loop, which might or might not lead to a routing loop. Figure 7-7 depicts such a configuration, in which three RRs are interconnected. In this hypothetical topology, R3 is made a client of R4, R5 is made client of R3, and R4 is made a client of R5. To alter the best-path selection, the default WEIGHT on R3 is changed to 100 to prefer R4.

Figure 7-7   *Example of a Routing Information Loop with RR*

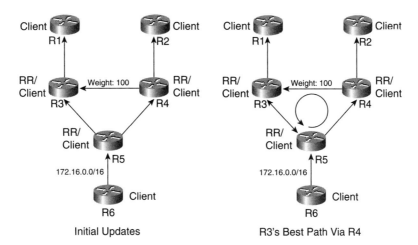

When R5 receives the prefix 172.16.0.0/16 from its client R6, it reflects to both R3 and R4.
The prefix is then reflected from R4 to R3. Now R3 has two paths for the prefix: one from
R5 and one from R4.

The best path is via R4, because R3 prefers the path with a higher WEIGHT. This causes
R3 to withdraw the route sent to R4 and readvertise the new best path to R5 and R1. So R5
receives the same route via R3 that it previously sent to R4. Without a loop-prevention
mechanism, R5 accepts the route and installs it into the BGP RIB, forming a routing
information loop.

To prevent routing information loops in an RR environment, as described in the previous
paragraphs, two BGP path attributes are specifically created: ORIGINATOR_ID and
CLUSTER_LIST.

ORIGINATOR_ID

Chapter 2 explained the ORIGINATOR_ID attribute and how it is set in an RR environment.
This chapter builds on that explanation to focus on how ORIGINATOR_ID prevents loops.

Consider the topology shown in Figure 7-8, in which two RRs of different clusters share
the same client. When the client R5 receives an update for 172.16.0.0/16 from external peer
R6, it readvertises the prefix via iBGP to R3 and R4. In turn, R3 and R4 readvertise the
prefix to each other. Because R3 and R4 are in different clusters (the default behavior in
IOS), the prefix from each other is accepted. Now both R3 and R4 have two paths to the
same destination. Now suppose a higher WEIGHT is set in R3 for the session with R4. R3
prefers the path via R4.

Figure 7-8 *How ORIGINATOR_ID Breaks a Loop*

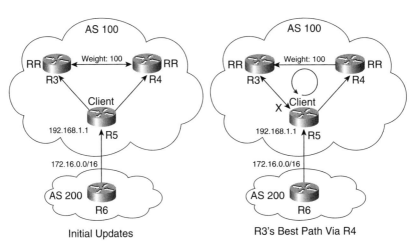

As soon as R3 selects R4 as the best path, it withdraws the route sent to R4. It also sends a new update to R5 to inform it of the new best path. R5 rejects this update from R3 because the update contains R5's ORIGINATOR_ID. Consequently, the loop is prevented.

In an RR environment, the first RR creates the ORIGINATOR_ID attribute and sets it to the BGP router ID of the router that originated the route. In Figure 7-8, R4 sets the ORIGINATOR_ID to R5's router ID, which is 192.168.1.1. This attribute is never modified by subsequent RRs. When R5 receives the update with its own ORIGINATOR_ID, it denies the update, breaking the routing information loop. This is shown in Example 7-2, as captured by the **debug ip bgp update** command.

Example 7-2 *ORIGINATOR_ID Breaks the Routing Information Loop on R5*

```
Local router is the Originator; Discard update
rcv UPDATE about 172.16.0.0/16 -- DENIED due to: ORIGINATOR is us;
```

CLUSTER_LIST

The CLUSTER_LIST is another BGP path attribute that helps break the routing informa-tion loop in an RR environment. It records the cluster in the reverse order the route has traversed. If the local CLUSTER_ID is found in the list, the route is discarded. Unlike the ORIGINATOR_ID, the CLUSTER_LIST is used only by RRs in loop prevention, because a client or nonclient (if it is not an RR itself) has no knowledge of which cluster it belongs to.

NOTE	The CLUSTER_LIST attribute is created or updated on an RR only during reflection—that is, when a route is reflected from one client to another client, from one client to a nonclient, or from a nonclient to a client. If an RR originates a route, the originating RR does not create the CLUSTER_LIST. When an RR advertises a route to an external peer, the existing CLUSTER_LIST is removed. When an RR advertises a route learned from an external peer to a client or nonclient, the RR does not create the CLUSTER_LIST.

Using the same configuration as shown in Figure 7-7, Figure 7-9 shows how the CLUSTER_LIST is used to break a routing information loop in an RR environment. The IP address next to each router is its RID. When R5 reflects the route to R3 and R4, it creates the CLUSTER_LIST with its own CLUSTER_ID, 192.168.1.1. By default, the CLUSTER_ID is the router ID. As R4 reflects the route to R2 and R3, it prepends its own CLUSTER_ID to the list. So at R3, there are two paths—one with a CLUSTER_LIST of 192.168.1.2, 192.168.1.1, and the other with a CLUSTER_LIST of 192.168.1.1. By default, R3 prefers the path with the shortest CLUSTER_LIST (for more information on BGP path selection, refer to Chapter 2), but because the path via R4 has a higher WEIGHT, the best path for R3 is via R4.

Figure 7-9   *How CLUSTER_ID Breaks a Loop*

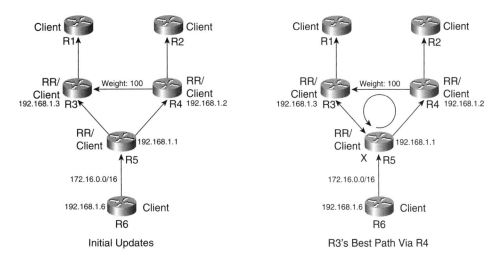

When R3 reflects the best path, it prepends its CLUSTER_ID, 192.168.1.3, to the update. When R5 receives the update, it notices its own CLUSTER_ID in the list, and the update is denied. Example 7-3 shows what happens on R5, as captured by the **debug ip bgp update** command.

Example 7-3 *CLUSTER_LIST Breaks the Loops on R5*

```
Route Reflector cluster loop; Received cluster-id 192.168.1.1
rcv UPDATE w/ attr: nexthop 192.168.1.6, origin i, localpref 100, metric 0,
   originator 192.168.1.6, clusterlist 192.168.1.3 192.168.1.2 0.0.0.0, path,
   community , extended community
rcv UPDATE about 172.16.0.0/16 -- DENIED due to: CLUSTERLIST contains our own
   cluster ID;
```

Hierarchical Route Reflection

Route reflection reduces the total number of iBGP sessions within a domain. However, because RRs must be fully meshed with each other, the potential still exists for a large number of iBGP sessions to be required in a very large network. To further reduce the number of sessions, RR hierarchies can be introduced.

Hierarchical route reflection architecture is characterized by having more than one level of RRs, with lower-level RRs serving as the clients of the RRs that are one level above. There is no limit on the number of levels, but levels of 2 to 3 have proven to make more practical sense. Figure 7-10 shows a two-level RR architecture, where dashed lines represent levels. Level 1 RRs are also clients of Level 2 RRs. Because they are clients themselves, Level 1 RRs do not need to be fully meshed with each other. This reduces the number of iBGP sessions within the domain.

Figure 7-10 *Hierarchical Route Reflection*

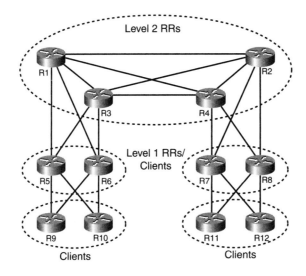

The top-level RRs, Level 2 RRs in Figure 7-10, must be fully meshed, because they are not clients of any RRs. The number of iBGP sessions in this example is 22, compared to 66 in a full mesh.

Rules for prefix advertisement for the hierarchical RRs are the same as for single-level RRs. Figure 7-11 shows an example. The prefix 172.16.0.0/16 is received by two border routers in AS 100. To simplify the discussion, the following focuses on one of the routers, R7.

Figure 7-11 *Prefix Advertisement Using Hierarchical Route Reflection*

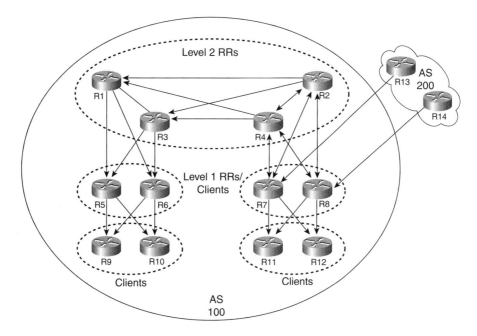

As a Level 1 RR, R7 advertises the prefix to its clients, R11 and R12. At the same time, R7 advertises the prefix to its nonclients, R2 and R4. Routers R2 and R4 reflect the prefix to each other, to the other client, and to other Level 2 RRs. Note that R1 and R3 do not advertise the prefix to each other, because they are regular iBGP peers with respect to the neighbors that advertised the prefix.

As RRs, R1 and R3 further propagate the prefix to their clients, R5 and R6. In turn, R5 and R6 advertise the prefix to their clients, R9 and R10. Now the entire domain is populated with the prefix.

It is important to remember that RRs reflect only the best path—not the entire path information. Even though hierarchical RRs behave the same as single-level RRs in this respect, the impact on path selection is more significant with a multilevel RR structure. For example, R1 in Figure 7-11 receives two paths for the prefix, but based on the BGP attributes and parameters local to the RR, R1 reflects the best path to R5 and R6. The same process occurs for R3. When R5 receives two paths, it evaluates the paths based on path attributes and parameters that are locally available. In turn, it reflects its best path to R9 and R10. If path attributes are not modified and comparable between RRs and clients, there should be no problems. Otherwise, suboptimal routing and route oscillation can occur. Examples of route oscillation because of improper RR designs are provided in the following sections.

So when should you consider using hierarchical route reflection? To answer this question, you should evaluate the following two factors:

- Size of the top-level mesh
- Number of alternative paths

In most cases, the primary concern is the size of the top-level iBGP mesh. If you think that the number of full-mesh sessions is administratively unmanageable, you should probably consider introducing RR hierarchy. As discussed in Chapter 3, "Tuning BGP Performance," the number of BGP peers configured on a router also has performance implications. The exact number of full-mesh sessions might depend on your requirements. The number of alternative paths has a direct impact on load sharing (if iBGP load sharing is enabled) and resource use. More hierarchies reduce the number of load-shared links but require fewer router resources.

Route Reflection Design Examples

This section presents extensive examples to demonstrate the best practices of RR designs and provides possible solutions for each problem.

When designing route reflection architectures, adhere to the following general guidelines:

- Keep logical and physical topologies congruent to increase redundancy and path optimization and to prevent routing loops.
- Use comparable metrics in route selection to avoid convergence oscillations.
- Set proper intra- and intercluster IGP metrics to prevent convergence oscillations.
- Use proper clustering techniques to increase RR redundancy.
- Modify the next hop with care, and do so only to bring RRs into the forwarding path.
- Use peer groups with RRs to reduce convergence time.

Keeping Logical and Physical Topologies Congruent

It is true that iBGP has no requirements for physical topology in building peer relations and forwarding packets as long as the IGP provides the reachability between peers and to the

BGP next hop. Physical topology presents less of an issue in a traditional iBGP environment than in an RR environment, because all the peers are fully meshed and have all the routing information in the domain.

In an RR environment, BGP speakers have only a partial view of the network topology—specifically, the exit paths to the neighboring autonomous systems. Therefore, designing an architecture with congruent logical and physical topologies becomes much more important. The following specific examples demonstrate why:

- Following physical topology
- Session between an RR and a nonclient should not traverse a client
- Session between an RR and its client should not traverse a nonclient

Following the Physical Topology

In an RR environment, it is important to keep physical and logical topologies congruent. When the two topologies are not congruent, several solutions can be considered:

- Changing the physical topology
- Modifying the logical topology
- Following the physical topology

The first solution to consider is changing the physical topology to fit the logical topology and thereby provide an optimal design. However, this solution might not always be acceptable because of circuit cost and geographic limitations.

Another solution is to modify the logical topology to follow the physical topology, perhaps resulting in a design that is less optimal but more cost-efficient. Because network design is often a compromise between various constraints and design goals, a set of possible solutions can be proposed. Which solution is preferable might depend on specific requirements for each problem.

Figure 7-12 shows an example of the need to maintain congruence between the two topologies. Both R1 and R2 are RRs, but their iBGP session goes through a client, R4. If there is any problem in R4 or links from R1 to R2, two RRs and their clients are isolated. One solution (shown in the center topology of Figure 7-12) is to have a direct physical link between R1 and R2.

Another solution is to follow the physical topology, as shown in the right topology in Figure 7-12. In this solution, R4 is an RR, and both R2 and R5 are clients of R4. Note that the session between R4 and R5 does not have a physical link, but because both R2 and R5 are clients and there is no physical redundancy, no additional risk is introduced.

Figure 7-12 *Following the Physical Topology*

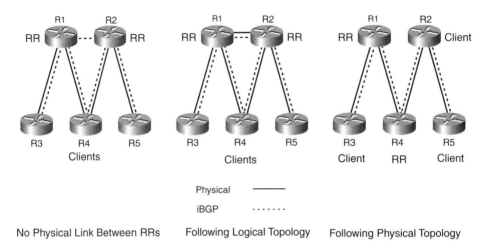

No Physical Link Between RRs   Following Logical Topology   Following Physical Topology

Figure 7-13 is another example of solving a problem by following the physical topology. Although there are redundant iBGP connections for clients to both RRs, there are no redundant physical links. If the physical link between R3 and R1 breaks, for example, R3's iBGP session with R2 also breaks. So the redundant iBGP connections do not really add any redundancy. One solution is to balance the logical connection with a physical link between the client and the redundant RR.

Figure 7-13 *Physical Topology Balances with the Logical Topology*

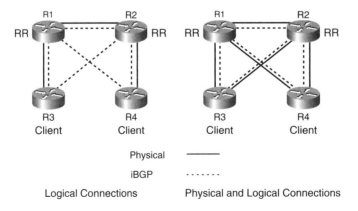

Logical Connections   Physical and Logical Connections

If the original design is used to allow redundant logical connections in an RR cluster (both R1 and R2 are in the same cluster), and additional physical links are not an option, the original design accomplishes the goal, with the caveat of no redundancy for R3 and R4. If R1 and R2 are in different clusters, redundant BGP sessions do not add much value without the physical links. Examples of clustering design are discussed in the following sections.

A Session Between an RR and a Nonclient Should Not Traverse a Client

The problem in Figure 7-14 is similar to that in Figure 7-12, except that the iBGP connection traversing the client is between an RR and a nonclient. Additionally, R2 peers with R4 (a client of R1) via iBGP.

Figure 7-14 *iBGP Session Between a Client and a Nonclient*

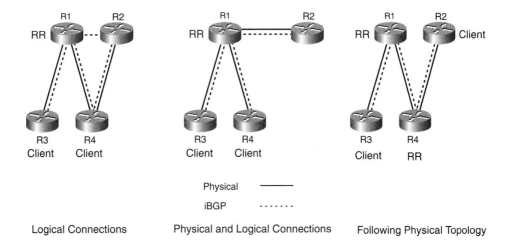

First of all, an iBGP peering between a client and a nonclient is generally not recommended. Because a client acts like a regular iBGP peer to another nonclient (Rule 3), routes received by the client from a nonclient are not advertised to other peers. Additionally, other clients would receive the routing information from RRs, which must peer with nonclients. Extra iBGP sessions also lead to extra paths on the client. Thus, the iBGP session between R2 and R4 is not recommended.

Similar to the problem shown in Figure 7-12, failure of the physical link between R1 and R4 breaks both BGP sessions: the session between R1 and R4 and the one between R1 and R2. This topology is also similar to the one that causes a persistent forwarding loop, as shown later in Figure 7-28.

One solution (as shown in Figure 7-14's center topology) is to move the link between R4 and R2 to between R1 and R2. This solution also removes the iBGP session between R4 and R2.

If the physical topology cannot be changed, another solution is to make R4 an RR and to make R2 a client of R4, as shown in the right topology in Figure 7-14. The session between R1 and R2 is removed.

A Session Between an RR and Its Client Should Not Traverse a Nonclient

In Figure 7-15, the iBGP session between R1 (RR) and R2 (client) traverses a nonclient R4. If inconsistent routing information exists between R4 and R2 (which could happen because clients do not have the complete routing information and RRs might have modified path attributes), packets might be looped. For a hypothetical example, assume that the following are true:

- R3 learns a prefix from an external neighbor and advertises it to R1.

- R2 learns the same prefix from another external peer and advertises it to R1 and R4.

- R1's best path to the prefix is via R3, and it reflects it to R2 and R4.

- R2 selects the path from R1 as the best because of its local administrative policy. Thus, R2 withdraws its previous advertisement to R1.

- R4 selects the path via R2 as the best path because of its local administrative policy.

Figure 7-15 *iBGP Session Between an RR and a Client Traverses a Nonclient*

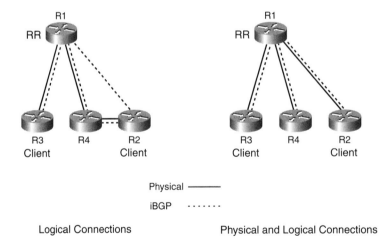

The conflict of BGP next hop between R4 and R2 in this topology leads to a routing loop as packets forwarded from R2 to the prefix are looped back to R2 from R4. One solution is to physically connect R1 and R2, as shown in Figure 7-15's right topology.

Figure 7-16 is another sample topology, in which two RR client sessions traverse non-clients. In this example, R5 is an RR that has two clients, R3 and R8. R6 is an RR that has two clients, R4 and R7. The session between R5 and R8 goes through R7, and the session between R6 and R7 goes through R8.

Figure 7-16 *Persistent Routing Loops*

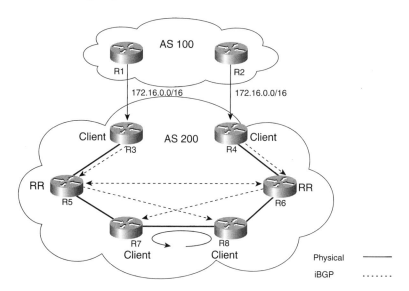

The prefix 172.16.0.0/16 is injected from AS 100 into two border routers in AS 200. Router R3 advertises the prefix to R5, which in turn reflects to R8 and R6. Assuming that R3 sets itself as the next hop, which is a common practice, the next hop for this prefix in R8 is R3. On the other side, R4 does the same thing. Eventually, R7 receives the prefix with the next hop pointing to R4.

When R8 attempts to forward traffic to the destination of 172.16.0.0/16, it looks up the IGP next hop to R3, which is R7. Then R8 forwards the traffic to R7. The same thing would happen in R7, so it would forward the traffic to R8. This forms a persistent routing loop between R7 and R8. The solutions to this problem are the same as previously discussed: Make the physical and logical topologies congruent. To follow logical topology, physical links should be provided between R5 and R6, between R5 and R8, and between R6 and R7. To follow physical topology, make R7 a client only of R5 and R8 a client only of R6.

Using Comparable Inter-AS Metrics in an RR Environment

Using comparable metrics is important for RR designs because RRs reflect only the best path. Anything that affects an RR's best-path selection that is inconsistent with other peers in the AS might cause inconsistent and nondeterministic results. The best example of incomparable metrics is MED. As discussed in Chapter 2, MED is a BGP metric that can be used to influence inter-AS path selection. MED by default is compared only among the paths from the same neighboring AS; thus, MEDs from different autonomous systems are not comparable. Chapter 2 also pointed out that, by default, the order in which paths are received might affect the outcome of the best-path selection. The following example demonstrates how these two default conditions can potentially lead to a persistent convergence oscillation in an RR environment.

Problem Description: Incomparable Inter-AS Metrics

Consider the topology shown in Figure 7-17. The prefix 172.16.0.0/16 is advertised by AS 400 to AS 200 and AS 300. When the prefix reaches R2 in AS 100 from R5, the MED is set to 10. In AS 300, R6 sets a MED of 5 and 6 in updates sent to R3 and R4, respectively, perhaps to influence the inbound traffic from AS 100 to use the R3-R6 link. Within AS 100, R1 is an RR with clients of R2, R3, and R4.

Figure 7-17 *Persistent Convergence Oscillation*

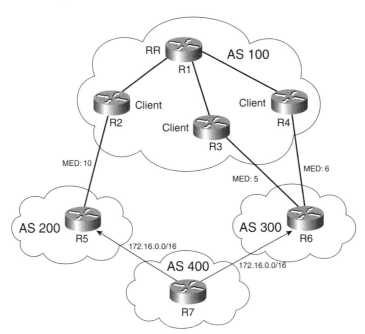

In Figure 7-17, all three border routers—R2, R3, and R4—set **next-hop-self** when announcing the prefix to R1. The values of WEIGHT and LOCAL_PREF are at their defaults. All links have an equal IGP metric of 10.

The neighbor and path information on R1 is shown in Table 7-1. To simplify the discussion, we will focus on R1 and R4 only.

Table 7-1   *Neighbor and Path Information on R1*

BGP Next Hop	Peer RID	AS_PATH	MED
R2	192.168.45.4	200 400	10
R3	192.168.45.5	300 400	5
R4	172.16.67.6	300 400	6

The following describes the steps of prefix advertisement that lead to a persistent convergence loop:

Step 1   All three border routers receive the prefix from their external neighbor. The prefix is installed into each router's BGP RIB, with the information as shown in Table 7-2.

Table 7-2   *Initial BGP Paths on All Three Border Routers*

Router	BGP Next Hop	AS_PATH	MED
R2	R5	200 400	10
R3	R6	300 400	5
R4	R6	300 400	6

Step 2   All three border routers advertise the prefix via iBGP to R1, as shown in Figure 7-18 (to simplify the figure, only routers in AS 100 are shown). The router R1 now has three paths for the prefix, as shown in Table 7-3. Note that the most recent path is listed at the top and the oldest path is listed at the bottom, assuming that the path from R3 is received first, followed by paths from R2 and R4.

NOTE   In the tables in this chapter, the best path is indicated with an asterisk (*).

Figure 7-18 *Prefix Propagation in Step 2*

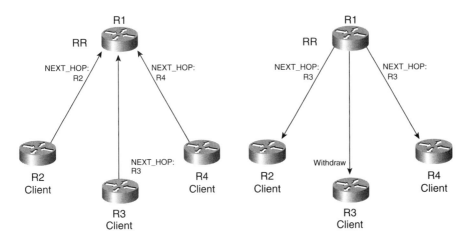

Table 7-3 *Initial Paths in R1*

Path	BGP Next Hop	AS_PATH	MED	RID
1	R4	300 400	6	172.16.67.6
2	R2	200 400	10	192.168.45.4
3*	R3	300 400	5	192.168.45.5

Using the steps described in Chapter 2, R1 selects the path via R3 as the best path. Here is what happens:

(a) R1 compares the top two paths.

(b) Because the paths are from different neighboring autonomous systems, MED is not compared.

(c) The tiebreaker is the router ID (RID). Because R4 has a lower RID, it is determined to be the better of the first two.

(d) R1 compares Path 1 and Path 3. Path 3 is determined to be the better path because it has a lower MED.

(e) R1 reflects its best path to its clients.

(f) Because the best path is via R3, R1 sends a withdraw message to R3 for the route.

(g) Routers R2 and R4 receive the path with R3 as the BGP next hop.

Prefix propagation is shown in Figure 7-18.

Step 3   With the new update from R1 and its previous path, R4 now has two paths to the prefix, as shown in Table 7-4. Path 1 is selected as the best path because it has a lower MED. Because of this selection, R4 must withdraw the route sent to R1, as shown in Figure 7-19.

Table 7-4   *New Path Information on R4*

Path	BGP Next Hop	AS_PATH	MED
1*	R3	300 400	5
2	R6	300 400	6

Figure 7-19   *Prefix Propagation in Steps 3 and 4*

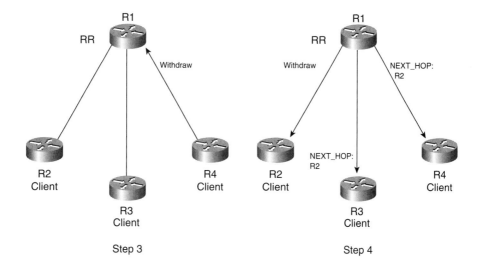

Step 4   After receiving the withdrawal message, R1 removes the path from R4. Now R1 has only two paths left, as shown in Table 7-5.

Table 7-5   *New Paths on R1*

Path	BGP Next Hop	AS_PATH	MED	RID
1	R2	200 400	10	192.168.45.4
2*	R3	300 400	5	192.168.45.5

Because the removed path is not the best path, BGP does not recalculate the best path yet. So Path 2 is still the best path. When the BGP scanner runs, the path-selection process is started. Because R2 has a lower RID, Path 1 is selected as the new best path.

Now R1 needs to update its clients about the new best path. So it sends updates to R3 and R4. For R2, it sends a withdrawal message. This is shown in Figure 7-19.

Step 5 With the new update from R1, R4 has a new BGP RIB, as shown in Table 7-6. Because Path 2 is learned via an external neighbor (R6), it is selected as the best path. Next, R4 sends the new path information to R1, as shown in Figure 7-20.

Table 7-6 *New Path Information on R4*

Path	BGP Next Hop	AS_PATH	MED
1	R2	200 400	10
2*	R6	300 400	6

Figure 7-20 *Prefix Propagation in Steps 5 and 6*

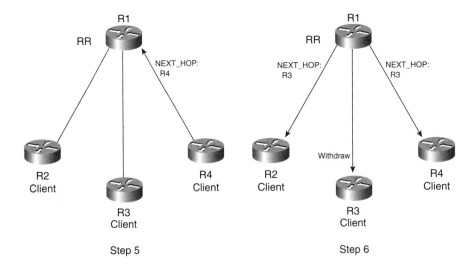

Step 6 After receiving the new update from R4, R1 now has three paths in its BGP RIB, as shown in Table 7-7. It steps through the path-selection process and selects Path 3 as the best path. Now R1 sends updates to its clients, as shown in Figure 7-20. Note that this is the same RIB as shown

in Step 2. What happens next is the same as what happened in Steps 2 through 6. This cycle continues indefinitely.

Table 7-7 *New Paths on R1*

Path	BGP Next Hop	AS_PATH	MED	RID
1	R4	300 400	6	172.16.67.6
2	R2	200 400	10	192.168.45.4
3*	R3	300 400	5	192.168.45.5

The problem of persistent convergence loops can be identified by observing the following two events:

- Ever-increasing BGP table version. Whenever there is a best-path change, the BGP table version is incremented.

- Constant next-hop change in the IP RIB for the destination. When there is a BGP best-path change, the IP RIB is updated with a new next hop.

Solutions to Incomparable Inter-AS Metrics

Because this problem is inherent in the architecture and the protocol, solutions have to come from design workarounds. Several options can be implemented individually or combined:

- Use a full iBGP mesh
- Enable **always-compare-med**
- Enable a **deterministic-MED** comparison
- Reset MEDs to 0s
- Use communities

These five solutions are explored in the following sections.

Using Full iBGP Mesh   When full mesh is used, all iBGP routers have the complete routing information, and a convergence loop is not formed. However, this option might be unacceptable if RRs were selected in the first place to increase scalability.

Enabling **always-compare-MED**   When MED is compared among all neighboring autonomous systems, the path with the lowest MED always wins. In Figure 7-17, for example, AS 100 will always prefer the path via R3. However, this **always-compare-MED** option has a couple issues:

- MEDs from different autonomous systems might not always be comparable. Making a comparison requires close coordination among all peering autonomous systems to associate the MED with consistent and meaningful metrics.

- Always preferring the path with the lowest MED might not be optimal, because this does not take into account the intra-AS topology. For example, R4 needs to forward traffic destined for 172.16.0.0/16 via R1 to R3 instead of directly to R6.

Enabling a **deterministic-MED** Comparison   When **deterministic-MED** is enabled, the order in which the paths are received is unimportant. (For more information, refer to Chapter 2.) Path selection is affected in Steps 2 and 3, as described in the section "Problem Description: Incomparable Inter-AS Metrics."

Table 7-8 shows the new BGP RIB on R1. Path 1 becomes the best path because it has a lower RID than Path 2. Now the path via R2 is sent to R4.

Table 7-8   *Initial Paths on R1*

Path	BGP Next Hop	AS_PATH	MED	RID
1*	R2	200 400	10	192.168.45.4
2	R3	300 400	5	192.168.45.5
3	R4	300 400	6	172.16.67.6

Step 7   Table 7-9 shows the new BGP RIB on R4. Path 2 is the best path because it is external.

Table 7-9   *New Path Information on R4*

Path	BGP Next Hop	AS_PATH	MED
1	R2	200 400	10
2*	R6	300 400	6

Notice that the best paths on R1 and R4 are not affected by new updates. So there is no best path oscillation. Because there is no negative impact, it is almost always a good practice to enable **deterministic-MED** in a network.

Resetting MEDs to 0s   One common solution for removing the impact of MED altogether on path selection is to reset incoming MEDs to 0s. Configurations are typically made on the edge of the network as updates are received from other autonomous systems.

Example 7-4 shows a configuration sample for R4 (only relevant commands are shown). An inbound route map named Med-reset is configured on R4's session with R6 (IP address 192.168.46.6). The route map resets MED to 0. Because similar configurations are made on R2 and R3, R1 has a consistent metric (0) in path selection.

Example 7-4 *BGP Configuration to Reset MED to 0 on R4*

```
neighbor 192.168.46.6 remote-as 300
neighbor 192.168.46.6 route-map Med-reset in
!
route-map Med-reset permit 10
 set metric 0
```

Using Communities   When communities are used to set BGP policies, MEDs are reset on the border routers, and the routing policy can be derived from the inbound community values. This effectively removes MED's impact. Because community is not evaluated in the path selection, a scheme of community values versus routing preference settings should be created and communicated to administrators of the neighboring autonomous systems. Chapter 9, "Service Provider Architecture," discusses how to design a coherent routing policy based on BGP communities.

Setting Proper IGP Metrics in an RR Environment

In the previous example, you learned that inconsistent inter-AS metric (MED) can cause persistent convergence loops. In this section, you will see that improper IGP metrics can also lead to persistent convergence loops in an RR environment.

In iBGP best-path selection, IGP metrics are often one of the tiebreakers. In a multicluster RR architecture, IGP metrics should be set in such a way that intracluster metrics are lower than intercluster metrics, which allows an RR to select an intracluster path over an intercluster path. Failure to set IGP metrics properly might lead to persistent convergence oscillation.

Problem Description: Improper IGP Metrics

Figure 7-21 shows a topology that potentially leads to an infinite convergence loop. This topology is similar to that shown in Figure 7-17, except that the IGP metrics are different and AS 100 has two RR clusters.

Figure 7-21 *Persistent Convergence Oscillation with Improper IGP Metrics*

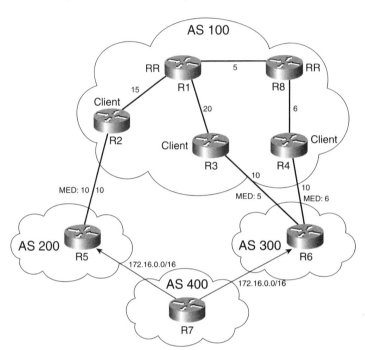

The following steps describe the process that leads to the convergence loop:

Step 1   All three border routers in AS 100 announce 172.16.0.0/16 with **next-hop-self**. The neighbor and path information is shown in Table 7-10.

Table 7-10   *Neighbor and Path Information on Three Border Routers*

Router	BGP Next Hop	AS_PATH	MED
R2	R5	200 400	10
R3	R6	300 400	5
R4	R6	300 400	6

Step 2   Initially, R1 has two paths in its BGP RIB, as shown in Table 7-11. The IGP metric is the cumulative link metric from the router to the BGP next hop.

Table 7-11   *Initial Paths on R1*

BGP Next Hop	AS_PATH	MED	IGP Metric
R2	200 400	10	15
R3	300 400	5	20

The initial BGP RIB on R8 is shown in Table 7-12.

Table 7-12   *Initial Path on R8*

BGP Next Hop	AS_PATH	MED	IGP Metric
R4	300 400	6	6

Step 3   With the update from R8, R1 has three paths, as shown in Table 7-13. To determine the best path, R1 first compares Path 1 and Path 2. Path 1 wins because it has a lower IGP metric. Then Path 1 is compared to Path 3, and Path 3 wins because it has a lower MED.

Table 7-13   *BGP Paths on R1*

Path	BGP Next Hop	AS_PATH	MED	IGP Metric
1	R4	300 400	6	11
2	R2	200 400	10	15
3[*]	R3	300 400	5	20

The best path is updated to all R1's neighbors, as shown in Figure 7-22. For R3, R1 sends a withdrawal message.

Figure 7-22 *Prefix Propagation in Steps 3 and 4*

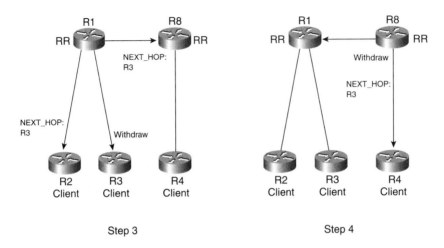

Step 3   Step 4

Step 4   Table 7-14 shows the new BGP RIB of R8. Path 1 is the best path because it has a lower MED. Figure 7-22 shows the updates sent to neighbors from R8. Because the path via R1 becomes the best path, R8 sends a withdrawal message to R1.

Table 7-14   *BGP Paths on R8*

Path	BGP Next Hop	AS_PATH	MED	IGP Metric
1*	R3	300 400	5	25
2	R4	300 400	6	6

Step 5   Table 7-15 shows the BGP RIB on R4. Path 1 is best because it has a lower MED. This causes R4 to send a withdrawal message to R8, as shown in Figure 7-23.

Table 7-15   *BGP Paths on R4*

Path	BGP Next Hop	AS_PATH	MED	IGP Metric
1*	R3	300 400	5	31
2	R6	300 400	6	10

Figure 7-23 *Prefix Propagation in Steps 5 and 6*

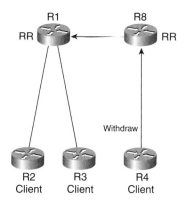

Step 5

Step 6 Table 7-16 shows the current BGP RIB on R8.

Table 7-16 *BGP Paths on R8*

Path	BGP Next Hop	AS_PATH	MED	IGP Metric
1*	R3	300 400	5	25

Step 7 Table 7-17 shows the new BGP RIB on R1. Path 1 is the best path because it has a lower IGP metric. Now R1 updates its neighbors with the new best path, as shown in Figure 7-24. Because R2 is the next hop, R1 sends a withdrawal message.

Table 7-17 *BGP Paths on R1*

Path	BGP Next Hop	AS_PATH	MED	IGP Metric
1*	R2	200 400	10	15
2	R3	300 400	5	20

Figure 7-24 *Prefix Propagation in Steps 7 and 8*

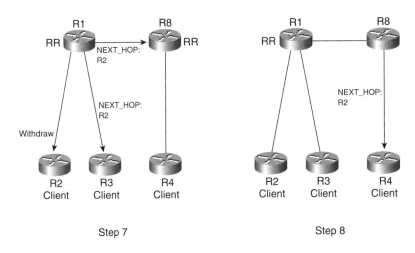

Step 7   Step 8

Step 8   The current BGP RIB on R8 is shown in Table 7-18. Next, R8 updates
R4 with the new path, as shown in Figure 7-24.

Table 7-18   *BGP Paths on R8*

Path	BGP Next Hop	AS_PATH	MED	IGP Metric
1*	R2	200 400	10	20

Step 9   With the new update from R8, the BGP RIB on R4 is shown in Table 7-19.
The best path is Path 2 because it is an external route. Next, R4 sends the
update to R8, as shown in Figure 7-25.

Table 7-19   *BGP Paths on R4*

Path	BGP Next Hop	AS_PATH	MED	IGP Metric
1	R2	200 400	10	26
2*	R6	300 400	6	10

Figure 7-25 *Prefix Propagation in Steps 9 and 10*

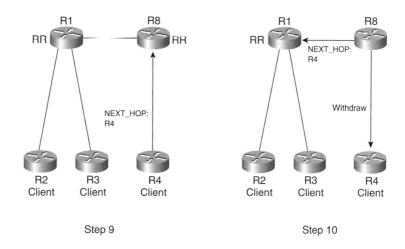

Step 10 Table 7-20 shows the updated BGP RIB on R8. Path 1 is the best because it has a lower IGP metric. Next, R8 sends updates to its neighbors, as shown in Figure 7-25.

Table 7-20 *BGP Paths on R8*

Path	BGP Next Hop	AS_PATH	MED	IGP Metric
1*	R4	300 400	6	6
2	R2	200 400	10	20

Step 11 With the update from R8, R1 now has three paths, as shown in Table 7-21. Notice that this is exactly the same BGP RIB as described in Step 3. From here, the same convergence cycle starts over again and continues indefinitely.

Table 7-21 *BGP Paths on R1*

Path	BGP Next Hop	AS_PATH	MED	IGP Metric
1	R4	300 400	6	11
2	R2	200 400	10	15
3*	R3	300 400	5	20

Solutions to Improper IGP Metrics

Of the several solutions possible, all but one were described in the section "Using Comparable Inter-AS Metrics in an RR Environment." The additional solution is to set proper IGP metrics. Because the result of enabling **deterministic-med** is more complex, this section focuses on these two solutions.

Enforcing Proper IGP Metric Settings   To set IGP metrics according to rules stated earlier (intracluster metrics are lower than intercluster metrics), the IGP metric between R1 and R8 is increased from 5 to 50. Now let's walk through the convergence steps again to see what happens:

Step 1   Each of the three border routers in AS 100 (refer to Figure 7-21) receives the prefix from external neighbors and announces the prefix internally with the next hop set to itself.

Step 2   The prefix is advertised from R2 and R3 to R1 and also from R4 to R8 to R1.

Step 3   The BGP RIB for R1 is given in Table 7-22. Path 1 is compared to Path 2, and Path 2 is found to be better because it has a lower IGP metric. Path 2 is then compared to Path 3, and Path 2 is found to be the best again because of the lower metric. Now R1 updates its neighbors with the new best path.

Table 7-22   *BGP Paths on R1*

Path	BGP Next Hop	AS_PATH	MED	IGP Metric
1	R4	300 400	6	56
2*	R2	200 400	10	15
3	R3	300 400	5	20

Step 4   Table 7-23 shows the new BGP RIB on R8. Path 2 is the best because it has a lower IGP metric. Thus, the best path on R8 is unaffected by the new update from R1.

Table 7-23   *BGP Paths on R8*

Path	BGP Next Hop	AS_PATH	MED	IGP Metric
1	R2	200 400	10	65
2*	R4	300 400	6	6

Step 5   The BGP RIB on R4 is unaffected, because R8 prefers the path via R4, so R4 still has only one entry, as shown in Table 7-24.

Table 7-24   *BGP Paths on R4*

Path	BGP Next Hop	AS_PATH	MED	IGP Metric
1[*]	R6	300 400	6	10

Step 6   For Step 6 and beyond, there is no best-path change. The network is converged. The best path for each router is shown in Figure 7-26. The arrows indicate the packet-forwarding direction. For example, the best path for R1 is consistently via R2.

Figure 7-26   *Packet Forwarding Directions with the Best Paths*

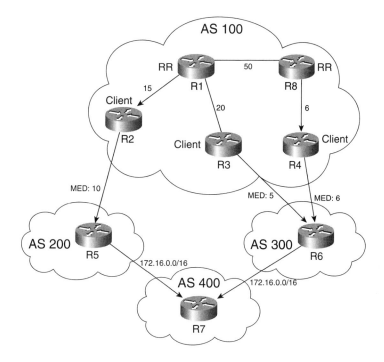

Enabling the **deterministic-MED** Option   The best path in this section is modified using a few steps from the previous scenario. The following steps describe the process:

Step 1   Each of the three border routers in AS 100 receives the prefix from external neighbors and announces the prefix internally with the next hop set to itself, respectively.

Step 2 The prefix is advertised from R2 and R3 to R1 and also from R4 to R8 to R1.

Step 3 Table 7-25 shows the new BGP RIB on R1. When comparing Path 2 and Path 3, the best path is Path 2, because it has a lower MED. Path 1 is the best path because it has a lower IGP metric than Path 2. Next, R1 updates its neighbors with information on this new best path.

Table 7-25 *BGP Paths on R1*

Path	BGP Next Hop	AS_PATH	MED	IGP Metric
1*	R2	200 400	10	15
2	R3	300 400	5	20
3	R4	300 400	6	11

Step 4 Table 7-26 shows the BGP RIB on R8. The best path is Path 2 because it has a lower IGP metric.

Table 7-26 *BGP Paths on R8*

Path	BGP Next Hop	AS_PATH	MED	IGP Metric
1	R2	200 400	10	20
2*	R4	300 400	6	6

No other steps are needed, because the network is now converged. The best path for each router is the same as shown in Figure 7-26.

Clustering Design

Proper clustering is very important to provide desired redundancy in an RR-based architecture. Consider the topology on the left side of Figure 7-27, in which two RRs use the same cluster ID. When the prefix 172.16.0.0/16 is advertised from R4, two RRs advertise to R1 and to each other. However, the updates between RRs are discarded because they are in the same cluster.

Obviously two RRs provide redundancy to clients, but is that enough? The answer depends on how RRs are configured, as explained in this section. R1 has two BGP paths to the destination—one learned from R2 and the other learned from R3. Between the two paths, R1 picks one best path—perhaps the path via R2 (it does not make any difference for this discussion which path is the best path).

Figure 7-27 *RR Clustering Design*

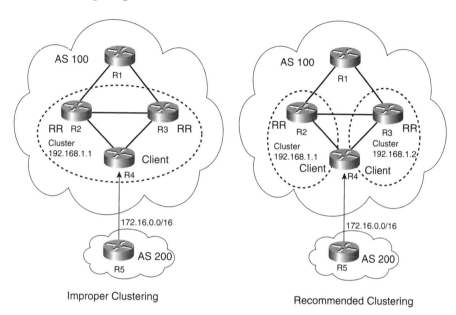

Now assume that the BGP next hop can be reached via two equal-cost IGP paths. R1 load-shares the packets using these two IGP paths. So far everything is fine. Now assume that the iBGP session between R4 and R3 is down, perhaps due to misconfiguration or administrative shutdown. While R2 continues to forward the traffic as before, the traffic via R3 is discarded because it has no path for the prefix, even though the physical link between R3 and R4 is still functioning. This results in about 50% packet loss.

To correct the problem, consider the design on the right of Figure 7-27. In this design, two RRs are in different clusters. In the case of iBGP session failure between R4 and R3, R3 continues to forward the traffic, because the prefix is also learned from R2. This design not only provides physical redundancy against a link failure but also provides logical redundancy against a failure of the iBGP session between a client and an RR. Note however that this design leads to more memory use due to the extra path.

Resetting the Next Hop

An iBGP speaker, including an RR, is required to preserve BGP attributes such as NEXT_HOP. The requirement is put in place to avoid routing loops when attributes are incorrectly modified. Consider the topology shown in Figure 7-28. When the prefix 172.16.0.0/16 is advertised to R1 (an RR), R2 sets itself as the BGP next hop, because it is configured with

next-hop-self. When R1 reflects the route to R3 and R4, suppose it resets the next hop to itself. R4 forwards the traffic to the destination of 172.16.0.0/16 to R1. Because R1 and R2 are not physically connected (an improper design, as indicated before), R1 forwards the packet to R2 via R4. This results in a routing loop.

Figure 7-28 *Improper Next-Hop Setting Leads to Routing Loops*

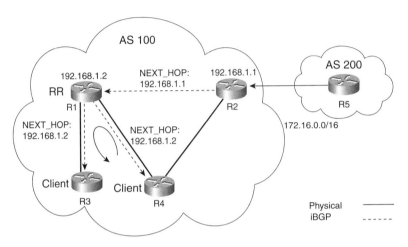

NOTE	The topology shown in Figure 7-28 uses an RR design that does not follow the basic RR design guidelines that were discussed previously. The topology is used here to demonstrate the importance of proper next-hop settings.

Under certain conditions, however, it might be desirable to reset the BGP next hop on RRs. One example is to bring RRs into the forwarding path. IOS provides methods to accomplish this. The following discusses how this can be done.

Basically, you can use two methods to set the BGP next hop at an RR:

- **neighbor next-hop-self** command
- Outbound route map

If the routes are learned from an external peer, you can reset next hops on RRs by using **next-hop-self** or an outbound route map to clients and nonclients. Note that RRs here are border routers. Figure 7-29 shows an example.

Figure 7-29 *Next-Hop Setting for Routes Learned from an External Neighbor*

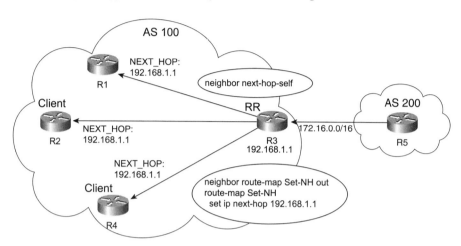

If routes are learned from an internal neighbor (nonclient or client), the next hop can be reset on RRs only using an outbound route map. Under this condition, the command neighbor next-hop-self is ignored. Figure 7-30 shows an example.

Figure 7-30 *Next-Hop Setting for Routes Learned from an Internal Neighbor*

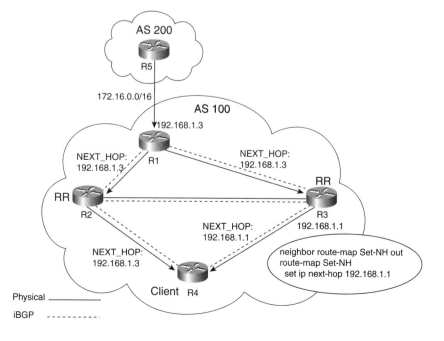

R1 receives the prefix 172.16.0.0/16 from an external peer, R5. The next hop is reset at R1 to itself, and the prefix is advertised to R2 and R3. Both R2 and R3 are RRs in different clusters, with R4 as a client. When R3 reflects the route to its client R4, it resets itself as the BGP next hop. This is accomplished in an outbound route map Set-NH. On R2, no next-hop reset is configured.

As a client to both R2 and R3, R4 receives two paths for the prefix. The path from R3 has the next hop set to R3, and the path from R2 has the next hop set to R1. So R4 uses the link with R3 to forward the traffic for the prefix (because of a lower IGP metric to the BGP next hop), unless the link between R4 and R3 is down or R3 fails. In both cases, R4 forwards the traffic to R2, which sends it to R1 to exit AS 100.

Two points deserve further discussion. First, what is the benefit of resetting the next hop at R3? Without the next hop reset, R4 might choose the link to R2 to forward traffic to 172.16.0.0/16. Suppose the policy dictates that the path via R3 is to be used for R4 during normal operation for one of the following reasons:

- The link between R3 and R4 has higher bandwidth or lower cost.
- The link between R2 and R4 has lower bandwidth or higher cost.
- The link between R1 and R2 is overutilized.

Resetting the next hop on R3 is one way to force the traffic to take the path via R3 (although changing the IGP metric might also accomplish the goal).

The second significant point is that the distinction between the two methods of setting the next hop is important, because RRs often set **next-hop-self** for externally learned routes. With that distinction, the next hop is not modified if routes are from an iBGP peer unless an outbound route map specifically changes it.

CAUTION Modifying next hops of iBGP routes at RRs using an outbound route map can cause routing loops. Use this feature with care.

Route Reflection with Peer Groups

The peer-group concept was discussed in Chapter 3 as a technique to increase update generation efficiency and thus shorten convergence time. This section does not restate the benefits of peer groups. Instead, it focuses on the peer-group behavior in an RR-based architecture.

All members of the peer group inherit the same outbound policy/updates. Likewise, all members of the peer group receive the same updates—even the original client that sources the prefix. Before Cisco IOS Release 12.0, peer groups cannot be used on RRs unless client-to-client reflection is turned off and all clients are fully meshed. This restriction can be explained by the following example. In Figure 7-31, the prefix 172.16.0.0/16 is advertised to R3 (RR) via two paths: through R1 (nonclient) and through R2 (client).

Figure 7-31 *Peer Groups with RR Before IOS 12.0*

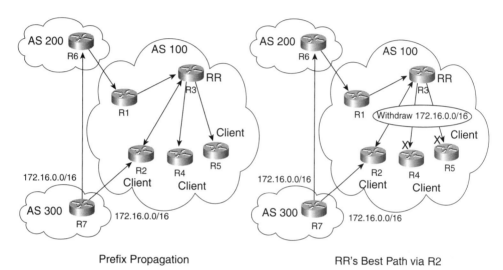

Prefix Propagation   RR's Best Path via R2

Assume that R3's best path is via R2 because it is a shorter AS_PATH. Because all clients are in the same peer group, R3 reflects the best path to all members of the peer group, including R2. Because the best path is via R2, R3 also needs to withdraw the route from R2. When all clients are in a peer group, R3 ends up sending the withdrawal message to R4 and R5 as well. This prefix is removed from the BGP RIB in R4 and R5. If R2, R4, and R5 are fully meshed and the default client-to-client reflection on R3 is turned off, R4 and R5 receive the prefix from R2 directly.

With Cisco IOS Release 12.0 and later versions, the restriction just described is lifted, because clients understand the RR-related attributes. When RR needs to withdraw a route from a client in a peer group, it does not send the withdrawal message. Instead, it sends the current best path to all its clients. At that point, all other members of the peer group are properly updated with the prefix. When R2 receives the update, it detects its own ORIGINATOR_ID and discards the update, as shown in Figure 7-32.

Figure 7-32 *Peer Groups with RR for IOS 12.0 or Later*

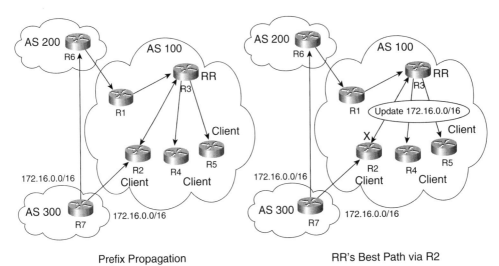

Prefix Propagation   RR's Best Path via R2

Confederation

As indicated in the previous section, route reflection solves the iBGP scalability issue by relaxing the iBGP advertisement rule for RRs. These routers can reflect routes between clients they serve and other iBGP peers; thus, clients need to peer only with RRs. Confederation approaches the same issue from a different angle. This section discusses various aspects of confederation and its design guidelines.

How Confederation Works

Confederation solves the full iBGP mesh issue by splitting a large AS into a number of smaller autonomous systems, called *member autonomous systems* or *subautonomous systems*. Because eBGP sessions are used among member autonomous systems, no full mesh is required. Within each member AS, however, the iBGP full-mesh requirement still applies.

The eBGP session within a confederation is slightly different from a regular eBGP session. To differentiate between the two, this type of eBGP session is called an *intraconfederation eBGP session*. When the session is initially brought up, it behaves exactly like an eBGP session. In other words, no verification is made on both peers to determine if the session is a true eBGP or confederation eBGP session. The difference comes in when propagating prefixes over the sessions. The intraconfederation eBGP session follows iBGP rules for prefix advertisement in some regards and eBGP rules in others. For example, NEXT_HOP, MED, and LOCAL_PREF are preserved, yet AS_PATH is modified when sending the updates.

To the external neighbors (peers outside the confederation), the sub-AS topology is invisible. That is, the AS_PATH modified within the confederation is stripped in updates sent to eBGP neighbors. To other autonomous systems, a confederation appears as a single AS.

Within each member AS, full iBGP mesh is required. Route reflection can also be deployed. One distinct advantage of confederation is that there is no requirement that member autonomous systems use the same IGP. It is not necessary for each member AS to reveal its internal topology to other member autonomous systems. When different IGPs are used, however, BGP next-hop reachability must be guaranteed within each member AS.

Figure 7-33 shows an example of confederation. A confederation has three types of peerings:

- External peerings, such as between R10 and R12
- Confederation external peerings, such as between R4 and R8
- Internal peerings, such as between R5 and R6 or R5 and R7

Figure 7-33 *BGP Confederation*

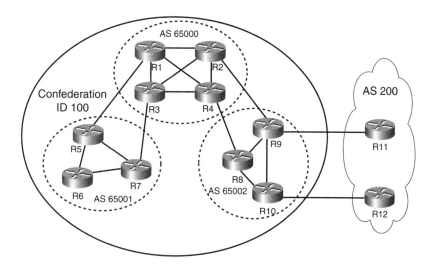

Special Treatment of AS_PATH

The loop-prevention mechanism inside a confederation is based on the AS_PATH attribute. Confederation introduces two new AS_PATH segment types:

- **AS_CONFED_SEQUENCE**—An ordered set of member AS numbers in the local confederation that the route has traversed.

- **AS_CONFED_SET**—An unordered set of member AS numbers in the local confederation that the route has traversed.

NOTE   In Cisco IOS software, member AS numbers are enclosed in parentheses in the output of **show ip bgp**.

How AS_PATH is updated within a confederation depends on the type of sessions. Figure 7-34 shows AS_PATH changes for three types of peerings (to simplify the figure, only one-way advertisement is shown):

Intraconfederation eBGP session—The member AS number is prepended to the AS_CONFED_SEQUENCE of the AS_PATH, such as from R4 to R2.

Internal BGP session—The AS_PATH is not modified, as in the path from R2 to R1.

External BGP session—The member AS numbers are removed from the AS_PATH, and the confederation number is prepended to the AS_PATH, as shown in the path from R3 to R6.

Figure 7-34 *AS_PATH with BGP Confederation*

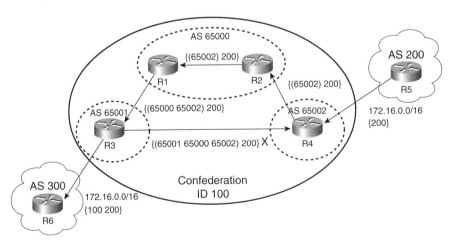

In confederation, the segments of AS_CONFED in the AS_PATH are used to prevent routing information loops among member autonomous systems. When R3 sends an update about 172.16.0.0/16 back to R4, the update is denied because 65002 is already present in the path.

Special Treatment of Communities

Chapter 2 discussed four types of well-known communities. Of the four, the LOCAL_AS well-known community applies to BGP confederations. Figure 7-35 demonstrates how these well-known communities can be used to set BGP policies in a confederation environment.

Figure 7-35 *Well-Known Communities Within BGP Confederation*

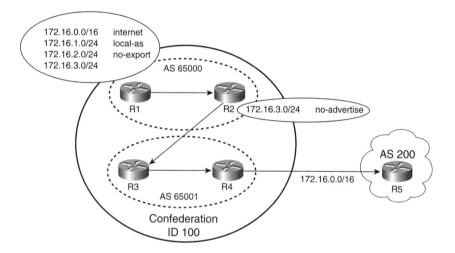

When four prefixes are advertised from R1 to R2 within the confederation member AS 65000, three well-known communities are attached to three prefixes, respectively. The community is not set for the fourth one.

The prefix 172.16.0.0/16 has a community value of **internet**; thus, no restriction is placed on the prefix. The prefix is received by R2, R3, R4, and R5.

The community for prefix 172.16.1.0/24 is **local-as**; thus, R2 does not advertise the prefix to AS 65001. This prefix is not seen on R3, R4, and R5.

Because the community for 172.16.2.0/24 is **no-export**, R2 advertises the prefix to R3. In turn, R3 advertises the prefix to R4, which does not advertise it to R5.

When the prefix 172.16.3.0/24 is advertised from R2 to R3, a community of **no-advertise** is attached to it. When R3 receives the prefix, it does not advertise the prefix further to R4. Thus, the prefix is not known on R4 and R5.

Confederation External and Confederation Internal Routes

A *confederation external route* is a route received from a confederation external peer, whereas a *confederation internal route* is received from an internal peer. From a path-selection perspective, there is no distinction between the two.

Private AS Numbers

The member AS numbers used within the confederation are never visible from outside the confederation. Thus, a private AS number (ranging from 64512 through 65535) is typically, but not necessarily, used to identify the member AS inside a confederation without the need to coordinate AS number assignment with an official AS delegation authority. In IOS, all member AS numbers are removed automatically at confederation borders, so no manual configuration is needed to remove the member AS number.

Confederation Design Examples

When designing a confederation architecture, you should follow certain guidelines to reduce complexity and routing issues. This section presents the following two design examples:

- Hub-and-spoke architecture
- Setting the proper IGP metrics for confederations

Hub-and-Spoke Architecture

A *hub-and-spoke confederation architecture* is one that has one member AS as the backbone and that also acts as a transit sub-AS that connects to all the other member autonomous systems. Figure 7-36 shows an example of this architecture, in which AS 65000 is the backbone transit AS for the confederation 100.

The benefits of this architecture are as follows:

- None of the other subautonomous systems have to be connected directly to each other, which reduces the number of intraconfederation eBGP sessions.
- The hub-and-spoke confederation results in a predictable and consistent AS_PATH within the confederation. For traffic from one nontransit member AS to any other nontransit member, autonomous systems always take two AS hops. For example, traffic from AS 65002 takes two hops to AS 65001, 65003, or 65004.

Figure 7-36 *Hub-and-Spoke Confederation Design*

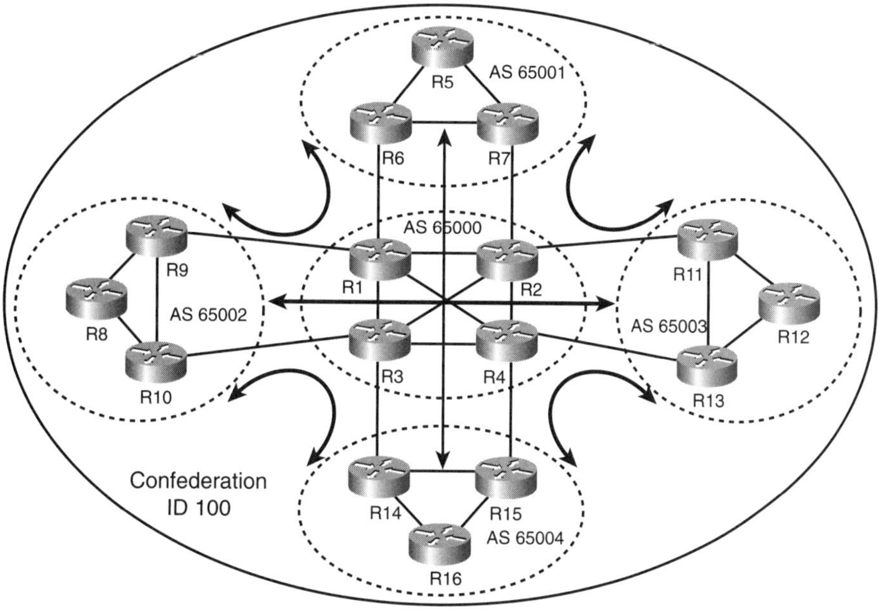

Setting Proper IGP Metrics for Confederations

The impact of IGP metrics on path selection in a confederation environment is quite similar to that in an RR-based environment that deploys multiple clusters, where MEDs are used to choose paths. In such an environment, IGP metrics should be set so that IGP metrics within the member AS are lower than those between them, which allows the router to prefer an intra-sub-AS path over an inter-sub-AS in path selection. Failure to set IGP metrics in this way might lead to persistent convergence oscillation.

Problem Description: Improper IGP Metrics Within Confederations

Figure 7-37 shows a topology that might lead to convergence oscillation in a confederation. IGP metrics are given for each link in confederation 100. Other routing information is similar to that shown in Figure 7-21. The problem description in this section is almost identical to that presented in the section "Problem Description: Improper IGP Metrics," because a member AS is quite similar to an RR cluster in terms of path selection. The only exception is AS_PATH. With confederation, sub-AS numbers are inserted into the AS_PATH sent to intraconfederation eBGP peers. However, the best path is not affected, because sub-AS is not considered in the path selection. This is why the process and the outcome are the same as in the previous cases involving RR clusters.

Figure 7-37 *Persistent Convergence Oscillation with Improper IGP Metrics in Confederation*

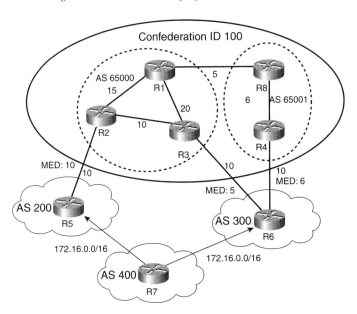

The following steps briefly describe the process that leads to persistent convergence oscillation:

Step 1   All three border routers in Confederation 100 announce 172.16.0.0/16 with next-hop-self. The neighbor and path information is shown in Table 7-27. The IGP metric is the cumulative link metric from the router to the BGP next hop.

Table 7-27 *Neighbor and Path Information from Three Border Routers*

Router	BGP Next Hop	AS_PATH	MED	IGP Metric
R2	R5	200 400	10	10
R3	R6	300 400	5	10
R4	R6	300 400	6	10

Step 2   Initially, R1 has two paths in its BGP RIB, as shown in Table 7-28.

Table 7-28 *Initial Paths on R1*

BGP Next Hop	AS_PATH	MED	IGP Metric
R2	200 400	10	15
R3	300 400	5	20

The initial BGP RIB on R8 is shown in Table 7-29.

Table 7-29   *Initial Path on R8*

BGP Next Hop	AS_PATH	MED	IGP Metric
R4	300 400	6	6

Step 3   With the update from R8, R1 has three paths, as shown in Table 7-30. To determine the best path, R1 compares Path 1 and Path 2 first. Path 1 wins because it has a lower IGP metric. Note that the member AS number is not considered in path selection. So for path selection, Path 1 and Path 2 have the same AS_PATH length. Then Path 1 is compared to Path 3, and Path 3 wins because it has a lower MED. Again, sub-AS 65001 is not considered in path selection.

Table 7-30   *BGP Paths on R1*

Path	BGP Next Hop	AS_PATH	MED	IGP Metric
1	R4	(65001) 300 400	6	11
2	R2	200 400	10	15
3*	R3	300 400	5	20

The best path is updated to all R1's neighbors. For R3, R1 sends a withdrawal message.

Step 4   Table 7-31 shows R8's new BGP RIB. Path 1 is the best path because it has a lower MED. The member AS number is not considered in path selection. A withdrawal message is sent from R8 to R1.

Table 7-31   *BGP Paths on R8*

Path	BGP Next Hop	AS_PATH	MED	IGP Metric
1*	R3	(65000) 300 400	5	25
2	R4	300 400	6	6

Step 5   Table 7-32 shows the BGP RIB on R4. Path 1 is best because it has a lower MED. R4 now withdraws the route sent to R8.

Table 7-32   *BGP Paths on R4*

Path	BGP Next Hop	AS_PATH	MED	IGP Metric
1*	R3	(65000) 300 400	5	31
2	R6	300 400	6	10

Step 6   Table 7-33 shows the current BGP RIB on R8.

Table 7-33   *BGP Paths on R8*

Path	BGP Next Hop	AS_PATH	MED	IGP Metric
1*	R3	(65000) 300 400	5	25

Step 7   Table 7-34 shows the new BGP RIB on R1. Path 1 is the best path because it has a lower IGP metric. R1 updates its neighbors with the new best path.

Table 7-34   *BGP Paths on R1*

Path	BGP Next Hop	AS_PATH	MED	IGP Metric
1*	R2	200 400	10	15
2	R3	300 400	5	20

Step 8   The current BGP RIB on R8 is shown in Table 7-35. Next, R8 updates R4 with the new path.

Table 7-35   *BGP Paths on R8*

Path	BGP Next Hop	AS_PATH	MED	IGP Metric
1*	R2	65000 200 400	10	20

Step 9   With the new update from R8, the BGP RIB on R4 is shown in Table 7-36. Path 2 is best because it is learned from an external peer. Next, R4 sends the update to R8.

Table 7-36   *BGP Paths on R4*

Path	BGP Next Hop	AS_PATH	MED	IGP Metric
1	R2	65000 200 400	10	26
2*	R6	300 400	6	10

Step 10   Table 7-37 shows the updated BGP RIB on R8. Path 1 is best because it has a lower IGP metric. Next, R8 sends updates to its neighbors.

Table 7-37   *BGP Paths on R8*

Path	BGP Next Hop	AS_PATH	MED	IGP Metric
1*	R4	300 400	6	6
2	R2	65000 200 400	10	20

Step 11 With the update from R8, R1 now has three paths, as shown in Table 7-38. Notice that this is exactly the same BGP RIB as in Step 3. From here, the same convergence cycle would start over again and continue indefinitely.

Table 7-38 *BGP Paths on R1*

Path	BGP Next Hop	AS_PATH	MED	IGP Metric
1	R4	65001 300 400	6	11
2	R2	200 400	10	15
3*	R3	300 400	5	20

Solutions: Setting Proper IGP Metrics Within Confederations

Because path selection does not consider member AS numbers, solutions to this problem are similar to those provided for route reflection. The following briefly describes each of the solutions:

- **Use full iBGP mesh**—As with route reflection, this solution might not be acceptable if confederation is used in the first place to increase iBGP scalability.

- **Enable always-compare-med**—Because MEDs are not modified by member autonomous systems, the same guidelines and caveats apply as for route reflection.

- **Enable deterministic-MED comparison**—It is almost always a good practice to enable deterministic MED comparison, although there might be cases in which this solution alone does not solve the problem.

- **Reset MEDs to 0s**—This eliminates MED as a decision-maker. The same guidelines apply as for route reflection.

- **Use communities**—Communities exchanged between external neighbors are primarily private community values, so the same guidelines apply as for route reflection.

- **Set proper IGP metrics**—If the intra-member-AS metric is set lower than the inter-member-AS, the intra-member-AS path is preferred over the inter-member-AS paths, with all other higher-order comparisons being equal. This stops the loops.

Confederation Versus Route Reflection

This chapter introduced two approaches to solve the iBGP scalability issue—confederation and route reflection. Each method has its strengths and weaknesses, so how do you determine which method to use during a network design? This section helps you answer that question by comparing and contrasting the two methods.

Table 7-39 lists some of the similarities and differences between route reflection and confederation.

Table 7-39   *Route Reflection and Confederation Comparison*

Parameter	Comparison
Multilevel hierarchy	Both methods support hierarchies to further increase scalability. Route reflection supports hierarchical route reflection. Confederation allows route reflection to be used within a member AS.
Policy control	Both provide routing policy control, although confederation might offer more flexibility.
Regular iBGP migration complexity	Migration complexity is very low for route reflection, because few changes to overall network configuration occur. However, migration from iBGP to confederation requires major changes to the configuration and architecture. Chapter 8 provides two case studies on how to migrate from an iBGP architecture to an RR- or confederation-based architecture.
Capability support	All routers within the confederation must support confederation capability, because all routers need to understand the confederation AS_PATH attribute. In a route reflection architecture, only RRs are required to support route reflection capability. With the new clustering design, however, clients must also understand RR attributes. Because both route reflection and confederation were introduced in IOS in very early releases, this feature comparison is not really important. In fact, it is better to have all the routers support route reflection even though you are not using the new clustering design, because that gives you the flexibility to use the design in the future.
IGP expansion	Route reflection requires a single IGP inside an AS, whereas confederation supports single or separate IGPs. This is probably the most distinctive advantage of confederation over route reflection. If your IGP is reaching its scalability limit or it is just too big to handle administration, confederation can be used to reduce the size of the IGP tables.
Deployment experience	Because many more service providers have deployed route reflection than confederation, much more experience has been gained for route reflection.
AS merge	AS merge is actually irrelevant to iBGP scalability, but it is included here because it is one of the benefits of confederation. An AS can be merged with an existing confederation by treating the new AS as a sub-AS of the confederation. AS merge in an RR environment is much more disruptive.

Table 7-39 spells out the comparative values of each method; its recommendations can be boiled down into the following two general guidelines:

- If you need to scale your IGP, you should use confederation.

- If you do not need to scale your IGP, select the route reflection method whenever you can to simplify migration and management.

Summary

This chapter provided a detailed discussion of two approaches to increasing iBGP scalability. The first approach, route reflection, gets around the full iBGP mesh requirement by relaxing the requirement for a group of routers called route reflectors (RRs). These routers can reflect routes between the clients they serve and other iBGP peers, or nonclients. Because clients need to peer only with RRs that serve them, the number of iBGP sessions is reduced.

The second approach for increasing iBGP scalability is confederation, which differs from route reflection in that it divides a large AS into a number of smaller autonomous systems, called member autonomous systems or subautonomous systems. Because eBGP is used between member autonomous systems, no full mesh is required.

The focus of the chapter was the design examples. For each example, proper design guidelines were presented, as well as the consequences of disregarding the guidelines. In addition, possible solutions were presented for each example. Chapter 8 contains four case studies on designing and implementing migration strategies involving route reflection and confederation.

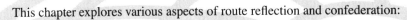

This chapter explores various aspects of route reflection and confederation:

- General migration strategies
- Case Study 1: iBGP Full Mesh to Route Reflection Migration
- Case Study 2: iBGP Full Mesh to Confederation Migration
- Case Study 3: Route Reflection to Confederation Migration
- Case Study 4: Confederation to Route Reflection Migration

CHAPTER 8

Route Reflection and Confederation Migration Strategies

This chapter covers the following migration strategies that are relevant to iBGP scalability:

- From iBGP full mesh to route reflection
- From iBGP full mesh to confederation
- From route reflection to confederation
- From confederation to route reflection

The subject of route reflection and confederation was discussed in Chapter 7, "Scalable iBGP Design and Implementation Guidelines." As networks expand, the need to migrate from one architecture to another arises to increase iBGP scalability. The focus of this chapter is the deployment of these migration techniques. Four case studies are provided in this chapter to demonstrate in detail how to migrate one architecture to another. Note that these procedures document only one of the ways to complete the migration. There are probably many ways to do this. Where appropriate, different migration methods are compared and contrasted. The procedures are written with the goal of minimizing network downtime and traffic loss.

General Migration Strategies

This section discusses the general migration strategies that apply to all four case studies in this chapter. To ensure a successful migration, you must take certain preparatory steps before the migration. Some common concerns of migrations are discussed in this section as well.

Preparatory Steps

Before you start the migration, certain preparatory steps are needed. The following are some of the points to consider:

- Verify that all loopback addresses, when used as peer addresses, are still reachable via IGP.
- Ensure that remote console access is available on all the routers in the AS.

- Follow the design guidelines presented in Chapter 7 on how to design a route reflector (RR) or confederation-based architecture.

- Schedule migration during maintenance windows. Migrate one point of presence (POP) during one maintenance window to minimize risks.

- Prepare a detailed backout-and-restore procedure in the event that migration cannot be completed.

Identifying the Starting and Final Network Topologies

Three types of network topologies are used in this chapter:

- iBGP full mesh

- Route reflection

- Confederation

Depending on the case study, one of the three topologies is used as the starting topology (before the migration). The final topology (after the migration) is either route reflection or confederation, depending on the case study. Consult Chapter 7 on when to use route reflection versus confederation to increase iBGP scalability.

Figure 8-1 shows the iBGP full-mesh topology. Within AS 100, seven routers simulate two POPs. The left POP has R1, R2, and R3, and the right POP has R4, R5, R6, and R7. The core routers are R1, R2, R4, and R5. An external peering is simulated between R1 and R8. All routers in AS 100 peer with each other in a full iBGP mesh.

Figure 8-1   *BGP Full-Mesh Topology*

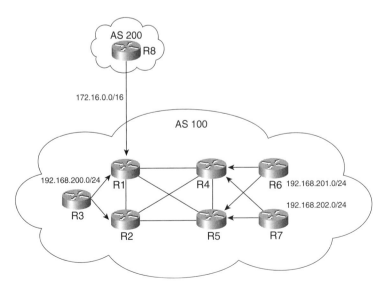

NOTE   Arrows indicate the directions in which prefixes are advertised. For clarity, arrows are
drawn only from the router that originates the prefix.

Figure 8-2 shows the topology based on route reflection. In this topology, all core routers
(R1, R2, R4, and R5) are RRs, with access routers (R3, R6, and R7) as their respective
clients. Clients peer only with RRs in the same POP. All core routers are fully meshed.

Figure 8-2   *RR-Based Topology*

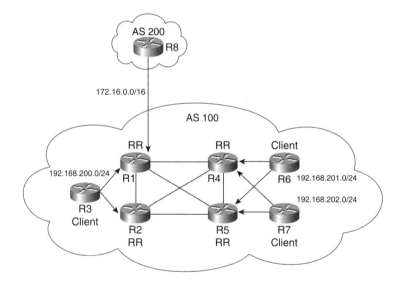

NOTE   Access routers here represent the ones that interconnect with customers or other networks.
Customer prefixes can be injected into BGP locally on access routers or exchanged via BGP
if customer routers are running BGP. To simplify the discussion, customer prefixes are
simulated in this chapter by injecting them statically on access routers.

Figure 8-3 shows the confederation topology, in which each POP is a member AS in
confederation 100. A core router peers with other core routers with which it has direct
physical connections. Within each member AS, all BGP speakers are fully meshed.

Figure 8-3 *Confederation-Based Topology*

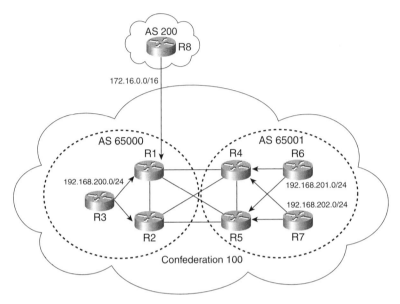

To simplify the addressing scheme, all the addresses within AS 100 are in the range of 192.168.0.0/16, and all link addresses are of /24 length. Router numbers are used as the corresponding link addresses (the third octet) and host addresses (the fourth octet). For example, the link between R1 and R2 has the address 192.168.**12**.0/24, with R1's and R2's addresses as 192.168.**12.1** and 192.168.**12.2**, respectively. As another example, the addresses of R4 and R7 for the link between them are 192.168.**47.4** and 192.168.**47.7**, respectively. Loopback addresses are in the range of 192.168.100.0/24, with the router ID as the host part of the addresses. For example, the loopback 0 interface address on R1 is 192.168.100.**1**/32. The loopback 0 address is used as the BGP router ID for that router.

All link addresses and loopback addresses are part of the IGP, which is IS-IS, in AS 100. A single level, Level 2, is used for this chapter. The loopback address for each router is used as its system ID.

To simulate external prefix advertisements, prefix 172.16.0.0/16 is advertised from AS 200 to AS 100. The prefix 192.168.200.0/24 is injected into BGP in R3 to simulate a customer route. Additionally, 192.168.201.0/24 and 192.168.202.0/24 are injected on R6 and R7, respectively.

Identifying the Starting Router

The starting router is the first router to be migrated to the new architecture. There are three choices; each has its own challenges:

- **A core router**—If a core router is migrated first, traffic can be black-holed during the migration. You can avoid the temporary traffic loss by moving the core router out of the forwarding path if redundant connections exist.

- **An access router**—If an access router is migrated first, the reachability of customer prefixes may be affected. If customer prefixes are originated from that router, these prefixes are unavailable unless they can be generated in other routers temporarily. If customer prefixes are exchanged via BGP, these prefixes are unavailable unless the customer is multihomed. In this chapter, access routers do not have eBGP sessions with customers.

- **A router with external peerings**—If an eBGP router is migrated first, connections to the external neighbors are affected unless multiple connections are available.

In the topologies presented in this chapter, redundant connections exist between the core and access routers, and each POP has at least one core router without a single-homed external connection. Thus, a core router is the most logical choice as the starting router for all case studies.

Minimizing Traffic Loss

During migration, traffic can be temporarily looped or black-holed. Traffic loops are generally caused by conflicting next-hop settings between routers. Two types of next hops are involved: BGP next hop and IGP next hop. BGP next hop is often recursively resolved to an IGP next hop. The case studies in this chapter discuss the cause of potential loops and ways to prevent them.

Traffic loss caused by *black-holing* occurs because a router on the forwarding path does not have the correct routing information. A router under migration drops all traffic for which it has not yet learned routing information. The solution to the problem is to move the router temporarily out of the forwarding path for all prefixes or to build additional BGP sessions in advance. Specifically, you can choose from the following options:

- Shut down all relevant links on the router under migration. This approach is simple to accomplish but might require remote console access to the router to ensure further migration. The other drawback of this method is that BGP sessions might not be able to form while some of the links are down.

- Change the IGP interface metrics so that the router under migration is not selected as an IGP next hop. While the router does not have transit traffic to forward, its BGP sessions can be established; thus, routing information can be exchanged. Undoing the metric changes puts the router back in the forwarding paths.

- Build temporary BGP sessions in advance so that routing information is still available during the migration process. These sessions can be removed after the migration. This approach is the most complex of all but might be useful when the router under migration cannot be removed from the forwarding path, such as in the cases that the path via the router is the only path or that the redundant paths via other routers are overloaded.

Traffic loss caused by routing information black holes occurs only during configuration changes and thus is temporary and short. The following case studies demonstrate in detail how to prevent or minimize traffic loss during migration.

Case Study 1: iBGP Full Mesh to Route Reflection Migration

This case study presents detailed procedures on how to migrate an iBGP fully meshed network to a route reflection-based architecture. The starting topology is as shown in Figure 8-1. The final topology after the migration is shown in Figure 8-2.

Starting Configurations and RIBs

This section shows BGP and IGP configurations before the migration. Examples 8-1 through 8-7 show the configurations for R1 through R7, respectively. All BGP speakers in AS 100 are fully meshed. A peer group called Internal is used for all the iBGP sessions.

There are three ways to make R8 reachable in AS 100: setting **next-hop-self** on R1, making the link between R1 and R8 part of the IGP domain in AS 100, or using a route map on R1 to reset the next hop to R1. In this case study, the BGP next hop on R1 is reset for all internal sessions using **next-hop-self**.

Example 8-1 *Relevant Configurations on R1*

```
router isis
 net 49.0001.1921.6810.0001.00
 is-type level-2-only
!
router bgp 100
 no synchronization
 bgp router-id 192.168.100.1
 bgp log-neighbor-changes
 neighbor Internal peer-group
 neighbor Internal remote-as 100
 neighbor Internal update-source Loopback0
 neighbor Internal next-hop-self
 neighbor 192.168.18.8 remote-as 200
 neighbor 192.168.100.2 peer-group Internal
 neighbor 192.168.100.3 peer-group Internal
 neighbor 192.168.100.4 peer-group Internal
```

Example 8-1 *Relevant Configurations on R1 (Continued)*

```
 neighbor 192.168.100.5 peer-group Internal
 neighbor 192.168.100.6 peer-group Internal
 neighbor 192.168.100.7 peer-group Internal
 no auto-summary
```

R2 is the other core router in the left POP. The same peer group Internal is used for all iBGP peers (See Example 8-2.)

Example 8-2 *Relevant Configurations on R2*

```
router isis
 net 49.0001.1921.6810.0002.00
 is-type level-2-only
 !
router bgp 100
 no synchronization
 bgp router-id 192.168.100.2
 bgp log-neighbor-changes
 neighbor Internal peer-group
 neighbor Internal remote-as 100
 neighbor Internal update-source Loopback0
 neighbor 192.168.100.1 peer-group Internal
 neighbor 192.168.100.3 peer-group Internal
 neighbor 192.168.100.4 peer-group Internal
 neighbor 192.168.100.5 peer-group Internal
 neighbor 192.168.100.6 peer-group Internal
 neighbor 192.168.100.7 peer-group Internal
 no auto-summary
```

R3 is an access router that injects customer routes into BGP. The prefix 192.168.200.0/24 is originated and advertised to other BGP peers. (See Example 8-3.)

Example 8-3 *Relevant Configurations on R3*

```
router isis
 net 49.0001.1921.6810.0003.00
 is-type level-2-only
 !
router bgp 100
 no synchronization
 bgp router-id 192.168.100.3
 bgp log-neighbor-changes
 network 192.168.200.0
 neighbor Internal peer-group
 neighbor Internal remote-as 100
 neighbor Internal update-source Loopback0
 neighbor 192.168.100.1 peer-group Internal
```

continues

Example 8-3 *Relevant Configurations on R3 (Continued)*

```
 neighbor 192.168.100.2 peer-group Internal
 neighbor 192.168.100.4 peer-group Internal
 neighbor 192.168.100.5 peer-group Internal
 neighbor 192.168.100.6 peer-group Internal
 neighbor 192.168.100.7 peer-group Internal
 no auto-summary
```

R4 is a core router in the right POP. It has similar BGP configurations as R2. (See Example 8-4.)

Example 8-4 *Relevant Configurations on R4*

```
router isis
 net 49.0001.1921.6810.0004.00
 is-type level-2-only
 !
router bgp 100
 no synchronization
 bgp router-id 192.168.100.4
 bgp log-neighbor-changes
 neighbor Internal peer-group
 neighbor Internal remote-as 100
 neighbor Internal update-source Loopback0
 neighbor 192.168.100.1 peer-group Internal
 neighbor 192.168.100.2 peer-group Internal
 neighbor 192.168.100.3 peer-group Internal
 neighbor 192.168.100.5 peer-group Internal
 neighbor 192.168.100.6 peer-group Internal
 neighbor 192.168.100.7 peer-group Internal
 no auto-summary
```

R5 is another core router in the right POP (see Example 8-5).

Example 8-5 *Relevant Configurations on R5*

```
router isis
 net 49.0001.1921.6810.0005.00
 is-type level-2-only
 !
router bgp 100
 no synchronization
 bgp router-id 192.168.100.5
 bgp log-neighbor-changes
 neighbor Internal peer-group
 neighbor Internal remote-as 100
 neighbor Internal update-source Loopback0
 neighbor 192.168.100.1 peer-group Internal
 neighbor 192.168.100.2 peer-group Internal
 neighbor 192.168.100.3 peer-group Internal
```

Example 8-5 *Relevant Configurations on R5 (Continued)*

```
 neighbor 192.168.100.4 peer-group Internal
 neighbor 192.168.100.6 peer-group Internal
 neighbor 192.168.100.7 peer-group Internal
 no auto-summary
```

As shown in Example 8-6, R6 is an access router that injects customer routes into BGP. The prefix 192.168.201.0/24 is originated and advertised to its BGP peers.

Example 8-6 *Relevant Configurations on R6*

```
router isis
 net 49.0001.1921.6810.0006.00
 is-type level-2-only
 !
router bgp 100
 no synchronization
 bgp router-id 192.168.100.6
 bgp log-neighbor-changes
 network 192.168.201.0
 neighbor Internal peer-group
 neighbor Internal remote-as 100
 neighbor Internal update-source Loopback0
 neighbor 192.168.100.1 peer-group Internal
 neighbor 192.168.100.2 peer-group Internal
 neighbor 192.168.100.3 peer-group Internal
 neighbor 192.168.100.4 peer-group Internal
 neighbor 192.168.100.5 peer-group Internal
 neighbor 192.168.100.7 peer-group Internal
 no auto-summary
```

R7 is another access router in the right POP that injects customer routes into BGP. The prefix 192.168.202.0/24 is originated and advertised to its BGP peers. (See Example 8-7.)

Example 8-7 *Relevant Configurations on R7*

```
router isis
 net 49.0001.1921.6810.0007.00
 is-type level-2-only
 !
router bgp 100
 no synchronization
 bgp router-id 192.168.100.7
 bgp log-neighbor-changes
 network 192.168.202.0
 neighbor Internal peer-group
 neighbor Internal remote-as 100
 neighbor Internal update-source Loopback0
```

continues

Example 8-7 *Relevant Configurations on R7 (Continued)*

```
 neighbor 192.168.100.1 peer-group Internal
 neighbor 192.168.100.2 peer-group Internal
 neighbor 192.168.100.3 peer-group Internal
 neighbor 192.168.100.4 peer-group Internal
 neighbor 192.168.100.5 peer-group Internal
 neighbor 192.168.100.6 peer-group Internal
 no auto-summary
```

The only router that is not part of AS 100 is R8. Its BGP configurations are shown in Example 8-8. The prefix 172.16.0.0/16 is generated locally and is advertised to AS 100.

Example 8-8 *Relevant Configurations on R8*

```
router bgp 200
 no synchronization
 bgp log-neighbor-changes
 network 172.16.0.0
 neighbor 192.168.18.1 remote-as 100
 no auto-summary
!
ip route 172.16.0.0 255.255.0.0 Null0
```

The following examples provide some sample outputs for a few selected routers. Example 8-9 shows the IP RIB on R1. Note that all the loopback addresses in AS 100 can be reached.

Example 8-9 *IP RIB on R1*

```
R1#show ip route
Codes: C - connected, S - static, I - IGRP, R - RIP, M - mobile, B - BGP
       D - EIGRP, EX - EIGRP external, O - OSPF, IA - OSPF inter area
       N1 - OSPF NSSA external type 1, N2 - OSPF NSSA external type 2
       E1 - OSPF external type 1, E2 - OSPF external type 2, E - EGP
       i - IS-IS, L1 - IS-IS level-1, L2 - IS-IS level-2, ia - IS-IS inter area
       * - candidate default, U - per-user static route, o - ODR
       P - periodic downloaded static route

Gateway of last resort is not set

i L2 192.168.46.0/24 [115/20] via 192.168.14.4, Serial7/0
C    192.168.12.0/24 is directly connected, Ethernet0/0
i L2 192.168.47.0/24 [115/20] via 192.168.14.4, Serial7/0
C    192.168.13.0/24 is directly connected, Ethernet1/0
C    192.168.14.0/24 is directly connected, Serial7/0
C    192.168.15.0/24 is directly connected, Serial8/0
i L2 192.168.45.0/24 [115/20] via 192.168.14.4, Serial7/0
```

Example 8-9 *IP RIB on R1 (Continued)*

```
                        [115/20] via 192.168.15.5, Serial8/0
i L2 192.168.25.0/24 [115/20] via 192.168.12.2, Ethernet0/0
                        [115/20] via 192.168.15.5, Serial8/0
i L2 192.168.24.0/24 [115/20] via 192.168.14.4, Serial7/0
                        [115/20] via 192.168.12.2, Ethernet0/0
i L2 192.168.57.0/24 [115/20] via 192.168.15.5, Serial8/0
B    172.16.0.0/16 [20/0] via 192.168.18.8, 00:38:51
i L2 192.168.56.0/24 [115/20] via 192.168.15.5, Serial8/0
B    192.168.200.0/24 [200/0] via 192.168.100.3, 00:20:34
B    192.168.201.0/24 [200/0] via 192.168.100.6, 00:20:02
B    192.168.202.0/24 [200/0] via 192.168.100.7, 00:19:31
i L2 192.168.23.0/24 [115/20] via 192.168.12.2, Ethernet0/0
                        [115/20] via 192.168.13.3, Ethernet1/0
     192.168.100.0/32 is subnetted, 7 subnets
i L2    192.168.100.4 [115/20] via 192.168.14.4, Serial7/0
i L2    192.168.100.5 [115/20] via 192.168.15.5, Serial8/0
i L2    192.168.100.6 [115/30] via 192.168.14.4, Serial7/0
                        [115/30] via 192.168.15.5, Serial8/0
i L2    192.168.100.7 [115/30] via 192.168.15.5, Serial8/0
                        [115/30] via 192.168.14.4, Serial7/0
C       192.168.100.1 is directly connected, Loopback0
i L2    192.168.100.2 [115/20] via 192.168.12.2, Ethernet0/0
i L2    192.168.100.3 [115/20] via 192.168.13.3, Ethernet1/0
C    192.168.18.0/24 is directly connected, Serial6/0
```

Example 8-10 shows the BGP summary table on R1. Note that R1 has sessions with R2 through R8.

Example 8-10 *BGP Summary Table on R1*

```
R1#show ip bgp summary
BGP router identifier 192.168.100.1, local AS number 100
BGP table version is 5, main routing table version 5
4 network entries and 4 paths using 548 bytes of memory
2 BGP path attribute entries using 120 bytes of memory
1 BGP AS-PATH entries using 24 bytes of memory
0 BGP route-map cache entries using 0 bytes of memory
0 BGP filter-list cache entries using 0 bytes of memory
BGP activity 4/8 prefixes, 4/0 paths, scan interval 60 secs

Neighbor        V    AS MsgRcvd MsgSent   TblVer  InQ OutQ Up/Down  State/PfxRcd
192.168.18.8    4   200      45      47        5    0    0 00:40:24            1
192.168.100.2   4   100      32      33        5    0    0 00:28:04            0
192.168.100.3   4   100      31      31        5    0    0 00:26:21            1
192.168.100.4   4   100      29      30        5    0    0 00:25:22            0
192.168.100.5   4   100      28      29        5    0    0 00:24:41            0
192.168.100.6   4   100      28      28        5    0    0 00:23:44            1
192.168.100.7   4   100      28      28        5    0    0 00:23:17            1
```

Example 8-11 shows the BGP RIB on R7. Note that all four prefixes are available. Note the next hops for all the prefixes.

Example 8-11 *BGP RIB on R7*

```
R7#show ip bgp
BGP table version is 5, local router ID is 192.168.100.7
Status codes: s suppressed, d damped, h history, * valid, > best, i - internal,
              r RIB-failure
Origin codes: i - IGP, e - EGP, ? - incomplete

   Network          Next Hop          Metric LocPrf Weight Path
*>i172.16.0.0       192.168.100.1          0    100      0 200 i
*>i192.168.200.0    192.168.100.3          0    100      0 i
*>i192.168.201.0    192.168.100.6          0    100      0 i
*> 192.168.202.0    0.0.0.0                0            32768 i
```

Example 8-12 shows the BGP RIB on R8. The three prefixes from AS 100 are properly installed.

Example 8-12 *BGP RIB on R8*

```
R8#show ip bgp
BGP table version is 5, local router ID is 192.168.18.8
Status codes: s suppressed, d damped, h history, * valid, > best, i - internal,
              r RIB-failure
Origin codes: i - IGP, e - EGP, ? - incomplete

   Network          Next Hop          Metric LocPrf Weight Path
*> 172.16.0.0       0.0.0.0                0            32768 i
*> 192.168.200.0    192.168.18.1                           0 100 i
*> 192.168.201.0    192.168.18.1                           0 100 i
*> 192.168.202.0    192.168.18.1                           0 100 i
```

Migration Procedures

When migrating a fully meshed network to an RR-based network, first migrate routers that are to become RRs, and then migrate client routers one at a time. When all the clients are moved to the new RR, migrate the remaining core routers to RRs. This minimizes downtime if access routers have redundant connections to the core.

NOTE   When access routers do not have redundant physical connections to the core, you should create additional BGP sessions to avoid traffic loss, as indicated previously in the section "Minimizing Traffic Loss." This approach works when the BGP process is not going to be replaced during the migration, as in this case study.

The following is a high-level summary of the steps involved:

Step 1   Select the starting core router, R4.

Step 2   Create a new peer group for clients, and enable route reflection.

Step 3   Move all access routers to the new peer group created for clients.

Step 4   Move the other core router, R5, to RR, and add access routers as clients. Repeat Steps 2 and 3 for R5.

Step 5   Remove iBGP sessions that are no longer needed.

Step 6   Repeat Steps 1 through 5 for the other POP.

Step 7   Verify BGP reachability for all prefixes.

NOTE   These steps are presented in such a way for easier discussion. In real migration, many of the steps might be completed simultaneously in one maintenance window.

The following sections illustrate the detailed procedures.

Step 1: Select the Starting Core Router

Step 1   Start the migration from a core router that will be an RR. R4 is selected.

Step 2: Create a New Peer Group for Clients, and Enable Route Reflection

On R4, create another peer group called Clients to represent all its clients. Example 8-13 shows a sample peer group configuration.

Example 8-13 *Peer Group for Clients*

```
neighbor Clients peer-group
neighbor Clients remote-as 100
neighbor Clients update-source Loopback0
neighbor Clients route-reflector-client
```

Step 3: Move All Access Routers to the New Peer Group

Move client peerings on R4 from the existing Internal peer group to the Clients peer group. Within the POP on the right, move R6 and R7, one at a time, from the Internal peer group to the Clients peer group. No configuration changes are needed on the clients.

This step is service-affecting during the changeover for any prefixes that have R4 as an IGP next hop. For example, the prefix 192.168.201.0/24 is originated by R6. That prefix is deleted from the BGP RIB on R4 when the peer group membership is changed from a regular iBGP session to a client-RR session. When traffic destined for 192.168.201.0/24 reaches R4, such traffic is dropped.

To avoid traffic loss, the following three approaches are available:

- Shutting down the links between R4 and other core routers so that R4 is removed from the forwarding paths for all the prefixes. This is probably the simplest method but typically isn't recommended because BGP sessions cannot form when the links are down.

- Increasing IGP metrics from other core routers to R4 so that traffic entering the right POP uses R5. Note that if IGP metrics between R4 and access routers in the same POP are not changed, R4 may still be used as an IGP next hop for traffic leaving the POP. If symmetric forwarding is desired, IGP metrics for all links of R4 should be increased.

- Building additional BGP sessions between R4 and R6 and between R4 and R7 using physical interface addresses or other loopback addresses. These temporary sessions allow R4 to maintain all the routing information during the migration so that R4 can share the traffic entering and leaving the POP.

NOTE   The traffic loss is short and temporary during the configuration change and until new routing information is learned.

This case study chooses to move R4 out of the forwarding paths for 192.168.201.0/24 and 192.168.202.0/24 by increasing the IS-IS link metrics between R1 and R4 and between R2 and R4. When R4 learns these two prefixes after the peer group changes, R4 can be put back in the forwarding paths by removing the metric changes.

Clients may receive additional paths for a prefix because the clients receive the prefix directly from the peer that announces the prefix. They also receive the prefix from R4. Example 8-14 shows the BGP RIB on R6 after the peer group membership change on R4. There are two paths for each prefix that is not originated locally. The additional path is reflected from R4.

Example 8-14 *BGP RIB on R6 as a Client of R4*

```
R6#show ip bgp
BGP table version is 5, local router ID is 192.168.100.6
Status codes: s suppressed, d damped, h history, * valid, > best, i - internal,
              r RIB-failure
```

Example 8-14 *BGP RIB on R6 as a Client of R4 (Continued)*

```
Origin codes: i - IGP, e - EGP, ? - incomplete

   Network          Next Hop          Metric LocPrf Weight Path
 * i172.16.0.0      192.168.100.1          0    100      0 200 i
 *>i                192.168.100.1          0    100      0 200 i
 * i192.168.200.0   192.168.100.3          0    100      0 i
 *>i                192.168.100.3          0    100      0 i
 *> 192.168.201.0   0.0.0.0                0         32768 i
 * i192.168.202.0   192.168.100.7          0    100      0 i
 *>i                192.168.100.7          0    100      0 I
```

NOTE   The direct path is selected as the best path because the reflected path has a longer cluster list.

Step 4: Move the Other Core Router to RR, and Add Access Routers as Clients

Repeat Steps 2 and 3 for R5. As soon as both R4 and R5 are RRs for R6 and R7, even more paths appear on clients. Example 8-15 shows the BGP RIB on R7. For each prefix that is not locally generated, R7 receives three paths: one from the originator, and one each from the two RRs.

Example 8-15 *BGP RIB on R7 After Both R4 and R5 Are Migrated to RRs*

```
R7#show ip bgp
BGP table version is 5, local router ID is 192.168.100.7
Status codes: s suppressed, d damped, h history, * valid, > best, i - internal,
              r RIB-failure
Origin codes: i - IGP, e - EGP, ? - incomplete

   Network          Next Hop          Metric LocPrf Weight Path
 * i172.16.0.0      192.168.100.1          0    100      0 200 i
 * i                192.168.100.1          0    100      0 200 i
 *>i                192.168.100.1          0    100      0 200 i
 * i192.168.200.0   192.168.100.3          0    100      0 i
 * i                192.168.100.3          0    100      0 i
 *>i                192.168.100.3          0    100      0 i
 * i192.168.201.0   192.168.100.6          0    100      0 i
 * i                192.168.100.6          0    100      0 i
 *>i                192.168.100.6          0    100      0 i
 *> 192.168.202.0   0.0.0.0                0         32768 i
```

Example 8-16 shows the detail path information for 192.168.201.0/24. The first path is reflected from R5, the second path is reflected from R4, and the third path is from R6 directly. The third path is selected as the best path.

Example 8-16 *Detailed Path Information for 192.168.201.0*

```
R7#show ip bgp 192.168.201.0
BGP routing table entry for 192.168.201.0/24, version 3
Paths: (3 available, best #3, table Default-IP-Routing-Table)
  Not advertised to any peer

  Local
    192.168.100.6 (metric 30) from 192.168.100.5 (192.168.100.5)
      Origin IGP, metric 0, localpref 100, valid, internal
      Originator: 192.168.100.6, Cluster list: 192.168.100.5
  Local
    192.168.100.6 (metric 30) from 192.168.100.4 (192.168.100.4)
      Origin IGP, metric 0, localpref 100, valid, internal
      Originator: 192.168.100.6, Cluster list: 192.168.100.4
  Local
    192.168.100.6 (metric 30) from 192.168.100.6 (192.168.100.6)
      Origin IGP, metric 0, localpref 100, valid, internal, best
```

Step 5: Remove iBGP Sessions That Are No Longer Needed

Remove unneeded BGP sessions. On migrated clients R6 and R7, remove all BGP sessions except for those to RRs in the POP R4 and R5. On all routers in the other POP, remove BGP sessions to the migrated clients, R6 and R7. The BGP RIB on a client now shows only reflected paths from RRs.

Example 8-17 shows the BGP summary table on R6. Now only two BGP sessions are left: one to R4, and the other to R5.

Example 8-17 *BGP Summary Table on R6 After Cleanup*

```
R6#show ip bgp summary
BGP router identifier 192.168.100.6, local AS number 100
BGP table version is 8, main routing table version 8
4 network entries and 7 paths using 668 bytes of memory
3 BGP path attribute entries using 180 bytes of memory
6 BGP rrinfo entries using 144 bytes of memory
1 BGP AS-PATH entries using 24 bytes of memory
0 BGP route-map cache entries using 0 bytes of memory
0 BGP filter-list cache entries using 0 bytes of memory
BGP activity 4/74 prefixes, 11/4 paths, scan interval 60 secs

Neighbor        V    AS MsgRcvd MsgSent   TblVer  InQ OutQ Up/Down  State/PfxRcd
192.168.100.4   4   100    1120    1119        8    0    0 17:12:34        3
192.168.100.5   4   100    1114    1111        8    0    0 00:07:35        3
```

Example 8-18 shows the BGP RIB on R7 after the session cleanup. For each prefix that is not locally originated, two paths are now available.

Example 8-18 *BGP RIB on R7 After Cleanup*

```
R7#show ip bgp
BGP table version is 8, local router ID is 192.168.100.7
Status codes: s suppressed, d damped, h history, * valid, > best, i - internal,
              r RIB-failure
Origin codes: i - IGP, e - EGP, ? - incomplete

   Network          Next Hop          Metric LocPrf Weight Path
 * i172.16.0.0      192.168.100.1          0    100      0 200 i
 *>i                192.168.100.1          0    100      0 200 i
 * i192.168.200.0   192.168.100.3          0    100      0 i
 *>i                192.168.100.3          0    100      0 i
 * i192.168.201.0   192.168.100.6          0    100      0 i
 *>i                192.168.100.6          0    100      0 i
 *> 192.168.202.0   0.0.0.0                0          32768 i
```

Example 8-19 shows the detailed path information for the prefix 172.16.0.0/16 on R7. Both paths are reflected, one from each RR.

Example 8-19 *Detailed Path Information for 172.16.0.0/16 on R7*

```
R7#show ip bgp 172.16.0.0
BGP routing table entry for 172.16.0.0/16, version 7
Paths: (2 available, best #2, table Default-IP-Routing-Table)
  Not advertised to any peer
  200
    192.168.100.1 (metric 30) from 192.168.100.5 (192.168.100.5)
      Origin IGP, metric 0, localpref 100, valid, internal
      Originator: 192.168.100.1, Cluster list: 192.168.100.5
  200
    192.168.100.1 (metric 30) from 192.168.100.4 (192.168.100.4)
      Origin IGP, metric 0, localpref 100, valid, internal, best
      Originator: 192.168.100.1, Cluster list: 192.168.100.4
```

Step 6: Repeat Steps 1 Through 5 for the Other POP

Repeat Steps 1 through 5 for the remaining POPs. In this case study, there is one remaining POP left to migrate.

Step 7: Verify BGP Reachability for All Prefixes

Verify that all sessions are up and that all routes are received correctly. The following examples show sample outputs.

Example 8-20 shows the BGP summary table on R1. There are five BGP sessions: one external with R8, three iBGP sessions to all other RRs, and one iBGP session with its client R3.

Example 8-20 *BGP Summary Table on R1*

```
R1#show ip bgp summary
BGP router identifier 192.168.100.1, local AS number 100
BGP table version is 9, main routing table version 9
4 network entries and 7 paths using 668 bytes of memory
2 BGP path attribute entries using 120 bytes of memory
5 BGP rrinfo entries using 120 bytes of memory
1 BGP AS-PATH entries using 24 bytes of memory
0 BGP route-map cache entries using 0 bytes of memory
0 BGP filter-list cache entries using 0 bytes of memory
BGP activity 5/41 prefixes, 10/3 paths, scan interval 60 secs

Neighbor        V    AS MsgRcvd MsgSent   TblVer  InQ OutQ Up/Down  State/PfxRcd
192.168.18.8    4   200    1151    1153        9    0    0 19:06:30            1
192.168.100.2   4   100    1152    1154        9    0    0 19:07:32            1
192.168.100.3   4   100      29      32        9    0    0 00:24:07            1
192.168.100.4   4   100    1153    1153        9    0    0 19:07:33            2
192.168.100.5   4   100    1153    1153        9    0    0 19:07:07            2
```

Example 8-21 shows the BGP RIB on R1. The redundant path for each internal prefix is received from the redundant RR.

Example 8-21 *BGP RIB on R1*

```
R1#show ip bgp
BGP table version is 9, local router ID is 192.168.100.1
Status codes: s suppressed, d damped, h history, * valid, > best, i - internal,
              r RIB-failure
Origin codes: i - IGP, e - EGP, ? - incomplete

   Network          Next Hop          Metric LocPrf Weight Path
*> 172.16.0.0       192.168.18.8           0               0 200 i
*  i192.168.200.0   192.168.100.3          0    100        0 i
*>i                 192.168.100.3          0    100        0 i
*  i192.168.201.0   192.168.100.6          0    100        0 i
*>i                 192.168.100.6          0    100        0 i
*  i192.168.202.0   192.168.100.7          0    100        0 i
*>i                 192.168.100.7          0    100        0 i
```

Verify that AS 200 still receives all three prefixes from AS 100. Example 8-22 shows the BGP RIB on R8. This shows the same BGP RIB as before the migration.

Example 8-22 *BGP RIB on R8*

```
R8#show ip bgp
BGP table version is 7, local router ID is 192.168.18.8
Status codes: s suppressed, d damped, h history, * valid, > best, i - internal,
              r RIB-failure
Origin codes: i - IGP, e - EGP, ? - incomplete

   Network          Next Hop          Metric LocPrf Weight Path
*> 172.16.0.0       0.0.0.0                0         32768 i
*> 192.168.200.0    192.168.18.1                        0 100 i
*> 192.168.201.0    192.168.18.1                        0 100 i
*> 192.168.202.0    192.168.18.1                        0 100 i
```

Final BGP Configurations

This section summarizes the relevant BGP configurations after the migration of a few selected routers. Two configurations are shown: one for an RR, and one for a client.

Example 8-23 shows the final BGP configurations on R1.

Example 8-23 *Final BGP Configurations on R1*

```
router bgp 100
 no synchronization
 bgp router-id 192.168.100.1
 bgp log-neighbor-changes
 neighbor Internal peer-group
 neighbor Internal remote-as 100
 neighbor Internal update-source Loopback0
 neighbor Internal next-hop-self
 neighbor Clients peer-group
 neighbor Clients remote-as 100
 neighbor Clients update-source Loopback0
 neighbor Clients route-reflector-client
 neighbor Clients next-hop-self
 neighbor 192.168.18.8 remote-as 200
 neighbor 192.168.100.2 peer-group Internal
 neighbor 192.168.100.3 peer-group Clients
 neighbor 192.168.100.4 peer-group Internal
 neighbor 192.168.100.5 peer-group Internal
 no auto-summary
```

Example 8-24 shows the final BGP configurations on R3.

Example 8-24 *Final BGP Configurations on R3*

```
router bgp 100
 no synchronization
 bgp router-id 192.168.100.3
 bgp log-neighbor-changes
 network 192.168.200.0
 neighbor Internal peer-group
 neighbor Internal remote-as 100
 neighbor Internal update-source Loopback0
 neighbor 192.168.100.1 peer-group Internal
 neighbor 192.168.100.2 peer-group Internal
 no auto-summary
```

Case Study 2: iBGP Full Mesh to Confederation Migration

This case study presents detailed procedures on how to migrate an iBGP fully meshed network into a confederation-based architecture. The starting topology before the migration is shown in Figure 8-1, and the final topology is shown in Figure 8-3. The same IGP (IS-IS) is used across the entire confederation. If different IGPs or IGP instances are used in different member autonomous systems, the IGP needs to be migrated as well. The IGP migration is outside the scope of this chapter.

Starting Configurations and RIBs

Because this case study uses the same starting topology that is used in Case Study 1, there are no changes to the basic configurations and RIBs that were presented in Case Study 1.

Migration Procedures

Because of significant architectural differences between the BGP confederation and fully meshed iBGP, expect disruption to the existing network. The goal of these procedures is to minimize the disruption while migrating to the new architecture.

The procedures described in this section take advantage of the feature that the BGP confederation ID can be the same as its member AS number. When the first router is migrated into a new member AS, the entire AS 100 should be changed to a confederation. This in effect changes the original AS 100 into a confederation 100 with two member autonomous systems—one of which is 100. The remaining procedures migrate routers from member AS 100 to the appropriate member autonomous systems.

Here is the high-level summary:

Step 1   Select R4 as the starting router, and move it out of the forwarding paths.

Step 2   Remove R4's BGP process, and replace it with the confederation configuration. Update all other routers with confederation configurations.

Step 3   Create iBGP mesh sessions and intraconfederation eBGP sessions.

Step 4   Update the configurations on R1 and R2 to peer with R4.

Step 5   Move R6 from member AS 100 to member AS 65001, and put R4 back in the forwarding paths.

Step 6   Move R7 from member AS 100 to member AS 65001, and move R5 out of the forwarding paths.

Step 7   Move R5 from member AS 100 to member AS 65001, and put R5 back in the forwarding paths.

Step 8   Update the peering with R5 on R1 and R2.

Step 9   Move R2 out of the forwarding paths, and migrate R2 from member AS 100 to member AS 65000.

Step 10 Update the peerings with R2, and put R2 back in the forwarding paths.

Step 11 Move R3 from member AS 100 to member AS 65000.

Step 12 Move R1 from member AS 100 to member AS 65000.

Step 13 Update the peering with R1.

Step 14 Verify BGP reachability for all prefixes.

The following sections illustrate the detailed procedures.

Step 1: Select R4 as the Starting Router and Move It out of the Forwarding Paths

Select the starting router, R4, in the right POP. If R4's BGP configurations are removed, traffic black-holes if R4 is on the forwarding path. For example, for traffic destined for 192.168.200.0/24 and 172.16.0.0/16 from R6 and R7, a black hole on R4 occurs if the IGP next hop is R4. To solve the problem, move R4 out of the forwarding path or build temporary iBGP sessions, as discussed previously. For simplicity, this case study chooses to move R4 out of the forwarding paths by increasing IS-IS link metrics toward R4.

Example 8-25 shows the Cisco Express Forwarding (CEF) path for 192.168.100.6 (the BGP next hop for 192.168.201.0/24) on R1 after R4 is moved out of the forwarding paths.

Example 8-25 *CEF Path for 192.168.100.6 on R1*

```
R1#show ip cef 192.168.100.6
192.168.100.6/32, version 44, epoch 0, cached adjacency to Serial8/0
0 packets, 0 bytes
  via 192.168.15.5, Serial8/0, 1 dependency
    next hop 192.168.15.5, Serial8/0
    valid cached adjacency
```

Example 8-26 shows the CEF path for 192.168.100.6 on R2 after R4 is moved out of the forwarding paths.

Example 8-26 *CEF Path for 192.168.100.6 on R2*

```
R2#show ip cef 192.168.100.6
192.168.100.6/32, version 33, epoch 0, cached adjacency to Serial10/0
0 packets, 0 bytes
  via 192.168.25.5, Serial10/0, 1 dependency
    next hop 192.168.25.5, Serial10/0
    valid cached adjacency
```

Step 2: Replace R4's BGP Process with the Confederation Configuration and Update All Routers

Migrate R4 by replacing the current BGP process with the member AS 65001, and configure a confederation using the current BGP AS number 100 as the confederation ID. Use 100 and 65000 as the member AS peers.

Example 8-27 shows the new confederation configuration on R4 as entered line by line.

Example 8-27 *BGP Confederation Configurations on R4*

```
R4(config)#no router bgp 100
R4(config)#bgp router 65001
R4(config-router)#bgp confederation identifier 100
R4(config-router)#bgp confederation peers 100 65000
```

NOTE   In a real migration, Steps 2 and 3 would be combined. Two steps are presented here for easier discussion.

Add confederation configurations to all other routers in AS 100—specifically, the **bgp confederation identifier 100** and **bgp confederation peers** commands. Consult the final topology to determine the member AS numbers to use.

Step 3: Create iBGP Mesh Sessions and Intraconfederation eBGP Sessions

Create a peer group called Internal for intramember AS peers, and assign R5, R6, and R7 to the peer group. Create additional peer sessions for intermember AS peers. Thus, R4 peers with R1 and R2. Physical addresses are used as peer IDs in this chapter, but loopback addresses can be used as well. During the changeover, R1, R2, R4, R5, R6, and R7 might complain that the peer is in the wrong AS. Ignore these messages; they are expected during this phase of the migration. Additionally, R3's iBGP session with R4 is down, as expected.

Example 8-28 shows the new BGP configurations on R4.

Example 8-28 *BGP Configurations on R4*

```
router bgp 65001
 no synchronization
 bgp router-id 192.168.100.4
 bgp log-neighbor-changes
 bgp confederation identifier 100
 bgp confederation peers 100 65000
 neighbor Internal peer-group
 neighbor Internal remote-as 65001
 neighbor Internal update-source Loopback0
 neighbor 192.168.14.1 remote-as 100
 neighbor 192.168.24.2 remote-as 100
 neighbor 192.168.100.5 peer-group Internal
 neighbor 192.168.100.6 peer-group Internal
 neighbor 192.168.100.7 peer-group Internal
 no auto-summary
```

Step 4: Update the Configurations on R1 and R2 to Peer with R4

Because R1 and R2 are already part of the confederation, the configuration modification is to change the current iBGP peering with R4 to eBGP peering, as shown in Example 8-29. Physical addresses are used for the peering addresses here.

You can use several methods to make R8 reachable in a different member AS inside confederation 100:

- Make the link between R1 and R8 part of the IGP if the entire confederation shares the same IGP. This is the recommended approach.

- Reset the next hop to R1 using a route map for external routes only, and leave the next hop of internal and confederation eBGP routes unchanged. This is probably the most flexible method.

- Set **next-hop-self** on R1 for all iBGP and confederation eBGP sessions. You should avoid this method when migrating a network to or from a confederation architecture, because temporary loops might form between routers in the confederation. This case study demonstrates the danger of using this method and ways to avoid loops.

Example 8-29 shows the modified BGP configurations on R1. This case study chooses to make R8's address reachable via the IGP, so the BGP next hop is not reset for the session between R1 and R4, and **next-hop-self** is removed from the Internal peer group. The danger of resetting the next hop to R1 for this session is demonstrated later in this case study. Similar configuration changes are made to R2 (not shown). Note that the iBGP sessions with R6 and R7 are still up and will be removed in a later step. After the sessions are up, R4 learns all the prefixes from R1 and R2.

Example 8-29 *BGP Configuration Changes on R1*

```
router bgp 100
 no synchronization
 bgp router-id 192.168.100.1
 bgp log-neighbor-changes
 bgp confederation identifier 100
 bgp confederation peers 65001
 neighbor Internal peer-group
 neighbor Internal remote-as 100
 neighbor Internal update-source Loopback0
 neighbor 192.168.14.4 remote-as 65001
 neighbor 192.168.18.8 remote-as 200
 neighbor 192.168.100.2 peer-group Internal
 neighbor 192.168.100.3 peer-group Internal
 neighbor 192.168.100.5 peer-group Internal
 neighbor 192.168.100.6 peer-group Internal
 neighbor 192.168.100.7 peer-group Internal
 no auto-summary
```

NOTE   In the configurations, a shaded line indicates that the line has been modified or added.

Figure 8-4 shows the current network topology. Although R4's configuration is complete, it is not yet in the forwarding paths (shown isolated in Figure 8-4). Within sub-AS 100, all routers are still fully meshed. Before proceeding to Step 5, verify that all the prefixes are still being received correctly on all the other routers.

Figure 8-4   *Current Network Topology*

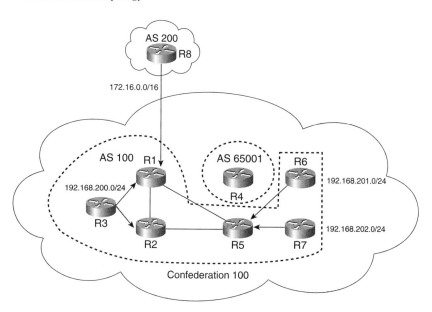

Step 5: Move R6 from Member AS 100 to Member AS 65001 and Put R4 Back in the Forwarding Paths

Move R6 into member AS 65001, which is service-affecting for the prefix originated locally on the router. Example 8-30 shows the new BGP configurations on R6. Note that R6 is not peered with any router in the other POP.

Example 8-30 *Current BGP Configurations on R6*

```
router bgp 65001
 no synchronization
 bgp router-id 192.168.100.6
 bgp log-neighbor-changes
 bgp confederation identifier 100
 bgp confederation peers 100 65000
 network 192.168.201.0
 neighbor Internal peer-group
 neighbor Internal remote-as 65001
 neighbor Internal update-source Loopback0
 neighbor 192.168.100.4 peer-group Internal
 neighbor 192.168.100.5 peer-group Internal
 neighbor 192.168.100.7 peer-group Internal
 no auto-summary
```

NOTE   When entire BGP configurations are changed, as in Example 8-30, no highlighting
(shading) is used.

After R4 learns the prefix from R6, put R4 back in the forwarding path so that the traffic
load can be shared between R4 and R5. Verify that the prefix 172.16.0.0/16 is available on
R4 and R6 and that the prefix 192.168.201.0/24 is available on all the routers in the member
AS 100 and on R8. Note that R4 already has the prefix 192.168.202.0/24 from Step 4.

NOTE   R4 can also be put back into the forwarding paths earlier, at the end of Step 4.

Verify that R1 learns all the prefixes correctly. Example 8-31 shows the BGP RIB on R1.
The prefix 192.168.201.0/24 is learned from member AS 65001.

Example 8-31 *BGP RIB on R1*

```
R1#show ip bgp
BGP table version is 11, local router ID is 192.168.100.1
Status codes: s suppressed, d damped, h history, * valid, > best, i - internal,
              r RIB-failure
Origin codes: i - IGP, e - EGP, ? - incomplete

   Network          Next Hop          Metric LocPrf Weight Path
*> 172.16.0.0       192.168.18.8           0            0 200 i
*>i192.168.200.0    192.168.100.3          0    100     0 i
*> 192.168.201.0    192.168.100.6          0    100     0 (65001) i
*>i192.168.202.0    192.168.100.7          0    100     0 i
```

Example 8-32 shows the current BGP RIB on R8. All three prefixes are received correctly
on R8, where the AS number is 100 and member AS numbers are not visible.

Example 8-32 *BGP RIB on R8*

```
R8#show ip bgp
BGP table version is 17, local router ID is 192.168.18.8
Status codes: s suppressed, d damped, h history, * valid, > best, i - internal,
              r RIB-failure
Origin codes: i - IGP, e - EGP, ? - incomplete

   Network          Next Hop          Metric LocPrf Weight Path
*> 172.16.0.0       0.0.0.0                0          32768 i
*> 192.168.200.0    192.168.18.1                        0 100 i
*> 192.168.201.0    192.168.18.1                        0 100 i
*> 192.168.202.0    192.168.18.1                        0 100 i
```

At this stage, there is no BGP redundancy in part of the network. This is because the sessions between R4 and R7, between R5 and R6, and between R4 and R5 are still down. The current topology is shown in Figure 8-5.

Figure 8-5   *Current Network Topology*

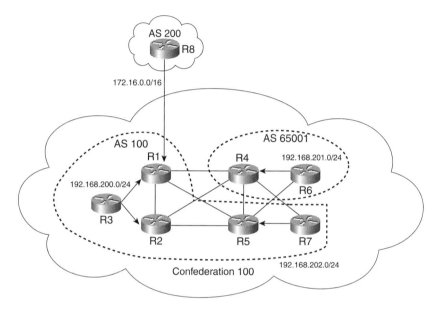

If **next-hop-self** is used for the session between R1 and R4 (the third option in Step 4), there is a potential forwarding loop between R1 and R4. Example 8-33 shows the BGP RIB on R4. Besides the route from R6, all other prefixes are learned via the member AS 100. Note that the BGP next hop for 192.168.202.0 is R1 for the path learned from R1 (the best path). A forwarding loop is formed between R1 and R4 for the prefix, because R4 is also one of the two IGP next hops from R1 to reach R7.

Example 8-33 *BGP RIB on R4*

```
R4#show ip bgp
BGP table version is 8, local router ID is 192.168.100.4
Status codes: s suppressed, d damped, h history, * valid, > best, i - internal,
              r RIB-failure, S Stale
Origin codes: i - IGP, e - EGP, ? - incomplete

   Network          Next Hop          Metric LocPrf Weight Path
*  172.16.0.0       192.168.100.1          0    100      0 (100) 200 i
*>                  192.168.14.1           0    100      0 (100) 200 i
*  192.168.200.0    192.168.100.3          0    100      0 (100) i
```

continues

Example 8-33 *BGP RIB on R4 (Continued)*

```
 *>                      192.168.14.1          0    100    0 (100) i
 *>i192.168.201.0        192.168.100.6         0    100    0 i
 *   192.168.202.0       192.168.100.7         0    100    0 (100) i
 *>                      192.168.14.1          0    100    0 (100) i
```

This temporary forwarding loop is formed only if the next hop is reset on R1 for all the pre-fixes, as indicated previously in Step 4. So the solution is to not reset next hops for sessions between member autonomous systems. You can do this by putting the link between R1 and R8 into IS-IS when the same IGP is used for the entire confederation, or by resetting the next hops only for eBGP learned routes on R1.

Step 6: Move R7 from Member AS 100 to Member AS 65001 and Move R5 out of the Forwarding Paths

Move R7 from member AS 100 to member AS 65001, which is service-affecting for the prefix originated locally on the router. Example 8-34 shows the new BGP configurations on R7.

Example 8-34 *BGP Configurations on R7*

```
router bgp 65001
 no synchronization
 bgp router-id 192.168.100.7
 bgp log-neighbor-changes
 bgp confederation identifier 100
 bgp confederation peers 100 65000
 network 192.168.202.0
 neighbor Internal peer-group
 neighbor Internal remote-as 65001
 neighbor Internal update-source Loopback0
 neighbor 192.168.100.4 peer-group Internal
 neighbor 192.168.100.5 peer-group Internal
 neighbor 192.168.100.6 peer-group Internal
 no auto-summary
```

To prepare the migration of R5 (in the next step) and to avoid traffic loss, you should move R5 out of the forwarding paths by increasing IGP metrics to R5. Because R4 has reachability to all prefixes, traffic forwarding is unaffected. The current network topology is shown in Figure 8-6.

CAUTION	A potential forwarding loop might form if **next-hop-self** is configured on R1 for the session between R1 and R4. As R5 learns prefix 192.168.201.0 from R1 with the BGP next hop reset as R1, a loop is formed when R5 is an IGP next hop for the prefix from R1. However, this loop is prevented when R5 is moved out of the forwarding paths.

Figure 8-6 *Current Network Topology*

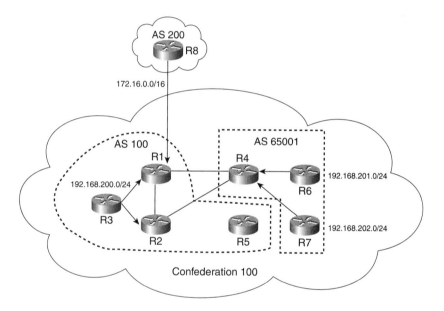

Step 7: Move R5 from Member AS 100 to Member AS 65001 and Put R5 Back in the Forwarding Paths

Move R5 from member AS 100 to member AS 65001. The warning messages on R4, R6, and R7 about the wrong AS should now stop. Example 8-35 shows the new BGP configurations on R5.

Example 8-35 *BGP Configurations on R5*

```
router bgp 65001
 no synchronization
 bgp router-id 192.168.100.5
 bgp log-neighbor-changes
```

continues

Example 8-35 *BGP Configurations on R5 (Continued)*

```
bgp confederation identifier 100
bgp confederation peers 100 65000
neighbor Internal peer-group
neighbor Internal remote-as 65001
neighbor Internal update-source Loopback0
neighbor 192.168.15.1 remote-as 100
neighbor 192.168.25.2 remote-as 100
neighbor 192.168.100.4 peer-group Internal
neighbor 192.168.100.6 peer-group Internal
neighbor 192.168.100.7 peer-group Internal
no auto-summary
```

After the routing information is learned, you can put R5 back in the forwarding paths by removing the IGP metric changes made in Step 6.

Step 8: Update the Peering with R5 on R1 and R2

On R1 and R2, update the peerings with R5. Remove the peering sessions with R6 and R7. Example 8-36 shows the new BGP configurations on R1.

Example 8-36 *BGP Configurations on R1*

```
router bgp 100
 no synchronization
 bgp router-id 192.168.100.1
 bgp log-neighbor-changes
 bgp confederation identifier 100
 bgp confederation peers 65001
 neighbor Internal peer-group
 neighbor Internal remote-as 100
 neighbor Internal update-source Loopback0
 neighbor 192.168.14.4 remote-as 65001
 neighbor 192.168.15.5 remote-as 65001
 neighbor 192.168.18.8 remote-as 200
 neighbor 192.168.100.2 peer-group Internal
 neighbor 192.168.100.3 peer-group Internal
 no auto-summary
```

This step completes the migration of the POP on the right. An updated topology is shown in Figure 8-7.

Figure 8-7   *Current Network Topology*

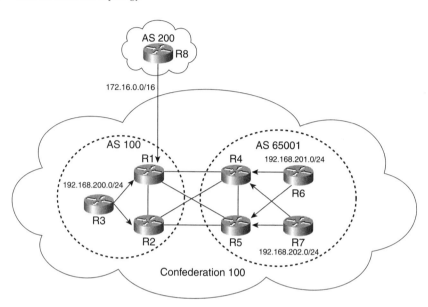

Step 9: Move R2 out of the Forwarding Paths, and Migrate R2 from Member AS 100 to Member AS 65000

Move R2 from the current member AS 100 to a new member AS 65000. To avoid black-holing traffic on R2, you should move R2 out of the forwarding paths until the migration of R2 is complete (in the next step). Example 8-37 shows R2's new BGP configurations.

Example 8-37 *BGP Configurations on R2*

```
router bgp 65000
 no synchronization
 bgp router-id 192.168.100.2
 bgp log-neighbor-changes
 bgp confederation identifier 100
 bgp confederation peers 65001
 neighbor Internal peer-group
 neighbor Internal remote-as 65000
 neighbor Internal update-source Loopback0
 neighbor 192.168.24.4 remote-as 65001
 neighbor 192.168.25.5 remote-as 65001
 neighbor 192.168.100.1 peer-group Internal
 neighbor 192.168.100.3 peer-group Internal
 no auto-summary
```

Figure 8-8 shows the updated topology. Note that R2 is not in the forwarding path for any prefix.

Figure 8-8 *Current Network Topology*

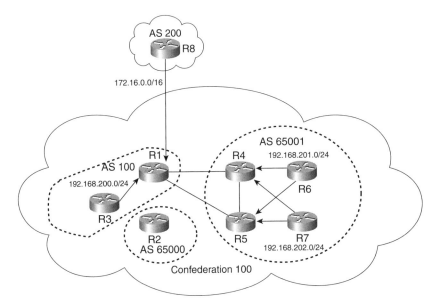

Step 10: Update the Peerings with R2 and Put R2 Back in the Forwarding Paths

On R4 and R5, update the peerings with R2. The updated BGP configurations on R4 are shown in Example 8-38. Make similar changes to the BGP configurations on R5 (not shown).

Example 8-38 *BGP Configurations on R4*

```
router bgp 65001
 no synchronization
 bgp router-id 192.168.100.4
 bgp log-neighbor-changes
 bgp confederation identifier 100
 bgp confederation peers 100 65000
 neighbor Internal peer-group
 neighbor Internal remote-as 65001
 neighbor Internal update-source Loopback0
 neighbor 192.168.14.1 remote-as 100
 neighbor 192.168.24.2 remote-as 65000
 neighbor 192.168.100.5 peer-group Internal
 neighbor 192.168.100.6 peer-group Internal
 neighbor 192.168.100.7 peer-group Internal
 no auto-summary
```

After the routing information is received on R2, put R2 back in the forwarding paths by removing the IGP metric changes made in Step 9.

Step 11: Move R3 from Member AS 100 to Member AS 65000

Move R3 from member AS 100 to member AS 65000, which is service-affecting for the prefix originated locally on the router. You can remove the unneeded sessions with routers on the other POP. Example 8-39 shows the new BGP configurations on R3.

Example 8-39 *BGP Configurations on R3*

```
router bgp 65000
 no synchronization
 bgp router-id 192.168.100.3
 bgp log-neighbor-changes
 bgp confederation identifier 100
 bgp confederation peers 65001
 network 192.168.200.0
 neighbor Internal peer-group
 neighbor Internal remote-as 65000
 neighbor Internal update-source Loopback0
 neighbor 192.168.100.1 peer-group Internal
 neighbor 192.168.100.2 peer-group Internal
 no auto-summary
```

Example 8-40 shows the current BGP summary table on R2. The down session with R1 (in Active state) is expected, because R1 is not updated with the correct peering with R2. This is not needed, because you migrate R1 next.

Example 8-40 *BGP Summary Table on R2*

```
R2#show ip bgp summary
BGP router identifier 192.168.100.2, local AS number 65000
BGP table version is 9, main routing table version 9
4 network entries and 7 paths using 668 bytes of memory
3 BGP path attribute entries using 180 bytes of memory
2 BGP AS-PATH entries using 48 bytes of memory
0 BGP route-map cache entries using 0 bytes of memory
0 BGP filter-list cache entries using 0 bytes of memory
BGP activity 5/35 prefixes, 9/2 paths, scan interval 60 secs

Neighbor        V    AS MsgRcvd MsgSent   TblVer  InQ OutQ Up/Down  State/PfxRcd
192.168.24.4    4 65001      32      27        9    0    0 00:12:50            3
192.168.25.5    4 65001      33      34        9    0    0 00:12:08            3
192.168.100.1   4 65000      37      37        0    0    0 never    Active
192.168.100.3   4 65000      39      43        9    0    0 00:02:27            1
```

Example 8-41 shows the new BGP RIB on R1. All routes are properly received and installed. The prefix 192.168.200.0 is received from R4 and R5 in member AS 65001, because the sessions between R1 and R3 and between R1 and R2 are not up. This is fine, because the forwarding still follows the IGP path from R1 to R3 directly.

Example 8-41 *BGP RIB on R1*

```
R1#show ip bgp
BGP table version is 15, local router ID is 192.168.100.1
Status codes: s suppressed, d damped, h history, * valid, > best, i - internal,
              r RIB-failure
Origin codes: i - IGP, e - EGP, ? - incomplete

   Network          Next Hop          Metric LocPrf Weight Path
*> 172.16.0.0       192.168.18.8           0             0 200 i
*  192.168.200.0    192.168.100.3          0    100      0 (65001 65000) i
*>                  192.168.100.3          0    100      0 (65001 65000) i
*  192.168.201.0    192.168.100.6          0    100      0 (65001) i
*>                  192.168.100.6          0    100      0 (65001) i
*  192.168.202.0    192.168.100.7          0    100      0 (65001) i
*>                  192.168.100.7          0    100      0 (65001) i
```

Figure 8-9 shows the current topology.

Figure 8-9   *R3 Moved to AS 65000*

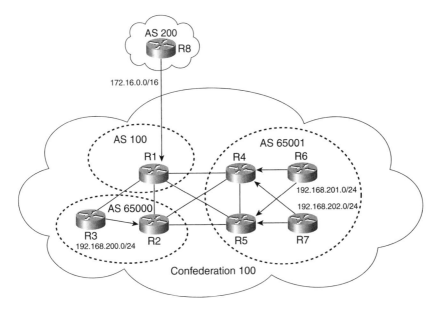

Step 12: Move R1 from Member AS 100 to Member AS 65000

Move R1 from member AS 100 to member AS 65000. This removes member AS 100 from the topology, which is service-affecting between AS 200 and confederation 100, unless redundant connections exist. Example 8-42 shows the new BGP configurations on R1.

Example 8-42 *BGP Configurations on R1*

```
router bgp 65000
 no synchronization
 bgp router-id 192.168.100.1
 bgp log-neighbor-changes
 bgp confederation identifier 100
 bgp confederation peers 65001
 neighbor Internal peer-group
 neighbor Internal remote-as 65000
 neighbor Internal update-source Loopback0
 neighbor 192.168.14.4 remote-as 65001
 neighbor 192.168.15.5 remote-as 65001
 neighbor 192.168.18.8 remote-as 200
 neighbor 192.168.100.2 peer-group Internal
 neighbor 192.168.100.3 peer-group Internal
 no auto-summary
```

Step 13: Update the Peering with R1

On R4 and R5, update the peerings with R1. Example 8-43 shows the new BGP configurations on R4. Similar changes are made to R5 (not shown). Now you can remove member AS 100 from the peer list.

Example 8-43 *BGP Configurations on R4*

```
router bgp 65001
 no synchronization
 bgp router-id 192.168.100.4
 bgp log-neighbor-changes
 bgp confederation identifier 100
 bgp confederation peers 65000
 neighbor Internal peer-group
 neighbor Internal remote-as 65001
 neighbor Internal update-source Loopback0
 neighbor 192.168.14.1 remote-as 65000
 neighbor 192.168.24.2 remote-as 65000
 neighbor 192.168.100.5 peer-group Internal
 neighbor 192.168.100.6 peer-group Internal
 neighbor 192.168.100.7 peer-group Internal
 no auto-summary
```

This step completes the migration process. The topology is the final topology, as shown earlier in Figure 8-4. In the next step, you verify the prefixes' reachability.

Step 14: Verify BGP Reachability for All Prefixes

Verify that all the sessions are up and that routes are properly received. The following examples show some of the sample outputs.

Example 8-44 shows the BGP summary table on R1.

Example 8-44 *BGP Summary Table on R1*

```
R1#show ip bgp summary
BGP router identifier 192.168.100.1, local AS number 65000
BGP table version is 5, main routing table version 5
4 network entries and 8 paths using 708 bytes of memory
3 BGP path attribute entries using 180 bytes of memory
2 BGP AS-PATH entries using 48 bytes of memory
0 BGP route-map cache entries using 0 bytes of memory
0 BGP filter-list cache entries using 0 bytes of memory
BGP activity 4/8 prefixes, 8/0 paths, scan interval 60 secs

Neighbor        V    AS MsgRcvd MsgSent   TblVer  InQ OutQ Up/Down   State/PfxRcd
192.168.14.4    4 65001      23      22        5    0    0 00:13:26            2
192.168.15.5    4 65001      24      23        5    0    0 00:12:25            2
192.168.18.8    4   200      18      19        5    0    0 00:13:55            1
192.168.100.2   4 65000      19      18        5    0    0 00:13:58            2
192.168.100.3   4 65000      18      18        5    0    0 00:13:59            1
```

Example 8-45 shows the BGP summary table on R5.

Example 8-45 *BGP Summary Table on R5*

```
R5#show ip bgp summary
BGP router identifier 192.168.100.5, local AS number 65001
BGP table version is 16, main routing table version 16
4 network entries and 8 paths using 708 bytes of memory
3 BGP path attribute entries using 180 bytes of memory
2 BGP AS-PATH entries using 48 bytes of memory
0 BGP route-map cache entries using 0 bytes of memory
0 BGP filter-list cache entries using 0 bytes of memory
BGP activity 6/45 prefixes, 14/6 paths, scan interval 60 secs

Neighbor        V    AS MsgRcvd MsgSent   TblVer  InQ OutQ Up/Down   State/PfxRcd
192.168.15.1    4 65000     149     152       16    0    0 00:16:06            2
192.168.25.2    4 65000     145     152       16    0    0 01:08:20            2
192.168.100.4   4 65001     145     146       16    0    0 02:13:49            2
192.168.100.6   4 65001     138     146       16    0    0 02:13:56            1
192.168.100.7   4 65001     138     146       16    0    0 02:13:29            1
```

Example 8-46 shows the BGP RIB on R5. Note that R5 receives three paths for 172.16.0.0 and 192.168.200.0: one from R4 via iBGP, one from R1 via intraconfederation eBGP, and one from R2 via intraconfederation eBGP.

Example 8-46 *BGP RIB on R5*

```
R5#show ip bgp
BGP table version is 16, local router ID is 192.168.100.5
Status codes: s suppressed, d damped, h history, * valid, > best, i - internal,
              r RIB-failure
Origin codes: i - IGP, e - EGP, ? - incomplete

   Network          Next Hop          Metric LocPrf Weight Path
 * i172.16.0.0      192.168.14.1           0    100      0 (65000) 200 i
 *>                 192.168.15.1           0    100      0 (65000) 200 i
 *                  192.168.100.1          0    100      0 (65000) 200 i
 *> 192.168.200.0   192.168.15.1           0    100      0 (65000) i
 * i                192.168.14.1           0    100      0 (65000) i
 *                  192.168.100.3          0    100      0 (65000) i
 *>i192.168.201.0   192.168.100.6          0    100      0 i
 *>i192.168.202.0   192.168.100.7          0    100      0 i
```

Example 8-47 shows the BGP RIB on R8. Note that all three prefixes from AS 100 are received correctly.

Example 8-47 *BGP RIB on R8*

```
R8#show ip bgp
BGP table version is 27, local router ID is 192.168.18.8
Status codes: s suppressed, d damped, h history, * valid, > best, i - internal,
              r RIB-failure
Origin codes: i - IGP, e - EGP, ? - incomplete

   Network          Next Hop          Metric LocPrf Weight Path
 *> 172.16.0.0      0.0.0.0                0           32768 i
 *> 192.168.200.0   192.168.18.1                          0 100 i
 *> 192.168.201.0   192.168.18.1                          0 100 i
 *> 192.168.202.0   192.168.18.1                          0 100 i
```

Case Study 3: Route Reflection to Confederation Migration

This case study presents detailed procedures on how to migrate an RR-based network to a confederation-based architecture. The starting topology is shown in Figure 8-2. The final topology is shown in Figure 8-3. In the final topology, the same IGP is used across the confederation member autonomous systems.

Because of some similarities between iBGP full mesh and route reflection (for example, neither has AS subdivision), many of the procedures described in this case study are similar to those in Case Study 2. Thus, detailed discussions in some steps are omitted for brevity. For completeness, all necessary steps are still retained.

Starting Configurations

Although some of the configurations were presented in Case Study 1 in the section "Final BGP Configurations," the complete BGP configurations for all the routers are presented here for reference in Examples 8-48 through 8-55.

The BGP next hop is reset on R1 so that the external prefix can be reached in AS 100. The other way to accomplish the reachability is to put the inter-AS link in IS-IS and configure passive interface on the link, as shown in Example 8-48.

Example 8-48 *BGP Configurations on R1*

```
router bgp 100
 no synchronization
 bgp router-id 192.168.100.1
 bgp log-neighbor-changes
 neighbor Internal peer-group
 neighbor Internal remote-as 100
 neighbor Internal update-source Loopback0
 neighbor Internal next-hop-self
 neighbor Clients peer-group
 neighbor Clients remote-as 100
 neighbor Clients update-source Loopback0
 neighbor Clients route-reflector-client
 neighbor Clients next-hop-self
 neighbor 192.168.18.8 remote-as 200
 neighbor 192.168.100.2 peer-group Internal
 neighbor 192.168.100.3 peer-group Clients
 neighbor 192.168.100.4 peer-group Internal
 neighbor 192.168.100.5 peer-group Internal
 no auto-summary
```

Configure route reflection on R1 and R2, with R3 as the only client. All core routers (RRs) are fully meshed. (See Example 8-49.)

Example 8-49 *BGP Configurations on R2*

```
router bgp 100
 no synchronization
 bgp router-id 192.168.100.2
 bgp log-neighbor-changes
 neighbor Internal peer-group
 neighbor Internal remote-as 100
 neighbor Internal update-source Loopback0
```

Example 8-49 *BGP Configurations on R2 (Continued)*

```
 neighbor Clients peer-group
 neighbor Clients remote-as 100
 neighbor Clients update-source Loopback0
 neighbor Clients route-reflector-client
 neighbor 192.168.100.1 peer-group Internal
 neighbor 192.168.100.3 peer-group Clients
 neighbor 192.168.100.4 peer-group Internal
 neighbor 192.168.100.5 peer-group Internal
 no auto-summary
```

R3 is a client that peers with both R1 and R2. (See Example 8-50.)

Example 8-50 *BGP Configurations on R3*

```
router bgp 100
 no synchronization
 bgp router-id 192.168.100.3
 bgp log-neighbor-changes
 network 192.168.200.0
 neighbor Internal peer-group
 neighbor Internal remote-as 100
 neighbor Internal update-source Loopback0
 neighbor 192.168.100.1 peer-group Internal
 neighbor 192.168.100.2 peer-group Internal
 no auto-summary
```

R4 is an RR in the right POP serving R7 and R8. It is fully meshed with other RRs. (See Example 8-51.)

Example 8-51 *BGP Configurations on R4*

```
router bgp 100
 no synchronization
 bgp router-id 192.168.100.4
 bgp log-neighbor-changes
 neighbor Internal peer-group
 neighbor Internal remote-as 100
 neighbor Internal update-source Loopback0
 neighbor Clients peer-group
 neighbor Clients remote-as 100
 neighbor Clients update-source Loopback0
 neighbor Clients route-reflector-client
 neighbor 192.168.100.1 peer-group Internal
 neighbor 192.168.100.2 peer-group Internal
```

continues

Example 8-51 *BGP Configurations on R4 (Continued)*

```
 neighbor 192.168.100.5 peer-group Internal
 neighbor 192.168.100.6 peer-group Clients
 neighbor 192.168.100.7 peer-group Clients
 no auto-summary
```

R5 is the other RR in the right POP. (See Example 8-52.)

Example 8-52 *BGP Configurations on R5*

```
router bgp 100
 no synchronization
 bgp router-id 192.168.100.5
 bgp log-neighbor-changes
 neighbor Internal peer-group
 neighbor Internal remote-as 100
 neighbor Internal update-source Loopback0
 neighbor Clients peer-group
 neighbor Clients remote-as 100
 neighbor Clients update-source Loopback0
 neighbor Clients route-reflector-client
 neighbor 192.168.100.1 peer-group Internal
 neighbor 192.168.100.2 peer-group Internal
 neighbor 192.168.100.4 peer-group Internal
 neighbor 192.168.100.6 peer-group Clients
 neighbor 192.168.100.7 peer-group Clients
 no auto-summary
```

R6 is an RR client of both R4 and R5. (See Example 8-53.)

Example 8-53 *BGP Configurations on R6*

```
router bgp 100
 no synchronization
 bgp router-id 192.168.100.6
 bgp log-neighbor-changes
 network 192.168.201.0
 neighbor Internal peer-group
 neighbor Internal remote-as 100
 neighbor Internal update-source Loopback0
 neighbor 192.168.100.4 peer-group Internal
 neighbor 192.168.100.5 peer-group Internal
 no auto-summary
```

R7 is the other client in the right POP. (See Example 8-54.)

Example 8-54 *BGP Configurations on R7*

```
router bgp 100
 no synchronization
 bgp router-id 192.168.100.7
 bgp log-neighbor-changes
 network 192.168.202.0
 neighbor Internal peer-group
 neighbor Internal remote-as 100
 neighbor Internal update-source Loopback0
 neighbor 192.168.100.4 peer-group Internal
 neighbor 192.168.100.5 peer-group Internal
 no auto-summary
```

The configurations on R8 remain the same. (See Example 8-55.)

Example 8-55 *BGP Configurations on R8*

```
router bgp 200
 no synchronization
 bgp log-neighbor-changes
 network 172.16.0.0
 neighbor 192.168.18.1 remote-as 100
 no auto-summary
```

Migration Procedures

Because the high-level summary is similar to that in the previous case study, only detailed procedures are provided in this section.

Step 1: Select R4 as the Starting Router and Move It out of the Forwarding Paths

Select R4 as the starting router. Because both clients R6 and R7 are served by two redundant RRs, moving R4 out of the RR architecture does not affect BGP reachability. As in Case Study 2, move R4 out of the forwarding path to avoid traffic loss.

Step 2: Migrate R4 from AS 100 to Member AS 65001 and Update All Other Routers with Confederation Configurations

Migrate R4 by replacing the current BGP process with member AS 65001, and configure the confederation using the current BGP AS number 100 as the confederation ID. Configure 100 and 65000 as member AS peers.

Example 8-56 shows the new confederation configuration on R4.

Example 8-56 *BGP Confederation Configurations on R4*

```
R4(config)#no router bgp 100
R4(config)#bgp router 65001
R4(config-router)#bgp confederation identifier 100
R4(config-router)#bgp confederation peers 100 65000
```

Add confederation configurations to all other routers in AS 100—specifically, the **bgp confederation identifier 100** and **bgp confederation peers** commands. Consult the final topology to determine the member AS numbers to use.

Step 3: Create Intramember and Intermember AS Sessions on R4

Create a peer group called Internal for intramember AS peers, and assign R5, R6, and R7 to the peer group. Create additional peer sessions for intermember AS peers. In other words, make R4 peer with R1 and R2. During the changeover, R1, R2, R4, R5, R6, and R7 might complain that the peer is in the wrong AS. Ignore these messages.

NOTE   In a real migration, Steps 2 and 3 would be combined. Two steps are presented here for easier discussion.

Example 8-57 shows the new BGP configurations on R4.

Example 8-57 *BGP Configurations on R4*

```
router bgp 65001
 no synchronization
 bgp router-id 192.168.100.4
 bgp log-neighbor-changes
 bgp confederation identifier 100
 bgp confederation peers 100 65000
 neighbor Internal peer-group
 neighbor Internal remote-as 65001
 neighbor Internal update-source Loopback0
 neighbor 192.168.14.1 remote-as 100
 neighbor 192.168.24.2 remote-as 100
 neighbor 192.168.100.5 peer-group Internal
 neighbor 192.168.100.6 peer-group Internal
 neighbor 192.168.100.7 peer-group Internal
 no auto-summary
```

Step 4: Update the Peering on R1 and R2

On R1 and R2, change the current iBGP peering with R4 to eBGP peering. To make R8 reachable within confederation 100, put the link between R1 and R8 as part of the IGP. Also remove the **next-hop-self** setting in both peer groups on R1. Consult Step 4 in Case Study 2 for the various options for setting BGP next hops.

Example 8-58 shows the modified BGP configurations on R1. Similar configuration changes are made to R2 (not shown).

Example 8-58 *BGP Configuration Changes on R1*

```
router bgp 100
 no synchronization
 bgp router-id 192.168.100.1
 bgp log-neighbor-changes
 bgp confederation identifier 100
 bgp confederation peers 65001
 neighbor Internal peer-group
 neighbor Internal remote-as 100
 neighbor Internal update-source Loopback0
 neighbor Clients peer-group
 neighbor Clients remote-as 100
 neighbor Clients update-source Loopback0
 neighbor Clients route-reflector-client
 neighbor 192.168.14.4 remote-as 65001
 neighbor 192.168.18.8 remote-as 200
 neighbor 192.168.100.2 peer-group Internal
 neighbor 192.168.100.3 peer-group Clients
 neighbor 192.168.100.5 peer-group Internal
 no auto-summary
```

Figure 8-10 shows the updated network topology.

Step 5: Move R6 from Member AS 100 to Member AS 65001 and Put R4 Back in the Forwarding Paths

Move R6 into member AS 65001, which is service-affecting for the prefix originated locally on the router. Example 8-59 shows the new BGP configurations on R6. Note that R6 has peer sessions with all other routers in the right POP.

Example 8-59 *Current BGP Configurations on R6*

```
router bgp 65001
 no synchronization
 bgp router-id 192.168.100.6
 bgp log-neighbor-changes
 bgp confederation identifier 100
 bgp confederation peers 100 65000
 network 192.168.201.0
```

continues

Example 8-59 *Current BGP Configurations on R6 (Continued)*

```
neighbor Internal peer-group
neighbor Internal remote-as 65001
neighbor Internal update-source Loopback0
neighbor 192.168.100.4 peer-group Internal
neighbor 192.168.100.5 peer-group Internal
neighbor 192.168.100.7 peer-group Internal
no auto-summary
```

Figure 8-10 *Current Network Topology*

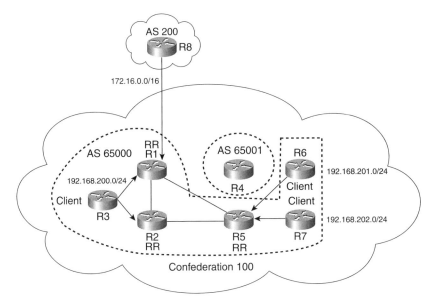

Now put R4 back in the forwarding paths. Verify that prefix 172.16.0.0/16 is available on R4 and R6 and that prefix 192.168.201.0/24 is available on all the routers in member AS 100 and on R8.

Example 8-60 shows the BGP summary table on R4. As expected, the sessions with R5 and R7 are still down. Ignore the messages about the wrong AS.

Example 8-60 *BGP Summary Table on R4*

```
R4#show ip bgp summary
BGP router identifier 192.168.100.4, local AS number 65001
BGP table version is 5, main routing table version 5
4 network entries and 7 paths using 668 bytes of memory
3 BGP path attribute entries using 180 bytes of memory
2 BGP AS-PATH entries using 48 bytes of memory
0 BGP route-map cache entries using 0 bytes of memory
0 BGP filter-list cache entries using 0 bytes of memory
```

Example 8-60 *BGP Summary Table on R4 (Continued)*

```
BGP activity 4/0 prefixes, 7/0 paths, scan interval 60 secs

Neighbor        V    AS MsgRcvd MsgSent  TblVer  InQ OutQ Up/Down  State/PfxRcd
192.168.14.1    4   100      10      10       5    0    0 00:01:13          3
192.168.24.2    4   100      12      11       5    0    0 00:01:06          3
192.168.100.5   4 65001     233     233       0    0    0 never    Idle
192.168.100.6   4 65001     231     232       5    0    0 00:03:54          1
192.168.100.7   4 65001     231     233       0    0    0 never    Idle
```

Example 8-61 shows the BGP RIB on R1. Note that the prefix 192.168.201.0/24 is learned from member AS 65001.

Example 8-61 *BGP RIB on R1*

```
R1#show ip bgp
BGP table version is 9, local router ID is 192.168.100.1
Status codes: s suppressed, d damped, h history, * valid, > best, i - internal,
              r RIB-failure
Origin codes: i - IGP, e - EGP, ? - incomplete

   Network          Next Hop          Metric LocPrf Weight Path
*> 172.16.0.0       192.168.18.8           0             0 200 i
*  i192.168.200.0   192.168.100.3          0    100      0 i
*>i                 192.168.100.3          0    100      0 i
*> 192.168.201.0    192.168.100.6          0    100      0 (65001) i
*>i192.168.202.0    192.168.100.7          0    100      0 i
```

Example 8-62 shows the current BGP RIB on R8. All prefixes from AS 100 are received correctly.

Example 8-62 *BGP RIB on R8*

```
R8#show ip bgp
BGP table version is 7, local router ID is 192.168.18.8
Status codes: s suppressed, d damped, h history, * valid, > best, i - internal,
              r RIB-failure
Origin codes: i - IGP, e - EGP, ? - incomplete

   Network          Next Hop          Metric LocPrf Weight Path
*> 172.16.0.0       0.0.0.0                0         32768 i
*> 192.168.200.0    192.168.18.1                        0 100 i
*> 192.168.201.0    192.168.18.1                        0 100 i
*> 192.168.202.0    192.168.18.1                        0 100 i
```

At this stage, there is no BGP redundancy in part of the network. The current topology is shown in Figure 8-11.

Figure 8-11 *Current Network Topology*

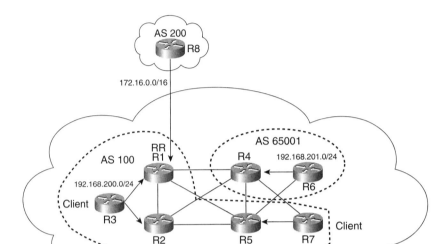

Step 6: Move R7 from Member AS 100 to Member AS 65001 and Move R5 out of the Forwarding Paths

Move R7 from member AS 100 to member AS 65001, which is service-affecting for the prefix originated locally on the router. Example 8-63 shows the new BGP configurations on R7.

Example 8-63 *BGP Configurations on R7*

```
router bgp 65001
 no synchronization
 bgp router-id 192.168.100.7
 bgp log-neighbor-changes
 bgp confederation identifier 100
 bgp confederation peers 100 65000
 network 192.168.202.0
 neighbor Internal peer-group
 neighbor Internal remote-as 65001
 neighbor Internal update-source Loopback0
 neighbor 192.168.100.4 peer-group Internal
 neighbor 192.168.100.5 peer-group Internal
 neighbor 192.168.100.6 peer-group Internal
 no auto-summary
```

To prepare the migration of R5 (in the next step) and to avoid traffic loss, you should move R5 out of the forwarding paths by increasing IGP metrics to R5. Because R4 has reachability to all prefixes, traffic forwarding is unaffected. The current network topology is shown in Figure 8-12.

Figure 8-12 *Current Network Topology*

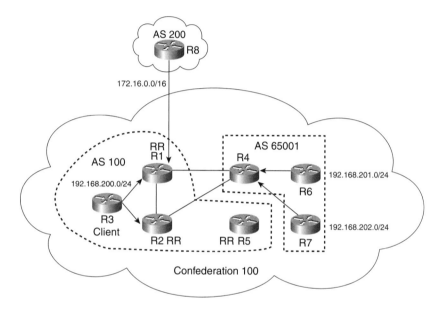

Step 7: Move R5 from Member AS 100 to Member AS 65001 and Put R5 Back in the Forwarding Paths

Move R5 from member AS 100 to AS 65001. The warning messages on R4, R6, and R7 about the wrong AS are now gone. When the correct routing information is learned, you can put R5 back in the forwarding paths. Example 8-64 shows the new BGP configurations on R5.

Example 8-64 *BGP Configurations on R5*

```
router bgp 65001
 no synchronization
 bgp router-id 192.168.100.5
 bgp log-neighbor-changes
 bgp confederation identifier 100
 bgp confederation peers 100 65000
 neighbor Internal peer-group
```

continues

Example 8-64 *BGP Configurations on R5 (Continued)*

```
 neighbor Internal remote-as 65001
 neighbor Internal update-source Loopback0
 neighbor 192.168.15.1 remote-as 100
 neighbor 192.168.25.2 remote-as 100
 neighbor 192.168.100.4 peer-group Internal
 neighbor 192.168.100.6 peer-group Internal
 neighbor 192.168.100.7 peer-group Internal
 no auto-summary
```

Step 8: Update the Peering with R5

On R1 and R2, update the peering with R5. Example 8-65 shows the current BGP
configurations on R1. Similar configuration changes are made to R2 (not shown).

Example 8-65 *BGP Configurations on R1*

```
router bgp 100
 no synchronization
 bgp router-id 192.168.100.1
 bgp log-neighbor-changes
 bgp confederation identifier 100
 bgp confederation peers 65001
 neighbor Internal peer-group
 neighbor Internal remote-as 100
 neighbor Internal update-source Loopback0
 neighbor Clients peer-group
 neighbor Clients remote-as 100
 neighbor Clients update-source Loopback0
 neighbor Clients route-reflector-client
 neighbor 192.168.14.4 remote-as 65001
 neighbor 192.168.15.5 remote-as 65001
 neighbor 192.168.18.8 remote-as 200
 neighbor 192.168.100.2 peer-group Internal
 neighbor 192.168.100.3 peer-group Clients
 no auto-summary
```

This step completes the migration of the POP on the right. An updated topology is shown
in Figure 8-13.

Figure 8-13 *Current Network Topology*

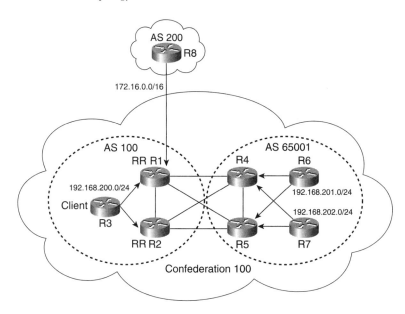

Step 9: Move R2 out of the Forwarding Paths and Migrate R2 from Member AS 100 to Member AS 65000

Move R2 from the current member AS 100 to the new member AS 65000. To avoid black-holing traffic by R2, you should move R2 out of the forwarding paths.

Example 8-66 shows R2's new BGP configurations. After the configuration change, R1, R3, R4, and R5 complain about the wrong AS to R2. Ignore these messages; they are expected during this phase of the migration.

Example 8-66 *BGP Configurations on R2*

```
router bgp 65000
 no synchronization
 bgp router-id 192.168.100.2
 bgp log-neighbor-changes
 bgp confederation identifier 100
 bgp confederation peers 65001
 neighbor Internal peer-group
```

continues

Example 8-66 *BGP Configurations on R2 (Continued)*

```
neighbor Internal remote-as 65000
neighbor Internal update-source Loopback0
neighbor 192.168.24.4 remote-as 65001
neighbor 192.168.25.5 remote-as 65001
neighbor 192.168.100.1 peer-group Internal
neighbor 192.168.100.3 peer-group Internal
no auto-summary
```

Figure 8-14 shows the updated topology.

Figure 8-14 *Current Network Topology*

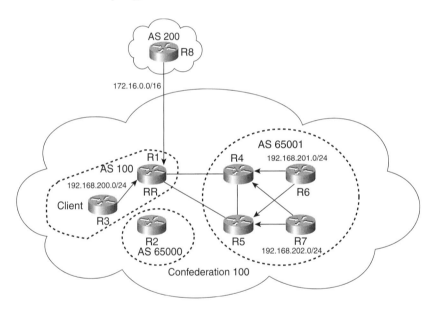

Step 10: Update the Peerings with R2, and Put R2 Back in the Forwarding Paths

On R4 and R5, update the peerings with R2. Example 8-67 shows the updated BGP
configurations on R4. Make similar changes to the BGP configurations on R5 (not shown).

Example 8-67 *BGP Configurations on R4*

```
router bgp 65001
 no synchronization
 bgp router-id 192.168.100.4
```

Example 8-67 *BGP Configurations on R4 (Continued)*

```
bgp log-neighbor-changes
bgp confederation identifier 100
bgp confederation peers 100 65000
neighbor Internal peer-group
neighbor Internal remote-as 65001
neighbor Internal update-source Loopback0
neighbor 192.168.14.1 remote-as 100
neighbor 192.168.24.2 remote-as 65000
neighbor 192.168.100.5 peer-group Internal
neighbor 192.168.100.6 peer-group Internal
neighbor 192.168.100.7 peer-group Internal
no auto-summary
```

After the routing information is received on R2, put R2 back in the forwarding paths by removing the IGP metric changes made in Step 9.

Step 11: Move R3 from Member AS 100 to Member AS 65000

Move R3 from member AS 100 to member AS 65000, which is service-affecting for the prefix originated locally on the router. In this case, the prefix 192.168.200.0/24 is temporarily unavailable during the configuration change on R3. Example 8-68 shows the new BGP configurations on R3.

Example 8-68 *BGP Configurations on R3*

```
router bgp 65000
 no synchronization
 bgp router-id 192.168.100.3
 bgp log-neighbor-changes
 bgp confederation identifier 100
 bgp confederation peers 65000
 network 192.168.200.0
 neighbor Internal peer-group
 neighbor Internal remote-as 65000
 neighbor Internal update-source Loopback0
 neighbor 192.168.100.1 peer-group Internal
 neighbor 192.168.100.2 peer-group Internal
 no auto-summary
```

Example 8-69 shows the current BGP summary table on R2. As expected, the session with R1 is down. This is fine, because R2 receives all routes correctly, and you will migrate R1 next.

Example 8-69 *BGP Summary Table on R2*

```
R2#show ip bgp summary
BGP router identifier 192.168.100.2, local AS number 65000
BGP table version is 5, main routing table version 5
4 network entries and 7 paths using 668 bytes of memory
3 BGP path attribute entries using 180 bytes of memory
2 BGP AS-PATH entries using 48 bytes of memory
0 BGP route-map cache entries using 0 bytes of memory
0 BGP filter-list cache entries using 0 bytes of memory
BGP activity 4/28 prefixes, 7/0 paths, scan interval 60 secs

Neighbor          V    AS MsgRcvd MsgSent   TblVer  InQ OutQ Up/Down  State/PfxRcd
192.168.24.4      4 65001      16      14        5    0    0 00:09:45           3
192.168.25.5      4 65001      16      17        5    0    0 00:09:50           3
192.168.100.1     4 65000      22      22        0    0    0 never      Idle
192.168.100.3     4 65000      14      16        5    0    0 00:09:06           1
```

Example 8-70 shows the new BGP RIB on R1. Note that prefix 192.168.200.0 is received from member AS 65001, because R1 has no sessions with R3 or R2. This is fine, because R3 is the next hop for both BGP and IGP. Traffic is forwarded directly to R3.

Example 8-70 *BGP RIB on R1*

```
R1#show ip bgp
BGP table version is 17, local router ID is 192.168.100.1
Status codes: s suppressed, d damped, h history, * valid, > best, i - internal,
              r RIB-failure
Origin codes: i - IGP, e - EGP, ? - incomplete

   Network          Next Hop            Metric LocPrf Weight Path
*> 172.16.0.0       192.168.18.8             0             0 200 i
*  192.168.200.0    192.168.100.3            0    100      0 (65001 65000) i
*>                  192.168.100.3            0    100      0 (65001 65000) i
*  192.168.201.0    192.168.100.6            0    100      0 (65001) i
*>                  192.168.100.6            0    100      0 (65001) i
*  192.168.202.0    192.168.100.7            0    100      0 (65001) i
*>                  192.168.100.7            0    100      0 (65001) i
```

Figure 8-15 shows the current topology.

Figure 8-15 *R3 Moved to AS 65000*

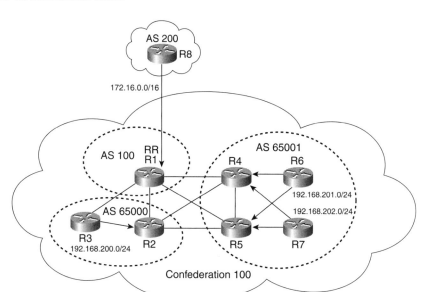

Step 12: Move R1 from Member AS 100 to Member AS 65000

Move R1 from member AS 100 to member AS 65000, which is service-affecting between AS 200 and confederation 100 unless redundant connections exist. This removes member AS 100 from the topology. Example 8-71 shows the new BGP configurations on R1.

Example 8-71 *BGP Configurations on R1*

```
router bgp 65000
 no synchronization
 bgp router-id 192.168.100.1
 bgp log-neighbor-changes
 bgp confederation identifier 100
 bgp confederation peers 65001
 neighbor Internal peer-group
 neighbor Internal remote-as 65000
 neighbor Internal update-source Loopback0
 neighbor 192.168.14.4 remote-as 65001
 neighbor 192.168.15.5 remote-as 65001
 neighbor 192.168.18.8 remote-as 200
 neighbor 192.168.100.2 peer-group Internal
 neighbor 192.168.100.3 peer-group Internal
 no auto-summary
```

Step 13: Update the Peerings with R1

On R4 and R5, update the peerings with R1. Example 8-72 shows the new BGP configurations on R4. Similar changes are made to R5 (not shown). Additionally, you can remove the intraconfederation peer 100 from the configurations in R4 and R5. Note that this does not affect service.

Example 8-72 *BGP Configurations on R4*

```
router bgp 65001
 no synchronization
 bgp router-id 192.168.100.4
 bgp log-neighbor-changes
 bgp confederation identifier 100
 bgp confederation peers 65000
 neighbor Internal peer-group
 neighbor Internal remote-as 65001
 neighbor Internal update-source Loopback0
 neighbor 192.168.14.1 remote-as 65000
 neighbor 192.168.24.2 remote-as 65000
 neighbor 192.168.100.5 peer-group Internal
 neighbor 192.168.100.6 peer-group Internal
 neighbor 192.168.100.7 peer-group Internal
 no auto-summary
```

Step 14: Verify All the Routing Information

Verify that all the sessions are up and that routes are properly received. This step completes the migration. The following examples show some sample outputs.

Example 8-73 shows the BGP summary table on R1.

Example 8-73 *BGP Summary Table on R1*

```
R1#show ip bgp summary
BGP router identifier 192.168.100.1, local AS number 65000
BGP table version is 5, main routing table version 5
4 network entries and 8 paths using 708 bytes of memory
3 BGP path attribute entries using 180 bytes of memory
2 BGP AS-PATH entries using 48 bytes of memory
0 BGP route-map cache entries using 0 bytes of memory
0 BGP filter-list cache entries using 0 bytes of memory
BGP activity 4/8 prefixes, 8/0 paths, scan interval 60 secs

Neighbor        V    AS MsgRcvd MsgSent   TblVer  InQ OutQ Up/Down  State/PfxRcd
192.168.14.4    4 65001      16      14        5    0    0 00:02:29            2
192.168.15.5    4 65001      16      14        5    0    0 00:01:50            2
192.168.18.8    4   200       9      10        5    0    0 00:04:32            1
192.168.100.2   4 65000      10       9        5    0    0 00:04:49            2
192.168.100.3   4 65000      10      10        5    0    0 00:05:01            1
```

Example 8-74 shows the BGP RIB on R1.

Example 8-74 *BGP RIB on R1*

```
R1#show ip bgp
BGP table version is 5, local router ID is 192.168.100.1
Status codes: s suppressed, d damped, h history, * valid, > best, i - internal,
              r RIB-failure
Origin codes: i - IGP, e - EGP, ? - incomplete

   Network          Next Hop          Metric LocPrf Weight Path
*> 172.16.0.0       192.168.18.8           0             0 200 i
*>i192.168.200.0    192.168.100.3          0    100      0 i
*  192.168.201.0    192.168.100.6          0    100      0 (65001) i
*                   192.168.100.6          0    100      0 (65001) i
*>i                 192.168.100.6          0    100      0 (65001) i
*  192.168.202.0    192.168.100.7          0    100      0 (65001) i
*                   192.168.100.7          0    100      0 (65001) i
*>i                 192.168.100.7          0    100      0 (65001) i
```

Example 8-75 shows the BGP RIB detail for 192.168.201.0/24 on R1. Three paths are from R5, R4, and R2.

Example 8-75 *BGP RIB Detail for 192.168.201.0/24 on R1*

```
R1#show ip bgp 192.168.201.0
BGP routing table entry for 192.168.201.0/24, version 4
Paths: (3 available, best #3, table Default-IP-Routing-Table)
  Advertised to non peer-group peers:
  192.168.14.4 192.168.15.5 192.168.18.8
  (65001)
    192.168.100.6 (metric 30) from 192.168.15.5 (192.168.100.5)
      Origin IGP, metric 0, localpref 100, valid, confed-external
  (65001)
    192.168.100.6 (metric 30) from 192.168.14.4 (192.168.100.4)
      Origin IGP, metric 0, localpref 100, valid, confed-external
  (65001)
    192.168.100.6 (metric 30) from 192.168.100.2 (192.168.100.2)
      Origin IGP, metric 0, localpref 100, valid, confed-internal, best
```

Example 8-76 shows the BGP RIB on R5. For the two prefixes that are not from the local AS, R5 receives three paths: one from R1, one from R4, and one from R2.

Example 8-76 *BGP RIB on R5*

```
R5#show ip bgp
BGP table version is 17, local router ID is 192.168.100.5
Status codes: s suppressed, d damped, h history, * valid, > best, i - internal,
              r RIB-failure
```

continues

Example 8-76 *BGP RIB on R5 (Continued)*

```
Origin codes: i - IGP, e - EGP, ? - incomplete

   Network          Next Hop         Metric LocPrf Weight Path
*>  172.16.0.0      192.168.15.1          0    100      0 (65000) 200 i
* i                 192.168.14.1          0    100      0 (65000) 200 i
*                   192.168.100.1         0    100      0 (65000) 200 i
*>  192.168.200.0   192.168.15.1          0    100      0 (65000) i
* i                 192.168.14.1          0    100      0 (65000) i
*                   192.168.100.3         0    100      0 (65000) i
*>i192.168.201.0    192.168.100.6         0    100      0 i
*>i192.168.202.0    192.168.100.7         0    100      0 i
```

Example 8-77 shows the BGP RIB on R8. Note that all prefixes from AS 100 are received correctly.

Example 8-77 *BGP RIB on R8*

```
R8#show ip bgp
BGP table version is 17, local router ID is 192.168.18.8
Status codes: s suppressed, d damped, h history, * valid, > best, i - internal,
              r RIB-failure
Origin codes: i - IGP, e - EGP, ? - incomplete

   Network          Next Hop         Metric LocPrf Weight Path
*>  172.16.0.0      0.0.0.0               0          32768 i
*>  192.168.200.0   192.168.18.1                         0 100 i
*>  192.168.201.0   192.168.18.1                         0 100 i
*>  192.168.202.0   192.168.18.1                         0 100 i
```

Case Study 4: Confederation to Route Reflection Migration

This case study presents detailed procedures on how to migrate a confederation-based network into a route reflection-based architecture. Because this case study is the reverse of Case Study 3, the final topology in Case Study 3 (refer to Figure 8-3) is used as the starting topology, and the starting topology in Case Study 3 (refer to Figure 8-2) is used as the final topology.

Starting Configurations

The starting BGP configurations for all the routers are shown in Examples 8-78 through 8-85.

The starting BGP configurations on R1 are slightly different from the final configurations in Case Study 3 (refer to Example 8-71). To demonstrate a different way to reset the BGP next hop inside the confederation, the BGP next hop on R1 is reset using a route map set-NH for sessions with the other member AS. For sessions within the same member AS, the BGP next hop is still reset using the **next-hop-self** method. (See Example 8-78.)

Example 8-78 *BGP Configurations on R1*

```
router bgp 65000
 no synchronization
 bgp router-id 192.168.100.1
 bgp log-neighbor-changes
 bgp confederation identifier 100
 bgp confederation peers 65001
 neighbor Internal peer-group
 neighbor Internal remote-as 65000
 neighbor Internal update-source Loopback0
 neighbor Internal next-hop-self
 neighbor 192.168.14.4 remote-as 65001
 neighbor 192.168.14.4 route-map set-NH out
 neighbor 192.168.15.5 remote-as 65001
 neighbor 192.168.15.5 route-map set-NH out
neighbor 192.168.18.8 remote-as 200
 neighbor 192.168.100.2 peer-group Internal
 neighbor 192.168.100.3 peer-group Internal
 no auto-summary
!
access-list 1 permit 192.168.18.8
!
route-map set-NH permit 10
 match ip route-source 1
 set ip next-hop 192.168.100.1
!
route-map set-NH permit 20
!
```

Within the route map set-NH, only routes from R8 (192.168.18.8) are reset with a next hop to R1 (192.168.100.1). As discussed in Case Studies 2 and 3, this is one of the methods to avoid forwarding loops during migration.

Example 8-79 shows the BGP configurations of R2.

Example 8-79 *BGP Configurations on R2*

```
router bgp 65000
 no synchronization
 bgp router-id 192.168.100.2
 bgp log-neighbor-changes
 bgp confederation identifier 100
 bgp confederation peers 65001
 neighbor Internal peer-group
```

continues

Example 8-79 *BGP Configurations on R2 (Continued)*

```
 neighbor Internal remote-as 65000
 neighbor Internal update-source Loopback0
 neighbor 192.168.24.4 remote-as 65001
 neighbor 192.168.25.5 remote-as 65001
 neighbor 192.168.100.1 peer-group Internal
 neighbor 192.168.100.3 peer-group Internal
 no auto-summary
```

R3 peers only with R1 and R2 in the same member AS. (See Example 8-80.)

Example 8-80 *BGP Configurations on R3*

```
router bgp 65000
 no synchronization
 bgp router-id 192.168.100.3
 bgp log-neighbor-changes
 bgp confederation identifier 100
 bgp confederation peers 65001
 network 192.168.200.0
 neighbor Internal peer-group
 neighbor Internal remote-as 65000
 neighbor Internal update-source Loopback0
 neighbor 192.168.100.1 peer-group Internal
 neighbor 192.168.100.2 peer-group Internal
 no auto-summary
```

R4 is a border router in member AS 65001. It peers with R1 and R2 using intraconfederation eBGP. (See Example 8-81.)

Example 8-81 *BGP Configurations on R4*

```
router bgp 65001
 no synchronization
 bgp router-id 192.168.100.4
 bgp log-neighbor-changes
 bgp confederation identifier 100
 bgp confederation peers 65000
 neighbor Internal peer-group
 neighbor Internal remote-as 65001
 neighbor Internal update-source Loopback0
 neighbor 192.168.14.1 remote-as 65000
 neighbor 192.168.24.2 remote-as 65000
 neighbor 192.168.100.5 peer-group Internal
 neighbor 192.168.100.6 peer-group Internal
 neighbor 192.168.100.7 peer-group Internal
 no auto-summary
```

R5 is the other border router in member AS 65001. It is fully meshed with other BGP speakers in the same member AS. (See Example 8-82.)

Example 8-82 *BGP Configurations on R5*

```
router bgp 65001
 no synchronization
 bgp router-id 192.168.100.5
 bgp log-neighbor-changes
 bgp confederation identifier 100
 bgp confederation peers 65000
 neighbor Internal peer-group
 neighbor Internal remote-as 65001
 neighbor Internal update-source Loopback0
 neighbor 192.168.15.1 remote-as 65000
 neighbor 192.168.25.2 remote-as 65000
 neighbor 192.168.100.4 peer-group Internal
 neighbor 192.168.100.6 peer-group Internal
 neighbor 192.168.100.7 peer-group Internal
 no auto-summary
```

R6 is an internal router and is fully meshed with all other routers in member AS 65001. (See Example 8-83.)

Example 8-83 *BGP Configurations on R6*

```
router bgp 65001
 no synchronization
 bgp router-id 192.168.100.6
 bgp log-neighbor-changes
 bgp confederation identifier 100
 bgp confederation peers 65000
 network 192.168.201.0
 neighbor Internal peer-group
 neighbor Internal remote-as 65001
 neighbor Internal update-source Loopback0
 neighbor 192.168.100.4 peer-group Internal
 neighbor 192.168.100.5 peer-group Internal
 neighbor 192.168.100.7 peer-group Internal
 no auto-summary
```

R7 is the other internal router in member AS 65001. (See Example 8-84.)

Example 8-84 *BGP Configurations on R7*

```
router bgp 65001
 no synchronization
 bgp router-id 192.168.100.7
 bgp log-neighbor-changes
```

continues

Example 8-84 *BGP Configurations on R7 (Continued)*

```
bgp confederation identifier 100
bgp confederation peers 65000
network 192.168.202.0
neighbor Internal peer-group
neighbor Internal remote-as 65001
neighbor Internal update-source Loopback0
neighbor 192.168.100.4 peer-group Internal
neighbor 192.168.100.5 peer-group Internal
neighbor 192.168.100.6 peer-group Internal
no auto-summary
```

Configurations on R8 are not changed during migration. (See Example 8-85.)

Example 8-85 *BGP Configurations on R8*

```
router bgp 200
 no synchronization
 bgp log-neighbor-changes
 network 172.16.0.0
 neighbor 192.168.18.1 remote-as 100
 no auto-summary
```

Migration Procedures

When the first router is migrated, a new member AS, AS 100, is created. This router also has confederation ID 100. This in effect changes the two-member-AS confederation into a three-member-AS confederation. The remaining procedures are to migrate routers from the other two member autonomous systems to the new member AS 100. When all the routers are moved to member AS 100, the migration is complete.

Here is a high-level summary of the steps:

Step 1 Select R4 as the starting router, and move it out of the forwarding paths.

Step 2 Migrate R4 to a new member AS 100, and make it a route reflector.

Step 3 On R1 and R2, add member AS 100 to the peers, and update the peerings with R4.

Step 4 Move R6 from member AS 65001 to member AS 100. Put R4 back in the forwarding paths.

Step 5   Move R7 from member AS 65001 to member AS 100, and move R5 out of the forwarding paths.

Step 6   Move R5 from member AS 65001 to member AS 100, as in Step 2.

Step 7   On R1 and R2, update the peerings with R5. Put R5 back in the forwarding paths.

Step 8   Move R2 out of the forwarding paths, and migrate R2 from member AS 65000 to member AS 100.

Step 9   Update the peering on R4 and R5, and put R2 back into the forwarding paths.

Step 10   Move R3 from member AS 65000 to member AS 100.

Step 11   Move R1 from member AS 65000 to member AS 100.

Step 12   Update the peering with R1.

Step 13   Remove the confederation from the configurations of all routers in AS 100.

Step 14   Verify BGP reachability for all prefixes.

The following sections illustrate the detailed procedures.

Step 1: Select R4 as the Starting Router and Move It out of the Forwarding Paths

Select R4 as the starting router. To avoid black-holing traffic on R4, move R4 out of the forwarding paths.

Step 2: Migrate R4 to a New Member AS 100 and Make It a Route Reflector

Move R4 from member AS 65001 to a new member AS 100 within confederation 100, with member autonomous systems 65000 and 65001 as confederation eBGP peers. Make R4 an RR. Create two peer groups: one for the intraconfederation eBGP sessions and one for the clients. The Peers peer group includes R1 and R2. The Clients peer group includes R6 and R7. The peering with R5 is unimportant at this point. Example 8-86 shows the new BGP configurations on R4.

Example 8-86 *BGP Configurations on R4*

```
router bgp 100
 no synchronization
 bgp router-id 192.168.100.4
 bgp log-neighbor-changes
 bgp confederation identifier 100
 bgp confederation peers 65000 65001
 neighbor Peers peer-group
 neighbor Peers remote-as 65000
 neighbor Clients peer-group
 neighbor Clients remote-as 100
 neighbor Clients update-source Loopback0
 neighbor Clients route-reflector-client
 neighbor 192.168.14.1 peer-group Peers
 neighbor 192.168.24.2 peer-group Peers
 neighbor 192.168.100.6 peer-group Clients
 neighbor 192.168.100.7 peer-group Clients
 no auto-summary
```

Error messages about wrong AS numbers are reported on R1, R2, R4, R6, and R7. Ignore them. Verify that all the prefixes are still properly received on routers other than R4. The following are some sample outputs.

Step 1   Example 8-87 shows the BGP RIB on R1. Both prefixes originated from the POP on the right are received correctly.

Example 8-87 *BGP RIB on R1*

```
R1#show ip bgp
BGP table version is 9, local router ID is 192.168.100.1
Status codes: s suppressed, d damped, h history, * valid, > best, i - internal,
              r RIB-failure
Origin codes: i - IGP, e - EGP, ? - incomplete

   Network          Next Hop            Metric LocPrf Weight Path
*> 172.16.0.0       192.168.18.8             0             0 200 i
*>i192.168.200.0    192.168.100.3            0    100      0 i
*  192.168.201.0    192.168.100.6            0    100      0 (65001) i
*>i                 192.168.100.6            0    100      0 (65001) i
*  192.168.202.0    192.168.100.7            0    100      0 (65001) i
*>i                 192.168.100.7            0    100      0 (65001) i
```

Example 8-88 shows the BGP RIB on R6. The external prefix and the prefix from the POP on the left are received correctly.

Example 8-88 *BGP Configurations on R6*

```
R6#show ip bgp
BGP table version is 9, local router ID is 192.168.100.6
Status codes: s suppressed, d damped, h history, * valid, > best, i - internal,
              r RIB-failure
Origin codes: i - IGP, e - EGP, ? - incomplete


   Network          Next Hop           Metric LocPrf Weight Path
*>i172.16.0.0       192.168.15.1            0    100      0 (65000) 200 i
*>i192.168.200.0    192.168.100.3           0    100      0 (65000) i
*> 192.168.201.0    0.0.0.0                 0          32768 i
*>i192.168.202.0    192.168.100.7           0    100      0 I
```

Step 3: On R1 and R2, Add Member AS 100 to the Peers and Update the Peerings with R4

On R1 and R2, update the peerings with R4. Example 8-89 shows the new BGP configurations on R1. Note that you must add member AS 100 to the confederation peer list. Without it, the session cannot be established. If R1 thinks R4 is attempting an eBGP session rather than a confederation eBGP session, the session is rejected because it conflicts with confederation 100. Similar changes are made to R2.

Example 8-89 *BGP Configurations on R1*

```
router bgp 65000
 no synchronization
 bgp router-id 192.168.100.1
 bgp log-neighbor-changes
 bgp confederation identifier 100
 bgp confederation peers 100 65001
 neighbor Internal peer-group
 neighbor Internal remote-as 65000
 neighbor Internal update-source Loopback0
 neighbor Internal next-hop-self
 neighbor 192.168.14.4 remote-as 100
 neighbor 192.168.14.4 route-map set-NH out
 neighbor 192.168.15.5 remote-as 65001
 neighbor 192.168.15.5 route-map set-NH out
 neighbor 192.168.18.8 remote-as 200
 neighbor 192.168.100.2 peer-group Internal
 neighbor 192.168.100.3 peer-group Internal
 no auto-summary
```

Figure 8-16 shows the updated topology.

Figure 8-16 *Current Network Topology*

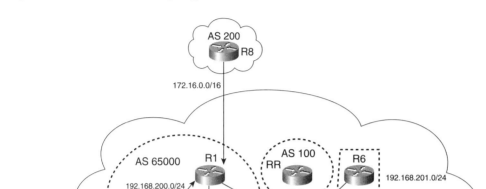

Step 4: Move R6 from Member AS 65001 to Member AS 100 and Put R4 Back in the Forwarding Paths

Move R6 from member AS 65001 to member AS 100. On R6, create a peer group called Internal for sessions with its future RRs, R4 and R5. Example 8-90 shows the new BGP configurations on R6. Note that R6 peers only with the two core routers in the same POP.

Example 8-90 *BGP Configurations on R6*

```
router bgp 100
 no synchronization
 bgp router-id 192.168.100.6
 bgp log-neighbor-changes
 bgp confederation identifier 100
 bgp confederation peers 65000 65001
 network 192.168.201.0
 neighbor Internal peer-group
 neighbor Internal remote-as 100
 neighbor Internal update-source Loopback0
 neighbor 192.168.100.4 peer-group Internal
 neighbor 192.168.100.5 peer-group Internal
 no auto-summary
```

The change made in this step is service-affecting on the router that originates prefixes. The prefix 192.168.201.0/24 is temporarily unavailable during the configuration change. R4 can be put back in the forwarding paths when all the routing information is learned correctly.

NOTE   As demonstrated in the previous two case studies, resetting the BGP next hop to R1 for confederation eBGP routes on the R1-R4 session can cause forwarding loops between the core routers in this step. The loops are avoided when the next hop is reset for only the external prefix on R1.

Example 8-91 shows the BGP summary table on R4. The session with R7 is down, as expected.

Example 8-91 *BGP Summary Table on R4*

```
R4#show ip bgp summary
BGP router identifier 192.168.100.4, local AS number 100
BGP table version is 5, main routing table version 5
4 network entries and 7 paths using 740 bytes of memory
4 BGP path attribute entries using 240 bytes of memory
3 BGP AS-PATH entries using 72 bytes of memory
0 BGP route-map cache entries using 0 bytes of memory
0 BGP filter-list cache entries using 0 bytes of memory
BGP activity 4/2 prefixes, 7/0 paths, scan interval 60 secs

Neighbor        V    AS MsgRcvd MsgSent   TblVer  InQ OutQ Up/Down  State/PfxRcd
192.168.14.1    4 65000      21      27        5    0    0 00:06:44        3
192.168.24.2    4 65000      23      24        5    0    0 00:05:39        3
192.168.100.6   4   100      84      87        5    0    0 00:15:53        1
192.168.100.7   4   100      97      99        0    0    0 never    Idle
```

Example 8-92 shows the BGP RIB on R4. The dual paths for prefixes from outside the local AS are received from R1 and R2.

Example 8-92 *BGP RIB on R4*

```
R4#show ip bgp
BGP table version is 5, local router ID is 192.168.100.4
Status codes: s suppressed, d damped, h history, * valid, > best, i - internal,
              r RIB-failure
Origin codes: i - IGP, e - EGP, ? - incomplete
```

continues

Example 8-92 *BGP RIB on R4 (Continued)*

```
    Network           Next Hop            Metric LocPrf Weight Path
*   172.16.0.0        192.168.100.1           0    100      0 (65000) 200 i
*>                    192.168.100.1           0    100      0 (65000) 200 i
*   192.168.200.0     192.168.100.3           0    100      0 (65000) i
*>                    192.168.100.3           0    100      0 (65000) i
*>i192.168.201.0      192.168.100.6           0    100      0 i
*>  192.168.202.0     192.168.100.7           0    100      0 (65000 65001) i
```

Example 8-93 shows the BGP RIB on R1. The prefix 192.168.201.0 is received from member AS 100.

Example 8-93 *BGP Summary Table on R1*

```
R1#show ip bgp
BGP table version is 11, local router ID is 192.168.100.1
Status codes: s suppressed, d damped, h history, * valid, > best, i - internal,
              r RIB-failure
Origin codes: i - IGP, e - EGP, ? - incomplete

    Network           Next Hop            Metric LocPrf Weight Path
*>  172.16.0.0        192.168.18.8            0              0 200 i
*>i192.168.200.0      192.168.100.3           0    100      0 i
*>  192.168.201.0     192.168.100.6           0    100      0 (100) i
*>  192.168.202.0     192.168.100.7           0    100      0 (65001) i
```

The current network topology is shown in Figure 8-17.

Figure 8-17 *R6 in AS 100 and R4 in the Forwarding Paths*

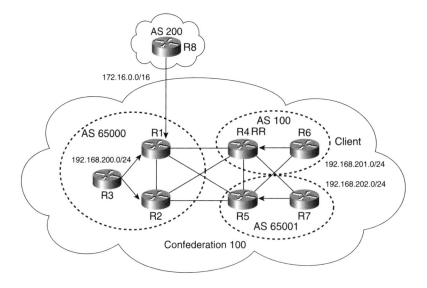

Step 5: Move R7 from Member AS 65001 to Member AS 100 and Move R5 out of the Forwarding Paths

Move R7 from member AS 65001 to member AS 100. Create a peer group called Internal for sessions with its future RRs, R4 and R5. Example 8-94 shows the new BGP configurations on R7. Note that there is no need to have 65001 in the peer list, because you will migrate R5 next.

Example 8-94 *BGP Configurations on R7*

```
router bgp 100
 no synchronization
 bgp router-id 192.168.100.7
 bgp log-neighbor-changes
 bgp confederation identifier 100
 bgp confederation peers 65000
 network 192.168.202.0
 neighbor Internal peer-group
 neighbor Internal remote-as 100
 neighbor Internal update-source Loopback0
 neighbor 192.168.100.4 peer-group Internal
 neighbor 192.168.100.5 peer-group Internal
 no auto-summary
```

The change made in this step is service-affecting on the router that originates prefixes. The prefix 192.168.202.0/24 is temporarily unavailable during the configuration change.

Before proceeding further, verify that all routes are properly received. Example 8-95 shows the BGP RIB on R1. Both prefixes from the POP on the right are received from member AS 100.

Example 8-95 *BGP RIB on R1*

```
R1#show ip bgp
BGP table version is 15, local router ID is 192.168.100.1
Status codes: s suppressed, d damped, h history, * valid, > best, i - internal,
              r RIB-failure
Origin codes: i - IGP, e - EGP, ? - incomplete

   Network          Next Hop            Metric LocPrf Weight Path
*> 172.16.0.0       192.168.18.8             0             0 200 i
*>i192.168.200.0    192.168.100.3            0    100      0 i
*> 192.168.201.0    192.168.100.6            0    100      0 (100) i
*> 192.168.202.0    192.168.100.7            0    100      0 (100) i
```

Figure 8-18 shows the updated topology.

Figure 8-18 *R7 in Member AS 100 and R5 out of the Forwarding Paths*

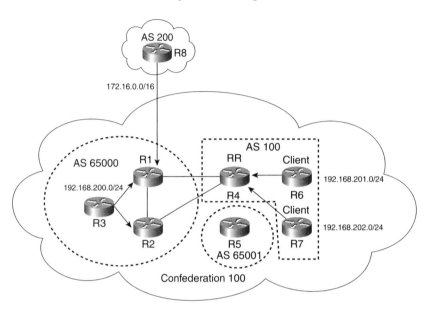

Step 6: Move R5 from Member AS 65001 to Member AS 100

Move R5 from member AS 65001 to member AS 100, as in Step 2. Create a new peer group called Internal for future peerings with all other RRs. Currently, only R4 is a member of the peer group Internal. Create a peer group called Clients that includes R6 and R7. Example 8-96 shows the new BGP configurations on R5.

Example 8-96 *BGP Configurations on R5*

```
router bgp 100
 no synchronization
 bgp router-id 192.168.100.5
 bgp log-neighbor-changes
 bgp confederation identifier 100
 bgp confederation peers 65000
 neighbor Peers peer-group
 neighbor Peers remote-as 65000
 neighbor Clients peer-group
 neighbor Clients remote-as 100
 neighbor Clients update-source Loopback0
 neighbor Clients route-reflector-client
 neighbor Internal peer-group
 neighbor Internal remote-as 100
 neighbor Internal update-source Loopback0
 neighbor 192.168.15.1 peer-group Peers
 neighbor 192.168.25.2 peer-group Peers
```

Example 8-96 *BGP Configurations on R5 (Continued)*

```
 neighbor 192.168.100.4 peer-group Internal
 neighbor 192.168.100.6 peer-group Clients
 neighbor 192.168.100.7 peer-group Clients
 no auto-summary
```

A similar peer group is created on R4 to peer with R5. Example 8-97 shows the new configurations on R4.

Example 8-97 *New BGP Configurations on R4*

```
router bgp 100
 no synchronization
 bgp router-id 192.168.100.4
 bgp log-neighbor-changes
 bgp confederation identifier 100
 bgp confederation peers 65000 65001
 neighbor Peers peer-group
 neighbor Peers remote-as 65000
 neighbor Clients peer-group
 neighbor Clients remote-as 100
 neighbor Clients update-source Loopback0
 neighbor Clients route-reflector-client
 neighbor Internal peer-group
 neighbor Internal remote-as 100
 neighbor Internal update-source Loopback0
 neighbor 192.168.14.1 peer-group Peers
 neighbor 192.168.24.2 peer-group Peers
 neighbor 192.168.100.5 peer-group Internal
 neighbor 192.168.100.6 peer-group Clients
 neighbor 192.168.100.7 peer-group Clients
 no auto-summary
```

Step 7: On R1 and R2, Update the Peerings with R5 and Put R5 Back in the Forwarding Paths

You need to update configurations on R1 and R2 to peer with R5. Example 8-98 shows the new BGP configurations on R1. Similar changes are made to R2 (not shown). Now you can put R5 back in the forwarding paths.

Example 8-98 *New BGP Configurations on R1*

```
router bgp 65000
 no synchronization
 bgp router-id 192.168.100.1
 bgp log-neighbor-changes
 bgp confederation identifier 100
 bgp confederation peers 100 65001
```

continues

Example 8-98 *New BGP Configurations on R1 (Continued)*

```
 neighbor Internal peer-group
 neighbor Internal remote-as 65000
 neighbor Internal update-source Loopback0
 neighbor Internal next-hop-self
 neighbor 192.168.14.4 remote-as 100
 neighbor 192.168.14.4 route-map set-NH out
 neighbor 192.168.15.5 remote-as 100
 neighbor 192.168.15.5 route-map set-NH out
 neighbor 192.168.18.8 remote-as 200
 neighbor 192.168.100.2 peer-group Internal
 neighbor 192.168.100.3 peer-group Internal
 no auto-summary
```

Figure 8-19 shows the updated network topology. This step completes the migration of the POP on the right.

Figure 8-19 *Current Network Topology*

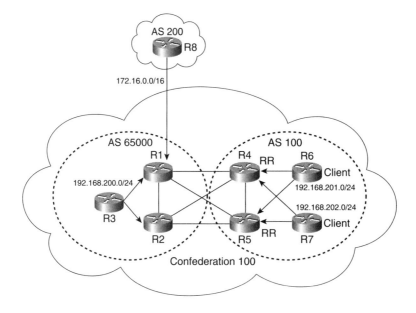

Step 8: Move R2 out of the Forwarding Paths and Migrate R2 from Member AS 65000 to Member AS 100

Move R2 from member AS 65000 to member AS 100. To avoid black-holing traffic on R2, you should move R2 out of the forwarding paths.

Example 8-99 shows the new configurations on R2.

Example 8-99 *New BGP Configurations on R2*

```
router bgp 100
 no synchronization
 bgp router-id 192.168.100.2
 bgp log-neighbor-changes
bgp confederation identifier 100
 bgp confederation peers 65000
 neighbor Internal peer-group
 neighbor Internal remote-as 100
 neighbor Internal update-source Loopback0
 neighbor Clients peer-group
 neighbor Clients remote-as 100
 neighbor Clients update-source Loopback0
 neighbor Clients route-reflector-client
 neighbor 192.168.100.1 peer-group Internal
 neighbor 192.168.100.3 peer-group Clients
 neighbor 192.168.100.4 peer-group Internal
 neighbor 192.168.100.5 peer-group Internal
 no auto-summary
```

Step 9: Update the Peering on R4 and R5 and Put R2 Back in the Forwarding Paths

Modify the peerings on R4 and R5 to reflect the changes on R2. Example 8-100 shows the new BGP configurations on R4.

Example 8-100 *New BGP Configurations on R4*

```
router bgp 100
 no synchronization
 bgp router-id 192.168.100.4
 bgp log-neighbor-changes
 bgp confederation identifier 100
 bgp confederation peers 65000 65001
 neighbor Peers peer-group
 neighbor Peers remote-as 65000
 neighbor Clients peer-group
 neighbor Clients remote-as 100
 neighbor Clients update-source Loopback0
 neighbor Clients route-reflector-client
 neighbor Internal peer-group
 neighbor Internal remote-as 100
 neighbor Internal update-source Loopback0
 neighbor 192.168.14.1 peer-group Peers
 neighbor 192.168.100.2 peer-group Internal
 neighbor 192.168.100.5 peer-group Internal
 neighbor 192.168.100.6 peer-group Clients
 neighbor 192.168.100.7 peer-group Clients
 no auto-summary
```

When all the routing information is correctly received, R2 can be put back in the forwarding paths. Example 8-101 shows the BGP summary table on R2. As expected, sessions with R1 and R3 are not up.

Example 8-101 *BGP Summary Table on R2*

```
R2#show ip bgp summary
BGP router identifier 192.168.100.2, local AS number 100
BGP table version is 1, main routing table version 1
4 network entries and 8 paths using 788 bytes of memory
3 BGP path attribute entries using 180 bytes of memory
4 BGP rrinfo entries using 96 bytes of memory
2 BGP AS-PATH entries using 48 bytes of memory
0 BGP route-map cache entries using 0 bytes of memory
0 BGP filter-list cache entries using 0 bytes of memory
BGP activity 4/8 prefixes, 8/0 paths, scan interval 60 secs

Neighbor        V    AS MsgRcvd MsgSent   TblVer  InQ OutQ Up/Down  State/PfxRcd
192.168.100.1   4   100       7       7        0    0    0 never    Idle
192.168.100.3   4   100       7       7        0    0    0 never    Idle
192.168.100.4   4   100       9       4        0    0    0 00:01:52        4
192.168.100.5   4   100       9       4        0    0    0 00:01:02        4
```

Figure 8-20 shows the current network topology.

Figure 8-20 *Current Network Topology*

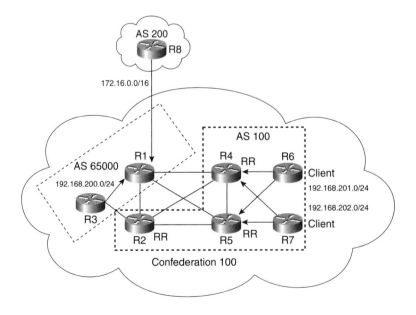

Step 10: Move R3 from Member AS 65000 to Member AS 100

Move R3 from member AS 65000 to member AS 100, which is service-affecting on the router that originates prefixes. The prefix 192.168.200.0/24 is temporarily unavailable during the configuration change. Example 8-102 shows the new BGP configurations on R3.

Example 8-102 *New BGP Configurations on R3*

```
router bgp 100
 no synchronization
 bgp router-id 192.168.100.3
 bgp log-neighbor-changes
 bgp confederation identifier 100
 bgp confederation peers 65000
 network 192.168.200.0
 neighbor Internal peer-group
 neighbor Internal remote-as 100
 neighbor Internal update-source Loopback0
 neighbor 192.168.100.1 peer-group Internal
 neighbor 192.168.100.2 peer-group Internal
 no auto-summary
```

Example 8-103 shows the current BGP RIB on R3. Note that the next hop for 172.16.0.0 is 192.168.100.1 because R3 learned the route from R2, which in turn learned it from R4 and R5.

Example 8-103 *BGP RIB on R3*

```
R3#show ip bgp
BGP table version is 5, local router ID is 192.168.100.3
Status codes: s suppressed, d damped, h history, * valid, > best, i - internal,
              r RIB-failure
Origin codes: i - IGP, e - EGP, ? - incomplete

   Network          Next Hop            Metric LocPrf Weight Path
*>i172.16.0.0       192.168.100.1            0    100      0 (65000) 200 i
*> 192.168.200.0    0.0.0.0                  0         32768 i
*>i192.168.201.0    192.168.100.6            0    100      0 i
*>i192.168.202.0    192.168.100.7            0    100      0 i
```

Example 8-104 shows the current BGP RIB on R1.

Example 8-104 *BGP RIB on R1*

```
R1#show ip bgp
BGP table version is 17, local router ID is 192.168.100.1
Status codes: s suppressed, d damped, h history, * valid, > best, i - internal,
              r RIB-failure
```

continues

Example 8-104 *BGP RIB on R1 (Continued)*

```
Origin codes: i - IGP, e - EGP, ? - incomplete

   Network            Next Hop          Metric LocPrf Weight Path
*> 172.16.0.0         192.168.18.8           0             0 200 i
*  192.168.200.0      192.168.100.3          0    100      0 (100) i
*>                    192.168.100.3          0    100      0 (100) i
*  192.168.201.0      192.168.100.6          0    100      0 (100) i
*>                    192.168.100.6          0    100      0 (100) i
*  192.168.202.0      192.168.100.7          0    100      0 (100) i
*>                    192.168.100.7          0    100      0 (100) i
```

Figure 8-21 shows the current network topology.

Figure 8-21 *R3 in AS 100*

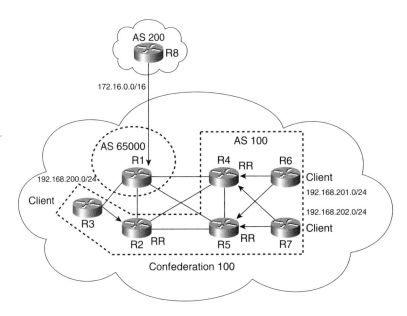

Step 11: Move R1 from Member AS 65000 to Member AS 100

Move R1 from member AS 65000 to member AS 100. The change in this step is service-affecting between AS 200 and confederation 100. Example 8-105 shows the new BGP configurations on R1.

Example 8-105 *BGP Configurations on R1*

```
router bgp 100
 no synchronization
 bgp router-id 192.168.100.1
 bgp log-neighbor-changes
 bgp confederation identifier 100
 neighbor Internal peer-group
 neighbor Internal remote-as 100
 neighbor Internal update-source Loopback0
 neighbor Internal next-hop-self
 neighbor Clients peer-group
 neighbor Clients remote-as 100
 neighbor Clients update-source Loopback0
 neighbor Clients route-reflector-client
 neighbor Clients next-hop-self
 neighbor 192.168.18.8 remote-as 200
 neighbor 192.168.100.2 peer-group Internal
 neighbor 192.168.100.3 peer-group Clients
 neighbor 192.168.100.4 peer-group Internal
 neighbor 192.168.100.5 peer-group Internal
 no auto-summary
```

NOTE   For both peer groups, **next-hop-self** is configured. The route map set-NH and the ACL are removed from the configuration. You can also continue to use the route map and the ACL to set the next hop for only the external routes. In an RR-based network, however, there is really not much difference.

Step 12: Update the Peering with R1

On R4 and R5, update the peerings with R1. Example 8-106 shows the new BGP configurations on R4. Similar changes are made to R5 (not shown).

Example 8-106 *BGP Configurations on R4*

```
router bgp 100
 no synchronization
 bgp router-id 192.168.100.4
 bgp log-neighbor-changes
 bgp confederation identifier 100
 bgp confederation peers 65000 65001
 neighbor Peers peer-group
 neighbor Peers remote-as 65000
```

continues

Example 8-106 *BGP Configurations on R4 (Continued)*

```
neighbor Clients peer-group
neighbor Clients remote-as 100
neighbor Clients update-source Loopback0
neighbor Clients route-reflector-client
neighbor Internal peer-group
neighbor Internal remote-as 100
neighbor Internal update-source Loopback0
neighbor 192.168.100.1 peer-group Internal
neighbor 192.168.100.2 peer-group Internal
neighbor 192.168.100.5 peer-group Internal
neighbor 192.168.100.6 peer-group Clients
neighbor 192.168.100.7 peer-group Clients
no auto-summary
```

Example 8-107 shows the updated BGP summary table on R1. All sessions are now up.

Example 8-107 *BGP Summary Table on R1*

```
R1#show ip bgp summary
BGP router identifier 192.168.100.1, local AS number 100
BGP table version is 5, main routing table version 5
4 network entries and 7 paths using 740 bytes of memory
2 BGP path attribute entries using 120 bytes of memory
5 BGP rrinfo entries using 120 bytes of memory
1 BGP AS-PATH entries using 24 bytes of memory
0 BGP route-map cache entries using 0 bytes of memory
0 BGP filter-list cache entries using 0 bytes of memory
BGP activity 4/8 prefixes, 7/0 paths, scan interval 60 secs

Neighbor        V    AS MsgRcvd MsgSent   TblVer  InQ OutQ Up/Down  State/PfxRcd
192.168.18.8    4   200      10      11        5    0    0 00:05:30           1
192.168.100.2   4   100      11      12        5    0    0 00:06:01           1
192.168.100.3   4   100      10      17        5    0    0 00:05:44           1
192.168.100.4   4   100      10      10        5    0    0 00:04:16           2
192.168.100.5   4   100       8       8        5    0    0 00:02:34           2
```

Example 8-108 shows the BGP RIB on R3. The dual paths are from redundant RRs in the POP.

Example 8-108 *BGP RIB on R3*

```
R3#show ip bgp
BGP table version is 10, local router ID is 192.168.100.3
Status codes: s suppressed, d damped, h history, * valid, > best, i - internal,
              r RIB-failure
Origin codes: i - IGP, e - EGP, ? - incomplete
```

Example 8-108 *BGP RIB on R3 (Continued)*

```
    Network          Next Hop         Metric LocPrf Weight Path
 * i172.16.0.0       192.168.100.1         0    100      0 200 i
 *>i                 192.168.100.1         0    100      0 200 i
 *> 192.168.200.0    0.0.0.0               0         32768 i
 *>i192.168.201.0    192.168.100.6         0    100      0 i
 * i                 192.168.100.6         0    100      0 i
 *>i192.168.202.0    192.168.100.7         0    100      0 i
 * i                 192.168.100.7         0    100      0 i
```

This step essentially completes the migration of routers from a confederation architecture to an RR-based architecture. In the next step, you perform the final configuration cleanup.

Step 13: Remove the Confederation from the Configurations of All the Routers in AS 100

Remove the confederation configurations from all routers in AS 100. Specifically, remove the two lines from the BGP configurations for R4 that are shown in Example 8-109. This is not service-affecting. After the configuration change in this step, routes that were classified as from confed-internal peers are now from internal peers.

Example 8-109 *Removing Confederation Configurations from R4*

```
R4(config)#router bgp 100
R4(config-router)#no bgp confederation peers 65000 65001
R4(config-router)#no bgp confederation identifier 100
```

Also remove the unneeded peer group Peers on R4 and R5.

Step 14: Verify BGP Reachability for All Prefixes

Verify that all sessions are up and that all routes are received correctly. The following examples show some sample outputs.

Example 8-110 shows the final BGP configurations on R1.

Example 8-110 *BGP Configurations on R1*

```
router bgp 100
 no synchronization
 bgp router-id 192.168.100.1
 bgp log-neighbor-changes
 neighbor Internal peer-group
```

continues

Example 8-110 *BGP Configurations on R1 (Continued)*

```
 neighbor Internal remote-as 100
 neighbor Internal update-source Loopback0
 neighbor Internal next-hop-self
 neighbor Clients peer-group
 neighbor Clients remote-as 100
 neighbor Clients update-source Loopback0
 neighbor Clients route-reflector-client
 neighbor Clients next-hop-self
 neighbor 192.168.18.8 remote-as 200
 neighbor 192.168.100.2 peer-group Internal
 neighbor 192.168.100.3 peer-group Clients
 neighbor 192.168.100.4 peer-group Internal
 neighbor 192.168.100.5 peer-group Internal
 no auto-summary
```

Example 8-111 shows the detailed information on the BGP prefix 192.168.200.0 on R7. Both paths are reflected from two RRs.

Example 8-111 *BGP Route for 192.168.200.0 on R7*

```
R7#show ip bgp 192.168.200.0
BGP routing table entry for 192.168.200.0/24, version 17
Paths: (2 available, best #2, table Default-IP-Routing-Table)
  Not advertised to any peer
  Local
    192.168.100.3 (metric 40) from 192.168.100.5 (192.168.100.5)
      Origin IGP, metric 0, localpref 100, valid, internal
      Originator: 192.168.100.3, Cluster list: 192.168.100.5, 192.168.100.1
  Local
    192.168.100.3 (metric 40) from 192.168.100.4 (192.168.100.4)
      Origin IGP, metric 0, localpref 100, valid, internal, best
      Originator: 192.168.100.3, Cluster list: 192.168.100.4, 192.168.100.1
```

Example 8-112 shows the BGP RIB on R8. All routes are received correctly.

Example 8-112 *BGP RIB on R8*

```
R8#show ip bgp
BGP table version is 23, local router ID is 192.168.18.8
Status codes: s suppressed, d damped, h history, * valid, > best, i - internal,
              r RIB-failure
Origin codes: i - IGP, e - EGP, ? - incomplete

   Network          Next Hop            Metric LocPrf Weight Path
*> 172.16.0.0       0.0.0.0                  0         32768 i
*> 192.168.200.0    192.168.18.1                       0 100 i
*> 192.168.201.0    192.168.18.1                       0 100 i
*> 192.168.202.0    192.168.18.1                       0 100 i
```

Summary

Migrating networks from one architecture to another is often a difficult task. Because of the size and complexity of many BGP networks, migration is typically a process where both old and new architectures exist side by side during migration. The goal of any migration procedure should be to minimize network downtime and traffic loss.

This chapter presented four migration strategies that are commonly confronted in real networks. Detailed procedures were provided for each of the four case studies to illustrate a step-by-step process.

This chapter explores various aspects of the service provider architecture:

- General ISP network architecture
- Transit and peering overview
- BGP community design
- BGP security features
- Case study: Distributed denial of service attack mitigation

CHAPTER 9

Service Provider Architecture

This chapter provides an overview of how an ISP network is architected from a BGP perspective. You can view this entire chapter as a case study, with the initial section detailing the physical infrastructure, design guidelines, and base configuration templates.

A BGP communities-based policy architecture is defined. This BGP community design provides efficient route filtering based on prefix origination, flexible customer-defined routing policy, and QoS-based service level definition.

The chapter concludes with a look at BGP security in an ISP network. That section covers TCP MD5 signatures, inbound route filtering, graded BGP dampening, public peering scenarios, and a dynamic traffic black-holing system for combating distributed denial-of-service (DDoS) attacks.

A final edge router configuration example is provided at the end of the chapter. It includes all the features that are discussed. The configurations for the core and aggregation routers remain unchanged from the initial example.

General ISP Network Architecture

This section describes the standard network architecture found in the vast majority of medium and large ISP networks. The basic network design is broken into several major components:

- Interior Gateway Protocol (IGP) layout
- Network layout
- Network addressing methodology
- Customer connectivity
- Transit and peering connections

These components form the basic architecture for an ISP network.

Interior Gateway Protocol Layout

The most common IGPs used in ISP networks are OSPF and IS-IS. The choice of which protocol to use is outside the scope of this book; however, both protocols can be deployed in a multiarea or single-area environment.

The purpose of the IGP in an ISP network is to support the BGP infrastructure. This includes providing reachability for the BGP peering sessions and next-hop resolution for BGP learned prefixes. The IGP should encompass only routers in the ISP network itself, not customer edge (CE) devices, even if those devices are managed by the ISP.

The number of devices in the average ISP network is typically small enough that a single area is used. Additional factors lead to ISPs using a single area, such as the need for MPLS traffic engineering and end-to-end IGP metric visibility.

Network Layout

The network design developed in this chapter employs several principles for building a stable and scalable network:

- **Hierarchy**—The most common method of enhancing a network's scalability is to introduce a hierarchy into the network. This distributes the network's complexity and reduces the concentration-of-scaling issue. Hierarchy is used in both the physical topology and the BGP peering layout.

- **Modularity**—Modularity in network design increases the network's extensibility. A modular design increases the network's predictability, providing a more deterministic traffic flow. It also increases the efficiency of troubleshooting network events.

- **Redundancy**—Redundancy provides the foundation for a fault-tolerant network. The use of redundancy reduces the impact of link or device failure. It is important to keep in mind that excess redundancy can create scaling issues by reducing the level of hierarchy in the network.

- **Simplicity**—Simplicity in network design results in fewer human mistakes and a reduced set of code issues. In ISP networks, the quantity of routing information puts additional stress on the routers, increasing the probability of encountering problems.

The overall design is developed in a hierarchical manner. The hierarchy is broken into three major components:

- The network core layer
- The aggregation layer
- The network edge layer

Each of these layers has a clearly defined role. A device's configuration is optimized for the layer in which it resides. The core is at the top of the hierarchy, followed by the aggregation layer, and then the edge layer at the bottom. This section covers each of these layers, defining that layer's role and BGP architecture. It also provides a BGP configuration template appropriate to that layer.

The Network Core Layer

The primary responsibility of the network core is switching packets at line rate. The network core consists of a small number of routers, usually fewer than 20, that are all connected in a dense partial mesh or full mesh. The network core is at the very top of the hierarchy, providing connectivity for the aggregation layer. Figure 9-1 shows a core network.

Figure 9-1   *Sample Network Core*

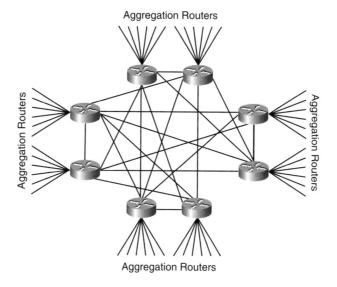

The core routers terminate two types of links: core links and aggregation uplinks. The core links form the actual core by interconnecting the core routers. These links are typically the highest-capacity links in the network. The aggregation uplinks provide connectivity for the aggregation layer into the network core. The core routers are not centrally located, because this would reduce the network's fault tolerance. A single location for all core routers would provide a single point of failure for the entire network.

It is uncommon to see policy application or packet filtering at the network core. The traffic levels on core devices present a scaling challenge for processing-intensive operations in the forwarding path.

The BGP architecture for the network reflects that the core is the top of the network hierarchy. The BGP deployment is based on a route reflector design. The iBGP full mesh is at the top of the hierarchy in a route reflector design.

The iBGP full mesh consists of all the core routers. Policy is not modified for BGP prefixes in the network core. A single peer group can be used for the entire iBGP mesh for the core peering sessions.

The network core is also responsible for providing connectivity to the aggregation layer. A second set of BGP sessions is required to all directly connected aggregation routers. An important rule for route reflection is that BGP peering sessions must follow the physical topology to avoid routing loops.

No connections external to the network are terminated on the core routers. This includes customer connections and peering or transit connections. The exception to this rule is for smaller ISPs that might have only a couple of core routers and two or three transit links.

Example 9-1 shows the BGP core router configuration template.

Example 9-1 *BGP Core Router Configuration Template*

```
router bgp <ISP ASN>
 no auto-summary
 no synchronization
 bgp log-neighbor-changes
 bgp router-id <ROUTER ID>
 !
 neighbor CORE_ROUTERS peer-group
 neighbor CORE_ROUTERS description Core iBGP Full Mesh
 neighbor CORE_ROUTERS version 4
 neighbor CORE_ROUTERS password <iBGP Password>
 neighbor CORE_ROUTERS update-source loopback0
 neighbor CORE_ROUTERS remote-as <ISP ASN>
 !
 neighbor AGG_ROUTERS peer-group
 neighbor AGG_ROUTERS description iBGP Sessions for Aggregation Routers
 neighbor AGG_ROUTERS version 4
 neighbor AGG_ROUTERS password <iBGP Password>
 neighbor AGG_ROUTERS update-source loopback0
 neighbor AGG_ROUTERS remote-as <ISP ASN>
 neighbor AGG_ROUTERS route-reflector-client
 ...
 !
```

The Aggregation Layer

The aggregation layer, shown in Figure 9-2, is in place primarily to reduce the complexity of the core routers by providing hierarchy. This includes distributing the circuit aggregation and reducing the number of BGP peering sessions terminating on the core routers. In smaller networks, this layer is often omitted. The access layer can be aggregated directly on the core routers. As the access layer grows, the aggregation layer becomes more important. The aggregation routers form the middle level of the network hierarchy.

Figure 9-2 *Aggregation Layer*

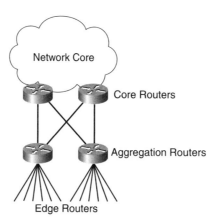

An aggregation router has two types of links: uplinks and downlinks. Uplinks are to the net-work core routers and the circuits to the edge routers. Typically, there are two uplinks for each aggregation router to two separate core routers. This provides uplink and core router redundancy. In addition to the physical redundancy, BGP redundancy is provided by having the aggregation router configured as a route reflector client to both directly connected core routers. Figure 9-2 shows only two aggregation routers connected to the two core routers, but a real network would have many more aggregation routers homed to the two core routers.

The aggregation routers have downlinks to the edge routers. The aggregation layer gets its name from providing aggregation to the edge routers. The use of an aggregation layer reduces the core routers' port density requirements and increases the network's extensibil-ity. Aggregation routers are not connected directly to other aggregation routers, because this reduces the predictability of traffic flow and can reduce the effectiveness of capacity planning.

The aggregation routers provide the second level of hierarchy in the BGP route reflection architecture. The aggregation routers are route reflector clients of the core routers and are route reflectors for the edge routers. The only BGP sessions on the aggregation routers are iBGP sessions, because external connections are terminated on the edge routers.

Two peer groups are required on the aggregation routers. The first peer group is the iBGP sessions to the upstream core routers. The second peer group is the iBGP sessions to the edge routers. The modularity provided allows the network to be expanded with minimal effort. The addition of new edge routers requires adding a BGP session to the edge router peer group and configuring the ports to terminate the uplink from the edge router.

Example 9-2 shows the BGP aggregation router configuration template.

Example 9-2 *BGP Aggregation Router Configuration Template*

```
router bgp <ISP ASN>
 no auto-summary
 no synchronization
 bgp log-neighbor-changes
 bgp router-id <ROUTER ID>
 !
 neighbor CORE_UPLINK peer-group
 neighbor CORE_UPLINK description iBGP Session to Core Routers
 neighbor CORE_UPLINK version 4
 neighbor CORE_UPLINK password <iBGP Password>
 neighbor CORE_UPLINK update-source loopback0
 neighbor CORE_UPLINK remote-as <ISP ASN>
 !
 neighbor EDGE_ROUTERS peer-group
 neighbor EDGE_ROUTERS description iBGP Sessions for Edge Routers
 neighbor EDGE_ROUTERS version 4
 neighbor EDGE_ROUTERS password <iBGP Password>
 neighbor EDGE_ROUTERS update-source loopback0
 neighbor EDGE_ROUTERS remote-as <ISP ASN>
 neighbor EDGE_ROUTERS route-reflector-client
 !
 neighbor PEER_ROUTERS peer-group
 neighbor PEER_ROUTERS description iBGP Sessions for Peering Routers
 neighbor PEER_ROUTERS version 4
 neighbor PEER_ROUTERS password <iBGP Password>
 neighbor PEER_ROUTERS update-source loopback0
 neighbor PEER_ROUTERS remote-as <ISP ASN>
 neighbor PEER_ROUTERS route-reflector-client
 neighbor PEER_ROUTERS route-map PARTIAL_ROUTES out
 ...
 !
 route-map PARTIAL_ROUTES permit 10
 match community 1
 !
 route-map PARTIAL_ROUTES deny 20
 !
 ip community-list 1 permit <Customer Routes Community>
 ip community-list 1 deny
 !
```

The peering routers are a special case of edge router. They require only partial routes, unlike the standard customer aggregation edge router that requires full routes. This subject is discussed in more detail in the later section "Public Peering Security Concerns."

The Network Edge Layer

The network edge, shown in Figure 9-3, is responsible for all external connectivity. This includes customer aggregation, transit, and peering connections. The network edge is the lowest level in the network hierarchy. Typically, an edge router has uplinks to two aggregation routers. This provides redundancy for the failure of an aggregation router or the uplink to the aggregation router.

Figure 9-3 *Network Edge*

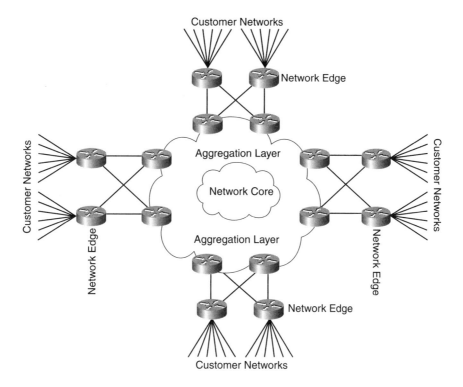

Services and policy are applied at the network edge. The traffic rates on the edge routers are much lower than at the aggregation and core routers. This improves the scalability of performing processor-intensive functions, because the processing load is distributed across a larger number of devices.

In a BGP architecture, the edge routers are route reflector clients of the aggregation routers. They also terminate eBGP peering sessions with customers. Several BGP functions are performed on the edge routers:

- **Route dampening**—The route dampening function works on only external prefixes. The edge routers contain externally learned prefixes from customers, transit, and peering. The suppression of prefixes at the network edge causes that prefix to be removed from the core and aggregation routers.

- **Route aggregation**—Prefix aggregation is also performed at the edge of the network. An ISP may have an /8 that is distributed to customers across the entire network. The specific prefixes are needed internally to provide reachability. However, the ISP will want to reduce the number of prefixes advertised externally by aggregating these longer customer prefixes into summaries.

- **Resetting the next hop**—Prefixes learned from an external peer have the next-hop attribute for that prefix set to the remote peer's address. The next hop for a prefix must be reachable for the path to be included in the BGP decision process. This situation is shown in Figure 9-4.

  The next-hop reachability requirements mean that the edge routers need to include the prefixes for the customer link in the IGP or reset the next hop for the BGP prefixes received. The most common method is to set **next-hop-self** on the iBGP session upstream to the aggregation routers. The inclusion of link addressing for all customer connections does not scale and dramatically increases the amount of information contained in the IGP.

- **Zeroing BGP Multi-Exit Discriminators (MEDs)**—If BGP MEDs are used, it is common practice to zero them on reception. This is because MEDs received from different autonomous systems have no relation to each other. Resetting the BGP MED of incoming prefixes prevents routing oscillation. If BGP MEDs are accepted, preventing routing oscillation requires you to configure **always-compare-med**, as discussed in Chapter 7, "Scalable iBGP Design and Implementation Guidelines."

- **Route information filtering**—All filtering of routing information is performed on the eBGP session. This includes filtering based on prefix lists, distribute lists, filter lists, and community lists.

- **Policy application**—The application of BGP policy is performed at the network edge. This includes attribute manipulation based on communities received from the customer, such as local preference or MEDs. This also includes setting communities for prefixes received to identify them for future policy application, such as filtering prefix advertisements to external peers.

Figure 9-4   *Next-Hop Attribute for Customer Prefixes*

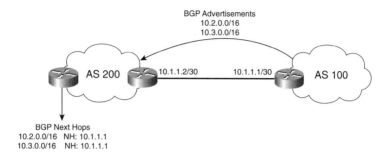

The network edge is where the vast majority of BGP policy is applied. The aggregation and core layers operate on the policy that is defined at the edge when performing best-path selection. Example 9-3 shows a sample network edge BGP configuration template.

Example 9-3   *BGP Edge Router Configuration Template*

```
router bgp <ISP ASN>
 no auto-summary
 no synchronization
 bgp dampening

 bgp log-neighbor-changes
 bgp router-id <ROUTER ID>
 !
 neighbor AGG_UPLINK peer-group
 neighbor AGG_UPLINK description iBGP Session to Aggregation Routers
 neighbor AGG_UPLINK version 4
 neighbor AGG_UPLINK password <iBGP Password>
 neighbor AGG_UPLINK update-source loopback0
 neighbor AGG_UPLINK next-hop-self
 neighbor AGG_UPLINK remote-as <ISP ASN>
 !
 neighbor CUST_GEN_ASN peer-group
 neighbor CUST_GEN_ASN description Customers using Generic ASN
 neighbor CUST_GEN_ASN version 4
 neighbor CUST_GEN_ASN password <Customer Password>
 neighbor CUST_GEN_ASN remote-as <Generic ASN>
 neighbor CUST_GEN_ASN remove-private-as
 neighbor CUST_GEN_ASN default-information originate
 !
 neighbor CUST_PRIV_ASN peer-group
 neighbor CUST_PRIV_ASN description Customer using Private ASN
 neighbor CUST_PRIV_ASN version 4
 neighbor CUST_PRIV_ASN password <Customer Password>
```

continues

Example 9-3 *BGP Edge Router Configuration Template (Continued)*

```
 neighbor CUST_PRIV_ASN remote-as 65000
 neighbor CUST_PRIV_ASN remove-private-as
 !
 neighbor CUST_PARTIAL peer-group
 neighbor CUST_PARTIAL description Customers Receiving Partial Routes
 neighbor CUST_PARTIAL version 4
 neighbor CUST_PARTIAL password <Customer Password>
 neighbor CUST_PARTIAL route-map PARTIAL_ROUTES out
 neighbor CUST_PARTIAL remove-private-as
 neighbor CUST_PARTIAL default-information originate
 !
 neighbor CUST_FULL peer-group
 neighbor CUST_FULL description Customers Receiving Full Routes
 neighbor CUST_FULL version 4
 neighbor CUST_FULL remove-private-as
 neighbor CUST_FULL password <Customer Password>
 ...
!
route-map PARTIAL_ROUTES permit 10
 match community 1
 !
route-map PARTIAL_ROUTES deny 20
 !
ip community-list 1 permit <Customer Routes Community>
ip community-list 1 deny
 !
```

The edge architecture template provides the basic BGP configuration for the edge. It does not include prefix filtering and BGP community application. These can be applied to the basic template. These topics are covered later in this chapter.

General BGP Settings

In the configuration templates provided in the previous sections, a couple settings are applied on all routers: autosummarization and BGP synchronization. This section briefly covers those commands.

BGP's autosummarization feature dates back to the days of classful routing. This feature should always be disabled in an ISP environment. If autosummarization is enabled, the router summarizes prefixes along their classful boundary when the prefixes are generated—typically at the point of redistribution. This means that if an ISP has a /19 allocation in traditional Class B space, autosummarization advertises the entire /16, even though the ISP has been assigned only one-eighth of that /16. This can result in the ISP's attracting traffic for which it is not the destination.

The BGP synchronization feature is intended for networks that are not running BGP on all contiguous routers in the forwarding path. The typical ISP runs BGP on all routers, so it does not need to run BGP synchronization. This feature is very seldom used in any network and should be disabled for ISP networks. A more detailed discussion of BGP synchronization is provided in Chapter 2, "Understanding BGP Building Blocks."

Network Addressing Methodology

The focus of this section on network addressing is specific to infrastructure addressing. The suggested IGP deployment is a single-area design. This provides no area border at which to aggregate infrastructure addressing. Infrastructure addressing consists of two types of addressing—loopback addresses and link addresses. These are discussed in the next sections. You'll then learn more about customer addressing.

Loopback Addressing

The loopback address provides an IP address that is independent of any physical interface. The router is the only device on the subnet, allowing a /32 to be used for optimal address efficiency. If IP multicast is deployed, an RP Anycast is used, as described in Chapter 11, "Multiprotocol BGP and Interdomain Multicast," and multiple loopback addresses are configured.

The loopback address that is not used for the RP Anycast should be explicitly configured as the BGP router ID. This prevents the possibility of BGP infrastructure failure from duplicate BGP router IDs existing in the network.

Link Addressing

The other aspect of infrastructure addressing is link addressing. The typical backbone connection is a point-to-point connection, with only two devices in a subnet. The /31 has been redefined without a network or broadcast address, making both IP addresses in the subnet usable. You should capitalize on /31 address efficiency when configuring link addressing.

The scarcity of IP address space and the difficulty of receiving additional allocations from the assigning authorities introduced the concept of using RFC 1918, or private addressing for link addresses. However, RFC 1918 specifically states that packets with private addressing in either the source or destination address should not be forwarded over interenterprise links. This means that they should not be forwarded across the Internet. A traceroute through an ISP using private addressing for infrastructure links generates packets sourced from private addresses.

If multiple ISPs use private addressing from the same subnets, there is the potential for configuration mistakes to cause inadvertent denial-of-service attacks. The accidental redistribution and advertisements of the private infrastructure addressing could interfere with other ISPs using the same address space for infrastructure addressing.

The solution is not to use private addressing in ISP networks. This is considered bad practice and is frowned on by the industry.

Customer Addressing

The standard model for handling customer prefixes is to carry them in BGP and not the IGP. The result is that there is no benefit to be had by internally aggregating or assigning address space on a regional basis. There is also the additional complication that customers often multihome or sometimes move and need to be rehomed. Maintaining a strict regional addressing scheme can very quickly become an administrative burden that is not supported by technical benefits.

Customer Connectivity

There are two common methods of handling prefix information from customer connections. The first method is BGP peering with the customer. The second method is static route configuration on the ISP edge router, redistributing the prefix into BGP. The later section, "Identifying Customer Prefixes," describes a method of identifying the source of BGP prefixes.

Customer BGP Peering

Customer BGP peering is used when the customer is either multihomed or requires the capability to dynamically advertise prefixes. In the case where the customer is multihomed to different ISPs, the customer must have a unique public autonomous system number (ASN) from an assigning authority. If the customer is multihomed to a single ISP or is not multihomed but requires the ability to dynamically advertise prefixes, two methods do not require the customer to obtain a public ASN. They are described next.

Generic Customer ASN

The ISP can obtain an ASN from an assigning authority to use as a generic customer ASN. This means that the ISP asks all customers to use this customer ASN. For example, the ISP has its own primary ASN of 100 and a second ASN of 101 for customer peering. ASN 101 is shared by all customers that require the capability to dynamically advertise prefixes to the ISP.

The main caveat is that prefix information sent by one customer using ASN 101 is not accepted by another customer running ASN 101. Initially, this might appear to present a problem; however, this method is used for customers that are not multihomed to multiple ISPs. The ISP only needs to originate the default to the customer to ensure full connectivity.

This method identifies customer prefixes by setting the originating ASN to 101.

Private ASN

The second method is to use an ASN in the range of 64512 to 65535. These ASN have been reserved for private use by the Internet Assigned Numbers Authority (IANA). These ASNs should not be advertised to the general Internet, which means that the ISP needs to remove the private ASN before propagating prefix information to the public Internet.

Static Route Redistribution

If a customer does not require the ability to dynamically advertise prefix information and is not multihomed, overhead for a BGP peering session is not needed. The customers aggregated onto a single edge router can number into the thousands. If a BGP peering session is used for every customer connection, this can place significant processing load on the router.

The most common way to provide customer connectivity is static route configuration on the ISP edge router. The customer router is configured with a static default route to the ISP. The static routes for the customer prefixes are then redistributed directly into BGP on the ISP edge router. When routes are injected into BGP through redistribution, the origin is set to Incomplete. ISPs often redistribute the routes through a route map to manually set the origin to IGP and perform any other BGP attribute manipulation, such as adding communities. The use of route maps to filter redistribution also helps reduce configuration mistakes.

Identifying Customer Prefixes

Chapter 6, "Internet Connectivity for Enterprise Networks," introduced the concept of advertising partial routes to a multihomed customer. Partial routes consist of the ISP's local routes and direct customers. An ISP must be able to identify what routes specifically are customer routes, as opposed to transit and peering routes, if it wants to offer partial routes. The use of static redistribution does not inherently provide a distinguisher like the generic customer ASN. Furthermore, attempting to filter based on a private ASN, a generic customer ASN, redistributed static routes, and customers with their own assigned ASNs can be cumbersome.

The solution is to define a specific BGP community for customer prefixes. This community is assigned to customer prefixes received via BGP and is added to static customer routes redistributed into BGP. Prefix advertisements to customers requesting partial routes can then be filtered based on community to block all routes except those with the ISP customer routes community.

Transit and Peering Overview

The focus so far has been on the ISP infrastructure and downstream connectivity for customer connections. This section discusses upstream ISP connectivity to the rest of the Internet. There are three primary types of upstream connectivity:

- Transit
- Peering—public and private
- ISP tiers and peering

The subject of upstream connectivity is one of the most political aspects of the ISP business, as you'll learn in the next sections.

Transit Connectivity

Transit connectivity is the most common form of connectivity available to small-to-medium-sized ISPs. Transit service essentially means buying full connectivity to the Internet from another ISP. An ISP sells transit service to its end customers. A transit connection means that the upstream provider lets the customer transit its network to reach any available destination on the Internet.

Peering

The term *peering* refers to both public and private peering. Peering in a general sense between two ISPs means that reachability to that ISP and its direct customers is provided over that connection. If ISP 1 and ISP 2 initiate a peering connection, they can reach each other but not ISP 3 if it is not a customer of either ISP 1 or ISP 2. Essentially, peering involves the exchange of partial routes between the two peering ISPs. The cost of peering is typically less than full transit service, because both ISPs peering expect to offload the traffic passing between their customers from their transit links.

Public Peering

Public peering occurs at one of the public peering points, such as Network Access Points (NAPs), Metropolitan Area Exchanges (MAEs), or Internet Exchange Points (IXPs). Typically, peering at a public peering point is done over a broadcast medium, such as Fast Ethernet or Gigabit Ethernet. Several of the major exchanges have started offering ATM service at the exchange points to provide quality of service (QoS) guarantees. An ISP obtains a port and can peer with anyone else at the exchange point who is interested over that port. The public exchanges have a reputation for being highly congested and having problems with packet loss.

Private Peering

Private peering involves two ISPs negotiating a peering agreement and establishing a private connection between the ISPs, such as a point-to-point circuit. These two ISPs are the only ones that peer across this circuit. The private peering model allows the ISPs to move away from congested exchanges, providing higher-quality connectivity.

ISP Tiers and Peering

The subject of ISP tiers is very hazy unless you have a good understanding of what each tier is. It is generally accepted that there are three tiers:

- Tier 1
  - Nationwide backbone
  - Does not purchase any transit
  - Relies completely on peering
- Tier 2
  - Nationwide backbone
  - Combination of peering and transit
- Tier 3
  - Regional or local network
  - Relies almost completely on transit
  - Might have some peering, but often does not

The major tier 1 providers rely entirely on peering without purchasing transit. They privately peer in eight U.S. locations, called the default-free zone. These locations are New York City, Washington D.C., Atlanta, Chicago, Dallas, Los Angeles, Seattle, and San Jose (Bay Area).

NOTE   A common sentiment about transit and peering is "Once a customer, never a peer." You should keep in mind this philosophy when determining where to purchase transit. After you become a customer of a particular ISP, it is very difficult to transition to a peering relationship with that ISP.

BGP Community Design

The BGP community attribute is one of the most powerful policy tools available in BGP. This attribute provides a way to assign prefixes to arbitrary groupings, or communities, as the name describes. Specific policies can then be applied to prefixes based on the community to which they belong. A prefix can carry multiple community attributes, allowing multiple policies to be applied to a prefix.

By default, there are only a few well-known communities:

- **no-export**—Do not advertise this prefix to an external peer.
- **no-advertise**—Do not advertise this prefix to any peers.
- **internet**—A regular prefix to be advertised globally.

The rest of the community space is available for ISPs to create custom communities and the associated policies. This section covers the popular custom communities that ISPs use to control routing policy and give customers flexibility in determining routing policy for their prefixes.

The configurations for deploying BGP communities across an ISP network are developed throughout this section. The final configurations provide the following functionality:

- Prefix origination identification
- Dynamic customer policy
- QoS-based service levels

The BGP community attribute is very flexible. The BGP community design presented in the next sections encompasses the most common usage of BGP communities; however, it is far from exhaustive with respect to what can be done. Another example of how BGP communities can be used to combat distributed denial-of-service attacks is provided in the case study near the end of the chapter.

Prefix Origin Tracking

The ISP's need to understand the origin of a particular prefix was discussed in the section "Identifying Customer Prefixes." An ISP network typically has three types of routes: transit, peering, and customer. The ISP does not want to send routing information indiscriminately. A sample community assignment based on prefix origin is shown in Table 9-1.

Table 9-1   *Prefix Origin-Based Community Assignment*

Route Type	Community Identifier
Transit prefixes	<ISP ASN>:1000
Peering prefixes	<ISP ASN>:2000
Customer prefixes	<ISP ASN>:3000

Example 9-4 shows the router configuration for assigning the prefix origin communities.

Example 9-4 *Prefix Origin Community Assignment*

```
route-map cust_inbound permit 10
  set community 100:3000 additive
!
route-map peer_inbound permit 10
  set community 100:2000 additive
!
route-map transit_inbound permit 10
  set community 100:1000 additive
!
```

These communities can be used to filter upstream prefix advertisements by permitting the advertisement of only prefixes with the community <ASN>:3000. This prevents the ISP from advertising peering routes over the transit connection and transit routes to peers. If the ISP does not filter prefix advertisements between the transit and peering connections, the ISP ends up providing transit service for its peers. Example 9-5 shows the outbound configuration for filtering based on the prefix origin communities.

Example 9-5 *Outbound Community-Based Filtering*

```
route-map peer_outbound permit 10
  match community 1
!
route-map peer_outbound deny 20
!
route-map transit_outbound permit 10
 match community 1
!
route-map transit_outbound deny 20
!
ip community-list 1 permit 100:3000
ip community-list 1 deny
!
```

The configurations provided in Examples 9-4 and 9-5 will be built upon in the remainder of this section. The resulting configuration will be a complete BGP community design.

Dynamic Customer Policy

It is common for customers to multihome to one or more providers. Customers choose providers for a variety of reasons and often have specific requirements for traffic policy.

A customer that is multihomed to the same provider might want traffic to load-balance between the two connections or might want to use the connections in a primary and backup scenario. If the ISP manually controls the traffic policy, this increases the support burden and the amount of configuration on the edge routers, increasing the likelihood of configuration errors.

A customer that is multihomed to multiple ISPs might want to use one of the ISPs for transit and the other just to reach locations local to that ISP. This can be complicated to configure on a per-customer basis. It is much easier to predefine communities for common customer policy requests that allow the customer to change its policy at any time without any manual intervention by the ISP.

The next two sections provide examples of how an ISP can define a policy to let customers dynamically influence traffic patterns upstream. This is accomplished through local preference manipulation in the upstream provider's network and by controlling aspects of the upstream provider's prefix advertisement.

Local Preference Manipulation

The customer can be given the ability to manipulate inbound policy through defining communities that change the local preference for received prefixes. This allows the customer that is multihomed to the same ISP to change its inbound routing policy without manual intervention from the ISP. Table 9-2 shows the community scheme.

Table 9-2   *Flexible Upstream Local Preference Communities*

Local Preference	BGP Policy Community
80	<ISP ASN>:80
90	<ISP ASN>:90
100 (default)	<ISP ASN>:100
110	<ISP ASN>:110
120	<ISP ASN>:120

The customer can use the communities listed in Table 9-2 to change the local preference of its routing information in the ISP network. The ISP configuration to implement flexible local preference is an extension of the inbound customer-facing route maps. The new route maps are shown in Example 9-6.

Example 9-6   *Flexible Local Preference Route Map Configuration*

```
route-map cust_inbound permit 10
  match community 10
  set community 100:3000 additive
  set local-preference 80
```

Example 9-6 *Flexible Local Preference Route Map Configuration (Continued)*

```
!
route-map cust_inbound permit 20
  match community 11
  set community 100:3000 additive
  set local-preference 90
!
route-map cust_inbound permit 30
  match community 12
  set community 100:3000 additive
  set local-preference 110
!
route-map cust_inbound permit 40
  match community 13
  set community 100:3000 additive
  set local-preference 120
!
route-map cust_inbound permit 50
  set community 100:3000 additive
  set local-preference 100
!
ip community-list 10 permit 100:80
ip community-list 10 deny
!
ip community-list 11 permit 100:90
ip community-list 11 deny
!
ip community-list 12 permit 100:110
ip community-list 12 deny
!
ip community-list 13 permit 100:120
ip community-list 13 deny
!
```

These route maps are an extension of the route maps defined in Example 9-4 on prefix
origin communities.

Controlling Upstream Prefix Advertisement

The ability to affect the ISP's advertisement of customer prefixes to upstream peers is
another policy aspect that can be made flexible through community usage. Two levels of
granularity are often defined. The first level requests suppression of advertisement to
upstream peers based on the peer type, transit, peering, or customer. The community
scheme for this is shown in Table 9-3.

Table 9-3   *Customer Advertisement Suppression Communities*

Suppression Target	BGP Community
Transit	\<ISP ASN>:210
Peering	\<ISP ASN>:220
Customer	\<ISP ASN>:230

The second level of granularity allows the customer to request AS prepending or complete suppression of advertisement on a per-AS basis. This is commonly not done for every ASN—only for major peers. The community scheme for this is shown in Table 9-4.

Table 9-4   *AS Prepending and Advertisement Suppression Communities*

BGP Community	How the ISP Policy Is Applied
65000:\<upstream ASN>	Suppresses advertisement to \<upstream ASN> peers.
65100:\<upstream ASN>	Prepends \<ISP ASN> one time to \<upstream ASN> peers.
65200:\<upstream ASN>	Prepends \<ISP ASN> two times to \<upstream ASN> peers.
65300:\<upstream ASN>	Prepends \<ISP ASN> three times to \<upstream ASN> peers.
65400:\<upstream ASN>	Prepends \<ISP ASN> four times to \<upstream ASN> peers.
65500:\<upstream ASN>	Prepends \<ISP ASN> five times to \<upstream ASN> peers.

The private ASN determines the action, and the upstream ASN is the upstream peer on which the action should be taken. This method, which is easy to use and remember, is used by at least one provider. The new route maps for controlling upstream prefix advertisement are shown in Example 9-7.

Example 9-7   *Route Maps for Controlling Upstream Prefix Advertisement*

```
route-map peer_outbound_AS1000 deny 10
 match community 20
!
route-map peer_outbound_AS1000 permit 20
 match community 21
 set as-path prepend 100
!
route-map peer_outbound_AS1000 permit 30
 match community 22
 set as-path prepend 100 100
!
route-map peer_outbound_AS1000 permit 40
 match community 23
 set as-path prepend 100 100 100
```

Example 9-7 *Route Maps for Controlling Upstream Prefix Advertisement (Continued)*

```
!
route-map peer_outbound_AS1000 permit 50
 match community 24
 set as-path prepend 100 100 100 100
!
route-map peer_outbound_AS1000 permit 60
 match community 25
 set as-path prepend 100 100 100 100 100
!
route-map peer_outbound_AS1000 permit 70
 match community 100:3000
!
route-map peer_outbound_AS1000 deny 80
!
ip community-list 20 permit 65000:1000
ip community-list 20 permit 100:220
ip community-list 20 deny
!
ip community-list 21 permit 65100:1000
ip community-list 21 deny
!
ip community-list 22 permit 65200:1000
ip community-list 22 deny
!
ip community-list 23 permit 65300:1000
ip community-list 23 deny
!
ip community-list 24 permit 65400:1000
ip community list 24 deny
!
ip community-list 25 permit 65500:1000
ip community-list 25 deny
!
```

These route maps are an extension of the prefix origin route maps defined in Example 9-5.

QoS Policy Propagation with BGP

A popular trend among ISPs is to offer multiple levels of service. These levels of service are typically differentiated by giving customers with a higher service level priority over lower service levels using IP precedence. This service level applies across the ISP's network, both inbound and outbound. The QoS Policy Propagation via BGP (QPPB) feature ensures that traffic in both directions is provided with the QoS level the customer has purchased. The ISP network in this example offers three levels of service: gold, silver, and bronze. These service levels and their associated communities are listed in Table 9-5.

Table 9-5 *Service Level Definitions*

Service Level	BGP Community
Gold	\<ISP ASN\>:500
Silver	\<ISP ASN\>:510
Bronze	\<ISP ASN\>:520

Inbound traffic from a customer is easy to handle. Policy marking can be configured on the inbound customer interface to mark all traffic to the appropriate service level. The difficulty is marking traffic destined for the customer coming into the ISP network from transit and peering links.

The solution is to mark customer prefixes with a community that identifies the service level for that destination prefix. This allows the use of the BGP table-map feature to populate the CEF table with the appropriate precedence for each destination prefix, enabling incoming precedence manipulation on a per-prefix basis. The BGP table map, as described in Chapter 4, "Effective BGP Policy Control," is a filter between the BGP table and the CEF table. Example 9-8 shows the extensions to the customer-facing route maps.

Example 9-8 *Community Route Map Extensions for QPPB*

```
! Gold Service Route Maps
route-map gold_cust_inbound permit 10
  match community 10
  set community 100:3000 100:500 additive
  set local-preference 80
!
route-map gold_cust_inbound permit 20
  match community 11
  set community 100:3000 100:500 additive
  set local-preference 90
!
route-map gold_cust_inbound permit 30
  match community 12
  set community 100:3000 100:500 additive
  set local-preference 110
!
route-map gold_cust_inbound permit 40
  match community 13
  set community 100:3000 100:500 additive
  set local-preference 120
!
route-map gold_cust_inbound permit 50
  set community 100:3000 100:500 additive
  set local-preference 100
!
! Silver Service Route Maps
route-map silver_cust_inbound permit 10
  match community 10
```

Example 9-8   *Community Route Map Extensions for QPPB (Continued)*

```
      set community 100:3000 100:510 additive
      set local-preference 80
 !
 route-map silver_cust_inbound permit 20
   match community 11
   set community 100:3000 100:510 additive
   set local-preference 90
 !
 route-map silver_cust_inbound permit 30
   match community 12
   set community 100:3000 100:510 additive
   set local-preference 110
 !
 route-map silver_cust_inbound permit 40
   match community 13
   set community 100:3000 100:510 additive
   set local-preference 120
 !
 route-map silver_cust_inbound permit 50
   set community 100:3000 100:510 additive
   set local-preference 100
 !
 ! Bronze Service Route Maps
 route-map bronze_cust_inbound permit 10
   match community 10
   set community 100:3000 100:520 additive
   set local-preference 80
 !
 route-map bronze_cust_inbound permit 20
   match community 11
   set community 100:3000 100:520 additive
   set local-preference 90
 !
 route-map bronze_cust_inbound permit 30
   match community 12
   set community 100:3000 100:520 additive
   set local-preference 110
 !
 route-map bronze_cust_inbound permit 40
   match community 13
   set community 100:3000 100:520 additive
   set local-preference 120
 !
 route-map bronze_cust_inbound permit 50
   set community 100:3000 100:520 additive
   set local-preference 100
 !
 ip community-list 10 permit 100:80
 ip community-list 10 deny
```

continues

Example 9-8 *Community Route Map Extensions for QPPB (Continued)*

```
!
ip community-list 11 permit 100:90
ip community-list 11 deny
!
ip community-list 12 permit 100:110
ip community-list 12 deny
!
ip community-list 13 permit 100:120
ip community-list 13 deny
!
```

The communities are set on the prefixes, identifying the service class that each belongs to. The remaining task is to configure the rest of the edge routers with the appropriate table map to translate the BGP service level communities into CEF-based policy marking. This configuration is provided in Example 9-9.

Example 9-9 *Precedence Marking Table-Map Configuration*

```
router bgp 100
table-map QOS_Policy
...
!
route-map QOS_Policy permit 10
 match community 50
 set ip precedence immediate
!
route-map QOS_Policy permit 20
 match community 51
 set ip precedence priority
!
route-map QOS_Polciy permit 30
 match community 52
 set ip precedence routine
!
ip community-list 50 permit 100:500
ip community-list 50 deny
!
ip community-list 51 permit 100:510
ip community-list 51 deny
!
ip community-list 52 permit 100:520
ip community-list 52 deny
!
```

The configuration shown in Example 9-9 needs to be applied to all edge routers in the network. The precedence on packets is set at the edge and is acted upon through precedence-aware queuing and congestion-avoidance mechanisms across the network.

Static Redistribution and Community Application

Customers that do not speak BGP must also have the appropriate communities applied for the peering filters and service levels to work correctly. The easiest method is to combine route tags with route maps to ensure that the appropriate BGP communities are assigned to each prefix when the static routes are redistributed into BGP. The route tags and service levels are shown in Table 9-6.

Table 9-6   *Service Levels and Associated Route Tags*

Service Level	Route Tag
Gold	500
Silver	510
Bronze	520

The route tags are specifically matched to the BGP communities for each service level to increase readability and maintain consistency. The redistribution route maps are shown in Example 9-10.

Example 9-10 *Static Redistribution Route Maps*

```
route-map STATIC_TO_BGP permit 10
 match tag 500
 set community 100:3000 100:500
 set origin igp
!
route-map STATIC_TO_BGP permit 20
 match tag 510
 set community 100:3000 100:510
 set origin igp
!
route-map STATIC_TO_BGP permit 30
 match tag 520
 set community 100:3000 100:520
 set origin igp
!
route-map STATIC_TO_BGP deny 40
!
```

The only prefixes allowed in the redistribution are those with a tag that specifically includes them in a particular service level.

BGP Security Features

Security on ISP networks can be very difficult because of the network's public nature. No firewalls protect routers, and device addressing is typically visible externally. This provides attackers with significant information about network devices and the ability to send packets unobstructed to those devices. The subject of ISP security is examined in this section from two angles.

The first angle is protecting the BGP infrastructure itself. The BGP infrastructure is the actual BGP peering sessions. The next section explains BGP MD5 and justifies its use.

The second angle is protecting against malicious BGP advertisements or advertisement patterns. Proper filtering and route dampening guidelines are provided in the following sections. The security issues surrounding public peering are covered, and three specific scenarios are explained that have been encountered in the field.

TCP MD5 Signatures for BGP Sessions

The BGP infrastructure can be directly attacked by attacking a BGP session's TCP layer. A TCP Reset that is accepted by the router for a BGP session results in a session reset. The source and destination addresses for an eBGP session can be determined through the use of traceroute.

The traceroute results provide the link address of one side of the peering connection. It is standard practice for eBGP sessions to peer using directly connected IP addresses in the same IP subnet. The IP address for both sides of the BGP session can be derived from one link address.

A TCP packet is considered valid for the session if the source address, destination address, source port, destination port, and TCP sequence numbers are correct. The attacker already knows the source and destination addresses and one of the ports, because BGP uses TCP port 179. Figure 9-5 shows the attack scenario.

Figure 9-5   *BGP TCP Reset Attack Scenario*

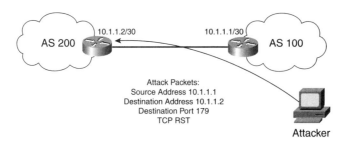

The attacker can use a "brute-force" method for the remaining TCP parameters. The attacker then sends the TCP reset packets, iterating through the various combinations until the session is reset. The TCP reset packets are sent, spoofing the source address of the TCP reset packets to make the BGP router under attack think they are arriving from the remote BGP peer.

The solution to the TCP reset attack is to enable the TCP MD5 signature option to protect the TCP session itself from attack. The TCP MD5 signature is an 18-byte value that is generated based on the data in the packet and a password that is configured on both peering routers. The addition of this MD5 signature dramatically increases the complexity of brute-force attacks against the TCP layer. The attack not only must know the TCP session parameters, but also must iterate through the entire 18-byte MD5 signature space.

The configuration to enable TCP MD5 signatures is

> **neighbor** *address* **password** *password*

CAUTION   It is important that the password remain confidential between the two peers. If the attacker knows the password, he can generate the correct MD5 signature for the attacking packets.

Peer Filtering

Routing information should not be accepted indiscriminately from customers or peers. Two classifications of prefixes should not be advertised on the Internet:

- Prefixes reserved for special use, such as RFC 1918 space.

- Unallocated address space. These prefixes are called *Martian addresses* or *bogons*.

The initial classification of prefixes (those that are reserved and should not be publicly routed) can be configured for every peering session. The prefix list for these networks is provided in Example 9-11.

Example 9-11 *Prefix List to Filter Reserved Addresses*

```
ip prefix-list MARTIAN seq 5 deny 0.0.0.0/8
ip prefix-list MARTIAN seq 10 deny 10.0.0.0/8
ip prefix-list MARTIAN seq 15 deny 127.0.0.0/8
ip prefix-list MARTIAN seq 20 deny 168.254.0.0/16
ip prefix-list MARTIAN seq 25 deny 172.16.0.0/12
ip prefix-list MARTIAN seq 30 deny 192.0.2.0/24
ip prefix-list MARTIAN seq 35 deny 192.168.0.0/16
ip prefix-list MARTIAN seq 40 deny 224.0.0.0/4
ip prefix-list MARTIAN seq 45 deny 240.0.0.0/4
```

This prefix list is also provided in Chapter 6, with a detailed explanation of each prefix.

The second classification is prefix blocks that IANA has not yet allocated to a registry for assignment. It is very common to see these prefixes advertised into the global BGP table; however, they are invalid. This list changes periodically as IANA allocates blocks to ARIN, APNIC, and RIPE. The current allocation status for the IPv4 address space is available at www.iana.org.

A sample bogon list is not presented here because of the list's dynamic nature. If an ISP will filter bogon prefixes, which is recommended, the appropriate prefix list should be built based on the allocation status from the IANA website.

Graded Route Flap Dampening

The BGP route dampening feature was discussed in Chapter 3, "Tuning BGP Performance." The default configuration for BGP dampening is a "flat and gentle" approach. All prefixes are treated equally, regardless of the prefix or its length. The reality, however, is that all prefixes are not equal and should not be treated equally. An /8 represents far more hosts than a /24. Even though a 60-minute maximum suppression time for a /24 might be reasonable, this same period might be unacceptable for an /8.

In addition, some prefixes are essential to the Internet's operation. These prefixes are for the DNS root servers. If access to the DNS root servers is lost, all name resolution fails, effectively cutting off Internet access. RIPE has made specific recommendations for deploying BGP route dampening that are sensitive to prefix length and the DNS system. The RIPE recommendation is RIPE-229. Although the specific address assignment of the DNS root servers is very stable, before the root server addresses are excluded from the dampening process, they should be verified on the RIPE website (www.ripe.net). The configuration is shown in Example 9-12.

Example 9-12 *Graded BGP Route Dampening Configuration*

```
router bgp 100
...
bgp dampening route-map graded-dampening
...
!
route-map graded-dampening deny 10
 match ip address prefix-list ROOTSERVERS
!
route-map graded-dampening deny 20
 match ip address prefix-list GTLDSERVERS
!
```

Example 9-12 *Graded BGP Route Dampening Configuration (Continued)*

```
route-map graded-dampening permit 30
 match ip address prefix-list SHORT_DAMP
 set dampening 10 1500 3000 30
!
route-map graded-dampening permit 40
 match ip address prefix-list MEDIUM_DAMP
 set dampening 15 750 3000 45
!
route-map graded-dampening permit 50
 match ip address prefix-list LONG_DAMP
 set dampening 30 820 3000 60
!
ip prefix-list ROOTSERVERS seq 5 permit 198.41.0.0/24
ip prefix-list ROOTSERVERS seq 10 permit 128.9.0.0/16
ip prefix-list ROOTSERVERS seq 15 permit 192.33.4.0/24
ip prefix-list ROOTSERVERS seq 20 permit 128.8.0.0/16
ip prefix-list ROOTSERVERS seq 25 permit 192.203.230.0/24
ip prefix-list ROOTSERVERS seq 30 permit 192.5.5.0/24
ip prefix-list ROOTSERVERS seq 35 permit 192.112.36.0/24
ip prefix-list ROOTSERVERS seq 40 permit 128.63.0.0/16
ip prefix-list ROOTSERVERS seq 45 permit 192.36.148.0/24
ip prefix-list ROOTSERVERS seq 50 permit 192.58.128.0/24
ip prefix-list ROOTSERVERS seq 55 permit 193.0.14.0/24
ip prefix-list ROOTSERVERS seq 60 permit 198.32.64.0/24
ip prefix-list ROOTSERVERS seq 65 permit 202.12.27.0/24
! Global Top Level Domain Servers
ip prefix-list GTLDSERVERS seq 5 permit 192.5.6.0/24
ip prefix-list GTLDSERVERS seq 10 permit 192.33.14.0/24
ip prefix-list GTLDSERVERS seq 15 permit 192.26.92.0/24
ip prefix-list GTLDSERVERS seq 20 permit 192.31.80.0/24
ip prefix-list GTLDSERVERS seq 25 permit 192.12.94.0/24
ip prefix-list GTLDSERVERS seq 30 permit 192.35.51.0/24
ip prefix-list GTLDSERVERS seq 35 permit 192.42.93.0/24
ip prefix-list GTLDSERVERS seq 40 permit 192.54.112.0/24
ip prefix-list GTLDSERVERS seq 45 permit 192.43.172.0/24
ip prefix-list GTLDSERVERS seq 50 permit 192.48.79.0/24
ip prefix-list GTLDSERVERS seq 55 permit 192.52.178.0/24
ip prefix-list GTLDSERVERS seq 60 permit 192.41.162.0/24
ip prefix-list GTLDSERVERS seq 65 permit 192.55.83.0/24
!
ip prefix-list LONG_DAMP seq 5 0.0.0.0/0 ge 24
!
ip prefix-list MEDIUM_DAMP seq 5 0.0.0.0/0 ge 22 le 23
!
ip prefix-list SHORT_DAMP seq 5 0.0.0.0/0 le 21
!
```

The dampening parameters have been adjusted to require four flaps before a prefix is dampened, instead of the default of three flaps. A failed code upgrade can result in three route flaps and a dampened prefix. The following sequence of events is an example of how a failed code upgrade can result in dampened prefixes:

1 The router restarts to load new code.

2 The router crashes.

3 The router reloads on a previous version of code.

The maximum suppression time is 60 minutes for prefixes that are /24 or longer, 45 minutes for /22 and /23, and 30 minutes for prefixes that are /21 or shorter.

Public Peering Security Concerns

Public peering points are a potential area of abuse by unethical network administrators. By manipulating routing information, it is possible to redirect traffic over other providers' networks. It is also possible to build tunnels over another provider's network, creating a virtual backbone circuit that offloads traffic from the offending ISP's network onto the unsuspecting peer.

This section describes the three most common abuses and the measures an ISP can take to prevent the theft of network resources:

- Pointing default
- Third-party next hop
- GRE tunneling

Pointing Default

The simplest method of peering point abuse is originating a default route into the ISP network from the peering router at the NAP. The default route at the NAP is pointed to another ISP. Traffic is then sent to the ISP's NAP router and to the unsuspecting ISP. This is shown in Figure 9-6.

In Figure 9-6, ISP1 points its default route at ISP2 on the NAP router. Traffic sent to the NAP router at ISP2 is unwittingly treated as transit traffic by ISP2. ISP1 can receive free transit over Fast Ethernet. This scenario is most common when ISP1 is much smaller than ISP2. The cost of the link to the NAP is cheaper than the transit connection.

The solution is not to carry full BGP routes on the NAP router. If ISP2 carries only customer routes on the NAP router, the traffic sent from ISP1 to ISP2 is black-holed, because ISP2 has no route for those destinations. A default route on the NAP router to null0 should also be configured to prevent any routing loops. However, traffic destined for ISP2's customers is still delivered.

Figure 9-6   *Transit Theft Through Default Routing*

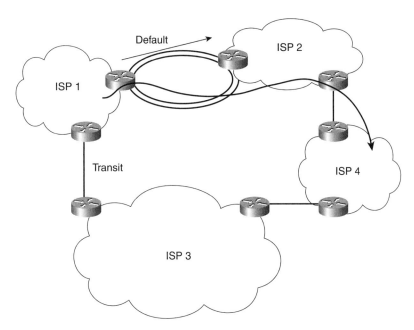

The purpose of the NAP router is to exchange customer prefixes with local peers. The NAP router does not need to know full routing tables, because transit services are not provided on a NAP router. The only traffic received inbound should be traffic destined for the ISP's customers.

Third-Party Next Hop

The third-party next-hop method is used to achieve traffic manipulation in the opposite direction of pointing default. Instead of offloading traffic outbound, the ISP attempts to redirect traffic inbound over a private peering link elsewhere to reduce traffic on the transit and backbone links. Because transit is more expensive than peering, this manipulation can save the unethical ISP significant transit and circuit costs. In Figure 9-7, the unethical ISP is ISP1.

In Figure 9-7, ISP1 BGP peers with ISP3 at the NAP. At this same NAP is ISP2, with which ISP1 is not peered. The BGP next-hop attribute is set to ISP2's interface address for prefixes advertised to ISP3 from ISP1. A private peering connection exists between ISP1 and ISP2. The traffic from ISP3 to ISP1 is sent to ISP2 and then is delivered to ISP1 over the private peering connection.

Figure 9-7 *Third-Party Next-Hop Traffic Manipulation*

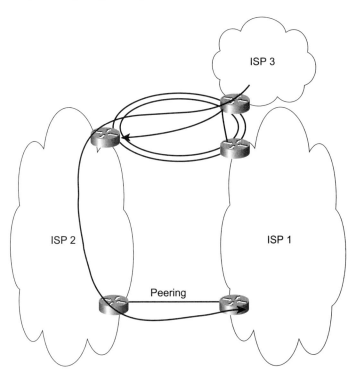

It would seem that ISP1 could have accepted the traffic from ISP3 at the NAP and back-hauled it over an infrastructure link. However, this increases the size of the circuit from the NAP router to ISP1's network. It is also a way for ISP1 to offload traffic from its backbone, reducing the internal bandwidth needed. The end result is the use of ISP2's network as a quasi-transit connection and bandwidth theft.

The solution to this issue is the same as with pointing default, even if the direction is different. If ISP2 does not carry full Internet routes on the NAP router, traffic sent from ISP3 to ISP2 for delivery to ISP1 is black-holed.

GRE Tunneling

The scenario in this section involves the use of GRE tunneling between peering routers. If ISP1 and ISP2 are at multiple NAPs, not necessarily peering, the unethical ISP1 can build a GRE tunnel across ISP2's network and use that tunnel as another virtual backbone link. This is shown in Figure 9-8.

Figure 9-8   *Virtual Backbone Links Using GRE*

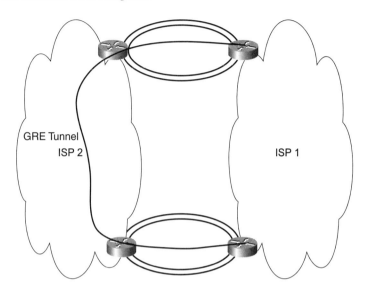

In Figure 9-8, ISP1 has built a GRE tunnel between its interface at NAP1 and its interface at NAP2, where both ISP1 and ISP2 are located. The NAP router for ISP1 has a static route configured as a /32 to the other end of the tunnel pointing to the interface on ISP2's router. This builds the tunnel over ISP2's network, on which ISP1 can run its IGP, treating that tunnel as a pseudo-wire.

The solution to this scenario goes back to how next hop for BGP prefixes is handled. The NAP router for ISP2 should reset the next hop for all BGP prefixes received on the NAP router from external peers. This removes any need to carry the NAP link addressing in the IGP. If ISP2 does not carry the NAP interface network in its IGP, the GRE tunnel does not form.

Case Study: Distributed Denial-of-Service Attack Mitigation

Distributed Denial-of-Service (DDoS) attacks have become an increasingly popular Internet attack mechanism because of the volume of traffic they can generate. The ISP providing connectivity to the victim host finds them difficult to deal with. The traffic enters the ISP from every upstream transit connection and peering point, making it very difficult to discard.

A popular solution for the ISP is to null-route the victim host on all the edge routers. This requires the ISP to touch every edge router to configure the null route. The null routes must later be removed from all routers to restore service to the victim host. If this is not done correctly, connectivity problems will result.

This case study explains a dynamic method for null-routing DDoS traffic on all the edge routers, with minimal configuration required during the actual attack. This DDoS mitigation design also provides the ability to redirect the DDoS traffic to a sink router, where it can be analyzed if needed.

The key to quickly mitigating the impact of a DDoS is to have the infrastructure and process in place before the attack happens. Unfortunately, as is the case with volume-based denial of service attacks, currently it is not possible to discard the attack traffic and leave valid traffic intact for the victim host.

Dynamic Black Hole Routing

The proposed solution to combating DDoS attacks is a dynamic black hole routing system. This system must be put in place before the actual DDoS attack. This system has two major design goals:

- Quickly initiate network-wide null routing for a prefix or network with minimal configuration

- Quickly initiate network-wide redirection of traffic for a prefix or network to a sink router with minimal configuration

The dynamic black hole system is based on the concept of advertising a BGP prefix and setting the next-hop attribute to an address that is covered by a null route, which is a route pointing toward null0. The null route is configured on every router. The victim's prefix or address is then advertised into BGP with the next hop set to the static null route. iBGP advertises the route to all the edge routers, and then the route is installed into the CEF table with a next hop of Null0. This effectively stops the DDoS traffic at the network edge.

You can extend this system to support a sink router by setting the prefix's next hop to the sink router instead of the prefix directed at Null0. The victim address or network should be injected on a special sinkhole router. If the route is configured on an edge router, the next hop is reset because of the **next-hop-self** setting on the BGP sessions to the aggregation routers, and all traffic is drawn to that edge router. It is inadvisable to make unnecessary configuration changes on core or aggregation routers or to inject routing information on these routers.

Example 9-13 shows the configuration for the static redistribution.

Example 9-13 *Dynamic Black Hole System Configuration*

```
ip route 192.0.2.0 255.255.255.0 null0
...
router bgp <ASN>
...
redistribute static route-map STATIC_TO_BGP
!
route-map STATIC_TO_BGP permit 40
 match tag 999
 set ip next-hop 192.0.2.1
 set community no-export
 set origin igp
!
route-map STATIC_TO_BGP permit 50
 match tag 998
set community no-export
 set origin igp
!
route-map STATIC_TO_BGP deny 60
!
```

The BGP community is set to **no-export** to ensure that the prefix is not advertised outside the local network. The Test Net prefix 192.0.2.0/24 can be used because it is completely internal to the network and is not externally visible.

The route tag is used to identify the prefix that is being black-holed without requiring prefix list configuration. The route that would be applied on the sinkhole router to activate black holing for prefix 10.0.0.0/8 is

ip route 10.0.0.0 255.0.0.0 null0 tag 999

This prefix is installed in the routing table and is advertised via iBGP to the entire network. The network is null-routed almost immediately. To send traffic to a sink router, the static route deployed would not use Null0 as the next hop. The following configuration directs traffic to the sink router if the sink router has an address of 192.168.1.1:

ip route 10.0.0.0 255.0.0.0 192.168.1.1 tag 998

The sink router address must also be advertised in the IGP to ensure next-hop reachability for BGP propagation of the victim prefix. The next hop is not manually set in the route map when using a sinkhole. This allows multiple sinkholes for various purposes based on the next-hop address configured in the static route.

Final Edge Router Configuration Example

The final edge router configuration for customer aggregation routers is provided in
Example 9-14.

Example 9-14 *Final Customer Aggregation Edge Router BGP Configuration*

```
router bgp 100
 no auto-summary
 no synchronization
 bgp dampening route-map graded-dampening
bgp log-neighbor-changes
 redistribute static route-map STATIC_TO_BGP
 bgp router-id <BGP Router ID>
 table-map QOS_Policy
 !
 neighbor AGG_UPLINK peer-group
 neighbor AGG_UPLINK description iBGP Session to Aggregation Routers
 neighbor AGG_UPLINK version 4
 neighbor AGG_UPLINK password <iBGP Password>
 neighbor AGG_UPLINK update-source loopback0
 neighbor AGG_UPLINK next-hop-self
 neighbor AGG_UPLINK remote-as 100
 !
 neighbor GOLD_CUST_FULL peer-group
 neighbor GOLD_CUST_FULL description Gold Full Routes Customers
 neighbor GOLD_CUST_FULL version 4
 neighbor GOLD_CUST_FULL password <Customer Password>
 neighbor GOLD_CUST_FULL route-map gold_cust_inbound in
 !
 neighbor SILVER_CUST_FULL peer-group
 neighbor SILVER_CUST_FULL description Silver Full Routes Customers
 neighbor SILVER_CUST_FULL version 4
 neighbor SILVER_CUST_FULL password <Customer Password>
 neighbor SILVER_CUST_FULL route-map silver_cust_inbound in
 !
 neighbor BRONZE_CUST_FULL peer-group
 neighbor BRONZE_CUST_FULL description Bronze Full Routes Customers
 neighbor BRONZE_CUST_FULL version 4
 neighbor BRONZE_CUST_FULL password <Customer Password>
 neighbor BRONZE_CUST_FULL route-map bronze_cust_inbound in
 !
 neighbor GOLD_CUST_PARTIAL peer-group
 neighbor GOLD_CUST_PARTIAL description Gold Partial Routes Customers
 neighbor GOLD_CUST_PARTIAL version 4
 neighbor GOLD_CUST_PARTIAL password <Customer Password>
 neighbor GOLD_CUST_PARTIAL route-map gold_cust_inbound in
 neighbor GOLD_CUST_PARTIAL route-map PARTIAL_ROUTES out
 neighbor GOLD_CUST_PARTIAL default-information originate
 !
 neighbor SILVER_CUST_PARTIAL peer-group
 neighbor SILVER_CUST_PARTIAL description Silver Partial Routes Customers
 neighbor SILVER_CUST_PARTIAL version 4
```

Example 9-14 *Final Customer Aggregation Edge Router BGP Configuration (Continued)*

```
  neighbor SILVER_CUST_PARTIAL password <Customer Password>
  neighbor SILVER_CUST_PARTIAL route-map silver_cust_inbound in
  neighbor SILVER_CUST_PARTIAL route-map PARTIAL_ROUTES out
  neighbor SILVER_CUST_PARTIAL default-information originate

  !
  neighbor BRONZE_CUST_PARTIAL peer-group
  neighbor BRONZE_CUST_PARTIAL description Bronze Partial Routes Customers
  neighbor BRONZE_CUST_PARTIAL version 4
  neighbor BRONZE_CUST_PARTIAL password <Customer Password>
  neighbor BRONZE_CUST_PARTIAL route-map bronze_cust_inbound in
  neighbor BRONZE_CUST_PARTIAL route-map PARTIAL_ROUTES out
  neighbor BRONZE_CUST_PARTIAL default-information originate
  ...
  !
route-map STATIC_TO_BGP permit 10
 match tag 500
 set community 100:3000 100:500
 set origin igp
!
route-map STATIC_TO_BGP permit 20
 match tag 510
 set community 100:3000 100:510
 set origin igp
!
route-map STATIC_TO_BGP permit 30
 match tag 520
 set community 100:3000 100:520
 set origin igp
!
route-map STATIC_TO_BGP deny 40
 !
route-map graded-dampening deny 10
 match ip address prefix-list ROOTSERVERS
 !
route-map graded-dampening deny 20
 match ip address prefix-list GTLDSERVERS
 !
route-map graded-dampening permit 30
 match ip address prefix-list SHORT_DAMP
 set dampening 10 1500 3000 30
 !
route-map graded-dampening permit 40
 match ip address prefix-list MEDIUM_DAMP
 set dampening 15 750 3000 45
 !
route-map graded-dampening permit 50
 match ip address prefix-list LONG_DAMP
 set dampening 30 820 3000 60
```

continues

Example 9-14 *Final Customer Aggregation Edge Router BGP Configuration (Continued)*

```
!
route-map PARTIAL_ROUTES permit 10
 match community 1
!
route-map PARTIAL_ROUTES deny 20
!
route-map QOS_Policy permit 10
 match community 50
 set ip precedence immediate
!
route-map QOS_Policy permit 20
 match community 51
 set ip precedence priority
!
route-map QOS_Polciy permit 30
 match community 52
 set ip precedence routine
!
! Gold Service Route Maps
route-map gold_cust_inbound permit 10
  match community 10
  set community 100:3000 100:500 additive
  set local-preference 80
!
route-map gold_cust_inbound permit 20
  match community 11
  set community 100:3000 100:500 additive
  set local-preference 90
!
route-map gold_cust_inbound permit 30
  match community 12
  set community 100:3000 100:500 additive
  set local-preference 110
!
route-map gold_cust_inbound permit 40
  match community 13
  set community 100:3000 100:500 additive
  set local-preference 120
!
route-map gold_cust_inbound permit 50
  set community 100:3000 100:500 additive
  set local-preference 100
!
! Silver Service Route Maps
route-map silver_cust_inbound permit 10
  match community 10
  set community 100:3000 100:510 additive
  set local-preference 80
!
route-map silver_cust_inbound permit 20
  match community 11
  set community 100:3000 100:510 additive
```

Example 9-14 *Final Customer Aggregation Edge Router BGP Configuration (Continued)*

```
   set local-preference 90
 !
route-map silver_cust_inbound permit 30
  match community 12
  set community 100:3000 100:510 additive
  set local-preference 110
 !
route-map silver_cust_inbound permit 40
  match community 13
  set community 100:3000 100:510 additive
  set local-preference 120
 !
route-map silver_cust_inbound permit 50
  set community 100:3000 100:510 additive
  set local-preference 100
 !
! Bronze Service Route Maps
route-map bronze_cust_inbound permit 10
  match community 10
  set community 100:3000 100:520 additive
  set local-preference 80
 !
route-map bronze_cust_inbound permit 20
  match community 11
  set community 100:3000 100:520 additive
  set local-preference 90
 !
route-map bronze_cust_inbound permit 30
  match community 12
  set community 100:3000 100:520 additive
  set local-preference 110
 !
route-map bronze_cust_inbound permit 40
  match community 13
  set community 100:3000 100:520 additive
  set local-preference 120
 !
route-map bronze_cust_inbound permit 50
  set community 100:3000 100:520 additive
  set local-preference 100
 !
! Community list for Partial Routes
ip community-list 1 permit 100:3000
ip community-list 1 deny
 !
! Inbound Customer Local Preference 80
ip community-list 10 permit 100:80
ip community-list 10 deny
 !
```

continues

Example 9-14 *Final Customer Aggregation Edge Router BGP Configuration (Continued)*

```
! Inbound Customer Local Preference 90
ip community-list 11 permit 100:90
ip community-list 11 deny
!
! Inbound Customer Local Preference 110
ip community-list 12 permit 100:110
ip community-list 12 deny
!
! Inbound Customer Local Preference 120
ip community-list 13 permit 100:120
ip community-list 13 deny
!
! Gold Service Community
ip community-list 50 permit 100:500
ip community-list 50 deny
!
! Silver Service Community
ip community-list 51 permit 100:510
ip community-list 51 deny
!
! Bronze Service Community
ip community-list 52 permit 100:520
ip community-list 52 deny
!
! Dynamic Black Hole Address
ip route 192.0.2.0 255.255.255.0 null0
!
! Prefix Lists for Graded Dampening
! Don't Dampen DNS Root Servers
ip prefix-list ROOTSERVERS seq 5 permit 198.41.0.0/24
ip prefix-list ROOTSERVERS seq 10 permit 128.9.0.0/16
ip prefix-list ROOTSERVERS seq 15 permit 192.33.4.0/24
ip prefix-list ROOTSERVERS seq 20 permit 128.8.0.0/16
ip prefix-list ROOTSERVERS seq 25 permit 192.203.230.0/24
ip prefix-list ROOTSERVERS seq 30 permit 192.5.5.0/24
ip prefix-list ROOTSERVERS seq 35 permit 192.112.36.0/24
ip prefix-list ROOTSERVERS seq 40 permit 128.63.0.0/16
ip prefix-list ROOTSERVERS seq 45 permit 192.36.148.0/24
ip prefix-list ROOTSERVERS seq 50 permit 192.58.128.0/24
ip prefix-list ROOTSERVERS seq 55 permit 193.0.14.0/24
ip prefix-list ROOTSERVERS seq 60 permit 198.32.64.0/24
ip prefix-list ROOTSERVERS seq 65 permit 202.12.27.0/24
! Global Top Level DNS Servers
ip prefix-list GTLDSERVERS seq 5 permit 192.5.6.0/24
ip prefix-list GTLDSERVERS seq 10 permit 192.33.14.0/24
ip prefix-list GTLDSERVERS seq 15 permit 192.26.92.0/24
ip prefix-list GTLDSERVERS seq 20 permit 192.31.80.0/24
ip prefix-list GTLDSERVERS seq 25 permit 192.12.94.0/24
ip prefix-list GTLDSERVERS seq 30 permit 192.35.51.0/24
ip prefix-list GTLDSERVERS seq 35 permit 192.42.93.0/24
ip prefix-list GTLDSERVERS seq 40 permit 192.54.112.0/24
```

Example 9-14 *Final Customer Aggregation Edge Router BGP Configuration (Continued)*

```
ip prefix-list GTLDSERVERS seq 45 permit 192.43.172.0/24
ip prefix-list GTLDSERVERS seq 50 permit 192.48.79.0/24
ip prefix-list GTLDSERVERS seq 55 permit 192.52.178.0/24
ip prefix-list GTLDSERVERS seq 60 permit 192.41.162.0/24
ip prefix-list GTLDSERVERS seq 65 permit 192.55.83.0/24
!
! Prefixes Longer than a /24
ip prefix-list LONG_DAMP seq 5 0.0.0.0/0 ge 24
! Prefixes that are a /22 or /23
ip prefix-list MEDIUM_DAMP seq 5 0.0.0.0/0 ge 22 le 23
! Prefixes that are a /21 or shorter
ip prefix-list SHORT_DAMP seq 5 0.0.0.0/0 le 21
!
```

A configuration example for a border or peering router is shown in Example 9-15.

Example 9-15 *Peering Router Sample BGP Configuration*

```
router bgp 100
 no auto-summary
 no synchronization
 bgp dampening route-map graded-dampening
 no bgp fast-external-fallover
 bgp log-neighbor-changes
 bgp router-id <BGP Router ID>
 table-map QOS_Policy
 !
 neighbor AGG_UPLINK peer-group
 neighbor AGG_UPLINK description iBGP Session to Aggregation Routers
 neighbor AGG_UPLINK version 4
 neighbor AGG_UPLINK password <iBGP Password>
 neighbor AGG_UPLINK update-source loopback0
 neighbor AGG_UPLINK next-hop-self
 neighbor AGG_UPLINK remote-as 100
 !
 neighbor <Peer Address> description Generic Peering Example to AS1000
 neighbor <Peer Address> version 4
 neighbor <Peer Address> password <Peer Password>
 neighbor <Peer Address> route-map peer_outbound_AS1000 out
 neighbor <Peer Address> prefix-list PEER_FILTER in
 neighbor <Peer Address> remote-as 1000
 ...
 !
 route-map graded-dampening deny 10
  match ip address prefix-list ROOTSERVERS
 !
 route-map graded-dampening deny 20
  match ip address prefix-list GTLDSERVERS
```

continues

Example 9-15 *Peering Router Sample BGP Configuration (Continued)*

```
!
route-map graded-dampening permit 30
 match ip address prefix-list SHORT_DAMP
 set dampening 10 1500 3000 30
!
route-map graded-dampening permit 40
 match ip address prefix-list MEDIUM_DAMP
 set dampening 15 750 3000 45
!
route-map graded-dampening permit 50
 match ip address prefix-list LONG_DAMP
 set dampening 30 820 3000 60
!
route-map peer_outbound_AS1000 deny 10
 match community 20
!
route-map peer_outbound_AS1000 permit 20
 match community 21
 set as-path prepend 100
!
route-map peer_outbound_AS1000 permit 30
 match community 22
 set as-path prepend 100 100
!
route-map peer_outbound_AS1000 permit 40
 match community 23
 set as-path prepend 100 100 100
!
route-map peer_outbound_AS1000 permit 50
 match community 24
 set as-path prepend 100 100 100 100
!
route-map peer_outbound_AS1000 permit 60
 match community 25
 set as-path prepend 100 100 100 100 100
!
route-map peer_outbound_AS1000 permit 70
 match community 1
!
route-map peer_outbound_AS1000 deny 80
!
route-map QOS_Policy permit 10
 match community 50
 set ip precedence immediate
!
route-map QOS_Policy permit 20
 match community 51
 set ip precedence priority
!
route-map QOS_Polciy permit 30
 match community 52
 set ip precedence routine
```

Example 9-15 *Peering Router Sample BGP Configuration (Continued)*

```
!
! Community list for Partial Routes
ip community-list 1 permit 100:3000
ip community-list 1 deny
!
ip community-list 20 permit 65000:1000
ip community-list 20 permit 100:220
ip community-list 20 deny
!
ip community-list 21 permit 65100:1000 100:3000
ip community-list 21 deny
!
ip community-list 22 permit 65200:1000 100:3000
ip community-list 22 deny
!
ip community-list 23 permit 65300:1000 100:3000
ip community-list 23 deny
!
ip community-list 24 permit 65400:1000 100:3000
ip community-list 24 deny
!
ip community-list 25 permit 65500:1000 100:3000
ip community-list 25 deny
!
! Gold Service Community
ip community-list 50 permit 100:500
ip community-list 50 deny
!
! Silver Service Community
ip community-list 51 permit 100:510
ip community-list 51 deny
!
! Bronze Service Community
ip community-list 52 permit 100:520
ip community-list 52 deny
!
! Dynamic Black Hole Address
ip route 192.0.2.0 255.255.255.0 null0
!
! Prefix Lists for Graded Dampening
! Don't Dampen DNS Root Servers
ip prefix-list ROOTSERVERS seq 5 permit 198.41.0.0/24
ip prefix-list ROOTSERVERS seq 10 permit 128.9.0.0/16
ip prefix-list ROOTSERVERS seq 15 permit 192.33.4.0/24
ip prefix-list ROOTSERVERS seq 20 permit 128.8.0.0/16
ip prefix-list ROOTSERVERS seq 25 permit 192.203.230.0/24
ip prefix-list ROOTSERVERS seq 30 permit 192.5.5.0/24
ip prefix-list ROOTSERVERS seq 35 permit 192.112.36.0/24
ip prefix-list ROOTSERVERS seq 40 permit 128.63.0.0/16
ip prefix-list ROOTSERVERS seq 45 permit 192.36.148.0/24
```

continues

Example 9-15 *Peering Router Sample BGP Configuration (Continued)*

```
ip prefix-list ROOTSERVERS seq 50 permit 192.58.128.0/24
ip prefix-list ROOTSERVERS seq 55 permit 193.0.14.0/24
ip prefix-list ROOTSERVERS seq 60 permit 198.32.64.0/24
ip prefix-list ROOTSERVERS seq 65 permit 202.12.27.0/24
! Global Top Level DNS Servers
ip prefix-list GTLDSERVERS seq 5 permit 192.5.6.0/24
ip prefix-list GTLDSERVERS seq 10 permit 192.33.14.0/24
ip prefix-list GTLDSERVERS seq 15 permit 192.26.92.0/24
ip prefix-list GTLDSERVERS seq 20 permit 192.31.80.0/24
ip prefix-list GTLDSERVERS seq 25 permit 192.12.94.0/24
ip prefix-list GTLDSERVERS seq 30 permit 192.35.51.0/24
ip prefix-list GTLDSERVERS seq 35 permit 192.42.93.0/24
ip prefix-list GTLDSERVERS seq 40 permit 192.54.112.0/24
ip prefix-list GTLDSERVERS seq 45 permit 192.43.172.0/24
ip prefix-list GTLDSERVERS seq 50 permit 192.48.79.0/24
ip prefix-list GTLDSERVERS seq 55 permit 192.52.178.0/24
ip prefix-list GTLDSERVERS seq 60 permit 192.41.162.0/24
ip prefix-list GTLDSERVERS seq 65 permit 192.55.83.0/24
!
! Prefixes Longer than a /24
ip prefix-list LONG_DAMP seq 5 0.0.0.0/0 ge 24
! Prefixes that are a /22 or /23
ip prefix-list MEDIUM_DAMP seq 5 0.0.0.0/0 ge 22 le 23
! Prefixes that are a /21 or shorter
ip prefix-list SHORT_DAMP seq 5 0.0.0.0/0 le 21
!
ip prefix-list PEER_FILTER seq 5 deny 0.0.0.0/8
ip prefix-list PEER_FILTER seq 10 deny 10.0.0.0/8
ip prefix-list PEER_FILTER seq 15 deny 127.0.0.0/8
ip prefix-list PEER_FILTER seq 20 deny 168.254.0.0/16
ip prefix-list PEER_FILTER seq 25 deny 172.16.0.0/12
ip prefix-list PEER_FILTER seq 30 deny 192.0.2.0/24
ip prefix-list PEER_FILTER seq 35 deny 192.168.0.0/16
ip prefix-list PEER_FILTER seq 40 deny 224.0.0.0/4
ip prefix-list PEER_FILTER seq 45 deny 240.0.0.0/4
ip prefix-list PEER_FILTER seq 50 deny any
!
```

Summary

This chapter covered the basic BGP architecture for an ISP network. The chapter began with basic BGP templates for the core, aggregation, and edge routers. The core and aggregation templates remained unchanged through the chapter. The core and aggregation layers serve to transit packets.

The edge router is broken into two separate types of edge routers: the customer aggregation router and the border or peering router. Both operate at the edge of the network, but they have different policy and BGP information requirements. The section "BGP Security

Features" identified problems associated with carrying full routes on the peering routers. The customer edge router, however, requires full routing tables for multihomed transit customers.

The edge router configuration changed considerably and became much more complex as services were added to the network. The final service added was a dynamic black-holing system to assist in the mitigation of denial-of-service attacks—specifically, distributed attacks. The last section provided the configuration for the edge routers, both customer aggregation and peering routers, after services deployment.

Implementing BGP Multiprotocol Extensions

This chapter explores the various aspects of multiprotocol BGP and MPLS VPN:

- BGP multiprotocol extension for MPLS VPN
- Understanding MPLS fundamentals
- Building MPLS VPN architectures
- VPNs across AS borders
- Deployment considerations

CHAPTER 10

Multiprotocol BGP and MPLS VPN

Multiprotocol Label Switching (MPLS) is a signaling and forwarding technology that uses labels to make forwarding decisions. MPLS virtual private networks (VPNs) deliver private network services over a shared MPLS infrastructure. BGP is extended to provide multiprotocol support, which allows BGP to carry VPN-IPv4 reachability information. An MPLS VPN built in such a manner is called a *Layer 3 VPN*.

This chapter discusses BGP multiprotocol support for MPLS VPN. The focus of this MPLS VPN discussion is BGP-based Layer 3 VPN.

BGP Multiprotocol Extension for MPLS VPN

The capability of a BGP speaker to support multiprotocol extensions for MPLS VPN is advertised to its peer during session setup. As discussed in Chapter 2, "Understanding BGP Building Blocks," the Capabilities Code 1 is for multiprotocol extension. Support for MPLS VPN is indicated with an address family identifier (AFI) of 1 (IPv4) and a subsequent address family identifier (SAFI) of 128.

The next sections describe the prefix format and attributes of VPN-IPv4.

Route Distinguisher and VPN-IPv4 Address

A VPN-IPv4 (VPNv4 for short) address has two components: an eight-octet Route Distinguisher (RD) and a four-octet IPv4 address. The purpose of an RD is to distinguish multiple VPN routes that have an identical IPv4 prefix. The prepending of an RD to an IPv4 address makes the same IPv4 address unique for different VPNs.

Although the format of an RD is a structured string consisting of a 2-byte Type field and a 6-byte Value field. As defined in RFC 2547bis, it has no mandatory semantics. In fact, when BGP compares two RDs, it ignores the structure and compares the entire 8-byte values. One common way of defining RD is to split it into two components: an AS number (4 bytes) and an assigned number (2 bytes). An example of an RD is 65000:1001, where 65000 represents an AS number and 1001 is a locally assigned number.

NOTE   The RD is not used to represent VPNs or to control route redistribution. It is only used to
make a VPNv4 address unique in an MPLS backbone even when IPv4 addresses are not.
RD assignments and best practices of RD design in an MPLS VPN are discussed in detail
in the later section "Design Guidelines for RDs."

Example 10-1 shows how a VPNv4 address is received by a multiprotocol BGP speaker. In
the example, the VPNv4 prefix 65000:1:10.0.0.1/32 is received from 192.168.1.1, where
65000:1 is the RD and 10.0.0.1/32 is the IPv4 prefix.

Example 10-1 *Output of* **debug ip bgp update**

```
...
23:48:33: BGP(1): 192.168.1.1 rcvd 65000:1:10.0.0.1/32
...
```

Extended Community Attribute

To control VPN route distribution, a new BGP attribute, extended community, is defined.
Comparing it to the standard BGP community attribute (attribute type 8), the extended
community attribute (attribute type 16) is extended from the standard 32 bits to 64 bits, and
it includes a Type field.

Currently, two extended communities are relevant to VPNv4:

● Route Target, Type 0x02
● Route Origin, Type 0x03

Route Target Extended Community

A Route Target (RT) extended community is used to identify a set of sites or VPNs. Asso-
ciating a certain RT with a VPNv4 route allows the route to be placed in VPNs/sites that
forward such traffic. As a result, RTs are used to control VPNv4 route redistribution.

A common way of assigning RTs to a route is to split an RT into two components: a 16-bit
AS number and a 16-bit assigned number. An example of an RT is 65000:100, where 65000
identifies an AS number and 100 is a locally assigned number that represents one VPN
or site. Examples of RT assignment in an MPLS VPN are presented in the later section
"Deployment Considerations."

NOTE	It is important to note that an RD has no association with an RT, even though they might have the same format and sometimes the same value. Additionally, a VPNv4 prefix might have only one RD but can have multiple RTs attached to it.

Example 10-2 shows RT as an attribute of a BGP VPNv4 prefix. The VPNv4 prefix 10:1:10.1.2.0/24 is received from 192.168.110.3, with an RT of 65000:100. The RD of the VPNv4 prefix is 10:1.

Example 10-2 *Output of* **debug ip bgp update**

```
...
23:48:51: BGP(1): 192.168.110.3 rcvd UPDATE w/ attr: nexthop 192.168.110.3,
  origin ?, path 10, extended community RT:65000:100
23:48:51: BGP(1): 192.168.110.3 rcvd 10:1:10.1.2.0/24
...
```

Route Origin Extended Community

Route Origin identifies the routers that inject the routes into BGP. This extended community is called Site of Origin (SOO) in Cisco IOS software. In an MPLS VPN that has multihomed connections, SOO is used to identify a customer site to prevent traffic from leaving the site from one point and being sent back to the same site from another point. The use of BGP in a Layer 3 MPLS VPN is discussed in the section "Building MPLS VPN Architectures." SOO is typically configured as a 16-bit AS number and a 16-bit assigned number. An example of SOO is 65000:100. The use of SOO in preventing routing information loops is discussed in the section "AS Override."

Multiprotocol Reachability Attributes

To advertise multiprotocol reachability information or Network Layer Reachability Information (NLRI) in BGP updates, two BGP attributes are created (refer to RFC 2858, *Multiprotocol Extensions for BGP-4*):

- Multiprotocol Reachable NLRI (MP_REACH_NLRI), Type 14
- Multiprotocol Unreachable NLRI (MP_UNREACH_NLRI), Type 15

MP_REACH_NLRI is used to advertise feasible routes. MP_UNREACH_NLRI is used to advertise, or rather withdraw, unfeasible routes. Each attribute has fields identifying AFI, SAFI, and NLRI. For VPNv4, AFI/SAFI are 1/128.

Within each NLRI, label mapping and VPNv4 prefix are carried in the following order (see RFC 3107, *Carrying Label Information in BGP-4*):

- Label
- RD
- IPv4 prefix

Note that the Label field can carry one or more labels. The following sections go into detail about how labels are generated and exchanged.

Understanding MPLS Fundamentals

MPLS is an IETF standard, as defined in a set of RFCs. Currently, MPLS is defined only for IP. Using a connection-oriented approach, packet forwarding in MPLS relies on preexisting paths. An MPLS forwarding path can also be thought of as a tunnel that goes from an MPLS ingress point to an MPLS egress point. Compared to conventional IP routing and forwarding, path selection and packet forwarding are separated in MPLS.

Figure 10-1 shows an example of an MPLS network. It consists of two types of devices:

- Edge Label Switch Router or Label Edge Router (LER)
- Label Switch Router (LSR)

Figure 10-1 *MPLS Network*

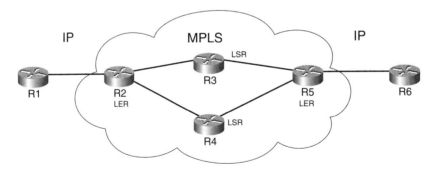

The function of an LER is to switch packets between the IP network and the MPLS network. In other words, switching can occur from an IP packet to a labeled packet, or from a labeled packet to an IP packet. The function of an LSR is to switch the packet with one label to a packet with another label.

The path from the ingress LER R2 to the egress LER R5 or the reverse is called a *Label Switched Path (LSP)*. Labels have local significance and are typically exchanged using a signaling protocol.

An IP packet is classified only once when entering the MPLS network. Thereafter, the original IP packet is encapsulated into a labeled packet and is switched based on the labels, not its IPv4 header. On the egress LER, the labeled packet is decapsulated into an IP packet and is delivered using conventional IP forwarding.

Rather than thinking of MPLS as a network service, MPLS is often considered more appropriately an enabling technology. MPLS provides a connection-oriented infrastructure that lets other service-oriented technologies be deployed. MPLS VPN is one such example. Additionally, traffic engineering (TE), quality of service (QoS), and Layer 2 simulation can be provisioned over MPLS.

The next sections provide an overview of the types of MPLS labels, how labels are exchanged between LSR pairs, and how labeled packets are processed.

MPLS Labels

MPLS labels can take a variety of forms, depending on the underlying links. With regards to label implementation, there are three general types of networks:

- Frame-based
- Cell-based
- Non-packet-based

Figure 10-2 shows the format of a label in a frame-based network such as Ethernet. The label value is a 20-bit field that carries the label's actual value. When a labeled packet is received, the label value at the top of the stack is looked up (a stack is a concatenation of one or more labels). From the lookup, the packet's next hop is learned, and the type of operation to be performed can be determined on the label stack before forwarding.

Figure 10-2 *Frame Label Header Format*

The following describes each of the fields in the frame-based label header:

- **Exp field**—The 3-bit Experimental Bits (Exp) field is typically used to convey the packet's class of service, as the Precedence bits do in the IPv4 header.

- **S field**—When the Bottom of Stack (S) bit is set to 1, the current label is on the bottom of the stack. This allows multiple labels to be encoded into the same packet to form a label stack. With this definition, an ordinary IP packet can be thought of as a labeled packet with zero depth of label stack.

- **TTL field**—The 8-bit Time to Live (TTL) field is used to encode a time-to-live value. If a labeled packet's outgoing TTL is 0, the packet's lifetime in the network is considered to have expired. The packet should not be forwarded further either labeled or unlabeled.

To create a labeled frame, a label is inserted into a section of the frame header that immediately precedes the Layer 3 header. This inserted label is often called the *shim header*. The shim header is used for links such as PPP, Packet over SONET (POS), Ethernet, and packet-based Asynchronous Transfer Mode (ATM) links.

To indicate a shim MPLS header, a new protocol number has been defined for MPLS. The MPLS protocol ID for PPP is 0x0281 for unicast and 0x0283 for multicast. The MPLS EtherType is 0x8847 for unicast and 0x8848 for multicast.

In a cell-based network such as ATM, cell headers are used to carry label information. Specifically, they are virtual path identifier (VPI) and virtual circuit identifier (VCI). An ATM LSR is typically a conventional ATM switch appended with a Layer 3 router.

When MPLS is applied to non-packet-based networks, such as optical networks, the definition of label is generalized. A generalized label can be a physical port, a wavelength, or a SONET or Synchronous Digital Hierarchy (SDH) circuit. This form of MPLS is now called Generalized MPLS (GMPLS).

In all three networks, there always exists a control channel between LSRs to initialize LSP setup. This channel is in the form of unlabeled packets in frame-based networks, a control virtual circuit (VC) in cell-based networks, or a special circuit in non-packet-based networks.

Label Exchange and LSP Setup

The labeled packets are forwarded along preestablished LSPs. An LSP is a forwarding path from the ingress LER to the egress LER that associates labels with destination prefixes and appropriate encapsulation information. To set up an LSP, label binding information must be exchanged among LSRs using the control channel. Here, label binding or mapping means the mapping of labels to prefixes and neighbors that advertised the labels.

There are several ways to exchange labels for unicast prefixes. For IGP prefixes, there is the standard Label Distribution Protocol (LDP) as well as Cisco's Tag Distribution Protocol (TDP). Multiprotocol BGP can carry label information for BGP prefixes. Resource Reservation Protocol (RSVP) is extended to exchange label information for MPLS traffic engineering tunnels.

NOTE	TDP and LDP are quite similar functionally, but they do not interoperate. As an example, TDP uses port 711, whereas LDP uses port 646 for neighbor discovery (using UDP) and session establishment (using TCP). When both are configured on the same link with **mpls label protocol both**, LDP is used to establish the adjacency.

Labels are distributed using the *downstream distribution* method. It has two variations:

- **Unsolicited downstream**—Sometimes simply called *downstream*, in this method, a downstream LSR sends its entire label space to the upstream LSRs. When it is ready to forward traffic for a labeled destination, the downstream LSR assigns an incoming (local) label to the destination and sends the label to all its upstream neighbors. This method is used for frame-based interfaces such as PPP, POS, and Ethernet.

- **Downstream on demand**—In this method, the upstream LSR explicitly requests a label binding for an FEC, and the downstream LSR returns a label binding for that FEC. This method is used for cell-based interfaces (ATM).

Labels are assigned downstream, and label bindings are distributed in the downstream-to-upstream direction. Here, downstream is per data forwarding, where the next-hop router is the downstream router.

In either method, label values 0 through 15 are reserved for special purposes. Table 10-1 lists some of the reserved labels. Currently, labels 4 through 15 are not used.

Table 10-1   *Some Reserved Labels and Their Meanings*

Label Value	LDP	TDP
0	IPv4 Explicit Null	IPv4 Explicit Null
1	Router Alert	IPv4 Implicit Null
2	IPv6 Explicit Null	Router Alert
3	IPv4 Implicit Null	IPv6 Explicit Null

Explicit Null is a unique label signaled by the egress (or ultimate) LER to the penultimate LSR (an upstream LSR that is directly connected to the egress LER) for label replacement during forwarding. Upon receiving such a labeled packet, the LER pops the Explicit Null label and forwards the packet based on the IPv4 header. The forwarding of labeled packets and the POP operation are discussed in detail in the next section.

Router Alert indicates that the router must inspect the packet. When a received packet contains this label value at the top of the label stack, the packet is processed locally. The actual packet forwarding is determined by the label beneath it in the stack.

When an egress LER advertises locally connected routes, it may advertise an Implicit Null label. This label is received only via the signaling path; it is never received from the forwarding path. An Implicit Null label directs the penultimate hop LSR to pop the top label during forwarding.

Figure 10-3 shows a simple example of how label exchange and LSP work. In this example, all routers are running IS-IS as the IGP to exchange IPv4 routing information. R2 through R5 are LSRs, and R1 and R6 support only IPv4.

Figure 10-3 *Label Distribution and LSP Setup*

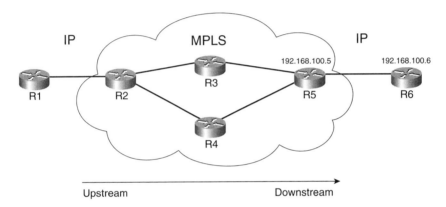

All links are Ethernet and have IP addresses assigned from 192.168.0.0/16, with the corresponding router IDs as the third and fourth octet addresses. For example, the address of R2 on the link with R4 is 192.168.24.2. All routers have loopback 0 interface addresses assigned from 192.168.100.x, where *x* is the router ID.

To simplify the discussion, the loopback addresses of R5 and R6 are selected as the prefixes of interest. Thus, the downstream direction points to R5 and R6. For example, R4 is considered an upstream LSR to R5.

All LSRs use LDP to exchange label binding information. LSRs use UDP to discover neighbors. Example 10-3 shows the neighbor discovery of R5 and R2 on R4. The LDP ID is expressed as a 4-byte router ID (192.168.100.4) and 2-byte label space (0). The label space defines the range of label values on an LSR. A 0 label space indicates that the labels are assigned from a single range (global to the platform). In contrast, labels can be inter-face-specific (where each interface has an independent label range), as in the case of an ATM interface.

Example 10-3 *Output of* **show mpls ldp discovery** *on R4*

```
R4#show mpls ldp discovery
 Local LDP Identifier:
   192.168.100.4:0
```

Example 10-3 *Output of* **show mpls ldp discovery** *on R4 (Continued)*

```
Discovery Sources:
Interfaces:
    Ethernet1/0 (ldp): xmit/recv
        LDP Id: 192.168.100.5:0
    Ethernet2/0 (ldp): xmit/recv
        LDP Id: 192.168.100.2:0
```

NOTE   The LDP router ID by default is the highest loopback IP address or the highest IP address of an up interface. This address must be routable. You can fix the router ID by configuring **mpls ldp router-id** *interface*. The change takes effect when the interface is up and when either the interface for the current ID is down or LDP is reset. To force the ID change immediately, append the command with the keyword **force**, which resets the LDP sessions.

Example 10-4 shows the two LDP sessions on R4. Note that an LDP session is established over TCP port 646. All available peer interface addresses are also listed per session.

Example 10-4 *Output of* **show mpls ldp neighbor** *on R4*

```
R4#show mpls ldp neighbor
    Peer LDP Ident: 192.168.100.5:0; Local LDP Ident 192.168.100.4:0
        TCP connection: 192.168.100.5.11013 - 192.168.100.4.646
        State: Oper; Msgs sent/rcvd: 22627/22644; Downstream
        Up time: 1w6d
        LDP discovery sources:
          Ethernet1/0, Src IP addr: 192.168.45.5
        Addresses bound to peer LDP Ident:
          192.168.100.5    192.168.56.5    192.168.35.5    192.168.45.5
    Peer LDP Ident: 192.168.100.2:0; Local LDP Ident 192.168.100.4:0
        TCP connection: 192.168.100.2.646 - 192.168.100.4.11745
        State: Oper; Msgs sent/rcvd: 20953/20956; Downstream
        Up time: 1w5d
        LDP discovery sources:
          Ethernet2/0, Src IP addr: 192.168.24.2
        Addresses bound to peer LDP Ident:
          192.168.100.2    192.168.12.2    192.168.24.2    192.168.23.2
```

NOTE   The default label exchange protocol in most Cisco IOS software releases is TDP, but you can change it to LDP either globally or per interface using the command **mpls label protocol ldp**. Neighbor relationships are formed between a pair of routers, not between individual interfaces.

As an egress LER for 192.168.100.5/32 and 192.168.100.6/32, R5 assigns local labels for these two prefixes and distributes them to its upstream neighbors, R3 and R4. Table 10-2 shows the label binding information on R5.

Table 10-2 *Label Bindings on R5*

Prefix	Local Label	Received Label	Next Hop
192.168.100.5/32	Implicit Null	None	R5
192.168.100.6/32	20	None	R6

The local label, also called in label, is assigned locally. The received label is received from its downstream neighbor. The received label is often an outgoing label in the forwarding path, except for the Implicit Null, as discussed previously.

Because 192.168.100.5/32 is local to R5, no outgoing label is received. With the default behavior on frame-based links, an Implicit Null local label is assigned for the prefix. The prefix 192.168.100.6/32 is a remote route from R6. R5 advertises a local label of 20. Because R6 is not running MPLS, R5 does not receive a label from R6.

Next, R5 distributes the local labels to its upstream neighbors. When R3 receives the two prefixes from R5, it assigns local labels and distributes them upstream to R2. Table 10-3 shows the label bindings on R3.

Table 10-3 *Label Bindings on R3*

Prefix	Local Label	Received Label	Next Hop
192.168.100.5/32	21	Implicit Null	R5
192.168.100.6/32	22	20	R5

Example 10-5 shows the output of **show mpls ldp bindings** on R3. Note that the label binding information from LDP or TDP is stored in the Label Information Base (LIB) or Tag Information Base (TIB). TSR stands for Tag Switch Router.

Example 10-5 *LIB on R3*

```
R3#show mpls ldp bindings
...
  tib entry: 192.168.100.5/32, rev 18
        local binding:  tag: 21
        remote binding: tsr: 192.168.100.2:0, tag: 20
        remote binding: tsr: 192.168.100.5:0, tag: imp-null
  tib entry: 192.168.100.6/32, rev 20
        local binding:  tag: 22
        remote binding: tsr: 192.168.100.2:0, tag: 21
        remote binding: tsr: 192.168.100.5:0, tag: 20
...
```

NOTE	The words *tag*, *label*, and *MPLS* are often used interchangeably in CLI and command outputs.

Table 10-4 shows a similar LIB on R4, except that R4 assigns 20 to 192.168.100.5/32 and 21 to 192.168.100.6/32.

Table 10-4   *Label Bindings on R4*

Prefix	Local Label	Received Label	Next Hop
192.168.100.5/32	20	Implicit Null	R5
192.168.100.6/32	21	20	R5

On R2, two paths are received for the two prefixes—one via R3 and one via R4. Table 10-5 shows the LIB on R2. For 192.168.100.5/32, for example, R2 receives label 20 from R4 and label 21 from R3. Note that the same label value 21 is received from R4 for 192.168.100.6/32. This is fine, because R2 keeps track of the bindings for each prefix in relation to the neighbor that advertises the label.

Table 10-5   *Label Bindings on R2*

Prefix	Local Label	Received Label	Next Hop
192.168.100.5/32	20	20	R4
		21	R3
192.168.100.6/32	21	21	R4
		22	R3

To summarize, there are two LSPs for each prefix from R2 (ingress) to R5 (egress): one from R2 to R5 via R3, and one from R2 to R5 via R4. Because the path cost is the same between these two LSPs, traffic is load-shared. This is shown in Example 10-6.

Example 10-6 *Output of* **traceroute** *for 192.168.100.6 on R2*

```
R2#traceroute 192.168.100.6

Type escape sequence to abort.
Tracing the route to 192.168.100.6

  1 192.168.24.4 [MPLS: Label 21 Exp 0] 32 msec
    192.168.23.3 [MPLS: Label 22 Exp 0] 52 msec
    192.168.24.4 [MPLS: Label 21 Exp 0] 40 msec
```

continues

Example 10-6 *Output of* **traceroute** *for 192.168.100.6 on R2 (Continued)*

```
 2 192.168.35.5 [MPLS: Label 20 Exp 0] 20 msec
   192.168.45.5 [MPLS: Label 20 Exp 0] 32 msec
   192.168.35.5 [MPLS: Label 20 Exp 0] 28 msec
 3 192.168.56.6 40 msec 32 msec *
```

Forwarding Labeled Packets

Three types of operations can be performed on a received packet:

- **Push**—Push, sometimes called *imposition*, is an operation performed by an LSR to create or add a label stack to a packet. This operation is often performed on an unlabeled packet or a labeled packet where the next-hop information indicates that a new label or labels should be inserted. Push is typically performed on an ingress LER.

- **Pop**—Pop is performed when a labeled packet is received and the next-hop information indicates that one or all label stack entries should be removed. Label popping, also called *label disposition*, is typically performed on a penultimate-hop LSR or an egress LER.

- **Swap**—When a labeled packet arrives, the top label is replaced by a another label. Label swapping is typically performed on a core LSR.

With the preceding three operations, four packet-switching paths are available:

- **IP to IP**—An incoming IP packet is switched to an outgoing IP packet. This is conventional IP routing and switching.

- **IP to label**—An unlabeled packet is pushed with one or more labels and is switched to an LSR.

- **Label to IP**—A labeled packet is popped, and a conventional IP packet is delivered.

- **Label to label**—An incoming label is swapped to an outgoing label, or the top label is popped, and one or more labels are available for forwarding.

To perform the preceding switching functions, many components must cooperate in a seamless fashion. Figure 10-4 shows the interaction of the Forwarding Information Base (FIB) and Label Forwarding Information Base (LFIB). Arrows indicate the directions of changes triggered from one component to another. As mentioned in Chapter 2, entries in the RIB provide the prefix entries in FIB. IP packets can be forwarded when the recursion is fully resolved and the encapsulation string is created in the adjacency table.

Figure 10-4 *Interaction of FIB and LFIB*

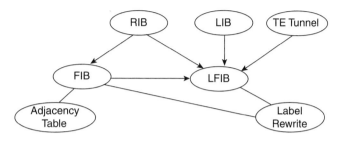

CEF is the preferred switching mechanism for IP packets and is the only method that supports MPLS. When MPLS is enabled, CEF also allows table lookup based on labels. The label forwarding information is stored in LFIB. Example 10-7 shows a sample LFIB.

Example 10-7 *Sample LFIB as Output of* **show mpls forwarding**

```
R2#show mpls forwarding
Local  Outgoing    Prefix            Bytes tag  Outgoing   Next Hop
tag    tag or VC   or Tunnel Id      switched   interface
16     Pop tag     192.168.45.0/24   0          Et2/0      192.168.24.4
17     17          192.168.56.0/24   0          Et2/0      192.168.24.4
       19          192.168.56.0/24   0          Et1/0      192.168.23.3
18     Pop tag     192.168.35.0/24   0          Et1/0      192.168.23.3
19     Pop tag     192.168.100.4/32  711        Et2/0      192.168.24.4
20     20          192.168.100.5/32  0          Et2/0      192.168.24.4
       21          192.168.100.5/32  0          Et1/0      192.168.23.3
21     21          192.168.100.6/32  0          Et2/0      192.168.24.4
       22          192.168.100.6/32  0          Et1/0      192.168.23.3
22     Untagged    192.168.100.1/32  2360       Et0/0      192.168.12.1
23     Pop tag     192.168.100.3/32  1143       Et1/0      192.168.23.3
```

This example shows three forms of labels on the outgoing side: a label, label popping (Pop tag), and no label (Untagged). If a label is indicated, label swapping is performed. If "Pop tag" is shown, the top label must be popped before forwarding. If "Untagged" is indicated, all labels are removed before forwarding.

NOTE   For an outgoing label to be installed in the LFIB for prefix *P*, in addition to having a remote binding from the next-hop neighbor for *P*, the next-hop IP address for the prefix (shown in **show ip route** *P* or **show ip cef** *P*) must also be in the set of addresses displayed for the neighbor in **show mpls ldp neighbor**.

IGP entries and tunnel interfaces created from MPLS TE tunnel configurations feed the LFIB. Labels for the FIB routes are provided from the LIB, which is created from information exchanged via LDP and TDP. Labels for TE tunnels are handled separately by the TE module. To encode label encapsulation, a label rewrite table is created.

As with the FIB, load sharing is also supported within the LFIB. A load-sharing structure is used to keep track of loads on available links. Because the load sharing is linked between the FIB and the LFIB, it is possible to have load sharing among links that are labeled and unlabeled. Table 10-5 provided an example of load sharing between a pair of label-switched paths. When multiple paths to the same destination exist, multiple label rewrite entries might be available.

When an IP packet is received, the FIB is consulted to determine its next hop. If the next-hop information indicates that it is to be switched untagged, conventional CEF switching is used to forward the packet. If the packet is to be switched labeled, the FIB uses the label rewrite to prepare the label stack encapsulation. The label load-sharing structure is consulted if multiple labeled paths to the destination exist. During the IP-to-label imposition, the IP Precedence field value is copied to the label EXP field in all label entries that are pushed onto the packet.

When a labeled packet is received, the in label is used as the lookup key. If the packet is to be switched labeled, appropriate label rewrite entries are used to push the label stack. During the label-to-label imposition, the EXP field value is copied to the EXP field in the swapped label entry and all the label entries that pushed onto the packet. If the packet is to be delivered untagged, the label stack is popped.

Special handling is required when the label is Implicit Null or Explicit Null. When an Implicit Null label is received via the signaling path, the penultimate hop LSR pops the top label during packet forwarding. This is called penultimate hop popping (PHP). It's the default behavior in IOS software for frame-based links. The purpose of PHP is to save one lookup on the ultimate hop and thus offload some of the processing burden on the LER.

When the out label is Explicit Null, the top label is swapped with the Explicit Null label. Upon receiving a packet labeled with Explicit Null, the ultimate hop or egress LER pops the label and forwards the packet based on the information below the label. TTL processing takes place before the label is popped. EXP bits are saved for QoS processing. The stack bit is checked to determine if there are more labels underneath. The Explicit Null can be used to retain EXP values up to the ultimate hop; with Implicit Null, the value of EXP in the top label would be lost.

Building MPLS VPN Architectures

With MPLS and multiprotocol extension for BGP in place, the foundation is set for MPLS VPN. Although you can build VPN services over an MPLS infrastructure in several ways, this chapter is concerned with Layer 3 VPNs.

The next sections describe the basic components of an MPLS VPN and the role of multi-protocol BGP in distributing VPNv4 information. The following subjects are covered:

- Components of an MPLS VPN
- Virtual routing and forwarding instance
- VPNv4 route and label propagation
- Automatic route filtering
- AS_PATH manipulation

Components of an MPLS VPN

Figure 10-5 shows the basic components of an MPLS VPN. Such a network has three types of devices:

- Customer edge (CE) router
- Provider edge (PE) router
- Provider (P) router

Note the similarity between Figure 10-5 and Figure 10-1. Typically a P device is a core LSR, and a PE device is an LER.

Figure 10-5 *Basic Components of an MPLS VPN*

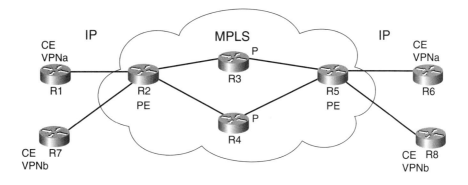

Central to the architecture are the PE devices. These devices maintain rules of route redistribution and the mappings of IPv4 prefixes in a VPN to VPNv4 prefixes in the core. In Figure 10-5, PE devices R2 and R5 provide connectivity to both VPNs, VPNa and VPNb. Configurations on these PE devices are made such that routes from VPNa are not redistributed to VPNb, and vice versa.

The P routers maintain LSPs among PE devices using LDP/TDP or other label distribution protocols and thus are unaware of any VPN information encapsulated inside LSPs. All provider devices, including P routers and PE devices, use an IGP so that all links and other local addresses can be reached within the provider network.

The CE routers are conventional IP routers. Neither VPN nor MPLS is needed on CE routers. These routers communicate only with routers in the same VPN, as dictated by the PE devices.

Multiprotocol BGP comes into play when PE devices communicate with each other. Specifically, PE devices use multiprotocol iBGP to advertise VPNv4 prefixes to each other. Similar to IPv4, route reflection and confederation can be used to increase iBGP scalability. The VPN routing information can be exchanged between a PE and a CE in several ways, including RIPv2, OSPF, BGP, EIGRP, and static routes.

NOTE   P routers do not need to run multiprotocol iBGP and do not maintain VPNv4 information.

The forwarding path is best illustrated by a layered approach, as shown in Figure 10-6. The packets between a CE and a PE are encapsulated in IP. In the IP layer, two CE devices and two PE devices are Layer 3 peers (this is why VPNs built in this way are called *Layer 3 VPNs*). On a PE, several layers are used. There are two layers of LSPs between the ingress PE and the egress PE:

- LSPv to identify the VPN
- LSPi to identify the remote PE

Thus, the original IP packet from the CE now carries a label stack of two entries. A P router has only one LSP, so the P router is unaware of the VPN LSP. All the P routers swap or pop the top label. The VPN label is popped by the egress PE, and the original packet is forwarded to the connected CE.

Figure 10-6 *Layered Visualization of the MPLS VPN Forwarding Path*

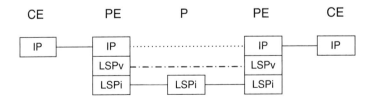

VPN Routing/Forwarding Instance

A fundamental concept of MPLS VPN implementation in IOS is VPN routing/forwarding instance (VRF). Each VRF can be associated with one VPN site (CE) via one or more interfaces. A PE router maintains one routing and forwarding table for each VRF that is configured locally. Additionally, a PE maintains a global routing and forwarding table that is not associated with any VRFs.

NOTE   A VRF is local to a PE device where it is configured. A VPN is a network-wide concept that consists of private routing and forwarding information. It may span multiple devices and VRFs.

To have unique VPNv4 addresses in the provider's network, each VRF has a locally unique RD (Route Distinguisher). When routes are received from a VPN site that belongs to this VRF, a PE router prepends the RD to the IPv4 prefixes before sending them to the remote PE.

To control VPN route redistribution, each VRF is also associated with one or more Route Targets (RTs). To attach an RT to a VPNv4 prefix is to export an RT. To allow a VPNv4 prefix with a certain RT to be installed into a VRF is to import the RT.

Example 10-8 shows a VRF configuration. A VRF is assigned a name that is locally signif-icant. Note that the VRF name is case-sensitive. When VPNv4 routes are advertised to the remote PE, an RT of 100:58 is attached (exported). VPNv4 routes from the remote PE devices are installed into VRF vpn58 only when they have an RT of 100:58.

Example 10-8 *Sample VRF Configuration*

```
ip vrf vpn58
 rd 100:58
 route-target export 100:58
 route-target import 100:58
```

The PE interface that is directly connected to a CE that belongs to a VRF is associated with the VRF using the interface command **ip vrf forwarding** *vrf-name*. To exchange routes between a PE and a CE, you can configure dynamic routing protocols or static routes on the PE.

NOTE   When the command **ip vrf forwarding** is entered under an interface, the existing IP address is automatically removed.

Example 10-9 shows a sample RIPv2 configuration. In Example 10-9, BGP AS 100 routes are redistributed into RIP. These are the routes received from the remote PEs. Before the redistribution, a VPNv4 prefix is filtered based on the RT import policy for the VRF.

Example 10-9 *Sample PE-CE Routing Protocol Configuration*

```
router rip
version 2
!
 address-family ipv4 vrf vpn58
 redistribute bgp 100 metric 3
 no auto-summary
 exit-address-family
```

Example 10-10 shows a sample BGP configuration for VPNv4. This example has two remote PE devices: 192.168.22.2 and 192.168.77.7. These are loopback addresses of the remote PE devices. For the IGP labels to be assigned properly, do not summarize the loopback addresses.

Example 10-10 *Sample BGP Configuration for VPNv4 Prefixes*

```
router bgp 100
 no synchronization
 neighbor 192.168.22.2 remote-as 100
 neighbor 192.168.22.2 update-source Loopback0
 neighbor 192.168.77.7 remote-as 100
 neighbor 192.168.77.7 update-source Loopback0
 no auto-summary
 !
 address-family ipv4 vrf vpn58
 redistribute rip
 no auto-summary
 no synchronization
 exit-address-family
!
 address-family vpnv4
 neighbor 192.168.22.2 activate
 neighbor 192.168.22.2 send-community extended
 neighbor 192.168.77.7 activate
 neighbor 192.168.77.7 send-community extended
 no auto-summary
 exit-address-family
```

There are three segments in the BGP configurations:

- Configurations under **router bgp**
- Configurations under an IPv4 address family for a VRF
- Configurations under the VPNv4 address family

All configurations directly under **router bgp** apply to IPv4 unicast only. Alternatively, these configurations can be made under the IPv4 address family in certain IOS releases using **address-family ipv4 unicast**. These configurations are still required even if only VPNv4 prefixes are exchanged, because the BGP neighbor relationships are still established over IPv4. If no IPv4 prefixes are to be exchanged for all peers, the IPv4 session can be disabled using the command **no bgp default ipv4-unicast**. Alternatively, IPv4 sessions can be disabled per neighbor using **no neighbor activate**.

To exchange VRF-specific routing information with a CE, configurations are needed under **address-family ipv4 vrf**. In this example, RIP routes from the CE are redistributed into BGP.

To activate the VPNv4 prefix exchange with other PEs, an address family for VPNv4 is needed. Each neighbor must be activated individually. Configurations are made in this segment to attach extended communities to the VPNv4 prefixes.

VPNv4 Route and Label Propagation

VPNv4 prefixes and VPN labels are propagated by multiprotocol BGP from one PE to another PE. As with IGP labels, BGP labels are distributed from a downstream PE to an upstream PE.

Consider Figure 10-7 for MPLS VPN route and label propagation. The prefix 172.16.0.0/16 can be reached on PE2 via a VPN static route. The VRF VPNa is associated with the prefix. The VPNv4 prefix 100:100:172.16.0.0/16 and its label (Lv) are advertised to PE1, with the BGP next hop (NH) set to itself. PE2's reachability (192.168.100.5) is advertised in the IGP and LDP. The link between PE2 and CE2 (192.168.56.0/24) is also redistributed into VPNa as a connected route (not shown in Figure 10-7).

Figure 10-7 *MPLS VPN Route and Label Propagation*

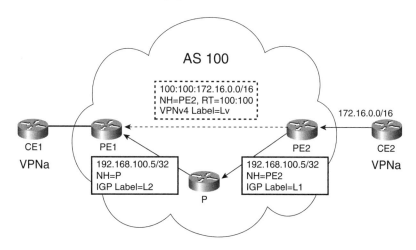

NOTE	In Figure 10-7 and subsequent figures in this chapter, solid boxes are used to contain the advertisement of IPv4 prefixes and labels, and dashed boxes are used for the advertisement of VPNv4 prefixes and labels.

The relevant configurations on PE2 are shown in Example 10-11. Note that a static route within VPNa is created with the next hop set to CE2.

Example 10-11 *Relevant Configurations on PE2*

```
ip vrf VPNa
 rd 100:100
 route-target export 100:100
 route-target import 100:100
!
ip cef
mpls label protocol ldp
!
interface Loopback0
 ip address 192.168.100.5 255.255.255.255
 ip router isis
!
interface Ethernet0/0
 ip address 192.168.35.5 255.255.255.0
 ip router isis
 tag-switching ip
!
interface Ethernet2/0
 ip vrf forwarding VPNa
 ip address 192.168.56.5 255.255.255.0
 ip router isis
!
router isis
 net 49.0001.1921.6810.0005.00
 is-type level-2-only
!
router bgp 100
 no synchronization
 bgp router-id 192.168.100.5
 bgp log-neighbor-changes
 neighbor 192.168.100.2 remote-as 100
 neighbor 192.168.100.2 update-source Loopback0
 no neighbor 192.168.100.2 activate
 no auto-summary
 !
 address-family ipv4 vrf VPNa
 redistribute connected
 redistribute static
 no auto-summary
 no synchronization
```

Example 10-11 *Relevant Configurations on PE2 (Continued)*

```
exit-address-family
!
address-family vpnv4
neighbor 192.168.100.2 activate
neighbor 192.168.100.2 send-community extended
no auto-summary
exit-address-family
!
ip route vrf VPNa 172.16.0.0 255.255.0.0 192.168.56.6
```

Example 10-12 shows the VPN prefixes on PE2. Local VPN routes are indicated by a [V] appended to the IPv4 prefix.

Example 10-12 *VPN Prefixes on PE2*

```
PE2#show mpls forwarding vrf VPNa
Local  Outgoing    Prefix           Bytes tag  Outgoing    Next Hop
tag    tag or VC   or Tunnel Id     switched   interface
25     Untagged    172.16.0.0/16[V] 0          Et2/0       192.168.56.6
26     Aggregate   192.168.56.0/24[V]   \
                                    2746
```

There are two types of VPN routes with regard to how an incoming VPN packet should be processed: aggregate and untagged. An aggregate label, such as for 192.168.56.0/24, is a special label used locally on PEs for prefixes that are destined for directly connected links (including loopback interfaces on the PE) and those aggregated by BGP. In Example 10-12, the prefix is a local address on the router. If the outgoing label field is untagged, all labels are popped before forwarding.

When a packet arrives at a PE with a label that corresponds to an outgoing aggregate label, two lookups are needed. The first lookup on the LFIB determines that it is an aggregate. An extra FIB lookup is needed to find the outgoing interface in the case of BGP aggregation or the outgoing MAC string in the case of a directly connected Ethernet.

There is no extra FIB lookup when routes can be reached via a CE router. They are shown as untagged in the LFIB. This is the case for the prefix 172.16.0.0/16.

Example 10-13 shows the VPN label assignment on PE1. The Out labels are assigned by PE2, which advertises the prefixes.

Example 10-13 *VPN Labels on PE1*

```
PE1#show ip bgp vpnv4 all labels
   Network          Next Hop      In label/Out label
Route Distinguisher: 100:100 (VPNa)
   172.16.0.0       192.168.100.5   nolabel/25
   192.168.56.0     192.168.100.5   nolabel/26
```

VPN labels are installed into the FIB for the VRF. Example 10-14 shows the VPN label for 172.16.0.0 in CEF on PE1. Note that the first label (19) is an IGP label (L2) to reach PE2 (192.168.100.5), and the second label (25) is the VPN label Lv.

Example 10-14 *VPN Label for 172.16.0.0 on PE1*

```
PE1#show ip cef vrf VPNa 172.16.0.0 detail
172.16.0.0/16, version 6, epoch 0, cached adjacency 192.168.23.3
0 packets, 0 bytes
  tag information set
    local tag: VPN-route-head
    fast tag rewrite with Et1/0, 192.168.23.3, tags imposed: {19 25}
  via 192.168.100.5, 0 dependencies, recursive
    next hop 192.168.23.3, Ethernet1/0 via 192.168.100.5/32
    valid cached adjacency
    tag rewrite with Et1/0, 192.168.23.3, tags imposed: {19 25}
```

To reach 172.16.0.0/16 in PE1, a recursive lookup of the BGP next hop (192.168.100.5) resolves the IGP next hop (192.168.23.3). When PE1 receives a packet from CE1 that is destined for 172.16.0.0/16, a label stack of 2 is imposed: the top label 19 to reach PE2 via P, and the bottom label 25 to reach 172.16.0.0/16 via VPNa. Upon receiving such a packet, P pops the top label (19) because of PHP. The packet is delivered to PE2 with the VPN label (25). When PE2 receives the packet, it removes the label and delivers the IP packet to CE2.

Automatic Route Filtering

To reduce memory use, PEs implement automatic route filtering (ARF). A PE accepts only VPN routes that are permitted from the VRFs configured locally. ARF is performed based on RTs and is enabled by default on a PE.

NOTE   If a PE is an RR for VPNv4, ARF is disabled by default.

Figure 10-8 shows an example of automatic route filtering on PE devices. As a PE with connections to two VRFs, VPNa and VPNb, R5 advertises to R1 and R2 VPNv4 prefixes that are from both CEs. Because R1 is connected only to VPNa, it rejects all the routes from VPNb. The same logic applies to R2, because it rejects routes for VPNa.

Figure 10-8 *Automatic Route Filtering on PEs*

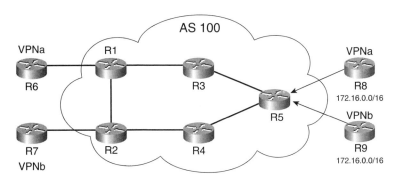

Example 10-15 shows debug output on R2. The prefix 100:200:172.16.0.0/16 from R5 has an RT of 100:200, whereas R2 is configured to import only 100:100 for VPNa. Thus, the prefix is denied automatically.

Example 10-15 *Output of* **debug ip bgp update in** *on R2*

```
*Dec 13 19:11:00.511: BGP(2): 192.168.100.5 rcvd UPDATE w/ attr: nexthop
  172.168.100.5, origin ?, localpref 100, metric 0
*Dec 13 19:11:00.511: BGP(2): 192.168.100.5 rcvd 100:200:172.16.0.0/16 -- DENIED
  due to:  extended community not supported;
```

NOTE   Changes made to the VRF configuration cause route refresh requests to be sent out.

AS_PATH Manipulation

When BGP is used between a PE and a CE, AS_PATH manipulation might be necessary to provide full connectivity among the VPN sites. This section discusses two ways to change the AS_PATH check on a PE: AS override and allow-AS.

AS Override

When BGP is used between PE and CE routers, the customer VPN might want to reuse the AS number in different sites. Figure 10-9 shows such a scenario. When the prefix 172.16.0.0/16 is advertised from PE2 to CE2, CE2 detects an AS_PATH loop, and the prefix is denied.

Figure 10-9 *AS_PATH Loop Scenario*

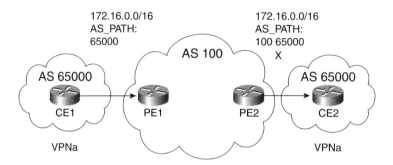

To provide connectivity between CE1 and CE2, a new procedure called *AS Override* must be implemented. When you configure AS Override on a PE, the PE replaces every occurrence of the connecting CE device's AS number in the entire AS_PATH with its own AS number before sending the updates to the CE.

NOTE   With AS Override, AS_PATH length is preserved.

Figure 10-10 shows the scenario in Figure 10-9 after AS Override is configured on PE2. When AS 65000 is replaced by AS 100, CE2 accepts the update. Note that a similar configuration must be made on PE1 if full connectivity is needed.

Figure 10-10 *AS Override Allows CE-CE Communication*

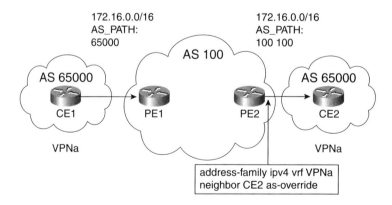

Use AS Override in conjunction with SOO to prevent routing information loops in a multi-homed site. Figure 10-11 shows such a scenario. Site 1 is connected as shown in Figure 10-9, but Site 2 is multihomed. To allow connectivity between Site 1 and Site 2, AS Override is configured on all three PE devices.

Figure 10-11 *Routing Loop Scenario with AS Override in a Multihomed Site*

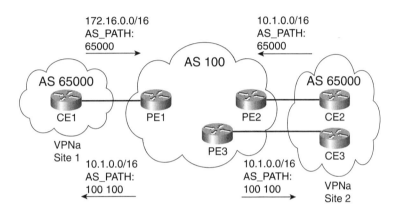

The prefix 10.1.0.0/16 is generated from Site 2 and is advertised from CE2 to PE2. When PE3 advertises the prefix back to CE3, the AS_PATH is changed to 100 100 because of AS Override. CE3 accepts this advertisement because there appears to be no AS_PATH loop. Thus, a routing information loop forms.

To break the loop, use the extended community SOO. On an inbound route map to Site 2 on both PE2 and PE3, you can configure a value of SOO representing Site 2 using the command **set extcommunity soo**. When the prefix 10.1.0.0 is advertised from PE2 to PE3, the SOO is attached. PE3 doesn't send the prefix back to Site 2, because PE3 detects the same SOO. Note that SOO loop detection is automatic (because of the configured inbound route map), and no outbound route map is needed. The prefix advertisement to Site 1 is unaffected.

Example 10-16 shows the **debug** output, where 192.168.47.7 is CE3. The prefix 10.1.0.0/16 is not advertised to CE3 because of the SOO loop. Note that the prefix 172.16.0.0/16 from CE1 is advertised as before.

Example 10-16 *Output of* **debug ip bgp update out** *on PE3*

```
*Dec 16 23:18:21.267: BGP(2): 192.168.47.7 soo loop detected for 10.1.0.0/16 -
  sending unreachable
*Dec 16 23:18:21.267: BGP(0): 192.168.47.7 send UPDATE (format) 172.16.0.0/16,
  next 192.168.47.4, metric 0, path 65000, extended community RT:100:100
```

Allow-AS

Allow-AS is another BGP feature that modifies the AS_PATH loop detection. It is used primarily in hub-and-spoke VPN scenarios, as shown in Figure 10-12.

Figure 10-12 *Hub-and-Spoke VPN*

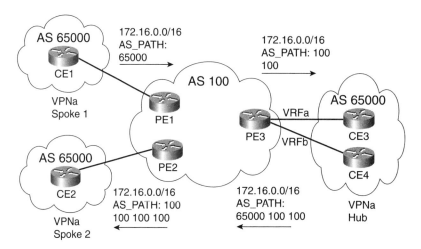

Three sites of VPNa are connected to AS 100: two spoke sites and one hub site. All spoke sites rely on the hub site for connectivity to other sites. Both spoke PE devices (PE1 and PE2) only exchange VPN routing information with PE3 for VPNa. The hub site has full routing knowledge of all other sites of the same VPN and is the central transit point between spoke sites. Spoke sites may also access central services that are available only in the hub site.

The hub site connects to the provider with two links, which belong to two different VRFs on PE3. One link is used to send updates to the hub site, and one is used to receive updates from the hub site. The ways to accomplish this using RTs are discussed in the section "Deployment Considerations." The focus here is to discuss the AS_PATH manipulation that is needed to provide full connectivity.

Because all sites use the same AS number, all three PEs must enable AS Override, as discussed in the preceding section. The prefix 172.16.0.0/16 is originated in Spoke 1. When the prefix is advertised from PE3 to CE3, the AS number is replaced with 100. When the prefix is advertised from the hub site back to PE3, the AS_PATH is 65000 100 100. The update is denied because PE3 detects its own AS number.

You can disable the AS_PATH loop check on PE3 using the command **neighbor CE4 allowas-in** under the VRFb address family. With this command, PE3 does not detect a loop if its own AS number occurs three times or less. Note that you can change the number of repeated occurrences by adding an optional number after this command. This number helps suppress routing information loops, because updates containing more occurrences of its AS number are denied.

When the prefix is advertised from PE2 to CE2, the AS_PATH is 100 100 100 100. This is because AS Override configured on PE2 replaces 65000 with 100.

VPNs Across AS Borders

The architecture of MPLS VPN presented so far requires that a single provider offer the VPN service. PE devices use multiprotocol iBGP to exchange customer VPNv4 prefixes. As the deployment of MPLS VPN expands, the single-provider requirement becomes a restriction.

Consider the scenario shown in Figure 10-13. A customer (VPNa) has two sites, Site 1 and Site 2, that need VPN connectivity. However, Site 1 is connected to AS 100, whereas Site 2 is connected to AS 200. Both providers support MPLS VPN. For the MPLS VPN connectivity between the two sites to work, the two providers need to exchange multiprotocol eBGP information between the two AS border routers (ASBRs). This is called *inter-AS VPN*, where providers are in a peer-to-peer relationship.

Figure 10-13 *MPLS VPN over Two Provider Backbones*

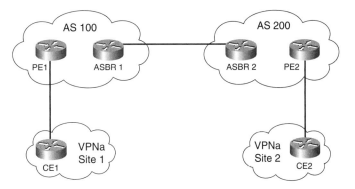

As another example, consider Figure 10-14. The same VPN connectivity is required between Site 1 and Site 2, as in Figure 10-13, but providers AS 100 and AS 200 do not have direct connectivity between them. Instead, they both connect to another provider, AS 300, which provides VPN services. Additionally, providers AS 100 and AS 200 intend to exchange full Internet tables between them. This is called Carrier Supporting Carrier (CSC), or carrier's carrier VPN, where providers are in a client/server relationship. Provider AS 300 is called the backbone carrier, and AS 100 and AS 200 are called customer carriers.

Figure 10-14 *MPLS VPN over a Common Transit VPN Backbone*

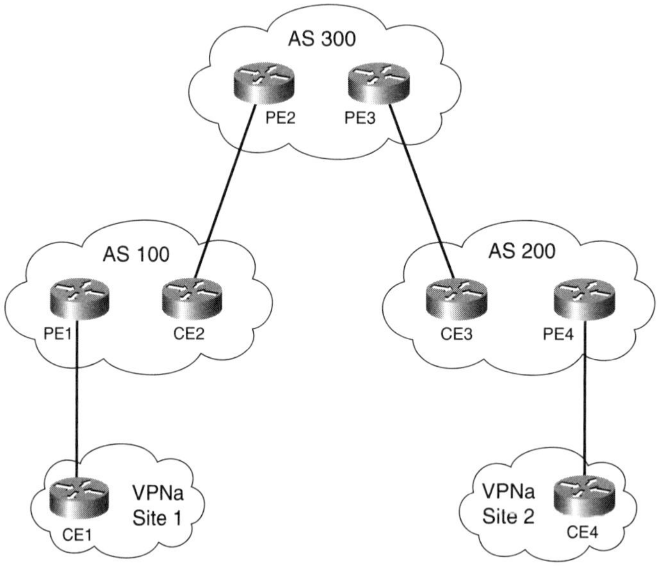

Inter-AS VPN

To achieve inter-AS VPN, you can choose from several options, depending on your design requirements. The following options are discussed in this section:

- Back-to-back VRF
- Single-hop multiprotocol eBGP for VPNv4
- Multihop multiprotocol eBGP for VPNv4
- Non-VPN transit provider for VPNv4

Back-to-Back VRF

The simplest method to achieve inter-AS VPN is back-to-back VRF. Consider the topology shown in Figure 10-15. Two sites, Site 1 and Site 2, are connected to two different providers, AS 100 and AS 200, respectively. The two providers have a connection between PE2 and PE3. The prefix 172.16.0.0/16 is advertised by CE2 in Site 2 and must be reachable by Site 1 in a VPN across the two providers.

Figure 10-15 *Sample Topology for Back-to-Back VRF*

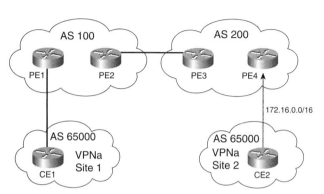

The back-to-back VRF handles the inter-AS VPNv4 connectivity by simply treating the other ASBR as a CE device. For example, a VRF named VPNa is configured on PE2, with the link between PE2 and PE3 as part of the VRF. On PE3, the same configuration is made so as to treat PE2 as a CE.

Figure 10-16 shows the VPN prefix and label advertisement. When the prefix 172.16.0.0/16 is advertised from CE2 to PE4, the BGP next hop is set to CE2. The VRF VPNa is configured with an RD of 200:200 and exports an RT of 200:200. When the VPNv4 prefix 200:200:172.16.0.0/16 is advertised toward PE3, the next hop is set to PE4, and an RT of 200:200 is attached. An in label, Lv1, is assigned for the prefix as well.

Figure 10-16 *VPN Prefix and Label Advertisement in Back-to-Back VRF*

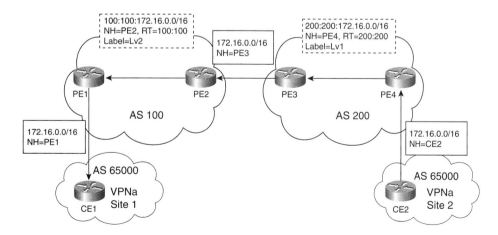

Example 10-17 shows the prefix information on PE3, where 192.168.67.7 is a next-hop P router (not shown in Figure 10-16) and 192.168.100.4 is PE4's loopback 0 address. Two labels are imposed: The top label 20 is the IGP label to reach PE4, and the bottom label 20 is the VPN label, Lv1. The advertisement of the IGP prefixes and labels is as shown previously in the section "Understanding MPLS Fundamentals."

Example 10-17 *Prefix and Label Information for 172.16.0.0 on PE3*

```
PE3#show ip cef vrf VPNa 172.16.0.0 detail
172.16.0.0/16, version 9, epoch 0, cached adjacency 192.168.67.7
0 packets, 0 bytes
  tag information set
    local tag: VPN-route-head
    fast tag rewrite with Et0/0, 192.168.67.7, tags imposed: {20 20}
  via 192.168.100.4, 0 dependencies, recursive
    next hop 192.168.67.7, Ethernet0/0 via 192.168.100.4/32
    valid cached adjacency
    tag rewrite with Et0/0, 192.168.67.7, tags imposed: {20 20}
```

The prefix is imported on PE3 into the VRF VPN A, because the VRF is configured to import prefixes with an RT of 200:200. As is done on a typical PE, the VPNv4 prefix is then converted to IPv4. Because PE3 considers PE2 to be a CE, the IPv4 prefix is advertised.

Example 10-18 shows the prefix information on PE2, where 192.168.100.2 is PE1 and 192.168.56.6 is PE3.

Example 10-18 *Output of* **show ip route vrf VPNa** *on PE2*

```
PE2#show ip bgp vpnv4 all 172.16.0.0
BGP routing table entry for 100:100:172.16.0.0/16, version 9
Paths: (1 available, best #1, table VPNa)
  Advertised to non peer-group peers:
  192.168.100.2
  200 65000
    192.168.56.6 from 192.168.56.6 (192.168.100.6)
      Origin IGP, localpref 100, valid, external, best
      Extended Community: RT:100:100
```

PE2 treats the prefix received from PE3 just like a prefix from a CE. The same process is repeated on PE2 as in PE4. When the prefix is advertised to PE1, the local RD for the VRF VPNa is prepended with an RT of 100:100. A new label, Lv2, is assigned for the VPNv4 prefix. A process similar to PE3 is performed on PE1. CE1 finally receives the IPv4 prefix.

Example 10-19 shows the prefix information on PE1, where 192.168.23.3 is a next-hop P router and 192.168.100.5 is PE2. Note that label 21 is the new VPN label, Lv2.

Example 10-19 *Prefix and Label Information for 172.16.0.0 on PE1*

```
PE1#show ip cef vrf VPNa 172.16.0.0 detail
172.16.0.0/16, version 8, epoch 0, cached adjacency 192.168.23.3
0 packets, 0 bytes
  tag information set
    local tag: VPN-route-head
    fast tag rewrite with Et1/0, 192.168.23.3, tags imposed: {17 21}
  via 192.168.100.5, 0 dependencies, recursive
    next hop 192.168.23.3, Ethernet1/0 via 192.168.100.5/32
    valid cached adjacency
    tag rewrite with Et1/0, 192.168.23.3, tags imposed: {17 21}
```

NOTE   To avoid the AS_PATH loop detection on CE1, you must configure AS Override on PE1.

For the back-to-back VRF approach to work, at least one inter-AS link (an interface or a subinterface) must be dedicated to each VPN. The same VPN must be configured on both ends of the link. Because of this restriction, the back-to-back VRF approach is unsuitable for interconnecting large numbers of VPNs.

Single-Hop Multiprotocol eBGP for VPNv4

You can use multiprotocol eBGP to exchange VPNv4 prefixes and labels across the AS boundary. No LDP/TDP is needed on the eBGP link. Thus, only VPN labels are exchanged between the eBGP peers. The inter-AS link is not associated with any VRF and is in the global table. To reduce memory use, it is recommended that you not configure any VRFs on the VPNv4 ASBRs.

To allow ASBRs to accept all VPNv4 prefixes, you must disable the default ARF. You do this by configuring **no bgp default route-target filter** on all VPNv4 ASBRs. Within the VPN address family, you must activate each VPNv4 ASBR neighbor. You can configure more granular policy control for each VPNv4 neighbor, as in IPv4 sessions.

All the multiprotocol eBGP peer addresses (IPv4) are installed automatically as connected /32 host routes in the local IP RIB of the receiving ASBR and thus in the LFIB (even though LDP/TDP is not configured between the two autonomous systems). A local IGP label is assigned for a /32 host route on the receiving ASBR. When receiving packets with these IGP labels, the top label is popped. These host routes are created only under the following conditions:

- The session is multiprotocol eBGP.
- The multiprotocol eBGP neighbor is directly connected.
- VPNv4 capability is supported on either peer.

All VPNv4 routes that need to be exchanged with the remote AS are stored in the BGP VPNv4 table and LFIB but not in the IP RIB or FIB. The in/out labels in the LFIB shown for these prefixes are top labels. The out label is the BGP (VPN) label if the route is from the remote AS; it is the IGP label (to reach the PE) if the route is from the local AS. To see the entire label stack, use **show mpls forwarding detail**. To see the BGP VPNv4 labels only, use **show ip bgp vpnv4 all labels**.

NOTE   Compared to the back-to-back VRF method, no VRFs are configured on the ASBRs using this method. Thus, the ASBRs do not function as traditional PEs.

Example 10-20 shows a sample LFIB on a VPNv4 ASBR. The two host routes are peer addresses. The first host route is of a PE in the local AS. The second host route is of a VPNv4 ASBR of the remote AS. There are two VPNv4 routes. The first VPNv4 route is from the PE in the local AS. The second one is from the VPNv4 ASBR from the remote AS. The out label 26 is the IGP label to reach the PE, and the out label 22 is the VPN label for the VPNv4 prefix.

Example 10-20 *Sample LFIB on a VPNv4 ASBR*

```
VPN-ASBR#show mpls forwarding
Local  Outgoing    Prefix             Bytes tag  Outgoing   Next Hop
tag    tag or VC   or Tunnel Id       switched   interface
16     Pop tag     192.168.10.4/32    0          Fa0/0      192.168.11.4
17     Pop tag     192.168.110.2/32   0          Fa3/0      192.168.110.2
22     26          10:1:10.1.2.0/24   3846       Fa0/0      192.168.11.4
23     22          1:1:10.1.1.0/24    1180       Fa3/0      192.168.110.2
```

When multiprotocol eBGP is used across the autonomous systems, the next hop is reset at the AS border, as in IPv4. As such, VPN labels are rewritten. The label assignment and exchanges are different, depending on how the next hop is set or reset.

As in IPv4, the BGP next hop for VPNv4 can be made reachable in the AS receiving the updates in the following two ways:

- The next hop is the advertising ASBR (of the AS that advertises the updates) and is carried unchanged inside the receiving AS. This is the default behavior. The advertising ASBR must be reachable within the receiving AS.

- The receiving ASBR resets the BGP next hop to itself when advertising to its iBGP neighbors. This is configured using the per-neighbor **next-hop-self** setting under the VPNv4 address family.

Next Hop Carried Unchanged Inside the Receiving AS

With the default behavior, the receiving ASBR does not reallocate a new VPN label for VPNv4 routes from the advertising AS. The address of the advertising ASBR (an IPv4 host route) can be made reachable in the receiving AS by redistribution (into the IGP) or by iBGP plus labels. When redistribution is used, these host routes are allocated IGP labels within the receiving AS. Thus, the remote ASBR becomes the PE devices' BGP next hop, and the BGP label assigned by that ASBR is used by PE devices. Using BGP to distribute labels for IPv4 prefixes is discussed in the section "Multihop Multiprotocol eBGP for VPNv4."

Figure 10-17 depicts a scenario using redistribution. When the next hop (NH) is reset at ASBR1, a new VPN label, Lv2, is assigned. The next hop is carried unchanged in AS 200 (the AS receiving the updates). Thus, Lv2 is still used by PE2 for the same VPN.

Figure 10-17 *Prefix and Label Distribution with the Next Hop Unchanged in the Receiving AS*

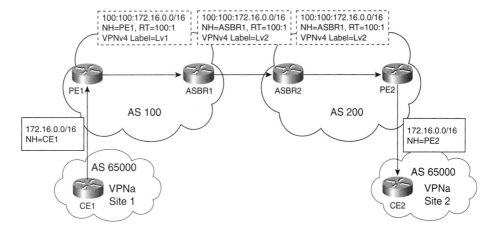

To allow inter-AS connectivity, the receiving VRF of the same VPN must import the same RT that is exported from the sending VRF.

Example 10-21 shows the label stack for 172.16.0.0/16 on PE2. The BGP next hop is ASBR1 (192.168.56.5), with a VPN label 25 (Lv2). To reach ASBR1, an IGP label 19 is used, with an IGP next hop of 192.168.47.7 (a P router toward ASBR2).

Example 10-21 *Label Stack for 172.16.0.0 on PE2*

```
PE2#show ip cef vrf VPNa 172.16.0.0 detail
172.16.0.0/16, version 13, epoch 0, cached adjacency 192.168.47.7
0 packets, 0 bytes
  tag information set
    local tag: VPN-route-head
    fast tag rewrite with Et1/0, 192.168.47.7, tags imposed: {19 25}
  via 192.168.56.5, 0 dependencies, recursive
    next hop 192.168.47.7, Ethernet1/0 via 192.168.56.5/32
    valid cached adjacency
    tag rewrite with Et1/0, 192.168.47.7, tags imposed: {19 25}
```

When the BGP next hop is unchanged in AS 200, ASBR2 is removed from the duty of VPN label distribution. This essentially extends the provider edge from ASBR2 to ASBR1 from the point of AS 200. One advantage of doing this is that ASBR2 does not need to maintain any VPN entries destined for AS 100, although it still maintains all the VPN entries for its own AS.

Example 10-22 shows a sample LFIB on ASBR2. The host route to reach ASBR1 is in the LFIB, with an outgoing label of Pop tag. Thus, a labeled packet with an incoming IGP label 21 is popped because of PHP. Note that the VPNv4 prefix 100:100:172.16.0.0/16 is not in the LFIB.

Example 10-22 *Sample LFIB on ASBR2*

```
ASBR2#show tag forwarding
Local   Outgoing     Prefix          Bytes tag  Outgoing    Next Hop
tag     tag or VC    or Tunnel Id    switched   interface
18      Pop tag      192.168.47.0/24 0          Et0/0       192.168.67.7
19      16           192.168.100.4/32 0         Et0/0       192.168.67.7
20      Pop tag      192.168.100.7/32 0         Et0/0       192.168.67.7
21      Pop tag      192.168.56.5/32 7670       Et1/0       192.168.56.5
```

Example 10-23 shows the LFIB on ASBR1. The incoming label for 100:100:172.16.0.0/16 is 25, which is the VPN label Lv2. A label stack is pushed, with the top label 16 to reach the IGP next hop of 192.168.35.3 (a P router toward PE1). The new VPN label (Lv1) is 21 (not shown).

Example 10-23 *LFIB on ASBR1*

```
ASBR1#show tag forwarding
Local   Outgoing     Prefix          Bytes tag  Outgoing    Next Hop
tag     tag or VC    or Tunnel Id    switched   interface
17      Pop tag      192.168.23.0/24 0          Et0/0       192.168.35.3
18      16           192.168.100.2/32 0         Et0/0       192.168.35.3
```

Example 10-23 *LFIB on ASBR1 (Continued)*

```
19      Pop tag     192.168.100.3/32  0            Et0/0      192.168.35.3
24      Pop tag     192.168.56.6/32   2360         Et1/0      192.168.56.6
25      16          100:100:172.16.0.0/16    \
                                      0            Et0/0      192.168.35.3
```

Figure 10-18 shows packet forwarding. A label stack of 2 is pushed on PE2. L1 is the IGP label toward ASBR1, and Lv2 is the VPN label. Because of PHP, ASBR2 pops the IGP label. On ASBR1, a label stack is swapped on, with the top label, L2, reaching PE1, and the bottom label, Lv1, as the new VPN label.

Figure 10-18 *Packet Forwarding in the Inter-AS VPN with the Next Hop Unchanged Inside AS 200*

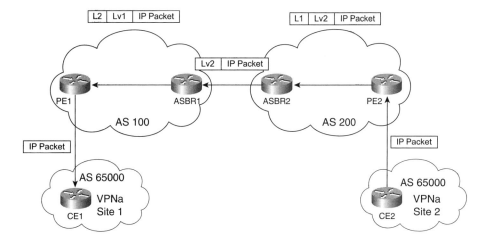

Next Hop Reset by next-hop-self

When the default BGP next hop is reset on the receiving ASBR with **next-hop-self**, the receiving ASBR assigns the VPNv4 prefix with a label stack. At the bottom of the stack, a new VPN label is created. The top label is the IGP label for PE devices within the AS to reach the ASBR's own loopback address, as in the case of a typical PE device.

Figure 10-19 shows a scenario with **next-hop-self** set on the receiving ASBR. In contrast to Figure 10-17, the next hop is changed to ASBR2 when the VPNv4 prefix is advertised to PE2. Because of the next-hop change, a new VPN label Lv3 is created on ASBR2.

Figure 10-19 *Inter-AS VPN with the* **next-hop-self** *Setting on the Receiving ASBR*

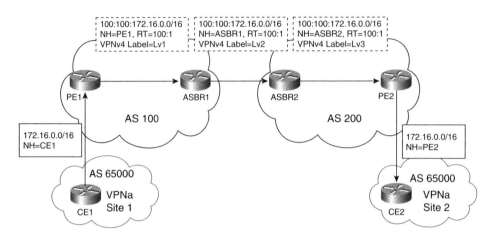

Example 10-24 shows a sample LFIB on ASBR2. The VPNv4 prefix 100:100:172.16.0.0/16 is in the LFIB. The incoming label 23 is Lv3, because of PHP in AS 200. The outgoing label 25 is Lv2. The function of ASBR1 remains unchanged from the previous case.

Example 10-24 *LFIB with the Next Hop Reset on ASBR2*

```
ASBR2#show tag forwarding
Local   Outgoing    Prefix            Bytes tag  Outgoing    Next Hop
tag     tag or VC   or Tunnel Id      switched   interface
16      Untagged    192.168.35.0/24   0          Et1/0       192.168.56.5
17      Untagged    192.168.100.5/32  0          Et1/0       192.168.56.5
18      Pop tag     192.168.47.0/24   0          Et0/0       192.168.67.7
19      16          192.168.100.4/32  0          Et0/0       192.168.67.7
20      Pop tag     192.168.100.7/32  0          Et0/0       192.168.67.7
21      Pop tag     192.168.56.5/32   7670       Et1/0       192.168.56.5
23      25          100:100:172.16.0.0/16   \
                                      0          Et1/0       192.168.56.5
```

Multihop Multiprotocol eBGP for VPNv4

Route reflection was discussed in Chapter 7, "Scalable iBGP Design and Implementation Guidelines," as a way to scale the iBGP connectivity for IPv4. Route reflection can also be used for VPNv4 for the same purpose. The use of route reflection to increase VPNv4 scalability is discussed in detail later in the section "Deployment Considerations." This section focuses on how route reflection is related to inter-AS VPN connectivity.

In an inter-AS VPN environment, route reflectors (RRs) might already maintain all the VPNv4 information for the AS. Therefore, it is logical to exchange the inter-AS VPN information directly between RRs, without burdening ASBRs. This reduces resource use on ASBRs. Figure 10-20 shows such a scenario. In each AS, a PE peers only with the RR in its own AS to exchange VPNv4 prefixes via multiprotocol iBGP. Two RRs exchange VPNv4 information via multihop multiprotocol eBGP. Two ASBRs exchange only IPv4 information, not VPNv4 information.

Figure 10-20 *Multihop Multiprotocol eBGP Using RRs*

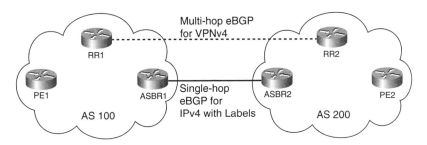

As seen previously in this chapter, any BGP next-hop change resets the label stack. To create an end-to-end LSP between two PE devices, the BGP next hop of the remote PE must not be changed when crossing AS borders. If the BGP next hop is reset on RRs, new label stacks have to be created. The solution to this problem is to force RRs to advertise VPNv4 prefixes without resetting the next hop. You do this by configuring **neighbor next-hop-unchanged** between the two RRs.

For both RRs to establish a BGP session, there must be IPv4 reachability between them. Within its respective AS, there is already an IGP LSP between a PE and an ASBR and between an RR and an ASBR. You need to connect the LSPs between the two autonomous systems.

Because eBGP for IPv4 is already running between the two autonomous systems, one obvious solution is to use BGP to carry labels for IPv4 prefixes. As indicated in Chapter 2, carrying labels for IPv4 prefixes is an option provided by the BGP multiprotocol capability. To send labels, use the BGP command **neighbor send-label** under the IPv4 address family.

To have an end-to-end LSP carry VPN traffic, the loopback addresses of the remote RRs and PEs must be reachable with proper labels by the local RRs and PEs. There are two ways to make this happen:

- ASBRs redistribute the loopback addresses of RRs and PEs that are in eBGP into the IGP in the local AS. This method is simple to accomplish but might be inappropriate if the addresses to be distributed are large and unstable. Proper filtering is required.

- ASBRs advertise the loopback addresses of remote RRs and PEs in IPv4 iBGP with labels to local RRs and PEs. This method isolates the local IGP from addresses in another AS. Because more labels are involved, this method is more complex to support.

Remote Addresses Redistributed into the Local IGP

Figure 10-21 shows how prefixes and labels are exchanged using redistribution in a sample topology. When RR1 advertises the VPNv4 prefix to RR2, the next hop is still PE1. The same next hop is maintained on PE2; thus, the VPN label, Lv, is the same from PE1 to PE2.

Figure 10-21 *Label Exchange with Multihop eBGP Between RRs Using Redistribution*

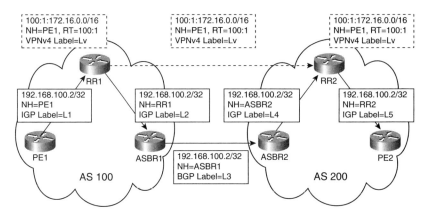

Example 10-25 shows the sample BGP configurations on RR1. There are two VPNv4 sessions on RR1: one to PE1 (192.168.100.2) and one to RR2 (192.168.100.7).

Example 10-25 *BGP Configurations on RR1*

```
router bgp 100
 no synchronization
 bgp router-id 192.168.100.3
 no bgp default ipv4-unicast
 bgp log-neighbor-changes
 neighbor Internal peer-group
 neighbor Internal remote-as 100
 neighbor Internal update-source Loopback0
 neighbor Internal activate
 neighbor 192.168.100.2 peer-group Internal
 neighbor 192.168.100.7 remote-as 200
 neighbor 192.168.100.7 ebgp-multihop 3
 neighbor 192.168.100.7 update-source Loopback0
 no auto-summary
 !
 address-family vpnv4
 neighbor 192.168.100.2 activate
 neighbor 192.168.100.2 route-reflector-client
 neighbor 192.168.100.2 send-community extended
 neighbor 192.168.100.7 activate
 neighbor 192.168.100.7 next-hop-unchanged
```

Example 10-25 *BGP Configurations on RR1 (Continued)*

```
neighbor 192.168.100.7 send-community extended
no auto-summary
exit-address-family
```

To establish eBGP connectivity between the two RRs, both RRs must have IPv4 reachability. Additionally, PE devices must have reachability across the AS border to build an end-to-end LSP. On ASBR1, the loopback addresses of PE1 and RR1 (reachable via local IGP, OSPF) are installed into the BGP RIB to be advertised to ASBR2.

Example 10-26 shows the OSPF and BGP configurations on ASBR1. The loopback addresses of PE1 (192.168.100.2) and RR1 (192.168.100.3) are advertised by BGP via the **network** command (they can also be redistributed from OSPF to BGP with proper filtering). These two addresses are advertised to ASBR2 (192.168.56.6) with eBGP labels.

Example 10-26 *OSPF and BGP Configurations on ASBR1*

```
router ospf 5
 log-adjacency-changes
 redistribute bgp 100 subnets
 passive-interface Ethernet1/0
 network 192.168.0.0 0.0.255.255 area 0
!
router bgp 100
 no synchronization
 bgp router-id 192.168.100.5
 bgp log-neighbor-changes
 network 192.168.100.2 mask 255.255.255.255
 network 192.168.100.3 mask 255.255.255.255
 neighbor 192.168.56.6 remote-as 200
 neighbor 192.168.56.6 route-map Fr_asbr2 in
 neighbor 192.168.56.6 route-map To_asbr2 out
 neighbor 192.168.56.6 send-label
 no auto-summary
!
ip prefix-list Adv_200 seq 5 permit 192.168.100.2/32
ip prefix-list Adv_200 seq 10 permit 192.168.100.3/32
!
ip prefix-list Rec_200 seq 5 permit 192.168.100.7/32
ip prefix-list Rec_200 seq 10 permit 192.168.100.4/32
!
route-map To_asbr2 permit 10
 match ip address prefix-list Adv_200
 set mpls-label
!
route-map Fr_asbr2 permit 10
 match ip address prefix-list Rec_200
 match mpls-label
```

An outbound route map, To_asbr2, is used to permit only PE1 and RR1 addresses. Additionally, labels are permitted by the **set mpls-label** clause. In the opposite direction, only addresses of RR2 and PE2 with labels are permitted into AS 100. These addresses are subsequently redistributed into the local OSPF process, thus connecting the LSPs in two autonomous systems. Similar configurations are used in AS 200 (not shown).

Example 10-27 shows the label stack for the VPN prefix 172.16.0.0/16 on PE2. The next hop is PE1 (192.168.100.2) for BGP and RR2 (192.168.47.7) for IGP. The VPN label 23, Lv, is as advertised by PE1.

Example 10-27 *Label Stack on PE2*

```
PE2#show ip cef vrf VPNa 172.16.0.0
172.16.0.0/16, version 22, epoch 0, cached adjacency 192.168.47.7
0 packets, 0 bytes
  tag information set
    local tag: VPN-route-head
    fast tag rewrite with Et1/0, 192.168.47.7, tags imposed: {19 23}
  via 192.168.100.2, 0 dependencies, recursive
    next hop 192.168.47.7, Ethernet1/0 via 192.168.100.2/32
    valid cached adjacency
    tag rewrite with Et1/0, 192.168.47.7, tags imposed: {19 23}
```

To reach PE1, PE2 uses an IGP label of 19 (L5). This label is replaced by 22 (L4) on RR2. On ASBR2, a BGP route is used to reach PE1. The outgoing BGP label is 19 (L3), as shown in Example 10-28. Note that the local BGP label 22 is passed on to LDP so that RR2 can have the correct IGP label.

Example 10-28 *BGP Label to Reach PE1 on ASBR2*

```
ASBR2#show ip bgp label
Network           Next Hop        In Label/Out Label
192.168.100.2/32 192.168.56.5     22/19
192.168.100.3/32 192.168.56.5     23/20
192.168.100.4/32 192.168.67.7     20/nolabel
192.168.100.7/32 192.168.67.7     21/nolabel
```

The LFIB on ASBR2 is shown in Example 10-29. Note that the BGP labels are installed for 192.168.100.2 (PE1).

Example 10-29 *LFIB on ASBR2*

```
ASBR2#show tag forwarding
Local  Outgoing   Prefix         Bytes tag  Outgoing   Next Hop
tag    tag or VC  or Tunnel Id   switched   interface
18     Pop tag    192.168.56.5/32  0          Et1/0      192.168.56.5
19     Pop tag    192.168.47.0/24  0          Et0/0      192.168.67.7
```

Example 10-29 *LFIB on ASBR2 (Continued)*

```
20      16          192.168.100.4/32  5076     Et0/0     192.168.67.7
21      Pop tag     192.168.100.7/32  2349     Et0/0     192.168.67.7
22      19          192.168.100.2/32  4690     Et1/0     192.168.56.5
23      20          192.168.100.3/32  1755     Et1/0     192.168.56.5
```

On ASBR1, the incoming BGP label is swapped with an IGP label 17 (L2). In this case, there is no outgoing BGP label. The LFIB is shown in Example 10-30. The IGP label 17 is later popped by RR1 because of PHP (not shown). The end-to-end LSP from PE2 to PE1 is now complete.

Example 10-30 *LFIB on ASBR1*

```
ASBR1#show tag forwarding
Local   Outgoing    Prefix            Bytes tag  Outgoing    Next Hop
tag     tag or VC   or Tunnel Id      switched   interface
17      Pop tag     192.168.56.6/32   2280       Et1/0       192.168.56.6
18      Pop tag     192.168.23.0/24   0          Et0/0       192.168.35.3
19      17          192.168.100.2/32  43690      Et0/0       192.168.35.3
20      Pop tag     192.168.100.3/32  124651     Et0/0       192.168.35.3
21      20          192.168.100.4/32  2016       Et1/0       192.168.56.6
22      21          192.168.100.7/32  522        Et1/0       192.168.56.6
```

Remote Addresses Carried in iBGP with Labels

When the loopback addresses of RRs and PE devices in the remote AS are carried directly in iBGP, you must enable the IPv4 label option on BGP sessions between RRs and their clients (PEs and ASBRs). Figure 10-22 shows label distribution in such an environment.

Figure 10-22 *Label Exchange with Multihop eBGP Between RRs Using iBGP with Labels*

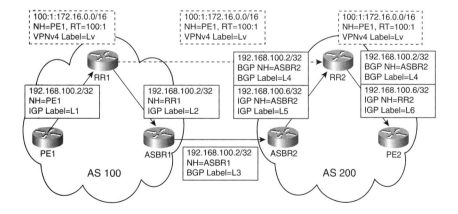

The VPNv4 label distribution is the same as in Figure 10-21. However, the way to make PE1 (192.168.100.2) and RR1 reachable in AS 200 is different. Within AS 100, these loopback addresses are reachable via IGP, as in Figure 10-21.

As in the previous example, ASBR1 advertises these loopback addresses in IPv4 with labels to AS 200 (Figure 10-22 shows only the advertisement of PE1's address). Instead of redistributing these eBGP prefixes into the IGP in AS 200, ASBR2 can advertise them via iBGP with labels.

When advertising a prefix in iBGP to RR2, ASBR2 can choose to advertise itself as the BGP next hop by setting **next-hop-self** (as shown in Figure 10-22) or by leaving the next hop unchanged and redistributing connected routes into the IGP (not shown in Figure 10-22). In either case, RR2 peers with ASBR2 and PE2 to exchange IPv4 prefixes and labels.

When the BGP next hop is reset on ASBR2, a new BGP label, L4, is assigned for the prefix 192.168.100.2/32 (PE1). Additionally, an IGP label, L5, is assigned to reach ASBR2 itself (192.168.100.6). PE1's loopback address (192.168.100.2) is reflected in iBGP by RR2 to PE2, and RR2 advertises ASBR2's loopback address in IGP to PE2, with an IGP label of L6. Thus, PE2 has a label stack of 3 for the VPN, as follows:

- The top label is the IGP label to reach ASBR2 (L6).
- The middle label is the BGP label to reach PE1 via ASBR2 (L4).
- The bottom label is the VPN label (Lv).

More detailed information on configurations, label exchange, and packet forwarding is provided in the case study near the end of this chapter.

Non-VPN Transit Provider for VPNv4

Inter-AS VPN can also be provided via a central transit provider that is running non-VPN MPLS. Figure 10-23 shows such a scenario.

Two client autonomous systems, AS 100 and AS 300, connect to the transit AS, AS 200. The client autonomous systems provide MPLS VPN, whereas the transit AS is running only MPLS. VPNv4 information between the two client autonomous systems is exchanged between RRs using a multihop eBGP.

As discussed previously, PE devices and RRs must have reachability and proper labels between the two client autonomous systems—namely, end-to-end LSPs from PE to PE. The client ASBRs can exchange IPv4 prefixes and labels with the ASBRs of the transit AS. Figure 10-24 demonstrates how PE1's address (192.168.100.2) in AS 100 is distributed to PE2 in AS 300.

Figure 10-23 *VPN via a Non-VPN Transit Provider*

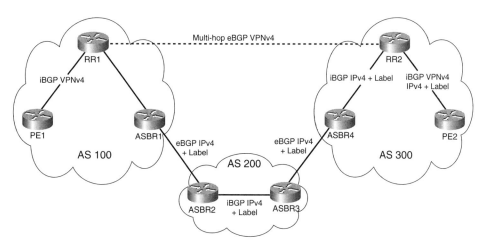

Figure 10-24 *Prefix and Label Distribution with a Non-VPN Transit AS*

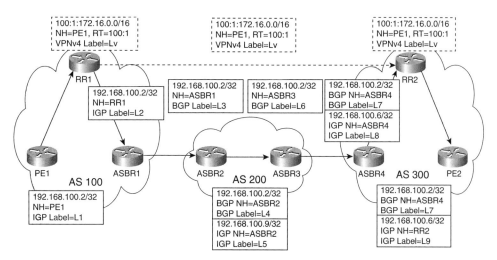

Table 10-6 shows the loopback addresses used in Figure 10-24.

Table 10-6 *Loopback Addresses Used in Figure 10-24*

Router	Loopback Address
PE1	192.168.100.2
ASBR2	192.168.100.9
ASBR4	192.168.100.6

PE1's loopback address is part of the IGP in AS 100 and is distributed via LDP, L1, and L2, to ASBR1. ASBR1 then advertises the address plus a new label, L3, to ASBR2 via eBGP, with ASBR1 as the BGP next hop.

Example 10-31 shows the BGP labels on ASBR2. To reach PE1 (192.168.100.2), an out label of 18 (L3) is used, and ASBR2 assigns a local label of 19 (L4). The BGP next hop for the prefix is ASBR1 (192.168.59.5).

Example 10-31 *BGP Labels on ASBR2*

```
ASBR2#show ip bgp label
Network           Next Hop          In Label/Out Label
192.168.100.2/32 192.168.59.5       19/18
192.168.100.3/32 192.168.59.5       20/19
192.168.100.4/32 192.168.100.10     21/21
192.168.100.7/32 192.168.100.10     22/22
```

ASBR2 advertises the prefix with a label, L4, via iBGP to ASBR3 by setting itself as the BGP next hop. Also, ASBR2 advertises via LDP an IGP label, L5, to reach itself (192.168.100.9). PE1's address and label (L4) are now in ASBR3's BGP RIB. In turn, ASBR3 advertises the prefix with a new label, L6, to ASBR4.

Example 10-32 shows the BGP labels on ASBR3. The value of L6, the in label, is 19. The BGP next hop is ASBR2 (192.168.100.9). Now ASBR4 (192.168.100.6) can set itself as the BGP next hop (using **next-hop-self**) and advertise the prefix with another label, L7, via iBGP. An IGP label, L8, is also generated and advertised in LDP.

Example 10-32 *BGP Labels on ASBR3*

```
ASBR3#show ip bgp label
Network           Next Hop          In Label/Out Label
192.168.100.2/32 192.168.100.9      19/19
192.168.100.3/32 192.168.100.9      20/20
192.168.100.4/32 192.168.106.6      21/18
192.168.100.7/32 192.168.106.6      22/19
```

When PE2 finally receives PE1's loopback address, there are two labels:

- One IGP label to reach ASBR4 via RR2 (L9), label value 17
- One BGP label to reach PE1 via ASBR4 (L8), label value 20

For the VPN prefix 172.16.0.0/16, there is also a third label, Lv, with a label value of 22. Example 10-33 shows the label stack on PE2, where 192.168.47.7 is RR2.

Example 10-33 *Label Stack on PE2*

```
PE2#show ip cef vrf VPNa 172.16.0.0
172.16.0.0/16, version 6, epoch 0, cached adjacency 192.168.47.7
0 packets, 0 bytes
  tag information set
    local tag: VPN-route-head
    fast tag rewrite with Et1/0, 192.168.47.7, tags imposed: {17 20 22}
  via 192.168.100.2, 0 dependencies, recursive
    next hop 192.168.47.7, Ethernet1/0 via 192.168.100.2/32
    valid cached adjacency
    tag rewrite with Et1/0, 192.168.47.7, tags imposed: {17 20 22}
```

Figure 10-25 shows packet forwarding with a non-VPN transit AS. To reach 172.16.0.0/16 from VPNa, PE2 performs a recursive lookup of the BGP next hop PE1 and resolves to a BGP next hop of ASBR4. One more lookup resolves to an IGP next hop of RR2. When PE2 receives a packet to 172.16.0.0/16 from VPNa, three labels are imposed:

- The top label (17) to reach ASBR4 via RR2
- The middle label (20) to reach PE1 via ASBR4
- The bottom label (22) to reach 172.16.0.0/16 in VPNa

Figure 10-25 *Packet Forwarding with a Non-VPN Transit AS*

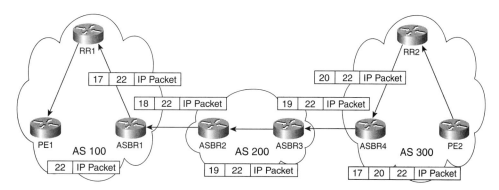

When ASBR3 receives the packet, it has two labels. The top label (19) is the BGP label L6, and the bottom label (22) is the VPN label Lv. The top label 19 is then replaced by another BGP label (19). Because of PHP, ASBR3 does not push an IGP label. Label swapping continues until PE1 receives the packet with Lv, and then an IP packet is delivered to the CE.

Comparison of Various Inter-AS VPN Options

So far, four inter-AS VPN options have been presented. Table 10-7 compares and contrasts them.

Table 10-7 *Comparison and Contrast of Four Inter-AS Options*

Option	Inter-AS Label	Inter-AS Filtering	Complexity	Scalability
Back-to-back VRF	Standard IPv4 without labels	PEs need to filter IPv4 routes from the remote AS per VRF.	Low Configurations are similar to the basic (same AS) VPN.	Low One VRF/interface is required per ASBR CE. ASBR PEs hold all (IPv4 and VPNv4) routing information.
Single-hop eBGP for VPNv4	VPNv4 labels	RTs should be filtered from the remote AS. ARF is disabled.	Medium VPNv4 labels are reset at ASBRs. BGP next hop can be made reachable at the receiving AS by redistribution or **next-hop-self**.	Medium Only one interface is required between ASBRs. No VRFs are required on ASBRs. ASBRs hold VPNv4 information for their own AS and might hold the VPNv4 information for the remote AS, depending on the next-hop configuration.
Multihop eBGP for VPNv4	IPv4 labels	IPv4 addresses and labels should be filtered for inbound and outbound.	High VPNv4 information is exchanged between RRs with the next hop unchanged. IPv4 with labels are exchanged on the inter-AS links.	High VPNv4 routes are exchanged between RRs. ASBRs are not involved in VPNv4 information exchange.

Table 10-7   *Comparison and Contrast of Four Inter-AS Options (Continued)*

Option	Inter-AS Label	Inter-AS Filtering	Complexity	Scalability
Non-VPN transit AS	IPv4 labels	IPv4 addresses and labels should be filtered for inbound and outbound.	Similar to the complexity of multihop eBGP for VPNv4, but there is the added complexity of coordinating among three autonomous systems.	High VPNv4 routes are exchanged between RRs. ASBRs are not involved in VPNv4 information exchange.

Carrier Supporting Carrier VPN

So far, the MPLS VPN discussion has assumed that VPN customers are end customers—that is, they are not service providers or carriers. In a case where VPN customers are themselves carriers, the resource use on PEs can increase significantly.

Consider the scenario shown earlier in Figure 10-14. If the two customer carriers are ISPs that carry full Internet routes between them, PE devices must hold these routes in a VRF. If more than one VPN customer is an ISP, the resources (memory and CPU) on PE devices become a severely limiting factor. This VPN model obviously is not scalable.

The CSC VPN model is developed for this purpose. Two scenarios are discussed in this section:

- Customer carriers exchange full Internet routes using a common VPN via the backbone carrier

- Customer carriers provide VPN services themselves via a common VPN from the backbone carrier, or hierarchical VPN

CSC for Full Internet Routes

Consider Figure 10-26, where AS 200 is the backbone VPN carrier that provides two-site connectivity for AS 100. AS 100 Site 2 receives full Internet routes from an upstream ISP, AS 400. An enterprise customer, AS 300, receives full Internet routes from its provider, AS 100, via Site 1. Within AS 100 (both sites), LDP is enabled on links among all the routers, and an IGP is used to advertise reachability for links and loopback addresses.

Figure 10-26 *Full Internet Routes via VPN*

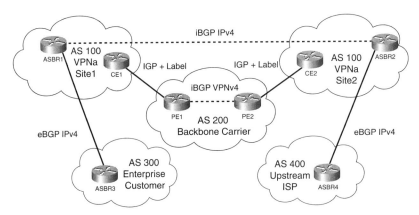

It is important to note here that the backbone carrier needs to carry two types of routes:

- Full Internet routes that are carried between ASBR1 and ASBR2
- IGP routes that are used to provide reachability within AS 100

The CSC solution is to extend the label switching from the PE devices' VRF interfaces to CE devices. Both CE devices advertise internal IGP routes to PE devices using an IGP or BGP, which redistribute them into multiprotocol iBGP to be advertised to the remote PE devices. Additionally, PEs and CEs exchange labels for these routes using LDP/TDP or BGP. Thus, an LSP is formed from CE1 to CE2, which completes the end-to-end LSP from ASBR1 to ASBR2.

An iBGP session is used between ASBR1 and ASBR2 to exchange the full Internet routes. Because of the end-to-end LSP, these routes do not need to be carried in any other routers. As a result, PE devices need to carry iBGP next-hop reachability information only for AS 100, not the full Internet routes.

NOTE   If AS 100 is not running MPLS, all routers in AS 100 must be BGP speakers and peer with each other in iBGP full mesh. Alternatively, RRs can be used to increase scalability.

Figure 10-27 shows prefix and label distribution. The BGP prefix 172.16.0.0/16 (simulating an Internet route) is received by ASBR2, which advertises, with the next hop reset to itself (192.168.100.4), to ASBR1. For ASBR1 to advertise the prefix to ASBR3 in AS 300, it needs to know how to reach ASBR2, the BGP next hop.

Figure 10-27 *Prefix and Label Distribution for CSC*

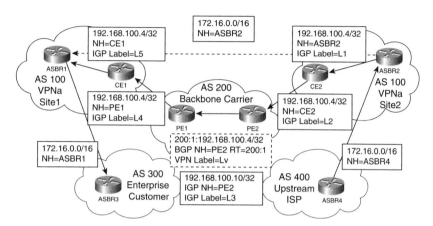

Because LDP is enabled, ASBR2 advertises an IGP label, L1, for its loopback address (192.168.100.4). The prefix is advertised by CE2 to PE2 in the common IGP between them. Additionally, CE2 advertises an IGP label using LDP, L2, to PE2. The example of using eBGP with labels between a PE and a CE is presented in the next section.

As the prefix 192.168.100.4/32 (ASBR2) from VPNa is redistributed into BGP on PE2, a VPN label, Lv, is advertised from PE2 to PE1. Additionally, PE2 advertises an IGP label, L3, for itself (192.168.100.10). After the VPNv4 prefix 200:1:192.168.100.4/32 is redistributed into a VRF for VPNa, PE1 advertises the prefix 192.168.100.4/32 to CE1. Additionally, an IGP label, L4, is advertised. In turn, CE1 advertises L5 to ASBR1. Now ASBR1 has an LSP to ASBR2. ASBR1's loopback address (192.168.100.2) is advertised the same way to ASBR2 (not shown).

Example 10-34 shows the LFIB on PE2, where 192.168.100.4 is ASBR2's loopback address and 192.168.106.6 is CE2. Label 31 is the local VPN label for 192.168.100.4 advertised to PE1 (Lv). Label 18 is a per-VRF IGP label received from CE2 (L2).

Example 10-34 *LFIB on PE2*

```
PE2#show tag forwarding
Local  Outgoing    Prefix           Bytes tag  Outgoing   Next Hop
tag    tag or VC   or Tunnel Id     switched   interface
16     Pop tag     192.168.106.6/32  0          Et1/0      192.168.106.6
17     18          192.168.59.0/24[V]  \
                                    0          Et0/0      192.168.109.9
18     Pop tag     192.168.100.9/32  0          Et0/0      192.168.109.9
19     Aggregate   192.168.106.0/24[V]  \
                                    0
```

continues

Example 10-34 *LFIB on PE2 (Continued)*

```
20      20        192.168.35.0/24[V]    \
                                      0       Et0/0      192.168.109.9
21      21        192.168.23.0/24[V]    \
                                      0       Et0/0      192.168.109.9
22      26        192.168.100.5/32[V]   \
                                      0       Et0/0      192.168.109.9
23      25        192.168.100.3/32[V]   \
                                   1521       Et0/0      192.168.109.9
24      22        192.168.100.2/32[V]   \
                                   2804       Et0/0      192.168.109.9
29      Pop tag   192.168.67.0/24[V]    \
                                      0       Et1/0      192.168.106.6
30      17        192.168.47.0/24[V]    \
                                   3528       Et1/0      192.168.106.6
31      18        192.168.100.4/32[V]   \
                                    310       Et1/0      192.168.106.6
32      Pop tag   192.168.100.6/32[V]   \
                                      0       Et1/0      192.168.106.6
33      19        192.168.100.7/32[V]   \
```

Example 10-35 shows the label binding information on PE1. The local label 31 (L4) is a per-VRF IGP label advertised to CE1 (which happens to have the same value as the local label on PE2, but they are not the same label), and label 23 is a local label for 192.168.100.4/32 on CE1 (192.168.100.5).

Example 10-35 *Label Binding Information on PE1*

```
PE1#show mpls ldp bindings vrf VPNa
  192.168.23.0/24, rev 23
        local binding:  label: 21
        remote binding: lsr: 192.168.100.5:0, label: 17
  192.168.35.0/24, rev 21
        local binding:  label: 20
        remote binding: lsr: 192.168.100.5:0, label: imp-null
  192.168.47.0/24, rev 44
        local binding:  label: 33
        remote binding: lsr: 192.168.100.5:0, label: 21
  192.168.59.0/24, rev 14
        local binding:  label: 18
        remote binding: lsr: 192.168.100.5:0, label: imp-null
  192.168.67.0/24, rev 42
        local binding:  label: 32
        remote binding: lsr: 192.168.100.5:0, label: 22
  192.168.100.2/32, rev 26
        local binding:  label: 22
        remote binding: lsr: 192.168.100.5:0, label: 18
  192.168.100.3/32, rev 28
        local binding:  label: 25
        remote binding: lsr: 192.168.100.5:0, label: 19
```

Example 10-35 *Label Binding Information on PE1 (Continued)*

```
192.168.100.4/32, rev 40
     local binding:  label: 31
     remote binding: lsr: 192.168.100.5:0, label: 23
192.168.100.5/32, rev 30
     local binding:  label: 26
     remote binding: lsr: 192.168.100.5:0, label: imp-null
192.168.100.6/32, rev 38
     local binding:  label: 30
     remote binding: lsr: 192.168.100.5:0, label: 24
192.168.100.7/32, rev 36
     local binding:  label: 29
     remote binding: lsr: 192.168.100.5:0, label: 25
192.168.106.0/24, rev 17
     local binding:  label: 19
     remote binding: lsr: 192.168.100.5:0, label: 20
```

To reach 172.16.0.0/16, ASBR1 recursively resolves for the next-hop address ASBR2. ASBR1 pushes an IGP label, L5, to the packet. This labeled packet is eventually replaced with a label stack, L3 and Lv, on PE1. The label stack is then replaced by L2 on PE2. With more label swapping and popping, eventually an IPv4 packet is delivered to AS 400.

Hierarchical VPN

When the customer carrier also provides MPLS VPN services, the CSC model becomes a hierarchical VPN, as shown in Figure 10-28. As before, AS 200 is a backbone VPN provider, and AS 100 is a customer provider that has two sites connected via VPNb. Now AS 100 also provides VPN services, where VPNa connects two sites. As another way to exchange labels between a customer carrier and a backbone carrier within VPNb, eBGP with IPv4 labels is used in this example. Thus, no IGP or LDP is needed between AS 100 CE devices and AS 200 PE devices. The example of using an IGP and LDP between a CE and a PE was presented in the previous section.

Figure 10-29 shows the process of prefix and label distribution, where 172.16.0.0/16 simulates an internal prefix within VPNa. Within AS 100, the RD for VPNa is 100:1. The customer prefix 172.16.0.0/16 is attached with an RT of 100:1. In AS 200, 200:1 is configured as the RD for VPNb. An RT of 200:1 is attached to the prefix of 192.168.100.4, which is PE4's loopback address.

Figure 10-28 *Hierarchical VPN*

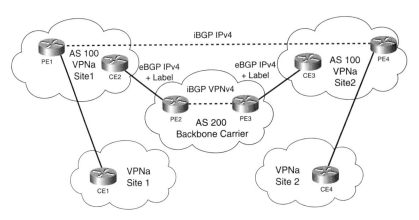

Figure 10-29 *Prefix and Label Distribution for Hierarchical VPN*

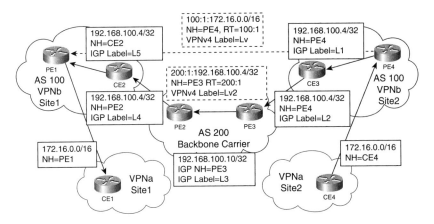

PE4 advertises the prefix 172.16.0.0/16 in VPNv4 to PE1, with a VPN label of Lv. For VPNa connectivity, an LSP must exist between PE1 and PE4. PE4's loopback address (192.168.100.4) is advertised with an IGP label, L1, to CE3.

As a PE router, PE3 advertises the PE4 address with a VPN label, Lv2. Additionally, PE3 advertises an IGP label, L3, to reach itself (192.168.100.10). Example 10-36 shows the BGP label information on PE2. Label 23 is Lv2.

Example 10-36 *Label Information on PE2*

```
PE2#show ip bgp vpnv4 all label
   Network           Next Hop       In label/Out label
Route Distinguisher: 300:1 (VPNa)
   192.168.23.0      192.168.59.5    21/16
   192.168.35.0      192.168.59.5    22/imp-null
   192.168.47.0      192.168.100.10  33/21
   192.168.59.0      192.168.59.5    23/aggregate(VPNa)
   192.168.67.0      192.168.100.10  32/22
   192.168.100.2/32 192.168.59.5     24/17
   192.168.100.3/32 192.168.59.5     25/18
   192.168.100.4/32 192.168.100.10   31/23
   192.168.100.5/32 192.168.59.5     26/imp-null
   192.168.100.6/32 192.168.100.10   30/30
   192.168.100.7/32 192.168.100.10   29/31
   192.168.106.0    192.168.100.10   28/32
   192.168.201.0    192.168.100.10   27/33
```

As another PE router within CSC, PE2 advertises a BGP label, L4, for PE4's address for VPNb. In label 31 in Example 10-36 is L4.

With regards to the customer prefix 172.16.0.0/16, CE2 is a P router; therefore, there is no need for CE2 to store any information for the customer prefix. CE2 only needs to maintain information for LSRs within AS 100.

An IGP label, L5, is advertised from CE2 to PE1. This completes the LSP from PE1 to PE4. The LSP from PE4 to PE1 is set up the same way (not shown). Example 10-37 shows the label stack on PE1. Label 21 is an IGP label used to reach PE4 (192.168.100.4) via CE2, whereas label 27 is Lv.

Example 10-37 *Label Stack on PE1*

```
PE1#show ip cef vrf VPNa 172.16.0.0
172.16.0.0/16, version 11, epoch 0, cached adjacency 192.168.23.3
0 packets, 0 bytes
  tag information set
    local tag: VPN-route-head
    fast tag rewrite with Et1/0, 192.168.23.3, tags imposed: {21 27}
  via 192.168.100.4, 0 dependencies, recursive
    next hop 192.168.23.3, Ethernet1/0 via 192.168.100.4/32
    valid cached adjacency
    tag rewrite with Et1/0, 192.168.23.3, tags imposed: {21 27}
```

When an IPv4 packet destined for 172.16.0.0/16 is received from CE1, PE1 pushes two labels to the packet, L5 and Lv. Upon receiving such a packet, CE2 replaces L5 with L4.

As a CSC PE, PE2 accepts labeled packets for which it has assigned labels. Because the labeled packet comes from VPNb, L4 is replaced with a label stack, L3 and Lv2. Now the packet has three labels—L3, Lv2, and Lv.

Assuming the default PHP, PE3 receives the packet with Lv2 and Lv. As a PE enabled with CSC, PE3 replaces the top label (Lv2) with L2. Example 10-38 shows the LFIB on PE3. Label 23 is Lv2, and label 18 is the BGP label L2 advertised by CE3.

Example 10-38 *LFIB on PE3*

```
PE3#show tag forwarding
Local   Outgoing    Prefix          Bytes tag   Outgoing    Next Hop
tag     tag or VC   or Tunnel Id    switched    interface
16      Pop tag     192.168.100.9/32  0          Et0/0       192.168.109.9
21      29          192.168.47.0/24[V]   \
                                      1298       Et1/0       192.168.106.6
22      32          192.168.67.0/24[V]   \
                                      0          Et1/0       192.168.106.6
23      18          192.168.100.4/32[V]   \
                                      16278      Et1/0       192.168.106.6
30      Pop tag     192.168.100.6/32[V]   \
                                      0          Et1/0       192.168.106.6
31      17          192.168.100.7/32[V]   \
                                      4295       Et1/0       192.168.106.6
32      Aggregate   192.168.106.0/24[V]   \
                                      1040
33      Pop tag     192.168.201.0/24[V]   \
                                      0          Et1/0       192.168.106.6
34      26          192.168.100.5/32[V]   \
                                      0          Et0/0       192.168.109.9
35      25          192.168.100.3/32[V]   \
                                      4685       Et0/0       192.168.109.9
36      24          192.168.100.2/32[V]   \
                                      10438      Et0/0       192.168.109.9
37      23          192.168.59.0/24[V]   \
                                      0          Et0/0       192.168.109.9
39      22          192.168.35.0/24[V]   \
                                      118        Et0/0       192.168.109.9
40      21          192.168.23.0/24[V]   \
                                      2360       Et0/0       192.168.109.9
```

At CE3, L2 is replaced with L1. Assuming the default PHP, PE4 receives the packet with one label, Lv. An IPv4 packet is then delivered to CE4.

BGP Confederations and MPLS VPN

So far the discussion on MPLS VPN across AS borders has centered on the use of multi-protocol eBGP. BGP confederation presents a similar situation, because the session between member autonomous systems is confederation eBGP, as discussed in Chapter 7. When MPLS VPN is used within a BGP confederation, two scenarios are possible, as described in the following list, depending on whether the BGP next hop is reset:

- When a single IGP is used, the BGP next hop is reachable across the confederation via the IGP. An end-to-end LSP using LDP can be maintained across member AS boundaries. There is no change to the regular VPN scenario.

- If each member AS uses its own IGP, the BGP next hop is reset at the member AS boundary. This is similar to the case of inter-AS VPN. When crossing member AS boundaries, the same inter-AS configuration options are available, as discussed earlier.

Figure 10-30 shows a scenario in which each member AS uses its own IGP, and the BGP next hop is reset at member AS borders. The BGP next hop is set to self for VPNv4 sessions between the two ASBRs. When the VPNv4 prefix is advertised from ASBR2 to ASBR1, the BGP next hop is thus ASBR2. A new VPN label, Lv2, is assigned.

Figure 10-30 *MPLS VPN Within a Confederation*

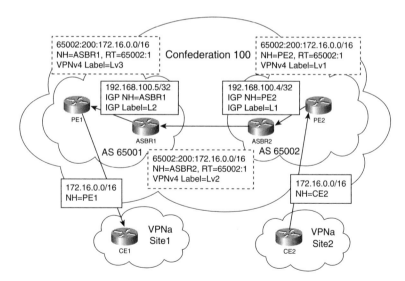

Example 10-39 shows the LFIB on ASBR1, where the outgoing label 22 is Lv2 and the local label 22 is Lv3.

Example 10-39 *LFIB on ASBR1*

```
ASBR1#show tag forwarding
Local  Outgoing    Prefix           Bytes tag  Outgoing   Next Hop
tag    tag or VC   or Tunnel Id     switched   interface
17     Pop tag     192.168.56.6/32  1770       Et1/0      192.168.56.6
18     Pop tag     192.168.23.0/24  0          Et0/0      192.168.35.3
19     17          192.168.100.2/32 0          Et0/0      192.168.35.3
20     Pop tag     192.168.100.3/32 0          Et0/0      192.168.35.3
22     22          65002:200:172.16.0.0/16  \
                                    0          Et1/0      192.168.56.6
```

When the VPNv4 prefix is advertised to PE1, ASBR1 resets itself (192.168.100.5) as the BGP next hop. This causes a new label stack to be created. Example 10-40 shows the label stack on PE1 for the VPNv4 prefix 172.16.0.0. The label 22 is Lv3.

Example 10-40 *Label Stack on PE1*

```
PE1#show ip cef vrf VPNa 172.16.0.0
172.16.0.0/16, version 15, epoch 0, cached adjacency 192.168.23.3
0 packets, 0 bytes
  tag information set
    local tag: VPN-route-head
    fast tag rewrite with Et1/0, 192.168.23.3, tags imposed: {18 22}
  via 192.168.100.5, 0 dependencies, recursive
    next hop 192.168.23.3, Ethernet1/0 via 192.168.100.5/32
    valid cached adjacency
    tag rewrite with Et1/0, 192.168.23.3, tags imposed: {18 22}
```

Deployment Considerations

This section focuses on various considerations in MPLS VPN deployment. Specifically, the following subjects are discussed:

- Scalability
- Route target design examples
- Convergence

Scalability

The subject of scalability is of special concern to MPLS VPN deployment, because VRF significantly increases resource consumption. When you design an MPLS VPN, carefully consider the following points:

- Minimizing resource consumption on PE devices, including proper RD design and RT policy to minimize PE memory use
- Separating VPNv4 and IPv4 routing information
- Using route reflection properly
- Filtering at inter-AS borders properly
- Using label maintenance methods

Many of these points are discussed throughout this chapter. This section concentrates on the following topics:

- Resource consumption on PE devices
- Route reflection with MPLS VPN
- Design guidelines for RDs

Resource Consumption on PE Devices

This discussion on resource consumption on PE devices focuses on CPU usage and memory consumption required to store various structures. This section describes factors that can affect resource consumption and some guidelines for consideration during actual evaluation. Follow current Cisco documentation on exact usage numbers, which can change from release to release.

The use of CPU resources is dependent on a variety of factors, including the following:

- **Number of backbone (toward P routers) BGP peers**—More peers lead to more processing. The use of peer groups reduces the per-peer processing overhead.
- **Number of provisioned VRFs**—A higher number of VRFs configured locally requires more maintenance.
- **Number of VPN routes**—More VPN routes require more processing.
- **PE-CE connectivity type**—Different protocols result in different processing overhead. For example, eBGP might require less processing than OSPF.
- **The type of CPU**—Higher-powered CPUs obviously have better performance.
- **Hardware platforms**—Hardware platforms might require different maintenance tasks to be performed.

Several structures can consume a significant amount of memory in a PE:

- A global IP RIB to hold the provider internal networks and Internet routes
- A VPN BGP table to hold VPNv4 structures
- CEF and LFIB for the global routes and VPN routes
- A VRF IP RIB to hold per-VRF routing information

Memory use on a PE is determined by the following factors:

- **Number of VRFs**—Each VRF structure consumes a certain amount of memory.

- **Number of local VPN routes**—Memory use increases with the number of local VPN routes.

- **Number of remote VPN routes**—Memory use increases with the number of remote VPN routes.

- **RD allocation schemes**—These schemes affect how VPN routes are stored. You'll read more about this topic in the section "Design Guidelines for RDs."

- **Number of CE neighbors and type of connectivity**—Neighbor structures use memory.

- **CE-PE protocol**—Different protocols use different structures and consume memory differently.

- **Number of iBGP peers**—Memory use increases with the number of peers.

- **Number of global routing table entries**—Memory use increases with the size of the table.

- **Hardware platform**—Hardware-specific structures use memory differently.

- **IOS release**—Different releases might store and cache the information differently.

If large numbers of routes, such as full Internet routes, are delivered in a VPN, the CSC model should be used. As another example, separation of IPv4 and VPNv4 routes and the use of RRs (discussed in the next section) reduce resource consumption. During capacity planning for PE devices, keep the following points in mind:

- The number of VRFs per PE is limited primarily by CPU, whereas the number of VRF routes is constrained by available memory.

- Do a baseline assessment before adding any VPN routes. Within the baseline, take into account the memory uses of the IOS image, backbone IGP routes, Internet routes (if any), and forwarding structures such as FIB and LFIB.

- Assess the extra requirements added by VRFs, considering overhead memory per VRF (about 60 to 70 KB) and memory use per VRF route (about 800 to 900 KB).

- Leave an additional amount of memory (about 20 MB) as transient memory.

Route Reflector Designs with MPLS VPN

Route reflection can be effectively used to reduce CPU and memory use in an MPLS VPN. An RR can selectively reflect routes between a group of PE devices with proper use of filtering. In an inter-AS environment, for example, the use of eBGP multihop peering between VPNv4 RRs reduces memory use in ASBRs.

When designing an RR-based MPLS VPN architecture, consider the following guidelines:

- Partition RRs.
- Move RRs out of the forwarding path.
- Use a high-end processor with maximum memory.
- Use peer groups.
- Tune RR routers for improved performance.

Some of these points have been discussed elsewhere. The following sections discuss RR partitioning and briefly RR router performance tuning.

Partitioning RRs

You can use a partition in an MPLS VPN environment to reduce the memory use on RRs. The partition can take several forms:

- Logical partition between RRs
- Selective filtering between a PE and an RR
- Selective filtering between RRs
- Separation of IPv4 and VPNv4 RRs

Logical partition refers to different RRs for different VPNs or PE devices. Dedicated RRs peer only with PEs that they serve. This method is simple to accomplish but requires more hardware and more management.

Selective filtering can be implemented between a PE and an RR in that an RR accepts only routes with a specific RT or RTs. This can be accomplished by using RR groups on the RR. By default, RRs accept all the VPNv4 routes advertised by all the PEs they peer with. With RR groups, an RR accepts only routes that are permitted by the configured RTs.

The RR group is configured under the VPNv4 address family with the command **bgp rr-group** *acl#*, where *acl#* is an ACL that specifies an extended community list. An extended community list is like a numbered community list and has standard (1 to 99) and expanded (100 to 199) formats. In the standard lists, only extended communities are accepted; in the expanded lists, regular expressions are allowed.

NOTE   Changes to the RR group cause route refresh requests to be sent out.

Example 10-41 shows a standard extended community list that permits VPNv4 routes that have RTs 100:1 and 100:2. This is an exact match, meaning that both RTs must exist for a prefix to be accepted.

Example 10-41 *Example of a Standard Extended Community List*

```
ip extcommunity-list 1 permit rt 100:1 rt 100:2
```

Figure 10-31 shows an RR design using RR groups, where two RTs designate two RR groups. The first group has two redundant RRs, which accepts only routes with an RT of 100:101. In the second group, two redundant RRs accept only routes with an RT of 100:102.

Figure 10-31 *Partitioning RRs with RR Groups*

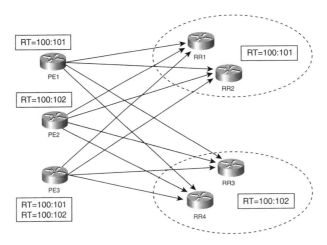

All PEs peer with all RRs to simplify configuration and management. In addition to existing RTs, PE1 also exports an RT of 100:101 (RR group 1). Thus, RR group 1 accepts routes from PE1. The additional RT exported by PE2 is 100:102; thus, RR group 2 accepts the routes from PE2. Routes from PE3 are accepted by both RR groups as both RTs are exported. From an RR perspective, RR1 and RR2 reflect routes from PE1 and PE3; RR3 and RR4 reflect routes from PE2 and PE3. Note that there is no full-mesh requirement between RRs of the different RR groups.

NOTE   The grouping of RRs with RTs does not necessarily coincide with RR clusters.

To further increase RR scalability, you can create hierarchies. Between different levels of RRs, you can use standard BGP communities to designate routes to be passed between different partitions. For example, PEs can attach a designated additional standard community to a subset of the VPNv4 routes that need to be made available in the other RR groups. The top-level RRs can then be configured to accept only the routes with the designated standard community, so only routes matching that community can be passed between RR groups.

Selective filtering between a PE device and an RR can also be accomplished on the PE side. An RT export map (discussed later, in the section "Route Target Design Examples") configured under a VRF can selectively export RTs that an RR will accept. A standard community filter can also be used on a PE device. When compared to outbound filtering on PE devices, inbound filtering on RRs generally requires less maintenance but increases CPU usage on RRs.

In a network that carries both IPv4 and VPNv4 routes, RRs for both types of prefixes can be used to increase scalability. When large numbers of Internet routes and VPN routes are carried, it is desirable to have dedicated RRs for each address family. On a VPNv4 RR, disable the default IPv4 prefix processing for all sessions.

Tuning an RR Router

Because an RR handles large numbers of routes, it is important that the router is at peak performance for receiving and processing updates. You can use the following two approaches:

- Increase input hold-queue size for all the interfaces
- Enable TCP path-MTU discovery.

Consult Chapter 3, "Tuning BGP Performance," for details.

Design Guidelines for RDs

One RD is configured on a PE router for each VRF. A common RD format is local AS number:customer ID. However, an RD might or might not be related to a site or a customer VPN. The assignment of RDs affects how VPNv4 routes are installed. This section discusses the implications for memory use.

Generally, there are three different ways to assign RDs in PE devices across the network:

- The same RD for the same VPN
- A unique RD for each VRF
- A unique RD for each VRF per site

The Same RD for the Same VPN

In this option, which is the simplest and most intuitive, the same RD is used for the same VPN regardless of the site or VRF. This option might not be possible, however, because some sites might belong to more than one VPN. In this case, two sites that belong to the same VPN have different RDs.

A drawback of this option is the limitation to do load sharing for the VPN traffic. When a VPNv4 prefix is processed for the BGP best path, the entire prefix, including the RD, is considered. Because an RR reflects only the best path, PEs have only one path.

NOTE   Load sharing can still occur if RRs are brought into forwarding paths. Also, in a VPN without RRs, PEs can still load-share when they have all the routing information.

A Unique RD for Each VRF

Using a unique RD for each VRF on the same VPN allows iBGP load sharing for VPNv4 prefixes. For example, if two PE devices advertise an identical IPv4 prefix but with different RDs to an RR, both VPNv4 prefixes are reflected. However, the drawback is increased memory consumption on PE devices.

When a VPNv4 prefix is installed in the BGP RIB, the prefix's RD is checked against the RDs configured locally on the PE. If the RDs are the same, one copy of the route is imported into the BGP RIB. When RDs are different, one copy is installed for each RD that permits the route. For example, if 100:1:172.16.0.0 is received on a PE that has an RD of 100:1, one copy of the route is installed. If the PE is configured with RDs of 100:2 and 100:3, one copy of the route is installed for each locally configured RD (assuming that the route passes the RT import policy), plus a copy for the original RD 100:1. The memory use can be significant if there are a large number of VRFs on the PE.

A Unique RD for Each VRF Per Site

Using a unique RD for each VRF per site lets you quickly identify the site that originated the route. This is true only when multiple CE sites of the same VPN are connected to the same PE. Each site can be associated with a different VRF. However, this option is undesirable because of the high cost in terms of memory consumption and the number of VRFs to be configured. Moreover, SOO and other BGP communities may be used to identify where the route originated.

Route Target Design Examples

This section presents some examples of how you can use RTs to achieve complex VPN solutions:

- Hub-and-spoke VPN
- Extranet VPN
- Management VPN

Hub-and-Spoke VPN Topologies

On the PE connecting to the hub site, create two VRFs for customer Cust1—Cust1-hub-in and Cust1-hub-out—as shown in Example 10-42. On Cust1-hub-in, import all spoke routes (RT 100:50); on Cust1-hub-out, export hub routes to spokes (RT 100:51).

Example 10-42 *RTs for the Hub PE*

```
ip vrf Cust1-hub-in
 rd 100:100
 route-target import 100:50

ip vrf Cust1-hub-out
 rd 100:101
 route-target export 100:51
```

On each spoke site, import all routes from Cust1-hub-out with 100:51, and export spoke routes as 100:50. Example 10-43 shows the sample configurations.

Example 10-43 *RTs for the Spoke PE*

```
ip vrf Cust1-spoke1
 rd 100:1
 route-target export 100:50
 route-target import 100:51
```

Extranet VPN

An extranet VPN is created when routing information is exchanged between certain sites of one VPN with certain sites of another VPN. In Example 10-44, Cust1 wants to allow access to a locally connected site to the current PE by Cust2. An additional RT of 100:100 is created for the extranet. Note that the configurations in this example allow the whole site to be accessible. If only some prefixes should be accessible, you can use route maps (import maps and export maps).

Example 10-44 *Extranet Example*

```
ip vrf Cust1
  rd 100:1001
  route-target import 100:1001
  route-target export 100:1001
  route-target import 100:100
  route-target export 100:100
!
ip vrf Cust2
  rd 100:1002
  route-target import 100:1002
  route-target export 100:1002
  route-target import 100:100
  route-target export 100:100
```

Management VPN

Providers sometimes might need to manage CE routers. You can create a management VRF to import an RT designated for the CE management. On each customer VRF, export the management RT. You can implement additional filtering with route maps to allow only CE addresses to be in the management VPN and only management stations to be in each customer VPN.

In Example 10-45, the management RT is 100:2000 for export and 100:2001 (RT from a customer VRF) for import. To limit the routes to be imported from other VPNs to only CEs, you can configure an import map. In this example, Fr_cust allows only routes that match the CE prefix list (addresses of the managed CEs). Note that both the **match extcommunity 2** clause and **route-target import 100:2001** are required to import 100:2001.

Example 10-45 *Management VPN Configurations*

```
ip vrf manage
 rd 100:2000
 import map Fr_cust
 route-target export 100:2000
 route-target import 100:2001
!
ip extcommunity-list 2 permit rt 100:2001
!
ip prefix-list CE seq 5 permit 192.168.100.1/32
ip prefix-list CE seq 10 permit 192.168.100.8/32
!
route-map Fr_cust permit 10
 match ip address prefix-list CE
 match extcommunity 2
```

NOTE   When a VPNv4 route is being imported, it is evaluated sequentially, first by the RT import policy (configured with the command **route-target import**) and then by the import map (configured with the command **import map**) if it's configured. For a route to be imported, it must pass both policies. If no RT import policy is configured, all routes are denied, even if they are permitted later by the import map policy. If no import map is configured, routes are imported based on the RT import policy.

On a customer VPN, routes with proper RTs must be exported. Example 10-46 shows a sample configuration. An export map Cust1_out is configured. If an address matches CE1, set an RT of 100:2001 (to be imported into the management VRF); if not, set an RT of 100:200 (to be imported into Cust1 VPN). The management RT 100:2000 is imported into each customer VRF. Additional filtering can be configured to permit only the management stations.

Example 10-46 *Customer VPNs for Management*

```
ip vrf Cust1
 rd 100:200
 export map Cust1_out
 route-target import 100:200
 route-target import 100:2000
!
ip prefix-list CE1 seq 5 permit 192.168.100.1/32
!
route-map Cust1_out permit 10
 match ip address prefix-list CE1
 set extcommunity rt  100:2001
!
route-map Cust1_out permit 20
 set extcommunity rt  100:200
```

NOTE   Unlike the import map, the export map performs no RT filtering function. If both the RT export and export map are configured, the export map takes precedence in setting the RT values. In fact, there is no need to configure an RT export if an export map is configured. If both policies are required, the keyword **additive** can be used in the export map's set clause.

Convergence

Convergence is the time it takes for routers in a routing domain to learn the complete topology and to recompute alternative paths to a particular destination after a network event. A converged network implies that all the routers within the same routing domain are synchronized in their view of the network. In an MPLS VPN, convergence can be assessed in two areas:

- Provider backbone convergence
- VPN site-to-site convergence

Provider Backbone Convergence

If the BGP next hop is unaffected, the convergence of the provider network because of up or down network events does not cause convergence between two VPN sites. However, traffic forwarding between the sites might be affected during these events. The convergence within the backbone can be dependent on a variety of factors, including the following:

- **Physical layer stability**—Physical layer stability can be increased with physical line protection, such as SONET protection schemes. With SONET Automatic Protection Switching (APS), for example, line failure is recovered within 50 ms from the point of failure detection.

- **Circuit or path protection**—With hot-standby circuits or paths, convergence can be improved. For example, using MPLS Fast Reroute, a feature of MPLS TE, can result in a failure recovery rate comparable to SONET APS.

- **IGP convergence**—The convergence of an IGP is variable but typically is completed in tens of seconds. With proper timer tuning, IGP convergence time can be greatly reduced.

- **LDP/TDP convergence**—Convergence of LDP/TDP is affected by how the labels are maintained. For example, liberal retention mode (the default for the frame-based MPLS) allows an LSR to keep all the label mappings received from its neighbors even though they are not used. When an LDP/TDP session is lost, however, the convergence takes longer.

The next section examines site-to-site convergence.

Site-to-Site Convergence

Site-to-site convergence is perhaps more critical to MPLS VPN convergence than provider backbone convergence. For a route to be propagated from one site to another site, several processes are involved. Each can contribute to the convergence.

Site-to-site convergence is the time it takes for a route to be advertised from a CE to a PE. This time is dependent on the routing protocol between the PE and the CE. For example, BGP advertisements are paced differently between eBGP and iBGP. You can change the default advertisement interval in BGP using the **neighbor advertisement-interval** command.

Routes received from a CE must be installed into a VRF and then redistributed into BGP on the PE. If the PE-CE protocol is eBGP, no redistribution is involved. Next, these routes are advertised via iBGP to remote PEs or RRs, which might be subjected to the advertisement pacing. iBGP's default advertisement interval is 5 seconds, but you can tune this between 0 and 600 seconds. The addition of each RR in the path increases the total time to reach the remote PE.

When the remote PE receives these routes, they are installed into the appropriate VRFs in each scan-time interval. By default, the VPNv4 import scanner runs every 15 seconds. You can change this interval to between 5 and 60 seconds using **bgp scan-time import** under the VPNv4 address family. Note that withdraws are processed immediately and next-hop deletion is processed at the general BGP scanner interval (60 seconds).

The last two components of site-to-site convergence are the time to advertise VPN routes from a PE to a CE and the time it takes for a CE to install these routes into its local routing protocol. Again, the advertisement might be paced if BGP is used.

In summary, the time for site-to-site convergence depends on PE-CE protocols, the number of hops that routes have to be advertised within the provider networks, and various timers. Proper timer tuning and testing are important in reducing the total convergence time.

NOTE   As with all convergence tunings, it is important to note that faster convergence often leads to less network stability and greater resource consumption. Any change to a default timer should be carefully evaluated in a simulated environment to discover its impact on convergence and stability.

Case Study: Inter-AS VPN Using Multihop eBGP Between RRs and IPv4 Labels

This case study demonstrates in detail how an inter-AS scenario works, as discussed in the section "Multihop Multiprotocol eBGP for VPNv4." The topology is shown in Figure 10-32. Inter-AS VPN is needed between AS 100 and AS 200 for VPNa. To reduce the resource use on ASBRs, two autonomous systems decide to peer between their RRs in a multihop eBGP for VPNv4 prefixes.

Figure 10-32 *Topology and BGP Sessions*

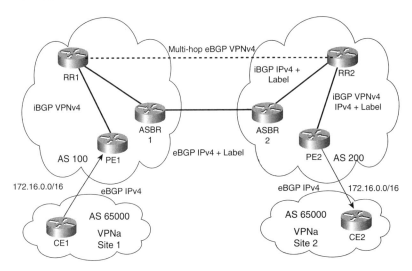

To have reachability between RRs and PEs, loopback addresses must be exchanged. AS 100 decides to use redistribution so that loopback addresses of RR2 and PE2 are redistributed on ASBR1 into its OSPF. AS 200 wants to isolate its OSPF from routes from AS 100 and decides to use iBGP. Loopback addresses of RR1 and PE1 are advertised in iBGP and in labels to RR2, which is an RR for both IPv4 and VPNv4 addresses. Both autonomous systems use LDP to distribute their IGP labels.

The BGP next hop for VPNv4 prefixes is not changed between the two VPNv4 RRs. Both autonomous systems also coordinate their RT policies so that routes within the same VPN are properly imported and exported. To simulate VPNv4 prefix advertisement and label distribution, 172.16.0.0/16 is generated in CE1.

Example 10-47 shows the relevant configurations on PE1. Under VRF VPNa, the RT import of 200:200 is for Inter-AS routes from AS 200. PE1 has two BGP sessions: one to CE1 (192.168.12.1) and one to RR1 (192.168.100.3). AS Override is configured with CE1.

Example 10-47 *Relevant Configurations on PE1*

```
ip vrf VPNa
 rd 100:100
 route-target export 100:100
 route-target import 100:100
 route-target import 200:200
!
ip cef
mpls label protocol ldp
```

Example 10-47 *Relevant Configurations on PE1 (Continued)*

```
!
interface Loopback0
 ip address 192.168.100.2 255.255.255.255
!
interface Ethernet0/0
 ip vrf forwarding VPNa
 ip address 192.168.12.2 255.255.255.0
!
interface Ethernet1/0
 ip address 192.168.23.2 255.255.255.0
 tag-switching ip
!
router ospf 2
 log-adjacency-changes
 network 192.168.0.0 0.0.255.255 area 0
!
router bgp 100
 no synchronization
 bgp router-id 192.168.100.2
 no bgp default ipv4-unicast
 bgp log-neighbor-changes
 neighbor 192.168.100.3 remote-as 100
 neighbor 192.168.100.3 update-source Loopback0
 no auto-summary
 !
 address-family ipv4 vrf VPNa
 neighbor 192.168.12.1 remote-as 65000
 neighbor 192.168.12.1 activate
 neighbor 192.168.12.1 as-override
 no auto-summary
 no synchronization
 exit-address-family
 !
 address-family vpnv4
 neighbor 192.168.100.3 activate
 neighbor 192.168.100.3 send-community extended
 no auto-summary
 exit-address-family
```

Example 10-48 shows the relevant configurations on RR1. There are two BGP sessions: one to PE1 (192.168.100.2) and one to RR2 (192.168.100.7). Both sessions are for VPNv4 only.

Example 10-48 *Relevant Configurations on RR1*

```
ip cef
mpls label protocol ldp
!
interface Loopback0
 ip address 192.168.100.3 255.255.255.255
```

continues

Example 10-48 *Relevant Configurations on RR1 (Continued)*

```
!
interface Ethernet0/0
 ip address 192.168.35.3 255.255.255.0
 tag-switching ip
!
interface Ethernet1/0
 ip address 192.168.23.3 255.255.255.0
 tag-switching ip
!
router ospf 3
 log-adjacency-changes
 network 192.168.0.0 0.0.255.255 area 0
!
router bgp 100
 no synchronization
 bgp router-id 192.168.100.3
 no bgp default ipv4-unicast
 bgp log-neighbor-changes
 neighbor Internal peer-group
 neighbor Internal remote-as 100
 neighbor Internal update-source Loopback0
 neighbor Internal activate
 neighbor 192.168.100.2 peer-group Internal
 neighbor 192.168.100.7 remote-as 200
 neighbor 192.168.100.7 ebgp-multihop 5
 neighbor 192.168.100.7 update-source Loopback0
 no auto-summary
 !
 address-family vpnv4
 neighbor 192.168.100.2 activate
 neighbor 192.168.100.2 route-reflector-client
 neighbor 192.168.100.2 send-community extended
 neighbor 192.168.100.7 activate
 neighbor 192.168.100.7 next-hop-unchanged
 neighbor 192.168.100.7 send-community extended
 no auto-summary
 exit-address-family
```

Example 10-49 shows the relevant configurations on ASBR1. There is one BGP session with IPv4 plus labels to ASBR2 (192.168.56.6). Two route maps (inbound and outbound) are configured to control the prefixes and labels exchanged between the two autonomous systems. Local loopback addresses are advertised to AS 200 via two **network** statements. Loopback addresses from AS 200 are redistributed from BGP into OSPF.

Example 10-49 *Relevant Configurations on ASBR1*

```
ip cef
mpls label protocol ldp
!
interface Loopback0
 ip address 192.168.100.5 255.255.255.255
!
interface Ethernet0/0
 ip address 192.168.35.5 255.255.255.0
 tag-switching ip
!
interface Ethernet1/0
 ip address 192.168.56.5 255.255.255.0
!
router ospf 5
 log-adjacency-changes
 redistribute bgp 100 subnets route-map bgp2ospf
 passive-interface Ethernet1/0
 network 192.168.0.0 0.0.255.255 area 0
!
router bgp 100
 no synchronization
 bgp router-id 192.168.100.5
 bgp log-neighbor-changes
 network 192.168.100.2 mask 255.255.255.255
 network 192.168.100.3 mask 255.255.255.255
 neighbor 192.168.56.6 remote-as 200
 neighbor 192.168.56.6 route-map Fr_200 in
 neighbor 192.168.56.6 route-map To_asbr2 out
 neighbor 192.168.56.6 send-label
 no auto-summary
!
ip prefix-list Adv_200 seq 5 permit 192.168.100.2/32
ip prefix-list Adv_200 seq 10 permit 192.168.100.3/32
!
ip prefix-list Rec_200 seq 5 permit 192.168.100.7/32
ip prefix-list Rec_200 seq 10 permit 192.168.100.4/32
!
route-map bgp2ospf permit 10
 match ip address prefix-list Rec_200
!
route-map To_asbr2 permit 10
 match ip address prefix-list Adv_200
 set mpls-label
!
route-map Fr_200 permit 10
 match ip address prefix-list Rec_200
 match mpls-label
```

Example 10-50 shows the relevant configurations on ASBR2. The configurations are similar to those of ASBR1. However, there is an additional BGP session with RR2 (192.168.100.7) to exchange IPv4 prefixes and labels. The BGP next hop is reset to ASBR2. Also, no redistribution is configured from BGP to OSPF.

Example 10-50 *Relevant Configurations on ASBR2*

```
ip cef
mpls label protocol ldp
!
interface Loopback0
 ip address 192.168.100.6 255.255.255.255
!
interface Ethernet0/0
 ip address 192.168.67.6 255.255.255.0
 tag-switching ip
!
interface Ethernet1/0
 ip address 192.168.56.6 255.255.255.0
!
router ospf 6
 log-adjacency-changes
 passive-interface Ethernet1/0
 network 192.168.0.0 0.0.255.255 area 0
!
router bgp 200
 no synchronization
 bgp router-id 192.168.100.6
 bgp log-neighbor-changes
 network 192.168.100.4 mask 255.255.255.255
 network 192.168.100.7 mask 255.255.255.255
 neighbor 192.168.56.5 remote-as 100
 neighbor 192.168.56.5 route-map Fr_asbr1 in
 neighbor 192.168.56.5 route-map To_asbr1 out
 neighbor 192.168.56.5 send-label
 neighbor 192.168.100.7 remote-as 200
 neighbor 192.168.100.7 update-source Loopback0
 neighbor 192.168.100.7 next-hop-self
 neighbor 192.168.100.7 send-label
 no auto-summary
!
ip prefix-list Adv_100 seq 5 permit 192.168.100.7/32
ip prefix-list Adv_100 seq 10 permit 192.168.100.4/32
!
ip prefix-list Rec_100 seq 5 permit 192.168.100.2/32
ip prefix-list Rec_100 seq 10 permit 192.168.100.3/32
!
route-map To_asbr1 permit 10
 match ip address prefix-list Adv_100
 set mpls-label
```

Example 10-50 *Relevant Configurations on ASBR2 (Continued)*

```
!
route-map Fr_asbr1 permit 10
 match ip address prefix-list Rec_100
 match mpls-label
```

Example 10-51 shows the relevant configurations on RR2. Besides the VPNv4 sessions with RR1 (192.168.100.3) and PE2 (192.168.100.4), RR2 also is an IPv4 RR for ASBR2 (192.168.100.6) and PE2 to reflect IPv4 prefixes and labels.

Example 10-51 *Relevant Configurations on RR2*

```
ip cef
mpls label protocol ldp
!
interface Loopback0
 ip address 192.168.100.7 255.255.255.255
!
interface Ethernet0/0
 ip address 192.168.67.7 255.255.255.0
 tag-switching ip
!
interface Ethernet1/0
 ip address 192.168.47.7 255.255.255.0
 tag-switching ip
!
router ospf 7
 log-adjacency-changes
 network 192.168.0.0 0.0.255.255 area 0
!
router bgp 200
 no synchronization
 bgp router-id 192.168.100.7
 bgp log-neighbor-changes
 neighbor 192.168.100.3 remote-as 100
 neighbor 192.168.100.3 ebgp-multihop 5
 neighbor 192.168.100.3 update-source Loopback0
 no neighbor 192.168.100.3 activate neighbor 192.168.100.4 remote-as 200
 neighbor 192.168.100.4 update-source Loopback0
 neighbor 192.168.100.4 route-reflector-client
 neighbor 192.168.100.4 send-label
 neighbor 192.168.100.6 remote-as 200
 neighbor 192.168.100.6 update-source Loopback0
 neighbor 192.168.100.6 route-reflector-client
 neighbor 192.168.100.6 send-label
 no auto-summary
```

continues

Example 10-51 *Relevant Configurations on RR2 (Continued)*

```
!
address-family vpnv4
neighbor 192.168.100.3 activate
neighbor 192.168.100.3 next-hop-unchanged
neighbor 192.168.100.3 send-community extended
neighbor 192.168.100.4 activate
neighbor 192.168.100.4 route-reflector-client
neighbor 192.168.100.4 send-community extended
no auto-summary
exit-address-family
```

Example 10-52 shows the relevant configurations of PE2. To accept the VPN routes from AS 100, an RT import of 100:100 is configured. The BGP session with RR2 (192.168.100.7) carries both IPv4 and VPNv4 prefixes. The BGP session with CE2 (192.168.48.8) is configured with AS Override.

Example 10-52 *Relevant Configurations on PE2*

```
ip vrf VPNa
 rd 200:200
 route-target export 200:200
 route-target import 200:200
 route-target import 100:100
!
ip cef
mpls label protocol ldp
!
interface Loopback0
 ip address 192.168.100.4 255.255.255.255
!
interface Ethernet0/0
 ip vrf forwarding VPNa
 ip address 192.168.48.4 255.255.255.0
!
interface Ethernet1/0
 ip address 192.168.47.4 255.255.255.0
 tag-switching ip
!
router ospf 4
 log-adjacency-changes
 network 192.168.0.0 0.0.255.255 area 0
!
router bgp 200
 no synchronization
 bgp router-id 192.168.100.4
 no bgp default ipv4-unicast
 bgp log-neighbor-changes
 neighbor 192.168.100.7 remote-as 200
 neighbor 192.168.100.7 update-source Loopback0
```

Example 10-52 *Relevant Configurations on PE2 (Continued)*

```
neighbor 192.168.100.7 activate
neighbor 192.168.100.7 send-label
no auto-summary
!
address-family ipv4 vrf VPNa
neighbor 192.168.48.8 remote-as 65000
neighbor 192.168.48.8 activate
neighbor 192.168.48.8 as-override
no auto-summary
no synchronization
exit-address-family
!
address-family vpnv4
neighbor 192.168.100.7 activate
neighbor 192.168.100.7 send-community extended
no auto-summary
exit-address-family
```

When the VPN prefix 172.16.0.0 is advertised from PE1 to RR1, a VPN label 24 is assigned, as shown in Example 10-53. (For a graphical representation of prefix and label distribution, refer to Figure 10-22.) The BGP next hop is CE1 but is reset to PE1 when the route is advertised to RR1 (shown next).

Example 10-53 *BGP Label for 172.16.0.0 on PE1*

```
PE1#show ip bgp vpnv4 all label
   Network          Next Hop      In label/Out label
Route Distinguisher: 100:100 (VPNa)
   172.16.0.0       192.168.12.1    24/nolabel
```

The same VPN label is used when RR1 advertises the prefix to RR2, as shown in Example 10-54. The BGP next hop is PE1. Also, RR2 advertises the same label when it advertises the prefix to PE2 (not shown).

Example 10-54 *BGP Label for 172.16.0.0 on RR1*

```
RR1#show ip bgp vpnv4 all label
   Network          Next Hop      In label/Out label
Route Distinguisher: 100:100
   172.16.0.0       192.168.100.2   nolabel/24
```

For this inter-AS VPN to work, loopback addresses of RRs and PEs must be reachable via an LSP in the remote AS. The following examines how PE1's loopback address plus labels are received on PE2, forming an end-to-end LSP.

Within AS 100, OSPF and LDP allow reachability of PE1's address in ASBR1, with LSPs between them. Example 10-55 shows the LFIB on ASBR1. An outgoing IGP label of 17 is used to reach PE1, which is then popped by RR1 because of PHP (not shown).

Example 10-55 *LFIB on ASBR1*

```
ASBR1#show tag forwarding
Local  Outgoing    Prefix         Bytes tag  Outgoing   Next Hop
tag    tag or VC   or Tunnel Id   switched   interface
16     Untagged    192.168.100.6/32  0        Et1/0      192.168.56.6
17     Pop tag     192.168.56.6/32   0        Et1/0      192.168.56.6
18     Pop tag     192.168.23.0/24   0        Et0/0      192.168.35.3
19     17          192.168.100.2/32  8880     Et0/0      192.168.35.3
20     Pop tag     192.168.100.3/32  10819    Et0/0      192.168.35.3
21     20          192.168.100.4/32  1592     Et1/0      192.168.56.6
23     21          192.168.100.7/32  1344     Et1/0      192.168.56.6
```

Between ASBR1 and ASBR2, the only label exchange method is BGP. When PE1's address is advertised in eBGP to ASBR2, a BGP label (19) is assigned to it. Note that this label is the local label in Example 10-55 for 192.168.100.2/32. Example 10-56 shows the BGP labels on ASBR2.

Example 10-56 *BGP Label on ASBR2*

```
ASBR2#show ip bgp label
Network          Next Hop        In Label/Out Label
192.168.100.2/32 192.168.56.5    24/19
192.168.100.3/32 192.168.56.5    25/20
192.168.100.4/32 192.168.67.7    20/nolabel
192.168.100.7/32 192.168.67.7    21/nolabel
```

When ASBR2 advertises PE1's address to RR2, the BGP next hop is set to ASBR2. Because iBGP plus labels is used in AS 200, the BGP label 24 is advertised for the address. RR2 does not modify the BGP next hop (standard RR practice). The same label is sent to PE2 via iBGP. Example 10-57 shows the BGP label on PE2. PE2 uses this label (24) to reach PE1 (192.168.100.2) via ASBR2 (192.168.100.6).

Example 10-57 *BGP Label on PE2*

```
PE2#show ip bgp label
Network          Next Hop        In Label/Out Label
192.168.100.2/32 192.168.100.6   nolabel/24
192.168.100.3/32 192.168.100.6   nolabel/25
```

In addition to the BGP prefixes, ASBR2 is also part of the OSPF domain in AS 200. It distributes an IGP label, Implicit-Null, to RR2. Example 10-58 shows the LFIB on RR2 for 192.168.100.6 (ASBR2), where PHP occurs.

Example 10-58 *LFIB on RR2*

```
RR2#show tag forwarding
Local  Outgoing    Prefix           Bytes tag  Outgoing   Next Hop
tag    tag or VC   or Tunnel Id     switched   interface
16     Pop tag     192.168.100.4/32 10898      Et1/0      192.168.47.4
17     Pop tag     192.168.56.0/24  2642       Et0/0      192.168.67.6
18     Pop tag     192.168.100.6/32 6672       Et0/0      192.168.67.6
```

Similarly, RR2 assigns an IGP label (18) to reach ASBR2 and distributes the binding to PE2. Example 10-59 shows the LFIB on PE2.

Example 10-59 *LFIB on PE2*

```
PE2#show tag forwarding
Local  Outgoing    Prefix           Bytes tag  Outgoing   Next Hop
tag    tag or VC   or Tunnel Id     switched   interface
16     Pop tag     192.168.100.7/32 0          Et1/0      192.168.47.7
18     Pop tag     192.168.67.0/24  0          Et1/0      192.168.47.7
19     17          192.168.56.0/24  0          Et1/0      192.168.47.7
20     18          192.168.100.6/32 0          Et1/0      192.168.47.7
```

Example 10-60 shows the label stack for the VPNv4 prefix 172.16.0.0 on PE2. The top label, 18, is used to reach ASBR2 via RR2 (192.168.47.7); the middle label, 24, is used to reach PE1 via ASBR2; and the bottom label, 24, is used to reach VPNa via PE1.

Example 10-60 *Label Stack on PE2*

```
PE2#show ip cef vrf VPNa 172.16.0.0
172.16.0.0/16, version 16, epoch 0, cached adjacency 192.168.47.7
0 packets, 0 bytes
  tag information set
    local tag: VPN-route-head
    fast tag rewrite with Et1/0, 192.168.47.7, tags imposed: {18 24 24}
  via 192.168.100.2, 0 dependencies, recursive
    next hop 192.168.47.7, Ethernet1/0 via 192.168.100.2/32
    valid cached adjacency
    tag rewrite with Et1/0, 192.168.47.7, tags imposed: {18 24 24}
```

Figure 10-33 shows the label-forwarding path from PE2 to PE1. Because of PHP, the top label is popped at RR1 and RR2.

Figure 10-33 *Label-Forwarding Path*

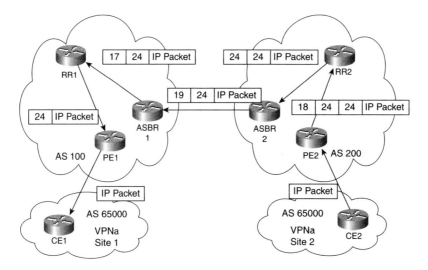

Summary

When BGP is extended with multiprotocol capabilities, VPNv4 prefixes can be carried within BGP. BGP multiprotocol extension makes it possible to support VPNv4 prefixes, extended communities, and BGP labels for IPv4 prefixes.

MPLS is a service-enabling technology that allows connection-oriented packet forwarding along a preestablished label path. MPLS VPN is a VPN service that is provisioned over an MPLS network.

Depending on the requirements, various VPN connection models are available. A basic Layer 3 VPN uses iBGP to exchange VPN information, yet an inter-AS VPN may involve a combination of iBGP and eBGP. The carrier's carrier VPN model allows a VPN provider to carry full Internet routes and provide hierarchical VPN services.

This chapter explores the various aspects of multiprotocol BGP and interdomain multicast:

- Multicast fundamentals
- Interdomain multicast
- Case study: Service provider multicast deployment

CHAPTER 11

Multiprotocol BGP and Interdomain Multicast

This chapter begins with an overview of the fundamentals of IP multicast that are the foundation of the coverage of Multicast Source Discovery Protocol (MSDP) and its counterpart, Multicast Extensions for Multiprotocol BGP. The chapter concludes with a case study detailing the deployment of interdomain multicast in a service provider network. The case study covers the internal architecture of the multicast deployment, the customer connectivity options for multicast services, and interdomain multicast connectivity.

Multicast Fundamentals

The traditional data delivery model for computer networks is unicast-based traffic streams. This model has a single receiver for the data stream. This data delivery method works very well for many types of communication, such as web pages and e-mail. However, with another class of communication, this data delivery model faces serious scaling issues. An example of this class of communication is real-time or live multimedia streaming. The inefficient traffic pattern shown in Figure 11-1 results in a linear increase in traffic on the network for each additional receiver that joins the stream. This inefficiency can be resolved through implementing Multicast Distribution Trees.

Multicast Distribution Trees

The concept of IP multicast is that sending source(s) and listeners form a group. A spanning tree connecting all the listeners or receivers that use the source as the root employs a different distribution model than unicast-based traffic streams. At each branch of the tree, the data is replicated and forwarded down each branch. This model of data delivery is shown in Figure 11-2.

Figure 11-1 *Unicast Delivery Model Inefficiencies*

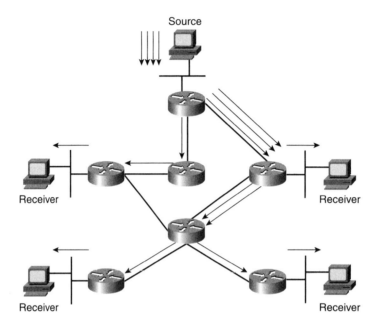

Figure 11-2 *Multicast Delivery Model Efficiency Gains*

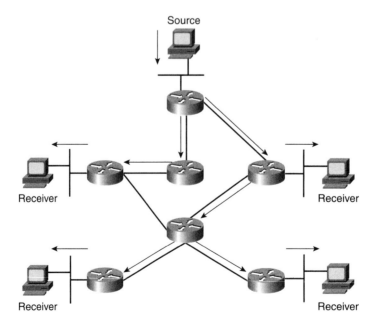

Using a Multicast Distribution Tree (MDT) results in a significant reduction of data traffic and solves the scaling issue of linear traffic growth across the network. The source itself is required to send only a single stream, which is replicated at each branch of the distribution tree. This process distributes the load of generating the additional data and optimizes the location of the data replication by moving it as close to the receiver as possible.

This doesn't mean that multicast-based delivery has no scaling issues. The primary issues are fan-out and packet replication, as shown in Figure 11-3.

Figure 11-3 *Multicast Data Replication*

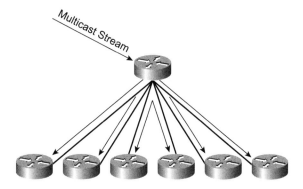

On many platforms, packet replication is handled in hardware, thereby minimizing the performance impact.

Multicast Group Notation

A multicast group is identified using a Class D IPv4 address that is in the range 224.0.0.0/4. The group is used in place of the destination address in the IPv4 packet. The source address field of the IPv4 packet is the IP address of the actual source of the stream.

There are two ways to define a particular multicast stream. The first is by group only. This is notated by (*,G), pronounced "star comma G." This notation refers to a particular group (G) and includes all sources sending to that group. This notation is used when working with a shared tree or an MDT that is shared by all sources sending to a single group.

The second way of identifying a stream is by the source and group pair. This is notated by (S,G), pronounced "S comma G." This is a more specific case of (*,G) in that it includes data from only a single source. The (S,G) notation is used when working with a source tree or with an MDT that is used by a single source sending to a specific group. It is common to use the term Shortest Path Tree (SPT) when discussing source trees.

In a router, it is not possible for (S,G) entries to exist without a (*,G). However, it is possible for (*,G) entries to exist without an (S,G). Traffic is forwarded using a matching (S,G) entry if it exists, because it is more specific than the (*,G) entry.

Shared Tree

The *shared tree* is a multicast distribution tree that is not specific to a single source. It is used by any source that does not have its own source-specific distribution tree. To build a shared tree, there must be a device that is the shared root for the tree, as shown in Figure 11-4.

Figure 11-4 *Shared Tree Distribution Tree*

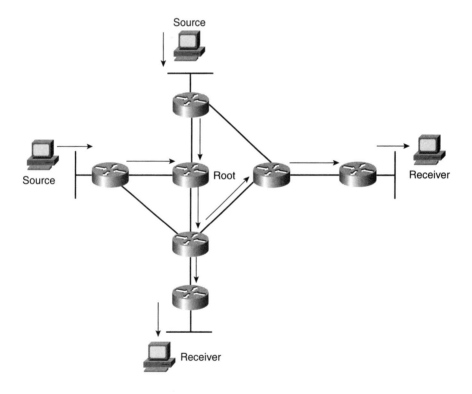

The shared tree is built from the receivers to the root. However, the traffic from the sources must arrive at the shared root before it can be forwarded down the shared tree. This topic is covered in greater detail during the discussion of Protocol-Independent Multicast Sparse Mode (PIM-SM). Traffic arrives at the router inbound from the interface that faces back toward the shared root. Traffic is delivered to the rest of the MDT ports other than the arrival interface.

Source Tree

A source tree, or SPT, is defined by an (S,G) entry in the multicast route table. This tree is specific to a single source, and only multicast packets from this source are forwarded down the source tree. Figure 11-5 shows an example of multiple sources each using their own SPT.

Figure 11-5 *Source Tree Distribution Tree*

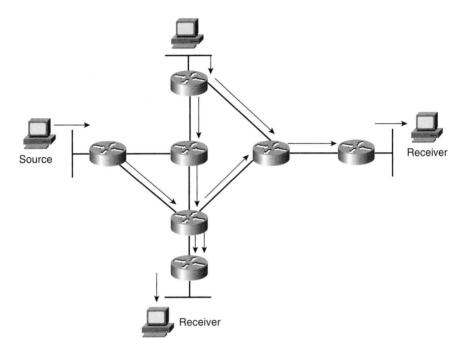

In Figure 11-5, each source has its own distribution tree. Even if some portions overlap, there are separate trees with separate forwarding information. These forwarding trees are not combined. Traffic arrives at the router on the interface that faces back toward the source. Traffic is sent out the interfaces in the MDT other than the interface on which it arrived. If an (S,G) does not exist, the (*,G) entry is used.

Building Multicast Distribution Trees

The primary protocol for building MDTs is Protocol-Independent Multicast (PIM). Unlike its predecessor, Distance Vector Multicast Routing Protocol (DVMRP), PIM relies on the unicast routing protocol to provide topological information. This chapter does not discuss DVMRP, because PIM is the recommended protocol for deploying IP multicast.

PIM has two modes of operation, Dense Mode and Sparse Mode. PIM Dense Mode is based on a flood-and-prune methodology, whereby IP multicast traffic is floodcd out all PIM adjacencies, and unwanted streams are pruned. PIM Sparse Mode is based on an explicit join methodology, whereby IP multicast traffic is forwarded down an adjacency only when it has been explicitly requested.

On each router, an MDT is composed of an Incoming Interface (IIF) and an Outgoing Interface List (OIL). The IIF is based on the Reverse Path Forwarding (RPF) information for the particular (*,G) or (S,G). The source address of arriving IP multicast packets is used for the RPF check, which is a paradigm shift from standard unicast routing. The RPF information for an (S,G) indicates which interface is used to send traffic to the source via the shortest path. This information is typically derived from the IGP. The RPF information for a (*,G) uses the address of the Rendezvous Point (RP) instead of the source address. The RP is the root of the shared tree in PIM-SM. Rendezvous points are covered in further detail in the "Sparse Mode" section. Figure 11-6 shows an example of RPF.

Figure 11-6 *Multicast Reverse Path Forwarding*

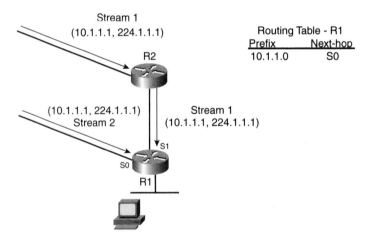

Figure 11-6 shows two copies of the same (S,G) arriving at R1. The first stream, Stream 1, arrives on port S1 on R1. The source is 10.1.1.1. The routing table on R1 says the next hop to 10.1.1.1 is through port S0. The stream arriving on port S1 fails the RPF check because it arrives on a different interface than the path back to the source. Stream 2 arrives on port S0 and passes the RPF check. R1 prunes Stream 1 and forwards Stream 2 to the locally connected receiver.

Dense Mode

When operating in dense mode, the PIM protocol uses a "push" methodology. Multicast traffic is flooded out all PIM-DM adjacencies every 3 minutes, creating state for every (S,G) in every router in the network. Unwanted traffic is pruned. This process repeats every 3 minutes.

The configuration to enable PIM-DM is minimal. Multicast routing must be enabled on every node in the network using the global configuration command **ip multicast-routing**.

Every interface in the network must have PIM-DM enabled to allow PIM adjacencies to form. The purpose of PIM adjacencies is very similar to IGP adjacencies, in that they define the available interfaces on which MDTs can be built. This is enabled with the interface configuration command **ip pim dense-mode**.

Another command also enables PIM-DM, but with the addition of an RP, the network converts to Sparse Mode (PIM-SM). This interface configuration command is **ip pim sparse-dense-mode**.

It is recommended that you enable PIM Sparse/Dense Mode rather than just PIM-DM, thereby allowing an RP to be configured to migrate the network to PIM-SM. With PIM-DM, traffic is forwarded down source trees. The RPF function is performed against the source address only, because a PIM-DM network has no shared root.

PIM-DM Example

This section describes the operation of a PIM-DM network. Figure 11-7 shows the network's initial topology. The focus of this example is at a high level. It doesn't delve too deeply into the state details.

Figure 11-7 *Initial Topology for the PIM-DM Network*

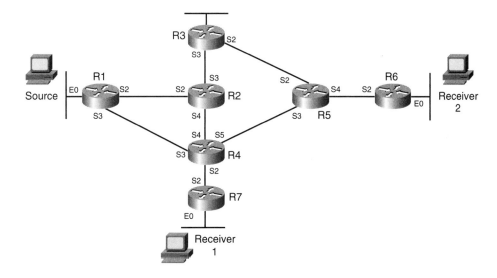

In the initial topology, two receivers are inactive, and there is a single inactive source. The first device to join the multicast group is Receiver 1. However, the upstream router does not know anything about the requested group. There is no source online, so no multicast traffic has been flooded to the router to create state. Example 11-1 shows the multicast state for the upstream router from Receiver 1.

Example 11-1 *Multicast State on R7 for Group 224.1.1.1*

```
R7#show ip mroute 224.1.1.1
IP Multicast Routing Table
Flags: D - Dense, S - Sparse, B - Bidir Group, s - SSM Group, C - Connected,
       L - Local, P - Pruned, R - RP-bit set, F - Register flag,
       T - SPT-bit set, J - Join SPT, M - MSDP created entry,
       X - Proxy Join Timer Running, A - Candidate MSDP Advertisement,
       U - URD, I - Received Source Specific Host Report, Z - Multicast Tunnel
       Y - Joined MDT-data group, y - Sending to MDT-data group
Outgoing interface flags: H - Hardware switched
 Timers: Uptime/Expires
 Interface state: Interface, Next-Hop or VCD, State/Mode

(*, 224.1.1.1), 00:00:15/00:02:46, RP 0.0.0.0, flags: DC
  Incoming interface: Null, RPF nbr 0.0.0.0
  Outgoing interface list:
    Serial2/0, Forward/Dense, 00:00:15/00:00:00
    Ethernet0/0, Forward/Dense, 00:00:15/00:00:00
```

In Example 11-1, the multicast state information for group 224.1.1.1 indicates the existence of the group with the (*,G) entry. However, the lack of an (S,G) means that this group has no source. This means that the receiver has joined the group, but no source is online.

The source comes online, sending traffic to its upstream router. This traffic is flooded through the network; Receiver 1 now receives the traffic stream. The flooded traffic is shown in Figure 11-8.

The traffic is sent to several routers that have no downstream receivers, either directly or indirectly. This traffic is pruned to ensure that traffic is forwarded down the tree to only listening stations. However, state is maintained in all routers for the multicast group. The PIM-DM pruning is shown in Figure 11-9.

Figure 11-8 *Initial Traffic Flooding in the PIM-DM Network*

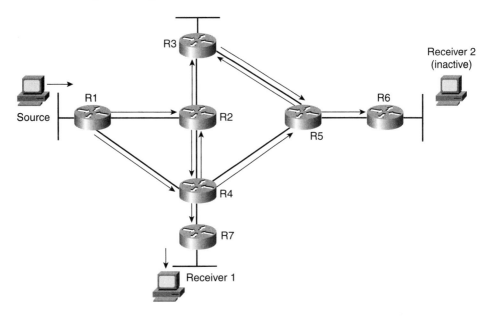

Figure 11-9 *PIM-DM Network Traffic Pruning*

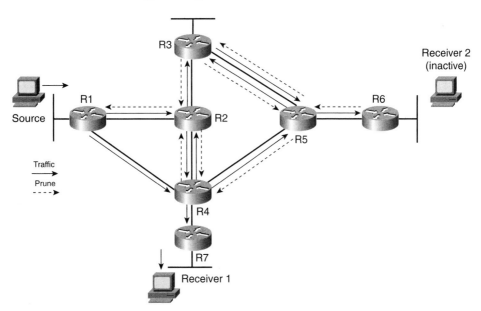

Example 11-2 shows the state for the (S,G) on Receiver 1's upstream. The traffic is forwarded out Ethernet0/0 to the receiver.

Example 11-2 *Operational MDT for Group 224.1.1.1*

```
R7#show ip mroute 224.1.1.1
IP Multicast Routing Table
Flags: D - Dense, S - Sparse, B - Bidir Group, s - SSM Group, C - Connected,
       L - Local, P - Pruned, R - RP-bit set, F - Register flag,
       T - SPT-bit set, J - Join SPT, M - MSDP created entry,
       X - Proxy Join Timer Running, A - Candidate MSDP Advertisement,
       U - URD, I - Received Source Specific Host Report, Z - Multicast Tunnel
       Y - Joined MDT-data group, y - Sending to MDT-data group
Outgoing interface flags: H - Hardware switched
 Timers: Uptime/Expires
 Interface state: Interface, Next-Hop or VCD, State/Mode

(*, 224.1.1.1), 00:05:35/stopped, RP 0.0.0.0, flags: DC
  Incoming interface: Null, RPF nbr 0.0.0.0
  Outgoing interface list:
    Serial2/0, Forward/Dense, 00:05:35/00:00:00
    Ethernet0/0, Forward/Dense, 00:05:35/00:00:00

(10.5.1.5, 224.1.1.1), 00:02:51/00:02:44, flags: T
  Incoming interface: Serial2/0, RPF nbr 10.2.1.25
  Outgoing interface list:
    Ethernet0/0, Forward/Dense, 00:02:51/00:00:00
```

In Example 11-2, the source has come online, and the traffic has been flooded. The updated state information shows the (S,G) entry as well as the (*,G) entry. The incoming interface for the (S,G) is Serial2/0. The (*,G) entry is not used to forward multicast traffic when PIM operates in dense mode. The incoming interface for the (*,G) is always Null.

Example 11-3 shows the state for the (S,G) on Receiver 2's upstream. The state exists, but the OIL is empty. This indicates that traffic for this (S,G) has been flooded to this router, but there is no local receiver. Nor is there a downstream receiver from this router.

Example 11-3 *Multicast State Maintained After Pruning*

```
R6#show ip mroute 224.1.1.1
IP Multicast Routing Table
Flags: D - Dense, S - Sparse, B - Bidir Group, s - SSM Group, C - Connected,
       L - Local, P - Pruned, R - RP-bit set, F - Register flag,
       T - SPT-bit set, J - Join SPT, M - MSDP created entry,
       X - Proxy Join Timer Running, A - Candidate MSDP Advertisement,
       U - URD, I - Received Source Specific Host Report, Z - Multicast Tunnel
       Y - Joined MDT-data group, y - Sending to MDT-data group
```

Example 11-3 *Multicast State Maintained After Pruning (Continued)*

```
Outgoing interface flags: H - Hardware switched
 Timers: Uptime/Expires
 Interface state: Interface, Next-Hop or VCD, State/Mode

(*, 224.1.1.1), 00:00:21/stopped, RP 0.0.0.0, flags: D
  Incoming interface: Null, RPF nbr 0.0.0.0
  Outgoing interface list:
    Serial2/0, Forward/Dense, 00:00:21/00:00:00

(10.5.1.5, 224.1.1.1), 00:00:21/00:02:42, flags: PT
  Incoming interface: Serial2/0, RPF nbr 10.2.1.29
  Outgoing interface list: Null
```

This flood-and-prune process repeats every 3 minutes for all multicast streams. When Receiver 2 comes online, R6 sends a Graft message upstream to build the MDT. This is possible because R6 maintains the (S,G) with the empty OIL from the flood-and-prune process, as shown in Example 11-3. The graft behavior is shown in Figure 11-10.

Figure 11-10 *New Receiver Grafting onto Source Tree*

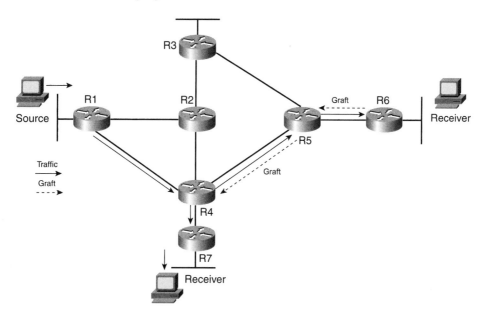

As shown in Example 11-4, the state on R6 is updated to forward traffic to Receiver 2 with the addition of the Ethernet0/0 interface to the OIL and the removal of the P flag (Prune) from the (S,G) entry.

Example 11-4 *Multicast State After Receiver 2 Joins 224.1.1.1*

```
R6#show ip mroute 224.1.1.1
IP Multicast Routing Table
Flags: D - Dense, S - Sparse, B - Bidir Group, s - SSM Group, C - Connected,
       L - Local, P - Pruned, R - RP-bit set, F - Register flag,
       T - SPT-bit set, J - Join SPT, M - MSDP created entry,
       X - Proxy Join Timer Running, A - Candidate MSDP Advertisement,
       U - URD, I - Received Source Specific Host Report, Z - Multicast Tunnel
       Y - Joined MDT-data group, y - Sending to MDT-data group
Outgoing interface flags: H - Hardware switched
 Timers: Uptime/Expires
 Interface state: Interface, Next-Hop or VCD, State/Mode

(*, 224.1.1.1), 00:02:12/stopped, RP 0.0.0.0, flags: DC
  Incoming interface: Null, RPF nbr 0.0.0.0
  Outgoing interface list:
    Ethernet0/0, Forward/Dense, 00:00:21/00:00:00
    Serial2/0, Forward/Dense, 00:02:12/00:00:00

(10.5.1.5, 224.1.1.1), 00:02:12/00:01:11, flags: T
  Incoming interface: Serial2/0, RPF nbr 10.2.1.29
  Outgoing interface list:
    Ethernet0/0, Forward/Dense, 00:00:21/00:00:00
```

The final multicast distribution tree is shown in Figure 11-11.

Figure 11-11 *Final MDT for the PIM-DM Network*

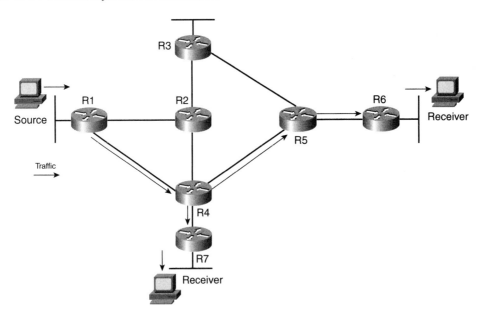

The flood-and-prune behavior is not graceful and can have a dramatic impact on network performance. A stable network has periodic traffic oscillations because of this flood-and-prune behavior. Also, PIM-DM does not work with MSDP and does not participate with interdomain multicast. It is generally recommended that you deploy PIM-SM and not PIM-DM for all environments.

Sparse Mode

The PIM protocol when operating in sparse mode (PIM-SM) uses an explicit join methodology with no periodic flood-and-prune. The flood-and-prune method of PIM-DM provides a way to inform all routers in the network of available multicast groups and sources. In PIM-SM, on the other hand, the concept of the Rendezvous Point (RP) is introduced as a way for sources and receivers to (as the name describes) rendezvous.

The RP knows about all sources and groups in the network. When a source begins sending, its immediate upstream router registers that (S,G) with the RP. When a receiver starts listening to a stream, if the upstream does not have a specific (S,G) or (*,G) for that stream, it builds a shared tree (*,G) back to the RP.

PIM-SM has a couple of advantages over PIM-DM. The flood-and-prune behavior is not used, thereby reducing network resource requirements. The second advantage is that, unlike PIM-DM, state is not maintained in every router for all (S,G)s, not even for those with no downstream listeners,.

The PIM-SM configuration is very similar to PIM-DM. Therefore, IP multicast routing must be enabled for the router with the global configuration command **ip multicast-routing**.

Every interface must be configured to enable the PIM protocol in sparse mode with the interface command **ip pim sparse-mode**.

In addition, every router must be configured with the RP's IP address by using the global command **ip pim rp-address** *address*.

It is very important that all routers agree on the same RP for any particular multicast group. Unlike PIM-DM, traffic can be forwarded using the (*,G) or a more specific (S,G). This means that for traffic forwarded using the shared tree, the RPF function is performed using the RP address. Traffic forwarded down a source tree using an (S,G) uses the source address for the RPF function.

PIM-SM Example

This example provides an overview of the operation of a PIM-SM network. Figure 11-12 shows the initial topology. This example focuses at a high level on how PIM-SM operates, without delving too deeply into the protocol state details.

Figure 11-12 *Initial Topology for the PIM-SM Network*

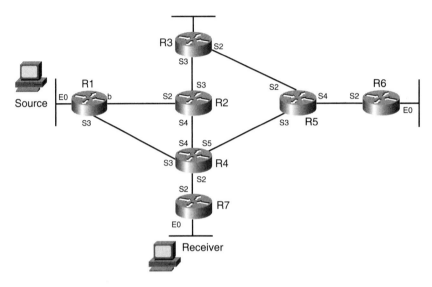

The first device to join the group is a receiver. The upstream router from the receiver knows the RP's address and builds the shared tree to the RP to allow any traffic for this group to flow to the receiver. Figure 11-13 shows the receiver's shared tree construction process.

Figure 11-13 *Receiver Joins the Shared Tree to the RP*

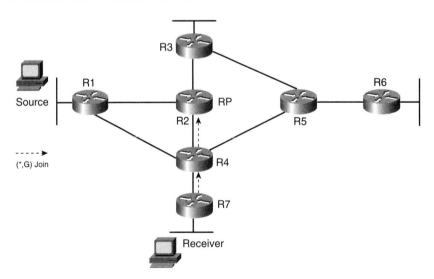

Example 11-5 shows the multicast state information for a router on the shared tree. R4 was chosen because it is where the shared tree and the source tree diverge. The OIL is populated, and the incoming interface is pointed back toward the RP. This state information is the shared tree being built from the receiver to the RP, where the receiver is expecting to rendezvous with a source.

Example 11-5 *Shared Tree State Information for 224.1.1.1 on R4*

```
R4#show ip mroute 224.1.1.1
IP Multicast Routing Table
Flags: D - Dense, S - Sparse, B - Bidir Group, s - SSM Group, C - Connected,
       L - Local, P - Pruned, R - RP-bit set, F - Register flag,
       T - SPT-bit set, J - Join SPT, M - MSDP created entry,
       X - Proxy Join Timer Running, A - Candidate MSDP Advertisement,
       U - URD, I - Received Source Specific Host Report, Z - Multicast Tunnel
       Y - Joined MDT-data group, y - Sending to MDT-data group
Outgoing interface flags: H - Hardware switched
 Timers: Uptime/Expires
 Interface state: Interface, Next-Hop or VCD, State/Mode

(*, 224.1.1.1), 00:00:28/00:03:06, RP 10.1.1.2, flags: S
  Incoming interface: Serial4/0, RPF nbr 10.2.1.10
  Outgoing interface list:
    Serial2/0, Forward/Sparse, 00:00:28/00:03:06
```

A source begins sending traffic to the multicast group. The first downstream router from the multicast source registers with the RP. The RP receives the special Register message that is sent via unicast, alerting it to the existence of a source. The Register message encapsulates the arriving multicast packets to ensure that no multicast packets are dropped while the RP is building the source tree to the source. The RP builds a source tree to the source. As soon as traffic begins to flow down the source tree to the RP, the RP sends a Register Stop message to end the registration process. At this point, the required MDTs for traffic delivery form. Figure 11-14 shows the register process and the construction of the SPT from the RP to the source. The traffic is sent from the RP down the shared tree to the receiver.

The MDT is shown in Figure 11-15.

Figure 11-14 *Source Register Process and RP Joins SPT to the Source*

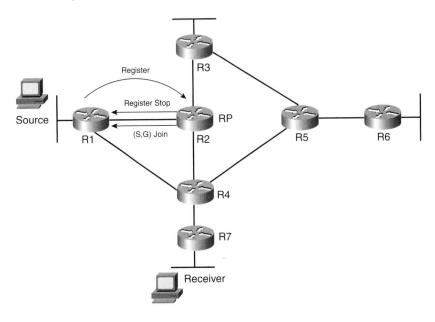

Figure 11-15 *Initial MDT*

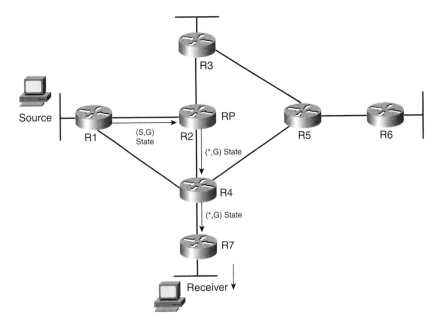

The multicast state information for R4 is shown in Example 11-6.

Example 11-6 *Multicast State for the Shared Tree and Source Tree on R4*

```
R4#show ip mroute 224.1.1.1
IP Multicast Routing Table
Flags: D - Dense, S - Sparse, B - Bidir Group, s - SSM Group, C - Connected,
       L - Local, P - Pruned, R - RP-bit set, F - Register flag,
       T - SPT-bit set, J - Join SPT, M - MSDP created entry,
       X - Proxy Join Timer Running, A - Candidate MSDP Advertisement,
       U - URD, I - Received Source Specific Host Report, Z - Multicast Tunnel
       Y - Joined MDT-data group, y - Sending to MDT-data group
Outgoing interface flags: H - Hardware switched
 Timers: Uptime/Expires
 Interface state: Interface, Next-Hop or VCD, State/Mode

(*, 224.1.1.1), 00:01:17/stopped, RP 10.1.1.2, flags: SF
  Incoming interface: Serial4/0, RPF nbr 10.2.1.10
  Outgoing interface list:
    Serial2/0, Forward/Sparse, 00:01:17/00:03:25

(10.5.1.5, 224.1.1.1), 00:00:16/00:03:16, flags:
  Incoming interface: Serial3/0, RPF nbr 10.2.1.5
  Outgoing interface list:
    Serial2/0, Forward/Sparse, 00:00:16/00:03:25
```

Example 11-6 contains an important detail in the incoming interface for the (*,G) and (S,G) for the 224.1.1.1 group. The (*,G) has an incoming interface of Serial4/0, whereas the (S,G) has an incoming interface of Serial3/0. This means that there is a more optimal path for the MDT for this particular source through a path different than down the shared tree. A process known as SPT switchover is used to transition traffic from the shared tree to the more optimal source tree. This divergence triggers the SPT switchover as soon as traffic rates reach a certain threshold. The default threshold is a single packet.

Because the optimal path for traffic destined for the receiver is not through the RP, the R4 is prompted to build an SPT directly to the source and prune this particular source from the shared tree. A special prune called an RP-bit prune is used to prune a single source from the shared tree or to prune from the (*,G) tree on an (S,G) basis. This special prune ensures that the entire shared tree is not pruned, because this would prevent the receiver from receiving any traffic sent down the shared tree from a new source. Figure 11-16 shows the SPT switchover process.

After the SPT switchover, the RP no longer forwards traffic from this particular source. The RP then prunes the SPT from the RP to the source. The new state information in Example 11-7 shows that the traffic has moved onto the SPT. You can see the indication that traffic is flowing down the SPT instead of the shared tree by comparing the flags for the (S,G) in Examples 11-6 and 11-7. The addition of the T flag means that the SPT switchover has occurred.

Figure 11-16 *SPT Switchover Process*

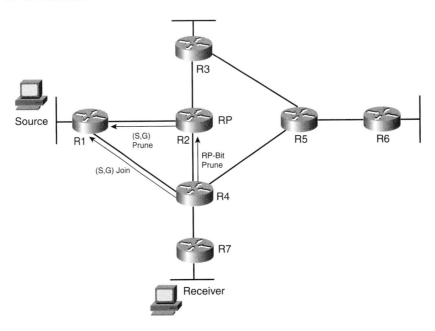

Example 11-7 *Source Tree State Information Indicates SPT Switchover on R4*

```
R4#show ip mroute 224.1.1.1
IP Multicast Routing Table
Flags: D - Dense, S - Sparse, B - Bidir Group, s - SSM Group, C - Connected,
       L - Local, P - Pruned, R - RP-bit set, F - Register flag,
       T - SPT-bit set, J - Join SPT, M - MSDP created entry,
       X - Proxy Join Timer Running, A - Candidate MSDP Advertisement,
       U - URD, I - Received Source Specific Host Report, Z - Multicast Tunnel
       Y - Joined MDT-data group, y - Sending to MDT-data group
Outgoing interface flags: H - Hardware switched
 Timers: Uptime/Expires
 Interface state: Interface, Next-Hop or VCD, State/Mode

(*, 224.1.1.1), 00:02:59/stopped, RP 10.1.1.2, flags: SF
  Incoming interface: Serial4/0, RPF nbr 10.2.1.10
  Outgoing interface list:
    Serial2/0, Forward/Sparse, 00:02:59/00:02:58

(10.5.1.5, 224.1.1.1), 00:01:58/00:03:25, flags: T
  Incoming interface: Serial3/0, RPF nbr 10.2.1.5
  Outgoing interface list:
    Serial2/0, Forward/Sparse, 00:01:58/00:02:58
```

The multicast state information on the RP indicates that the SPT to the source 10.5.1.5 has been pruned. The pruning is shown in Example 11-8 where the (S,G) has the P flag set, and no OIL. The RP must maintain information about this particular source so that other receivers can join. State is maintained to allow the RP to rebuild the SPT to the source, if needed, much like grafts in PIM-DM.

Example 11-8 *Multicast State Information on the RP Indicates That SPT Has Been Pruned After SPT Switchover*

```
R2#show ip mroute 224.1.1.1
IP Multicast Routing Table
Flags: D - Dense, S - Sparse, B - Bidir Group, s - SSM Group, C - Connected,
       L - Local, P - Pruned, R - RP-bit set, F - Register flag,
       T - SPT-bit set, J - Join SPT, M - MSDP created entry,
       X - Proxy Join Timer Running, A - Candidate MSDP Advertisement,
       U - URD, I - Received Source Specific Host Report, Z - Multicast Tunnel
       Y - Joined MDT-data group, y - Sending to MDT-data group
Outgoing interface flags: H - Hardware switched
 Timers: Uptime/Expires
 Interface state: Interface, Next-Hop or VCD, State/Mode

(*, 224.1.1.1), 00:04:33/stopped, RP 10.1.1.2, flags: S
  Incoming interface: Null, RPF nbr 0.0.0.0
  Outgoing interface list:
    Serial4/0, Forward/Sparse, 00:04:33/00:02:41

(10.5.1.5, 224.1.1.1), 00:03:33/00:01:34, flags: PT
  Incoming interface: Serial2/0, RPF nbr 10.2.1.1
  Outgoing interface list: Null
```

The final MDT is shown in Figure 11-17.

Figure 11-17 *Final MDT for the PIM-SM Network*

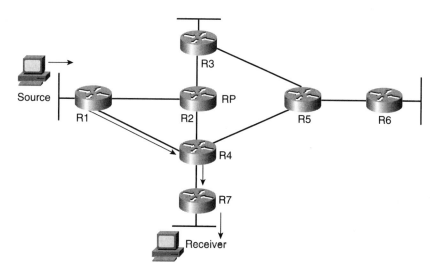

The topic of IP multicast is extensive. This section provided a high-level overview of how multicast routing works intradomain. The purpose of this overview was to cover the fundamentals you need to learn more about interdomain multicast.

Interdomain Multicast

In a multicast domain, the RP has knowledge of all active sources for that domain. When moving beyond a single multicast domain, knowledge of active multicast sources must be distributed to other domains. A possible solution is to have a global RP that is shared by the entire Internet. However, this would not scale for both technical and administrative reasons.

An initial solution located all RPs adjacent to each other at a Multicast Internet Exchange (MIX) running PIM-DM between them. This solution caused periodic flooding of multicast source information. However, this solution does not scale and places specific constraints on RP location. Figure 11-18 shows an example of using a MIX for interdomain multicast.

Figure 11-18 *Multicast Internet Exchange*

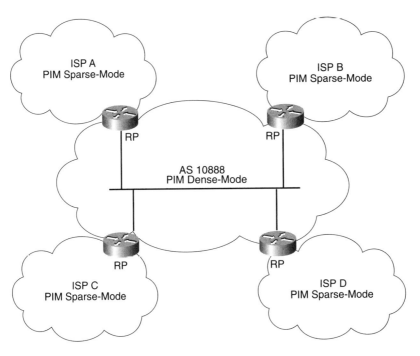

The next solution devised was to advertise active sources between RPs across multiple domains. This new paradigm spurred the development of Multicast Source Discovery Protocol (MSDP). The sole purpose of MSDP is to advertise the existence of remote (S,G)

information. This solution allows RPs to be located anywhere in the network and lets providers have independent RPs.

The other challenge is that not all autonomous systems in the Internet support multicast traffic. This means that an alternative source of RPF information besides the unicast routing table needs to be available for building MDTs. If the RPF for a specific (S,G) pointed toward an AS that does not support multicast, the MDT could not be built back to the source, and IP multicast would not function for that (S,G). The solution was the introduction of IPv4 multicast NLRI in BGP as a new SAFI. This multicast NLRI would provide an alternative database for performing RPF checking.

Multicast Source Discovery Protocol

The MSDP protocol provides a mechanism for interdomain multicast connectivity. The functionality provided by MSDP is the advertisement of active (S,G) information to remote domains. In a PIM-SM domain, the RP has information on all active (S,G) entries for that domain. The interdomain (S,G) advertisement challenge boils down to advertising active (S,G) entries between RPs in all participating PIM-SM domains.

MSDP is specified to operate over both TCP and UDP on port 639; however, all implementations use TCP. The control information advertised through MSDP is called a Source Active (SA) message. An SA contains three primary pieces of information:

- Address of the multicast source
- Multicast group address the source is sending to
- IP address of the originating RP

The RP for a particular (S,G) is the only router that can originate the SA message for that (S,G). A non-RP router is unable to originate SA messages and can provide only SA transit. The mechanism in MSDP to prevent the looping of SA messages is called *peer-RPF*. The peer-RPF function differs from RPF with respect to MDT creation. The peer-RPF function ensures that only SA messages received from an MSDP that is logically closer to the originator of the SA are accepted. When an MSDP router receives a new SA that passes the peer-RPF check, it floods that SA to all the MSDP peers other than the one on which it was received. The MSDP router caches all received SA messages. If an SA is received that is already in the cache, the MSDP router does not flood that SA. This prevents periodic reflooding of the same SA information.

The ability to perform peer-RPF requires MSDP to understand the logical topology back to the originating RP. This understanding of the logical topology allows MSDP to determine which peer is closest to the originating RP. MSDP does not contain any information internally to provide this topology; instead, MSDP relies on BGP. For MSDP to rely on BGP for topology determination, the MSDP peering topology should mirror the BGP peering topology. The peer-RPF rules are presented in the section "mBGP/MSDP Interaction."

Like multicast, the actual configuration of MSDP is deceptively simple. The configuration is simple, but the actual layout of the MSDP peering sessions is where the difficulty lies. The rule of thumb for MSDP peering session design is to mirror the BGP topology. This ensures proper SA propagation. The configuration of an MSDP peer is as follows:

ip msdp peer {*remote-address*} [**connect-source** *local-interface*] [**remote-as** *AS*]

remote-address is the remote peering address, and connect-source is the local peering address. This is analogous to BGP, with the neighbor address and update-source configuration settings. The **remote-as** value is optional, because MSDP can automatically derive that value based on the BGP peering information.

If only a single MSDP peering is used, a default peer can be configured. Using a default peer removes the need to perform peer-RPF checking, because there is no possibility of SA loops. The configuration of a default peer is

ip msdp default-peer *remote-address*

If multiple default peers are defined in the configuration, they are used for redundancy. The first one in the configuration is used. If it is unable to establish, the second one in the configuration is used. Multiple default peers are not all concurrently established. Only one is active.

Multicast NLRI in MP-BGP

The deployment of interdomain multicast is not pervasive, meaning that not all domains have deployed multicast. The lack of pervasiveness in multicast deployment results in noncongruent unicast and multicast topologies from an AS perspective. This lack of congruency can create scenarios in which an MDT attempts to form across a unicast-only domain. If the best path to a remote source is through a unicast domain, the MDT attempts to form in that direction using the normal RPF mechanisms. However, an MDT cannot form across a network that does not have multicast enabled, thereby breaking the interdomain multicast functionality.

The solution is to enable BGP through the MP-BGP extensions to carry separate NLRI specifically for use in performing RPF functions. This allows different path selection for the same prefix in the unicast RIB (uRIB) and the multicast RIB (mRIB), which maintains consistent unicast forwarding and allows interdomain multicast to function correctly. The mRIB is never used for unicast forward, but the uRIB can be used for multicast RPF checking. When performing the multicast RPF check, the mRIB is checked first. If there is no entry, the uRIB is checked. The multicast NLRI is carried in MP-BGP using an address family identifier (AFI) of 1, which indicates IPv4, and a subsequent address family identifier (SAFI) of 2, which indicates multicast NLRI.

The address family style of configuration is used when advertising multicast NLRI. This topic is covered in Chapter 10, "Multiprotocol BGP and MPLS VPN," for MPLS-VPN deployment. Configuration examples are provided later in this chapter, in the case study.

mBGP/MSDP Interaction

MSDP and BGP operate hand in hand. The acronym (m)BGP is used here to refer to a BGP session that is carrying either unicast, multicast, or unicast/multicast NLRI. This is because both multicast and unicast NLRI can be used for peer-RPF checking, with multicast NLRI taking precedence over unicast NLRI. The MSDP peering topology should mirror the BGP peering topology to ensure that proper peer-RPF checks are made.

There are six major peer-RPF rules for incoming SA messages based on the BGP and MSDP peering congruency. These rules are discussed in detail in the next sections. These six rules are broken down into three cases where a peer-RPF check is not required and three specific peer-RPF scenarios.

The peer-RPF check is not required when any of the following conditions are met:

- The sending MSDP peer is the originating RP for the SA.
- The sending MSDP peer is a mesh group peer.
- The sending MSDP peer is the only MSDP peer.

The peer-RPF check rules depend on the MSDP and (m)BGP peering congruency. The (m)BGP session with the same address as the MSDP peering session is identified. The type of BGP session, internal or external, is used to determine the criteria for performing the peer-RPF check. The following rules are used for the peer-RPF check:

- Rule 1: The sending MSDP peer is also an i(m)BGP peer.
- Rule 2: The sending MSDP peer is also an e(m)BGP peer.
- Rule 3: The sending MSDP peer is not an (m)BGP peer.

It should be noted that because the third rule indicates that there is no (m)BGP peer, the MSDP peering address does not match any of the (m)BGP peer addresses. There must still be an (m)BGP NLRI on the router for the SA messages to pass the peer-RPF check. This third rule just deals with the lack of a congruent MSDP and (m)BGP topology.

The next three sections examine these peer-RPF rules in more detail.

Peer-RPF Checking Rule 1: i(m)BGP Session

The router looks for the best path to the originating RP for the MSDP SA message. The mRIB is checked first, followed by the uRIB. If the path is not found, the RPF check fails.

If the path is found, the IP address of the BGP peer that sent the best path is compared to the MSDP peer address that sent the MSDP SA to the router that is performing the RPF check. If the peer addresses are the same, the RPF check succeeds. If they are different, the check fails.

Figure 11-19 shows an RPF check that succeeds.

Figure 11-19 *Successful iBGP-Based MSDP SA RPF*

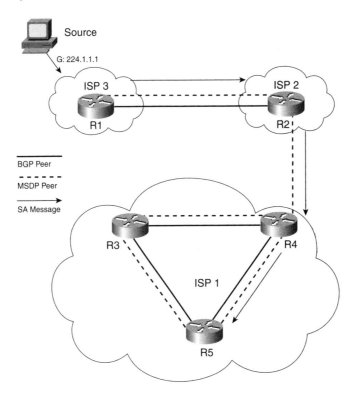

The MSDP SA shown in Figure 11-19, for the group 224.1.1.1, is received by R5 from R4, which are iBGP peers, using the loopback0 interface for both the iBGP and MSDP peering. The debug for the received MSDP SA is shown in Example 11-9. Using an i(m)BGP neighbor for the RPF, the RPF check passes for the SA received from R4.

Example 11-9 *MSDP Debugs Show That SA RPF Succeeds*

```
*Mar  3 09:21:19.691: MSDP(0): 10.1.0.4: Received 20-byte msg 31 from peer
*Mar  3 09:21:19.691: MSDP(0): 10.1.0.4: SA TLV, len: 20, ec: 1, RP: 10.1.0.1
*Mar  3 09:21:19.691: MSDP(0): 10.1.0.4: Peer RPF check passed for 10.1.0.1,
  used IMBGP peer
```

In Example 11-10, the BGP path information for the originating RP, 10.1.0.1, indicates that the best path was received from 10.1.0.4, or R4. According to the rules for RPF using an i(m)BGP peer, the source of the MSDP session needs to be 10.1.0.4, which it is, as indicated by the MSDP debugs shown in Example 11-9.

Example 11-10 *mBGP Best Path Selection for the Originating RP*

```
R5#show ip mbgp 10.1.0.1
BGP routing table entry for 10.1.0.1/32, version 4
Paths: (1 available, best #1, table Default-MBGP-Routing-Table)
  Not advertised to any peer
  2 3
    10.2.1.1 (metric 128) from 10.1.0.4 (10.1.0.4)
      Origin IGP, localpref 100, valid, internal, best
```

Figure 11-20 shows an RPF check that fails.

Figure 11-20 *Failed iBGP-Based MSDP SA RPF*

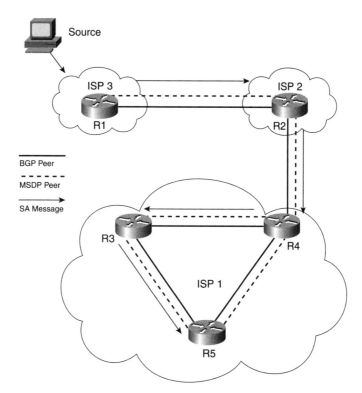

R4 receives the MSDP SA message for group 224.1.1.1. R4 then advertises this SA to both R3 and R5, which both accept the SA, because it passes the RPF check. However, there is also an MSDP peering between R3 and R5. R3 advertises the SA to R5, which you see in the debugs shown in Example 11-11. In this example, the RPF check fails. Example 11-10 indicates that the best path to the originating RP, 10.1.0.1, was received from 10.1.0.4 and not from 10.1.0.3, which is why the RPF check fails for the SA received from R3. The SA check was looking for a peer of 10.1.0.4 (R4) to pass the RPF check.

Example 11-11 *MSDP Debug for a Failed SA RPF Check*

```
*Mar  3 09:21:18.499: MSDP(0): 10.1.0.3: Received 20-byte msg 29 from peer
*Mar  3 09:21:18.499: MSDP(0): 10.1.0.3: SA TLV, len: 20, ec: 1, RP: 10.1.0.1
*Mar  3 09:21:18.499: MSDP(0): 10.1.0.3: Peer RPF check failed for 10.1.0.1,
  used IMBGP route's peer 10.1.0.4
```

Peer-RPF Checking Rule 2: e(m)BGP Session

The router looks in the BGP table for the best path to the originating RP. The mRIB is checked first, followed by the uRIB. If a path to the originating RP is not found, the SA fails the RPF check.

If the best path is found and the MSDP peer is the same IP address as an eBGP peer, the first AS in the AS_PATH for the best path to the originating RP is compared to the ASN for the eBGP peer that matches the MSDP peer. If they are the same ASN, the RPF check succeeds. If they are a different ASN, the RPF check fails. Essentially, this ensures that the upstream AS toward the originating RP is the same as the MSDP peer from which the SA was received.

Figure 11-21 shows an example of an RPF check that succeeds.

R5 receives the MSDP SA for group 224.1.1.1. This SA is received from R4 in AS 4. The MSDP SA RPF function is performed against an e(m)BGP peer. The MSDP debug shown in Example 11-12 shows that the RPF check for the SA received from 10.3.1.10 (the link address on R4) passes.

Example 11-12 *MSDP Debug for a Successful SA RPF Check on R5*

```
R5#
*Mar  3 09:58:18.291: MSDP(0): 10.3.1.10: Received 20-byte msg 101 from peer
*Mar  3 09:58:18.291: MSDP(0): 10.3.1.10: SA TLV, len: 20, ec: 1, RP: 10.1.0.1
*Mar  3 09:58:18.291: MSDP(0): 10.3.1.10: Peer RPF check passed for 10.1.0.1,
  used EMBGP peer
```

Figure 11-21 *Successful eBGP-Based MSDP SA RPF*

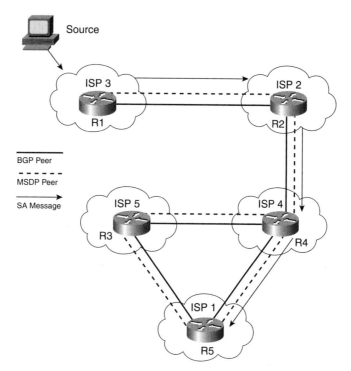

When the MSDP peer address is the same as the address of an EBGP peer, the RPF function is to ensure that the SA is received from the MSDP peer in the AS from which the best path to the originating RP is received. In Example 11-13, the first AS in the AS_PATH to the originating RP is 4. The MSDP peer from which the SA was received is 10.3.1.10, which is also the address of the EBGP peering with AS 4.

Example 11-13 *mBGP Information for the Originating RP*

```
R5#show ip mbgp 10.1.0.1
BGP routing table entry for 10.1.0.1/32, version 2
Paths: (2 available, best #2, table Default-MBGP-Routing-Table)
  Advertised to non peer-group peers:
  10.3.1.5
  5 4 2 3
    10.3.1.5 from 10.3.1.5 (10.1.0.3)
      Origin IGP, localpref 100, valid, external
  4 2 3
    10.3.1.10 from 10.3.1.10 (10.1.0.4)
      Origin IGP, localpref 100, valid, external, best
```

Figure 11-22 shows an RPF check that fails.

Figure 11-22 *Failed eBGP-Based MSDP SA RPF*

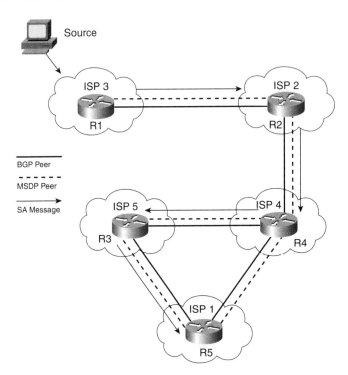

R4 sends the SA to R5 in AS 1 and to R3 in AS 5. R3 in AS 5 accepts the SA and advertises it to R5 in AS 1. The debug shown in Example 11-14 shows that this SA fails the RPF check. The reason is that the first AS in the AS_PATH to the originating RP is AS 4. The relevant BGP path information is shown in Example 11-13. The MSDP peer on which the SA was received matches an e(m)BGP peer with AS 5, failing the RPF check.

Example 11-14 *MSDP Debug for a Failed SA RPF Check*

```
*Mar  3 09:57:57.499: MSDP(0): 10.3.1.5: Received 20-byte msg 99 from peer
*Mar  3 09:57:57.499: MSDP(0): 10.3.1.5: SA TLV, len: 20, ec: 1, RP: 10.1.0.1
*Mar  3 09:57:57.499: MSDP(0): 10.3.1.5: Peer RPF check failed for 10.1.0.1,
  EMBGP route/peer in AS 4/5
```

Peer-RPF Checking Rule 3: No (m)BGP Session

If there is no matching (m)BGP peer when the check is performed on the IP address of the sending MSDP peer, a different set of criteria is used. The router checks for a best path to the originating RP. The mRIB is checked first, followed by the uRIB. If no path is found, the RPF check fails.

If a path to the originating RP is found, the BGP table is checked for a path to the MSDP peer. The mRIB is checked first, followed by the uRIB. If no path is found, the RPF check fails.

The originating (last) AS from the path to the MSDP peer is compared to the first AS in the path to the originating RP. If they are the same, the RPF check succeeds. If they are different, the RPF check fails. This procedure ensures that the MDT built to the domain originating the (S,G) passes through the AS from which the MSDP SA was received.

Figure 11-23 shows an RPF check that succeeds.

Figure 11-23 *MSDP SA RPF Succeeds Without Matching the BGP Session*

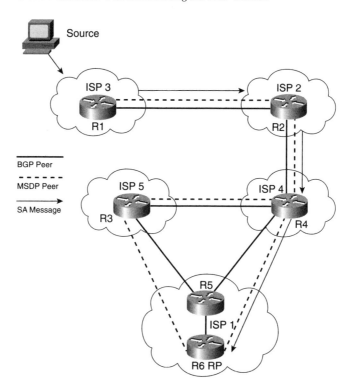

In Figure 11-23, there is an MSDP session between R6 and R4; however, there is no BGP session between these routers. An RPF check that requires the MSDP peer to match with a BGP peer would fail. However, the topology can be checked to prevent loops by ensuring that the next AS in the path to the RP is the AS in which the MSDP peer that sent the SA resides.

The MSDP debugs for the RPF check are shown in Example 11-15, which specifies e(m)BGP as the RPF mechanism. There are no e(m)BGP sessions on R6; the RPF check, however, passes.

Example 11-15 *MSDP Debug for a Successful SA RPF Check*

```
*Mar  3 10:22:35.739: MSDP(0): 10.1.0.4: Received 20-byte msg 13 from peer
*Mar  3 10:22:35.739: MSDP(0): 10.1.0.4: SA TLV, len: 20, ec: 1, RP: 10.1.0.1
*Mar  3 10:22:35.739: MSDP(0): 10.1.0.4: Peer RPF check passed for 10.1.0.1,
  used EMBGP peer
```

The condition to pass an RPF check without a direct relationship between an MSDP and BGP peering is that the first AS in the path to the originating RP must be the same as the last AS in the path to the MSDP peer that sent the SA. Example 11-16 shows the BGP path information. The first path in the AS_PATH for the originating RP is AS 4. The debug shown in Example 11-15 shows that the MSDP peer that the SA was received from is 10.1.0.4. The prefix for 10.1.0.4 originates in AS 4. Hence, the RPF check passes.

Example 11-16 *mBGP Best Path for Originating RP and MSDP Peers*

```
R6#show ip mbgp 10.1.0.3
BGP routing table entry for 10.1.0.3/32, version 4
Paths: (1 available, best #1, table Default-MBGP-Routing-Table)
  Not advertised to any peer
  5
    10.3.1.5 (metric 128) from 10.1.0.5 (10.1.0.5)
      Origin IGP, metric 0, localpref 100, valid, internal, best
R6#show ip mbgp 10.1.0.4
BGP routing table entry for 10.1.0.4/32, version 5
Paths: (1 available, best #1, table Default-MBGP-Routing-Table)
  Not advertised to any peer
  4
    10.3.1.10 (metric 128) from 10.1.0.5 (10.1.0.5)
      Origin IGP, metric 0, localpref 100, valid, internal, best
R6#show ip mbgp 10.1.0.1
BGP routing table entry for 10.1.0.1/32, version 2
Paths: (1 available, best #1, table Default-MBGP-Routing-Table)
  Not advertised to any peer
  4 2 3
    10.3.1.10 (metric 128) from 10.1.0.5 (10.1.0.5)
      Origin IGP, localpref 100, valid, internal, best
```

Figure 11-24 shows an RPF check that fails.

Figure 11-24 *MSDP SA RPF Fails Without Matching the BGP Session*

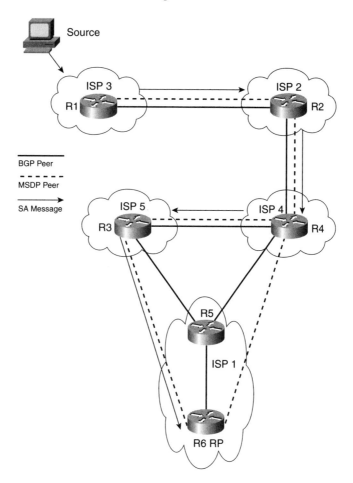

The MSDP SA for group 224.1.1.1 originated by the RP 10.1.0.1 is also received by R6 from R3 in AS 5. The MSDP debugs for the SA reception are shown in Example 11-17, where the RPF check fails. The SA is received from MSDP peer 10.1.0.3, for which R6 has no matching BGP session. The first AS in the AS_PATH for the originating RP (10.1.0.1) is AS 4, as shown in Example 11-16. The originating AS for MSDP peer 10.1.0.3 is AS 5. These do not match, which results in the RPF check's failing.

Example 11-17 *MSDP Debug for the Failed SA RPF Check*

```
*Mar  3 10:22:44.847: MSDP(0): 10.1.0.3: Received 20-byte msg 15 from peer
*Mar  3 10:22:44.847: MSDP(0): 10.1.0.3: SA TLV, len: 20, ec: 1, RP: 10.1.0.1
*Mar  3 10:22:44.847: MSDP(0): 10.1.0.3: Peer RPF check failed for 10.1.0.1,
  EMBGP route/peer in AS 5/0
```

Mesh Groups

In complex deployments, especially when RP Anycast is used, there might be a significant number of MSDP peering sessions in a single domain. The use of Anycast RP is covered in the case study. MSDP mesh groups optimize SA flooding within a domain. Figure 11-25 shows MSDP mesh groups in action. Configuration examples are provided in the case study.

Figure 11-25 *MSDP SA Flooding with Mesh Groups*

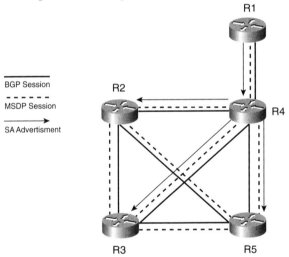

The concept of mesh groups is built on the assumption that all peers in the mesh group are fully meshed. This means that when a router receives an SA from a mesh group peer, it can assume that the sending MSDP peer also sent the SA to all other peers in that mesh group. It then floods the SA to any other MSDP peers that are not part of the mesh group on which the SA was received. The RPF check is not performed on SA messages received from a mesh group peer.

It is possible to have multiple mesh groups on a router. It is also possible to form mesh group loops that will result in a routing information loop. MSDP SA messages are not RPF-checked when they are received from an MSDP mesh group peer. An MSDP mesh group loop can be formed with three routers that are peers with each other in a full mesh, which is three MSDP peering sessions. If each MSDP peering session is configured as a different mesh group peer, a loop forms. The mesh group definitions are local to the router.

Route Reflection Issues

The use of route reflection can create problems with MSDP SA RPF checking. This is because the BGP peering addresses are used for the RPF check. Figure 11-26 shows how route reflection can interfere with MSDP SA RPF checking by diverging the (m)BGP and MSDP peering topology.

Figure 11-26 *Route Reflection's Impact on MSDP SA RPF*

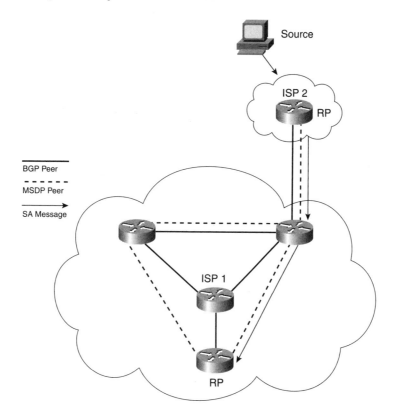

The main issue to watch out for with route reflection and MSDP peering is that the MSDP peering session does not correspond with the iBGP peer unless the RR is also part of the MSDP topology. In this case, the No BGP Session RPF rule is used instead of the iBGP

Session rule, which results in a peer-RPF failure. The AS_PATH to the originating RP is 2, and the AS_PATH to the MSDP peer is "". This results in a failure on the peer-RPF check, per Rule 3.

Case Study: Service Provider Multicast Deployment

This case study looks at the three aspects of deploying IP multicast.

The first aspect is the internal architecture. A deployment with a single RP is not redundant, because the RP is a single point of failure. The concept of RP Anycast is introduced to provide redundancy, using mesh groups to optimize SA flooding.

The second aspect is customer connectivity. There are multiple options for providing multicast service, depending on the level and type of redundancy. There is also the consideration of whether the customer has his or her own RP or will be using upstream ISPs RP.

The third aspect is interdomain connectivity. This section covers extending the local multicast service to allow customers to receive nonlocal multicast traffic streams and to allow remote access to customer-generated multicast data streams.

Anycast RP

So far, we have assumed a static configuration of RPs in all the routers. The need for RP redundancy is addressed by Cisco's Auto-RP, Bootstrap Router (BSR), and the development of MSDP, Anycast RP. The recommended method is Anycast RP, which is covered here.

The concept of Anycast RP is to configure multiple routers with the same IP address, making this address the network's RP. This results in a network with all routers agreeing on the RP's identity, but multiple routers acting as that RP. Sources register to the nearest RP, and the receiver's upstream routers build the shared tree to the nearest RP.

The problem is that the RPs used are not always the same. A receiver attempting to join a group might end up with a shared tree to an RP that does not know about the active source, which registered with a different RP.

The solution to this problem is to use MSDP between all the RPs to ensure that every RP contains all the active source information for the domain. Figure 11-27 shows a small core network with four RPs and the MSDP peering needed to provide a working deployment.

Figure 11-27 *RP Anycast Network Core*

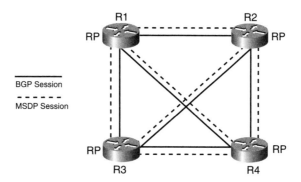

Example 11-18 shows the configuration using mesh groups from R1.

Example 11-18 *Mesh Groups from R1*

```
hostname R1
!
ip multicast-routing
!
interface Loopback0
 description RP Interface
 ip address 100.1.1.1 255.255.255.255
!
interface Loopback1
 description Router ID and Peering Source
 ip address 100.1.0.1 255.255.255.255
!
interface Serial2/0
 ip address 100.2.1.1 255.255.255.252
 ip pim sparse-mode
!
interface Serial3/0
 ip address 100.2.1.5 255.255.255.252
 ip pim sparse-mode
!
interface Serial4/0
 ip address 100.2.1.9 255.255.255.252
 ip pim sparse-mode
```

continues

Example 11-18 *Mesh Groups from R1 (Continued)*

```
!
router ospf 100
 router-id 100.1.0.1
 log-adjacency-changes
 network 0.0.0.0 255.255.255.255 area 0
!
router bgp 100
 no synchronization
 bgp router-id 100.1.0.1
 bgp log-neighbor-changes
 network 100.1.1.0 mask 255.255.255.0
 network 100.1.1.0 mask 255.255.255.255
 neighbor CORE_MESH peer-group
 neighbor CORE_MESH remote-as 100
 neighbor CORE_MESH update-source Loopback1
 neighbor 100.1.0.2 peer-group CORE_MESH
 neighbor 100.1.0.3 peer-group CORE_MESH
 neighbor 100.1.0.4 peer-group CORE_MESH
 no auto-summary
 !
 address-family ipv4 multicast
 neighbor CORE_MESH activate
 neighbor 100.1.0.2 peer-group CORE_MESH
 neighbor 100.1.0.3 peer-group CORE_MESH
 neighbor 100.1.0.4 peer-group CORE_MESH
 no auto-summary
 network 100.1.1.0 mask 255.255.255.0
 network 100.1.1.0 mask 255.255.255.255
 exit-address-family
!
ip pim rp-address 100.1.1.1
ip msdp peer 100.1.0.2 connect-source Loopback1 remote-as 100
ip msdp peer 100.1.0.3 connect-source Loopback1 remote-as 100
ip msdp peer 100.1.0.4 connect-source Loopback1 remote-as 100
ip msdp mesh-group CORE_MESH 100.1.0.2
ip msdp mesh-group CORE_MESH 100.1.0.3
ip msdp mesh-group CORE_MESH 100.1.0.4
!
```

In the configuration, the mesh group is a full mesh with the other RPs. The MSDP peering is sourced from the non-RP addressed loopback. This is essential to ensure that the MSDP sessions can form. It is also important to ensure that the BGP sessions are not sourced from the RP interface.

NOTE   This deployment has four routers, each configured with a loopback interface of the same address. If the RP address is used for the Router-ID, BGP sessions do not form, and the IGP might not converge. The BGP Router-ID and IGP Router-ID must be explicitly configured to avoid potential network impact.

Customer Configurations

The most common scenarios for providing customer connectivity are described here, with configuration examples. The scenario in which the customer uses the ISP's RP is not covered, because no MSDP/mBGP peering is involved.

The customer connectivity scenarios are

- MSDP default peer
- Multiple links, same upstream provider
- Multiple ISPs, dedicated unicast and multicast
- Multiple upstream ISPs, redundant multicast

MSDP Default Peer

As shown in Figure 11-28, this scenario illustrates a customer who has his own RP and a single link to his upstream provider.

Figure 11-28 *MSDP Single Peer Customer Connection*

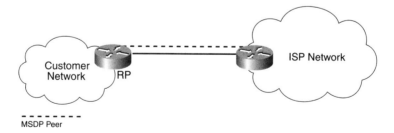

The customer configuration is shown in Example 11-19.

Example 11-19 *Customer Router Configuration*

```
hostname Customer
!
ip multicast-routing
!
interface Loopback0
 ip address 10.1.0.1 255.255.255.255
!
interface Ethernet0/0
 ip address 10.100.1.1 255.255.255.0
 ip pim sparse-mode
!
interface Serial2/0
 ip address 10.1.1.1 255.255.255.252
 ip pim sparse-mode
!
ip pim rp-address 10.1.0.1
ip msdp peer 10.1.1.2 connect-source Serial2/0
ip msdp default-peer 10.1.1.2
```

The provider configuration is shown in Example 11-20.

Example 11-20 *Provider Router Configuration*

```
hostname Provider
!
ip multicast-routing
!
interface Loopback0
 ip address 100.1.0.2 255.255.255.255
!
interface Serial2/0
 ip address 10.1.1.2 255.255.255.252
 ip pim sparse-mode
 no fair-queue
!
!
router bgp 100
 ...
 address-family ipv4 multicast
 ...
 network 10.100.1.0 mask 255.255.255.0
 network 10.1.0.1 mask 255.255.255.255
!
ip pim rp-address 100.1.0.2
ip msdp peer 10.1.1.1 connect-source Serial2/0
ip route 10.1.0.1 255.255.255.255 10.1.1.1
ip route 10.100.1.0 255.255.255.0 10.1.1.1
!
```

There is no need for (m)BGP, because there is a single MSDP peer, and no RPF checking is performed on the MSDP SA messages. The provider must inject the customer's networks into mBGP to ensure that RPF checking will work. The provider does not need to perform peer-RPF on the SA messages received from the customer, because the customer is the originating RP.

Multiple Links, Same Upstream Provider

As shown in Figure 11-29, this scenario illustrates a customer who has his own RP and multiple links to the same upstream ISP. The customer wants to use only one of the links for multicast.

Figure 11-29 *Multiple Links, Same Upstream Customer Connection*

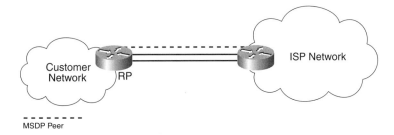

The customer configuration is shown in Example 11-21.

Example 11-21 *Customer Router Configuration*

```
hostname Customer
!
ip multicast-routing
!
interface Loopback0
 ip address 10.1.0.1 255.255.255.255
!
interface Serial2/0
 ip address 10.1.1.1 255.255.255.252
!
interface Serial3/0
 ip address 10.1.2.1 255.255.255.252
 ip pim sparse-mode
!
router bgp 65000
 no synchronization
 bgp log-neighbor-changes
```

continues

Example 11-21 *Customer Router Configuration (Continued)*

```
network 10.1.0.1 mask 255.255.255.255
network 10.1.100.0 mask 255.255.255.0
neighbor 10.1.1.2 remote-as 100
neighbor 10.1.2.2 remote-as 100
no auto-summary
!
address-family ipv4 multicast
neighbor 10.1.2.2 activate
no auto-summary
network 10.1.0.1 mask 255.255.255.255

network 10.1.100.0 mask 255.255.255.0
exit-address-family
!
ip pim rp-address 10.1.0.1
ip msdp peer 10.1.2.2 connect-source Serial3/0
ip msdp default-peer 10.1.2.2
!
```

The provider configuration is shown in Example 11-22.

Example 11-22 *Provider Router Configuration*

```
hostname Provider
!
ip multicast-routing
!
interface Loopback0
 ip address 100.1.0.2 255.255.255.255
!
interface Serial2/0
 ip address 10.1.1.2 255.255.255.252
!
interface Serial3/0
 ip address 10.1.2.2 255.255.255.252
 ip pim sparse-mode
!
router bgp 100
 ...
 neighbor 10.1.1.1 remote-as 65000
 neighbor 10.1.2.1 remote-as 65000
 !
 address-family ipv4 multicast
 ...
 neighbor 10.1.2.1 activate
 exit-address-family
!
ip pim rp-address 100.1.0.2
ip msdp peer 10.1.2.1 connect-source Serial3/0
!
```

There are two separate BGP sessions to the provider: an MP-BGP session for the multicast link (Serial3/0) and a regular BGP session for the unicast link (Serial2/0). The MSDP session is sourced from the multicast link's interface address. The mBGP NLRI ensures that the RPF function builds the MDT over the multicast-enabled link. The customer router injects the local prefix into BGP along with its RP address for remote RPF checks. The provider does peer-RPF against the e(m)BGP session to the customer. The customer doesn't need to do a peer-RPF check, because it has only a single MSDP session.

Multiple ISPs, Dedicated Unicast and Multicast

As shown in Figure 11-30, this scenario illustrates that the customer has his or her own RP and is connected to multiple ISPs. Only one of the ISPs offers multicast service. MSDP is deployed with mBGP to the ISP offering multicast service. Regular BGP is deployed with the ISP that does not offer multicast service.

Figure 11-30 *Multiple Upstreams, Dedicated Multicast*

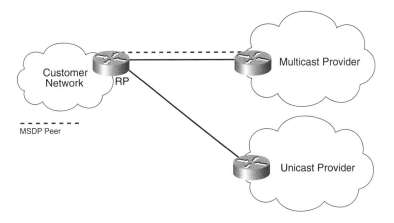

The configurations for this scenario are almost identical to the preceding scenario, except that the BGP sessions go to different providers instead of being attached to different links on the same router.

The use of mBGP ensures that the RPF resolves to the multicast-enabled ISP, which allows the MDT to form correctly.

Multiple Upstream ISPs, Redundant Multicast

As shown in Figure 11-31, this scenario illustrates that the customer has his or her own RP and is multihomed to two ISPs that provide multicast service. The customer wants to use both ISPs for multicast, using whichever ISP has the best path.

Figure 11-31 *Multiple Upstreams, Redundant Multicast*

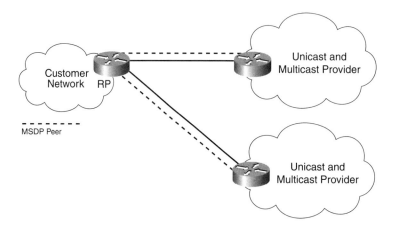

The customer's configuration is shown in Example 11-23.

Example 11-23 *Customer Router Configuration*

```
hostname Customer
!
ip multicast-routing
!
interface Loopback0
 ip address 10.1.0.1 255.255.255.255
!
interface Serial2/0
 ip address 10.1.1.1 255.255.255.252
 ip pim sparse-mode
!
interface Serial4/0
 ip address 10.1.3.1 255.255.255.252
 ip pim sparse-mode
!
router bgp 65000
 ...
 network 10.1.0.1 mask 255.255.255.255
 network 10.1.100.0 mask 255.255.255.0
 neighbor 10.1.1.2 remote-as 100
 neighbor 10.1.3.2 remote-as 200
 !
address-family ipv4 multicast
 ...
 neighbor 10.1.1.2 activate
 neighbor 10.1.3.2 activate
 network 10.1.0.1 mask 255.255.255.255
 network 10.1.100.0 mask 255.255.255.0
```

Example 11-23 *Customer Router Configuration (Continued)*

```
 exit-address-family
 !
ip pim rp-address 10.1.0.1
ip msdp peer 10.1.1.2 connect-source Serial2/0
ip msdp peer 10.1.3.2 connect-source Serial4/0
 !
```

The configuration for Provider A is shown in Example 11-24.

Example 11-24 *Provider A Router Configuration*

```
hostname ProviderA
!
ip multicast-routing
!
interface Loopback0
 ip address 100.1.0.2 255.255.255.255
!
interface Serial2/0
 ip address 10.1.1.2 255.255.255.252
 ip pim sparse-mode
!
router bgp 100
 ...
 network 100.1.0.2 mask 255.255.255.255
 neighbor 10.1.1.1 remote-as 65000
 !
 address-family ipv4 multicast
 ...
 neighbor 10.1.1.1 activate
 network 100.1.0.2 mask 255.255.255.255
 exit-address-family
!
ip pim rp-address 100.1.0.2
ip msdp peer 10.1.1.1 connect-source Serial2/0
!
```

The configuration for Provider B is shown in Example 11-25.

Example 11-25 *Provider B Router Configuration*

```
hostname ProviderB
!
ip multicast-routing
!
interface Loopback0
 ip address 20.1.0.3 255.255.255.255
```

continues

Example 11-25 *Provider B Router Configuration (Continued)*

```
!
interface Serial4/0
 ip address 10.1.3.2 255.255.255.252
 ip pim sparse-mode
!
router bgp 200
 ...
 network 20.1.0.3 mask 255.255.255.255
 neighbor 10.1.3.1 remote-as 65000
 !
 address-family ipv4 multicast
 ...
 neighbor 10.1.3.1 activate
 network 20.1.0.3 mask 255.255.255.255
 exit-address-family
!
ip pim rp-address 20.1.0.3
ip msdp peer 10.1.3.1 connect-source Serial4/0
!
```

The customer has MP-BGP sessions and MSDP sessions with both providers so that he can use whichever upstream ISP is closest to the multicast source, based on standard BGP path selection. The use of multiple MSDP peers requires the use of MP-BGP for MSDP SA RPF checking. The customer with two e(m)BGP sessions performs peer-RPF based on Rule 2.

Interdomain Connections

The interdomain MSDP sessions are handled by having the MSDP peering session form between the remote domain's RP and the border router with the connection to the remote domain. The border routers then MSDP peer with the RP, as shown in Figure 11-32.

The general rule of thumb for deploying MSDP is to run (m)BGP and ensure a congruent peering topology. This ensures that failures are handled correctly to ensure continued connectivity when external peering sessions fail.

Figure 11-32 *Interdomain Multicast Peering Placement*

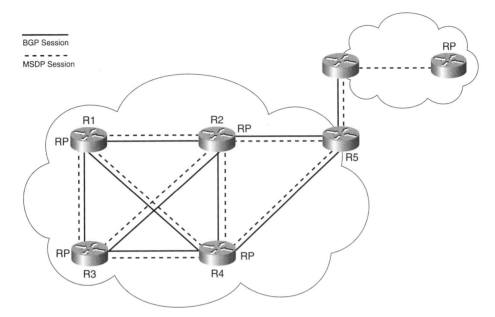

Summary

This chapter provided an overview of basic multicast operation, with a look at PIM Dense Mode and PIM Sparse Mode. The foundation for interdomain multicast is provided by the PIM-SM functionality. A protocol overview of MSDP and mBGP was also presented, with emphasis on their interaction and dependencies. The chapter concluded with a case study on deploying interdomain IP multicast in a service provider network.

This chapter focused on MSDP and mBGP from a deployment standpoint. A detailed discussion of IP multicast and PIM protocol internals is outside the scope of this book. Further information on IP multicast deployment can be found in the Cisco Press publication, *Developing IP Multicast Networks*, by Beau Williamson.

This chapter covers the following topics:

- IPv6 enhancements
- IPv6 addressing
- MP-BGP extensions for IPv6 NLRI
- Configuring MP-BGP for IPv6
- Case study: Deploying a dual-stack IPv4 and IPv6 environment

CHAPTER 12

Multiprotocol BGP Support for IPv6

The IPv4 protocol suite was developed in the late 1970s and early 1980s. It was designed for use in a moderately sized network. The network requirements of today are different from when IPv4 was designed. It is not so much that these requirements have changed, but that they have been increased because of the nature of the global Internet.

The primary goals during the design of IPv4 were to provide global reachability and fault-tolerant traffic routing. The nature of the Internet creates a need to provide increased levels of traffic differentiation for varying levels of traffic handling through quality of service (QoS), enhanced security requirements, a larger address space, improved address administration, and more efficient data handling in the forwarding path.

The IPv6 project began as an effort to resolve the potential for address exhaustion in the IPv4 address space and developed into providing a foundation for the next-generation Internet, capable of providing a worldwide communications and commerce medium. The migration to IPv6 will be the most significant transition for the Internet and corporate networks to date.

This chapter starts by covering IPv6 to provide a basis for understanding the BGP-specific information. The primary enhancements of IPv6 over IPv4 are discussed, followed by a look at IPv6 addressing. After a brief examination of IPv6 addressing, the BGP extensions to support IPv6 network layer reachability information (NLRI) are covered, including caveats that result from IPv4 information that is required for protocol operation. This chapter concludes with a case study on IPv4 and IPv6 in a dual-stack deployment.

IPv6 Enhancements

The development of IPv6 is an evolutionary step from IPv4. The last 20 years have brought to light a number of areas for improvement. The IPv6 protocol is very similar to IPv4 in most aspects. The enhancements can be classified into the following general categories:

- Expanded addressing
- Autoconfiguration
- Header simplification
- Security
- QoS

The next sections compare IPv4 and IPv6 in each of these categories.

Expanded Addressing Capabilities

In IPv4, addresses are 32 bits long. This creates the potential for approximately 4.2 billion addresses. However, a combination of factors have resulted in a significant inefficiency in address utilization:

- Subnet sizing
- Current address allocations
- Classful deployments
- One-eighth of the address space is reserved (Class E) or designated for multicast (Class D)

The IETF formed a working group, Address Lifetime Expectation (ALE), to determine the expected lifetime of the IPv4 address space in the early 1990s. The ALE working group predicted that the IPv4 address space would be exhausted between 2005 and 2011. The use of Network Address Translation (NAT) has extended this timeframe. The need for additional address space is felt most strongly outside the U.S.

IPv6 addresses are 128 bits long. Only one-eighth of the address space is assigned for unicast addressing. However, even one-eighth of the available address space is still virtually limitless from the perspective of network-addressable devices.

Autoconfiguration Capabilities

The IPv4 protocol was not designed with inherent address autoconfiguration capabilities. This prompted the IETF to develop Dynamic Host Configuration Protocol (DHCP) to decrease the administrative overhead involved in managing a large network. Automatic Private IP Addressing (APIPA) was added eventually to allow a host to automatically configure itself with a locally routable address. However, these autoconfigured addresses cannot be routed over the global Internet.

The IPv6 protocol lets a host automatically configure itself with a globally routable address. The autoconfiguration capabilities involve the use of Internet Control Message Protocol version 6 (ICMPv6) to determine the local subnet. The host then automatically configures a 64-bit portion of the address, called the *interface identifier*, to form a unique address, which can be globally routed.

Header Simplification

The IPv4 header format allows various options to be included directly in the IPv4 header. This results in increased processing during the forwarding of IPv4 packets.

In IPv6, the main header is a fixed 40 bytes in length. Additional extension headers and routing headers can be added after the main IPv6 header. The fixed header lengths provide simplified header formats and more efficient forwarding of IPv6 packets. This design also lets extensions to the IPv6 protocol be handled gracefully instead of hacking into the main header.

Security Enhancements

IPv4 does not contain built-in authentication or data encryption. The IPv4 protocol provides the ability to include checksum information to allow validation of data integrity. The ability to perform payload encryption is not inherent and is managed above the network layer.

IPv6 provides an Authentication Header (AH) to perform authentication, with the use of IPSec for data encryption using the Encapsulating Security Payload (ESP) Header. The ESP Header also can provide authentication, removing the need for both an AH and ESP Header when performing encryption and authentication. The ability to provide IPSec-based encryption is required for IPv6-capable hosts. The ability to carry a checksum is maintained at the transport layer with TCP or UDP. This provides authentication, encryption, and data integrity validation.

QoS Capabilities

IPv4 allows limited QoS information to be carried in the IP header. This QoS information is contained primarily in the 3 Precedence bits and 3 type of service (TOS) bits. The combined use of Precedence bits and TOS bits is called Differentiated Services Code Points (DSCPs), allowing a maximum of 64 DSCPs.

IPv6 provides 8 bits to store differentiated services information, which allows for 256 different classifications. This increased granularity for differentiating traffic improves traffic classification and more specialized data handling for advanced queuing and packet discard schemes.

IPv6 also provides a 20-bit Flow Identifier field, which can be combined with the IP source address to uniquely identify a particular data flow. This allows routers in the forwarding path to provide specialized treatment to an entire data flow without having to delve deeply into the packet headers to obtain enough information to differentiate between data flows. In IPv4, several fields at the network and transport layers are required to uniquely identify a data flow, increasing data processing in the forwarding path.

IPv6 Addressing

IPv4's addressing format is very simple compared to IPv6. IPv4 has unicast, multicast, and broadcast addresses. Unicast addresses are divided into classes, which are defined by the address's 3 high-order bits. These classes are relevant only when classful routing is performed. Multicast addresses occur when the address's 3 high-order bits are all 1s.

The IPv6 addressing format includes an increased level of aggregation, which is reflected in the addresses themselves using Aggregator Level fields. IPv6 has unicast, multicast, and anycast addresses. The broadcast address type has been removed. The additional bits in an IPv6 address allow much more information about the actual use and assigning authorities to be reflected in the address itself.

Anycast Address Functionality

The concept of an anycast address is formalized in IPv6. An anycast address has no special notation or format; it is a unicast address that has been assigned to multiple interfaces or devices. Data sent to any anycast address is delivered to the closest instance of that address as determined by the routing protocol. Informally, anycast functionality is available in IPv4, as discussed in Chapter 11, "Multiprotocol BGP and Interdomain Multicast."

General Address Format

In IPv4, addresses are 32 bits or 4 bytes in length and are typically represented in a dotted-quad format. In IPv6, addresses are 128 bits or 16 bytes and are represented in a colon-delimited fashion, with eight sequences of hexadecimal digits in 2-byte increments, as follows:

```
2001:0400:AAAA:BBBB:CCCC:DDDD:1234:5678
```

Working with IPv6 addresses is more cumbersome because of their length. It is much more difficult to differentiate between addresses at a glance. To make it easier to work with IPv6 addresses, you can abbreviate them when they contain two or more consecutive 0s. Here's a sample address with consecutive 0s:

```
2001:0400:0000:0000:0000:0000:1234:5678
```

The abbreviated form of this address is

```
2001:0400::1234:5678
```

You can abbreviate only a single sequence of consecutive 0s in an IPv6 address. If you tried to abbreviate multiple sequences of consecutive 0s, you would have no way to determine how many 0s should be inserted when expanding the address to its full length.

Another form of abbreviation is to leave out the leading 0s in each octet. An IPv6 address with leading 0s might look like this:

```
2001:0400:00AA:00BB:00CC:00DD:1234:5678
```

The abbreviated form of the address looks like this:

```
2001:400:AA:BB:CC:DD:1234:5678
```

You can abbreviate leading 0s only. You can't abbreviate trailing 0s. This is because if both leading and trailing 0s could be abbreviated, IPv6 devices would not know where to add back the 0s when expanding an abbreviated address to its full length.

There's another way to abbreviate an IPv6 address that contains a significant number of 0s. With multiple strings of consecutive 0s, one is compressed to a double colon, and the other has leading 0s compressed.

Here is an IPv6 address with multiple strings of consecutive 0s and leading 0s:

```
2001:0400:0000:0000:ABCD:0000:0000:1234
```

Here's the abbreviated address:

```
2001:400:0:0:ABCD::1234
```

Figure 12-1 shows the general format of an IPv6 address.

Figure 12-1 *Format of an IPv6 Address*

n bits	m bits	128 − m − n bits
Global Routing Prefix	Subnet ID	Interface Identifier

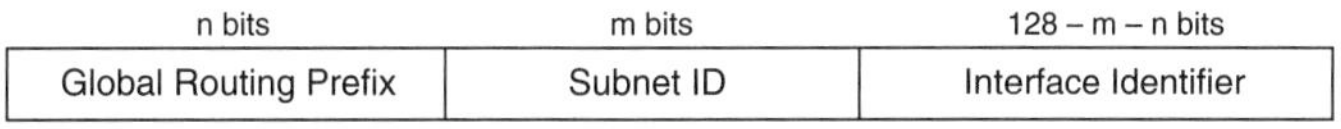

The actual type of IPv6 address defines the values for m and n in Figure 12-1. These fields are not a fixed length, but the total number of bits for each address is 128 bits. The type of address is defined by the prefix itself.

IPv6 has several types of addressing, such as link-local, site-local, globally aggregatable, and addressing formats for IPv4 and IPv6 compatibility. In IPv4, the entire address space is divided into Class A, B, C, D, and E space. An address's class is indicated in the first 4 bits of the address. The use of class membership for an address for the purpose of autosummarization is deprecated with classless routing and Classless Interdomain Routing (CIDR). Table 12-1 shows the original address classes for IPv4.

Table 12-1 *IPv4 Address Space*

Address Class	High-Order Byte	Address Space
Class A	0*XXXXXXX*	0.0.0.0/1
Class B	10*XXXXXX*	128.0.0.0/2
Class C	110*XXXXX*	192.0.0.0/3
Class D	1110*XXXX*	224.0.0.0/4
Class E	1111*XXXX*	248.0.0.0/4

The type of an IPv6 address can be determined by the high-order bits. The number of bits used to determine an address's type is variable. This set of high-order bits is also called the format prefix. The primary divisions of the IPv6 address space are shown in Table 12-2.

Table 12-2 *IPv6 Address Space*

Address Type	Binary Prefix	IPv6 Notation
Unspecified	00...0 (128 bits)	::/128
Loopback	00...1 (128 bits)	::1/128
Multicast	11111111	FF00::/8
Link-local unicast	1111111010	FE80::/10
Site-local unicast	1111111011	FEC0::/10
Global unicast	(Everything else)	—

Anycast addressing is taken from global unicast addressing and is no different from a unicast address syntactically.

Aggregatable Global Unicast Addresses

The term *aggregatable global unicast addresses* is really just a fancy term for normal unicast addressing using a globally routable prefix. Until recently, there was a complex hierarchical structure for aggregating global unicast addresses based on Top-Level Aggregators (TLAs), Next-Level Aggregators (NLAs), and Site-Level Aggregators (SLAs). However, this structure was recently deprecated by RFC 3587.

Local Addressing

IPv6 has two types of local addressing: link-local and site-local. Link-local addressing was designed to be used on a single link, which might be a point-to-point connection with only two hosts or a broadcast medium with hundreds of hosts. Packets containing a source or destination address with link-local scope are not to be forwarded to another subnet. The purpose of link-local addressing is to provide local connectivity, address autoconfiguration, and neighbor discovery on networks without a router present. The format of a link-local address is shown in Figure 12-2.

Figure 12-2 *Link-Local Addressing Format*

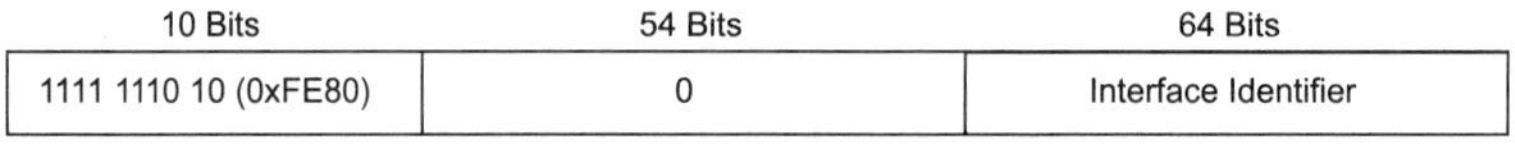

10 Bits	54 Bits	64 Bits
1111 1110 10 (0xFE80)	0	Interface Identifier

The value 0xFE80 in the first 10 bits of the link-local address is the global prefix that is allocated for link-local addressing. All link-local addresses begin with this prefix.

Site-local addressing was designed for use within a site. A site may consist of only a single link, or it might have thousands of links and devices. Site-local addressing is not globally routable, and there is no guarantee that a host with a site-local address is unique outside the scope of the site it resides in. Site-local addressing is the IPv6 equivalent of private addressing in IPv4. IPv6 traffic with a site-local source or destination address must not be forwarded outside the site. The format of a site-local address is shown in Figure 12-3.

Figure 12-3 *Site-Local Addressing Format*

10 Bits	38 Bits	16 Bits	64 Bits
1111 1110 11 (0xFEC0)	0	Subnet ID	Interface Identifier

The value 0xFEC0 in the first 10 bits of the site-local address is the global prefix that is allocated for site-local addressing. All site-local addresses begin with this prefix.

Interface Identifiers

Interface Identifiers are a component of unicast IPv6 addresses. The Interface ID is used to identify an interface on a link. The Interface ID must be unique over the subnet. Although it isn't required, it is recommended that the Interface ID be unique over the link. The case where an Interface ID may not be unique over a link is when multiple subnets are assigned to a single link.

All unicast addresses that do not begin with a binary format prefix of 000 must have a 64-bit Interface ID, which is constructed in Modified EUI-64 format. The construction of Modified EUI-64-based Interface ID is described in RFC 3513. When possible, the Interface ID is based on the 48-bit MAC address.

Special Addresses

Two special addresses have been defined for IPv6: the *unspecified address* and the *loopback address*. The unspecified address is 0:0:0:0:0:0:0:0, or :: in abbreviated form. Never assign the unspecified address to a node, because it indicates the absence of an address. A node may source packets with the unspecified address before it has fully initialized and obtained its own address. This is done as part of an address configuration process. Packets with a source or destination address set to the unspecified address should not be forwarded by an IPv6 router. The unspecified address should never be used as a destination address.

The loopback address is 0:0:0:0:0:0:0:1, or ::1 in abbreviated form. A node may use this address to send packets to itself. This address should be considered to have link-local scope over a virtual link from the node back to itself. Packets should never be sent by a node with either the source or destination addresses set to the loopback address. An IPv6 router should not forward packets that contain the loopback address as either the source or destination address.

MP-BGP Extensions for IPv6 NLRI

The deployment of IPv6 in a global network requires an Exterior Gateway Protocol (EGP) to provide full global reachability. The decision was to include support for IPv6 NLRI and to allow IPv6 transport for MP-BGP. This allowed the reuse of operational experience gained through years of work with BGP. The BGP extension to carry various types of routing information is called multiprotocol BGP, or MP-BGP. This functionality is discussed in Chapter 2, "Understanding BGP Building Blocks," in the section "BGP Capabilities."

The difference between BGPv4 and MP-BGP is the ability to carry prefix information for multiple protocols, such as IP multicast, CLNS, MPLS labels, IPv4 VPN, and IPv6. This information is advertised using address families. Prefix information is advertised using the BGP attribute MP_REACH_NLRI and is withdrawn using the MP_UNREACH_NLRI attribute.

The Address Family Identifier (AFI) for IPv6 is 2, and the Subsequent Address Family Identifiers (SAFIs) are 1 for unicast, 2 for multicast, and 3 for both unicast and multicast.

The next two sections discuss the concept of a dual-stack deployment with IPv4 and IPv6 running concurrently and the protocol impact of integrating IPv6 support into MP-BGP.

Dual-Stack Deployment

The term *dual stack* is frequently used when discussing IPv6 deployment. Dual stack refers to running IPv4 and IPv6 concurrently in the router or device. This is commonly considered the preferred method for migrating from IPv4 to IPv6.

The use of a dual-stack deployment places additional load on the routers in the network. There are increased resource requirements to maintain both the IPv4 and IPv6 routing tables. This includes separate RIBs and FIBs. Most likely, you will also need multiple IGPs.

In the case of BGP, there are increased memory requirements to maintain the additional prefix information. There is also additional processing to maintain more BGP peering sessions. You should configure separate BGP sessions for IPv4 and IPv6 prefix information. This ensures next-hop reachability for each address family.

MP-BGP for IPv6 Deployment Considerations

The mechanisms and techniques provided by BGPv4 are also available in MP-BGP for handling IPv6 NLRI. The decision process, scalability mechanisms, and policy features are not specific to IPv4 NLRI; they apply quite well to IPv6 NLRI. This means that route reflection, route dampening, BGP confederations, Multi-Exit Discriminator (MED), and outbound route filtering (just to name a few) are all unchanged for MP-BGP.

In general, BGP is protocol-agnostic. It runs on top of TCP, which is the same in IPv4 and IPv6. This means that the underlying network layer protocol can be either IPv4 or IPv6 without requiring any changes to BGP. However, two fields in BGP messages are IPv4-specific—router ID and cluster ID. Both are 4 bytes long.

The BGP Open message contains a field for the router ID. This field is 4 bytes long. There is no particular requirement that this address be reachable or even an actual IPv4 address, only that it be a unique 32-bit number.

The router generates the router ID automatically based on IPv4 addressing configured on the router, the address configured on the loopback interface, or, if there is no loopback, the highest IPv4 address on any of the interfaces.

In a pure IPv6 deployment, no IPv4 addressing is configured, providing nothing for the router to use in building a router ID. In this case, the router ID must be manually configured under the BGP process. If there is no router ID, BGP sessions do not form.

The other component of BGP that requires a unique 4-byte number is the cluster ID, used on route reflectors. The cluster ID is carried with the NLRI in the BGP UPDATE messages. If a router ID is configured, this value is used for the cluster ID. The cluster ID can also be configured independent of the router ID. The originator ID attribute is also a 4-byte value that is used with route reflection. The manual configuration of a 4-byte router ID provides the value for the originator ID.

The concept of autosummarization along classful boundaries does not exist in IPv6. Because IPv6 does not use address classes, the **auto-summary** command in BGP has no effect on IPv6 prefix information.

Configuring MP-BGP for IPv6

The BGP configuration for IPv4 and IPv6 is very similar. However, when you configure IPv6, the address family-style (AF-style) configuration is required. The AF-style configuration is used for all address families besides IPv4.

IPv6 forwarding is not enabled by default. This must be done explicitly in global configuration mode with the command **ipv6 unicast-routing**. Do this before configuring IPv6 routing.

BGP Address Family Configuration

BGP AF-style configuration is based on the concept of defining all the peering relationships or neighbors in the main BGP router configuration. These neighbors are then activated under the address family for each NLRI type that will be carried in this peering session. The IPv4 NLRI is on by default for all BGP sessions. You can disable the default behavior of carrying IPv4 NLRI on all BGP sessions using the **no bgp default ipv4-unicast** command. Example 12-1 shows a pure IPv6 deployment.

Example 12-1 *AF-Style Configuration for IPv6*

```
router bgp 65000
 no synchronization
 bgp router-id 10.1.1.5
 no bgp default ipv4-unicast
 bgp log-neighbor-changes
 neighbor 2001:400:0:1234::1 remote-as 65000
 neighbor 2001:400:0:1234::1 update-source Loopback1
 neighbor 2001:400:0:1234::2 remote-as 65000
 neighbor 2001:400:0:1234::2 update-source Loopback1
no auto-summary
 !
 address-family ipv6
 no synchronization
 neighbor 2001:400:0:1234::1 activate
 neighbor 2001:400:0:1234::2 activate
 network 2001:400:0:ABCD::/64
 exit-address-family
 !
```

Injecting IPv6 Prefixes into BGP

The process of injecting IPv6 prefix information into BGP is the same as for IPv4; however, it must be done under the IPv6 AF configuration. You can redistribute prefix information from another routing protocol or inject prefixes from the routing table using the **network** command.

Prefix Filtering for IPv6

The two primary methods of matching and filtering prefix information are access control lists (ACLs) and prefix lists.

ACLs are the most common form of prefix or packet filtering. When building ACLs for IPv6 prefix information, you must use named ACLs, because numbered ACLs are not supported. The initial implementation of ACLs for IPv6 supported only matching against source and destination addresses. However, in Cisco IOS Releases 12.2(13)T and 12.0(23)S, support was added to match against additional information. Table 12-3 shows the fields that the two implementations support. When you use ACLs for prefix filtering, only the source and destination addresses are relevant. It is also important to note that wildcard bits are not supported.

Table 12-3   *IPv6 ACL Field Matching*

Field	Before Releases 12.2(13)T and 12.0(23)S	Releases 12.2(13)T or 12.0(23)S and Later
Protocol		X
Source Address	X	X
Destination Address	X	X
Source Port		X
Destination Port		X
Flow-label		X
Fragment Header		X
Timeout		X
Routing Header		X
Sequence		X
DSCP		X

The prefix list functionality has been extended to support IPv6 route filtering. Prefix lists with IPv6 are used only for prefix filtering, not for packet filtering, just like IPv4 prefix lists. Example 12-2 shows an IPv6 prefix list.

Example 12-2 *IPv6 Prefix List Example*

```
ipv6 prefix-list FILTER_IN seq 5 permit 2001:400::/29
ipv6 prefix-list FILTER_IN seq 10 permit 2001:600::/29
ipv6 prefix-list FILTER_IN seq 15 permit 2001:800::/29
ipv6 prefix-list FILTER_IN seq 20 permit 3FFE::/16
ipv6 prefix-list FILTER_IN seq 25 permit 2002::/16
ipv6 prefix-list FILTER_IN seq 30 permit ::/80
ipv6 prefix-list FILTER_IN seq 35 deny ::/0
```

NOTE   Cisco IOS software automatically abbreviates IPv6 addresses if possible.

The preferred method of prefix filtering is the use of prefix lists. ACLs are used primarily for packet filtering.

Case Study: Deploying a Dual-Stack IPv4 and IPv6 Environment

This case study begins with a simple IPv4 network in a route-reflection environment. The steps to deploy IPv6 in a dual-stack configuration are discussed, and configuration examples are provided.

Initial IPv4 Network Topology

The initial IPv4 network is built using a route reflection environment. The network has three core routers—R1, R2, and R3. They are route reflectors and have a full iBGP mesh. The network also has three route reflector clients—R4, R5, and R6. The physical topology is shown in Figure 12-4.

Figure 12-4 *Physical Network Topology*

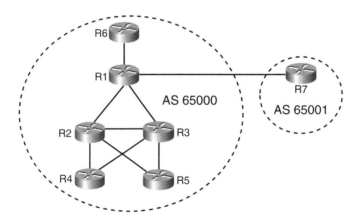

Each router has an IPv4 loopback address for the iBGP sessions. The addressing scheme for the loopback addressing is 10.1.1.*X*/32, where *X* is the router number.

The IGP used for internal reachability for the BGP sessions is IS-IS. This IGP was chosen because it can offer IPv6 functionality in an integrated fashion. The IS-IS routing protocol does not run over IPv4 or IPv6, but directly over the data link. This allows IPv4 and IPv6 prefix information to be carried in the same protocol, with the network topology being built independent from the IP version.

Initial Configurations

This section shows the initial IPv4 BGP configurations. These configurations provide the foundation on which IPv6 is deployed in this case study. The configuration shown in

Example 12-3 provides the basic route reflector configuration in the case study network. Peer groups are used, and there is a single eBGP client, R7.

Example 12-3 *R1 BGP Configuration*

```
router bgp 65000
 no synchronization
 bgp log-neighbor-changes
 neighbor IPv4_RR peer-group
 neighbor IPv4_RR remote-as 65000
 neighbor IPv4_RR update-source Loopback0
 neighbor IPv4_RRC peer-group
 neighbor IPv4_RRC remote-as 65000
 neighbor IPv4_RRC update-source Loopback0
 neighbor IPv4_RRC route-reflector-client
 neighbor 10.1.1.2 peer-group IPv4_RR
 neighbor 10.1.1.3 peer-group IPv4_RR
 neighbor 10.1.1.6 peer-group IPv4_RRC
 neighbor 192.168.1.1 remote-as 65001
 no auto-summary
 !
```

Example 12-4 shows the configuration of R6.

Example 12-4 *R6 BGP Configuration*

```
router bgp 65000
 no synchronization
 bgp log-neighbor-changes
 network 10.6.0.0 mask 255.255.0.0
 neighbor 10.1.1.1 remote-as 65000
 neighbor 10.1.1.1 update-source Loopback0
 no auto-summary
 !
```

Planned IPv6 Overlay

The IPv6 BGP deployment follows the same topology as the IPv4 network. The core routers (R1, R2, and R3) act as route reflectors for the IPv6 prefix information. The edge routers (R4, R5, and R6) are route reflector clients.

The following steps outline the process of configuring the IPv6 BGP network:

Step 1   If IPv6 forwarding is not enabled, IPv6 packets will not be routed. It is possible to configure IPv6 routing and have IPv6 routing information in the routing table, but packets will not be forwarded if forwarding is not enabled. The command is **ipv6 unicast-routing** in global configuration mode.

Step 2   The BGP router ID should be manually set for every router. This ensures
that if IPv4 is ever removed from the network, the IPv6 BGP sessions
will remain active. While IPv4 addresses are configured on the router,
this does not cause a problem. However, the removal of IPv4 can result
in a failure of all IPv6 BGP sessions if the BGP router ID is not set. The
command is **bgp router-id** *x.x.x.x* under the BGP router configuration.

Step 3   Configure a loopback with an IPv6 address. This addressing is used to
form the MP-BGP sessions, just like the IPv4 sessions. It is not required
to configure addressing on all the internal links, because link-local
addressing can be used for forwarding. To use link-local addressing on
the physical links, configure the command **ipv6 enable** under each
interface to initiate the autocreation of link-local addresses. Global
addressing is used for external-facing links to provide a reachable next-
hop address.

Step 4   Enable the IPv6 IGP. This step provides reachability across the entire
network for IPv6 packets, which allows the IPv6 BGP sessions to form
after they have been configured. In this case study, because IS-IS is used,
you can do this by configuring **ipv6 router isis** under each interface,
including the loopback interface.

Step 5   With the foundation in place, you can configure the IPv6 BGP sessions.
You do this under the main BGP configuration. After you configure the
BGP sessions, you must activate them in the IPv6 address family
configuration mode.

The IPv6 BGP network is now ready to advertise prefix information. IPv6 prefix information should be injected under IPv6 address family configuration mode using redistribution
or network statements. Also, BGP synchronization must be disabled for IPv6 and IPv4 if
synchronization is not being used.

IPv6 Network Topology

The IPv6 loopback addresses configured on each router are in the form of 2001:0400:0:
1234::*X*/128, where *X* is the router number. IPv6 prefixes are injected into BGP on each of
the edge routers for IPv6 reachability testing.

The output from **show bgp ipv6 summary** on R1 is shown in Example 12-5. The output
should be familiar to you from working with IPv4.

Example 12-5 **show bgp ipv6 summary** *Output*

```
R1#show bgp ipv6 summary
BGP router identifier 10.1.1.1, local AS number 65000
BGP table version is 5, main routing table version 5
4 network entries and 6 paths using 948 bytes of memory
```

Example 12-5 show bgp ipv6 summary *Output (Continued)*

```
2 BGP path attribute entries using 120 bytes of memory
4 BGP rrinfo entries using 96 bytes of memory
1 BGP AS-PATH entries using 24 bytes of memory
0 BGP route-map cache entries using 0 bytes of memory
0 BGP filter-list cache entries using 0 bytes of memory
BGP activity 15/22 prefixes, 32/21 paths, scan interval 60 secs

Neighbor        V    AS MsgRcvd MsgSent   TblVer  InQ OutQ Up/Down  State/PfxRcd
2001:400:0:701::701
                4 65001     29      33        5    0    0 00:06:26            1
2001:400:0:1234::2
                4 65000     53      54        5    0    0 00:05:39            2
2001:400:0:1234::3
                4 65000     53      53        5    0    0 00:05:48            2
2001:400:0:1234::6
                4 65000     52      63        5    0    0 00:05:14            1
```

The output from **show bgp ipv6 summary** lists the BGP peers and their current state. If the peers are in a state other than Established, that state is identified. In Example 12-5, all the peers are in an Established state.

IPv6 prefix information carried in BGP is shown with the **show bgp ipv6** command, as shown in Example 12-6.

Example 12-6 *IPv6 BGP Table Display*

```
R5#show bgp ipv6
BGP table version is 19, local router ID is 10.5.1.1
Status codes: s suppressed, d damped, h history, * valid, > best, i - internal,
              r RIB-failure
Origin codes: i - IGP, e - EGP, ? - incomplete

   Network          Next Hop            Metric LocPrf Weight Path
*>i2001:400::/29    2001:400:0:1234::4
                                             0    100      0 i
*  i                2001:400:0:1234::4
                                             0    100      0 i
*  i2001:400:0:1234::7/128
                    2001:400:0:701::701
                                             0    100      0 65001 i
*>i                 2001:400:0:701::701
                                             0    100      0 65001 i
*> 2001:500::/29    ::                       0         32768 i
*  i2001:600::/29   2001:400:0:1234::6
                                             0    100      0 i
*>i                 2001:400:0:1234::6
                                             0    100      0 i
```

The **show bgp ipv6** output shows the BGP path information in the IPv6 RIB. The prefix 2001:500::/29 is a locally generated path, which is indicated by the unspecified address :: being used as the next hop.

Example 12-7 shows BGP path information about a specific prefix.

Example 12-7 *IPv6 BGP Path Information on a Specific Prefix*

```
R5#show bgp ipv6 2001:600::/29
BGP routing table entry for 2001:600::/29, version 3
Paths: (2 available, best #1, table Global-IPv6-Table)
  Not advertised to any peer
  Local
    2001:400:0:1234::6 (metric 30) from 2001:400:0:1234::2 (10.1.1.2)
      Origin IGP, metric 0, localpref 100, valid, internal, best
      Originator: 10.1.1.6, Cluster list: 10.1.1.2, 10.1.1.1
  Local
    2001:400:0:1234::6 (metric 30) from 2001:400:0:1234::3 (10.1.1.3)
      Origin IGP, metric 0, localpref 100, valid, internal
      Originator: 10.1.1.6, Cluster list: 10.1.1.3, 10.1.1.1
```

The detailed path information for 2001:600::/29 shows the influence of MP-BGP's 32-bit dependencies. The cluster ID and originator ID (derived from the router ID) are shown as IPv4 addresses.

Final Configurations

The final BGP configurations are shown in the following examples. The final configurations have IPv4 and IPv6 running in a dual-stack configuration.

Example 12-8 shows the final BGP configuration for R1.

Example 12-8 *R1 Final BGP Configuration*

```
router bgp 65000
 no bgp default ipv4-unicast
 no synchronization
 bgp log-neighbor-changes
 neighbor IPv4_RR peer-group
 neighbor IPv4_RR remote-as 65000
 neighbor IPv4_RR update-source Loopback0
 neighbor IPv4_RR activate
 neighbor IPv4_RRC peer-group
 neighbor IPv4_RRC remote-as 65000
 neighbor IPv4_RRC update-source Loopback0
 neighbor IPv4_RRC route-reflector-client
 neighbor IPv4_RRC activate
 neighbor IPv6_RR peer-group
 neighbor IPv6_RR remote-as 65000
 neighbor IPv6_RR update-source Loopback0
```

Example 12-8 *R1 Final BGP Configuration (Continued)*

```
 neighbor IPv6_RRC peer-group
 neighbor IPv6_RRC remote-as 65000
 neighbor IPv6_RRC update-source Loopback0
 neighbor IPv6_RRC route-reflector-client
 neighbor 10.1.1.2 peer-group IPv4_RR
 neighbor 10.1.1.3 peer-group IPv4_RR
 neighbor 10.1.1.6 peer-group IPv4_RRC
 neighbor 2001:400:0:701::701 remote-as 65001
neighbor 2001:400:0:1234::2 peer-group IPv6_RR
 neighbor 2001:400:0:1234::3 peer-group IPv6_RR
 neighbor 2001:400:0:1234::6 peer-group IPv6_RRC
 neighbor 192.168.1.1 remote-as 65001
 no auto-summary
 !
 address-family ipv6
 neighbor IPv6_RR activate
 neighbor IPv6_RRC activate
 neighbor IPv6_RRC route-reflector-client
 neighbor 2001:400:0:701::701 activate
 neighbor 2001:400:0:701::701 prefix-list FILTER_IN in
 neighbor 2001:400:0:1234::2 peer-group IPv6_RR
 neighbor 2001:400:0:1234::3 peer-group IPv6_RR
 neighbor 2001:400:0:1234::6 peer-group IPv6_RRC
 no synchronization
 exit-address-family
 !
 !
 ipv6 prefix-list FILTER_IN seq 5 permit 2001:400::/29
 ipv6 prefix-list FILTER_IN seq 10 permit 2001:600::/29
 ipv6 prefix-list FILTER_IN seq 15 permit 2001:800::/29
 ipv6 prefix-list FILTER_IN seq 20 permit 3FFE::/16
 ipv6 prefix-list FILTER_IN seq 25 permit 2002::/16
 ipv6 prefix-list FILTER_IN seq 30 permit ::/80
 ipv6 prefix-list FILTER_IN seq 35 deny ::/0
 !
```

The R1 configuration uses peer groups for the iBGP peers. IPv4 and IPv6 must be in separate peer groups because of update replication, as discussed in Chapter 3, "Tuning BGP Performance." Also, an external peer with a prefix list is applied inbound to permit only prefixes from currently assigned address blocks.

Example 12-9 shows the final BGP configuration of R6.

Example 12-9 *R6 Final BGP Configuration*

```
router bgp 65000
 no bgp default ipv4-unicast
 no synchronization
 bgp log-neighbor-changes
```

continues

Example 12-9 *R6 Final BGP Configuration (Continued)*

```
 bgp router-id 10.1.1.6
 network 10.6.0.0 mask 255.255.0.0
 neighbor 10.1.1.1 remote-as 65000
 neighbor 10.1.1.1 update-source Loopback0
 neighbor 10.1.1.1 activate
 neighbor 2001:400:0:1234::1 remote-as 65000
 neighbor 2001:400:0:1234::1 update-source Loopback0
no auto-summary
 !
 address-family ipv6
 neighbor 2001:400:0:1234::1 activate
 network 2001:600::/29
 no synchronization
 exit-address-family
 !
```

The R6 configuration has only a single peer for IPv4 and IPv6, because it is a nonredundant route reflector client. Under the IPv6 address family, a prefix is injected into BGP.

Summary

This chapter provided a high-level overview of IPv6 and using MP-BGP for IPv6 prefix information. The subject of IPv6 is extensive, and many standards detail its operation. The focus of this chapter was to help you understand how BGP has been modified to work with IPv6 from an operational perspective.

The core of the BGP protocol remains the same with the MP-BGP extensions, allowing you to leverage your BGP experience when you transition to IPv6. In many cases, the only significant change is the format of the addressing. This chapter concluded with a case study on deploying IPv6 alongside IPv4 in a dual-stack deployment, which is expected to be the primary method of deploying IPv6.

PART V

Appendixes

This appendix covers the following topics:

- DCN scalability

- DCN architecture

- BGP-based DCN network design

- Multiprotocol BGP for CLNS configuration example

- CLNS support caveats

Multiprotocol BGP Extensions for CLNS Support

The use of BGP has expanded beyond the IP environment. BGP's ability to manage large amounts of routing information efficiently can be capitalized on elsewhere. A primary example of where BGP can be leveraged is in the Data Communications Network (DCN) environment. The DCN is a management network for Synchronous Optical Network (SONET) and Synchronous Digital Hierarchy (SDH) network elements (NEs). The Connectionless Network Service (CLNS) is used to manage the NEs, with File Transfer Access Method (FTAM) and Common Management Interface Protocol (CMIP).

This appendix covers the general design for DCN management networks and how BGP can best be used. The details of the CLNS protocol and the IS-IS routing protocol are outside the scope of this book, so only very brief coverage is provided. This appendix is primarily intended for engineers who are familiar with DCNs and who are looking at BGP as a scalability mechanism.

DCN Scalability

The primary scalability challenge that IP networks face is the amount of prefix information that must be advertised. This is also the case in the DCN environment; however, the number of nodes in the network has created additional constraints.

The DCN environment network is composed of SONET or SDH network elements (NEs), typically add/drop multiplexers (ADMs). The number of NEs in a single SONET/SDH ring averages around 10 but can range from 3 to 40. A typical DCN can have well over a thousand rings, resulting in tens of thousands of NEs. This would not pose a problem, except that each NE acts like an intermediate system (IS) and not an end system (ES).

SONET rings have a control channel, called the Data Communications Channel (DCC), which is used to send control messaging between network elements. This control channel has a bandwidth of 192 kbps. Bellcore specifies the architecture for the SONET DCC to run an HDLC-based protocol that provides the equivalent of a point-to-point connection between each adjacent network element, forming a ring architecture. (ITU-T does likewise for SDH.)

The result of this specification is that each network element must be able to forward packets to adjacent network elements via the DCC. The NEs must act as ISs instead of ESs, which requires them to be part of the Layer 3 topology. Therefore, they must participate in routing.

DCN Architecture

The common Layer 3 architecture in the DCN is for each ring to be its own Level 1 (L1) area. The NE that connects to the management network is called the gateway network element (GNE). Smaller rings may have only a single GNE; however, it is common for larger rings to have two GNEs to provide redundancy.

The management router is a Level 1/Level 2 (L1/L2) router that is responsible for aggregating connections to the GNEs and providing connectivity to the L2 backbone. The management router can connect to multiple areas using the IS-IS multiarea (IS-IS MA) feature. If the management router does not support the IS-IS MA feature, a separate L1/L2 router is required for each ring. The management router connects to the GNE via an L1 adjacency and connects to L2-only aggregation routers via an L2 adjacency.

Typically, low-end routers are used in the DCN because of their small form factor and the scarcity of rack space in the CO. This limits the size of the L2 network to approximately 200 routers, or about 100 to 150 COs. It is not uncommon for a single network to consist of several hundred COs.

This scalability constraint results in the creation of multiple routing domains, which must all be interconnected. Typically, a core network is built and the L2-only aggregation routers are connected to the core network using static routing or Interior Gateway Routing Protocol for CLNS (ISO-IGRP). Static routing and ISO-IGRP do not provide the scalability required for today's largest DCNs and certainly will not scale to support future networks that might result from organic network growth or mergers between current DCNs. It was to solve this scalability issue that support was added to BGP for CLNS routing information. The use of BGP for CLNS routing scales better than static routes from an administrative perspective and better than ISO-IGRP from a prefix advertisement perspective.

BGP-Based DCN Network Design

The implementation of CLNS support in BGP relies on TCP, not Transport Protocol 4 (TP4), to provide the transport layer connection. Peering sessions are built between IP addresses, not Network Service Access Points (NSAPs). This adds complexity regarding the BGP next hop for NSAPs, which is covered in the section "BGP Next-Hop for CLNS Prefixes." This also necessitates the introduction of IP into the network to let the TCP sessions for BGP form.

IS-IS Area Layout

Each SONET or SDH ring in the network is typically its own IS-IS L1 area. Figure A-1 shows an example of a four-node ring. The IS-IS adjacencies are shown together with the level in which they reside.

Figure A-1   *SONET/SDH Ring with IS-IS Adjacency Information*

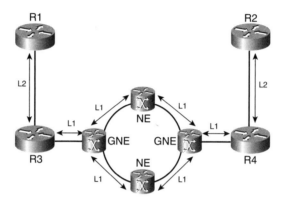

The connections between the NEs are all L1 adjacencies. The GNE nodes connect to the gateway routers R3 and R4, which reside in the CO. Using the IS-IS multiarea feature, it is possible to aggregate a number of rings on the same gateway routers. The gateway routers connect to the aggregation routers R1 and R2 via L2 IS-IS adjacencies. Typically, 150 gateway routers can be terminated on the aggregation routers, depending on the model of router used for the aggregation routers.

The gateway routers are usually lower-end routers, which is what limits the overall size of the L2 network to approximately 200 routers. The L1 areas are usually limited to a single ring per area, or a couple of rings if they are small. This is because of the limited bandwidth on the DCC for Link State Protocol (LSP) Data Unit flooding.

BGP Peering Relationships

The classic architecture uses only IS-IS, or a combination of IS-IS and static routing, or ISO-IGRP.

In a BGP architecture, the core network consists of a full iBGP mesh. Route reflectors can be used if BGP peering scalability is an issue. Confederations are not supported for CLNS prefix information. The aggregation routers peer with the core network using eBGP. Figure A-2 shows a sample topology with two COs and a small core network.

Figure A-2 *BGP Peering Layout with Two Central Offices*

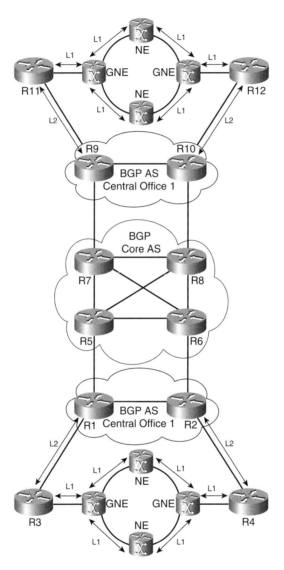

It is a common practice to originate a CLNS default from the core network via eBGP to the aggregation routers. The aggregation routers advertise the area addresses in their autonomous system to the core routers via eBGP. In the DCN environment, the goal is not optimal routing from any to any. The purpose is to provide fault-tolerant routing from the management stations to all the NEs. It usually isn't necessary to advertise all the NSAP prefixes from the core autonomous systems into the aggregation domains.

The traffic flow from an NE to the management station is straightforward. The data from the NE is sent toward the closest L1/L2 routers by following the attach bit (ATT bit) in the L1 area. When the packet reaches the L1/L2 router, the CLNS default route, not the ATT bit, is followed into the core autonomous system. The specific CLNS route to the management station is used in the network core. The traffic flow from the management station can follow a specific NSAP prefix back to the network element being managed.

BGP Next Hop for CLNS Prefixes

An interesting caveat comes with using BGP to transport CLNS prefix information. The recursive routing functionality that BGP uses with respect to next-hop information is not conducive to CLNS operation. IP addressing is per-link, whereas CLNS addressing is per-node. This section looks at how the addressing paradigm for CLNS creates a complication for using BGP.

The BGP protocol can establish a connection between the two peers because they share an IP subnet, which means that each router knows how to reach the other router to which it is directly connected. However, in CLNS, addressing is done on a per-node basis, not a per-link basis. The result is that in a CLNS network, two directly connected routers do not share any addressing information to provide unicast reachability between them without some discovery mechanism. Figure A-3 shows an example.

Figure A-3   *CLNS Next-Hop Reachability*

As shown in Figure A-3, both routers have IP reachability through the 10.1.1.0/30 subnet. However, both routers are in different CLNS areas because of the different area addresses. R1 is in area 47.5678, and R2 is in area 47.1234.

In an IS-IS network, two nodes send out Hello packets and discover each other, resulting in an adjacency's being formed. However, if in the DCN example the aggregation routers were to form L2 adjacencies with the core routers, the result would be one very large L2 domain, which is the initial problem that BGP is being used to solve.

A solution is to form an End System-to-Intermediate System (ES-IS) adjacency between the aggregation router and the core router. An ES-IS adjacency is used to allow routers to send data packets to ESs, or hosts. Using an ES-IS adjacency allows each router to learn about the other router without merging the L2 routing domains.

This solution is not without complications. The core routers and aggregation routers are all L2-only routers, which are not permitted to advertise an ES-IS adjacency according to

ISO/IEC 10589. The behavior of IS-IS cannot be modified to automatically advertise ES-IS adjacencies in L2 LSPs without potentially creating other problems. The general operation of IS-IS must remain compliant with the specification.

The practical implementation of this solution is for R1 to form an ES-IS adjacency with R2 and for R2 to form an ES-IS adjacency with R1. This is achieved through enabling CLNS on the interface, not IS-IS, using the **clns enable** command. This means that R1 thinks it is an IS and that R2 is an ES, whereas R2 thinks it is an IS and that R1 is an ES. An eBGP peering session is formed between R1 and R2 using the 10.1.1.0/30 network to provide reachability for the peering session.

The CLNS prefix information that R2 receives from R1 has a BGP next hop of R1's NSAP. The next hop is reachable via an ES-IS adjacency, so the prefix passes the next-hop reachability requirement in the BGP best-path algorithm. This allows the prefix to be installed into the BGP RIB and, assuming it is the best path for that prefix, the routing table.

A complication appears when an eBGP learns that NSAP is advertised via iBGP. Figure A-4 shows an example.

Figure A-4   *BGP Next Hop Complication with iBGP*

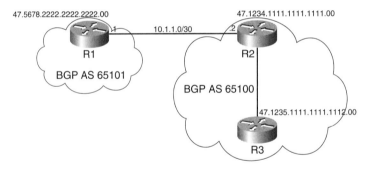

If R1 advertises an NSAP via eBGP to R2, which in turn advertises it to R3 via iBGP, R3 receives the NSAP with a next hop of R1. R2 is unable to advertise the NSAP for R1, which it knows via ES-IS, because it is L2-only and its adjacency with R3 is L2-only. This is seen by R2 and R3 being in different areas—R2 in area 47.1234 and R3 in area 47.1235.

This complication is resolved by having R2 automatically include the prefix for R1 in its L2 LSP if the following three conditions are met:

- An ES-IS adjacency exists between the two eBGP peers.

- A BGP Update message is received that contains an MP_REACH_NLRI with the NSAP address family identifier.

- The next-hop address in the MP_REACH_NLRI is identical to the NSAP of the eBGP neighbor.

These conditions are met automatically if CLNS is enabled on the interface between the routers and the eBGP session is formed between them, with NLRI exchange taking place.

The inclusion of R1's NSAP in R2's L2 LSP provides R3 with next-hop reachability for any iBGP learned prefixes that use R1 as the next hop. If the ES-IS adjacency or eBGP peering session between R1 and R2 goes down, the prefix for R1's NSAP is removed from R2's L2 LSP.

Multiprotocol BGP for CLNS Configuration Example

This example focuses specifically on BGP configuration aspects. A four-router core network and two aggregation routers in different autonomous systems provide the sample topology, as shown in Figure A-5.

Figure A-5   *Sample Network Topology*

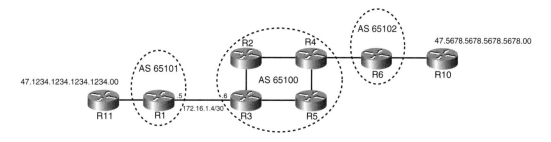

The NSAP addressing is shown in Table A-1.

Table A-1   *CLNS Addressing for the Sample Network*

Router	NSAP
R1	47.1111.1111.1111.1111.00
R2	47.2222.2222.2222.2222.00
R3	47.3333.3333.3333.3333.00
R4	47.4444.4444.4444.4444.00
R5	47.5555.5555.5555.5555.00
R6	47.6666.6666.6666.6666.00
R10	47.5678.5678.5678.5678.00
R11	47.1234.1234.1234.1234.00

The IP addressing for the loopback interfaces in the network core is shown in Table A-2.

Table A-2 *IP Addressing for Core Network Loopback Interfaces*

Router	Loopback Address
R1	10.1.1.1/32
R2	10.1.1.2/32
R3	10.1.1.3/32
R4	10.1.1.4/32
R5	10.1.1.5/32

The core network consists of a full iBGP mesh with all iBGP sessions sourced from the loopback interfaces. Each aggregation router connects to the core network via eBGP.

The core routers send only a CLNS default prefix to the aggregation routers. The aggregation routers send a couple prefixes each to the network core.

Network Verification

First, you verify if ES-IS adjacency exists between the core router and the aggregation router. This is shown in Example A-1 for core router R3 and in Example A-2 for aggregation router R1.

Example A-1 *ES-IS Adjacency with R1 on Core Router R3*

```
R3#show clns neighbor
System Id         Interface   SNPA        State  Holdtime  Type Protocol
1111.1111.1111 Se3/0         *HDLC*      Up     282       IS   ES-IS
R2                Se2/0         *HDLC*      Up     28        L2   IS-IS
R5                Se4/0         *HDLC*      Up     27        L2   IS-IS
```

Example A-2 *ES-IS Adjacency with R3 on Aggregation Router R1*

```
R1#show clns neighbor
System Id         Interface   SNPA        State  Holdtime  Type Protocol
3333.3333.3333 Se3/0         *HDLC*      Up     267       IS   ES-IS
R11               Se2/0         *HDLC*      Up     25        L2   IS-IS
```

ES-IS adjacency is active on both R1 and R3, which allows the forwarding of CLNS packets between the two routers.

The BGP peering sessions should be active. Example A-3 shows the summarized peering information from R3.

Example A-3 *BGP Peering Summary for CLNS Peers*

```
R3#show bgp nsap summary
BGP router identifier 10.1.1.3, local AS number 65100
BGP table version is 14, main routing table version 14
8 network entries and 8 paths using 1584 bytes of memory
4 BGP path attribute entries using 240 bytes of memory
2 BGP AS-PATH entries using 48 bytes of memory
0 BGP route-map cache entries using 0 bytes of memory
0 BGP filter-list cache entries using 0 bytes of memory
BGP activity 23/22 prefixes, 24/16 paths, scan interval 60 secs

Neighbor        V    AS MsgRcvd MsgSent   TblVer  InQ OutQ Up/Down  State/PfxRcd
10.1.1.2        4 65100     110     114       14    0    0 00:42:51            1
10.1.1.4        4 65100     116     116       14    0    0 00:41:49            3
10.1.1.5        4 65100     107     112       14    0    0 00:42:52            1
172.16.1.5      4 65101     118     131       14    0    0 00:42:33            2
```

The iBGP sessions between the core routers are all established, and the eBGP session with R1 (peer 172.16.1.5) is also established. The eBGP session with R1 shows that at least one UPDATE message has been received, which means that R3 should be originating information in its L2 LSP for R1 to provide next-hop reachability. This is shown in Example A-4.

Example A-4 *eBGP-Neighbor Route Based on ES-IS Adjacency*

```
R3#show clns route
Codes: C - connected, S - static, d - DecnetIV
       I - ISO-IGRP, i - IS-IS, e - ES-IS
       B - BGP,       b - eBGP-neighbor
b  47.1111.1111.1111.1111.00 [15/10]
       via 1111.1111.1111, Serial3/0
```

Example A-4 shows only the relevant routing entry. The rest of the CLNS routing information was removed for clarity. CLNS routes received by standard BGP are marked with a B. The special eBGP-neighbor route that is injected into CLNS routing and the IS-IS L2 LSP is shown with a b. This prefix appears only as an eBGP-neighbor route in the router that terminates the eBGP session. This prefix appears as a normal IS-IS route in the rest of that routing domain.

In this example, each aggregation autonomous system originates a prefix from the gateway routers. In AS 65101, NSAP 47.1234 is originated, and in AS 65102, NSAP 47.5678 is originated. Both of these NSAPs can be seen in the core router's BGP table, as shown in Example A-5, taken from R5.

Example A-5 *CLNS Routing Information in the Network Core for Remote CLNS Prefixes*

```
R5#show bgp nsap 47.1234
BGP routing table entry for 47.1234, version 29
Paths: (1 available, best #1)
  Not advertised to any peer
  65101
    47.1111.1111.1111.1111.00 (metric 10) from 10.1.1.3 (10.1.1.3)
      Origin IGP, localpref 100, valid, internal, synchronized, best
R5#show bgp nsap 47.5678
BGP routing table entry for 47.5678, version 34
Paths: (1 available, best #1)
  Not advertised to any peer
  65102
    47.6666.6666.6666.6666.00 (metric 10) from 10.1.1.4 (10.1.1.4)
      Origin IGP, localpref 100, valid, internal, synchronized, best
```

The BGP core network sends only the default prefix to the aggregation routing domains.
All specific prefix information is filtered out. The aggregation router—R1, for instance—
redistributes the default prefix into IS-IS. To verify connectivity, a CLNS ping can be sent
across the network. In Example A-6, R11 sends a ping to the NSAP for R10; they are
located across the core from each other. R10 and R11 are not running BGP.

Example A-6 *CLNS Routing Information for the Default Prefix*

```
R11#show clns route
Codes: C - connected, S - static, d - DecnetIV
       I - ISO-IGRP, i - IS-IS, e - ES-IS
       B - BGP,      b - eBGP-neighbor

C  47.1234.1234.1234.1234.00 [1/0], Local IS-IS NET
C  47.1234 [2/0], Local IS-IS Area
i  Default Prefix [110/10]
     via R1, Serial2/0
i  47.3333.3333.3333.3333.00 [110/10]
     via R1, Serial2/0
i  47.1111 [110/10]
     via R1, Serial2/0

R11#ping clns 47.5678.5678.5678.5678.00
Type escape sequence to abort.
Sending 5, 100-byte CLNS Echos with timeout 2 seconds
!!!!!
Success rate is 100 percent (5/5), round-trip min/avg/max = 32/54/120 ms
```

Configuration Summary

The configurations for the topology are shown for two of the routers. The first
configuration, in Example A-7, is for R1.

Example A-7 *Aggregation Router Configuration for R1*

```
!
version 12.2
!
hostname R1
!
clns routing
clns filter-set DEFAULT_ONLY deny 47...
clns filter-set DEFAULT_ONLY permit default
!
!
interface Loopback0
 ip address 10.1.1.1 255.255.255.255
!
interface Serial2/0
 ip address 172.16.1.2 255.255.255.252
 clns router isis
!
interface Serial3/0
 ip address 172.16.1.5 255.255.255.252
 clns enable
!
router isis
 net 47.1111.1111.1111.1111.00
 is-type level-2-only
 redistribute bgp 65101 clns route-map BGP_TO_ISIS
!
router bgp 65101
 no synchronization
 no bgp default ipv4-unicast
 bgp log-neighbor-changes
 neighbor 172.16.1.6 remote-as 65100
 no auto-summary
 !
 address-family nsap
 neighbor 172.16.1.6 activate
 network 47.1234
 network 47.1111.1111.1111.1111.00
 no synchronization
 exit-address-family
 !
!
route-map BGP_TO_ISIS permit 10
 match clns address DEFAULT_ONLY
 !
```

The **clns filter-set** is used to create an NSAP filter that blocks all NSAPs except the default NSAP. The NSAP filter is used to control the redistribution of BGP into IS-IS.

The Serial3/0 interface is the connection to the core network. It requires the **clns enable** interface configuration command to enable the CLNS ES-IS process on that interface.

In the BGP NSAP address family configuration, network statements are used to inject NSAPs from the IS-IS routing table into BGP, and the neighbor is activated to advertise CLNS information. The BGP network statements for CLNS NSAPs can specify just the area address or the full NSAP, depending on the granularity needed.

The configuration for the core router R3 is shown in Example A-8.

Example A-8 *Core Router Configuration for R3*

```
!
version 12.2
!
hostname R3
!
clns routing
clns filter-set DEFAULT_OUT deny 47...
clns filter-set DEFAULT_OUT permit default
!
interface Loopback0
 ip address 10.1.1.3 255.255.255.255
!
interface Serial2/0
 ip address 172.16.1.14 255.255.255.252
 ip router isis
 clns router isis
!
interface Serial3/0
 ip address 172.16.1.6 255.255.255.252
 clns enable
!
interface Serial4/0
 ip address 172.16.1.9 255.255.255.252
 ip router isis
 clns router isis
!
router isis
 net 47.3333.3333.3333.3333.00
 is-type level-2-only
 passive-interface Serial3/0
 passive-interface Loopback0
!
router bgp 65100
 no synchronization
 no bgp default ipv4-unicast
 bgp log-neighbor-changes
 neighbor 10.1.1.2 remote-as 65100
 neighbor 10.1.1.2 update-source Loopback0
```

Example A-8 *Core Router Configuration for R3 (Continued)*

```
 neighbor 10.1.1.4 remote-as 65100
 neighbor 10.1.1.4 update-source Loopback0
 neighbor 10.1.1.5 remote-as 65100
 neighbor 10.1.1.5 update-source Loopback0
 neighbor 172.16.1.5 remote-as 65101
 no auto-summary
 !
 address-family nsap
 neighbor 10.1.1.2 activate
 neighbor 10.1.1.4 activate
 neighbor 10.1.1.5 activate
 neighbor 172.16.1.5 activate
 neighbor 172.16.1.5 default-originate
 neighbor 172.16.1.5 prefix-list DEFAULT_OUT out
 network 47.3333.3333.3333.3333.00
 no synchronization
 exit-address-family
 !
```

clns filter-set DEFAULT_OUT is applied to the BGP peering session to prevent any prefixes from being advertised from the core to the aggregation routing domains except the default.

The core network has IS-IS enabled in Integrated mode, which means that it is used for both CLNS and IP routing, unlike in the aggregation routing domains, where IS-IS was in CLNS-only mode. The reason for adding IP support in the core network is to provide IP reachability for the BGP peering sessions.

The BGP NSAP address family configuration activates all the iBGP neighbors in the core and the eBGP neighbor to R1. The default prefix is originated to R1 using the **neighbor 172.16.1.5 default-originate** command. All other NSAPs are blocked with the prefix list DEFAULT_OUT, which is defined in Example A-8 using the **clns filter-set** command.

CLNS Support Caveats

BGP support for CLNS prefix information was first included in Cisco IOS software Release 12.2(8)T. This feature is available only in the Service Provider and Telco feature sets. The following BGP features and commands are not supported for CLNS prefix information:

- BGP confederations
- BGP extended communities

- Unsupported commands:

  — **auto-summary**

  — **neighbor advertise-map**

  — **neighbor distribute-list**

  — **neighbor soft-reconfiguration**

  — **neighbor unsuppress-map**

Additional information on CLNS routing and IS-IS is available in the Cisco Press publication, *IS-IS Network Design Solutions*, by Abe Martey and Scott Sturgess.

Matrix of BGP Features and Cisco IOS Software Releases

This appendix provides a matrix of various BGP features and the relevant Cisco IOS software releases for easy reference (see Table B-1). Keep the following in mind when using this matrix:

- The IOS Release column lists the first IOS releases that introduced the feature. All subsequent releases may automatically inherit the features. For easy reference, a simplified IOS release train roadmap is shown in Figure B-1 at the end of this appendix.

- Not all releases are included in the IOS Release column, and not all hardware platforms are supported for each feature.

- No attempt has been made to individually verify each release for the integration of the indicated feature.

- You should always consult the Cisco online documentation for accurate and up-to-date information.

- Cisco bug ID numbers are provided as additional sources of information for some features when the release-note information is available. A bug toolkit is available at www.cisco.com/cgi-bin/Support/Bugtool/home.pl. Note that you need a username and password to access this site.

- Consult Appendix D, "Acronym Glossary," for a complete list of acronyms.

Table B-1   *Matrix of BGP Features and IOS Releases*

Feature	IOS Release	Notes
Allow AS in	12.0(10)ST and 12.0(7)T	
AS override	12.0(7)T	
BGP maximum AS limit	12.0(16.3)S, 12.0(16.3)ST, and 12.1(4.1)T	This command was introduced in CSCdr54230 and made visible in 12.0(23)S, 12.2(12.7), 12.2(12.8)S, and 12.2(12.7)T.

continues

Table B-1   *Matrix of BGP Features and IOS Releases (Continued)*

Feature	IOS Release	Notes
Cisco Express Forwarding (CEF)	11.1(17)CC	
Communities	10.3(1)	
Conditional advertisement	11.2(7)	
Conditional injection	12.0(14)ST and 12.2(4)T	12.2(4)T3 adds support for 7500s.
Cost community	12.0(24)S	CSCdu53928
Carrier supporting Carrier (CsC)	12.0(14)ST and 12.2(8)T	12.0(16)ST supports GSR E0 line cards. 12.0(21)ST adds support for E2 line cards.
CsC IPv4 label	12.0(21)ST, 12.0(22)S, and 12.2(13)T	12.0(23)S adds support for additional GSR line cards.
Default **no auto-summary**	12.2(8.4)S, 12.2(7.6)T, and 12.0(20.3)ST3	CSCdu81680
Default **no synchronization**	12.2(8.4)S, 12.2(7.6)T, and 12.0(20.3)ST3	CSCdu81680
DMZ link bandwidth	12.2(2)T and 12.0(24)S	
Dynamic peer group	12.0(24)S	
EIBGP multipath	12.2(4)T and 12.0(24)S	12.2(4)T3 adds support for 7500 series routers. 12.2(13)T1 fixes more bugs.
Graceful restart	12.0(22)S	
IBGP multipath	12.2(2)T	
Inter-AS IPv4 label	12.0(21)ST, 12.0(22)S, and 12.2(13)T	12.0(23)S adds support for additional GSR line cards.
Inter-AS VPN	12.1(5)T	12.0(16)ST adds support for GSR E0 cards. 12.0(17)ST adds support for E2 line cards.
IPv6 unicast routing	12.0(21)ST, 12.0(22)S, and 12.2(2)T	
Label Distribution Protocol (LDP)	12.0(10)ST, 12.1(2)T, 12.1(8a)E, and 12.2(2)T	12.2(4)T3 adds support for Cisco 7500 series routers.
Local AS	12.0(5)S and 12.2(8)T	CSCdt35109 adds the **no-prepend** keyword.

Table B-1   *Matrix of BGP Features and IOS Releases (Continued)*

Feature	IOS Release	Notes
Maximum prefix limit	11.2(10)	CSCdj43952 adds thresholds. CSCds61175 adds the **restart** keyword.
MIB support for per-peer received routes	12.0(21)S and 12.2(13)T	
MPLS-aware NetFlow	12.0(24)S	
MPLS label switch controller	12.0(5)T	
MPLS LDP MIB	12.2(2)T	
MPLS Label Switch Router (LSR) MIB	12.2(2)T	
MPLS or tag switching	11.1(17)CT and 12.0(3)T	
MPLS VPN	12.0(11)ST, 12.0(22)S, and 12.0(5)T	
MPLS VPN scan import timer	12.0(7)T	
MPLS VPN support for EIGRP as PE-CE protocol	12.0(22)S	
Multicast Source Discovery Protocol (MSDP)	12.0(7)T	
Multicast routing support	11.1(20)CC	
Multiprotocol BGP for IPv6	12.0(21)ST, 12.0(22)S, and 12.2(2)T	
Multiprotocol BGP for multicast	12.0(7)T	
Named community list	12.0(10)S, 12.0(16)ST, 12.1(9)E, and 12.2(8)T	
Next hop reset on route reflector	12.0(16)ST, 12.0(22)S, and 12.2(3)T	CSCdr80335
Next hop unchanged	12.0(16)ST, 120(22)S, and 12.2(3)T	This feature was introduced in CSCdr80335. CSCdu02357 changes to the current keyword.
Outbound Route Filtering (ORF)	12.0(11)ST and 12.2(4)T	12.2(4)T3 adds support for 7500 series routers. The current CLI was introduced in 12.0(18)ST.
Peer group	11.0(1)	

continues

Table B-1 *Matrix of BGP Features and IOS Releases (Continued)*

Feature	IOS Release	Notes
Peer-group restriction change	11.3(3.1), 11.1(17.5)CC, 11.3(3.1)T, and 11.1(17.5)CT	CSCdj70944
Peer template	12.0(24)S	
Policy accounting	12.0(9)S, 12.0(17)ST, and 12.2(13)T	
Policy accounting enhancement	12.0(22)S	
Policy list	12.0(22)S	
Prefix list	11.1CC	Introduced in CSCdj61356. CSCdk60284 expanded the functionality.
QoS Policy Propagation via BGP (QPPB)	11.1(20)CC	
Remove private AS	11.1(06)CA	CSCdi64489
IP RIB installation failure for BGP routes	12.2(08.05)T and 12.0(25.01)S	Introduced in CSCdp12004 (to be compliant with the RFC), but the behavior was reversed by CSCdy39249. The new command introduced in CSCdy39249, **bgp suppress-inactive**, achieves the same behavior as in CSCdp12004.
Route dampening	11.0(3)	
Route refresh	12.0(7)T and 12.0(2)S	12.0(22)S adds support for VPNv4 and IPv6 AFIs.
Route-map continue/goto	12.0(24)S	CSCdx90201
Session restart after maximum prefix limit	12.0(22)S	
Soft reconfiguration	11.2(1)	
TCP MD5 authentication	11.0(1)	
TDP	11.1CT	
Update group	12.0(24)S	
Update packing	12.0(18)S01, 12.0(18.06)ST, 12.0(18.06)SP, and 12.0(18.06)S	

Table B-1   *Matrix of BGP Features and IOS Releases (Continued)*

Feature	IOS Release	Notes
VPN IPv4 labels for Inter-AS	12.0(19.03)ST and 12.2T	CSCdp99739
VRF maximum routes	12.0(7)T	
VRF multipath import	12.0(25)S and 12.2(12)T	CSCdu11016

For easier reference, a simplified IOS release train roadmap is provided in Figure B-1. Only a subset of the release trains that are relevant to this book is included. An arrow's direction indicates the feature inheritance of the child-to-parent relationship. Always consult the Cisco online documentation for detailed and up-to-date information.

Figure B-1   *Simplified IOS Release Train Roadmap*

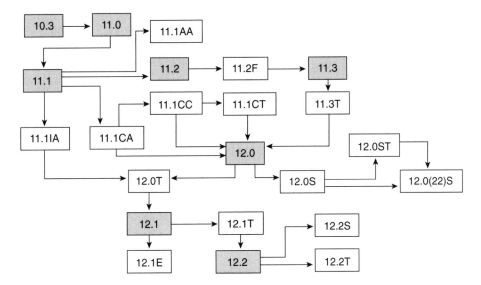

Additional Sources of Information

This appendix lists additional resources for information, including RFCs, URLs, books, and papers.

The Internet RFCs can be readily obtained from the IETF site at www.ietf.org. Some documents on the Cisco website (www.cisco.com) might require certain user privileges to access. If URLs have been updated, use the site's search tool.

RFCs

- RFC 1771, *A Border Gateway Protocol 4 (BGP-4)*. Y. Rekhter and T. Li.

- RFC 1997, *BGP Communities Attribute*. R. Chandra, P. Traina, and T. Li.

- RFC 1998, *An Application of the BGP Community Attribute in Multi-home Routing*. E. Chen and T. Bates.

- RFC 2385, *Protection of BGP Sessions via the TCP MD5 Signature Option*. A. Heffernan.

- RFC 2439, *BGP Route Flap Damping*. C. Villamizar, R. Chandra, and R. Govindan.

- RFC 2519, *A Framework for Inter-Domain Route Aggregation*. E. Chen and J. Stewart.

- RFC 2545, *Use of BGP-4 Multiprotocol Extensions for IPv6 Inter-Domain Routing*. P. Marques and F. Dupont.

- RFC 2796, *BGP Route Reflection—An Alternative to Full Mesh IBGP*. T. Bates, R. Chandra, and E. Chen.

- RFC 2918, *Route Refresh Capability for BGP-4*. E. Chen.

- RFC 3031, *Multiprotocol Label Switching Architecture*. E. Rosen, A. Viswanathan, and R. Callon.

- RFC 3032, *MPLS Label Stack Encoding*. E. Rosen, D. Tappan, G. Fedorkow, Y. Rekhter, D. Farinacci, T. Li, and A. Conta.

- RFC 3036, *LDP Specification*. L. Andersson, P. Doolan, N. Feldman, A. Fredette, and B. Thomas

- RFC 3063, *MPLS Loop Prevention Mechanism*. Y. Ohba, Y. Katsube, E. Rosen, and P. Doolan.

- RFC 3065, *Autonomous System Confederations for BGP*. P. Traina, D. McPherson, and J. Scudder.

- RFC 3107, *Carrying Label Information in BGP-4*. Y. Rekhter and E. Rosen.

- RFC 3345, *Border Gateway Protocol (BGP) Persistent Route Oscillation Condition*. D. McPherson, V. Gill, D. Walton, and A. Retana.

- RFC 3392, *Capabilities Advertisement with BGP-4*. R. Chandra and J. Scudder.

Cisco Systems URLs

- Achieve Optimal Routing and Reduce BGP Memory Consumption. www.cisco.com/warp/public/459/41.shtml.

- BGP Best Path Selection Algorithm. www.cisco.com/en/US/tech/tk365/tk80/technologies_tech_note09186a0080094431.shtml.

- BGP Internetwork Design Guidelines. www.cisco.com/univercd/cc/td/doc/cisintwk/idg4/nd2003.htm#xtocid54.

- BGP Samples and Tips. www.cisco.com/pcgi-bin/Support/browse/psp_view.pl?p=Internetworking:BGP&s=Implementation_and_Configuration#Samples_and_Tips

- BGP Troubleshooting Steps and Tools. www.cisco.com/pcgi-bin/Support/browse/psp_view.pl?p=Internetworking:BGP&s=Verification_and_Troubleshooting#Known_Problems.

- Configuring an Inter-AS MPLS VPN Using VPNv4 eBGP Sessions Between ASBRs. www.cisco.com/en/US/tech/tk436/tk428/technologies_configuration_example09186a0080094472.shtml.

- Field Notice: Endless BGP Convergence Problem in Cisco IOS Software Releases. www.cisco.com/warp/public/770/fn12942.html.

- How BGP Routers Use the Multi-Exit Discriminator for Best Path Selection. www.cisco.com/en/US/tech/tk365/tk80/technologies_tech_note09186a0080094934.shtml.

- How to Troubleshoot the MPLS VPN. www.cisco.com/en/US/tech/tk436/tk428/technologies_tech_note09186a0080093fcd.shtml.

- Internet Connectivity Options. www.cisco.com/en/US/tech/tk436/tk428/technologies_white_paper09186a00801281f1.shtml.

- Monitor and Maintain BGP. www.cisco.com/univercd/cc/td/doc/product/software/ios120/12cgcr/np1_c/1cprt1/1cbgp.htm#5646.

- MPLS Troubleshooting. www.cisco.com/en/US/tech/tk436/tk428/technologies_tech_note09186a0080094b4e.shtml.

- Route Selection in Cisco Routers. www.cisco.com/warp/public/105/21.html.

- Troubleshooting CEF Routing Loops. www.cisco.com/en/US/tech/tk827/tk831/technologies_tech_note09186a00800cdf2e.shtml.

- Troubleshooting High CPU Caused by the BGP Scanner or BGP Router Process. www.cisco.com/warp/public/459/highcpu-bgp.html.

- Troubleshooting Incomplete Adjacencies with CEF. www.cisco.com/en/US/tech/tk827/tk831/technologies_tech_note09186a0080094303.shtml.

- Troubleshooting Load Balancing Over Parallel Links Using Cisco Express Forwarding. www.cisco.com/en/US/tech/tk827/tk831/technologies_tech_note09186a0080094806.shtml.

- Troubleshooting Prefix Inconsistencies with Cisco Express Forwarding. www.cisco.com/en/US/tech/tk827/tk831/technologies_tech_note09186a00800946f7.shtml.

Books

- Alwayn, V. *Advanced MPLS Design and Implementation*. Cisco Press. 2001.

- Bollapragada, V., R. White, and C. Murphy. *Inside Cisco IOS Software Architecture.* Cisco Press. 2000.

- Doyle, J. and J. D. Carroll. *Routing TCP/IP, Volume II*. Cisco Press. 2001.

- Halabi, S. and D. McPherson. *Internet Routing Architectures*, Second Edition. Cisco Press. 2000.

- Parkhust, W. R. *Cisco BGP-4 Command and Configuration Handbook*. Cisco Press. 2001.

- Pepelnjak, I., and J. Guichard. *MPLS and VPN Architectures*. Cisco Press. 2002.

- Van Beijnum, I. *BGP*. O'Reilly. 2002.

- Zinin, A. *Cisco IP Routing*. Addison-Wesley. 2002.

Papers

- Dube, R. "A Comparison of Scaling Techniques for BGP." *ACM Computer Communications Review*, 29(3). 1999.

- Labovitz, C., R. Malan, and F. Jahanian. "Internet Routing Stability." *IEEE/ACM Trans. Networking*, Vol. 6, pp. 515–528. 1998.

Acronym Glossary

This appendix lists and defines the common acronyms used in this book.

ACL   access control list. A form of IOS filter designed for packet and route classification and control.

AF   address family. Types of IP addresses that share the same characteristics, such as IPv4 and IPv6.

AFI   address family identifier. A value that represents an address family.

ARF   automatic route filtering. Automatic filtering of routes by matching RTs received versus those configured locally in an MPLS VPN network.

ARP   Address Resolution Protocol. An IETF protocol to map an IP address to a MAC address.

AS   autonomous system. A BGP routing domain that shares the AS number.

ASBR   autonomous system border router. A router that interfaces with other routing domains.

ATM   Asynchronous Transfer Mode. An international standard for cell relay.

BGP   Border Gateway Protocol. An interdomain routing protocol for exchanging reachability information among autonomous systems.

CE   Customer Edge or Customer Edge router. This device is typically located at the customer site and connects to the service provider network.

CEF   Cisco Express Forwarding. A packet-forwarding mechanism in IOS that is based on topology information.

CLI   command-line interface. An user interface that is purely based on commands.

CLNS   Connectionless Network Service. An ISO network layer protocol.

CoS class of service. A classification of traffic to allow differentiated processing using prioritization, queuing, and other QoS features.

CSC Carrier Supporting Carrier. An MPLS VPN architecture in which service providers are in a client/server relationship.

DMZ demilitarized zone. A part of a network that interfaces with another network.

eBGP External Border Gateway Protocol. A form of BGP used between different autonomous systems.

EGP Exterior Gateway Protocol. Primarily a type of routing protocol for exchanging interdomain reachability information.

eiBGP External-Internal BGP. A term used only for BGP multipath within an MPLS VPN network.

EIGRP Enhanced Interior Gateway Routing Protocol. A type of IGP developed by Cisco.

EXP Experimental bits in an MPLS header.

Exp-Null explicit null. One of the reserved labels.

FEC Forwarding Equivalence Class. A group of destination addresses that have the same forwarding characteristics.

FIB forwarding information base. A database for packet forwarding.

GMPLS Generalized Multiprotocol Label Switching. An IETF protocol for extending the packet/cell-based MPLS to other forms of networks.

GRP Gigabit Route Processor. A type of route processor used in Cisco's 12000 series routers.

GSR Gigabit Switch Router. A Cisco 12000 series router.

iBGP Internal Border Gateway Protocol. A form of BGP used to exchange reachability information between routers of the same AS.

ICMP Internet Control Management Protocol. An IETF protocol for IP control and management.

IGP   Interior Gateway Protocol. A type of routing protocol for exchanging routing information within a domain.

IGRP   Interior Gateway Routing Protocol. An IGP developed by Cisco.

Imp-Null   implicit null. One of the reserved labels used in LDP and TDP.

I/O   input/output. A BGP process.

IP   Internet Protocol. An IETF network layer protocol.

IPC   Inter-Process Communication. A mechanism to exchange messages among different processes in a system.

IPv4   IP version 4. The current version of IP used in most networks.

IS-IS   Intermediate System-to-Intermediate System. An IETF and ISO protocol to disseminate interior routing information.

ISP   Internet service provider. A service provider that delivers Internet connectivity.

LDP   Label Distribution Protocol. An IETF protocol to distribute label binding information between LSRs.

LER   Label Edge Router. A router that performs label imposition or disposition.

LFIB   Label Forwarding Information Base. A database for labeled packet processing.

LIB   Label Information Base. A database used by an LSR to store labels learned from other LSRs, as well as labels assigned by the local LSR.

LSP   Label Switched Path. A sequence of hops in which a labeled packet travels by means of label-switching mechanisms.

LSR   Label Switch Router. A router that forwards a packet based on the value of a label encapsulated in the packet.

MAC   Media Access Control. An IEEE protocol that deals with Layer 2 control and encapsulation.

MD5   Message Digest 5. A one-way hashing algorithm that produces a 128-bit hash.

MED Multi-Exit Discriminator. A BGP attribute exchanged among autonomous systems to affect inbound traffic flows.

MPLS Multiprotocol Label Switching. An IETF standard for packet forwarding using labels.

MSDP Multicast Source Discovery Protocol. A mechanism to connect multiple PIM sparse-mode domains.

MTU maximum transmission unit. The maximum packet size, in bytes, that a particular interface can transmit.

NH next hop. The IP address of the next router to be used to reach a specific destination.

NLRI Network Layer Reachability Information. Prefixes exchanged among BGP speakers.

NSF Non-Stop Forwarding. A mechanism in which a router continues to forward or receive packets forwarded during transient failure conditions.

ORF Outbound Route Filtering. A form of filtering performed by a sender to suppress the routing information that will later be denied on the receiver.

OSPF Open Shortest Path First. An IETF protocol for exchanging interior routing information.

P Provider router. A provider core router device in an MPLS VPN network.

PE Provider edge router. This device connects to one or more customer sites in the service provider network.

PHP Penultimate Hop Popping. The top label is popped by the router that is one hop immediately prior to the edge label switch router.

PIM Protocol-Independent Multicast. An IETF protocol to disseminate multicast routing information. PIM is unicast routing protocol-independent. It can operate in different modes, such as sparse mode and dense mode.

POP point of presence. The part of a service provider network that provides interconnections to customers and other networks.

POS Packet over SONET. An IETF protocol to carry packets over SONET.

PPP Point-to-Point Protocol. An IETF protocol to exchange packets over a point-to-point link.

QoS Quality of Service. A mechanism to provide differential treatment to traffic.

QPPB QoS Policy Propagation via BGP. A mechanism to use BGP's attributes to propagate QoS policies over a network.

RD Route Distinguisher. An 8-byte value prepended to an IPv4 prefix so that it becomes a unique VPN-IPv4 prefix.

RIB Routing Information Base. A database that stores routing information from various routing sources.

RIP Routing Information Protocol. An IGP that uses hop count as its primary routing metric.

RR route reflector. An iBGP speaker that can reflect routes between its clients and other iBGP speakers.

RT route target. An extended BGP community attached to a VPNv4 prefix for routing policy control.

SAFI Subsequent Address Family Identifier. A value that is used to further identify an address group within an address family.

SDH Synchronous Digital Hierarchy. An ITU protocol that is equivalent to SONET.

SOO site of origin. An extended BGP community to indicate the site that generates the route.

TDP Tag Distribution Protocol. A Cisco protocol for tag-binding distribution.

TE traffic engineering. A technique or process used to cause routed traffic to travel through the network on a path that might be different from one that is provided by a routing protocol.

TFIB Tag Forwarding Information Base. A database that is used to forward tagged packets.

UDP User Datagram Protocol. An IETF protocol that provides connectionless packet delivery.

VCI   Virtual Circuit Identifier. A value to identify a circuit in ATM.

VPI   virtual path identifier. A value to identify a path in ATM.

VPN   Virtual Private Network. A framework that provides private IP networking over a public infrastructure such as the Internet.

VPNv4   Virtual Private Network-Internet Protocol version 4. A keyword in commands to indicate VPN-IPv4 prefixes. These prefixes are VPN addresses.

VRF   VPN routing/forwarding instance. Consists of an IP routing table, a forwarding table, a set of interfaces that use the forwarding table, and a set of rules and routing protocols that determine what goes into the forwarding table.

INDEX

Numerics

0.0.0.0/8 addressing, 230
16-8-8 data structure, 40
256-way mtrie, 40
8-8-8-8 mtrie structure, 40

A

access routers
    as starting router for network migration, 311
    migration concerns, 318
    moving to new peer groups, 319
ACLs, filtering classless routing updates, 115
address families (AFs), 28
address space, provider-based summarization, 237
addressing
    anycast, 564
    IPv6
        address format, 564–565
        aggregatable global unicast addresses, 566
        local addressing, 566
        special addresses, 567
    ISP networks, 397
adjacency tables, 40
administrative policies, 8
ADMs (add/drop multiplexers), 583
advertisement suppression communities, 405
advertisements
    AFs, 28
    aggregates, 230
    conditional, 123
        examples, 124, 127–129
        forms, 124
    SAFIs, 28

AFs (address families), 28
aggregatable global unicast addresses, 566
aggregation, 230
    aggregate prefix, default attributes, 130
    BGP policy control, 130–133
    remote site (BGP enterprise core), 192
aggregation layer (ISP networks), 390
aggregation routers, 391
Allow-AS, 460
American Registry for Internet Numbers (ARIN), 226
anycast, 564
Anycast RP, 548
APNIC (Asia Pacific Network Information Centre, 226
architectures
    DCNs, 584
    enterprise network core design, 160
        eBGP, 168–178
        iBGP, 161–167
        internal/external BGP, 178–189, 192
    migration. See migration
    MPLS VPNs, 449
are, 599
ARIN (American Registry for Internet Numbers, 226
ARP table (Address Resolution Protocol), 33
AS (autonomous systems), 294
AS Override, 457–458
AS path lists, 117
ASBRs (AS border routers), 461, 476
AS_PATH attribute, 18, 21
    disabling, 460
    iBGP confederation, 296
    looping, 458

C

M

Q

R

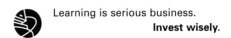

Cisco Press

Learning is serious business.

Invest wisely.

CCIE®

Cisco LAN Switching
Kennedy Clark, Kevin Hamilton
1-57870-094-9 • **Available Now**

This book is essential for preparation for the CCIE Routing and Switching exam track. As well as CCIE preparation, this comprehensive volume provides readers with an in-depth analysis of Cisco LAN Switching technologies, architectures, and deployments. Product operational details, hardware options, configuration fundamentals, spanning tree, source-route bridging, multilayer switching, and other technology areas related to the Catalyst series switches are discussed.

CCIE Routing and Switching Exam Certificatin Guide
Anthony Bruno
1-58720-053-8 • **Available Now**

CCIE Routing and Switching Exam Certification Guide is a comprehensive study and assessment tool. Written and reviewed by CCIEs, this book helps you understand and master the material you need to know to pass the test. The companion CD-ROM includes over 200 practice exam questions in a simulated testing environment, customizable so you can focus on the areas in which you need the most review.

CCIE Practical Studies, Volume I
Karl Solie, CCIE
1-58720-002-3 • **Available Now**

CCIE Practical Studies, Volume I, provides you with the knowledge to assemble and configure all the necessary hardware and software components required to model complex, Cisco-driven internetworks based on the OSI reference model-from Layer 1 on up.

BGP-4 Command and Configuration Handbook
William R. Parkhurst, Ph.D.
1-58705-017-X Available Now

The comprehensive, hands-on guide to all Cisco IOS Software BGP-4 commands. *Cisco BGP-4 Command and Configuration Handbook* is an exhaustive practical reference to the commands contained within BGP-4. For each command/subcommand, author Bill Parkhurst explains the intended use or function and how to properly configure it. Then he presents scenarios to demonstrate every facet of the command and its use, along with appropriate show and debug commands. Through the discussion of functionality and the scenario-based configuration examples, *Cisco BGP-4 Command and Configuration Handbook* will help you gain a thorough understanding of the practical side of BGP-4.

Data Center Fundamentals
Mauricio Arregoces and Maurizio Portolani
1-58705-023-4 Available December 2003

Master the basics of data centers to build server farms that enhance your website performance. Today's market demands that businesses have an Internet presence through which they can perform e-commerce and customer support, and establish a presence that can attract and increase their customer base. Underestimated hit ratios, compromised credit card records, perceived slow website access, or the infamous "Object Not Found" alerts make the difference between a successful online presence and one that is bound to fail.

Internet Routing Architectures, Second Edition
Sam Halabi
1-57870-233-X • Available Now

The industry's leading resource for Internet routing solutions scenarios. *Internet Routing Architectures*, Second Edition explores the ins and outs of interdomain routing network designs with emphasis on BGP-4 (Border Gateway Protocol Version 4)—the de facto interdomain routing protocol.

Learning is serious buisiness. **Invest wisely.**

BGP-4 Command and Configuration Handbook
William R. Parkhurst, Ph.D.
1-58705-017-X Available Now

The comprehensive, hands-on guide to all Cisco IOS Software BGP-4 commands. *Cisco BGP-4 Command and Configuration Handbook* is an exhaustive practical reference to the commands contained within BGP-4. For each command/subcommand, author Bill Parkhurst explains the intended use or function and how to properly configure it. Then he presents scenarios to demonstrate every facet of the command and its use, along with appropriate show and debug commands. Through the discussion of functionality and the scenario-based configuration examples, *Cisco BGP-4 Command and Configuration Handbook* will help you gain a thorough understanding of the practical side of BGP-4.

Data Center Fundamentals
Mauricio Arregoces and Maurizio Portolani
1-58705-023-4 Available December 2003

Master the basics of data centers to build server farms that enhance your website performance. Today's market demands that businesses have an Internet presence through which they can perform e-commerce and customer support, and establish a presence that can attract and increase their customer base. Underestimated hit ratios, compromised credit card records, perceived slow website access, or the infamous "Object Not Found" alerts make the difference between a successful online presence and one that is bound to fail.

Internet Routing Architectures, Second Edition
Sam Halabi
1-57870-233-X • Available Now

The industry's leading resource for Internet routing solutions scenarios. *Internet Routing Architectures*, Second Edition explores the ins and outs of interdomain routing network designs with emphasis on BGP-4 (Border Gateway Protocol Version 4)—the de facto interdomain routing protocol.

Internetworking Technologies Handbook,
Fourth Edition
Cisco Systems, Inc.
1-58705-119-2 Available Now

The updated edition of the best-selling all-in-one networking reference provides coverage of essential and cutting-edge technologies. *Internetworking Technologies Handbook*, Fourth Edition, is a comprehensive reference that enables networking professionals to understand and implement contemporary internetworking technologies. Master the terms, concepts, technologies, and devices used in today's networking industry. Learn how to incorporate internetworking technologies into a LAN/WAN environment. With new and updated chapters on security, storage, optical networking, scalability, and speed, this book is a complete and up-to-date reference to the topics that are essential to all networking professionals, regardless of expertise.

Readers will obtain a greater understanding of LAN and WAN networking, particularly the hardware, protocols, and services involved. Fundamental technology information is provided on a broad range of integral systems and services, including detailed descriptions, review questions to ensure concept comprehension and retention, and additional resources for further study. Coverage is also extended not only to new networking concepts, but also to older, legacy systems, providing a more realistic picture of the real-world networking environments in which professionals operate. Tools and guidelines for optimizing system performance will increase productivity and improve efficiency, helping the reader make more intelligent, cost-efficient decisions for their networks.

Designing Network Security, Second Edition
Merike Kaeo
1-58705-117-6 Available Now

Master the design of secure networks with the updated edition of this best-selling security guide. *Designing Network Security*, Second Edition is a practical guide designed to help you understand the fundamentals of securing your corporate network infrastructure. In addition, it provides a complete description of Cisco security products and useful implementation examples.

You will gain a thorough understanding of basic cryptography and the most widely deployed security technologies. You will be able to guide the architecture and implementation of a security policy for a corporate environment by knowing possible threats and vulnerabilities, and understanding the steps required to perform a risk management assessment.

OSPF Network Design Solutions, Second Edition
Tom Thomas
1-58705-032-3 Available Now

The comprehensive reference for Open Shortest Path First (OSPF) network design and deployment. One of the most prevalent Interior Gateway Protocols (IGPs), OSPF is in use in numerous networks across the globe. OSPF is also one of the most widely tested protocols if you choose to pursue a networking certification. From a technical perspective, the overwhelming presence of OSPF ensures that you will encounter it at some point in your career. As a result, every networking professional should understand how OSPF operates, how to configure and troubleshoot this important protocol, and most importantly how to design a network that uses OSPF.

IF YOU'RE USING

CISCO PRODUCTS,

YOU'RE QUALIFIED

TO RECEIVE A

FREE SUBSCRIPTION

TO CISCO'S

PREMIER PUBLICATION,

PACKET™ MAGAZINE.

Packet delivers complete coverage of
cutting-edge networking trends and
innovations, as well as current product
updates. A magazine for technical, hands-on
Cisco users, it delivers valuable information
for enterprises, service providers, and
small and midsized businesses.

Packet is a quarterly publication. To
start your free subscription, click on the
URL and follow the prompts:
www.cisco.com/go/packet/subscribe

☐ YES! I'm requesting a **free** subscription to *Packet*™ magazine.

☐ No. I'm not interested at this time.

☐ Mr.
☐ Ms.

First Name (Please Print) _____ Last Name _____

Title/Position (Required) _____

Company (Required) _____

Address _____

City _____ State/Province _____

Zip/Postal Code _____ Country _____

Telephone (Include country and area codes) _____ Fax _____

E-mail _____

Signature (Required) _____ Date _____

☐ I would like to receive additional information on Cisco's services and products by e-mail.

1. Do you or your company:
- A ☐ Use Cisco products
- B ☐ Resell Cisco products
- C ☐ Both
- D ☐ Neither

2. Your organization's relationship to Cisco Systems:
- A ☐ Customer/End User
- B ☐ Prospective Customer
- C ☐ Cisco Reseller
- D ☐ Cisco Distributor
- E ☐ Integrator
- F ☐ Non-Authorized Reseller
- G ☐ Cisco Training Partner
- I ☐ Cisco OEM
- J ☐ Consultant
- K ☐ Other (specify): _____

3. How many people does your entire company employ?
- A ☐ More than 10,000
- B ☐ 5,000 to 9,999
- C ☐ 1,000 to 4,999
- D ☐ 500 to 999
- E ☐ 250 to 499
- F ☐ 100 to 249
- G ☐ Fewer than 100

4. Is your company a Service Provider?
- A ☐ Yes
- B ☐ No

5. Your involvement in network equipment purchases:
- A ☐ Recommend
- B ☐ Approve
- C ☐ Neither

6. Your personal involvement in networking:
- A ☐ Entire enterprise at all sites
- B ☐ Departments or network segments at more than one site
- C ☐ Single department or network segment
- F ☐ Public network
- D ☐ No involvement
- E ☐ Other (specify): _____

7. Your Industry:
- A ☐ Aerospace
- B ☐ Agriculture/Mining/Construction
- C ☐ Banking/Finance
- D ☐ Chemical/Pharmaceutical
- E ☐ Consultant
- F ☐ Computer/Systems/Electronics
- G ☐ Education (K–12)
- U ☐ Education (College/Univ.)
- H ☐ Government—Federal
- I ☐ Government—State
- J ☐ Government—Local
- K ☐ Health Care
- L ☐ Telecommunications
- M ☐ Utilities/Transportation
- N ☐ Other (specify): _____

CPRESS

PACKET

Packet magazine serves as the premier publication linking customers to Cisco Systems, Inc. Delivering complete coverage of cutting-edge networking trends and innovations, *Packet* is a magazine for technical, hands-on users. It delivers industry-specific information for enterprise, service provider, and small and midsized business market segments. A toolchest for planners and decision makers, *Packet* contains a vast array of practical information, boasting sample configurations, real-life customer examples, and tips on getting the most from your Cisco Systems' investments. Simply put, *Packet* magazine is straight talk straight from the worldwide leader in networking for the Internet, Cisco Systems, Inc.

We hope you'll take advantage of this useful resource. I look forward to hearing from you!

Cecelia Glover
Packet Circulation Manager
packet@external.cisco.com
www.cisco.com/go/packet